SECOND EDITION

INTRODUCTION TO CANADIAN BUSINESS

Brian E. Owen ■ University of Manitoba

Frederick A. Starke ■ University of Manitoba

John A. Reinecke ■ University of Southern Mississippi

William F. Schoell ■ University of Southern Mississippi

ALLYN AND BACON, INC.
Toronto ■ Boston ■ London ■ Sydney

Canadian Cataloguing in Publication Data

Main entry under title:

Introduction to Canadian business

Includes index.
ISBN 0-205-08188-6

1. Business.   2. Canada—Commerce.   I. Owen, Brian E., 1943–

HF5351.I57   1984   380.1′0971   C84-098333-6

Library of Congress Cataloging in Publication Data

Main entry under title:

Introduction to Canadian business.

Includes index.

1. Industrial management — Canada.   2. Business enterprises — Canada.   I. Owen, Brian E.
HD70.C2I57   1984   658′.00971   84-453
ISBN 0-205-08188-6

Printed in the United States of America.

10 9 8 7 6 5 4 3 2 1 89 88 87 86 85 84

Photo Credits

page 3: NFB Photothèque/Photo by Ted Grant/Miller Services Ltd.

page 33: Bert Hoferichter/Miller Services Ltd.

page 65: NFB Photothèque/Photo by Cedric Pearson

page 97: NFB Photothèque/Photo by George Hunter

page 131: NFB Photothèque/Photo by Tom Bochsler

page 169: NFB Photothèque/Photo by Tom Bochsler/Miller Services Ltd.

page 207: Alex Kalnins/Miller Services Ltd.

page 247: NFB Photothèque/Photo by George Hunter

page 253: Larry Lawfer/The Picture Cube

page 293: Olivier Rebbot/Woodfin Camp & Associates

page 303: Neil Newton/Miller Services Ltd.; NFB Photothèque/Photo by Gar Lunney/Miller Services Ltd.

page 389: Sepp Seitz/Woodfin Camp & Associates

page 334: Courtesy of CPT Corporation

page 342: NFB Photothèque/Photo by Julien LeBourdais

page 368: Courtesy of FMA/Puma.

page 369: Courtesy of Richardson Greenshields of Canada Limited

page 370: Courtesy of Manitoba Milk Producers' Marketing Board

page 371: Courtesy of Ben Moss Jewellers

page 372: Courtesy of Canadian Life and Health Insurance Association, Inc.

page 385: Larry Lawfer/The Picture Cube

page 413: Ellis Herwig/The Picture Cube

page 417: Courtesy of NCR

page 421: Courtesy of International Business Machines, Inc. (magnetic disk pack, magnetic tape, punched cards); courtesy of Media Division, Memorex, a Burroughs Company (floppy disk)

page 422: Courtesy of Burroughs Corp. Business Machines

page 424: Courtesy of the IBM Corp.

page 449: R. Smith/Image Finders Photo Agency

page 489: George Gooderham/Miller Services Ltd.

page 519: NFB Photothèque/Photo by Cliff Baskin

page 549: Courtesy of CPT Corporation

page 589: Peter Thomas/Miller Services Ltd.

page 613: NFB Photothèque/Photo by Brian King

page 643: NFB Photothèque

Cover Photograph: Tibor Bognar/Miller Services

CONTENTS

3 Forms of Business Ownership 65

SECTION TWO □ MANAGEMENT AND ORGANIZATION 95

4 Management Functions and Decision Making 97

5 Organizing the Firm 131

SECTION THREE □ HUMAN RESOURCES AND PRODUCTION MANAGEMENT   167

6 Personnel Management   169

7 Labour Relations   207

8 Producing Goods and Services   247

SECTION FOUR □ MARKETING MANAGEMENT   291

9 The Marketing Concept   293

10 Marketing Decisions   329

SECTION FIVE □ ACCOUNTING, COMPUTERS, AND INFORMATION MANAGEMENT   383

11 Accounting   385

19 The Political Environment   643

PREFACE

IN DEVELOPING THE FIRST EDITION OF *INTRODUCTION TO CANADIAN Business*, we began with an excellent basic text written by John Reinecke and William Schoell and revised it for Canadian students. In some chapters dealing with universal concepts such as those of management, marketing, finance, production, and personnel, basic theory was maintained and Canadian business practice in these areas was described. In other chapters, particularly those dealing with the environment of Canadian business, completely new material was added. Between these two extremes a number of chapters, including those on business ownership, financial institutions, labour relations, and international business, were extensively revised.

Our objective in this second Canadian edition is an improved text for students of Canadian business that retains the outstanding features of the first edition. *Introduction to Canadian Business*, Second Edition, reveals the excitement, meaning, and challenge found in modern business. Our goal is to convey to students a basic understanding of contemporary business concepts and how they are applied to the real world.

IMPROVEMENTS IN THE SECOND EDITION

The second edition of *Introduction to Canadian Business* has been reorganized into nineteen more carefully integrated chapters—in eight sections, rather than five, as in the first edition. This reorganization means a somewhat longer text, but we believe that breaking down the material into smaller, more manageable units improves the text for instructors and students alike.

Each chapter has been updated and new material added, including some completely new features. This revised and additional material gives students a fuller understanding of the Canadian business scene. Each chapter contains the following features:

Learning objectives. The list of objectives at the beginning of each chapter ties together the text and the Instructor's Resource Manual. Each item in the Test Bank (included in the Instructor's Resource Manual) is linked to a specific and identified learning objective.

Key concepts. The list of key concepts at the beginning of each chapter, identifying the most important terms in the chapter, helps to build business vocabulary. The key concepts, which appear in the margins, are defined in boldface in the text. The terms are also defined in the expanded Glossary at the end of the book.

Career profile. Each chapter contains a career profile of a man or woman who is currently working in a job that is related to the material in that chapter. The career profiles give an idea of some of the practical aspects of careers in specific areas.

Real-world examples. Real-world examples of contemporary business practice are found throughout each chapter. These, like the incidents and case studies at the end of each chapter, help build interest and link the chapter content to contemporary business practices in the area covered.

Boxed inserts. Several types of boxed inserts elaborate on the discussion in each chapter. *What Do You Think?* boxes require a decision on a contemporary business problem. *Point of View* boxes present various perspectives on contemporary business issues. *Authors' Commentary* boxes present the authors' opinions and/or predictions about current business questions.

Advertisements, photographs, and business documents. Contemporary advertisements dramatize major business concepts and practices. Photos and reproductions of actual business documents add a visual dimension that livens up the presentation.

Summary and look ahead. This feature not only summarizes the chapter in a concise manner, but also introduces the subject matter that follows in the next chapter or section. This continues the strategy of tying together the major ideas from chapter to chapter and from section to section.

Questions for review and discussion. The questions at the end of each chapter relate directly to the chapter's factual material and encourage students to explore and analyze the issues in the chapter.

Incidents and case studies. At the end of each chapter are several short incidents and usually one or more longer case studies. These focus on issues in contemporary business. Their real-world orientation helps you to build your analytical skills and to apply what you have learned in the chapter to realistic business situations.

ACKNOWLEDGMENTS

We owe special thanks to our production editor, Barbara Willette, and to our series editor, Jerry Smith, for their dedicated efforts toward helping us to meet our goal of significantly improving on the first edition. We also want to thank Pam Poulson for help in securing permissions. Special thanks go to Diana Sokolowski and Maryann Urban, who helped us tremendously in the typing of the manuscript. Thanks also go to our families for bearing with us, and for encouraging us, throughout the revision process.

Many changes in this second edition were inspired by the readers of the previous edition. We want to continue to learn from them, for they are our best possible critics.

The following people helped by reviewing the material herein and/or by graciously offering suggestions, either on their own or in reply to questionnaires distributed by Allyn and Bacon sales representatives. Their comments were gratefully received, carefully read, and implemented wherever possible.

Harold Best, Mohawk College of Applied Arts and Technology;
G. Edward Bissell, British Columbia Institute of Technology;
Philip Bomeisl, Bergen County Community College;
Sonya Brett, Macomb County Community College;
Don R. Brown, Northern Arizona University;
Harold Buck, Mohawk College;
Frank Collom, Queen's University;
Kathy Hegar, Mountain View College;
Bradley B. Hill, St. Lawrence College;
Murray Hilton, University of Manitoba;
Robert Litro, Mattatuck Community College;
James C. Manning, Dawson College;
John Marts, University of Southwest Louisiana;
Donald Mask, Dawson College;
John McCallum, University of Manitoba;
Jack Miller, St. Petersburg Junior College;
Robert Nelson, University of Illinois at Urbana-Champaign;
Tariq Nizami, Champlain Regional College;
Robert Ristau, Eastern Michigan University;
Donald Sedik, Harper College;
Dr. S.P. Sethi, University of Toronto;
Douglas R. Sherk, Seneca College of Applied Arts and Technology;
Denis C. Stephenson, Sheridan College of Applied Arts and Technology;
James Wallace, Loyola College;
Anthony K. Wensley, University of Waterloo;
Ian A. Wilson, St. Lawrence College

Section One

Our study of business begins with a discussion of economic systems and the economic problem, the business firm's role in the market economy, and the forms of business ownership.

In Chapter 1 we examine what an economic system is and why it exists. The main purpose of any economic system is to cope with the overall economic problem—how to satisfy unlimited wants with limited resources—which confronts all people. Economic systems differ widely in how they address the economic problem. At the two ends of the spectrum are collectivism and capitalism in their pure forms. In Canada we have a "mixed" economic system.

In Chapter 2 we take a look at the market forces of supply and demand in our economic system, the factors that underlie them, and how they determine prices. We look at the business firm, the basic building block for organizing production in our system, and how it does so to take advantage of market opportunity.

Chapter 3 describes the forms of business ownership. Although many people think mainly of corporations when they think of business firms, there are other forms of ownership. In fact, the majority of Canadian firms are not corporations, although corporations conduct most of the business activity in Canada.

OUR BUSINESS SYSTEM

After reading this chapter, you should be able to:

1. Define and discuss the economic problem and how we cope with it.
2. Distinguish between needs and wants.
3. Identify and explain the two basic concepts of value.
4. Discuss how an economic system's performance is measured.
5. List and define the factors of production.
6. State the basic purpose of an economic system.
7. Compare and contrast the collectivist and capitalist economic systems.
8. List and discuss the chief characteristics of a capitalist economic system.
9. Explain the characteristics of our mixed economy.

KEY CONCEPTS

In reading the chapter, look for and understand these terms:

the economic problem
specialization
exchange
utility
value in exchange
standard of living
Gross National Product (GNP)
inflation
Disposable Personal Income (DPI)
factors of production
land
labour
capital

entrepreneurship
entrepreneur
mercantilism
laissez faire
capitalism
mixed economic system
collectivism
central planning
individualism
Protestant ethic
capital formation
consumer power
consumerism

ALL ECONOMIC SYSTEMS SHARE THE problem that human wants are unlimited while the resources with which to satisfy them are limited. You confront this problem every day and cope with it by assigning priorities to your wants and spending your limited income accordingly.

In our economic system, business firms try to anticipate what their target customers want and produce goods and services they hope will satisfy these wants. Business people can profit if they produce things consumers want, but they assume the risk of losing their investment if they produce things that consumers do not want.

A different situation exists in some other types of economic systems. Although these economic systems must also cope with unlimited human wants and limited productive resources, they allow individual consumers and businesspeople very little voice in coping with the economic problem. In the Soviet Union, for example, the State Planning Committee (GOSPLAN) sets a plan every five years to govern the workings of the economic system. The Committee determines what goods and services will be produced and the prices at which they will be sold. It also sets production quotas for workers, in effect telling each citizen how much of which good or service he or she must produce. The central planners decide what will be produced and what will be available for consumers to buy.

CHAPTER ONE

The Economic Problem and Our Economic System

THE PROBLEM OF DEALING WITH LIMITED RESOURCES TO SATISFY unlimited wants is not new. Human beings have always been "wanting" animals. Even early cave dwellers had to satisfy their unlimited needs and wants with the limited resources available to them.

In contrast to the cave people who lived in small, independent groups, modern people live with others in large, interdependent social and economic systems. In advanced systems we learn to want many more things than we really need in order to survive. Our natural resources, however, have not increased to the same degree as our wants. Thus the economic problem has been brought into sharper focus.

Our limited resources consist of land, labour, capital, and entrepreneurship—the factors of production. By specializing and exchanging our limited resources, we can satisfy more of our wants. This raises our standard of living because we can produce more goods and services to consume. Recently an increasing number of people have been questioning whether we really are better off. They question whether a greater output of goods and services really improves the quality of life.

An economic system is a framework for satisfying human wants. Collectivism and capitalism are two different types of systems. We will discuss both in their pure and real-world forms. We will also discuss the nature and functioning of the Canadian "mixed" economic system. A major similarity among the various types of economic systems—that is, the one thing that they all have in common—is that they must all cope with the economic problem.

THE ECONOMIC PROBLEM

the economic problem

Because our wants are unlimited and our resources are limited, we face a problem. It is the economic problem. **The economic problem is concerned with how we can satisfy our unlimited wants with our limited resources.** This problem exists for nations, individuals, business firms, and nonbusiness organizations.

We must deal with the questions of: What goods and services to produce and in what quantities? How to produce goods and services? How to allocate the goods and services among members of society?

We have always had to face the economic problem. Our material progress depends on our ability to cope with it. Today in Canada, for example, we have to make decisions on how our scarce natural resources are to be used to satisfy our wants.

Specialization

specialization

Sharing in the task to provide basic needs means that people do not have to provide for all their needs alone. In earliest times each person had to hunt and cook alone. Later, each person had more freedom to do only one task—either to hunt or to cook. This is an example of specialization in a simple economic system. **Specialization means concentrating effort on a specific task instead of dividing one's effort among a greater number of tasks.** By specializing, better use is made of each person's limited time. For the cave dwellers, for example, this means one person would specialize in hunting, and the other would specialize in cooking.

A modern example of specialization is the assembly line in an automobile plant. Each worker on the assembly line performs a highly specialized task.

Exchange

exchange

Specialization is pointless, however, unless specialists can exchange. **Exchange means trade, or giving up one thing to get another thing.**

Let's assume that the man specializes in hunting and the woman specializes in cooking. The man exchanges part of his hunt for part of the meal prepared by the woman. Specialization and exchange, of course, can be extended beyond the family—and have been.

Over time we have come to live in larger groups. From the simple family, we have progressed to more complex groups such as tribes, villages, towns, cities, and nations. Production has become organized in shops, stores, and factories. Thus, the specialization and exchange process now includes a great many people. Each person is dependent on an increasing number of people to satisfy his or her wants. The process of exchange organizes people into groups. An economic system is the result. Although there are many different types of economic systems, all have one element in common—they exist to satisfy human wants.

NEEDS AND WANTS

An isolated person has basic needs like food, clothing, and shelter. These needs must be satisfied if the person is to survive. However, once the person relates to other people, specialization and exchange begin and result in new needs which are learned. These new needs are not needs in the sense that a person must satisfy them in order to survive. They are wants.

A person needs food to survive. He or she can satisfy this need by eating wild berries. But a person may also learn, as a result of coming into contact with other people, to want fancy cuts of meat and pastries. Many other wants are also learned. No one really needs a television set, a piano, an automatic dishwasher, or a car in order to survive. But a lot of us want them and many other products and services as well.

Satisfaction of Wants

A want is satisfied by consuming an object or a service which is useful in relation to the want. If a good can satisfy a certain want, then it has utility. **Utility means usefulness.**

Wants are very specific to individuals. A list of wants made by one person would probably be somewhat similar to that made by another. Basic wants such as food would appear in both lists. Beyond these, however, there would be many differences in the types of wants.

In a modern economy, people have different wants. Thus, different goods have different degrees of utility for different persons. Suppose two people have the same want. Even then, we could not assume that a certain good that satisfies the want would have the same utility to both people.

If something has utility for someone, it is valuable to that person. All of us must breathe. Thus, air has value to all of us. Although it has value, people will not ordinarily pay anything for air. It is too plentiful. It has value in use, but it does not have value in exchange. **Something has value in exchange when it can command something else in return for it.** These two concepts of value — value in use and value in exchange — are important to any economic system.

An example will help to illustrate the meaning of value in exchange. Mr. Green has some apples. Mr. Smith has some oranges. Suppose both men want apples and oranges. Mr. Green can exchange some apples for some oranges. Mr. Smith can exchange some oranges for some apples. Exchange would occur if both men thought they would benefit from it. Mr. Green, since he already has apples, values them less than Mr. Smith, who has none. Mr. Smith, since he already has oranges, values them less than Mr. Green, who has none.

The exchange does not involve things of equal value. Mr. Green's apples are worth less to him than the oranges he gets in return. Mr. Smith's oranges are worth less to him than the apples he gets in return. How much anything is worth to a person depends partly on how much of it he or she already has. The more a person has of it, the less that person wants (and is willing to pay) to get more units. This is the principle of diminishing marginal utility.

One of the important functions of an economic system is to determine what goods and services to produce to satisfy people's wants.

Standard of Living

The purpose of an economic system is to satisfy human wants. It is, therefore, desirable to measure the system's performance. Comparisons of different systems may be made by a measure called the standard of living. **The standard of living is a measure of economic well-being.** It indicates how much income is available to allocate to all members of society.

The standard of living helps us compare the well-being of one society with that of another society. It also helps us to observe change in well-being over time. The standard of living estimates the value of all goods and services produced by a country during a period of time. This figure is then divided by the population. The result is a measure of the economic well-being of an average person in that country.

Gross National Product (GNP)

A popular measure of the standard of living is Gross National Product (GNP). **The Gross National Product is the sum of the values of all goods and services produced in a nation during a given year.** Canada measures its GNP in billions of dollars. Recently our GNP was $349.9 billion. (See Figure 1.1.) In recent years much of the increase in GNP has been due to inflation. **Inflation means an increase in the prices of goods and services over a period of time that effectively reduces the purchasing**

inflation

Figure 1.1
Gross National Product of Canada (Source: Bank of Canada Review, December 1982, pp. S120–S122.)

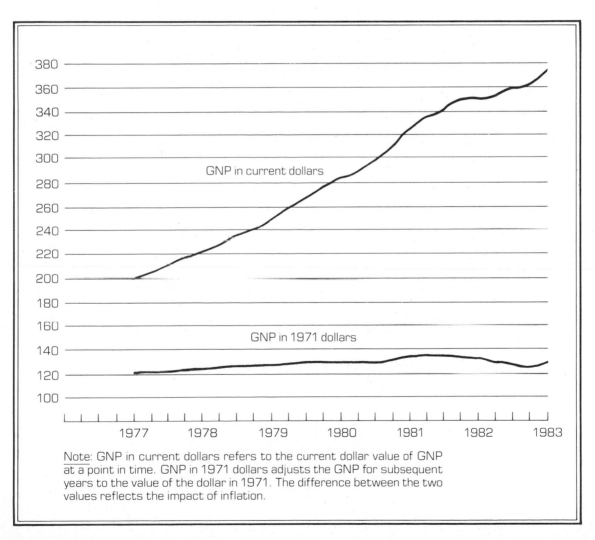

Note: GNP in current dollars refers to the current dollar value of GNP at a point in time. GNP in 1971 dollars adjusts the GNP for subsequent years to the value of the dollar in 1971. The difference between the two values reflects the impact of inflation.

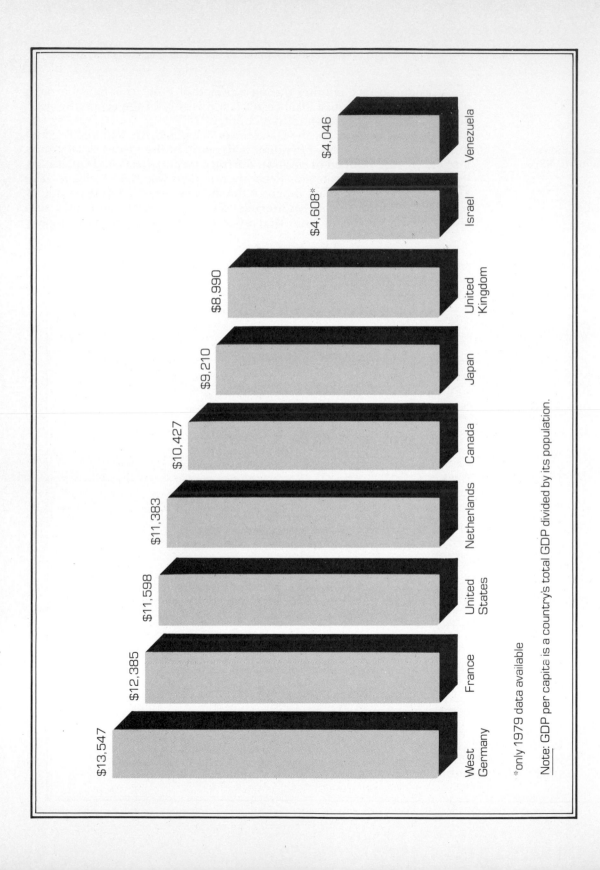

$13,547 — West Germany

$12,385 — France

$11,598 — United States

$11,383 — Netherlands

$10,427 — Canada

$9,210 — Japan

$8,990 — United Kingdom

$4,608* — Israel

$4,046 — Venezuela

*only 1979 data available

Note: GDP per capita is a country's total GDP divided by its population.

Table 1.1 Canadian Consumer Price Index (1981 = 100)

Year	Consumer Price Index
1971	42.2
1972	44.2
1973	47.6
1974	52.8
1975	58.5
1976	62.9
1977	67.9
1978	73.9
1979	80.7
1980	88.9
1981	100.0
1982	110.8

Source: Reproduced by the Minister of Supply and Services Canada.

power of a nation's currency. It is a serious problem in Canada and in most other countries. Inflation is one reason why the prices of new homes and new cars are so high, as reflected in the consumer price index. (See Table 1.1.)

Figure 1.2 compares the GDP (GNP) of Canada with that of several other countries. It shows per capita GDP for each of the countries in U. S. dollars. (Per capital GDP is a country's total GDP divided by its population.)

Disposable Personal Income (DPI)

Some people think that Disposable Personal Income (DPI) is a better measure of the people's welfare. **Disposable Personal Income is a smaller amount than GNP. It indicates the total amount of buying power from current sources available to the nation's people. It is equal to their incomes minus the taxes they pay.**

Quality of Life

Measures such as GNP and DPI, however, do not indicate the quality of life in a nation. There are side effects of high productivity which are not measured by GNP. These include pollution, congested cities, and rapid depletion of basic natural resources. They may have a strong negative effect on our enjoyment of our productive efforts. In other words, the value of things is subjective — it depends on the judgment of the people who possess or consume them.

Are we really better off simply because we produce more goods and services, or do we also have to look beyond quantity and consider the overall

Figure 1.2
Gross Domestic Product per capita for selected countries (in 1980 U.S. dollars)
(Source: prepared from Worldwide Economic Indicators, Comparative Summary of 131 Countries, 1982 Annual. Copyright 1982 by Business International Corporation, Online Services Department, One Dag Hammarskjold Plaza, New York, N. Y. 10017.)

WHAT DO YOU THINK?

**How Do You Measure
the Quality of Life?**

A study for the Economic Council of Canada by D.W. Henderson on social indicators indicated three basic goals related to the quality of life. These were (1) material well-being, (2) sociocultural well-being, and (3) equity of opportunity with respect to the first two.

These three were further subdivided into nine different major areas of socioeconomic concern.

1. Individual rights and responsibilities (legal rights and participation in public decision making)
2. Social rights and national identity (domestic social rights and international relations)

3. Command over knowledge and skills (basic and higher education, etc.)
4. Health (mortality, morbidity, and positive health)
5. Natural environment (soil, water, and air)
6. Humanmade environment (social and political)
7. Production and consumption of final goods and services (inputs, outputs, and efficiency)
8. Employment (labour-management relations, job security and satisfaction, etc.)
9. Financial status (income and assets)

Is this listing of concerns useful in measuring the "quality of life"? WHAT DO YOU THINK?

Reproduced by permission of the Minister of Supply and Services Canada.

---

quality of our lives? There is some evidence that some of us are becoming more conscious of and concerned with the quality of life. Some business firms, for example, are finding it harder to transfer their employees to other areas, even when it means promotions and pay raises for the employees. These individuals are considering quality of life; that is, they are concerned with areas of well-being other than promotions and pay raises.

THE FACTORS OF PRODUCTION

factors of production

Limited resources must be wisely used to achieve a high standard of living. **These limited resources are the factors of production: (1) land, (2) labour, (3) capital, and (4) entrepreneurship. The factors of produc-**

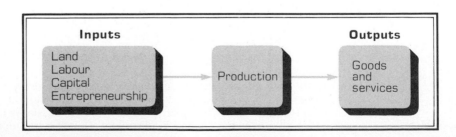

Figure 1.3
The productive system

tion are the inputs of the productive system. One of the issues addressed in any economic system is how the factors of production are combined to produce outputs. The outputs are the goods and services produced to satisfy human wants. (See Figure 1.3.)

Land

land

Land, as a factor of production, means natural resources. Examples are petroleum, iron ore, and farmland. In the long run, all natural resources can run out. With proper management, some will last for a very long time (air, water, forests). Others, however, are nonrenewable (petroleum, uranium, other metals). Physical land is limited, too. We have a choice between thoughtless and rapid use of these resources and carefully planned resource use.

Labour

labour

Labour means human mental and physical effort. Much of our economic progress results from substituting mental effort for physical effort. Mental effort leads to technological breakthroughs which result in greater output from the same physical effort. This enables us to get more satisfaction from a given quantity of natural resources. For example, if such progress enables us to get 10 percent more energy from a ton of coal, the effect is the same as adding 10 percent to the coal supply.

Capital

capital

Capital, as a factor of production, means tools and machinery or anything made by humans that aids in producing and distributing goods. It is humanmade productive capacity.

A CONTEMPORARY ISSUE

Oil Shortage or Glut?

Until quite recently Canadians were worried about an oil shortage. Alternative energy sources such as solar power, wind power, coal generators, and nuclear power plants were constantly in the news.

It then became fashionable to talk about an oil glut. Prices at the pumps would drop from 44 cents a litre to 25 cents a litre within a few days. This was the result of neighbourhood stations competing for customers in order to reduce large inventories.

Are we currently moving toward an oil glut or an oil shortage? Should we continue exploring alternative energy sources? If so, what types of energy sources? WHAT DO YOU THINK?

WHAT DO YOU THINK?

How Do We Deal with Limited Natural Resources?

Two ways of dealing with the growing scarcity of natural resources (land as a factor of production) are to limit wants and/or to increase the capacity of natural resources to satisfy our wants.

Government can adopt policies to limit consumption. For example, to discourage consumption of gasoline, it could be rationed or prices could be raised.

Another approach is to use the other factors of production to help us to expand the want-satisfying capacity of our natural resource base. Human mental effort (labour) leads to new technology. Entrepreneurs put this technology to work by building new plants and equipment (capital) based on that technology. To get more miles per gallon from gasoline, for example, technological advances are made in engineering and producing cars. Which approach is better? WHAT DO YOU THINK?

To add to its capital equipment, an economy must produce more than it currently consumes. But how much of its output can a country devote to its productive facilities? This depends largely on the willingness and ability of its people to postpone consumption.

Entrepreneurship

entrepreneurship

entrepreneur

Bringing land, labour, and capital together and managing them productively to produce a good or service to make a profit is entrepreneurship. An entrepreneur is a person who assumes the risk of organizing and managing a business in the hope of making a profit.
People who go into business for themselves have no guarantee of earning a profit. They assume the risk of losing what they invest in their firms. Their willingness to assume the risk depends a lot on how healthy they think the economy will be in the future, the past political stability of the country, and their expected profit from undertaking the risk.

The factors of production can be combined and used in many ways to produce many different things. The amount and variety of goods produced depends mainly on the way economic life is organized.

THE PURPOSE OF AN ECONOMIC SYSTEM

The purpose of an economic system is to provide a framework for satisfying human wants. The functions of an economic system are to determine what products to produce, how to produce them, and how to allocate income among members of society. In Canada, most productive economic activities (producing and selling) are channelled through business firms. They operate through the market system. Historically, there have been different types of economic systems.

In ancient Greece, for example, producing goods for sale was not common. Agriculture was the main economic activity. Business, economic activity, and profit seeking were considered acceptable but lowly activities.

During the Middle Ages, the Church taught that people should not seek economic betterment but should concentrate on salvation. Although there was a great deal of economic activity, it was considered worldly and often sinful.

mercantilism

The next major "age," as far as economic philosophy is concerned, was the age of mercantilism. **Mercantilism is an economic philosophy which advocates building strong national states (nations) from warring feudal kingdoms. A major goal of mercantilism is to increase the government's holdings of precious metals.** Foreign trade between two countries was viewed as involving a gain for one and a loss for the other. The nation with the greatest supply of precious metals was considered the strongest. The citizens could be poor, but as long as gold was in the state treasury, the state was considered wealthy.

laissez faire

Mercantilism was followed by a period of "laissez faire" economics in Europe and, later, in the United States. **Laissez faire means let people do as they please. When applied to business, it means let the owners of business set the rules of competition without government regulation or control.** More generally, it means absence of intervention in the operation of the economic system. This new economic philosophy began in France, but it was first presented in a complete form in 1776 by Adam Smith in his book, *The Wealth of Nations.* Smith believed in free competition and capitalism.

capitalism

Capitalism is an economic system based on private ownership of the factors of production. The major features of capitalism are individualism, private property, profit incentive, consumer sovereignty (or consumer power), freedom to compete, occupational freedom, freedom of contract, and limited role of government.

TWO POINTS OF VIEW

Socialism

Collectivist systems are egalitarian in that they seek to equalize incomes and achieve a uniform standard of living for their people.

Socialists in Canada want to do the same. They see government's social programs as the equalizing and levelling force in society. Through these programs, they believe, the "have-nots" will have more and the "haves" will have less. This redistribution of income and wealth would continue until there is total equality. The socialist movement has a lot of appeal to some groups in our society.

Critics of socialism argue that a socialist system cannot exist in a capitalist-based economy because equal wealth would destroy the profit incentive.

Can those who favour socialism and those who oppose it resolve their differences? WHAT DO YOU THINK?

Collectivism, or socialism, is another type of economic means of production and distribution by society (the state) rather than by private individuals. Collectivism is characterized by features such as government ownership, joint decision making, and central planning.

Our Canadian economic system has its roots in the philosophy of laissez faire capitalism. However, at present we are far from a pure capitalist economic system. **In Canada we have a "mixed" economic system, characterized by an active market economy with significant direct and indirect involvement by government in economic decision making.**

mixed economic system

Some portions of the Canadian economy can be accurately described in terms of the features which characterize capitalism. There is also, however, a substantial portion of the economic activity in this country owned and operated by governments.

There are also many significant government involvements in the Canadian economy which stop short of direct ownership and control. There are a wide range of regulations, regulatory boards, incentive programs, tariffs, taxes, and other government influences.

In the sections below we discuss the characteristics of pure collectivist and pure capitalist economic systems. The mixed Canadian economic system is then discussed in greater depth.

COLLECTIVISM

In any economic system decisions are made about the alternative uses of resources and how the goods produced from those resources are to be distributed (see Figure 1.4). In a purely collectivist system, the government controls social and economic decision making. **Collectivism means government ownership of the factors of production and government control of all economic activities.** There is little or no private property. The government determines such things as the economy's rate of growth, the amount of investment, the actual allocation of resources, and the division of output. Direct government means are used to achieve the desired results. Wage rates, production volumes, and prices of goods are set by the government as well.

collectivism

The government likely also practises central planning. **Central planning means that the government drafts a master plan of what it wants to accomplish and directly manages the economy to achieve the plan's objectives.** The total supply of goods available for household consumption is fixed. This supply is distributed to households in limited amounts and at fixed prices. There is no guarantee, however, that the goods produced are what consumers want. Thus, consumers spend their fixed incomes on fixed amounts of goods at fixed prices.

central planning

A collectivist system seeks to achieve what it alleges to be the "greatest good for the greatest number." People contribute to it on the basis of their abilities. They receive from it on the basis of their needs. The individual is of less importance than the system, and the government largely determines each person's role in the system.

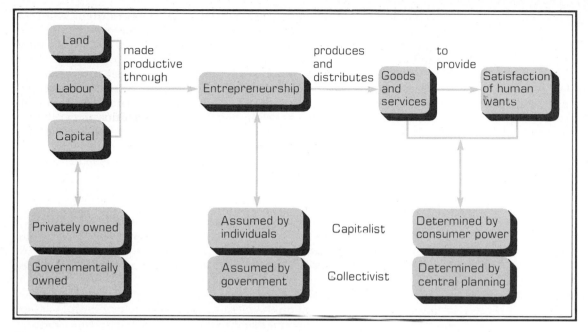

Figure 1.4
Characteristics of capitalist and collective economic systems

Collectivist systems, however, stress social and economic equality among their citizens. They seek to eliminate differences in economic welfare among people of different occupations, races, and backgrounds. A uniform standard of living is sought in order to eliminate friction among the various classes of people.

CAPITALISM

Individualism

individualism

The basic idea underlying capitalism is individualism. **Individualism is the idea that the group, the society, and the government are necessary but are of less importance than the individual's self-determination.** The ancient Greeks valued the dignity and uniqueness of the individual. Although this value was lost sight of during some of the darker periods of history since the Greeks, the idea of individualism remains a cornerstone of most of the Western democracies.

Capitalism is based upon the strength of individual self-interest. The basic belief is that a person will, if left alone, seek his or her economic betterment. It is assumed that this will lead to the economic betterment of the whole society and a more economical use of resources.

The full development of individual initiative and some other basic ideas of capitalism required a shift in Christian philosophy from medieval notions of "other-worldliness" and distrust for business to the more practical Protestant ethic. **The Protestant ethic is a tradition which emphasizes the value of hard work, accumulation of property, and self-reliance.** Its most extreme form existed in the United States during the nineteenth century. It became a belief in the survival of the economically fittest. It gave the mark of Christian respectability to the rugged individualists who dominated that country's economic growth in the latter half of the nineteenth century.

Private Property

Related to individualism is the right of private property. This is an individual's right to acquire, to use, to accumulate, and to dispose of things of value. The right to own and accumulate property is felt to be a contributing factor to individual initiative.

Private property has existed in most cultures. In any society, certain limitations must be placed on the right of ownership. For example, a person who owns a house may not use it to conduct illegal activities. Nor may the owner set fire to it. In Canada one is restricted from selling certain properties to foreigners subject to approval by the Foreign Investment Review Agency. A balance is struck between the individual's private property rights and the society's "common good."

An important aspect of private property is that a person can accumulate it and use it as he or she pleases within the very broad limits set by society.

Profit Incentive

The success of a capitalistic system in contributing to a high standard of living depends on having many people use their private property to generate more property. They invest it to make a profit. The incentive to invest lies in the chance of getting a return—making a profit—from it. If people could not profit, they would have little reason to use their property in such a way. Instead, they would use up or consume their property. If people did not make a profit from investing or going into business, they would not bother to accumulate property.

The right to pursue profits involves risk. The degree of risk depends on the use to which property is put. When people willingly risk their private property, such as their savings, by going into business, they do so to try to make a profit. This process of putting money into business firms in order to try to make more money is called investment.

Investment is necessary for a nation's economic growth. The more complex forms of productive business activity require large amounts of equipment, tools, land, and other things. Capital formation is another way

capital formation

to describe the process of investment. **Capital formation is the process of adding to an economy's productive capacity.** The profit incentive encourages investment in a capitalistic economic system.

Consumer Power

Unless a firm can cultivate a group of customers, it will not survive. It must have buyers for its products or services. In our system the consumer enjoys a position of great influence. **The consumer power concept means that, because consumers are free to do business with whomever they choose, businesses must consider consumer needs and wants in making decisions.** By doing this, businesses may earn a profit. Consumers, therefore, decide the economic fate of a firm through their individual decisions to buy from one firm or another. This is another way in which individualism is so important in our economic system. (See Table 1.2.)

consumer power

consumerism

Consumerism is a movement to strengthen the power of product users in relation to the power of product makers and sellers. It has become a deep-seated force in our business system. Examples of consumerist concerns are product safety and truth in advertising. Several government agencies have been set up to protect consumers. Examples are the federal Department of Consumer Affairs and various provincial government Departments of Consumer Affairs.

Perhaps you have heard the concept of consumer power expressed in terms of "casting dollar votes in the marketplace." Firms that do not provide want-satisfying products and services will not receive "dollar votes" from consumers. Consumers will not buy what these firms offer for sale and the firms will lose out in the struggle for customers.

Businesses, of course, do what they can to influence our buying decisions. Canadian firms, for example, spend millions of dollars every year on advertising to inform us about their products and to persuade us to buy them.

Table 1.2　Government vs. Consumer Control over Economic Decision Making

Collectivism	Capitalism
1. Government practises central planning.	1. The individual makes independent choices.
2. Central planning determines how resources will be allocated.	2. These choices determine how resources will be allocated.
3. Resources are allocated so as to achieve the goals set by government.	3. Resources are allocated in response to decisions made by consumers.
4. Government determines: (a) what will be produced. (b) how it will be produced. (c) how much will be produced. (d) how the products and services will be distributed.	4. Through the market consumers contribute to decisions about: (a) what will be produced. (b) how it will be produced. (c) how much will be produced. (d) how the products and services will be distributed.

Freedom to Compete

A person who is free to compete can risk his or her private property in the hope of earning a profit. Within very broad limits, that person can go into any business. This is true no matter how much those already in the same type of business would like to keep the field to themselves.

Competition among firms benefits both consumers and firms. When competitors stand ready to take sales away from a firm, that firm has a strong incentive to remain efficient and to please its customers. Thus, both the firm and its customers benefit when rivals seek to earn the customer's favour.

Occupational Freedom

Still another example of individual freedom is the freedom of occupational choice. You are free to start up a new firm — go into business for yourself and become your own boss. You are also free to work for someone else. The choice of occupation is a highly personal one. No one forces a person to be a plumber, a teacher, or a lawyer. The choice is made by each person. Individuals make this choice guided by their own best economic interests and within the limits of their talents and education.

In some economic systems, however, central planning determines the need for persons to fill various job categories. People are trained for, and assigned to, those jobs. The choice of a job is not made by the person. It is made by the government.

Freedom of Contract

One of the most important freedoms is freedom of contract. This enables a person to enter into contracts with one or more other persons. The contract may involve relationships like that between an employer and an employee or that between a seller and a buyer. As long as a contract is legal, it is protected by law and is legally enforceable.

Limited Role of Government

A basic characteristic of a capitalist economic system is the limited role of governments. In general, the government is permitted to step in only when the welfare of citizens is threatened. The manner in which government regulates can be hotly debated.

Closely related to the concept of limited role of government is a belief that price is the basic regulator of the economic system.

Table 1.3 compares some of the basic ideas which underlie capitalism and collectivism, the two ends of the spectrum of economic systems.

Table 1.3 Basic Ideas Underlying Capitalism and Collectivism

Capitalism	Collectivism
1. The individual is of primary importance	1. The individual is less important than the system, which seeks equality for all of its citizens
2. Private property	2. No private property
3. Profit incentive	3. No recognition of profit
4. Consumer power	4. Central control over social and economic decision making
5. Freedom to compete	5. Competition results in economic waste
6. Occupational freedom	6. Central planning determines the need for various types of occupations
7. Freedom of contract	7. Little freedom of contract
8. Limited role of government	8. The government is the primary decision maker

THE CANADIAN MIXED ECONOMY

In Canada, as mentioned previously, we have neither a purely capitalist nor a collectivist economy. We have a "mixed" economy. In a speech given in January, 1976, to the Canadian Club in Ottawa, Prime Minister Trudeau said, "The fact is that for over 100 years, since the government stimulated the building of the Canadian Pacific Railway by giving it Crown land, we have not had a free market economy in Canada, but a mixed economy—a mixture of private enterprise and public enterprise."

Sectors of our economy are characterized best as capitalist. Examples of these include the retail and service industries, the printing industry, newspapers, sporting goods, and small business in general.

We have a significant number of business-related activities which are government-owned. According to the 1982 Public Accounts of Canada, the total assets controlled by federal Crown corporations in 1981 amounted to $64.4 billion for 43 Crown corporations. In Canada, the federal government has been responsible for a large number of Crown corporations for many years. They operate, for example, in transportation (Canadian National Railway [CNR], Air Canada, Eldorado Aviation Ltd., Northern Transportation Company Ltd., St. Lawrence Seaway, and more recently VIA Rail Canada, Inc.), communications (CBC and Telsat), housing (Central Mortgage and Housing Corporation), and many others such as the Farm Credit Corporation and National Arts Centre Corporation. In addition, many provincial governments have established Crown corporations. The most prominent of these are involved in the generation and distribution of hydro-electricity.

Between the sector of the economy which is government-owned and that which is best characterized as free enterprise or capitalist, there are varying degrees and types of government intervention. In its November 1976 issue, the magazine *Canadian Insurance/Agent and Broker* records Professor D. H. Thain of the University of Western Ontario as referring to a medium amount of government involvement and a public utility type of system as different degrees of government involvement between the two ends of the spectrum. The medium amount of government involvement

Assets of Canadian Crown Corporations for 1978 and 1981

	1978 $000,000	1981 $000,000
Air Canada	1,333.5	1,869.9
Atlantic Pilotage Authority	1.9	1.7
Atomic Energy of Canada	1,859.2	1,362.8
Bank of Canada	15,105.6	19,153.9
Canada Deposit Insurance Corporation	147.6	232.5
Canadian Arsenals Ltd.	24.5	n/a
Canadian Broadcasting Corporation	452.6	522.1
Canadian Commercial Corporation	129.5	226.3
Canadian Dairy Commission	151.6	240.6
Canadian Film Development Corporation	2.9	2.0
Canadian Livestock Feed Board	1.0	3.6
Canadian National Railway System	4,531.1	6,140.2
Canadian National (West Indies) Steamship	0.6	n/a
Canadian Patents & Developments Ltd.	0.9	2.6
Canadian Saltfish Corporation	10.0	12.9
Canadian Wheat Board	1,695.2	3,720.5
Cape Breton Development Corporation	146.4	197.7
Central Mortgage & Housing Corporation	10,101.9	10,797.1
Crown Assets Disposal Corporation	8.9	0.7
Defence Construction (1951) Ltd.	0.6	0.6
Eldorado Aviation Ltd.	0.7	—
Eldorado Nuclear Ltd.	314.9	618.4
Export Development Corporation	2,359.2	4,269.8
Farm Credit Corporation	2,869.7	3,483.1
Federal Business Development Bank	1,631.7	2,046.5
Freshwater Fish Marketing Corporation	17.7	20.9
Great Lakes Pilotage Authority	3.1	2.9
Jacques Cartier & Champlain Bridges, Inc.	33.1	31.3
Laurentian Pilotage Authority	4.4	5.1
Loto Canada, Inc.	41.4	n/a
National Battlefields Commission	2.5	0.08
National Capital Commission	365.4	369.1
National Harbour Board	526.8	682.3
Northern Canada Power Commission	205.1	206.2
Northern Transportation Company Limited and subsidiary companies	58.7	75.0
Pacific Pilotage Authority	2.6	2.8
Petro-Canada	3,348.9	6,612.5
Royal Canadian Mint	48.3	72.2
The St. Lawrence Seaway Authority	663.6	667.3
The Seaway International Bridge Corporation Ltd.	0.2	0.3
Teleglobe Canada	259.2	332.1
Uranium Canada Ltd.	103.9	—
VIA Rail Canada, Inc.	75.3	373.1
Totals	48,641.9	64,358.68

Source: Receiver General for Canada, Government of Canada, *Public Accounts of Canada, 1979 & 1982.* Reproduced by permission of the Minister of Supply and Services Canada.

was referred to as a "welfare state based on an industrial system with a high degree of free enterprise"; he said, "this is what has been going on in Canada for the last twenty or thirty years and involves a continual expansion of government involvement, regulation and planning to achieve a higher level of employment and welfare services for the redistribution of wealth."

Thain refers to the next stage as the public utility stage. At this stage companies must report some intended decisions to regulatory agencies for prior approval. This takes away the autonomy of companies to make independent decisions about those issues for which prior approval is required. It also puts a company in a position of being subject to an arbitrary decision of a regulatory agency. There are numerous examples of individual company decisions which must receive prior approval. One very general example was the wage-and-price-controls program initiated in November, 1975, and phased out beginning in 1978. Under this program many companies could not change prices or finalize a wage settlement with employees before receiving approval from the Anti-Inflation Board. This act turned many companies into quasi-public utilities. The relationships between business and government are expanded upon in Chapter 19.

The economic systems of many other countries also cannot be categorized as either purely capitalist or collectivist.

MODERN COLLECTIVISM

Just as our economic system is mixed and not purely capitalist, neither are the economic systems of all communist countries purely collectivist. Pure collectivism involves setting exact rates of growth, exact control of investment, exact prices and wages, and so on.

Some forms of collectivism now recognize how hard it is to set exact prices and objectives through strict central planning. Increasingly, they settle for approximations.

In some collectivist countries there is a degree of self-management of business firms. Managers are expected to earn a profit. They, not the government, determine what consumer goods will be produced. Competition among firms in these nations is a fact of economic life. Wage rates, and even the prices of the goods the firms sell, are essentially determined in the market. The firms pay taxes, and part of their profits are distributed to the workers and managers. Since the consumers buy those goods and services they desire, firms have an incentive to produce them efficiently. This involves making decisions about how the factors of production will be combined and employed. Those firms that anticipate consumer demand for various products and services and offer them for sale are the ones that profit most.

There are, of course, still examples of strict collectivism, such as that found in the People's Republic of China, where economic freedom is severely limited. In the Soviet Union itself, the degree of freedom is much smaller than it is in some of the satellite countries (Romania, Hungary, Czechoslovakia) or the "independent" communist nation of Yugoslavia. (See Figure 1.5.)

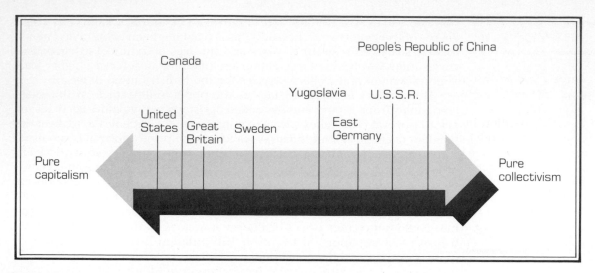

Figure 1.5
Some socioeconomic systems in the world today

MODERN CAPITALISM

The socioeconomic systems of some Western European nations are not easy to categorize as capitalist or collectivist. These systems might be lumped under the heading of "democratic socialism." Through peaceful, democratic means these nations have adopted some rather severe restrictions of the classic capitalist freedoms. In many cases, the practice of medicine and ownership of certain basic industries are in the hands of the government. Other economic activities are highly regulated by government. Advertising is restricted and consumption of goods is sometimes controlled by rationing. Taxation is, in many of these nations, much heavier than it is in Canada.

Even the United States is far from pure capitalism. Public utilities such as telephone and power companies are strictly regulated. Today many forms of regulation and taxation further distinguish the United States from the capitalist ideal. Progressive income taxes, laws against price discrimination, the Small Business Administration (through which the federal government gives aid to small firms), and many other governmental activities represent a retreat (or an advance?) from pure capitalism.

THE POSTINDUSTRIAL SERVICES ECONOMY

During the 1950s and 1960s, the North American economy began undergoing a basic change from an industrial economy based on the manufacture of tangible products to a *postindustrial economy* based on the creation of *intangible services*. The effects of this change still are being felt in the Canadian economy.

AUTHORS' COMMENTARY

Improving Productivity in the Postindustrial Services Economy

A lot of attention has been paid recently to increasing the productivity of businesses. For example, many industries now use computerized robots on the assembly line.

However, in our postindustrial services economy, such basic manufacturing activities actually account for a declining proportion of the GNP. So, if we are to increase the over-all productivity of our labour force, we will have to focus more attention on nonmanufacturing operations.

Some progress has been made in office automation. Desk-top word and data processing terminals and electronic mail systems are being used increasingly by clerical workers. Beyond that, we can expect greater focus on improving the productivity of executives and professionals like attorneys, accountants, and physicians through office automation.

The tremendous growth of our economy during the 1950s and 1960s contributed to record high levels of Disposable Personal Income, and consumers began buying huge amounts of intangible services. Recreation, entertainment, travel, and other service industries began growing faster than many of our manufacturing and research industries. One of the most dramatic examples of this growth in service industries is the spread of restaurants such as The Keg and Mothers Pizza.

We will discuss the implications of this shift from an industrial to a postindustrial services economy at several places in this book.

WHAT DO YOU THINK?

Are Our Capitalist Freedoms Declining?

According to some people, many of the characteristics of capitalism were more evident during our early history than they are now. Individualism and individual self-determination have taken a back seat to the collective well-being of society. The right of private property has diminished due to government programs such as the Foreign Investment Review Act. The profit incentive has been dealt a heavy blow by progressive income taxes and, from time to time, governmentally enforced price and wage controls. The government does not, it is argued, play a limited role in the economy.

Some believe that the only characteristic of capitalism that has been strengthened is consumer sovereignty. Our governments are more committed to protecting the consumer in the marketplace. But this has been accomplished at the expense of some of the other freedoms.

On the other hand, some people argue that these freedoms were never really characteristic of our mixed economic system. Are capitalist freedoms declining in Canada? WHAT DO YOU THINK?

CAREER PROFILE

MY NAME IS MICHAEL BURNS, AND I AM AN executive. Unlike some others I am the chief executive of a number of companies. Adjectives I use to describe my executive role include temporary; intermittent; and interim executive. I DO THINGS!

In addition to being on the board of directors of seventeen organizations in the last year, I was the chief executive of four organizations. These include: Interim General Manager of Expo 86, the 1986 World's Fair in Vancouver; a working director and part-time permanent President of Metro Canada International, a company that sells urban transportation systems; President of Campbell River Land Company, a land development company which is developing single- and multi-family residential property; and President of Inland Fibre Specialties Ltd., a company that makes fibreglass items such as water slides, satellite receiving dishes, and boats.

I have a significant equity position in the last two companies and intend to have it grow significantly in the coming years. The other two organizations generate the cash flow to support current expenses.

In addition, I am very active in British Columbia provincial politics in an operating

role as the coordinator of fund raising for the Social Credit party.

My job in all the organizations I run (business, nonprofit, and political) is simply stated

SUMMARY AND LOOK AHEAD

Economic systems help us to satisfy our unlimited wants with our limited resources. Because our wants are so varied and because our resources, in many instances, have become more scarce, the economic problem today is more complex than it was in the past.

Several elementary concepts (utility, value, specialization, exchange, standard of living, diminishing marginal utility, and the factors of production) were introduced. These concepts are relevant in any type of economic system.

The major ideas underlying a capitalist private-enterprise system are individualism, private property, profit incentive, consumer power, freedom to compete, occupational freedom, freedom of contract, and limited role of government.

as doing what is necessary to see that they operate as they should to obtain desired results. I have full responsibility and accountability for the organizations I run. I operate only at their top levels, concentrating upon strategic management. My aim is to build competent management teams in all the organizations and delegate operating responsibility to them.

Twenty years of experience with IBM in line marketing and executive management positions provide the background training and experience for my current activities. When I left IBM I was Vice-President for Western Canada. A reluctance to move my family again after nine career moves was important in my decision to leave the large corporate environment for my current entrepreneurial role.

My current second career is only available to me because of a successful first career. Only some large company executives are able to make the conversion to successful entrepreneurial activity. A key to success in my current activities has been an ability to build many of the organizational and management support resources for smaller companies that were available from a large company like IBM.

I have found great personal satisfaction with both my "careers." The only major problem I have now is organizing the time to do all the things I am involved with. There are many rewards in my current activities. They include earnings, a great variety of activities and experiences, interesting people and events, and an immense degree of personal satisfaction. For example, I felt great satisfaction on the day of the Expo 86 flag-raising ceremony, after having been associated with that project from its inception.

Another point I would like to emphasize is how important I feel it is to put something back into our Canadian society which presents such great opportunities for us all. This is a primary reason for my involvement in political activity. It also motivates my involvement on a hospital board, the Symphony board, and the Canadian Council of Christians and Jews. I feel there is a responsibility for talented people to get more involved in public activities. Too many public institutions are run by the willing rather than by the most able. My role in public agencies involves use of the same skills I employ to operate my business organization.

In summary, my career has been built upon development of skills over a period of years. It has been important to learn in detail, and strive for excellence in each job I have undertaken at each stage of my career. This cumulative training and experience is the base which allows me to undertake the many interesting activities that I am currently engaged in.

The type of economic system most unlike the capitalist system is the collectivist system. In this type of system, private property and the other institutions and ideas of the private-enterprise system are largely absent. Central planning by government replaces individual freedoms and initiative.

Most economic systems in the world today fall somewhere between the two extremes of pure capitalism and pure collectivism. In Canada we have a "mixed" economic system.

In the next chapter we will see how people use the freedoms accorded them under our economic system to form business firms. We will discuss the business firm and its role in our market economy. We will also examine the market forces of supply and demand and how they determine market prices. ∎

1. Has the economic problem become more complex in modern times than it was in earlier times? Explain.
2. Discuss the processes of specialization and exchange and their relationship to the economic problem.
3. Distinguish between needs and wants.
4. Should comparisons of the standards of living in different countries be based on per capita GNP? Explain?
5. List and define the factors of production.
6. What is the basic purpose of (a) a capitalist economic system and (b) a collectivist economic system?
7. List and discuss the major features of capitalism.
8. In what ways does pure capitalism differ from pure collectivism?
9. In what ways has our Canadian economic system changed over the last century?
10. Capital formation is necessary for fuller economic development. How does it occur in the absence of private property and profit incentive?
11. What is the basic motivation for business firms to produce want-satisfying products and services for consumers?
12. How do you as an individual cope with the economic problem?
13. Should future generations of people be considered when we cope with the economic problem?
14. Individual initiative is important in our system. What factors determine a person's initiative?
15. Does consumer power guarantee that consumer welfare is maximized?
16. One of the features of capitalism is freedom to compete. When should limitations be placed on this freedom? In Canada, do we need more limitations on the freedom to compete than there are at present?
17. What is profit? What determines how much profit a business firm will make?

INCIDENTS

Dome Petroleum Ltd.'s Federal Bail-Out

Dome Petroleum Ltd. is Canada's largest oil company with approximately $10 billion in assets; but it also has 7.3 billion in debts.

In the fall of 1982 the federal government helped Dome avoid bankruptcy by negotiating a deal which could eventually allow Ottawa and the banks to purchase up to $1 billion in debentures convertible to Dome stock at $2.50 per share. If fully exercised, two-thirds ownership and control of Dome would transfer to these banks and the federal government from the original investors.

Questions:
1. Should the federal government interfere with firms that are having trouble staying in business?
2. Why do you think the federal government decided to bail out Dome?

3. Were the federal government's actions fair to the original shareholders?
4. Would this happen in a purely capitalistic economic system? Explain.

Jane Patterson

Jane Patterson, a first-year student in business administration at a community college, was recently asked by a friend why she chose business as her course of study. This friend, Charles Smith, was also a student, majoring in political science.

Actually, Charles's question was preceded by a friendly debate with Jane. It seems that Charles is really down on "the system." He told Jane that there is no excuse for our system's failure to solve all our social problems. "Canada is one of the richest nations in the world, but still diseases remain unconquered, pollution is a problem, poverty remains in the midst of plenty, and our country even threatens to break up."

Questions:
1. Do you think Charles's negative sentiments about "the system" are justified? Why or why not?
2. Suppose you were Jane. How would you answer Charles's question as to why you are studying business?

Anthony B. Mark

Anthony B. Mark, a syndicated columnist whose column appears in newspapers across Canada, has for years been a leading social critic of contemporary life in North America. On one of his numerous speaking engagements Mr. Mark commented that too many of our wants are frivolous and result in a misallocation of our resources. Millions and millions of dollars are spent every year by Canadians buying the latest gadgets, such as new automobiles, when the previous year's models are still capable of transporting people. Even home appliances, such as dishwashers, refrigerators, and washing machines, now go through annual model changes in an attempt to induce the buying public to become dissatisfied with older models which still perform the job they were bought to perform. Millions of dollars are spent every year by men and women on cosmetics which, in some cases, are actually dangerous to their health.

Mr. Mark believes that our wants have to be channelled in new directions. "As our resources become increasingly scarce, it is idiotic to waste what remains on frivolous forms of consumption."

Questions:
1. How do you think Mr. Mark would define "frivolous wants"?

2. Do you think that the "frivolous wants" to which he refers are learned wants? How do we learn them?
3. How do you think Mr. Mark would have us go about "channelling our wants in new directions"? What "directions" do you think he has in mind?

CASE STUDY

AUTOMOBILE INSURANCE IN CANADA

IN CANADA WE HAVE TWO DIFFERENT TRADITIONS FOR MAKING automobile insurance available to the public. In British Columbia, Saskatchewan, Manitoba, and Quebec automobile insurance coverage or parts of automobile insurance coverage are available through government-operated organizations. In Canada's other provinces automobile insurance is offered through the more common private system.

The basic purpose of any system of automobile insurance is to provide coverage against the risk of having an accident and the hazards that can accompany an automobile accident. The basic types of risks against which motorists are protected are bodily injury and property damage. Coverage is available for your own or your family's bodily injury and your own automobile. Third-party coverage protects against bodily injury to another individual, or to damage of another person's vehicle or other property.

In effect, the auto insurance function is performed by insured subjects paying money into a central fund or number of funds; then, when an accident occurs that results in a claim, the money is withdrawn or paid out from the fund. This necessitates a variety of activities. Basically, these activities can be grouped into two different types: those associated with assembling the funds, and those associated with paying out the funds.

One activity associated with assembling funds is deciding upon the type of rating structure that will be used. In other words, will all insured people pay the same rate, or will an attempt be made to have higher-risk individuals pay more money than lower-risk individuals? A distribution function is also necessary. This involves contact between the insuring organization and the public who desires insurance. In a private system this may be called a sales force. Typically, agents are involved in the distribution of the product.

After individuals are contacted and they decide that they desire insurance, it is necessary to underwrite them. This involves making sure that the individual is assigned to the correct rating group. When these functions have all been performed correctly the individual will pay his or her premium and receive a policy which provides coverage against the specific hazards indicated in the policy. The insurance company, on the other hand, has the money, held in a fund which it will invest in various types of securities.

The other basic activity involves paying out money. When a subject has an accident covered by his or her policy, he or she will make a claim against the insurance company. When an accident occurs, the claims department will assess the amount of damage and determine how much money will be paid to the various parties involved, based upon the type of coverage that was held. Claims settlement requires that a certain amount of money be taken out of the fund to pay the injured subject's insured claim. The more money an insurance organization pays out in settlement of claims, the less money it has remaining in its fund to invest and to meet operating expenses.

There is a considerable amount of debate over which automobile insurance system is more appropriate—public or private.

Advocates of the public automobile insurance system argue that it is superior because of one or more of the following advantages they say are associated with it:

1. It is easier to be certain that all motorists are covered. This eliminates problems associated with having an accident with someone who does not carry insurance.
2. With public insurance it is easier to standardize insurance coverage and rates throughout a province.
3. Public insurance is a monopoly system. It is therefore easier to subsidize and thereby lower the cost for high-risk drivers, like young beginning drivers, at the expense of lower-risk older drivers.
4. There are potential economies of scale associated with public insurance. These are in the form of lower costs for distribution of the product, administration of claims settlements, and general administration of the firm.
5. It is stated that it is much easier to centralize claims services. You can have drive-in claims centers because, by virtue of being the only insurer in a jurisdiction, you can insist that motorists come to your claim center in order to file a claim and have their automobile damage assessed.
6. Some people claim that it is possible to control investment of the fund and direct it to more local or public investments with a public automobile insurance company.
7. Overall, the claim is that public auto insurance is less expensive than private automobile insurance because of the economies of scale associated with operating a monopoly operation such as this.

On the other hand, there are strong proponents of the argument that private automobile insurance is a more desirable system than public automobile insurance. Their argument includes:

1. Private companies are more efficient than a government-sponsored organization. The private companies keep their costs lower than public companies.
2. Different private companies will offer different types of insurance policy features. This gives insured motorists a much greater variety of coverages from which to choose. Customers will be able to configure whatever insurance package they themselves would like to have.

3. There is an argument that competition among insurance companies is a very healthy situation. This ensures that the latest techniques and technologies will be applied to the insurance business and that costs will be much more subject to control.
4. An argument against public insurance companies and for private companies is that governments can have a great deal of difficulty in controlling and overseeing the operation of a monopoly public company.
5. The argument has been made that because they are guaranteed by the government, public insurance companies do not have to abide by the same rules and regulations regarding reserves that private companies do. Therefore, they are being subsidized by the government.
6. The argument is made that there is a much better insurance service when there is an active sales agent network. This will ensure that more attention is paid on an individual basis to customers and that insured motorists get better service.
7. The argument is made that many of the economies of scale such as drive-in claim centers can be offered by private companies as well as by public companies.

A choice between public and private insurance is a choice between more and less government involvement in our economic system.

Questions:
1. What is your view of this situation?
2. Should there be more automobile insurance offered by government-owned companies, or should it be offered exclusively by the private sector? ∎

1. Explain what a mixed market economy is and how it works.
2. Define the "law of demand" and the "law of supply."
3. Discuss the factors that influence the overall levels of supply and demand.
4. Explain how the concepts of supply, demand, and price influence the allocation of resources for production of goods and services in a free-market economy.
5. Draw supply and demand curves.
6. Explain the significance of the intersection of a supply and a demand curve on a graph.
7. Discuss reasons why governments become involved in decisions about what goods and services to produce.
8. Discuss how governments become involved in decisions about how to produce goods and services.
9. Discuss the reasons why people form business firms.
10. Define profit and give examples of ways firms try to increase their profits.
11. Discuss the role of top management of a business firm.
12. Understand the concept of business strategy.
13. Differentiate between strategy formulation and strategy implementation.
14. Explain why business owners assume risk.

KEY CONCEPTS

In reading the chapter, look for and understand these terms:

market economy	supply curve
price	business firm
demand	profit
law of demand	opportunity
discretionary income	risk
real income	business policy
supply	strategy
law of supply	strategy formulation
demand curve	implementation of strategy

IN OUR ECONOMY, BUSINESS FIRMS seek to identify market opportunity and to use their resources and capabilities to profit from it. Apple Computer, Inc., the personal computer company founded in 1975, is a good example. Steven Jobs and Stephen Wozniak, the entrepreneurs who started the company, recognized opportunity in the computer field, despite the fact that the industry was dominated by giants like IBM. Jobs and Wozniak started the personal computer industry.

Market opportunity for a business firm arises from the environment of that firm. It can be the result of a variety of factors. In this chapter we discuss some of the non-price environmental factors that increase demand, thereby creating business opportunities. We will see how business firms must organize their resources in order to take advantage of such opportunities. We will then discuss the nature of business firms and their motivation, as well as the strategic decision processes which match

CHAPTER TWO

The Market Economy and the Business Firm

organizational capability to market opportunity.

The ability to recognize market opportunity is vitally important for success in business. Businesspeople must always be alert to it. Consider, for example, how changes in our lifestyles can create problems and opportunities for business. Colour TV was a growth industry during much of the 1960s, but its growth slowed toward the end of the decade. Most people who wanted and could afford a colour TV had already bought one and were spending their "entertainment dollars" away from home—dining out, going to theatres, travelling, and so on.

Recently, environmental factors such as high inflation, advances in technology, and higher gasoline prices are causing many people to rely on in-home entertainment. This change did not go unnoticed. Atari, First Choice, and marketers of video cassette recorders and video disc players recognized a market opportunity in our changing lifestyle.

BECAUSE OUR RESOURCES ARE LIMITED, WE MUST CHOOSE HOW THEY will be used. Under our economic system, independent decisions made by consumers and producers, guided by the price system, determine what will and what will not be produced.

Business firms are the basic building blocks for the production of goods and services. Most economic activity in our system is chanelled through business firms, which gather and organize resources for production. They do so in the hope of making a profit by supplying products that their present and potential customers want. Doing so, however, requires that they be willing to assume the risk of going into business. Let's begin with a look at how our market economy works.

THE MIXED MARKET ECONOMY

Although, as we indicated in Chapter 1, ours is a "limited" market economy, market forces are extremely important to us, both within Canada and internationally as we trade with other countries. Therefore, a sound understanding of the market and the market forces of supply and demand is essential to any prospective businessperson.

The term *market* has many meanings. To some people it might mean the place where they shop for groceries. To others it might mean the stock market. To a manufacturer of women's dresses it might mean the current level of demand for dresses.

In this chapter we will think of a market as a set of economic forces (supply and demand) which together form a price. Supply forces tend to bring goods and services into production. Demand forces tend to result in consumption of those goods and services. Supply and demand interact to form a price.

market economy

A market economy is an economic system in which prices determine how resources will be allocated and how the goods and services produced will be distributed. Markets exist to form prices.

Prices

Prices induce or limit production and consumption. Were it not for the price consumers have to pay to get things, they could consume as much as they want. Since consumers have limited income and limited buying power, however, they must limit the amount they buy. The supplier of an item, on the other hand, would have no incentive to supply it without being paid for it. Price, therefore, must be at a level such that some producers are willing to produce goods and services for sale and some consumers are willing to buy them for consumption.

In a very simple economy, prices as we know them would not exist. Mr. Green might decide to trade his apples for the oranges produced by Mr. Smith. The two traders would agree on a rate of exchange of apples for oranges. This simple type of trading is called *barter.* Goods and services are exchanged directly for other goods and services. Barter still exists and has increased in recent years. Individuals sometimes barter goods and services in order to avoid the need for cash transactions.

price

Nevertheless, money facilitates or simplifies exchange by serving as a medium of exchange; it is the common measure of value for apples and oranges and thousands of other goods and services. **Price, therefore, is the quantity of money (or other goods and services) that is paid in exchange for something else.**

All economic systems must have a way of determining

- which goods and services will be produced
- how much of each will be produced
- the methods of producing them
- how they will be divided among the people

In a market economy these decisions are made through a pricing process in markets. The prices of different goods and services determine how resources will be allocated among alternative ends. Those prices also determine the kinds of goods and services that will be produced, their quantities, and the amounts that are made available to customers. A market economy, therefore, also can be called a *price system.* To understand how all this works, let's study the forces of demand and supply.

Demand

As we have seen, the basic human needs are for food, clothing, and shelter. We express these needs when we demand to buy a can of Sun Ripe apple juice, a red coat, or a new house.

Because your income is limited, you must choose which wants you will try to satisfy. Price helps you choose. By comparing prices of different things, you decide how much of item A must be given up to get one unit of item B. Price is the yardstick for comparisons. It is a major guide to production and consumption decisions.

In a modern economy new wants are always appearing and new goods and services are always being offered to satisfy those wants. Suppliers of these goods and services try to get consumers to spend money on them. In this way both the consumer's desire for want satisfaction and the supplier's desire for profit are supposed to be satisfied.

In business demand means much more than desire on the part of a would-be buyer. For example, perhaps everyone in your class would like to own a new Corvette. But General Motors will not rush into the production of Corvettes to satisfy the desire of you and your classmates, because GM is concerned with demand in the economic sense, not desire by itself.

demand

Demand for a good or a service exists when there are people who

- **desire the good or service**
- **have the buying power to purchase it**
- **are willing to part with some buying power in order to buy it**

Each of these requirements must be met in order for an effective demand (or market) for a good or a service to exist.

As we will see in the marketing chapters later on, firms do what they can to increase the demand for their goods and services. They use advertising to build the desire and willingness to spend. They often offer credit to increase consumer buying power.

For most products a greater number of units are demanded at a lower price than at a higher price. One of the reasons for this is the principle of diminishing marginal utility, mentioned in Chapter 1. A third pair of boots, for example, gives you less additional satisfaction than the first pair did. You may be better off with three pairs of boots than with only one, but you probably are not three times better off. As additional units lose something (marginal utility, or usefulness), you are willing to pay less and less to get them. Another reason is that your buying power is limited. **The inverse**

law of demand

relationship between price and quantity demanded is the "law of demand"—as price goes up, the quantity demanded goes down.

We can talk about demand from different points of view. The overall demand for all goods and services in an economy is called the *aggregate demand.* We can also refer to the total demand for a specific product class, such as the demand for cars. Narrowing it further, we could discuss the demand for a specific brand, such as Chevrolet Corvettes. An especially important distinction is *industry* and *firm demand.* The demand for cars is an example of industry demand, and the demand for GM cars is an example of firm demand.

The concept of demand, however, involves more than a relationship between quantity and price. Among the many non-price factors underlying demand are

- buying power
- willingness to spend
- population changes
- population shifts
- changes in tastes and cultural values
- presence and price of substitute goods and services

We will discuss each of these environmental factors in turn.

Buying Power

As Figure 2.1 shows, buying power comes from

- current income
- accumulated wealth
- credit

Figure 2.1

Current income, credit, and accumulated wealth are the three major sources of buying power

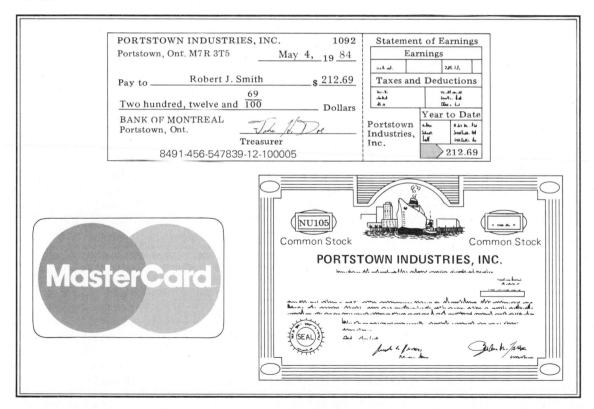

Current income is the major source of buying power for Canadians. Your current income is your salary or wages plus interest on savings accounts, rental income, dividends on stock, and interest on bonds. But you cannot spend it all because you have to pay taxes. Disposable income is your current income minus the taxes you pay. **Discretionary income is what remains of your disposable income after you have bought your necessities.** It is available to spend on "luxuries." **Finally, your real income is your income expressed in terms of buying power; it is your income adjusted for the decline in buying power due to inflation.** Suppose your income doubles over a ten-year period. Unless you can buy twice as much at the end of ten years as you could at the beginning, your real income does not really double.

discretionary income

real income

Table 2.1 shows that the median Canadian family earned an estimated $22,313 before taxes in 1979. (The median is the middle number of a group of numbers ranked from the smallest to the largest.) The corresponding figure in 1971 was $9,347. When we adjust the $22,313 figure for federal income tax and inflation it becomes $10,062 in 1971 dollars. This is disposable income expressed in real terms.

Our federal and provincial income taxes also affect the way income is *distributed* in our country. The income tax takes money from higher-income people and redistributes it, through government spending, to lower-income people. This results in less demand for luxuries and more demand for basic food, clothing, and shelter. Aggregate consumer demand, however, increases because people with lower incomes tend to spend a greater proportion of their income than people with higher incomes. People with higher incomes tend to save a greater proportion of their income.

Accumulated wealth can be liquid or nonliquid. Liquid wealth can be converted quickly into a known amount of cash for making purchases. Money in regular savings accounts is an example. It can be withdrawn easily and quickly to buy or make down payments on major purchases such as homes, cars, and home appliances. Canada Savings Bonds are another example of liquid wealth.

An example of nonliquid wealth is equity in a home, the difference between its current market value and what is owed on the mortgage. You

Table 2.1　Median Family Incomes Before and After Taxes

Year	Median Family Income	Income Taxes Deducted	After-Tax Income	
			Current Dollars	Constant (1971) Dollars
1971	$ 9,347	$1,239	$ 8,108	$ 8,108
1973	11,533	1,550	9,983	8,848
1975	15,065	1,906	13,159	9,470
1977	18,565	2,438	16,127	10,027
1978	20,463	2,676	17,787	10,170
1979	22,313	3,099	19,214	10,062

Source: Statistics Canada, *Income Distribution by Size In Canada,* Cat. 13–207, p. 33; and Statistics Canada, *Income After Tax, Distribution by Size in Canada,* Cat. 13–210, p. 41. Reproduced by permission of the Minister of Supply and Services Canada.

can look at your bank book and determine how much money you have on deposit. But it is much harder to put a dollar value on the equity in a house because its true current market value must be determined. Loan companies, banks, and savings and loan associations often are willing to grant loans to people on the basis of their equity in their homes. This frees this nonliquid wealth for current use.

There are two basic types of credit. *Instalment credit* involves making regular monthly payments (instalments) on credit purchases. It is very important in the purchase of consumer durables such as cars. *Non-instalment credit* involves paying in full for your charge purchases at the end of the credit period, usually thirty days. Both types of credit have expanded greatly in our economy during recent years, especially instalment credit. In fact, ours often is referred to as a credit economy. Without credit, many Canadians would have a much lower standard of living.

Willingness to Spend

How much income and other types of buying power people have affects their ability to buy. But we also have to consider their willingness to buy. In general, consumers are more willing to buy when they have confidence in the economy. When they lack confidence, they tend to spend less and to save more.

During recent years, however, this general pattern has not always held true, and periods of low consumer confidence have been accompanied by high levels of consumer spending. Part of the explanation for this is the very high rate of inflation. Apparently when consumers expect inflation to continue, they reason that tomorrow's prices will be even higher than today's. This is called *inflationary psychology.* Since the buying power of the dollar declines, saving money loses much of its appeal, and many consumers prefer to buy products they hope will increase in value such as jewelry, furs, silverware, antiques, and fine china. They look upon these purchases as investments.

On the other hand, the onset of a recession is often accompanied by a decline in consumer willingness to spend. Consumers postpone some purchases, particularly purchases of durable goods, in the hope that prices will come down. This contributes to lengthening the recession because consumer spending accounts for two-thirds of our Gross National Product.

Population Changes

Population changes also affect demand. When the population increases, sales of essential goods and services tend to increase. A declining birthrate, on the other hand, means a decline in the demand for baby food. Changes in the age distribution of the population also affect demand. For example, the proportion of children and teenagers in our population will decline during the coming decades. This means a decline in demand for child-oriented toys and elementary and secondary education. A decline in the number of teenagers could mean declining sales of soft drinks because teenagers are their biggest consumers.

The proportion of people sixty-five years and older will increase. This means increased demand for digestive aids, decaffeinated coffee, and bran

AUTHORS' COMMENTARY

Price Changes and Our Lifestyles

Changes in the prices of goods and services can affect our lifestyles and the way firms do business. Consider the housing industry. During much of the 1960s and 1970s, inflation and fixed interest rates on long-term mortgages helped make the purchase of a new home a good investment.

Between 1971 and 1981 the median price of newly constructed one-family homes rose over 150 percent. Mortgage interest rates reached record high levels in 1981. A typical $60,000 mortgage at 18 percent interest meant the homebuyer had a monthly interest charge of $900 before any principal repayment. New housing starts fell to the lowest level in years.

Lenders were developing new financing plans to help would-be homebuyers. Instead of a fixed interest rate, many started offering variable interest rate mortgages. Thus, if infla-

tion and high interest rates came down, the mortgage payment the homebuyer paid would be reduced.

Homebuilders also searched for new ways to cut building costs. Assembly-line construction, of mobile homes, for example, replaced much on-site construction. Meanwhile, zoning officials in many communities were having to rethink their minimum square-footage requirements because many of the newer homes were much smaller than the typical homes of past years.

The coming of age of the baby boom generation — those born between 1946 and 1964 — was expected to contribute to a big increase in homebuyers during the 1980s. However, many of these people were unable to buy homes because of the high prices and interest rates. Some people who could afford new housing were buying lower-cost mobile homes instead of conventional homes.

cereals. Perhaps you have noticed that older people are being featured more in commercials and advertisements. By the year 2000 the median age of Canadians is projected to be 35, up from 28 in 1970 and 30 in 1980.

Population Shifts

Population shifts also can affect demand. During recent years there has been some movement of people and industry from eastern Canada to Alberta and British Columbia. Quebec, in particular, has had a net out-migration of population.

Changes in Tastes and Cultural Values

Changes in consumer tastes and cultural values can affect demand as well. Recently, the demand for products like beef, sugar, and tennis racquets has declined. Many people who used to consume large quantities of sugar and beef have reduced their consumption, in part because of reports that those products allegedly contribute to health problems. Tennis has lost some of its popularity while racquetball has gained popularity.

The growing acceptance of a singles lifestyle has increased the demand for goods and services designed for the "singles market." Examples include

Campbell's Soup for One and housemate matching agencies for singles who want to share living space.

The rising divorce rate creates two households in place of one and therefore increases the demand for housing and household appliances. The women's rights movement has increased the demand for child-care centres, business clothing, and convenience foods. We will discuss other changes in our cultural values and how they affect business in Chapter 18.

Presence and Price of Substitutes

Finally, substitute products and services and their prices can affect demand. The demand for dry cleaning, butter, train tickets, tooth powder, and shaving soap declined when new clothing fabrics, margarine, air travel, toothpaste, and electric shavers were introduced. There have been some big shifts in demand for some goods and services in recent years due to shortages of some basic resources and resulting price jumps. The high cost of electricity and natural gas has increased the demand for alternative energy sources.

Supply

supply

The other half of the price system is supply. **The supply of a good or a service results from the effort of producers. The quantity supplied is the number of units of a good or a service that producers will offer for sale at a certain price.**

law of supply

In most cases, more higher-priced units will be offered for sale than lower-priced ones because producers perceive more profit potential. Price and quantity vary in the same direction. **This is the "law of supply"—as price goes up, the quantity supplied goes up.**

Like the concept of demand, the concept of supply involves much more than a relationship between quantity and price. Among the many factors underlying supply are

- the outlook for the economy
- the outlook for the industry
- the firm's objectives
- technological progress
- expected profitability of producing other goods and services
- the nature of competition
- government spending policies and regulations
- other environmental factors

The Outlook for the Economy

The aggregate supply of all goods and services is affected by many of the same things that affect overall demand. For example, producers who expect consumer buying power to increase may step up production in order to satisfy the expected increase in demand. When economic forecasters predict good times ahead, producers are optimistic and are willing to produce in anticipation of orders from customers.

POINT OF VIEW

Demand versus Supply Management

Between the 1930s and 1980 the most popular view of the workings of an economic system was based on Keynesian economics. According to the late British economist, John Maynard Keynes, the key to managing an economic system is to manage demand. The basic idea is that an economy can be managed by adjusting the demand side of the supply-and-demand equation. Thus, to reduce inflation, Keynesians favour tax hikes in order to reduce demand (consumer spending). To reduce unemployment, Keynesians favour tax cuts to increase demand (consumer spending).

During the early 1970s, however, an economic condition known as stagflation existed. Both inflation and unemployment were simultaneously at unacceptably high rates and some economists started talking about *supply-side economics.* The basic idea is that an economy can be managed by adjusting the supply side of the supply-and-demand equation. Tax cuts would leave consumers with more money to spend and business people with more money to invest. Thus the economy would expand, employment would increase, supply would increase, demand would adjust to supply, and prices would stabilize. The election of President Reagan in the United States brought supply-side economics to the forefront. The so-called "Reaganomics" has both strong supporters and strong detractors.

Part of the theory of supply-side economics involves the widely discussed Laffer curve, named for its developer, Professor Arthur B.

Laffer. The basic idea that the curve purports to show is that a lower tax rate can generate as much tax revenue or more tax revenue than a higher rate.

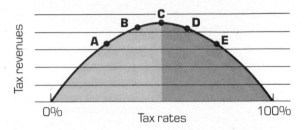

The Laffer curve portrays the presumed relationship between tax rates and tax revenues. Revenues are zero, of course, when the tax rate is zero. But they are also zero when tax rates rise to 100 percent; the tax base depends upon production and income, and at a 100 percent tax rate there would be no incentive to produce. Revenues are maximized at some intermediate point, labeled "C" in the diagram. Beyond that point, in the darker shaded zone, rising taxes discourage effort to such an extent that revenues fall—the higher rates are more than offset by reduced output. The curve is hypothetical, and nobody knows either its shape or the location of point C. These will vary with the type of tax; it is not likely either that the true curve is symmetrical or that the point of maximum revenue will lie at a tax rate halfway between 0 percent and 100 percent.

(*Source: The Chase Economic Observer,* The Chase Manhattan Bank, N.A., March/April 1981, p. 8.)

The Outlook for the Industry

The outlook for a particular industry affects supply in that industry. For example, if November and December car sales indicate that consumers are not in a buying mood, car makers will cut back on production. They will not produce as many units as they would have if the buying response were greater. When car makers cut back on production, they cut back on their orders for steel and the many other products that are used to make cars. This can affect the production plans of firms like INCO Ltd. that produce nickel, which is used in steel production.

The Firm's Objectives

A firm's objectives also affect how much it is willing to supply. A firm's market share is its percentage of total sales. Some firms have an objective of increasing their market share by producing and selling in large volumes, often at prices that are lower than those charged by their competitors. Other firms are more concerned with building an image by providing high-quality products. They may offer fewer units for sale in order to help build a reputation for "quality rather than quantity."

Technological Progress

Technological progress also affects supply. From both a cost and a quality standpoint, colour TVs can be made more efficiently today than fifteen years ago. The same is true for computers, pocket calculators, and photocopying machines. This induces suppliers to supply more.

Expected Profitability of Producing Other Products and Services

The supply of a product will decrease when a firm thinks it can make more profit by shifting its resources to another product. This is especially true when a firm can make the switch easily. General Electric and General Motors stopped making many types of small home appliances because they believed they could profit more by making other products. In recent years Xerox has re-entered the office of the future market with products such as personal computers.

The Nature of Competition

The nature of the competition in an industry also affects supply. When only three or four firms produce essentially the same product, the firms tend to recognize their interdependence. They know if they flood the market, all of them could end up with less profit because price will tend to fall due to excess supply.

Government Spending Policies and Regulations

Government spending policies and regulations also can stimulate or depress the supplies of some products and services. Tax incentives in the 1970s induced oil companies to search harder for new oil reserves; the National Energy Policy reduced petroleum exploration. Many home insulation producers expanded their production capacity when government programs provided rebates for homeowners who added insulation to their houses.

Other Environmental Factors

There are other environmental factors that can affect supply. Mounting product liability risk, for example, has led some drug manufacturers to stop

Table 2.2 Price and Quantity Supplied

Price (cents per unit)	Quantity supplied (units)
6	100
28	200
50	300
67	400
89	500
As price increases . . .	. . . quantity supplied increases

producing certain types of live virus for diseases like measles and mumps. The cost of product liability insurance is high and, in some cases, potential suppliers of high-risk products prefer not to offer them for sale.

THE DETERMINATION OF MARKET PRICES

To see how supply and demand determine prices, let us study the supply and demand for plastic rulers. Table 2.2 shows the relationship between price and quantity supplied. Table 2.3 shows the relationship between price and quantity demanded. Putting the law of supply and the law of demand into graphical form gives us Figure 2.2.

The demand curve (D) shows how many units are demanded at various
demand curve   prices. **A demand curve is a line that shows the number of units that will be demanded (bought) at each price at a given point in time. Fewer units are demanded at higher prices than at lower prices.**

The supply curve (S) shows how many units are supplied at various
supply curve   prices. **A supply curve is a line that shows the number of units that will be supplied (offered for sale) at each price at a given point in time. Fewer units are supplied at lower prices than at higher prices.**

The supply and demand curves in Figure 2.2 cross at a price of 50 cents per unit. Only at this price is the quantity suppliers are willing to offer exactly equal to the quantity buyers are willing to buy. At higher prices, suppliers would be willing to supply more units than buyers would be

Table 2.3 Price and Quantity Demanded

Price (cents per unit)	Quantity demanded (units)
75	100
62	200
50	300
37	400
25	500
As price decreases . . .	. . . quantity demanded increases

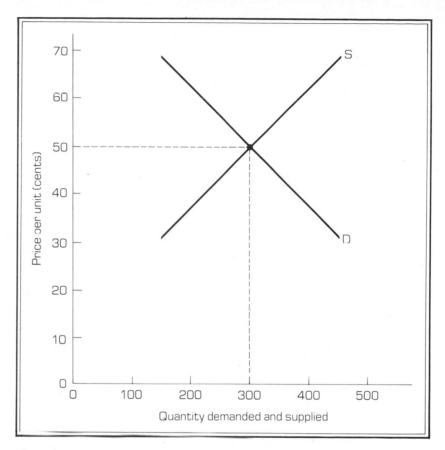

Figure 2.2
Determination of market price

willing to buy. At lower prices, buyers would be willing to buy more units than suppliers would be willing to supply.

At any rate, Figure 2.2 gives us a basic insight into the nature of price. Whether we are talking about the price we pay for hamburgers or cars, the price we get for our labour (wage), or the price we pay to borrow money (interest), the forces of supply and demand are at work. For some items, for example, primary products such as grains and minerals, the market forces of supply and demand are the primary determinants of price. Even in instances such as public utility price regulation, where prices are administered, the concepts of supply and demand underlie the final decisions made.

Figure 2.3 shows shifts in the demand and supply curves. The shifts are due to changes in the underlying forces of supply and demand. The shift from D_0 to D_1 means that, at any given price, demand is greater than it was before the shift. A firm advertises its product in the hope that it will shift its

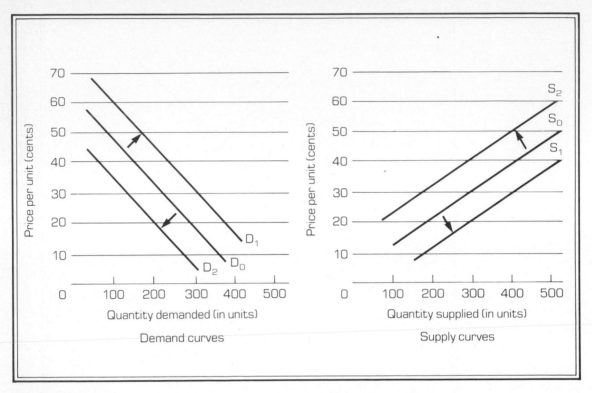

Figure 2.3
Shifts in demand and supply curves

demand curve up and to the right. More units are demanded at any given price.

The shift from D_0 to D_2 means that, at any given price, demand is smaller than it was before the shift. One real example is men's hats. Over the years, the demand for men's hats has shifted down and to the left. Fewer units are demanded at any given price.

The shift from S_0 to S_1 means that, at any given price, supply is greater than it was before the shift. More units are supplied at any given price. The shift from S_0 to S_2 means that, at any given price, supply is smaller than it was before the shift. Fewer units are supplied at any given price.

Table 2.4 explains several concepts of supply and demand.

However, supply and demand are not always the only factors influencing the establishment of prices. One example of such a situation is rail freight rates for grain. For years the Crow's Nest rates established in federal legislation kept the returns to Canada's railway companies for handling grain at a level below what would be established by supply and demand. This situation will change with changes to the Crow's Nest rates. After the energy crisis, when the world price of oil rose dramatically, Canadian federal and provincial governments followed policies that artificially kept the

Table 2.4 Demand and Supply Concepts

Change in demand. Means that a greater or lesser number of units is bought without changing price. This means a shift in the demand curve. If it shifts up and to the right, a greater number of units is demanded at any given price. If it shifts down and to the left, a lesser number of units is demanded at any given price.

Change in supply. Means that a greater or lesser number of units is supplied without changing price. This means a shift in the supply curve. If it shifts up and to the left, a lesser number of units is supplied at any given price. If it shifts down and to the right, a greater number of units is supplied at any given price.

Change in quantity demanded. Means that a greater or lesser number of units is bought because of a change in price. An increase in quantity demanded means that a greater number of units is bought because the price has been lowered. We are moving down a particular demand curve. A decrease in quantity demanded means that a lesser number of units is bought because the price has been raised. We are moving up a particular demand curve.

Change in quantity supplied. Means that a greater or lesser number of units is supplied because of a change in price. An increase in quantity supplied means that a greater number of units is supplied because the price has been raised. We are moving up a particular supply curve. A decrease in quantity supplied means that a lesser number of units is supplied because the price has been lowered. We are moving down a particular supply curve.

price of oil in this country below the world level. The intention was to bring the Canadian oil price up to the world level gradually, rather than allow it to move up all at once with the resulting pressures on industrial and personal customers.

It is also argued that large companies, large unions, and some large marketing boards have the power to set prices independently of the forces of supply and demand. The OPEC cartel is an example of a group that attempted, with some success, to control the world price of a commodity.

Resource Allocation

In a strictly free-market economy resources are allocated to the production of certain goods and services by the price system. For example, if the market price of a product is high in relation to the cost of producing it, as determined by the prices of inputs, a substantial profit can be made on it. This will motivate people to allocate resources to the production of this product. An example is the number of companies that allocated resources to the production of personal computers when their profit potential initially became known. Another example is the increased investment in home video stores in response to growing demand for these products in the 1980s.

The price system in a free-market economy also influences the way the various factors of production are combined. For example, if the cost of producing an item can be reduced by substituting machinery (a capital input) for labour, this action will be taken. In this sense the price system, which establishes the prices of the factors of production, would determine how goods and services are to be produced. Chapters 9 and 18 contain further discussion of the various types of market structures which can

WHAT DO YOU THINK?

Government Economic Decision Making

In June, 1978, the Cabinet of Canada's federal government was debating a $200 million proposal for 4,000 new (grain) hopper cars and rehabilitation of 5,000 grain cars. This decision was to be made by the government rather than the railway companies (Canadian National and Canadian Pacific) because, as a company spokesman said, "the government controls the purse strings" in determining what the railways can charge for moving grain. "And it's up to it to determine what happens to the grain fleet."

Another railway company spokesman said the company isn't "making a nickel moving grain now so it just isn't logical that it would put money into grain car repairs." Another spokesman said that his company, although continuing to make minor repairs to grain cars, hadn't undertaken major repairs of grain cars for at least two years because there's no money to be made in moving grain.

Officials of both CN and CP had indicated that their companies would be willing to undertake grain car repair programs almost immediately if the government agreed to underwrite the cost of repairs.

The issue was heightened because there had been recent criticism of the rail companies by grain companies. The grain companies had questioned the railways about withholding cars when all available resources are needed to move export grain to waiting ships at Thunder Bay and Vancouver.

WHAT DO YOU THINK? Should the federal government invest this money? Should the government be involved in making this type of decision or should it be left to the market?

exist. For example, oligopoly and monopoly markets are discussed in addition to perfect competition.

Many decisions about what goods and services to produce and how to produce them are made after consideration of social, ecological, and/or political factors as well as economic ones. The Canadian Broadcasting Corporation is an example of a service that would not be offered if the only consideration were economic. The corporation annually records significant deficits. A government decision has been made that the service offered by the corporation is valuable to Canadians for social reasons.

Actions like tax incentives and the formulation of regulations also influence the manner in which resources are combined to produce goods and services. These actions are taken by the federal, provincial, and municipal governments.

THE BUSINESS FIRM

business firm

Business firms play an integral role in our economic system. **A business firm is an entity (thing) which seeks to make a profit by gathering and allocating productive resources to satisfy demand.** Both public (government) and private organizations can be defined as business firms. Most private organizations, with the exception of those that are specifically nonprofit, are business firms. Government organizations which are intended to be self-supporting (i.e., make a profit or break even) also qualify as business firms. This means that firms such as Air Canada, Canadian National Railways, The Saskatchewan Government Insurance Office, and provincially owned telephone and hydro-utilities will be viewed as business firms even though they are government-owned.

On the other hand, the Canadian Broadcasting Corporation, which is not viewed as self-supporting, is not a business firm. Services offered to the public that are not intended to break even are public services. In addition to the CBC illustration above, public education (elementary, secondary, and post-secondary), police and fire services, hospitals, garbage collection, roads, parks, the Mint, the postal service, and so on are examples of public services. Many people are employed by organizations offering public services, and they account for a major share of governments' budgets and of Gross National Expenditure. Many of the concepts of accounting, personnel, labour relations, production, finance, and marketing are as applicable to public services as they are to business firms. Also, there is considerable scope for innovation and improvement in these services. However, they are not the focus of this text.

The business firm is the basic building block for economic decision making in our system. Through it, resources are organized for production. Land, labour, and capital are gathered and converted into products or services which can be sold. This activity is directed and guided by managers in business firms.

Business activity, regardless of whether the firm conducting it is publicly or privately owned, requires decision making to produce and sell goods and services at a profit. It requires buying as well as selling. Thus, the market plays a role. How resources are used depends mainly on choices made by firms and consumers. Both are primarily guided by market prices. The firm is the key to the market's operation. It guides the flow of resources through the marketplace. The firm is an input-output system. The inputs are productive resources which the firm buys in the market. The outputs are the goods it makes and sells in the market. Both input and output depend on market prices. In some instances, decisions will be guided by social and political considerations in addition to economic ones. (See Figure 2.4.)

Resources and the goods made from them are both scarce. Thus, they command prices. The firm's costs of doing business (converting resources from one form to another) must be less than its returns if it is to earn a profit. To determine how profitable it is, a firm must keep records of its costs and sales. Accounting traces the effects of resource flows on its profits. **Profit is the difference between the cost of inputs and the revenue from outputs.**

profit

It is hard to define some of the terms used in modern business. The following statements, however, summarize some key points:

1. A business firm is an entity (thing) which seeks to make a profit by gathering and allocating productive resources to satisfy demand.
2. Most economic activity in our system is channelled through

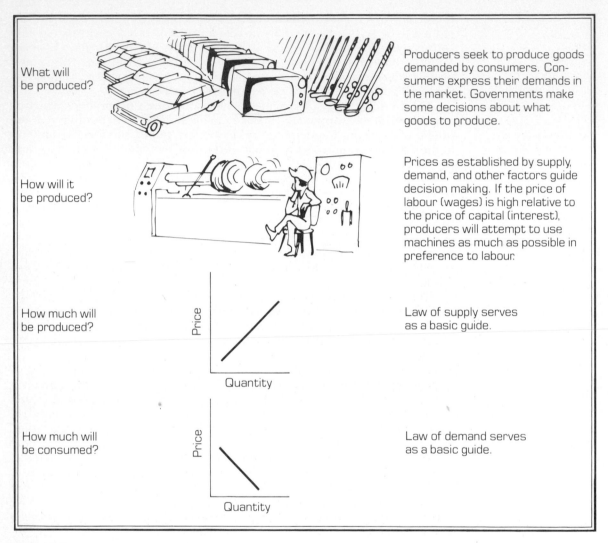

What will be produced?

Producers seek to produce goods demanded by consumers. Consumers express their demands in the market. Governments make some decisions about what goods to produce.

How will it be produced?

Prices as established by supply, demand, and other factors guide decision making. If the price of labour (wages) is high relative to the price of capital (interest), producers will attempt to use machines as much as possible in preference to labour.

How much will be produced?

Law of supply serves as a basic guide.

How much will be consumed?

Law of demand serves as a basic guide.

Figure 2.4
Economic decision making by business firms is guided primarily by price

privately owned business firms, although some is conducted by publicly owned firms.

3. Business activity involves gathering and allocating resources to make a profit.
4. Since resources are scarce and choices must be made, business activity requires that costs be recognized.
5. Producer and consumer choices are primarily guided by prices.
6. Most prices are determined by the price system.
7. Business activity requires that demand is present and saleable goods or services can be supplied to satisfy buyers.

Table 2.5 The nature of business activity

Effort	is exerted to exploit	Opportunity
Supply	is created to satisfy	Demand
Most prices	are determined in	Markets
Entrepreneurship	is concerned with	Risk assumption
Risk	is assumed in the hope of	Profit
Profit	involves a recognition of	Costs
Decision making	is necessary because of the	Choice process
Production activity	is primarily guided by the	Price system
Land ⎫ Labour ⎬ Capital ⎭	are made productive through	Entrepreneurship
Factors of production (inputs)	are converted to	Marketable goods and services (outputs)
Marketing activity	is primarily guided by the	Price system
Markets	exist because of	Specialization and exchange

You might find it helpful to study Table 2.5.

The Motivation of the Firm

People form business firms to produce and sell want-satisfying goods and services so that they can make a profit. Profit, however, does not appear until it is earned. In our system there is no guarantee that a firm will make a profit. It is the hope for profit that leads people to start and operate businesses. By providing products and services that satisfy customers, a firm may make a profit. (See Figure 2.5.)

Suppose Tommy Fields, age seven, opens a lemonade stand because he hopes to make a profit. During the first week he sells twenty cups of lemonade at 5 cents per cup. Is his profit for the week $1?

The answer depends on many things. If the cost of sugar, lemons, and cups is 2 cents per cup, Tommy's profit is not $1 but 60 cents—the difference between $1 in revenue and 40 cents in costs (2 cents per cup times 20 cups). If his mother wanted to be paid for the things she supplied him, Tommy would realize that they are scarce resources. His profit is sales revenue minus the cost of doing business.

If revenues are greater than costs, a profit is earned. Profit may be increased by raising prices, lowering costs, or selling more units. But most firms cannot raise prices very much without reducing sales. Most of them try to increase profit by cutting costs and/or increasing the number of units sold.

If a firm's revenues and costs are equal, it earns no profit. It only breaks even. Very few people, however, go into business to break even. This is especially true if there is no "owner's salary" included in the firm's list of expenses. Firms that just break even give their owners no economic return from being in business.

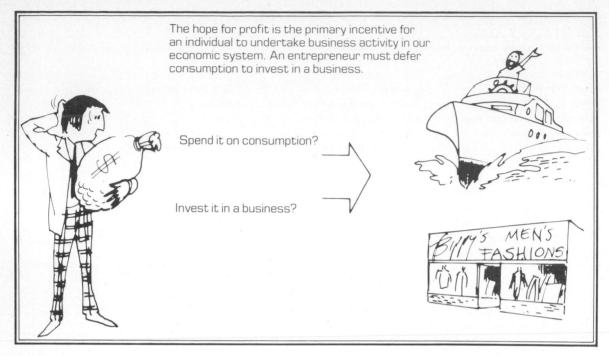

Figure 2.5
Profit

Any after-tax profit earned by a firm is reinvested in the firm and/or is distributed to its owners. For many firms, reinvested profit is the major source of funds to finance their growth. The owners, in effect, are willing to reinvest their profit in the firm rather than taking it out and spending it on consumption.

WHAT DO YOU THINK?

What Is the Social Responsibility of Business?

The business firm is the basic building block for organizing production in our system. The decisions made by businesspersons affect all of us. Business touches our lives in our various roles as consumers, employees, taxpayers, and citizens. We all have a stake in those decisions.

A private individual goes into business hoping to make a profit. That person can stay in business only by continuing to make a profit over the long haul. This is a simple fact of business life in our economic system.

But should the "reason for being" for one of our most basic institutions be so self-serving? Should a person engage in business activity only to make a profit, or does that person owe something to society? WHAT DO YOU THINK?

A HEALTHY ATTITUDE TOWARD BUSINESS

Most people who have attended college work for businesses. Some are there because they couldn't find anything else and needed to earn a living. Some are very unhappy, because their only reason for staying in their jobs is to earn a living. This situation is unfortunate, because these people are not nearly as productive or happy as they would be if they were doing work that really gave them satisfaction.

If you're going to work in business, it helps to start with the right attitude toward business itself and toward your particular job and employer. Most people who are taking this course in business administration already have a generally favourable attitude toward business. They know that it is a worthwhile activity. They know that: (1) business is the chief provider of goods and services to our nation; (2) business is working hard now to improve opportunities for all and to eliminate discrimination among workers and managers; (3) business has to be flexible, inventive, and open to new ideas if it is to grow; and (4) business holds the key to economic growth and technological development. In short, business can be exciting and satisfying for most people.

If you are going to be motivated in the specific firm and job you choose, however, you must examine your own values and attitudes. In some cases, values and attitudes are only loosely held; that is, you don't have a very strong basis for holding them. If this is true about some of your presently held reasons for accepting or rejecting a career, you'd better get informed. There is nothing like knowing the facts to repair distorted or biased attitudes and values. A good example is the female graduate of a western Canadian university. She nearly turned down a job offer in Toronto because she had some very bad impressions of the city. This was due to her exposure to some people who had previously lived and worked in Toronto and did not like the city. It was also due in part to the fact that none of her friends and classmates were going there. After flying down for one interview, she discovered her previous perceptions were wrong. She took the job and eventually found a rewarding career as a director of personnel for a large electronics firm.

You may need to get more facts, too, so that the values you employ in choosing a job are reasonable ones. Don't assume that all advertising people are phonies or that all accountants are dull or any of the clichés about occupations. Get the facts. They will strengthen your system for evaluation.

Governments also have profitability in mind when they form business firms. However, they also take into account other social and political factors.

Profit Opportunity and Organized Effort

It is an accepted fact in capitalist-based economies that all types and sizes of business firms seek profit. There is some argument, however, whether profit should be their only objective. Later in our book, we will discuss the concept of the social responsibility of business. At any rate, it's one thing to seek profit and another to make it.

THINK ABOUT IT!

The Importance of Profit to You

The profits earned by business are important to you in many ways. Profits reinvested in firms for growth create jobs. Business profits are an important source of federal and provincial tax revenues. These tax payments by businesses help to pay for schools, hospitals, and other social services.

Not only does profit reward a firm's current owners, but it also attracts new investors. This stimulates investment, creates more jobs, and raises our standard of living.

Profitable firms can afford to set up programs to train people who want to work but cannot find jobs because they lack job skills. Profitable firms can afford to invest in costly pollution control devices. Unprofitable firms cannot.

In other words, business profits are important to all of us. THINK ABOUT IT!

A firm must find a way to use its scarce resources to its advantage by converting them into saleable goods. It must both identify an opportunity for profit and use its resources to try to make that profit.

opportunity

Before a market opportunity can be exploited, it must exist and be recognized. **An opportunity exists where there is a "set of circumstances" which may enable a firm to make a profit.** This set of circumstances can be the result of decisions made by persons inside or outside the firm or it can be mostly good luck.

An announcement in a town's newspaper that a large factory will soon be located there can represent opportunity for many firms. The expected inflow of workers may lead True Realty Company to build a new apartment complex. This is an externally created opportunity for True Realty. The decision to locate the factory in the town was not made by True Realty but by the firm which is moving into town.

For an example of internally created opportunity, consider the case of Gem Chemical Company. It recently discovered a new cleaning compound. This set of circumstances was the result of decisions made by Gem's management. Their own research has made profit more likely.

Exploiting opportunity, however, need not involve developing new products. A grocer is doing it simply by staying open an hour longer than the competitors in order to satisfy late-night shoppers. In any case, exploiting opportunity requires an ability to meet it with organized effort and productive resources. Unless the firm can do this, that opportunity will be lost.

The Role of Risk

risk

It is the hope of profit that motivates people to go into business. Since hopes are not always realized, risk is present. **Risk is the chance of loss.** The hope for profit explains risk assumption. The person thinks the expected profit is worth the risk involved. The greater the reward a business owner expects, the more risk he or she is likely to take.

WHAT DO YOU THINK?

Risks of New Product Development

In his monograph, *Winning the New Product Game,* Professor Robert G. Cooper, of the Faculty of Management at McGill University, reported that "huge sums could be lost" if efforts to develop and introduce new products failed. In the course of a survey of 150 companies in Ontario and Quebec, he reported that "in more than one case a new product failure had actually resulted in corporate bankruptcy, while several firms had been forced to refinance with new owners because of substantial losses from a new product failure."

Only 6 percent of the firms studied thought their new product development programs were "extremely successful." Almost 60 percent of the 150 firms rated their product development activities as only "moderately successful" or worse. Only 49.4 percent of new products were considered a commercial success in another study conducted by Professor Cooper.

On the other hand, successful new product development had very attractive rewards associated with it. For successful new products the "median ratio of profits returned to dollars risked was over five to one"! WHAT DO YOU THINK? Are the risks of investment in new product development worth taking?

People see risk differently. What one person sees as a very risky investment, another may see as "quite safe." This perception of risk is important in understanding why people are willing to risk their money in the hope of profit. Each year, thousands of new firms are started in Canada. Their owners invest their money in them in the hope of making a profit from serving customer wants.

Much of our material progress is due to our stable political and economic systems. This helps to reduce the amount of risk seen in a possible investment. Thus, a person is more likely to invest in Canada than in a country where frequent and violent revolutions occur. (See Figure 2.6.)

Top Management of Business Firms

business policy

The study of top management of business firms is the subject of business policy. The major types of decisions of a business firm discussed in this chapter are made by a firm's top management. These include, among others, the decisions about what business to be in (what products to produce); what markets to serve (geographical area to sell in); what methods of production to employ (how to produce); where to locate production facilities; what profit goals to aspire to; what level of risk to accept; and how to distribute the firm's revenues, among employees, dividends to owners, and reinvestment in the firm (allocation of income).

All firms, large and small, have top management which is responsible for these types of major corporate decisions. The job of top management will differ between smaller and larger businesses. In small businesses the top manager, who will usually also be an owner of the firm, will tend to be involved in all aspects of the firm's operation.

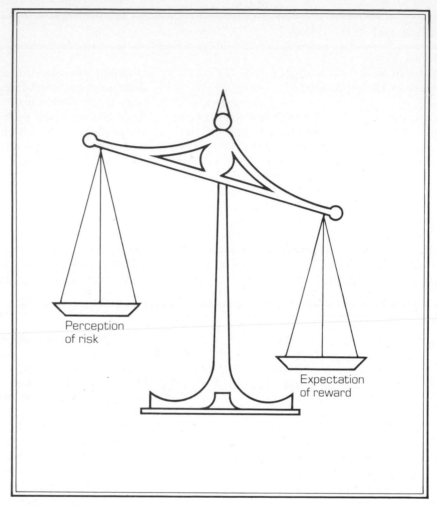

Figure 2.6
The businessperson weighs perceived risk against the expected reward—profit.
When the expected profit outweighs the perceived risk, the business opportunity
probably will be undertaken.

In large, functionally organized, single-product firms, the top management job tends to be one of coordination of the various functional activities of the firm. In large, multi-product (diversified) firms, which have a large number of operating units, top management will be primarily involved in finance, control, and provision of advice to the operating divisions.

For all types of firms the key concept of business policy is strategy. **A firm's strategy is what it is currently doing, what it intends to do in the future (its goals), and how it intends to achieve these goals.** A firm's

strategy

strategy formulation

strategy embodies its decisions about what products or services to produce, how to produce and distribute them, the goals and objectives the firm aspires to, and the intended plan of action for achieving these goals.

As the term implies, **strategy formulation is the activities (formal and/or informal) determining what a firm's strategy is to be. Formulating a strategy involves matching company strengths with environmental opportunity.** The corporate top management strategist must have a good understanding of the environment. He or she must anticipate and cope with market conditions and trends with political, social, and technological developments. The top manager must also have a good understanding of the strengths and limitations of the resources at his or her disposal. A strength is present when a firm has a competitive advantage over other firms in an industry. A strength can be any of a large number of things. For example, a firm could have a strength by being superior to others in terms of lower production costs, faster delivery, higher quality, better financial structure, more skilled work force, good corporate image, better marketing force, or many others.

KNOW YOUR STRENGTHS

Few of you will be responsible for general management decisions in the near future. The concepts of strategy and strategy formulation can, however, be immediately useful to you in making career decisions.

In making a decision about a career it is important, as it is in establishing a new business venture, to be aware of both the opportunities available and the strengths you possess to exploit these opportunities.

A good understanding of a wide range of available opportunities can be obtained from information gleaned from a number of sources. These might include discussions with professors, recent graduates, businesspersons, civil servants, and others. Other information can be obtained from libraries and from contacting the various industry associations and organizations indicated in this book.

It is sometimes harder to assess your own strengths than it is to obtain information about job opportunities. You start from the premise that every individual has things he or she is better at than other things.

Your grades and intellectual ability should

be one thing you consider. However, you must not neglect your interpersonal and other types of skills. Also, assess your motivation and desire when you are considering your strengths.

You must, however, be objective and neither underrate nor overrate yourself. Self-analysis can be a difficult thing. One way to approach the task is to list in two columns your strengths and your weaknesses. Another way is to sit down and draft a hypothetical letter of reference for yourself for a variety of different types of jobs. You will find these tasks difficult but useful.

After you have completed your analysis of strengths and opportunities, you will find that you have more information on which to base a career choice. Remember, the potential is greater when you attempt to apply strength to opportunity than when you attempt either to apply strength to an area where there is no opportunity or to take advantage of an opportunity even though you are weak in the area and are unwilling to develop the appropriate strength.

CAREER PROFILE

MY NAME IS DONA HARVEY. I AM THE Managing Editor of *The Province,* A Vancouver daily newspaper with a circulation of 140,000. *The Province* has recently converted to a tabloid format in an effort to build a more distinctive readership base and thus bring in more advertising revenue.

As a child growing up in Vancouver, I always wanted to be in the newspaper business. I worked on school papers as a student. When I completed high school in Everett, Washington, I immediately began work with the *Everett Herald.* I got my university Arts degree while working with the *Herald.* I subsequently worked with the *Edmonton Journal* (where I moved from writing and copy editing to management) and with the *Winnipeg Tribune* as Editor. After the *Winnipeg Tribune* folded I joined *The Province* on January 1, 1981.

As Managing Editor I am head of the Editorial Department, and am responsible for all news and features except the editorial page. I report to the Publisher — the Chief Executive Officer — of the paper, as do the heads of other departments including advertising and circulation.

My job as Managing Editor is multifaceted. It involves administration, acting as senior editor, chairing news conferences, coordinating with other departments, and liaison with the public.

Administration encompasses all staffing matters related to the 115 employees I am responsible for. It involves decisions about hiring,

The skill of the strategist lies in the capacity to identify strengths, identify opportunities, match the two, and take decisive and appropriately timed action. In matching strength to opportunity, top managers must also take into account their personal desires and aspirations. There is great scope for innovation and creativity in formulating strategies. The various aspects of the firm and the environment will be discussed throughout the remainder of this book.

After a strategy is formulated, top management must ensure that it is implemented. The tools available to top management for strategy implementation are discussed in detail in later chapters. Basically, however, **top management can influence implementation of strategy by design of organizational structure; by design and management of various or-**

implementation
of strategy

firing, and leaves of absence. It also involves negotiating and administering our collective agreement. Administration of our seven million dollar budget is also an important task.

As senior editor I must act on questions or problems involving news judgment. This could involve questions of taste, libel, or fairness of coverage. Any news matter in dispute between different levels of staff can be referred to me. In most cases decisions must be made very rapidly because of deadlines.

I chair two major staff news conferences every day. The objectives of these are: in the first conference to keep everyone informed of developments; in the second to make judgments regarding priority of coverage including where stories are placed.

Coordination with other departments, with and through the publisher, is the forum for short- and long-range planning. This is the forum in which the strategic decision to change from the traditional broadsheet format to the tabloid was made.

In liaison with the public, I make every effort to be available by telephone, by mail, and in person. I answer my own telephone, try to answer every letter I get and undertake regular public speaking engagements.

My major problems have been directly related to the fact that our newspaper has been losing money. We have been fighting for survival. Mounting losses due to the recession led to layoffs last fall. There was a lot of tension and bitterness because of this. Morale was very low. We have dealt with our uncertain future at a strategic level by moving to the tabloid format. The move to the new format has enabled us to overcome much of the morale problem. It has created an injection of hope for the future and for most staff an enthusiastic commitment to making it work.

Other problems involve tough judgment calls about how to handle certain news stories. When do you put a sensitive story on page one? When do you go against your lawyer's advice and publish a story?

My primary rewards come from the joy of producing a newspaper. The highs come from the people on the paper working together to produce an outstanding product. The way we worked together the evening of the last federal budget—moving from initial chaos, to a fine finished paper, and then seeing it out on the streets a few hours later—made me feel very satisfied, and proud.

In summary, I would suggest to students that people in an organization who are willing to make the commitment to go the extra mile and put in the extra effort stand out head and shoulders above the others. Also, anyone who wishes to get into management must realistically assess his or her own weaknesses and strengths and learn both how to build on the strengths and what to do about the weaknesses. You have to think about where you want to be in five to ten years and build toward that goal.

ganizational systems such as accounting and control, planning, reward/punishment, staffing, training, and the like; and by the personal leadership style used in dealings with others in the firm.

The essence of the top management job is to relate the firm to the environment in which it operates. The firm must be positioned so that it exploits market opportunities which arise in the environment while at the same time coping with other economic as well as political, social, technological, and ecological environmental factors.

The remainder of this text will provide you with a framework for understanding the various functional aspects of a business firm. It will also indicate the different environmental factors a Canadian business manager must take into account.

Ours is a market-based economy. The market determines opportunities available to business firms. The market forces of demand and supply determine prices. Environmental factors underlying supply and demand also determine prices. In many instances, relative prices determine how limited resources will be used to satisfy unlimited wants. Because resources are limited, choices must be made about what will be produced. Many of these choices are made by consumers and producers working through the price system. In other instances, governments determine what goods and services will be provided.

Prices induce or limit production and consumption. The price system helps firms decide which goods will be produced, how much will be produced, how they will be produced, and how they will be distributed.

The law of demand means that more of a given good is demanded at lower prices than at higher prices. The law of supply means that more of a given good is offered for sale at higher prices than at lower prices. These forces of supply and demand work to determine prices.

The firm is the basic building block for organizing production in our economy. It gathers productive resources (inputs) and converts them into saleable products or services (outputs). Both input and output depend on the price system.

The hope of profit motivates people to go into business. They earn profit from identifying opportunity and exploiting it through organized effort. But risk is always present. One role of top management is to identify opportunities and use the resources of the firm to take advantage of these opportunities.

Now that we know what a firm is and why it exists, we can go on to discuss the different forms of legal ownership of business firms. ∎

1. What is a market economy? Is it the same as a price system? Explain.
2. Contrast demand and quantity demanded, state the "law of demand," and draw a demand curve.
3. What are the three main sources of buying power?
4. Contrast disposable income, discretionary income, and real income.
5. Contrast supply and quantity supplied, state the "law of supply," and draw a supply curve.
6. What is the significance of (a) the intersection of a supply curve and a demand curve on a graph, and (b) shifts in demand and supply curves?
7. Are supply and demand forces the only ones that affect prices? Explain.
8. What can a firm do to increase its profits?
9. In what two basic ways can a firm use its after-tax profit?
10. What is "business opportunity"?
11. Why is risk present in business activity?
12. Can goods or services really be overpriced?
13. Is the concept of the social responsibility of business at odds with its need to make a profit?

14. What is a "favorable business climate"?
15. The chapter said that the hope of profit is the main reason business people undertake risk. What other reasons for going into business can you identify?
16. Are there any types of business opportunity in your community that are not being exploited? If there are, why are they not being exploited?
17. Why do people perceive risk differently?
18. Is it true that all businesses must serve their customers if they are to survive?
19. How can factors underlying supply and demand create business opportunities?

INCIDENTS

Supply and Demand in the Cattle Industry

The cattle industry provides a good example of how the laws of supply and demand work. When beef is plentiful, the price drops and some consumers will want to buy more beef. Ranchers, however, will want to supply less beef because of the low price and they will start sending their breeding cows to slaughterhouses. This means that beef supplies will become tighter and the price of beef will start to rise. Ranchers also will be encouraged to rebuild their herds. This cycle tends to repeat itself every eight years.

Questions:
1. When the price of beef drops and consumers want to buy more, is this an increase in demand for beef or an increase in the quantity demanded of beef?
2. In the cycle we have described, what encourages ranchers to want to supply more beef or less beef?
3. In the cycle we have described, what encourages consumers to demand more beef or less beef? What other factors might underlie consumer demand for beef?
4. Is any risk present in the cattle industry? Discuss.

Indexing Income Taxes

Suppose a household's income in one year is $20,000 and it pays $2,000 in income taxes. It pays 10 percent of its income in income taxes.

Now, assume that the Consumer Price Index (CPI) for the next year shows that consumer prices rose 12 percent. Further, assume that the household's income rises 12 percent to keep up with inflation.

Theoretically, the household will be able to buy the same quantity of goods and services it could have bought in the previous year. At the end of the year the household will find that its 12 percent increase in income paid for the higher prices of the goods and services it bought.

If the 12 percent increase in income shifted the household to a higher tax bracket, it will end up having less buying power than it did in the previous year. Although it may have broken even by using its 12 percent increase in income to pay prices that were 12 percent higher, it is also in a higher tax bracket, which means that it will pay more than 10 percent of its income in income taxes.

Income tax exemptions in Canada were automatically indexed to the CPI prior to 1983. Budgetary changes eliminated automatic indexation at that time.

Questions:
1. What effect would indexation of income tax exemption have had on a household's real income?
2. How would indexing income taxes probably affect a typical household's willingness to spend?
3. Is indexing income tax exemptions a good idea? Why or why not?

After reading this chapter, you should be able to:

1. Identify the reasons for the growth in public ownership of the factors of production in Canada.
2. List and define the four major forms of legal ownership of business firms.
3. Discuss the relative advantages and disadvantages of each major form of legal ownership of business firms.
4. List and define the different types of partnerships and partners.
5. List and define the different types of corporations.
6. Discuss the relative importance of the four major forms of legal ownership in terms of the number of firms.
7. Draw up a partnership agreement.
8. Explain how a corporation is formed and who controls it.
9. Identify and discuss other business structures in addition to the four major forms.
10. Understand the co-operative form of business ownership.
11. Discuss the advantages and disadvantages of large-scale operations.

KEY CONCEPTS

In reading the chapter, look for and understand these terms:

sole proprietorship	cumulative voting
unlimited liability	proxy
partnership	board of directors
corporation	corporation bylaws
stockholders	co-operative
common stock	professional managers
preferred stock	countervailing power

BIG CORPORATIONS ARE OFTEN IN THE news because their actions help to make the news. We frequently see giant firms like Bell Telephone, Imperial Oil, Stelco, and Canadian Tire in the news.

Before 1800 most industries were composed of small firms, often one-person or family operations. Large firms have existed in Canada for at least the last one hundred years—the Canadian Pacific Railway was one of the earliest. Large firms continue to make the news. In recent years an attempt by Power Corporation to buy control of Argus Corporation led to a federal government Royal Commission to investigate corporate concentration in Canada.

CHAPTER THREE

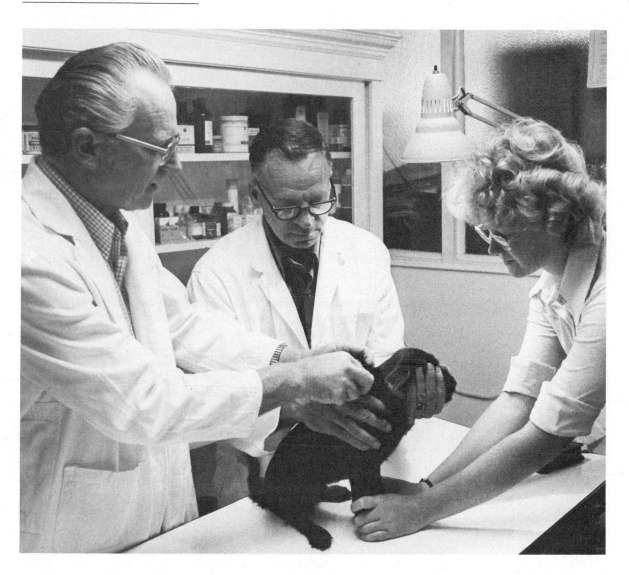

Forms of Business Ownership

BUSINESSES VARY IN SIZE FROM SINGLE-OWNER FIRMS TO GIANT corporations owned by thousands of people. The type of ownership is important. For example, some types of opportunity can be exploited only by large corporations. It would be hard to imagine a single-owner firm undertaking a project as vast as building a ship for the Canadian navy. Furthermore, a firm's growth is affected by its type of ownership. There are limits to expansion of single-owner firms.

We begin by briefly comparing private and public ownership. The majority of the chapter is devoted to an analysis of the four common forms of business ownership in Canada—sole proprietorships, partnerships, corporations, and co-operatives.

PUBLIC VERSUS PRIVATE OWNERSHIP

In our capitalist system a person has the right to save and to invest money to make more money. The same right holds for a group of people. Persons, alone or in groups, can risk their money by going into business to try to make a profit. Private ownership of the means of production is a basic part of our economic system. Private ownership, however, is not the only form. Public or government ownership has become important in recent years.

Public ownership of the means of production may be undertaken for many reasons. When private investors are unwilling to assume the risk in some types of investment, the government may do it. In other cases, the investment needed may be too great for private investors and/or the potential payoff may be too intangible. Or, the government may wish to provide employment in an area and will therefore set up a government-owned firm to accomplish this goal. The government might also believe that certain businesses in the private sector are not providing a product or service properly, or are charging too high a price for it, so they will become competitors to those firms. Canadian National Railway, for example, competes with Canadian Pacific, a private corporation.

If we compared the growth rates of the private and the public sectors of our economy, we would find that the public sector has grown faster. Because the founders of our country feared too much government interference and control, they resisted public ownership. However, the Great Depression, which began in 1929, caused us to reexamine the basic reasons for distrusting government. During the depression, many people questioned the ability of the capitalist system to survive.

Today most Canadians accept the idea of some form of government ownership. Private ownership, however, still dominates society. The four most common legal forms of private ownership are the sole proprietorship, the partnership, the corporation, and the co-operative.

THE SOLE PROPRIETORSHIP

sole proprietorship

The sole proprietorship is the oldest and still the most common form of legal ownership in Canada. **A sole proprietorship is a business owned and managed by one person. That person, however, may have help from others in running the business.** The sole proprietor is the classic case of the entrepreneur. Only a sole proprietor can say, "I am the company" or "This is my business."

Advantages of the Sole Proprietorship

Suppose Alice Stone wants to go into the florist business. She might find that sole proprietorship is the easiest way for her to start. There are no general laws that regulate the setting up of a sole proprietorship. Of course, the business activity must be legal and there may be local and provincial laws that require licences and permits. The sole proprietor is required to register the firm's name. This prohibits two firms from operating under the same name. (Other licence and permit requirements are discussed in Chapter 15.) Otherwise, Alice can go into business any time she pleases. Simplicity in starting the business is a major advantage of the sole proprietorship.

As sole owner, Alice owns the firm outright. She is the sole owner of any profits (or losses). Alice gets personal satisfaction out of seeing her firm grow under her direct guidance. She does what she believes is best for her firm and makes decisions without required approval from anyone else.

Because Alice is the firm, she pays only personal income taxes on the firm's profits. There is no income tax on the firm as a separate entity. If Alice wants to go out of business, she simply sells her inventory and equipment. She needs permission from no one. A sole proprietorship is easy to dissolve.

The sole proprietorship's major advantages, therefore, are

- simplicity in starting the business
- ownership of all the profits
- enjoyment gained from a great deal of personal involvement and satisfaction from being one's own boss
- the ability to make management decisions without approval being required from anyone else
- no tax on profits of the business as a separate entity, only on the owner's personal income
- simplicity in dissolving the business

Disadvantages of the Sole Proprietorship

unlimited liability

Because Alice is the firm, she is legally liable for all its debts. She has unlimited liability. **Unlimited liability means that a proprietor is liable for claims against the business that go beyond the value of his or her**

ownership in the firm. The liability extends to his or her personal property (furniture, car, and personal savings) and, in some cases, real property (home and other real estate). If Alice goes out of business and stills owes her business creditors $10,000 after selling her inventory, equipment, and other business property, those creditors can legally lay claim to Alice's nonbusiness property.

Thus business creditors can force Alice to withdraw money from her personal savings account, sell her car and other personal property, and (in some provinces) sell her home to pay off the creditors. This unlimited liability exists because there is no legal distinction between Alice and her business. She risks losing everything she owns. There is no limit to her financial liability.

The amount of money Alice is able to invest in the firm is limited to what she has and what she can borrow. In many cases the difficulty of raising more money discourages this type of ownership.

As the firm grows Alice may find that she is spreading herself too thin. A sole proprietor usually takes on the entire task of running the business. The entire burden of management is borne by the owner.

If Alice were to die, go to prison, or go insane, the business would be legally terminated. The business may be passed on to a son or daughter, but when this occurs a new proprietorship is formed. The built-in impermanence of a sole proprietorship makes it hard for the firm to grow and to attract employees who want a permanent job.

The sole proprietorship's major disadvantages, therefore, are

- unlimited financial liability for business debts
- difficulty in raising funds for expansion
- no sharing of the burden of management
- impermanence of the business firm

THE PARTNERSHIP

partnership

A partnership comes into being when two or more individuals agree to combine their financial, managerial, and technical abilities for the purpose of operating a company for profit. The partnership came about to overcome some of the more serious disadvantages of the sole proprietorship. It also dates back to ancient times.

There are several different types of partnerships. (See Table 3.1.) Our discussion, however, focuses on the most common type — the general partnership.

Advantages of the Partnership

Instead of a proprietorship, suppose Alice decided to form a partnership with Joe Gunn. Getting started requires that the partners agree on their

Table 3.1 Types of Partnerships and Partners

Types of partnerships

General partnership	All partners have unlimited liability for the firm's debts.
Limited partnership	This partnership has at least one general partner and one or more limited partners. The latter's liability is limited to their financial investment in the firm.

Types of partners

General partner	Actively involved in managing the firm and has unlimited liability.
Secret partner	Actively participates in managing the firm and has unlimited liability. A secret partner's identity is not disclosed to the public.
Dormant partner	Does not actively participate in managing the firm. A dormant partner's identity is not disclosed to the public. Has unlimited liability.
Ostensible partner	Not an actual partner but his or her name is identified with the firm. Usually an ostensible partner is a well-known personality. Promotional benefits accrue from using that name for which the person is usually paid a fee. Has unlimited liability.
Limited partner	Liability is limited to the amount invested in the partnership.

duties, distribution of profits, and other features of the proposed association. While the agreement may be written or oral, a written agreement is superior, since it helps avoid future disagreement between partners. Like a sole proprietorship, a partnership is easy to set up.

Since Alice and Joe are in business together, they can pool their funds and invest more than either one could invest alone. They have a greater ability to borrow money, since their combined personal and real property are available to creditors. They can also pool their talents and divide the tasks of the business. This brings the advantages of specialization to the firm.

Like a proprietorship, a partnership is not taxed as a business separate from its owners. The owners, not the firm, are taxed.

The partnership's major advantages, therefore, are

- simplicity in starting the business
- the pooling of funds and talents of the partners
- greater borrowing power than a sole proprietorship
- more opportunity for specialization than a sole proprietorship
- like the sole proprietor, the partners' enjoyment of personal involvement and satisfaction in running the business
- no tax on profits of the business as a separate entity, only on the owners' personal incomes

PARTNERSHIP AGREEMENT

THIS PARTNERSHIP AGREEMENT made and entered into this first day of January, 1984, and between Alice Stone of Victoria, B.C., and Joseph Gunn of Victoria, B.C.

WITNESSETH:

1. The parties hereby agree to form a partnership.
2. The name of the partnership shall be S & G Florists.
3. The business to be conducted shall be a florist business.
4. The principal place of business of the partnership shall be at 807 East Main Avenue.
5. The capital of the partnership is to consist of the sum of $30,000.00.
   Alice Stone is to contribute $15,000 in cash and Joseph Gunn is to contribute $15,000 in cash. No interest shall be paid to the partners on any contributions to capital.
6. Whenever required, additional capital shall be contributed by the partners in the proportion of the initial capital contribution.
7. The net profits of the partnership shall be divided equally and the partners shall equally bear the net losses.
8. Each partner shall be entitled to a drawing account as may be mutually agreed upon.
9. Neither partner shall receive a salary.
10. Each partner shall have an equal right in the management of the partnership.
11. Alice Stone shall devote her entire time and attention to the business. Joseph Gunn shall devote his entire time and attention to the business.
12. Either partner may retire from the partnership after giving the other partner at least 90 days' written notice of his or her intention so to do. The remaining partner shall have the option of purchasing the retiring partner's interest or to terminate and liquidate the business. The purchase price shall be the balance in the retiring partner's capital account based upon an audit by an independent public accountant to the date of retirement. The purchase price shall be payable 50 per cent in cash and the balance in 36 equal monthly instalments and shall not bear interest.
13. Upon the death of a partner, the surviving partner shall have the option to either purchase the interest of the decedent or to terminate and liquidate the business. The purchase price and payment shall be the same as above set forth.
14. The partnership shall begin the tenth day of January, 1984, and shall continue until dissolved by retirement or death of a partner or by mutual agreement of the partners.

IN WITNESS WHEREOF, the parties have signed this agreement.

Witnesses:

Roger Allen

Vernon Collins

Alice Stone   (SEAL)

Joseph Gunn   (SEAL)

Figure 3.1
A partnership agreement

Disadvantages of the Partnership

Partners, like sole proprietors, have unlimited financial liability for the partnership's debts. It is a *joint liability*. This means that Alice is responsible for business debts incurred by Joe and vice versa.

Suppose Alice and Joe's business fails and, after selling the partnership's property to pay off the creditors, they still owe them $50,000. The partnership agreement in Figure 3.1 shows that Alice and Joe each contributed $15,000 in cash (see #5) to start the business and that they agreed to bear equally any losses (see #7). But suppose that after selling off all his personal and real property, Joe can pay off only $20,000 of his $25,000 share of the unpaid debt. Alice will be liable for paying her $25,000 share plus the $5,000 that Joe is unable to pay.

In forming a partnership, one must choose one's partner(s) with great care. Personal disagreements have caused many failures. For example, disagreement can occur over how long the partners intend to be in business; the amount of money each is to invest; their salaries; how profits or losses will be shared; the duties of each; the procedure for admitting new partners; and the procedure for dissolving the partnership. This is why the partnership agreement should be in writing.

A partnership is legally terminated upon the death, withdrawal, or insanity of a partner. Although an heir of a deceased partner might step in and help run the business, this is not the same partnership. In some cases partners will buy partnership insurance and enter into a buy-and-sell agreement. This ensures that money will be available upon the death of one partner so that the other(s) will be able to buy out his or her share from the deceased partner's estate. The buy-and-sell agreement spells out the value of the partnership shares and preserves the business for surviving partners.

Furthermore, a partner cannot simply withdraw his or her investment in the business. He or she must find an outsider (or a present partner) who

---

WHAT DO YOU THINK?

How Should Partners Deal with Personal Disagreements?

Personal disagreements between partners are a major cause of partnership failures. Even with a written partnership agreement, conflict will arise from time to time. But disagreement can be healthy if the partners can resolve their differences to the benefit of the firm.

Deep-seated personality differences which lead to endless petty arguments, however, can wreck a partnership. Unfortunately, these differences usually do not surface until after the partners are in business. The saying, "You really don't know a person until you live with that person," applied to a partnership, becomes, "You really don't know a person until you go into a partnership with that person." Do you agree? How should partners deal with personal disagreements? WHAT DO YOU THINK?

is willing to buy in and that person must be acceptable to the remaining partner(s). In a sense each partner's investment is frozen in the business.

The partnership's major disadvantages, therefore, are

- unlimited and joint financial liability
- the potential for personal disagreements between the partners
- impermanence of the business firm
- the freezing of each partner's investment in the business

THE CORPORATION

corporation

A corporation has been defined as "an artificial being, invisible, intangible, and existing only in contemplation of law." Unlike a sole proprietorship or partnership, the corporation has a legal existence apart from its owners. It can buy, hold, and sell property in its own name, and it can sue and be sued.

Originally, the corporate form of ownership was used most frequently for charitable, educational, or public purposes. In order to incorporate, a charter was required from the federal government. That is why the corporation is legally separate from its owners. It is a creation of governmental authority.

Formation of the Corporation

Although there are a number of different ways to form a corporation, the two most widely used avenues are federal incorporation under the Canada Business Corporations Act and provincial incorporation under any of the provincial Incorporations Acts. The former is used if the company is going to operate in more than one province; the latter is used if the founders intend to carry on business in only one province.

Except for banks and certain insurance and loan companies, any company can be federally incorporated under the Canada Business Corporations Act. To do so, Articles of Incorporation must be drawn up. These articles include such information as the name of the corporation (which must not already be in use), the type and number of shares to be issued, the number of directors the corporation will have, and the location of the company's operations. All companies must attach the word "Limited" (Ltd.) or "Incorporated" (Inc.) to the company name to clearly indicate to customers and suppliers that the owners have limited liability for corporate debts.

Provincial incorporation takes one of two forms. In certain provinces (British Columbia, Alberta, Saskatchewan, Manitoba, Ontario, Newfoundland, Nova Scotia, and the two territories) the registration system or its equivalent is used. Under this system, individuals wishing to form a corporation are required to file a memorandum of association. This document contains the same type of information as required under the Canada Business Corporations Act discussed above. In the remaining provinces the equivalent document is called the letters patent. The specific procedures and information required varies from province to province. The basic differences between these incorporation systems is that the registration system forms corporations by authority of parliament, while the letters-patent system forms corporations by royal prerogative.

Types of Corporations

Corporations can be found in both the private and the public sector in Canada, although our emphasis is on the private sector. The different types of public and private corporations and examples of each kind are indicated in Table 3.2.

Table 3.2 Types of Corporations

	Definition	*Examples*
1. Crown Corporations		
a. Departmental	Responsible for administrative, supervisory, and/or regulatory government services	Atomic Energy Control Board, Economic Council of Canada, Unemployment Insurance Commission
b. Agency	Management of trading or service operations on a quasi-commercial basis	Atomic Energy of Canada Ltd., Loto Canada, Royal Canadian Mint
c. Proprietary	Management of lending or financial operations; management of commercial or industrial operations	Air Canada, CBC, Central Mortgage & Housing Corp., St. Lawrence Seaway Authority
2. Business Corporations		
a. Private	Formed to carry on production of goods and/or services at a profit; number of shareholders limited to 50; board of directors must approve transfer of shares; stock cannot be traded on the open market	Eaton's, many other less well-known companies
b. Public	Formed to carry on production of goods and/or services at a profit; none of the restrictions on private corporations applies	Neonex, Massey-Ferguson, Steel Co. of Canada, Imperial Oil, many others

Figure 3.2
Ownership in Alcan Aluminium is shown by stock certificate

The Stockholders

stockholders

Stockholders are persons who own the common and preferred stock of a corporation. The number of votes a stockholder has depends on the number of shares he or she owns. It is not a case of "one person, one vote." This is why many small stockholders do not vote their shares in large corporations. For example, a person who owns ten shares of INCO may choose not to vote. Control of such a corporation can be effective if a group of stockholders pools their votes to get a voting majority. In some cases, a person with 10 percent or even less of a corporation's stock can exercise much control over its affairs. A stock certificate is shown in Figure 3.2.

Most corporations have thousands of shares and hundreds of stockholders. Some, however, remain quite small in terms of number of owners and the number and market value of shares outstanding.

A stockholder need not, and generally does not, participate in managing the corporation. Ownership and management are separate. Most of the stockholders in Canada do not participate in managing the corporations of which they are part owners. The stockholders come from many backgrounds — schoolteachers, plumbers, salaried executives, and so forth.

Stockholders are the direct owners of a corporation. There are, however, millions of other people who have an indirect ownership in many corporations. For example, the members of many labour unions make payments to their union pension funds. Some of this money is used to buy stock in corporations. Thus, the union members are indirect owners of stock.

A stockholder owns a partial interest in the whole corporation. Suppose you own one share of stock in Norcen Energy Resources. You are not entitled to walk into the corporation's headquarters and demand to see the "property" you own. The property is owned by the corporation. What you own is a small part of the entire corporation. The value of that part varies

---

YOU BE THE JUDGE!

Do We Need a Co-Determination Act in Canada?

In July, 1976, West Germany passed a "co-determination law" which gives workers in about 600 to 650 major companies a nearly equal voice with stockholders in running the companies. The idea is to extend political democracy to economic life. Other terms for this type of legislation are "worker participation" and "industrial democracy."

Worker participation in company decision making exists at two levels in West Germany. At the top, workers are represented on supervisory boards which are similar to boards of directors in Canadian firms. At the bottom, there is worker representation on the plant level in works councils. These councils have an equal voice with management in decisions about hiring, firing, and working conditions. The basic idea of worker participation has existed for a number of years. The West German coal and steel industries have operated under worker participation since 1951, and big firms in other industries have been required

since 1952 to allot one-third of supervisory seats to labour. The 1976 law raises the percentage to half for the largest firms.

In the United States in 1976, the United Auto Workers (UAW) asked Chrysler Corporation to give the union two seats on Chrysler's board but dropped the idea when Chrysler resisted. Later Chrysler relented, and the head of the UAW was given a seat on the board of directors. Except for the UAW, most North American unions oppose the idea for a number of reasons. Some union people see worker participation as a threat to union strength because board members representing labour might be independent of *unionized* labour. Some unionists also contend that union workers already enjoy enough participation through the collective-bargaining process. Do we need a co-determination act in Canada? WHAT DO YOU THINK?

Source: James Furlong, *Labor in the Boardroom: The Peaceful Revolution* (Princeton, N. J.: Dow Jones & Company, Inc., 1977).

with changes in the value of the shares of stock which you own. This is determined by the supply of, and demand for, the shares on the market.

There are two basic types of stock, common stock and preferred stock.

common stock

Common stock is a certificate showing ownership in a corporation. It is voting stock and all common stockholders enjoy the same rights. Common stockholders have a right to earnings that remain (residual earnings) after the corporation has met the prior claims of bondholders and preferred stockholders. The actual payment of a common stock dividend from these residual earnings does not occur until the board of directors declares a common stock dividend. If the corporation goes bankrupt, the common stockholders are the last to receive any proceeds from the sale of the corporation's property. Creditors, bondholders, and preferred stockholders share in the proceeds before the common stockholders. Thus common stockholders are the residual owners of a corporation.

preferred stock

Preferred stock is a certificate that also shows ownership in a corporation. Preferred stockholders usually cannot vote their shares, but they do enjoy certain preferences with respect to dividends and assets. As we have seen, they have a right to receive the dividend indicated on their stock certificates before common stockholders receive any dividends. This dividend also is not owed until declared by the corporation's board of directors. If the corporation goes out of business and pays off its debts, preferred stockholders have the right to receive their share of any remaining assets before the common stockholders receive anything.

The number of votes a stockholder has in elections of board members and other business voted on at stockholders' meetings depends on the number of shares he or she owns. Each share of common stock carries one vote; thus, a person with twenty shares has twenty votes.

cumulative voting

To give small stockholders more power in electing the board of directors, some provinces require cumulative voting. **With cumulative voting the number of votes a stockholder has is the number of his or her shares times the number of directors to be elected.** Thus, if 5 directors are to be elected, a person with 20 shares would have 100 votes (20 shares $\times$ 5 directors). These votes may be cast all for one person or allocated in whatever way the stockholder desires.

proxy

The corporate secretary must notify stockholders of the date, time, and place of stockholders' meetings. Since many stockholders are unable or unwilling to attend, a proxy form is usually included along with the meeting notice. **A proxy is a person who is appointed to represent another person. By signing a proxy form, a stockholder transfers his or her right to vote at a stockholders' meeting to someone else.** A stockholder who does not attend the meeting or does not return the proxy form loses voting rights in that meeting.

In addition to electing the board of directors, stockholders regularly vote on such business as the choice of an independent auditor or a proposal to change the corporation's name. Recently, some stockholders have raised thorny questions about corporate social responsibility, including such concerns as hiring and promotion policies for women and minorities, conservation, pollution, and doing business in countries that allegedly violate the human rights of their citizens.

Figure 3.3
The corporate structure

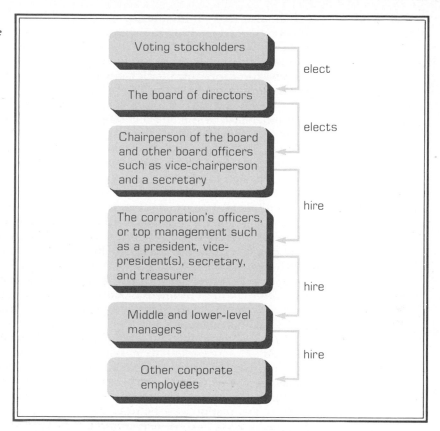

Voting stockholders	
	elect
The board of directors	
	elects
Chairperson of the board and other board officers such as vice-chairperson and a secretary	
	hire
The corporation's officers, or top management such as a president, vice-president(s), secretary, and treasurer	
	hire
Middle and lower-level managers	
	hire
Other corporate employees	

The Board of Directors and Corporate Officers

board of directors

A corporation's board of directors is elected by its stockholders. (See Figure 3.3.) **The board of directors is a group of people who are given the power to govern the corporation's affairs and to make general policy. This power comes from the corporate charter and the corporation's stockholders.** In small corporations the major stockholders often manage the business. But in larger corporations, with thousands of stockholders, the board of directors is accountable for guiding the affairs of the business. It's easy for a board to keep itself in power as long as it does a good job in the opinion of voting stockholders. Unseating a board member can be tough.

The board of directors elects its own officers. These *board officers* usually include a chairperson of the board, a vice-chairperson, and a secretary. The board also holds periodic meetings.

corporation bylaws

Although the stockholders have the authority to draw up the corporation's bylaws, they usually leave it up to the board. **Corporation bylaws are the rules by which the corporation will operate. They include**

- •place and time of meetings
- •procedure for calling meetings
- •directors' pay
- •duties of the corporate officers
- •regulations for new stock issues
- •procedure for changing the bylaws

Another task of the board is selecting the *corporation's officers,* or its top managers, who include the president, vice-president(s), secretary, and treasurer. The corporation's officers are employees of the board and they also are the corporation's top management. These officers, in turn, hire other, lower-level managers to help in running the corporation. In actual practice boards sometimes select only the president, or chief executive officer (CEO), and he or she then selects the other corporate officers.

The board is accountable to the stockholders for the actions of the corporate officers. In other words, the board performs the function of a "watchdog." As such, the board usually has the authority to accept or reject the officers' actions in managing the corporation.

In some corporations the board plays a very active role in managing the corporation. It holds frequent meetings and has a lot of say about the firm's day-to-day management. This is especially likely to be the case in small, closely held corporations.

On the other hand, some boards are content to select the company president. The president then selects other corporate officers and the board merely acts as a "review board" for the president and the other officers' decisions. In fact, the president pretty much runs the entire corporation subject to "rubber stamp" approval by the board.

Thus the distinctions between the board and the corporate officers often are blurred. In some corporations the chairperson of the board is also the company's president. The corporation's other top managers also may be on the board. In such a case the board members who are not corporate officers are called *outside directors.*

Board members have certain legal obligations. They must act in the best interest of the stockholders and be reasonable and prudent in doing their jobs. They must be as careful in managing the corporation's affairs as they are in managing their personal affairs. In the past, board members have been held liable for illegal acts and fraud, but not for poor judgment. More recently, however, some courts have held directors liable for using what the courts consider to be poor judgment.

Advantages of the Corporation

A corporation's stockholders are not the corporation. They have only limited financial liability. A corporation's debts are separate and distinct from those of its owners. If you purchased stock in a corporation, the most you could lose is what you paid for the stock.

Let's return to Alice and Joe's business discussed previously. Suppose the partnership is doing well and the owners want to expand. They have little money to finance it, and they have borrowed up to their credit limit. A logical step would be for them to incorporate. This would give them access to people who might want to buy shares in the new corporation. Suppose Alice and Joe need $500,000 to expand. They might find it easier to get 1,000 persons to invest $500 each than to borrow a lump sum of $500,000 or to find another partner willing to put up such a large sum. Thus, corporations usually find it easier to get money for expansion.

A corporation, for all practical purposes, can exist forever. The death, insanity, or imprisonment of a stockholder or a corporate officer has no direct effect on the corporation's existence.

A proprietor may have a lot of trouble selling his or her business. Selling one's interest in a partnership requires the approval of the other partners. But transfer of ownership is simple in a corporation. Stockholders simply sell their shares of stock. No permission from anyone else is needed. All that is needed is a buyer and a seller. Organized stock exchanges make it easy for them to get together. Millions of shares in hundreds of corporations are traded each day. In most cases, buyers and sellers never see each other. They deal through their stockbrokers. This is discussed in Chapter 13.

The benefits of specialization are apparent in a corporation. Corporations are more easily able to hire specialists to do specific types of work because of their typically larger size. This applies to workers and managers. Of course, the same is true for the few proprietorships and partnerships which are very large.

The corporation's major advantages, therefore, are

- •its existence as a separate legal entity
- •the limited financial liability of the owners
- •the long life of the business
- •easy transfer of ownership
- •greater financial capability

Disadvantages of the Corporation

A major disadvantage is that a corporation is subject to double taxation. As an entity separate from its owners, a corporation pays federal and provincial taxes on its profits. When the after-tax profits are paid to stockholders as dividends, they pay income taxes on them. Thus, corporate profits are taxed twice.

Another disadvantage is that corporations must conform to precise legal requirements to be granted a charter. Thus, they are more complicated and expensive to form than proprietorships and partnerships. To sell its shares of stock nationally, a corporation must get prior approval from a Securities Commission. In addition, federal and provincial regulation of corporations has increased over the past several decades.

Another disadvantage relates to the separation of ownership and management. Some people believe this makes a corporation's management too conservative. The proprietor who assumes risk stands to gain all the rewards. The hired manager of a corporation stands to gain less of the re-

Table 3.3   Relative Advantages and Disadvantages of the Sole Proprietorship, Partnership, and Corporate Forms of Ownership

Sole proprietorship	Partnership	Corporation
Advantages		
Simplest to start	Few restrictions on starting	Separate and legal entity
Proprietor owns all profits	Pooling of funds and talents of partners	Limited financial liability of owners
Personal involvement		Long life
Sole decision maker	Greater borrowing power than sole proprietorship	Easy transfer of ownership
No tax on the business as distinct from owner	More opportunity for specialization than sole proprietorship	Greater financial capability
Easy to dissolve	Personal involvement	
	No tax on the business as distinct from owners	
Disadvantages		
Unlimited financial liability	Unlimited and joint financial liability	Special and double taxation
Difficulty in raising funds for expansion	Potential for personal disagreements	Complicated and costly to form
Proprietor assumes entire burden of management	Relative impermanence	Government regulation and reporting requirements
Impermanence	Frozen investment	Lack of secrecy in operations

wards from risk assumption. A hired manager does not own the business but tends to be blamed for all that goes wrong. He or she may avoid going out on a limb even when that may be best for the firm. This tendency toward conservatism in management, where it exists, may be a disadvantage of the corporation. Of course, this is less likely in a very small corporation where the president owns a large percentage of the outstanding stock.

The separation of ownership and management also reduces personal contact between owners and managers and makes managers even more conservative. Lack of personal contact between managers and workers also tends to make workers feel "outside" the business. How serious a problem this is depends mainly on the corporation's size.

Finally, there is less privacy in a corporation in terms of its financial performance. Whereas proprietorships and partnerships need not publish yearly financial statements for public consumption, corporations must do so. Since knowledge of how well or poorly the firm is doing can be useful to competitors, this publishing of financial data is considered to be a disadvantage.

The corporation's major disadvantages, therefore, are

•special and double taxation
•complicated and costly formation
•considerable government regulation and reporting requirements
•lack of secrecy in operations

Table 3.3 is a summary of the advantages and disadvantages of the three forms of ownership discussed to this point. Figure 3.4 on page 82 indicates the percentage distribution of different forms of business ownership, and Table 3.4 discusses other business structures.

Table 3.4 Other Business Structures

Form	Nature	Example
Joint venture	A special type of temporary partnership set up for a specific purpose and ends when that purpose is accomplished. The death or withdrawal of a partner does not end the joint venture. Usually one partner manages the venture and has unlimited liability. The other partners have limited liability. Sometimes called a syndicate.	Several brokerage firms get together to sell a new stock issue for a client. These firms make up an underwriting syndicate.
Business trust	A trustee (or trustees) is created by an agreement. The trustees hold property, run the business, and accept funds from investors. Investors receive trust shares but they do not vote for trustees. Investors have limited liability.	A mutual fund accepts funds from investors. It pools their investment dollars and uses them to buy stock in other companies.
Mutual company	A firm which is owned by its user-members.	A life insurance company that is owned by its policyholders.
Holding company	A firm which holds enough of the stock of another firm(s) to control it or them. The controlled firm is called a holding company subsidiary.	Firm *A* buys controlling interest in Firms 1 and 2. Firm *B* buys controlling interest in Firms 5 and 6. *A* is a holding company and 1 and 2 are its subsidiaries. *B* is a holding company and 5 and 6 are its subsidiaries. If Firm *C* buys out controlling interest in *A* and *B*, *C* becomes the holding company.
Conglomerate	A firm which controls a number of firms in unrelated fields of business activity. A temporary decline in business in one industry will not have a large effect on the conglomerate's performance because its operations are spread out into several different industries. It is highly diversified.	International Telephone and Telegraph (ITT) Corporation's business activities include space, defence, industrial products, consumer products, natural resources, and telecommunications.

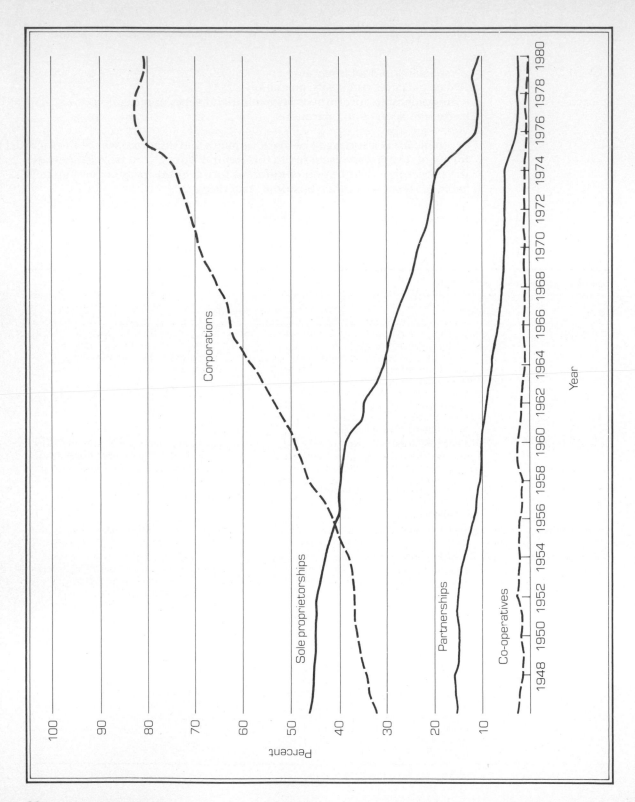

82

CO-OPERATIVES

co-operative

A co-operative is an organization which is formed to benefit its owners in the form of reduced prices and/or the disbursement of surpluses at year-end. The process works like this: suppose a group of farmers felt they could get cheaper fertilizer prices if they formed their own company and purchased in large volume. They might then form a co-operative (either federally or provincially chartered) and operate it. Prices are generally lower to buyers, and at the end of the fiscal year any surpluses are distributed to members on the basis of how much they have purchased. If Farmer Jones bought 5 percent of all co-op sales, he would receive 5 percent of the surplus.

Voting rights are markedly different from those in a corporation. In the co-operative, each member is entitled to one vote, irrespective of how many shares he or she holds. This voting system is entirely consistent with the egalitarian view generally held by co-op members, but it may be a disadvantage, since others who do not hold that view may not become members in the co-op. This system may also be plagued with poor management. It does, however, prevent voting and financial control of the business by a few wealthy individuals.

Types of Co-operatives

There are hundreds of different co-operatives, but they generally function in one of five main areas of business:

1. Consumer co-operatives — these organizations sell goods to both members and the general public (e.g., co-op gasoline stations, agricultural implement dealers).
2. Financial co-operatives — these organizations operate much like banks, accepting deposits from members, giving loans, and providing chequing services (e.g., credit unions).
3. Insurance co-operatives — these organizations provide many types of insurance coverage such as life, fire, liability, etc. (e.g., the Co-operative Hail Insurance Company of Manitoba).
4. Marketing co-operatives — these organizations sell the produce of their (farm) members and also purchase inputs for the production process (e.g., seed and fertilizer).
5. Service co-operatives — these organizations provide members with services, such as recreation.

Figure 3.4
Percentage distribution of manufacturing establishments by form of ownership
(Source: Statistics Canada Stat. 31-203. Reproduced by permission of the Ministry of Supply and Services Canada.)

In terms of number of establishments, co-operatives are the least important form of ownership. (See Figure 3.4.) However, they are important to society and to their members, since they may provide services that are not readily available or that cost more than the members would otherwise be willing to pay.

THE EFFECTS OF SIZE

The relative advantages of the four forms of ownership we have discussed relate basically to the *form of ownership.* While we usually think of sole proprietorships as very small firms and corporations as very large firms, this is not always accurate. Some sole proprietorships, for example, are as large or larger than some small corporations. In other words, the *size* of a business firm has no necessary relationship to its *form of ownership.*

It is also true, however, that when we talk about "big business," we are talking about big corporations. Some of our biggest corporations, however, have very little in common with small corporations. Small, locally owned corporations have more in common with sole proprietorships and partnerships than they have with Canadian Pacific, Imperial Oil, and other huge corporations. In fact, in discussing "business interests" we often find vast differences of opinion among big corporations, medium-size corporations, and small corporations, sole proprietorships, and partnerships regarding what is "good" for businesses. Table 3.5, on pages 86–87, shows the forty largest industrial corporations in Canada.

Advantages of Large-scale Operations

The larger a firm's size, the more likely it can afford to set up research and development, product testing, marketing research, and advertising departments and hire specialists such as engineers, chemists, market researchers, and advertising copy writers to staff them. A small firm usually cannot afford this degree of specialization. It may have one manager in charge of all production operations instead of separate managers for warehousing, traffic, production scheduling, and product quality control.

Large firms also are able to borrow more money and get favourable interest rates. The prime interest rate which often is reported in the news is the rate banks charge their most creditworthy customers—the big corporations. It is lower than the rate most smaller firms pay to borrow money.

Large firms tend to be more permanent, which helps them in hiring managers and workers who value permanence in employment. **Professional managers are people whose profession or career is management. Such a person participates in managing a firm in which he or she is not a major owner.** Sole proprietors, partners, and the owners of small corporations usually are *owner-managers.* Only larger firms can afford to hire professional managers. Partners in successful partnerships, however, can attract high-quality personnel who might expect to be offered

professional managers

a chance to buy into the firm. This practice is common in law and accounting firms.

The advantages of large-scale operation, regardless of the form of ownership, are

- greater opportunity for specialization by workers and managers
- greater borrowing power
- greater access to investment money
- greater availability of managerial talent

Disadvantages of Large-scale Operations

Some economists, government regulators, small-business owners, politicians, and labour leaders believe that businesses can be too big and result in reduced competition and greater concentration of economic power in the economy. Some of them would like to see giant corporations like Gulf Oil and GM broken up.

countervailing power   **In order to counter the power of big business, big labour and big government also are part of our business system. The overall balancing of power between them is called countervailing power.** Hopefully, the size and power of each of these three will prevent any one of them from becoming too powerful and dominant in our society.

In any large organization, there is some tendency toward impersonality. In some of our largest corporations, for example, the lack of personal contact between workers and managers may lower the morale of the

WHAT DO YOU THINK?

When Is A Corporation Too Big?

The corporation is one of our most basic business institutions. Without it, business activity as we know it would be impossible.

Large corporations can afford to invest in costly research and development. This leads to new manufacturing techniques, improvements to established products, and the introduction of new products. Large-scale operations are also economical. The classic example is the modern assembly line in manufacturing. As a greater number of units are produced, the manufacturing cost per unit tends to decline.

This can lead to lower prices for consumers.

However, some people believe that corporations can be too big. They argue that the tremendous size of some corporations contributes to reduced management efficiency, which, in turn, leads to lower profits and higher prices to consumers.

Other people are critical of corporations from a different point of view. Bigness, to them, is "badness." Many of these critics believe that the huge size and economic power of some corporations lead to reduced competition among firms and greater concentration of economic power. When is a corporation too big? WHAT DO YOU THINK?

Table 3.5   The Forty Largest Industrial Corporations in Canada

Rank		Company	Sales	Assets		Liabilities/ Equity	Current Ratio	Net Income		
81	80		$000	$000	Rank			$000	Rank	% Return on Equity
1	1	Canadian Pacific[1]	12,336,266	16,330,185	1	3.2	1.4	485,579	2	13.8
2	2	General Motors of Canada	10,416,050	3,479,547	16	3.0	1.1	−10,300	378	n.a.
3	—	Canadian Pacific Enterprises[2]	8,559,000	11,241,000	3	3.1	1.6	405,000	5	16.2
4	6	Imperial Oil	7,765,000	7,096,000	7	0.8	2.8	465,000	3	12.3
5	3	George Weston[3]	7,428,609	1,898,090	38	2.2	1.4	79,172	41	15.0
6	7	Bell Canada[4]	7,389,100	12,452,000	2	2.2	1.3	550,700	1	15.9
7	4	Ford Motor Co. of Canada	7,206,600	2,172,600	31	2.1	1.0	−98,900	392	12.5
8	5	Alcan Aluminium	5,990,000†	7,515,000	5	1.4	2.3	313,000	7	10.7
9	—	Loblaw Cos.[2,5]	5,794,531	1,033,634	73	2.3	1.2	40,592	72	14.6
10	9	Shell Canada	4,751,000	3,778,000	15	0.8	2.1	236,000	10	11.8
11	8	Gulf Canada	4,583,000	4,468,000	14	1.1	2.3	299,000	8	15.5
12	13	Texaco Canada	4,352,442	2,879,063	21	0.9	2.2	316,306	6	24.7
13	10	Hudson's Bay[6]	4,172,000	3,410,000	17	1.8	1.2	3,733	285	4.3
14	14	TransCanada PipeLines	3,404,897	4,586,300	12	2.9	0.8	154,072	16	15.9
15	20	Provigo[7]	3,293,960*	624,525	107	3.1	1.1	19,637	134	17.1
16	23	Canada Development Corp.	3,136,351	7,093,162	8	4.6	1.7	85,103	37	6.4
17	15	Simpsons-Sears[8]	3,129,625*	1,741,258	41	2.0	2.8	31,937	92	5.6
18	16	Noranda Mines	3,030,394	5,248,644	9	0.8	2.0	164,806	15	8.2
19	11	Massey-Ferguson[9]	2,955,000†*	3,004,000	19	3.4	2.2	−233,700	393	n.a.
20	17	Canada Packers[10]	2,943,000	544,700	110	1.0	1.3	30,000	99	12.0
21	32	Total Petroleum (North America)	2,822,000†*	1,302,173	58	2.9	1.0	−75,400	391	n.a.
22	25	Steinberg Inc.[11]	2,806,409	1,041,332	70	2.2	1.4	40,642	71	13.6
23	18	Canada Safeway[12]	2,711,889	718,318	95	0.5	2.3	66,473	47	16.2

Table 3.5 *(continued)*

Rank		Company	Sales	Assets		Liabili-ties/ Equity	Current Ratio	Net Income		
81	*80*		*$000*	*$000*	*Rank*			*$000*	*Rank*	*% Return on Equity*
24	29	Nova, An Alberta Corp.	2,669,551	5,003,919	10	3.7	1.0	129,862	20	12.7
25	21	International Thomson Organi-sation	2,665,000[13]	1,640,000	44	3.3	0.8	98,200	31	37.9
26	19	Dominion Stores[14]	2,594,337	1,269,562	62	2.0	1.2	23,821	117	11.9
27	28	Hiram Walker Re-sources[15]	2,578,000[16]	4,918,238	11	1.3	1.9	250,061	9	15.7
28	30	Northern Telecom	2,570,875	2,147,300	33	1.5	1.8	120,700	23	16.6
29	31	Chrysler Canada	2,480,600	759,900	90	n.a.	1.2	−54,800	390	n.a.
30	55	Dome Petro-leum	2,238,800*	10,208,700	4	5.5	n.a.	199,100[17]	12	n.a.
31	12	Inco	2,236,000†*	4,474,000	13	1.9	2.7	−5,785	373	n.a.
32	22	MacMillan Bloedel	2,230,136*	2,172,138	32	1.3	1.8	−26,690	386	n.a.
33	27	Moore Corp.	2,228,000†	1,290,000	60	0.5	3.0	136,800	19	18.1
34	33	Seagram Co.[18]	2,212,000†[19]	7,390,000	6	1.6	2.5	416,600	4	32.4
35	26	Stelco Inc.	2,173,775	2,909,602	20	0.9	3.0	82,842	39	5.3
36	24	Genstar	2,145,922	2,858,794	22	2.0	1.1	109,532	25	11.8
37	36	Oshawa Group[20]	1,896,569	380,026	147	2.0	1.4	15,310	156	13.2
38	47	AMCA Inter-national	1,865,000	1,437,000	52	2.3	1.7	83,260	38	21.0
39	40	IBM Canada	1,845,000	1,030,000	75	0.7	1.3	148,000	17	27.5
40	34	Alberta and Southern Gas	1,767,668	382,757	145	49.3	0.4	796	337	11.7

FOOTNOTES

  * Net sales
  † Figures converted from US $
n.a. Not available or not applicable
  1. Consolidates CP Enterprises (rank 3)
  2. Not listed separately last year
  3. Consolidates Loblaw Cos. (rank 9)
  4. Consolidates Northern Telecom (rank 28)
  5. 52 weeks ended Jan. 2, 1982

  6. Fiscal year ended Jan. 31, 1982
  7. Fiscal year ended Jan. 30, 1982
  8. 52 weeks ended Feb. 3, 1982
  9. Fiscal year ended Oct. 31, 1981
  10. 52 weeks ended Mar. 27, 1982
  11. 52 weeks ended July 25, 1981
  12. 53 weeks ended Jan. 3, 1981
  13. Figures converted from UK £
  14. Fiscal year ended Mar. 20, 1982

  15. Fiscal year ended Sept. 30, 1981
  16. Excludes $367 million excise taxes & duties
  17. Includes extraordinary item
  18. Fiscal year ended July 31, 1981
  19. Excludes $1.2 billion excise and sales taxes
  20. 52 weeks ended Jan. 23, 1982

Source: Canadian Business, July, 1982 (Used with permission)

CAREER PROFILE

MY NAME IS BROCK CORDES, AND I AM president of Seabrook Industries, Ltd. Seabrook is a holding company with 100 percent ownership of Web Graphics West, Ltd. and Reliance Press, Ltd. These two firms are involved in publishing and printing community newspapers and circulars. Seabrook also owns 50 percent of Edan Restaurants, Ltd., the subfranchisor of Country Kitchen for Manitoba and Saskatchewan. We currently employ approximately forty people.

I received a Bachelor of Arts in Political Science from the University of Alaska, and an MBA in Marketing from the University of Oregon. My first full-time position was teaching Marketing and Management at the University of Manitoba during the years 1968 through 1972. Later on I was a Branch Manager of a life insurance agency for Monarch Life Assurance, Ltd.

My entrepreneurial motivation has always been quite strong, so in 1974 I went into business for myself. After considerable discussion, two business associates and I decided to invest in the community newspaper business. We did not have equal money or motivation to manage such a business, so we decided to form a limited company. Had we formed a partnership everyone would have had equal rights and liability to the limit of their net worth, and we felt that this would not adequately reflect our different contributions to the business. Each of us put different amounts of money into the holding company; this money was used to buy shares of several other companies that were in the newspaper and printing business (e.g., Kingdon Press, Ltd., Garry Press, Ltd., and Reliance Press, Ltd.). These were all private corporations at the time, i.e., they had only a few shareholders and their shares were not traded on public stock exchanges. We also borrowed money from the bank using the assets of these acquired companies as collateral. The

workers. They may have trouble identifying with the corporation, its owners, and its managers. There is a lot more personal contact in small firms.

In smaller corporations, manager's accomplishments can be observed more easily than in large corporations, where there are many levels of managers. In large corporations, therefore, hired managers may get less of the rewards from assuming risk. Some may become overly conservative and avoid taking risks, even when that is best for the firm.

The disadvantages of large-scale operation, regardless of the form of ownership, are:

•the potential for too much concentration of economic power
•the potential for reduced management efficiency

goal of all this was to increase the size of these companies and to achieve economies of scale that would not have been possible had they remained as individual business entities.

There are several rewards that I have experienced as a result of my involvement in Seabrook. The most important one is that I am in control of the business. Along with my partners, I make major decisions that can make or break the company, and this is important to me. I also get a great deal of satisfaction out of planning a strategy that will make the company profitable. Since we used a form of ownership that limits liability, I am not risking my whole fortune in the business. Because of the limited liability provision, I don't have to worry about my personal assets being taken if something goes wrong with the business. If I had gotten involved in a partnership this would not have been true. The business I'm in has also allowed me to develop professional relationships with accountants, bankers, lawyers, and mentors. I wouldn't have been able to do this if I worked for a large organization. I have also been able to avoid a lot of the organizational infighting (politics) that occurs in bigger organizations as people try to work their way up the management hierarchy.

There are several problems associated with running a business like this. The major one for us is undercapitalization. When we set up a business plan, various things can go wrong that we have no control over. For example, labour rates may go up sharply or a recession may occur. When these things happen, they disrupt the best laid plans. What is usually required to resolve these unexpected problems is more money, but in the present uncertain economic environment, this is often difficult to get. Another major problem concerns disagreements with the two other individuals who formed the company with me. When three entrepreneurs get together and try to run a business, there is almost certain to be friction between them because, by definition, each of them has very strong views about how things should be done. This can be overcome to some extent by giving people clearly defined responsibilities in the different functional areas of the business. However, these individualistic tendencies can never be totally removed. (In fact, the stresses in our business were great enough that I eventually bought out the other two people and I now run the business on my own.) Another problem that I have had to face is that information systems had to be developed from scratch. As the scale of operations of the business increased, we found that we often had very little marketing or financial information that we could use to determine how well we were doing. We had great problems controlling and developing information on things like union wage rates, staff responsibilities, marketing success, and so on. One way we overcame this problem was by the use of a mini-computer.

Overall, the rewards of this business have exceeded the challenges. It is exciting to be involved in a limited corporation that is small enough so that I can have a real feeling of freedom to make decisions I think will benefit the business.

- some tendency toward impersonality
- the potential for overconservatism in management

SUMMARY AND LOOK AHEAD

The four major legal forms of business ownership are the sole proprietorship, the partnership, the corporation, and the co-operative. These are all forms of private ownership in contrast to public ownership. Private ownership is the most common form of ownership in Canada, but there is more public ownership today than there was fifty years ago.

Most privately owned firms are sole proprietorships. Most of these are small and employ only a handful of people. In many, the owner is the only employee.

A partnership is a firm owned by two or more persons who voluntarily go into business together. Like the proprietorship, it also dates back to ancient times.

A corporation is something separate and distinct from its owners. It is a creation of governmental authority. It comes into existence when its owners are granted a corporate charter by the provincial or federal government. Ownership is shown by shares of stock.

A co-operative is formed expressly for the benefit of its owners. It is premised on the belief that members should directly share in the benefits of the co-operative's existence.

What form is "best" depends on the circumstances in each situation. In no sense is one form of ownership always better than another.

In the next two chapters, we view the firm as an organization. As we will see, a firm has both formal and informal dimensions. ■

**QUESTIONS
FOR REVIEW
AND DISCUSSION**

1. What are some of the reasons for public ownership of the means of production?
2. List the business firms with which you did business in the past week. Which were proprietorships, which were partnerships, which were corporations, and which were co-operatives? Why do you think that form of ownership existed in each case?
3. Do you think the president of Canada Packers gets less personal satisfaction from his job than the proprietor of a small business? Why or why not?
4. What, in your opinion, is the most serious disadvantage of the partnership form of legal ownership? Why?
5. If you decided to form a business organization and had already made up your mind to form a partnership, what factors would you consider in the selection of a partner?
6. Suppose that you own one share of stock in MacMillan Bloedel. Exactly what do you "own"?
7. What problems, if any, do you think go along with the separation of ownership and management in the typical corporation?
8. Which form of legal ownership is "best"? Why?
9. What is the function of the board of directors?
10. Do you think that the hired managers of a corporation are likely to assume more social responsibility than the sole proprietor or partner? Explain.
11. Who really "controls" the corporation?
12. Do you think the profit incentive is as important to the manager in a corporation as it is to the sole proprietor? Why or why not?
13. What do you think is the primary concern of a stockholder in a "widely held" corporation?
14. Why are most big businesses corporations?
15. Why do people join co-operatives?
16. What are the advantages of large-scale operations? The disadvantages?

The Paluzzi Brothers

Georgo and Tony Paluzzi are brothers studying business administration at a community college in Ontario. They are energetic, industrious, and want to put to good use what they are learning in school. They have a hobby of developing new recipes for Italian foods. Not too long ago they came up with a dish which proved to be very popular among some of their friends at college. In fact, word of the "new food" spread so fast that the brothers find that their hobby has grown into something of a business. No other Italian food on the market is quite like theirs.

Thus, they are considering going into business on a somewhat larger scale. They are convinced that there are many people in the area who would buy their product if it could be canned and distributed to grocery stores. They also believe that it's a product which would appeal to almost all Canadians.

They are very enthusiastic about going ahead with plans to can and sell the new product. The only obstacles now seem to be money and "know-how."

Questions:
1. What would you advise the brothers to do at this point in their new venture?
2. What are the relative advantages and disadvantages of the four forms of legal ownership as far as this business is concerned?

Ted Adkins

Ted Adkins, a sole proprietor, has been in the business of installing carpets for the past five years. He gets a lot of jobs from two local carpet retailers who also sell other home and building supplies. These retailers do not want to employ their own installers. When they sell a carpet, they recommend Ted to the buyer. Because he has a fine reputation for quality work in the community, Ted also gets business from word-of-mouth advertising. Ted has only two employees who help him install the carpets.

Business is doing so well that Ted finds himself having to turn away customers. Being a perfectionist about his work, he won't let anybody else do a job for him unless he personally oversees the installation. He refuses to hire more employees because of the experience of some other installers who had thriving businesses until they hired more employees to do the actual installing while the owners concentrated on drumming up new business. Their reputations as quality installers suffered, and they lost customers as a result.

Questions:
1. Do you think that Ted is really a businessman or more like a craftsman who takes great pride in the quality of his work? Explain.
2. Why do you think the other installers ran into trouble?
3. Do you think Ted's business is typical of many small proprietorships? Why or why not?

CASE STUDY

PAUL MURRAY

WHILE PAUL MURRAY WAS GROWING UP IN VANCOUVER, HE SPENT A lot of time "tinkering" in his father's workshop. As a result, he developed great skill in wood-working, carpentry, and whittling. At age ten, he sold his first wooden toy. By the time he was sixteen, he was making and selling various items for sale to friends and relatives.

After he graduated from high school, Paul borrowed $2,000 from his uncle, Grant Murray. This interest-free loan enabled him to rent a garage in his neighbourhood. It also enabled him to buy the basic equipment he needed to make up to 500 toys per month in five basic models. He sold these to stores in Vancouver — three variety stores, a novelty shop, and a large toy store.

Paul's sister Heather had recently graduated from a community college where she studied accounting. She agreed to keep his financial records on a part-time basis for a wage of $6 per hour. She became his first employee.

Paul also got help from a lawyer he hired to check sales contracts. A local banker helped him set up a chequing account for the business and arranged for a short-term loan. The bank loan made it possible for Paul to buy wood and paint in larger quantities and to hire a shop assistant.

In the first year, after expanding the shop, sales grew a little and, despite the added wages and interest cost, Paul was able to pay his uncle back one-fourth of his original loan. By the end of the year, Paul got a year-long trial contract with a national toy distributor (Browning) to supply them with 1,000 units each of two of his toy models.

Within several months, Browning indicated that it wanted to negotiate with Paul for a longer-term contract for 5,000 units each of three of his most popular toys. Paul recognized the opportunity here, and he wanted to close the deal.

Paul's only problem was his shortage of funds. This is common in many small businesses like Paul's. He could not afford to buy the additional equipment and materials needed to meet the production requirements called for in the proposed contract. Although he reinvested all his profit in his business, he still needed more money for expansion.

Furthermore, he found that he needed more employees. Although he had three full-time production workers, he knew that the new contract would require hiring at least two more workers.

Browning offered Paul a $15,000 loan if he would agree to sign the proposed contract. Paul figured the loan would be adequate to enable him to "tool up" for the new order. Because Browning was convinced that it could make a large profit from sales of Paul's products, it was willing to lend the money at a very low rate of interest. Paul is seriously considering the offer.

Meanwhile, Paul's uncle approached him with a proposal to take him in as a general partner. Since Grant is quite wealthy, the new partnership would have no financial problems. Besides what Grant could contribute in cash, his being a partner would make the company a much better credit risk for any potential creditors.

Finally, Paul was also approached by three Vancouver investors who wanted to make the company a corporation. They assured Paul that they were seriously interested investors who would gladly invest in the firm as stockholders.

Questions:
1. Why do you think Browning was willing to lend Paul $15,000?
2. Why did Paul reinvest all his profit in his firm?
3. What are the relative advantages and disadvantages of the sole proprietorship, partnership, and corporation in Paul's case?
4. Would you advise Paul to take Uncle Grant in as a general partner, to form a corporation, or to take the loan from Browning? Or should he do something else? Explain the reasons for your recommendations.
5. What other sources of funds are available to Paul Murray?
6. What potential problems exist for Paul Murray if the company continues to grow? ■

Section Two

In this section we place the business firm under a microscope in order to get a sharper focus on how it is managed and organized. In Chapter 4 we look at the nature and functions of management and examine the decision-making process in which all managers engage.

Chapter 5 studies the firm as an organization. Its goals can be achieved only if its human, financial, and physical resources are meaningfully related to each other and if firm and personal objectives can be integrated. We look at types of formal structure and at informal groups within the firm. Both formal and informal organization is important to the firm's success.

MANAGEMENT AND ORGANIZATION

OBJECTIVES

After reading this chapter, you should be able to:

1. Distinguish between managerial work and nonmanagerial work and relate these types of work to the echelons of management.
2. List and discuss the managerial skills and relate these skills to the echelons of management.
3. Discuss the sources of stress on the job and how managers and workers can deal with stress.
4. List and define the functions of management and tell why they are interdependent.
5. Discuss the concept of management by objectives.
6. Interrelate the systems concept to the practice of management.
7. Contrast Theory X managers and Theory Y managers.
8. Contrast motivational factors and maintenance factors in the motivation-hygiene theory and the theory's relationship to job enrichment.
9. Contrast the "great person" theory of leadership to "traitist theory" and discuss several different types of leadership styles.
10. Illustrate the control process by means of a chart.
11. Discuss the stages in the decision-making process and identify the basic types of decisions.

KEY CONCEPTS

Look for these terms as you read the chapter:

manager	directing
management	participative management
echelons of management	communication
managerial skills	motivation
functions of management	job enrichment
planning	leadership
strategic planning	controlling
operational planning	decision-making process
management by objectives (MBO)	routine decision
organizing	nonroutine decision
systems concept	management by exception
staffing	

IN THE EARLY 1980s, SLUGGISH SALES of new cars resulted in reduced tire sales to auto makers. Sales of replacement tires also fell because many people switched to radial tires which last a lot longer than bias-ply tires.

Partly because of these conditions, B. F. Goodrich Company diversified into new businesses such as industrial chemicals and plastics. The firm's top management also decided to stop selling tires to car makers for installation on their new cars because price competition among tire sellers was driving down the price of tires sold to auto makers.

On the other hand, Goodyear Tire & Rubber Company's top management decided to increase their investment in the tire business. The firm built new plants, modernized older ones, and invested heavily in new product development in the tire business, rather than diversifying into other businesses.

Thus the top managements of two firms in the same industry made dramatically different decisions, even though the environment facing them was similar.

CHAPTER FOUR

Management Functions and Decision Making

MANAGERS ARE NEEDED IN ALL ORGANIZATIONS WHETHER THEY ARE large or very small. In fact, much of what business is all about comes under the heading of management. We got some hint of this in Chapter 3. The owner is the top manager in a sole proprietorship, partners share that role in a partnership, and the board of directors and corporate officers are the top management of a corporation.

If you turn back to the Table of Contents at the front of this book, you will notice the term *management* appears quite often. Whether we are talking about production, marketing, information, finance, or personnel — management is necessary. Thus there are production managers, marketing managers, information managers, finance managers, personnel managers, and other managers in most large businesses. They help carry out the decisions made by top managers. In the process, they also make decisions.

In this chapter we will discuss the nature of management. We will look at the type of work managers do, the skills they need, the functions of management, and the decision-making process.

THE NATURE OF MANAGEMENT

There are two basic types of work in any organization:

- nonmanagerial work
- managerial work

Assembly-line workers who make home appliances perform operative tasks such as tightening bolts; and football players block, punt, and tackle. But the president of Canadian General Electric or the head coach of the Toronto Argonauts ordinarily do not perform such tasks. They spend their time planning company and team strategy and performing the other functions of management.

manager

A manager is a person who works through other people (subordinates), and "brings together" their efforts to accomplish goals. Of course, nonhuman resources, such as money and materials, are also involved.

management

Management can mean the process of managing, a collection of managers, or an area of study. **Our primary definition of management is the process of achieving goals through the efforts of others.** Management is necessary in any organization that seeks to accomplish objectives. Without it, an organization becomes a collection of individuals, each going in his or her own direction with no unifying guidance toward organizational goals. The most important ingredient in a firm's ability to reach its goals is

Table 4.1 What a Worker Expects of Management

Job and Working Conditions	Concern with Individual Rights and Compensation	Opportunity for Advancement
A job that is safe	To be treated with dignity	Opportunity to learn new skills
A job that is not monotonous and boring	To feel important and needed	Equal opportunity for promotion
A job that enables a worker to use his or her acquired skills	To be managed by supervisors who can work with people	Training and development programs
A healthy job environment	The right to be heard	Recognition for past accomplishments
Reasonable hours of work	The right to participate in decision making that will affect him or her	Opportunity to improve his or her standard of living
Adequate physical facilities	To know what is expected in terms of performance	A job with a future
Stable employment	Objective basis for evaluating performance	
	No favouritism	
	Fair compensation system	
	Fringe benefits	
	Pay that reflects his or her contribution to the firm	

the quality of its managers. To look at it from another angle, poor management is the basic cause of business failures.

Because a manager must work through others to accomplish goals, how those "others" view management is important to a manager's effectiveness. Some of the major things a worker expects of management are listed in Table 4.1.

Management is partly a science, because managers use organized knowledge in carrying out their functions. Production and marketing managers use formulas developed by statisticians to manage inventories, to schedule production, and to plan and control the distribution of their products. They also use knowledge in the fields of sociology and psychology in managing people. They borrow knowledge from other disciplines to improve their managerial skills.

But management also is an art. Through experience, managers develop judgment, insight, intuition, and a general "feel" for the management job. These are subjective skills which are learned through training and experience.

Figure 4.1
*The management
pyramid*

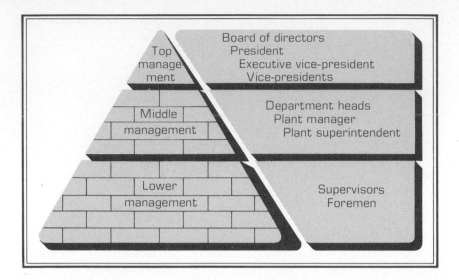

In general, management tends to be more science at the lower echelons and more art at the upper echelons. Staffpersons, for example, who advise top managers supply them with the "facts" they need to make decisions. In making their decisions, however, top managers often have to temper the objective facts with subjective judgment.

The Echelons of Management

Figure 4.1 shows three levels of management that are found in most medium-sized and large firms — top, middle, and lower management. In very small firms, the owner usually is the only manager. In very large firms, there may be more than three levels of management. **The different layers, or levels, of management in an organization are called the echelons of management.**

echelons of
management

Members of top management work through a greater number of subordinates than middle- and lower-level managers, and they seldom perform operative tasks. Members of middle management report to top management. They are accountable for carrying out top management's plans. Their perspective is more short-run than top management's because they arc closer to the firm's day-to-day activities. They also perform more operative tasks than top managers. Members of lower management report to middle management. Operating managers are the managers closest to the operative tasks in the firm. Foremen on assembly lines, for example, may get some grease on their hands and clothing. It is very unlikely that a top-level manager would.

In other words, the higher the level of management, the more time a manager spends performing managerial work. The lower the level of management, the more time a manager spends performing nonmanagerial tasks (See Figure 4.2).

Figure 4.2
*The relative importance
of managerial and
nonmanagerial work
at various levels
of the management
hierarchy*

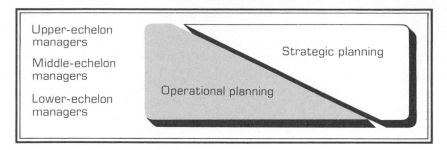

Managerial Skills

managerial skills

All managers, regardless of their level, must have three basic managerial skills:

- **conceptual skills**
- **"people" skills (human relations, communication, motivation, and leadership skills)**
- **technical skills**

Conceptual skills give a manager the ability to see the organization as a whole—to see it as a complex of interacting and interdependent parts. Such skills also allow a manager to see how an organization is related to its environment.

Managers with these skills can think creatively, analytically, and imaginatively. They can identify and solve problems and come up with new approaches to the management process. Conceptual skills are crucial for long-range planning and are most important at the upper echelons of management.

People skills include human relations skills—the manager's ability to get along and work with people, including both superiors and subordinates. Managers have to work effectively as group members in order to build a team effort. People skills also include communication, motivation, and leadership skills. They are the most important of the managerial skills and are discussed in more detail later in this chapter.

Effective managers view their subordinates as human assets and strive to create a work environment in which subordinates will put forth their best efforts to reach the firm's goals. Developing this human resource is a crucial task for all managers. People skills are equally important at all echelons of management.

Technical skills are the manager's ability to understand and use techniques, methods, equipment, and procedures—to understand how "things" operate. These skills are most important at the lower management level. Foremen, for example, must know how to operate the machinery their subordinates use. As a manager moves up the management hierarchy, technical skills become less important relative to the conceptual and people skills.

Technical skills are the most difficult to transfer from one industry to another. It is harder for lower-level managers, whose major skill is technical skill, to move from one industry to another than it is for higher-level managers. Conceptual and people skills are more transferable.

The higher a manager is in the management hierarchy, the more important it is to have knowledge in many areas. One of the toughest tasks for some younger managers is to broaden their outlook, to stop looking at their job from the viewpoint of their former job. Fortunately each of the managerial skills can be developed if a person is willing to work hard to learn them. They do not have to be "inborn."

Effective managers are willing to learn. They keep up with developments in their field and in related fields and seek to apply useful knowledge to the management job. Considerable progress has been made recently in automating office operations. This can free clerical workers and secretaries from a great deal of routine work. Many managers see this as an opportunity for them to retrain these people to assume some of the more routine managerial tasks. This, in turn, frees managers to devote more time to conceptual work.

Other Aspects of Managerial Work

Effective managers can set goals and put forth the effort needed to accomplish them. They also have a high achievement need and recognize the value of time. They can cram more into a 24-hour day than people with a lower need for achievement. Managerial work also is a stress-creating type of work.

Actually, nonmanagerial and managerial work both involve stress because individuals must subordinate, to some degree, their individuality and personal goals to the organization. Because managers must work through the efforts of subordinates, they must help them to manage their stress. Personality conflicts, the potential for conflict between different departments, and the conflict between labour and management are only a few of the sources of organizational conflict.

Conflict can disrupt the smooth functioning of a firm and contribute to stress among workers and managers. Conflict, however, also can benefit the firm; it often leads to new ways of doing things, and it brings deep-seated problems to the surface where they can be dealt with. The accompanying tension often stimulates the flow of creative new ideas. Management, therefore, should try to control conflict, not eliminate it.

A person who perceives an assigned task as important but too demanding experiences stress. People who have a high degree of self-confidence will usually perceive less difficulty in accomplishing a task than people who lack self-confidence.

Stress on the job can come from within a person or from his or her work environment. Internal sources of stress include low self-confidence, poor health, low tolerance for frustration, and a tendency to set unattainable goals for oneself. Examples of external sources are boring and

WHAT DO YOU THINK?

What Causes Some Managers to Burn Out?

During the 1970s the term "job burnout" crept into our vocabulary. Among the types of work often associated with burnout are teaching, politics, social work, nursing, and police work. These jobs involve a high degree of stress and coping with other peoples' problems. The people who hold these jobs experience burnout when the problems they deal with become overwhelming. The following excerpt discusses five stages of progressive burnout.

Burnout is progressive, occurring over a period of time. Authors Robert Veninga and James Spradley define five stages that lead from a stressful job to a burnt out case. 1) The Honeymoon — intense

enthusiasm and job satisfaction that, for all but a few dynamos, eventually give way to a time when valuable energy reserves begin to drain off. 2) Fuel Shortage — fatigue, sleep disturbances, possibly some escapist drinking or shopping binges and other early-warning signals. 3) Chronic Symptoms — exhaustion, physical illness, acute anger and depression. 4) Crisis — illness that may become incapacitating, deep pessimism, self-doubt, obsession with one's own problems. 5) Hitting the Wall — career and even life threatened. (Lance Morrow, "The Burnout of Almost Everyone," *Time,* Sept. 21, 1981)

Burnout also has become more common among managers in business firms. What causes some managers to burn out? WHAT DO YOU THINK?

monotonous work, too much responsibility, too little time to do the assigned work, and poor supervision.

In recent years many managers and their companies have become more aware of the importance of coping with stress and strengthening the cardiovascular system. Approaches and techniques range from exercise and recreation to biofeedback. Many firms have employee exercise plans. Some firms have their own gyms and some pay all or part of the cost of individual membership in fitness clinics.

THE FUNCTIONS OF MANAGEMENT

functions of management

Managerial work consists of performing the functions of management:

- **planning**
- **organizing**
- **staffing**
- **directing**
- **controlling**

Dividing managerial work into functions helps us to understand its nature, but, in the real world, managerial work cannot be divided into component parts. These functions are performed at the same time and are interdependent. (See Figure 4.3.)

Figure 4.3
The functions of management

Planning

planning

Planning means preparing a firm to cope with the future. It involves setting the firm's objectives over different time periods and deciding on the methods of achieving them.

Setting Objectives

Because a firm is an economic and social organization, its objectives are both economic and social. An economic objective of most firms is to produce and sell goods or services that satisfy customer wants at a profit to the firm. Other examples of economic objectives are:

- to maximize profits
- to achieve a 15 percent rate of return on investment
- to increase market share by 10 percent

Greater awareness of the social responsibility of business has led to growing attention to social objectives. Large corporations especially recognize that cooperation in attaining social objectives is in their long-run interest. Some examples of social objectives are:

- to provide employment opportunities for the disadvantaged unemployed
- to support the arts
- to improve ethnic relations in the community

Plans can be long-range, intermediate-range, or short-range. These periods, however, are not easily defined in terms of years or months. Long-range planning for large companies may cover a period of ten or more years. Long-range planning for a small apparel store may cover a period of six months to one year. How far ahead a firm plans (its planning horizon) depends on the particular industry a firm is in, its technology, and its products.

Long-range planning makes it easier for a firm to adapt to a changing environment. The purpose is not to show how well the firm can predict the future but to gain insight into the actions the firm has to take in the present to help ensure that it will, in fact, have a future.

There are basically two different types of planning: strategic planning and operational planning. (See Figure 4.4.)

Figure 4.4
The relative importance of strategic and operational planning at various levels of the management hierarchy

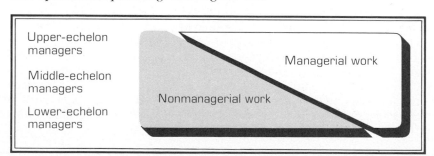

Upper-echelon managers

Middle-echelon managers

Lower-echelon managers

Managerial work

Nonmanagerial work

strategic planning

Strategic planning is concerned with a firm's long-range future and its overall strategy of growth. This is the type of planning for which top-level managers are responsible. For example, RCA Corporation's decision to introduce SelectaVision was a result of top management's strategic planning.

operational planning

Operational planning is planning for the day-to-day survival of the firm. Middle and lower-level managers engage mainly in this type of planning. For example, middle- and lower-level managers might plan the sales training program that distributors use to train their dealers' salespeople.

Regardless of the time frame for a particular objective, it is generally accepted that sound objectives should

- be specific
- be measurable
- identify expected results

TWO POINTS OF VIEW

Management by Objectives (MBO)

Supervisor A:

"This MBO is for the birds. Why should I let my subordinates help to set the goals they are supposed to accomplish? This mutual goal-setting lets them tell me what they should be trying to accomplish. But my job is to tell them what to accomplish.

"What is worse is that MBO lets workers help decide what acceptable levels of performance are. You can bet that it results in lower employee performance.

"Periodic meetings with each worker to discuss his or her progress toward reaching goals is another requirement of MBO which wastes both my time and my workers' time. Then we're supposed to meet again at the end of the period during which the worker is supposed to have accomplished the mutually agreed-upon goals. The big joke is that the worker and I are supposed to evaluate his or her performance and set new goals for the next period. Thus, not only does a worker help to set goals, a worker also helps evaluate his or her own performance. It's a never-ending cycle of giving away authority to make decisions."

Supervisor B:

"MBO is the best possible way to motivate subordinates. By letting them participate in setting their goals, they know what is expected of them. By letting them participate in evaluating their performance, they know how their performance will be evaluated. In other words, MBO improves boss-worker communication. It is at the heart of participative management. I think it shows workers that their ideas and opinions count.

"MBO helps each worker to better understand how his or her performance is related to the firm's accomplishment of its objectives. It also puts an end to the notion that promotions and pay raises are based on favouritism. Each worker knows what goals he or she is supposed to be working toward and how his or her performance will be evaluated. Supervisors who believe that MBO is no good assume that workers are lazy, unconcerned about accomplishing goals, and indifferent about performance evaluation."

•be reachable with reasonable effort

•be expressed within a time frame for accomplishing them

The person or department responsible for accomplishing objectives should have the necessary authority to accomplish them in order to prevent buck passing.

management by objectives (MBO)

Recently, many managers have been adopting the management by objectives (MBO), or managing by results, approach. The manager meets with each subordinate to set his or her objectives. The subordinate participates in goal setting and, if the objectives are accomplished, the subordinate is considered to have performed well. It's the result that counts!

MBO offers the following advantages:

•subordinates know at the beginning of a planning period what is expected of them, thereby reducing their uncertainty about what they are supposed to accomplish

•subordinates often enjoy participating with superiors in determining a method for measuring their performance, which increases their motivation to reach the objective

•subordinates are given more opportunity to use new approaches to reaching their objectives since MBO does not predetermine the means for reaching objectives

•managers have more confidence in future planning and predicting results

Managers who use the MBO approach assume that their subordinates (1) have higher-level needs which they desire to satisfy through their work, (2) are creative and have ideas and knowledge to bring to the job, and (3) will work harder to accomplish goals which they help to set.

Among the potential problems in implementing the MBO approach are (1) subordinate suspicion that the real purpose of MBO is to get more work out of them, (2) desire to "beat the system" by setting very minimal objectives to make their performance look good, (3) desire to "please management" by setting unrealistically high objectives, and (4) desire to avoid spending time with the boss discussing and writing objectives. Other problems may arise in integrating the various individuals' goals with those of the organization, setting a priority of objectives, and time-scheduling to accommodate them.

Deciding How to Reach Objectives

In planning, managers rely on knowledge of past and present conditions in their environment. They use this to forecast probable future developments and to plan a course of action in accordance with this forecast. Because no one knows for sure what the future holds, managers operate under conditions of uncertainty. The future, however, is not completely uncertain. Some conditions can be more or less taken for granted and projected into the future, thereby reducing the number of planning "unknowns."

For example, millions of babies were born during the baby boom years 1946–1964. Firms that sell houses, home appliances, and furniture knew years ago that when those people reached their twenties and thirties they would be good prospects as buyers. But those firms could not have predicted as easily the high interest rates, high inflation, and high unemployment of the early 1980s that prevented many of those people from buying new houses.

Planners, therefore, plan in the face of something more than complete uncertainty and something less than complete certainty. They plan under conditions of risk; they have knowledge (or a good guess) about the likelihood of occurrence of some factors, but not all.

Planning and decision making are bound up in a future filled with risk. This is why some managers avoid planning. They argue that it takes them away from "doing" and accomplishing results. They do not try to foresee problems; they "cross those bridges when they come to them." This, of course, is very shortsighted.

Usually there is more than one way to reach an objective, but there is no sure way of identifying the "best" way. Most managers will choose the approach they predict will yield the highest return relative to cost. This type of analysis is called *cost-benefit analysis.*

In other words, we set out the various plans that could be used to reach an objective. Underlying each plan is a set of planning premises, or assumptions about the future. Probabilities, or odds, are assigned to each set of premises to indicate our "best guess" as to which ones will become reality. Each plan's expected profit along with its probability of success also are estimated. The plan most likely to be chosen is based on the most realistic planning premises and offers the highest return, given the estimated probability of success in carrying out the plan.

Organizing

organizing

A firm becomes a structured organization through the process of organizing. **Organizing is the management function of relating people, tasks (or activities), and resources to each other so that an organization can accomplish its objectives.** Plans are carried out by the organizing process. Like planning, organizing also is a dynamic process. This means that changes in objectives and plans usually lead to changes in the organization's structure. We will discuss organizing in greater detail in Chapter 5.

The Systems Concept

systems concept

According to the systems concept, a firm is not the accounting department or the marketing department. It consists of a network of interrelationships among the various departments and their environment. The marketing research department is a *subsystem* of the firm. However, the firm is a subsystem of its industry, and the industry is a subsystem of the total economic system, and so on. Top management must integrate the various subsystems so that overall systems performance can be improved. Top management also must work for acceptance of this view by others in the firm.

The systems view underscores the need for top management to set clearly defined goals and to communicate them to lower-level managers and workers. In judging their effectiveness, credit managers tend to think in terms of reducing bad debts, while sales managers tend to think in terms of annual dollar sales increases. They often view the firm from different perspectives, but they should be striving to accomplish common goals.

The more that company personnel view the firm as a system, the less their actions will conflict and the more efficient the firm will become. The credit manager recognizes that some bad debts are acceptable in order to increase sales. The sales manager recognizes the need to deny credit to customers with poor credit ratings in order to keep bad-debt losses down. This is the essence of the systems view. Another indicator of systems thinking is a firm's responsiveness to social problems. When a firm accepts social responsibility, it is viewing itself as a subsystem of the larger socio-economic system.

Staffing

staffing

An organization is meaningless without people. The quality of its managers and workers probably is a firm's single most important asset. **Staffing includes the recruitment, selection, training, and promotion of personnel to fill both managerial and nonmanagerial positions in a company.** Because staffing is so important, we will study it in detail in Chapter 6.

Directing

directing

Assume that we have developed plans, created an organization structure, and staffed it. It now must be stimulated to action through the management function of directing. **Directing means encouraging subordinates to work toward achieving company objectives. It sometimes is called leading, guiding, motivating, or actuating.**

A manager's opinion of subordinates affects how they will be directed. Managers who think subordinates are lazy, irresponsible, and immature rely on rewards and punishments and use formal authority to get things done. Managers who think subordinates are responsible and are striving to achieve goals will likely "let them work." The amount and type of directing that are needed depend largely on the manager's view of his or her subordinates.

The discussion that follows focuses on four basic concepts that relate to the directing function:

- participation
- communication
- motivation
- leadership

Participation

Managers who practise participative management do not rely only on their formal authority to issue orders to subordinates. **Participative management means that the manager encourages and allows his or her subordinates to involve themselves directly in the decision making that will affect them.**

Douglas McGregor has suggested that there are two types of managers, *Theory X managers* and *Theory Y managers* (Douglas McGregor, *The Human Side of Enterprise.* New York: McGraw-Hill, 1960). Theory X managers assume that the average person

- inherently dislikes work
- is, by nature, lazy, irresponsible, and self-centered
- is security oriented and indifferent to the needs of the organization
- wants to avoid responsibility and has little ambition

Because they make these assumptions, Theory X managers believe they must threaten, coerce, and control in order to motivate the average person to work toward company goals.

Theory Y managers make the opposite assumptions about the average person. Theory Y managers assume that the average person is capable of

- developing interest in his or her work
- committing himself or herself to working to reach company goals
- working productively with a minimum of control and threat of punishment

According to McGregor, workers who fit the Theory X manager's set of assumptions do so because of the nature of their work and the supervision they receive. In other words, their jobs and the supervision they receive tend to make the workers dislike their work, become irresponsible, and so on.

Many managers believe that participative management is the key to building *employee morale,* the worker's attitudes about the job and employer. The more that workers view the firm as the source of their need satisfaction, the higher their morale is likely to be.

Some workers, however, *do* fit the Theory X assumptions. A manager who assumes they fit Theory Y assumptions probably will fail to motivate them. Furthermore, good employee morale is no guarantee of high employee productivity. Employees could be very happy on the job and still produce very little. They also could be very unhappy and have low morale and yet be very productive because they are afraid they will be fired!

For participative management to work effectively,

- there must be adequate time to anticipate problems and make plans, because participation requires more time than authoritarian decision making
- subordinates must be assured that their participation is genuine or else they will not see any personal benefit from participating

•managers must believe in it and trust their subordinates

•managers must understand that it involves accountability to their subordinates as well as to their superiors, because they are no longer merely passing "orders" down the chain of command

Communication

communication

Communication is a transfer of information between people that results in a common understanding between them. When workers believe that they not only are "talked down to" but also can talk up to their supervisors, two-way communication exists. Workers feel more important when their voice is heard.

Modern managers recognize the advantages of two-way communication. Communication of orders may be initiated at the top. But feedback (the receiver's response) from people lower in the firm is critical to the planning and control functions because these people are closer to the situation than upper-level managers. A production manager who recently installed new machinery on the assembly line wants feedback from foremen regarding the machinery's performance. Foremen, in turn, want feedback from assembly-line workers.

Motivation

motivation

Motivation is the result of the drive to satisfy an internal urge. Managers must structure jobs so that they provide incentives that will satisfy workers' needs if those workers apply effort on the job. By doing this, managers can motivate their subordinates to work toward company objectives. The more effectively organizational and personal objectives are integrated, the more motivated workers are to achieve the organizational objectives.

For many years money has been used as the "carrot" (incentive) to motivate workers. Money is an effective motivator as long as workers are focusing on satisfying only their lower-level needs, such as the needs for food, clothing, and shelter. But for many modern workers today, money has ceased to be the all-powerful motivator.

The Hawthorne Experiments mark the beginning of modern research into employee motivation and the human relations movement in management. In these experiments, researchers studied the effects of the physical work environment on worker productivity. For example, it seemed reasonable to assume that better lighting would lead to greater employee productivity. The researchers found, however, that production increased when the lighting level was raised *or* lowered. The apparent explanation for this surprising result was that the workers felt important because they were being studied by management.

The human relations movement brought new approaches to motivating and leading employees. Managers have come to understand that workers are not machines and that people on the job have the same needs as people off the job. As we will see in Chapter 5, if their higher-level needs are not satisfied by the former organization, workers will create an informal organization to satisfy them.

All managers are responsible for motivating their subordinates, but managers are limited in what they can do. Foremen are limited by company policies on wage scales and fringe benefits, and the company's president may be limited by policies set by the board of directors. Because the typical employee is said to work at about 30 percent of capacity, however, motivating them to become more productive is a big challenge for all managers.

An interesting view of motivation has given managers added insight into how to motivate employees. Frederick Herzberg's research led him to conclude that many factors managers often rely on to motivate workers are not true motivators (Frederick Herzberg, *Work and the Nature of Man.* Cleveland: World Publishing Co., 1966). He divides job factors into two groups:

- maintenance factors (hygiene factors), such as pay, working conditions, job security, and the nature of supervision
- motivational factors (motivators), such as achievement, recognition, responsibility, advancement, and growth potential

Maintenance factors occur as part of the work environment. They are job context, or extrinsic, factors that are not part of the work itself. If they are absent or inadequate, they tend to be *dissatisfiers.* Their presence, however, only helps to avoid worker dissatisfaction. Thus poor pay and poor working conditions are dissatisfiers but improving them will *not* provide true motivation.

Motivational factors occur as part of the work itself. They are job content, or intrinsic, factors. Motivational factors make work rewarding in and of itself — they are *satisfiers.*

job enrichment

Herzberg's motivation-hygiene theory has helped in focusing management attention on job content factors in motivating workers. **Job enrichment is the process of redesigning jobs to satisfy higher-level needs and organizational needs by improving worker satisfaction and task efficiency. It gives workers more responsibility, authority, and autonomy in planning and doing their work.**

Some managers believe that job enlargement and job rotation can help in providing more satisfying work for subordinates. *Job enlargement* involves adding new tasks to a job in order to make it less boring and more challenging. It is especially useful for assembly-line jobs that are repetitive and monotonous and do not involve the worker's mental process.

Job rotation among management trainees has been practised for many years to give them an overall view of the firm's operations and to prepare them for promotion. This practice has been used at the operative level in recent years. Workers periodically are assigned to new jobs in order to reduce boredom. The new job usually does not require the worker to learn a major new skill; but it does, for example, give assembly-line workers a better understanding of the total production process. They can relate their specialized jobs to the creation of a finished product.

Quite recently, a lot of attention has focused on quality-of-work-life programs. As we will see in Chapter 5, the goals are to increase job satisfaction and to improve productivity.

leadership

Leadership

Leadership is a manager's ability to get subordinates to develop their capabilities by inspiring them to achieve. It is a means of motivating them to accomplish goals. Leadership is practised in different degrees by the people in a firm. The president is ultimately responsible for directing the entire firm. He or she sets the style of leadership in the firm. If the president is a dictator, other managers are likely to be dictators, too.

One of the earliest leadership theories was the "great person" theory. It assumed that certain persons were gifted with leadership talent and that they would arise as great leaders in any situation. Examples of these "born leaders" are Alexander the Great, Napoleon, Abraham Lincoln, and Queen Elizabeth I.

Another theory is the "traitist" theory. The "traitists" believe that leadership traits don't have to be inborn. They feel that leadership ability can be acquired through experience and learning. For years the "traitists" have been searching for common traits among leaders, but there are striking differences among the lists compiled by various researchers. Some of the more common leadership traits, however, are intelligence, dependability, high tolerance for frustration, persistence, imagination, and cooperativeness.

Most of the newer research on leadership has focused on leadership styles. Figure 4.5, for example, presents a continuum of possible leadership styles. At the left is the boss-centered leader and at the right is the subordinate-centered leader. Most managers feel that the more subordi-

Figure 4.5
A continuum of leadership behaviour

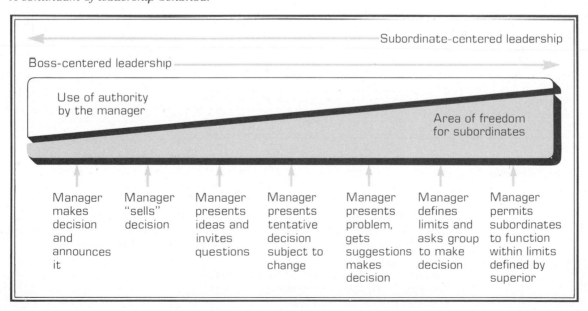

Autocratic leader		Democratic leader
No	Willing to delegate?	Yes
No	Believes in two-way communication?	Yes
No	Believes in participative management?	Yes
No	Trusts subordinates?	Yes
No	Willing to let followers learn by their mistakes?	Yes
No	Believes subordinates' ideas are important?	Yes
No	Believes subordinates seek to do a good job?	Yes
No	Interested in subordinates' higher-level needs?	Yes
Yes	Believes subordinates are naturally lazy?	No
Yes	Believes subordinates must be "watched" at all times?	No
Yes	Believes subordinates are uninterested in their work?	No
Yes	Believes money is all that is necessary to motivate workers?	No
Yes	Believes that subordinates have to be treated like children?	No

Figure 4.6
Styles of leadership

nate-centered leadership styles are more effective than the more boss-centered styles. Figure 4.6 presents this continuum in a different format. Other commonly used terms to describe leadership styles are

- autocratic, dictatorial, or authoritarian
- democratic, or participative
- laissez-faire, or free rein

POINT OF VIEW

What Is Management?

A lower-level manager:

"I'm a supervisor on a production line. To me, management means attending to detail—making sure that my subordinates do exactly as they are told. The really important work that can't be left up to somebody else to do is what it's all about. I spend a lot of time working right along with my subordinates. I'm not afraid to get my hands dirty!

"As far as management functions go, and I'll admit I never thought of management in those exact terms, most of my time is spent on directing. Controlling would come in second. My job is to get production out of my workers and that means getting them to do a good job and making sure that they do it."

A top-level manager:

"I'm president of a large firm that manufactures sporting goods. To me, management means keeping yourself free of detail work so that you can concentrate on thinking about your company's future—where your company will be ten to fifteen years from now. Of course, thinking by itself won't accomplish the job. That's why I've spent several years bringing together the best possible group of executives to carry out my plans for the future.

"Undoubtedly, my most important function is planning."

Autocratic leaders keep all decision-making authority to themselves, while democratic leaders share it with their subordinates. Laissez-faire leaders try to delegate total responsibility for decision making to their subordinates. They do not want to share their decision-making authority; they want to join the group for decision-making purposes.

As we suggested earlier, many modern managers regard the more participative styles of leadership as desirable because participative leadership

- permits subordinates to satisfy their higher-level needs (competence, knowledge, self-confidence, feelings of achievement, esteem) through the job
- is an approach to motivating subordinates
- permits managers to receive feedback from operatives at the lowest levels in the firm

In the final analysis, the "best" style of leadership depends on the three elements in the leadership environment:

- the leader
- the followers
- the situation

Participation will not work if the leader cannot inspire subordinates to participate or if the subordinates do not want to participate. Situations that call for quick decisions limit the time available for true participation of subordinates.

Fred Fiedler has developed a *contingency theory of leadership,* which makes it clear that there is no one "best" leadership style (Fred E. Fiedler, *A Theory of Leadership Effectiveness.* New York: McGraw-Hill, 1967). For example, situations that are either very easy or very difficult are handled best by task-oriented leaders. Situations that are only moderately difficult are handled best by subordinate-oriented leaders.

Controlling

controlling

Managers must always monitor operations (evaluate performance) to see if the firm is achieving its goals. This is the management function of controlling. **Controlling involves**

- **setting standards of performance**
- **measuring actual performance and comparing it to performance standards to detect deviations from standards**
- **taking corrective action when significant deviations exist**

As we suggested in our discussion of MBO, planning and controlling are closely related. When spouses prepare a budget, they are planning *and* setting up a control device. Suppose the budget plan is to save $1,000 by the end of the year. If their savings account shows a balance of $200 on July 1, the standard is not being met. Awareness of this should lead to corrective action. The earlier they discover the deviation from their saving standard, the quicker they can take corrective action.

Examples of controlling are an office manager's efforts to keep expenditures for typing paper in line with the budget or a plant manager's efforts to keep the number of rejects down to an acceptable minimum. First there must be a definite idea of what we want to accomplish (a standard). The office manager, for example, cannot exceed the budget for paper. In practice, setting standards is not always simple. How should management evaluate the production department's performance? On the basis of the number of rejects? On the basis of the average time required to produce an average unit of output? On the basis of the average cost of producing an average unit of output? Actually, all are important. A three percent reduction in rejects along with tripled production costs probably is not desirable. But whether it is or is not depends on the relative importance of avoiding rejects and avoiding cost increases.

Second, a manager measures actual performance and compares it to the established standard. Measurement is not so simple either. There are many problems in measuring employee performance. In some jobs only quantitative results (number of units produced) are important. In other jobs qualitative results (quality of the units produced) are the crucial basis for comparison.

The final element of control is taking corrective action. It is desirable to detect deviations from standards quickly. The longer that corrective action takes, the more it will cost. (See Figure 4.7.)

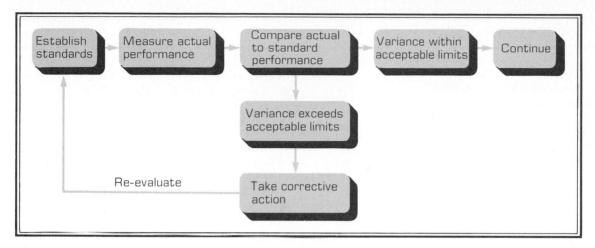

Figure 4.7
The control process

THE DECISION-MAKING PROCESS

Everything a firm does is the result of decisions made by managers. Examples are deciding on the firm's goals, what products to make, what equipment to buy, what advertising appeals to use, where to get funds, and where to sell its products. Decision making is a very complex process. The management functions are involved at each stage.

Stages in the Decision-Making Process

decision-making
process

The stages in the decision-making process are as follows:

- recognizing an opportunity or a problem
- gathering information
- developing alternatives
- analyzing alternatives
- choosing the best alternative
- implementing the decision
- evaluating the decision

Recognizing an Opportunity or a Problem

A business opportunity must be recognized before it can be exploited. Because a firm's resources are limited, management must decide what types of opportunity can be exploited. Exploiting the opportunity also requires decision making.

Decision making also is needed when management recognizes a problem. Often this is little more than a feeling that "something is not right."

AUTHORS' COMMENTARY

Japanese and Canadian Management Styles Will Become More Similar

Japanese managers are more likely than Canadian managers to practise participative management; they seek to manage by consensus. The goal of consensus management is to encourage subordinates to participate in the decision making that will affect them in order to get their commitment to the decision. There is more stress in Japan on "group think." Thus performance in Japanese firms tends to be evaluated more on group, or team, accomplishments than in Canadian firms, where performance tends to be evaluated more on the individual's accomplishments.

Although it ordinarily takes Japanese managers longer than Canadian managers to make decisions, the Japanese can usually implement their decisions more quickly because most of the opposition to a decision will have been eliminated before it is made. Canadian managers make decisions more quickly but typically spend more time implementing them.

It is likely that Japanese and Canadian styles of management will become more similar as firms in these two nations compete more aggressively for sales in the global business environment. Productivity will play a major role in determining which features of Japanese and Canadian management styles will remain and which ones will be modified or discarded.

Decisions must be made regarding a clear definition of the problem and whether or not anything will be done about it.

Gathering Information

After recognizing the opportunity or problem, the decision maker's next step is to gather information about it. This involves talks with company personnel and outsiders who might provide greater insight. Company records and secondary sources of information such as libraries also might be investigated.

Because of the tremendous capacity of computers to store data, many firms now have *management information systems.* These systems are made up of people and machines. People feed in the data needed for decision-making purposes, and these data are processed, summarized, and reported to decision makers who need it.

Developing Alternatives

After developing a good "feel" for the opportunity or problem and its setting, the decision maker begins to formulate alternative courses of action. The support of others might be sought in brainstorming sessions in which the participants offer ways to deal with the opportunity or problem. Freewheeling creativity is important here, so no evaluation is made of the alternatives offered at this stage. The goal is to stimulate new ways of looking at the opportunity or problem and to develop alternative ways of dealing with it. If there is only one alternative, there is no decision to make!

Analyzing Alternatives

After making a list of alternatives, the decision maker begins to analyze them critically. Alternatives that are unlikely to pay off are eliminated along with those that involve high risk in comparison to expected payoff. Those that remain often are ranked in terms of their expected payoff. The payoff could be stated in terms such as least cost, maximum profit, or maximum customer service.

This process might involve analyzing the projected consequences of each of the remaining alternatives, which is always tough because it involves forecasting the future. Nevertheless, the thought process required here helps to ensure that the decision maker considers the future consequences of present decisions.

Choosing the Best Alternative

In choosing the best alternative, a decision maker establishes a decision criterion and a decision rule. If the goal is to improve delivery service to customers, the decision criterion might be "fastest delivery." The decision rule would be to choose the transportation method that provides the fastest delivery to customers. The decision criterion, however, could have been "lowest cost." Choosing decision criteria requires good judgment concerning the firm's goals and an understanding of the risks involved.

Implementing the Decision

Once the decision has been made (the best alternative or a combination of several of the initial alternatives has been selected), the decision maker must move toward implementing it. Implementation, of course, also requires decision making in performing the management functions.

Evaluating the Decision

After implementing the decision, the decision maker must evaluate it. Operations must be monitored, or checked, to see whether the decision is being implemented properly. Monitoring also gives the decision maker

---

THINK ABOUT IT!

A Sure Way to Fail in Management

Decision making is needed in the performance of every management function, but decision making takes courage. In our dynamic business world, a manager seldom, if ever, has all the information he or she would like to make decisions. Nevertheless, some managers postpone making critical decisions on the grounds that they don't have enough information.

In many cases, getting all the information is practically impossible. In other cases it would cost more to get than it would be worth. Regardless, the manager who continually puts off decisions will fail as a manager. THINK ABOUT IT!

CAREER PROFILE

MY NAME IS GRANT RITCHIE, AND I AM president of Food Systems Management, Ltd. My company manages cafeterias in schools, office buildings, factories, and other institutional settings. I grew up in a family that had been involved in many facets of the fast-food business. However, I originally had no interest in carrying on the family business. After graduating from high school, I enrolled in the B. Comm. programs at two different universities, but I dropped out of school because I wanted to get started on a career. I went to work for Beneficial Finance, but while there I realized that there was very little security working for a big corporation. I felt that I might as well work for myself. After considering several business opportunities, I chose the food service business because it took very little financing to get into it. (I had only $200.00 and a small car with monthly payments.)

My key function as president of the company is to coordinate the various aspects of the business (sales, finance, warehousing, cafeteria performance evaluation, hiring of key personnel, public relations, etc.). I don't get involved in the day-to-day management of any of the cafeterias, but I do visit them regularly so that the manager or administrator who awarded the contract to our firm sees that I am concerned that the cafeteria is run properly. My key expertise is in sales. I attain business in

two ways: (1) I approach companies that are unhappy with their present caterer and discuss ways that my firm might improve their cafeteria; and (2) I generate totally new business by simply looking for opportunities.

Each cafeteria is headed by a supervisor who has several workers reporting to him or

feedback that helps in assessing whether the "right decision" was made and if corrective actions are needed.

Types of Decisions

routine decision

One type of decision is the routine decision. **A routine decision is a recurring decision. It is a decision that must be faced over and over.** You probably do not consciously decide the route you will take to class each day. For most of us, this is a routine decision. Because we face that decision so many times, we develop a routine decision for it.

her. I have three people reporting directly to me (the warehouse manager, the executive chef, and an office manager). The supervisors of the various cafeterias report to area managers. Except where the cafeteria is very large, each area manager is responsible for eight to ten cafeterias in several different settings. In this way each area manager gets wide experience. This allows the area manager to change positions without having to be retrained.

In the food service business there are several interesting problems that I must face. First, if a company where one of my cafeterias is located goes bankrupt, I automatically lose the business. Thus, in hard economic times such as those experienced in 1982 and 1983, I lost some business, not because I didn't run my cafeterias well, but because the business that it was located in went bankrupt. Secondly, it is often difficult to motivate people who work in food service. This is because 75 percent of the people who work for me do it as a sideline. Because we are unable to satisfy their monetary requirements due to lower salaries than in most industries, it is necessary to motivate them on a nonmonetary basis. This involves demonstrating appreciation for the work that they have performed. Thirdly, since the cost of food fluctuates rapidly, it is hard to give long-term guarantees to companies regarding the price structure for menu items in the cafeteria. As well, in most companies we have only short-term contracts, so they can terminate us on thirty-days notice. This makes long-range planning difficult. Fourthly, on various occasions the supervisor or operator of a cafeteria will begin to feel that he or she can run the cafeteria; that person will often approach the management of the company and suggest this. Management may go along with it because they personally know the supervisor or operator and because they have day-to-day contact with that person. When this happens, our firm could lose the contract for that particular company.

There are also many opportunities in the food service business. One positive aspect about this business is that the cash flow is substantial. We do not have an accounts receivable problem because the employees of each organization where the cafeterias are located pay cash. Another advantage is that being diversified into manufacturing, educational, government, and office type institutions, we are not tied to one location and so a problem in one company or sector of the economy (e.g., manufacturing) will not affect our total business much. The major reward of working in this business is that I have somewhat more control of my own destiny which I wouldn't have working for another company. I am also able to spend evenings and weekends with my family because I operate cafeterias in firms that operate mainly Monday through Friday. Another advantage is that the travelling I do helps me to meet people from other business organizations. This gives me a broader outlook on the economy, and also allows me to examine how they do things and perhaps apply it to my operation.

Managers also face routine decisions. These are often set up as policies and standard operating procedures. An office manager who sets up a policy of "no smoking in the office" does away with the need to make a decision actively each time an officeworker asks if it is all right to smoke in the office.

nonroutine decision

Another important type of decision is the nonroutine decision. **A nonroutine decision is a nonrecurring decision.** There are two types of nonroutine decisions, strategic and tactical. Strategic decisions are made by top-level management. Examples are decision making regarding the types of opportunity a firm will attempt to exploit (what business the firm will be in) and whether or not the company should buy out another company which is currently a competitor. Strategic decisions have an important and long-run effect.

MANAGEMENT AS A CAREER

To become a manager is to accept responsibility, to work through others, and to make an organization work. The skills needed include human relations skills, the ability to plan, and the ability to make and stand by your decisions. Managers must also have the self-discipline needed to take orders.

Many of these managerial skills are transferable across a wide range of businesses and in many nonbusiness enterprises. Specific areas include heavy industry, transportation, petroleum exploration, agribusiness, insurance, electronics, the hospitality industry, the health-care industry, local and federal government, and many others. In every case the manager organizes, plans, staffs, directs, and controls.

In nearly every field there are several levels of managers' jobs. It is normal to be promoted through the ranks. However, except in those rare cases where promotion depends mostly on seniority, the promotions get much tougher as you near the top of the organization. It is near the top that the exceptional management skills begin to show. This is where toughness of character, vision, and capacity to absorb and interpret complex information are required.

These days there is increasing emphasis on formal training for management. This usually means taking courses that will help you to better understand what management is all about. In many companies, you will find it easier to get a job if you have a degree or certificate in a business-related program from a university or community college.

Tactical decisions have less long-run effect. An example is a decision about where to locate a new warehouse. The dividing line between strategic and tactical decisions, however, is often an arbitrary one.

One important reason for distinguishing between routine and non-routine decisions involves the concept of management by exception.
According to the concept of management by exception (or the exception principle), higher-level management should be involved only with exceptional, nonroutine decisions. Routine decisions should be pushed as far down in the firm as possible. By granting authority to lower-level managers to make routine decisions, higher-level managers can devote more time to nonroutine decisions.

management by exception

Management by exception is related to the control function. It requires a well-developed system for monitoring operations. It also requires setting standards of performance, measuring actual performance, and comparing actual to standard performance. The idea is to allow subordinates to review performance against set standards and bring to the manager's attention only those cases that involve exceptions to normal or acceptable performance. This frees the manager from reviewing performance in situations where performance is in line with standards. He or she can concentrate on cases of exceptionally good performance and exceptionally poor performance. By studying these cases, he or she can develop ideas for improvement.

There are several potential drawbacks to management by exception. For example, advancing technology may make old standards obsolete. Unless they are reevaluated from time to time, managers may assume incorrectly that performance is acceptable and operations are going along as planned when, in fact, they are not. If some aspects of operations that are critical to success are not identified in advance, they will go unmeasured by the subordinate. There also is a measurement problem, especially for factors such as human behaviour. It may be next to impossible for such a system to call attention, for example, to a situation where employee morale is on the decline.

SUMMARY AND LOOK AHEAD

Businesses are living things that seek to accomplish objectives. Through the performance of nonmanagerial work and managerial functions, a firm moves toward the realization of its objectives. The three managerial skills required for effective performance of these functions are conceptual, people, and technical skills.

Managerial and nonmanagerial work can cause stress on the job. Firms do what they can to help control stress, but how a person deals with it is basically a personal decision.

The functions of management—planning, organizing, staffing, directing, and controlling—are performed by managers in the process of achieving goals by bringing together people and other resources. Management is necessary whenever results depend on group effort. There are different echelons (levels) of management in a firm. A firm's success or failure is traceable to the effectiveness of its managers. Likewise, there are different styles of management. For example, some managers practise participative management to a greater extent than others.

In reality, management cannot be broken down into a series of separate functions. It is a process. This becomes clear when we think of the firm as a system.

We can also view the management task in terms of decision making. Managers make decisions in performing their functions. There are seven stages in the decision-making process: (1) recognizing an opportunity or a problem, (2) gathering information, (3) developing alternatives, (4) analyzing alternatives, (5) choosing the best alternative, (6) implementing the decision, and (7) evaluating the decision.

Decisions can be routine or nonroutine. Nonroutine decisions can be either strategic or tactical. Truly strategic decisions are made by top management. Management by exception helps to ensure that upper-level managers will have adequate time to devote to strategic decisions.

The next chapter looks at the firm as an organization. We will see how management goes about organizing a business. ∎

QUESTIONS FOR REVIEW AND DISCUSSION

1. Since managers typically do not directly produce or sell anything, is management productive? Explain.
2. As a living organism, the business organization seeks to survive and grow. Explain how these objectives are accomplished.
3. Why did we describe management as a "process"?
4. List and describe the five functions of management.

5. When is management necessary?
6. Discuss the similarities and differences between operational and strategic planning. Which is more important? Why?
7. Picking apart the management process and breaking it down into its various functions is a convenient way to build a basic understanding of the nature of management. The danger in this approach is that we might come to "see the trees but not the forest." How might we avoid this danger?
8. It has been said that the president of a company need not be a good manager. All the president need do is possess an ability to select well-qualified subordinates. Do you agree? Why or why not?
9. In general, people in upper-management positions need to possess relatively few technical skills, whereas operatives must possess such skills. Does this mean that people in top management positions can transfer more easily from one type of industry to another than operatives can? Explain.
10. Do you think that a company president should direct subordinates in the same way that the boss of a work crew would direct subordinates? Discuss.
11. How are the management functions of planning and controlling related?
12. List and describe the seven stages in the decision-making process.
13. "If there is only one alternative, there is no decision." Do you agree? Why or why not?
14. Distinguish between a routine decision and a nonroutine decision. Identify two types of nonroutine decisions.
15. Explain how the functions of management are related to the decision-making process.

INCIDENTS

Marsha Thompson

Several years ago, Marsha Thompson quit her job with a large manufacturing firm and decided to go into business for herself. Although she was making a good salary as director of the firm's research department, she thought that she was required to do too much unnecessary "paperwork" which prevented her from applying her talents fully to her "real" job.

Marsha has been on her own for five years. Her firm has grown rapidly as a result of several big contracts, in addition to several patented processes which she developed in the field of pollution control.

Although Marsha's firm is very successful, she is not as happy as she once was. She and two other scientists formed the nucleus of her company, which has grown to include about one hundred employees. Originally Marsha employed only a handful of employees and could devote most of her time to research. She now finds herself having to devote too much time to the affairs of her company.

Questions:
1. Why did Marsha quit her job as director of the research department in the manufacturing firm?
2. Is Marsha a good manager? Why or why not?
3. Why do you think Marsha is growing dissatisfied with her present situation?

Motivating Employees

In carrying out the directing function, Canadian managers focus a lot of effort on motivating their subordinates to perform well. Japanese managers, however, focus less attention on motivating their subordinates. One reason is that larger firms in Japan and their employees tend to look at their employer-employee relationship as extending over a lifetime. A newly hired worker in such a firm tends to expect that he or she will be working for that employer until retirement. As a result, employees view their future well-being as directly tied to that of their employers. They reason that the more productive they are, the more the employer and the employees benefit.

Japanese firms like Nissan, Honda, Toyota, Hitachi, Sanyo, and Sharp with plants in Canada sometimes have management problems related to employee motivation. Japanese managers in those plants sometimes find Canadian employees less dedicated to the company than Japanese employees. Thus, these managers begin to focus more attention on motivating their workers.

Questions:
1. Which of the three basic managerial skills are most needed when a manager seeks to motivate workers? Explain.
2. Would a Japanese manager more likely be a Theory X or a Theory Y manager? Explain.
3. Do you think the concept of lifetime employment is beneficial to employers and employees? Why or why not?

Phil and Pete

Philip Herman is the director of environmental studies of a large oil company, and Peter Lucido is the vice-president of production. Phil and Pete have both been with the company for about ten years. Although they are very close friends, they have their differences concerning what management is all about. In fact, they have had many "friendly" debates.

Phil is a rather relaxed character. He is good-natured, draws people to him, has a cheerful outlook on life, and has a "live-for-today" philosophy of life. His subordinates respect him both as a manager and as a person. Phil believes that, given the chance, employees will want to advance themselves.

Pete, in many respects, is the opposite. Pete is best described as cautious and rather nervous. He attributes his ulcer to the fact that he doesn't know how to take it easy. He is a constant worrier. He is not nearly so sure as Phil that the average worker would pull his or her own weight if not coerced into doing so by a boss.

Despite their different personalities and outlooks on life, Phil and Pete are generally regarded as good managers by their superiors and their subordinates.

Questions:
1. Do you think that two persons who are so different can both be effective managers? Why or why not?
2. What similarities and differences would you expect between Phil's and Pete's performance of the functions of management? Discuss each function separately.

CASE STUDY*

CHAMPLAIN FOODS LTD.

ON JANUARY 30, 1981, KEN PARKER, ONTARIO AREA MANAGER FOR Champlain Foods, was reviewing the operating statement for period seven (December 20, 1980–January 17, 1981) of the Piccadilly Restaurant in Toronto, one of four in his region. To his surprise the statement showed revenues under budget by almost $20,000, or 20 percent, while food, beverage, and labour costs were 74.5 percent of sales versus the budgeted allowance of 66.3 percent. This was the second successive period of declining sales and increasing costs just when it appeared that Bill Fletcher, Unit Manager, finally had things under control. Ken wondered what had gone wrong and what should be done now to bring the operation back into line.

GENERAL BACKGROUND

Champlain Foods started operations in 1970 with one unit in Windsor, Ontario. During the period 1970–1980, the company had opened three additional units in Ontario and expanded into Western Canada. The most recent addition was the Piccadilly Restaurant in Toronto which was opened early in 1980. At that time, Bill Fletcher was appointed Unit Manager. The company's fiscal year was divided into 13 four-week periods from June to May. Total revenue for the fiscal year ended May 1980 totalled $8.0 million. Each unit consisted of a full service restaurant offering a good variety of menu choice, dining lounge, Pub and Wine Bar. The principal characters in this situation are shown in Exhibit 1 on page 128.

UNIT MANAGER'S RESPONSIBILITIES

Each unit was evaluated as a profit center. The manager was held responsible for revenues, food, beverage and labour costs and some outside services like equipment maintenance, laundry, etc. While the total variety of menu choices, prices and quality of food were prescribed by Head Office, each Unit Manager was free to choose the particular set of appetizers, entrees and desserts and to negotiate with Head Office any

*This case was written by William M. Braithwaite during the 1981 Case Writing Workshop. Case material of the School of Business Administration is prepared as a basis for classroom discussion. Copyright © 1981, School of Business Administration, The University of Western Ontario.

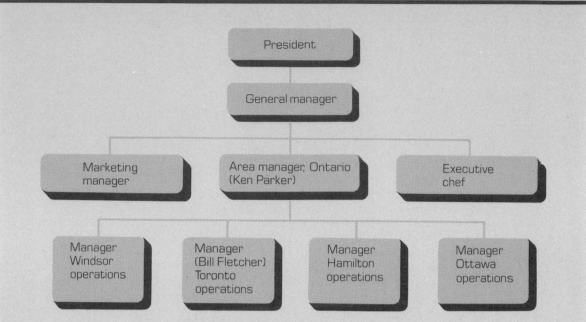

Exhibit 1   Organization Chart, Champlain Foods Ltd.

price changes he/she* felt appropriate for his local market. In addition, since the relative food costs vary with the choice of menu items (e.g., chicken offers the lowest price and the highest margin on many menus) the manager had some control over his relative food cost. Purchases of major food items from national distributors were made by Head Office but the Unit Manager determined the quantity and time of delivery; he was free to purchase perishable foods like dairy products and fresh produce from the best available source. Each manager had full control over the hiring of staff, wages paid and the amount of outside services purchased. Each manager was also responsible for preparing his own budget. This budget was forwarded to the Area Manager for approval. No change could be made in the budget without the approval of the Unit Manager. Differences of opinion were settled through negotiation. Once approved, the budget was sent to the General Manager for final approval and to be consolidated into the total budget for the company.

UNIT REPORTING AND ANALYSIS

Each Unit Manager was required to keep his own record of sales and costs and to prepare an operating statement for each period as shown in Exhibit 2. This was done to force the manager to look clearly at his own figures, and to initiate corrective action as soon as possible

*Future references will use the masculine pronoun for convenience only.

128

Exhibit 2 Piccadilly Restaurant, Toronto, 1981

Period	Revenue		Food Cost[1]		Beverage Cost[2]		Labour Cost[3]		Total of Food, Beverage, Labour Cost (%)	
	Budget	Actual	Budget	Actual	Budget	Actual	Budget	Actual	Budget	Actual
1	105,000	112,667	40.00	39.37	36.00	36.26	27.30	31.05	66.31	69.63
2	100,000	104,937	40.00	42.32	36.00	37.58	27.30	28.27	66.31	69.40
3	120,000	123,873	40.00	44.79	36.00	36.25	27.30	28.51	66.31	71.21
4	110,000	109,235	40.00	44.94	36.00	38.10	27.30	32.37	66.31	75.65
5	110,000	104,541	40.00	38.63	36.00	34.25	27.31	28.29	66.31	65.83
6	109,000	93,344	40.00	38.16	36.00	33.16	27.31	32.93	66.31	69.72
7	108,000	90,803	40.00	41.61	36.00	33.92	27.30	34.92	66.31	74.53

[1]Percent of total food sales
[2]Percent of total beverage sales
[3]Percent of total revenue

whenever actual costs exceeded the budgeted amounts by more than 1 percent.

This statement was normally completed within three days of period end. If actual results were below expectations, the manager was required to prepare an operating statement each week, and to do a detailed cost and sales analysis until the problem could be identified and changes made.

The information on revenues and costs was also sent to Head Office where it was entered into the computer. About the tenth day after period end the Area Manager received a computer print-out of each unit's operating statement and each Unit Manager received a copy of his own statement. The Area Manager used this statement to review the performance of each unit. The Unit Manager compared the computer print-out to his own figures to make sure no significant errors had been made in recording the information.

CONCLUSION

As he sat in his office, Ken Parker recalled the discussions he had had with Bill last fall over his results in Periods 3 and 4 (see Exhibit 2). Bill had responded well to some of his suggestions and the results for Period 5 showed a dramatic improvement on the cost-side without a major effect on revenues. It was, therefore, very disconcerting to Ken to see that the results for Period 7 were even worse than Period 4.

What went wrong, he wondered, and what should he do now to correct the situation? ∎

After reading this chapter, you should be able to:

1. Tell the difference between personal and organizational objectives and explain how they are integrated.
2. Draw a figure that illustrates the hierarchy of organizational objectives.
3. List and give an example of the different bases for departmentation.
4. List and explain the factors that affect a manager's optimum span of management.
5. List and explain the three actions involved in the delegation process.
6. Relate the delegation process to the degree to which a firm is centralized or decentralized.
7. Compare the line, line and staff, and committee organization structures and discuss the matrix organization and quality-of-work-life programs.
8. Tell the difference between line function and staff function and line managers and staff people.
9. Draw an organization chart and tell what it indicates and does not indicate.
10. Discuss the hierarchy of human needs.
11. Compare formal and informal organizations.

KEY CONCEPTS

Look for these terms as you read the chapter:

organization
hierarchy of organizational
  objectives
departmentation
span of management
delegation
responsibility
authority
accountability
centralization
decentralization
organization chart

line authority
line functions
staff functions
staff
functional authority
matrix organization
quality-of-work-life (QWL)
  programs
hierarchy of needs
informal groups
informal organization

THE COCA-COLA COMPANY HAS HAD a long history as a rather conservatively and closely managed company in which authority was largely centralized at company headquarters in the U.S. In 1980, Mr. Roberto Goizueta took over as chairman and chief executive officer and things started to change.

One of Mr. Goizueta's first actions as chief executive officer was to issue a corporate "vision" statement in which he outlined Coke's plans to remain the "dominant force in the soft-drink industry" around the world.

According to Mr. Goizueta, "The day of the one-man band is gone...My job is to pick the people, then give them the responsibility and authority to get the job done."

Mr. Don Keough, Coke's president, echoes the same philosophy. "We're giving

CHAPTER FIVE

Organizing the Firm

our division managers around the world a lot of authority, and we're holding them responsible."

The Coca-Cola Company, a very large organization that is over one hundred years old, has been undergoing some organizational changes since Mr. Goizueta took over. It has become a much more decentralized organization.

AN ORGANIZATION IS A COMBINATION OF HUMAN, FINANCIAL, AND physical resources put together by management so that certain goals can be accomplished. All firms have goals that can be reached only if their human, financial, and physical resources are tied together logically. This is why businesses are formally structured.

Individuals can accomplish their own personal objectives and help to achieve company objectives if both types of objectives are carefully integrated. Otherwise, a person will not get much satisfaction from the organization. Thus, the formal organization is the structure that helps a firm and its employees achieve their goals.

People are the most important resource of any organization. An organization can also be viewed in terms of how the people in the organization behave. A firm, or any other type of organization, contains a collection of smaller, informal groups. These informal groups are not created by management but by the group members themselves to satisfy some of their needs. The entire set of these small groups is the informal organization of a firm. It is separate and distinct from the formal organization.

WHAT IS AN ORGANIZATION?

Imagine two cars travelling in opposite directions on the same street. They approach an intersection with four stop signs. Both stop. No other cars are present. Suppose the driver of car A signals for a turn that will put his car in the path of the other car. Both drivers must interact to avoid a wreck. Avoiding a wreck is an objective of both parties. Traffic signals and rules lend structure so that one driver will always let the other pass first.

In the above example the elements of organization are present. They are (1) human interaction, (2) actions toward an objective, and (3) structure. The two drivers must interact, and their activities must be structured to avoid a wreck.

Now consider the case of a firm whose objective is to make a profit. Its employees' objective is to make a living. Workers interact with one another and with the tools of production. They perform those tasks necessary for the firm to make a profit and for the employees to earn a living. These elements — people, tasks, and physical resources — must be "meshed together" into a structure. The structure permits both the firm and the employees to achieve their goals.

We have seen two examples. Both are examples of organization but of two very different types. They vary in size, length of life, complexity, and formality. In the first example there are only two drivers, who interact briefly and informally. The second example involves a greater number of people who interact over a longer period of time on the basis of rules and procedures. There is a more formal structuring of the relationships among people, activities, and physical resources in the second case. In a business, accomplishing objectives requires continuing patterns of inter-action instead of only one interaction. Remember, though, both cases are examples of organization. **When a group of people and things interact to reach objectives and their behaviour is structured, we call this an organization.**

organization

Why Do People Join Organizations?

People belong to organizations because they believe they can achieve their goals better within the organization. You might join the marketing club, for example, because you would have more social functions to attend than you would if you were not a member. Most of us belong to many organizations because we have so many different goals. No one organization could satisfy them all.

In a business firm, people have some needs that are similar and that therefore can be satisfied through the firm. All employees can earn a living and perhaps receive bonuses for doing exceptionally good work, for example. But, as we'll see, individuals on the job may have other social needs that are not being satisfied by the firm. A woman may be earning a living by doing the tasks assigned to her by her boss. But she also may want to "feel important" and be well-liked by her co-workers. As a result, people on the job often form informal groups that help them satisfy wants that are not being satisfied by the formal structure of the firm. People tend to remain in an organization only if it helps them satisfy their goals.

Personal and Organizational Objectives

People contribute to an organization if they think it helps to satisfy their personal objectives. Integrating various personal objectives into a unified statement of the firm's objectives is not easy. For example, an employee may easily accept a company's objective "to make a profit." Doing so may provide money to be shared in the firm's profit-sharing plan. But that same employee may not accept a company objective "to be a good community citizen." Doing so could cause the firm to invest in pollution control equip-ment and to make contributions to the local symphony orchestra. These "extra costs" might leave less money for pay raises.

Ideally, an organization would meet all the personal objectives of all the people associated with it. Personal goals, however, often conflict. As a result, a firm's objectives usually are something other than the sum of the personal

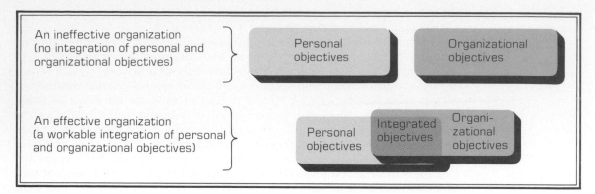

Figure 5.1
Personal objectives, organizational objectives, and organizational effectiveness

objectives of its different publics (employees, suppliers, owners, creditors, customers, and so on).

Formal organizations like business firms *suboptimize* objectives. This means they settle for less than the total achievement of all the objectives of their publics. Not all the personal goals of all their publics will be fully satisfied. Nor will company goals be completely achieved. For example, an employee may want to grow on the job — to be given the opportunity to learn new skills and be promoted to a higher-level job. But the firm may need his or her services in a very specialized job. The worker's desire for more varied tasks conflicts with the firm's objectives. The reason that every employee is never totally satisfied with his or her employer is that the personal and organizational objectives are never in total harmony. There is always some degree of conflict. (See Figure 5.1.)

A *trade-off* is necessary. Neither the worker's objective nor the firm's objective will be achieved 100 percent. A compromise is worked out whereby the firm and the worker each get something, but not all that each might want. The employee's job might be broadened to include a greater variety of tasks. This increases his or her job satisfaction. The employee becomes more productive and the firm, of course, benefits. The management by objectives approach discussed in Chapter 4 can help in integrating personal and organizational objectives.

ORGANIZATION AS STRUCTURE

All firms are structured to help achieve company and personal goals. How complex and formal this structure is depends on many things. Firms with only a handful of employees, for example, require a less formal structure than firms with many employees. Large firms require more attention to structure because there are more workers, greater specialization of labour, and a greater number of levels of managers.

For example, an owner-manager of a women's dress shop selects and orders merchandise from dress manufacturers, determines prices, and sets credit policies. He or she may have several salespeople, a bookkeeper, and perhaps a credit manager and a delivery driver. These people are in face-to-face contact, and the owner personally runs the business. But in a large department store there are many more salespeople, several delivery drivers, an entire credit department, an accounting department, and managers (buyers) for each separate department. It's almost impossible for one person to run such a large business alone.

What Is Being Structured?

An organizational structure is created to achieve goals. Within that structure, activities are performed to help achieve those goals. Organizational "structuring," therefore, focuses first on these activities.

For example, the primary goal of your school is to educate students. Another goal is that it be a good education. Relationships among the activities needed to reach these goals must be structured. The two essential activities here are teaching and learning; and they require people, books, and classrooms for their performance.

Teachers must be assigned to courses, textbooks must be related to courses, and classrooms must be assigned. Of course, students also must be assigned to teachers and courses. In other words, three basic components must be related to each other through the process of organizing:

- people
- activities
- physical resources

Organizing to Reach Objectives

In an organization, objectives are the ends that we want to accomplish. In order to accomplish them, certain activities must be performed by people working with other resources. In other words, these activities are the means for accomplishing the organization's objectives. These activities are also the connecting link between an organization's structure and its objectives. It is through the organizational structure that management coordinates those activities of workers that are required to reach the organization's objectives.

But what objective tells Harry the janitor to sweep the floor? The overall company objective "to supply customers with a quality product at a reasonable price" does not tell Harry what he should do to help the firm reach its goals. The company objective is too broad to provide a specific objective for Harry.

hierarchy of
organizational
objectives

Figure 5.2 shows a **hierarchy of organizational objectives. This concept involves breaking down broad company goals into specific goals for each person in the organization.** More specifically, broad company goals are first broken down into goals for company divisions. These, in turn, are broken down into departmental goals. Departmental goals are then

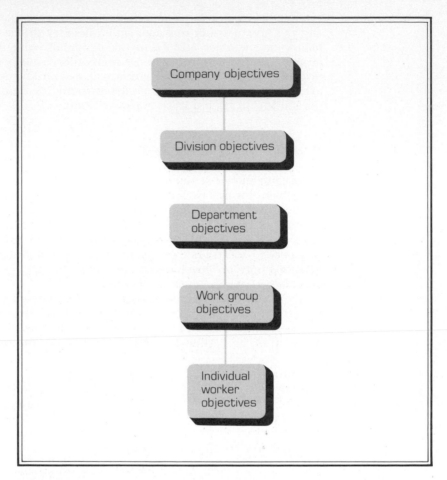

Figure 5.2
The hierarchy of organizational objectives

broken down into goals for work groups within each department. Finally, work-group goals are broken down into goals for each individual worker. This lets each employee know what activities he or she must perform. The number of levels of objectives depends on the firm's size and complexity. There are fewer levels in very small firms than in very large ones.

As an example of this process, consider a manufacturing firm that has two divisions—industrial products and consumer products. The overall organizational objective might be "to profitably serve both the consumer and the industrial market." The consumer division's objective would be stated more specifically and would deal strictly with the consumer market. The various departments within the consumer products division would have even more specific objectives. At the lowest level of the organization, each individual worker would have very specific objectives which would be consistent with the overall organizational objectives.

Identifying, Grouping, and Assigning Activities

The first step in building an organizational structure is to analyze the major activities that must be performed to help the organization reach its objectives. For a manufacturer these activities usually are production, marketing, and finance. Each activity is assigned to a separate department within the firm.

departmentation

Firms are broken down into departments through the process of departmentation. **Departmentation means identifying, grouping, and assigning activities to specialized departments within an organization.**

There are two basic approaches to identifying activities. One approach is to observe workers and classify their activities, such as assembling parts, buying raw materials, and pricing products. The other approach is to start with company goals and determine which activities are needed to reach those goals. This method is the only one available to a brand-new firm.

Next, activities are grouped and assigned. There are seven major bases upon which an organization could be departmentalized:

- function
- geography
- product
- customer
- process
- type of equipment
- time

POINT OF VIEW

Work Groups and the Organizational Structure

The concept of the hierarchy of organizational objectives says that individual workers, work groups, departments, divisions, and the company itself have objectives. An organizational structure is needed to help the business firm and its employees accomplish their objectives. But, as we have seen, some conflict always exists between the organization's objectives and those of its employees. Conflict also often exists among individual employees.

Many experts on organization are now focusing on work groups in their efforts to build effective organizations. The idea is to build work groups that are made up of individuals who see their personal goals as being essentially the same as those of the group as a whole. For this approach to organizing to be effective, however, management must be willing and able to allow work groups to participate in the decision making that will affect them. It cannot succeed if managers insist upon practising Theory X management.

Table 5.1 Bases for Departmentalizing

Basis	Example
1. Function	1. A manufacturing firm might be departmentalized into "producing" and "selling" departments; a retailing firm into "buying" and "selling" departments; a charitable organization into "collecting" and "disbursing" departments.
2. Geography	2. A manufacturing firm might organize its sales efforts in the Maritimes, Ontario, and the Prairie provinces.
3. Product	3. A company might have a manager in charge of sales for each major product produced.
4. Customer	4. A large meat-packing firm might have one sales department serving retail accounts and another serving institutional accounts.
5. Process	5. A brewery might have "cooking" and "aging" departments.
6. Type of equipment	6. Machines of one type might be grouped into one department and those of another type into another department; e.g., grinding machines in one department and polishing machines in another.
7. Time	7. Some employees might work the day shift and others the night shift.

These bases are discussed in Table 5.1.

Many firms use several bases for departmentation. A firm might be divided by function into production, marketing, and finance departments. The marketing department could be divided into a domestic sales organization and a foreign sales organization (geography). Decisions of this type are influenced by the relative advantages of the different approaches and the experience, preferences, and judgment of top management.

Many factors can affect departmentation decisions. One is technology. For example, the increasing importance of computer technology in business has led many firms to create specialized data processing departments. The faster pace of technological change also has led many firms to create specialized research and development departments.

Top management's decisions about the types of business opportunity the firm will seek to exploit also affect how a firm is departmentalized. When top management decides to diversify its operations outside the business it is currently in, it might decide to set up a new department to search for new types of business opportunity.

Departmentation is not intended to create "walls" around departments. For example, when problems arise that involve two or more departments, personnel from the departments involved work together to solve them. Engineering, production, finance, and marketing personnel, for example, might try to modify a product that, due to faulty design, is causing customer complaints. After the problem is solved, the work group is dissolved.

Activities are departmentalized to make work more efficient and to provide a means for controlling operations. Sometimes a firm will change the manner in which it is departmentalized to increase efficiency. IBM, for example, used to have three major sales divisions: data processing, general systems, and office products. As a result, some customers were called upon by three different IBM salespeople, each of whom was selling different IBM products. IBM now has two divisions, each of which sells all of IBM's products. The national accounts division sells to large accounts and the national marketing division sells to intermediate, small, and new accounts.

An obvious reason for departmentation is the simple fact that the number of subordinates a manager can manage is limited. Without departmentation a firm's size would be limited to the number of persons the top manager could supervise directly. Let's discuss this concept of the span of management.

THE SPAN OF MANAGEMENT

span of management

Span of management refers to the number of persons an individual manager supervises. The nature of the work that a manager's subordinates perform affects the span of management. If subordinates perform very similar and routine tasks, the manager's span of management is likely to be wide. Thus many lower-level managers, such as assembly-line fore-

---

PRINCIPLES OF MANAGEMENT

During the twentieth century, many business managers and academics have spend a lot of time trying to develop some fundamental principles of managing people and things. Some of these "principles of management" are:

1. *Unity of command:* Subordinates should generally have no more than one boss so they will not run the risk of receiving conflicting orders.
2. *Management by exception:* Managers should not be continually checking to see if subordinates are or are not performing their jobs. Only if something exceptional occurs should the manager become involved.
3. *Separation of doing and checking:* The people producing a product or a service should not have authority over the people

who check to see if it has been done satisfactorily. For example, quality control inspectors should not be subordinate to production-line foremen.
4. *Delegation:* Wherever possible, authority should be delegated to the lowest level possible in the organization, consistent with effective performance.
5. *Span of management (control):* The number of subordinates managers can handle should be kept within reasonable limits, given the job that is being done.
6. *Scalar chain:* There should be a clear line of authority from the top of the organization to the bottom. All people in the organization will, therefore, understand who they have authority over and to whom they report.

men, have wide spans of management because they do not spend much time supervising any one subordinate.

On the other hand, a manager whose subordinates perform very different, nonroutine types of work must spend considerable time supervising each subordinate. Thus top-level managers have narrow spans of management. This is why large firms usually have several echelons of management.

The personal characteristics of managers and their subordinates can also play a role in determining a manager's span of management. We discussed Theory X and Theory Y managers in Chapter 4. Theory X managers tend to have narrower spans of management than Theory Y managers because Theory X managers do not trust their subordinates and will supervise them more closely than Theory Y managers.

As we saw earlier in this chapter, technology can affect the departmentation process. It can also affect a manager's span of management. For example, big retail chains like Kmart, Woolco, and Canadian Tire are using computers to record sales of various products in each outlet. The computer simplifies store managers' decisions about what to buy for their stores and enables a district manager to supervise a greater number of store managers.

In their efforts to increase productivity, many firms have turned to automation, especially in production work, as we will see in Chapter 8. This has helped them trim their labour costs. Recently there has been growing interest in cutting management costs. Firms try to have fewer echelons of management and to increase the managers' spans of management.

Although there is no single, generally accepted formula for determining the optimum span of management, there are several factors that managers should consider:

- how well-defined the subordinates' jobs are and the complexity of their work
- the subordinates' training and ability to work with others
- the subordinates' motivation
- the pace of technological change in the industry
- the ability of the manager and subordinate to communicate effectively with each other
- the manager's capability
- the manager's willingness and ability to plan, to delegate, and to evaluate subordinates' job performance

The Delegation Process

delegation

Without delegation, a firm could not be departmentalized. **Delegation means entrusting part of a superior's job (or activities) to a subordinate. Three actions are involved in the delegation process:**

- **assigning responsibility**
- **granting authority**
- **establishing accountability**

responsibility

authority

Responsibility is the obligation of a subordinate to perform an assigned task. In delegating activities the superior assigns a responsibility to subordinates to carry out their assigned tasks.

Authority is the counterpart of responsibility. **Authority is the right to take the action necessary to accomplish an assigned task.** Authority and responsibility must be balanced if subordinates are to perform their assigned tasks.

One view of authority holds that the right to manage springs from the right of private property. Authority flows from a firm's owners down to its managers. It's a "top-down" flow. (See Figure 5.3.) Another view, the "acceptance" view, holds that a manager has authority over a subordinate only because the subordinate accepts the manager's authority.

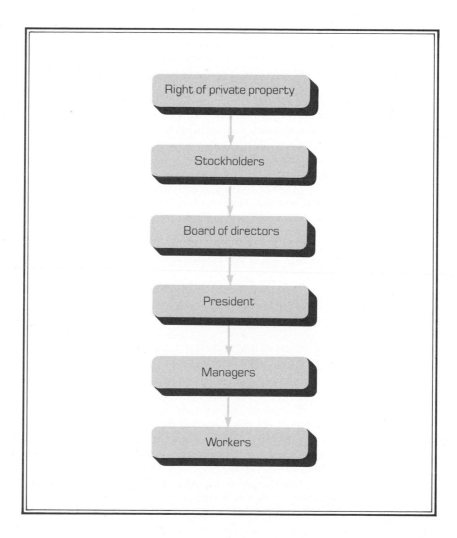

Figure 5.3
One view of authority in a corporation

Authority often is enjoyed by people because of personal qualities or expertise in a given area. A worker with "charisma" enjoys authority over co-workers. Likewise, the "old hand" who advises the new supervisor enjoys some degree of authority.

accountability   **Accountability is the act of holding subordinates, who have been delegated adequate authority to fulfill their responsibilities, liable for performing their assigned tasks and for reporting results to their superiors.** The subordinates are accountable to their superiors.

Roy manages a car tire shop. Sam removes old tires, Tom switches them on the rims, and Bill balances and remounts them. Roy assigned *responsibility* to them for performing these tasks. He also granted them *authority* to use the necessary tools to accomplish their tasks. Roy also established *accountability* in that the subordinates are answerable to him for results.

Delegation, however, does *not* relieve Roy of the responsibility for seeing to it that his subordinates do their jobs. If a customer's tires wear out because of faulty balancing, it is Roy's responsibility. In other words, the final responsibility rests with the person who is delegating.

The fact that delegation does not relieve a manager of responsibility makes some managers afraid to delegate. Theory X managers are especially unlikely to delegate. To delegate effectively, managers must have faith in their subordinates' abilities, be willing to let them learn by their mistakes, and be willing to follow up on how well they are doing their jobs. Managers, therefore, should select qualified subordinates who are capable of performing their assigned tasks.

Span of management and delegation are closely related. Except for very small firms, no firm could function effectively without some delegation. Managers who are afraid to delegate do everything themselves. Their span of management is likely to be very narrow. A sole proprietor, for example, who refuses to delegate limits the size of his or her firm. It cannot expand beyond what the proprietor is capable of doing alone.

Centralization versus Decentralization of Authority

centralization   The amount of delegation in a firm determines how much the power to decide (authority) is concentrated. **Centralization of authority means that decision-making authority is concentrated in the hands of a few people at the top level of a firm. Such a firm is said to be relatively centralized.** Its managers believe that this centralization makes it easier to coordinate and control the firm's activities.

decentralization   **Decentralization of authority means that decision-making authority is given to people in addition to those in top management. Such a firm is said to be relatively decentralized.** Middle- and lower-level managers have more decision-making authority than those in more centralized firms. This frees top-level managers to devote more time and effort to long-range planning.

YOU BE THE JUDGE!

Who Is Right Here?

Anna Scavo is a regional vice-president of sales for a large paint manufacturing firm. She is having some trouble with one of her district sales managers, Jim Clark.

This problem came to a head recently when several of Jim's sales representatives went "over his head" and complained to Anna. As they put it, "Jim has one rule of management—if it's an important decision, he'll make it. If it's a minor decision, he'll delegate it."

Anna talked this over with Jim. Jim's final statement on the matter was, "Delegation is a joke. You tell me to grant more authority to my subordinates. If I do it and they mess up, I get the blame. If I'm going to get the blame when things go wrong, I'm going to make the decision. At least that way I won't be taking the rap for somebody else's mistakes."

Despite her best efforts, Anna could not sell Jim on the delegation process. She even pointed out what she delegates to Jim. Jim agreed but said, "Sure, but you know I'll do what's right."

Last week, Anna hit on a new approach for dealing with Jim. She decided that the best way to "teach" Jim to delegate was to make his work load so heavy that he would have to delegate some decisions to his subordinates. Is Anna's approach sound? YOU BE THE JUDGE!

As we saw in Chapter 4, participative management means the manager encourages and allows subordinates to involve themselves directly in the decision making that will affect them. Firms that encourage participative management are less centralized than those which do not. So are firms that practice management by exception and management by objectives.

Centralization and decentralization of authority have nothing necessarily to do with geography. A firm with plants in many cities is not decentralized if decision-making power is concentrated at headquarters. But the degree to which a firm is centralized or decentralized does affect its organizational structure.

TYPES OF ORGANIZATIONAL STRUCTURES

organization chart

A firm's structure can be quite complex. **An organization chart graphically depicts a firm's formal structure at a given point in time.** It indicates

- the functions (production, marketing, etc.) that must be performed if the firm is to achieve its goals
- the lines of authority (chain of command)
- how the firm is departmentalized
- how the departments relate to each other
- the various positions and standing committees in the firm
- the titles of those positions

How complex these charts are depends on what management wants them to show. Generally, the larger the firm, the more complex the chart will be.

There are many things an organization chart does not show. It does not tell the degree to which authority is delegated, what the organizational objectives are, or the importance of various jobs in the organization. It also does not indicate the informal relationships which develop between people as they do their jobs. This is a real disadvantage of organization charts, because many important activities are done through the informal organization. This will be discussed shortly.

There are three basic types of organization structures:

- the line organization
- the line and staff organization
- the committee organization

The Line Organization

The line organization is the oldest and simplest type of organization structure. It has been used by military organizations and the Roman Catholic Church, and by business firms. In the military, the general gives orders to the colonel; the colonel gives orders to the major; the major gives orders to the captain; the captain gives orders to the lieutenant; the lieutenant gives orders to the sergeant; and the sergeant gives orders to the private. The Pope is the head of the Roman Catholic Church, and the chain of command extends downward through cardinals, archbishops, bishops, and priests.

line authority

From one point of view, line authority is the authority relationship that exists between superiors and subordinates. **Line authority is the right to direct subordinates' work.** In the line organization, as we have seen, the chain of command extends from the top to the bottom of the organization. At any given position in the chain, a person takes orders from people higher in the chain and gives orders to people lower in the chain.

Each superior has direct line authority over his or her subordinates, and each person in the organization reports directly to one boss. Each superior also has total authority over his or her assigned tasks. (See Figure 5.4.)

The major advantages of the line organization are:

- the organizational structure is easy to understand
- each person has only one direct supervisor
- decisions may be made faster because each supervisor is accountable to only one immediate supervisor
- authority, responsibility, and accountability are defined clearly and exactly, which makes it hard to "pass the buck" to someone else

Despite its advantages, the line organization suffers from some disadvantages which restrict its use in modern business to very small firms. The major disadvantages are:

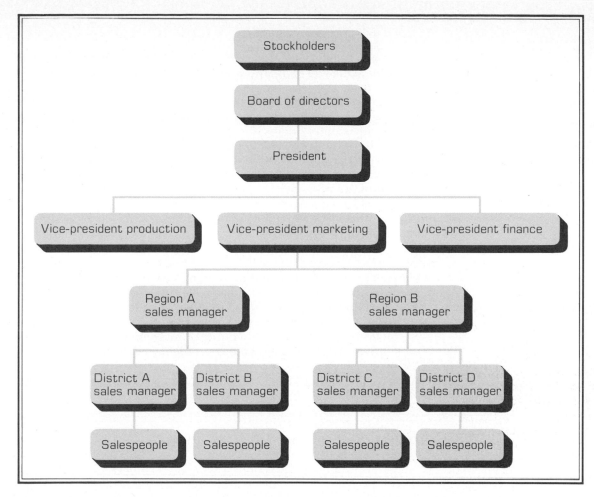

Figure 5.4
A simplified line organization

- each supervisor must be an expert in all aspects of his or her subordinates' work because there are no "specialists" or advisors to turn to
- the paperwork required in directly supervising each subordinate is a burden on each supervisor's time
- there is potential for the organization to become too inflexible and too bureaucratic

The Line and Staff Organization

line functions

Another view of authority involves the distinction between line functions and staff functions. **Line functions contribute directly to reaching primary firm goals.** For example, consider the case of a manufacturing firm whose primary goal is "to make a quality product and sell it at a fair price." The line functions are "production" and "marketing." For a retailer, "purchasing" and "selling" are the line functions. They are most directly concerned with achieving company goals. In a personal finance company, "lending" and "collecting" are the line functions.

staff functions

Staff functions help the line to achieve primary firm goals. In the manufacturing firm above, "quality control" and "market research" are staff functions. Quality control helps the production manager to produce a quality product. Market research helps the marketing manager to sell it.

staff

The use of staff is one way to divide up the work of line managers. **Staff are people who advise and assist line managers in their work of achieving company objectives.**

The personal staff performs duties at the request of his or her line boss. The duties can range from opening the line manager's mail to representing the line manager at company meetings. Personal staff usually have the title of "assistant to."

Specialized staff serve the entire firm — not just one line manager. They have a high degree of expertise in their area of specialization. The marketing manager (a line executive) seeks advice from the director of marketing research (a staff executive) concerning whether or not to introduce a new product. The director of marketing research might also supply information to the production manager (a line executive) concerning sales forecasts so that production scheduling might be more efficient.

LINE OR STAFF?

Let's assume you have resisted the urge to start your own business. Let's assume further that you choose to work for a medium- to large-size firm. This chapter discusses what staff and line positions are. What are *you*, a lineperson or a staffperson?

The big difference is that linepersons make the decisions and control the "mainstream" activities of the firm — producing and selling goods and services. Starting with the first-line supervisor and working up the organization, being "in the line" takes self-confidence and decisiveness — not unlike what it takes to run your own business. It takes a large measure of skills in human relations, too. The higher you get, the more breadth of vision it takes — being able to see the whole picture.

Staff positions are not so easy to describe because they are so varied. A personal staff-assistant position often requires helping to deal with important people and important prob-

lems, but only with those problems your boss (line) assigns you and without making major decisions of your own. If you are an efficient follower and don't mind "avoiding the limelight," a staff-assistant position may be for you.

If you have attained a special skill — as a lawyer, an accountant, a statistician, or creative artist — you may fill a staff-specialist position. This means you do special tasks a line officer hasn't the expertise or the time to do. You might have to write technical reports to help a line manager decide whether to sign an important contract or not. As you progress as a staff specialist, you might head a department of your own, such as the market research department of a firm. This will require more than a specialized skill in that area. It will take some of the same skills in human relations the lineperson needs.

What are you likely to be best at — line or staff work?

How staff sees line:
1. They get all the credit when things go right — we get the blame when things go wrong.
2. They have the final word, although we're trained experts in our fields.
3. They don't even want to try to see things from our point of view.
4. We may spend months developing recommendations, but they refuse even to listen to our advice, much less accept it.
5. They're older people who have been with the company so long that they're afraid to try new methods of doing things.
6. They resist change no matter what.

How line sees staff:
1. After all, I am the one who has the final word — they only give out advice.
2. There's only one right way — their way.
3. They can't even talk in ordinary language — it's always technical talk.
4. What he's doing now used to be part of my job.
5. They're know-it-all young college graduates who are always looking to change the way we do things around here.
6. They want to jump the gun without thinking through their ideas and recommendations.

Figure 5.5
Some potential sources of line-staff conflict

Staff people serve and advise line managers. In recent years there has been a tendency in many firms to add new staff positions. Computer specialists, tax-law experts, and other advisors and analysts are examples. These staff people cannot issue orders to line managers. They can only give line managers advice and assistance. But the head of a staff department, such as the director of marketing research, does have the necessary line authority to run the marketing research department.

As you might suspect from the above discussion, there is a lot of potential for line-staff conflict in a business firm. Figure 5.5 on page 147 discusses the nature of this conflict.

There are several ways to reduce this conflict. Some firms require line managers to consult staffpersons before making decisions on matters in the staff's area of expertise. In some cases, the line manager need only discuss the matter and is not required to follow the staff's advice. In other cases, the line manager must get the approval of the staff before making certain types of decisions. Thus, a production manager has to clear new recruits with the personnel department before hiring them.

functional authority | **In still other cases, the staff has authority to issue orders directly to line personnel. This is functional authority. It is granted only in the staff's area of expertise and only if it will benefit the firm.** Thus, a plant manager's authority over safety matters may be removed by superiors and given to a safety inspector who has authority to shut down the plant if dangerous working conditions exist.

Automation and computers enable some firms to eliminate some lower-level management jobs. Suppose a computer can do the same tasks

---

AUTHORS' COMMENTARY

Identifying the Need for Staff Personnel

Business's increasing complexity provides a legitimate explanation for the growth of staff personnel in many firms. Production managers, for example, recognize the importance of automation in increasing productivity, but because they often lack the needed technical expertise, they turn to experts on robotics. Industrial safety laws create a need for specialized staff to help the firm comply with the laws.

There are other, less legitimate, explanations for the growth in staff personnel, however. Theory X managers, for example, distrust their subordinates and want staff personnel to check on their performance. Incompetent or inexperienced managers need staff people to help compensate for their shortcomings. Some line managers also measure their importance in the firm in terms of the number of staff specialists reporting to them, the amount of paperwork they can generate and receive, and the amount of budget increases for which they can get approval. Paraphrasing two of Professor C. Northcote Parkinson's "laws" on bureaucracy: (1) work expands to fill the time allowed for completing it, and (2) as budgets increase, work expands to fit them (C. Northcote Parkinson, *Parkinson's Law and Other Studies in Administration*. Boston: Houghton Mifflin, 1957).

There is no doubt that increasingly productivity-conscious top managers will require their line managers to justify their need for staff personnel more carefully.

as a lower-level manager at a lower cost. Chances are that the manager will be replaced. Because upper-level managers often lack the technical know-how for using computers, they hire specialists (staff) to advise them. Thus, instead of starting at the bottom of the line organization, many young technicians start in a staff position directly advising upper-level managers. Staff status does *not* mean inferior status. Many staff specialists enjoy more pay and prestige than line managers.

The top box in Figure 5.6 shows the person who has final responsibility for the firm's management. In this case it is the president, but it could have been the chairperson of the board of directors. The vice-presidents of

Figure 5.6
The line and staff organization

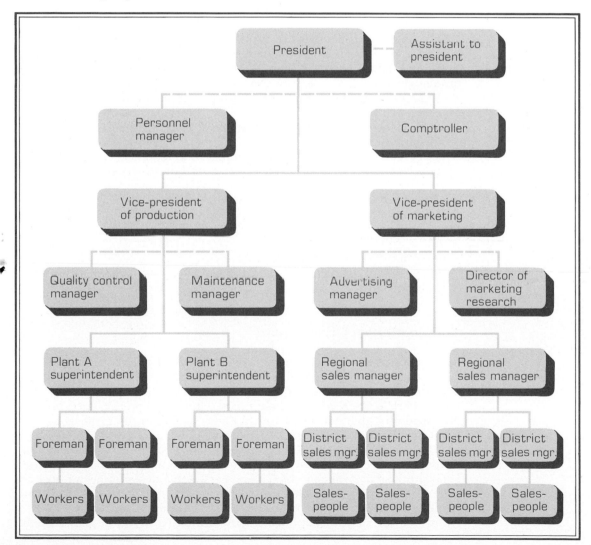

production and marketing report directly to the president. Plant superintendents A and B report directly to the vice-president of production. The other reporting relationships (the chain of command, or line authority) are indicated by the solid line. Notice the different echelons (levels) of management and the wider spans of management as we move down from the top.

The staff organization is described by means of a broken line. The assistant to the president is personal staff. That assistant serves only the president. The personnel manager and the comptroller are specialized staff. They serve the entire firm. There is no functional authority in this firm. If the quality control manager did have functional authority over the plant superintendents, it would be shown on the chart by a dotted line.

From the chart we can infer something about the top-down delegation of authority. The president delegates to the vice-presidents of production and marketing who, in turn, delegate to the plant superintendents and regional sales managers.

An organization chart by itself does not tell the degree to which authority is delegated. A manager might be a manager in name only. Nor does it tell us anything about the *informal organization*, which we will discuss shortly.

The line and staff organization's major advantages are:

- staff specialists are available to advise, support, and serve line executives
- line executives need not get bogged down in technical matters and can devote more time and energy to their line functions

The line and staff organization is the most widely used form of organization in contemporary business, especially among middle-sized and larger firms. But it does have some potential disadvantages:

- the potential for line-staff conflict
- the potential for going overboard in creating and filling unneccessary staff positions

The Committee Organization

In the committee organizational structure, several people share authority and responsibility for accomplishing an objective. Instead of reporting to one manager, subordinates may report to several. This form of organization, where it does exist, usually exists *within* the overall line and staff organization. Other names for committee organization are project management, program management, team management, and group management.

Some committees, such as company policy committees, are standing, or permanent, committees. Others are ad hoc committees that are formed to accomplish a particular objective and are disbanded after accomplishing it. An example is a committee formed to select the site for a new plant.

Many manufacturing firms have new product committees. Such a committee is made up of line and staff executives from various departments within the firm—accounting, finance, production, marketing, and engineering. The committee's job is to come up with new product ideas and develop them into marketable new products.

The major advantages of the committee form of organization are

- decisions are based on the combined expertise and judgment of committee members
- participation by persons in different departments may increase their commitment to committee decisions
- there is less chance of one person's biases affecting committee decisions

The major disadvantages of the committee form of organization are

- there is a greater potential for buck-passing
- there is a tendency to take a long time in making a decision
- decisions often represent a compromise among the members rather than what might be best for the firm

Other Approaches to Organization

Some critics of the traditional line and staff organization say that it often is too inflexible. It is built on hierarchies of power in which orders are passed down the chain of command. People at the lower levels have to wait for orders from people at the higher levels, which may tend to reduce their initiative on the job. Meanwhile, rapid changes in technology, market conditions, and government regulations are taking an increasing amount of top management's time, which slows down their passing of orders down the chain of command.

Some of the newer ideas on organization have led to some modifications of the traditional line and staff organization. Typical examples of these modifications are

- wider spans of management
- greater decentralization
- less rigid chains of command
- authority based on knowledge instead of position

Matrix Organization

matrix organization

One of the newer approaches to organization which is still evolving is the matrix organization. **A matrix organization includes horizontal reporting requirements in addition to the traditional vertical chain of command. Organizational activities are structured in both functional and project arrangements and functional and project managers have authority over the same subordinates.** Large firms are using the matrix organization to regain some of the flexibility of smaller firms. They are pushing decision-making power down in the organization by structuring

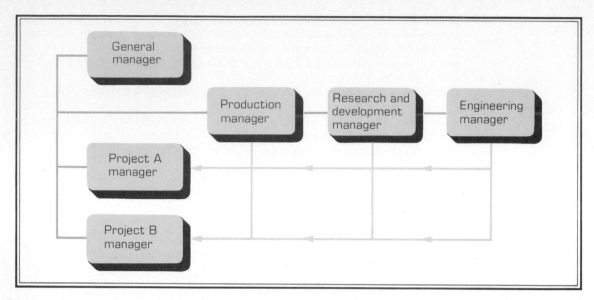

Figure 5.7
A matrix organization

their organizations around *objectives* rather than authority relationships and by placing emphasis on teamwork.

For example, a firm that builds engineering equipment may have a production manager, a research and development (R&D) manager, and an engineering manager. (See Figure 5.7.) These are permanent functional departments. Under these managers are production specialists, research scientists, and engineers, respectively. Suppose the firm has two projects underway. Project A requires the services of two engineers and a research scientist. These people are transferred temporarily from their functional departments to Project Manager A until the project is completed. They are under Project Manager A's direction while they are assigned there.

Project B requires the services of two production specialists and one engineer. These people are transferred temporarily from their functional departments to Project Manager B until the project is completed. They are under Project Manager B's direction while they are assigned there.

By being able to reassign personnel based on task needs, the firm is able to make better use of its personnel. But the matrix structure can cause conflict and uncertainty because there may be dual and even triple lines of authority. In other words, a subordinate may be accountable to two or three superiors.

Quality-of-work-life Programs

quality-of-work-life
(QWL) programs

Quality-of-work-life (QWL) programs have received a lot of attention in recent years. The underlying idea is that worker and manager participation in decisions at the bottom level of the organization through problem-solving committees will result in increased job satisfaction and raise both product quality and labour productivity.

QWL programs facilitate the flow of communication from workers to managers by involving workers more directly in their jobs. These various programs represent an effort to modify traditional ideas about work organization. They result in wider spans of management, greater decentralization, and less rigid chains of command, and recognize that authority can be based on knowledge as well as position.

If quality-of-work-life programs are to succeed, workers must perceive some benefit in participating. They may come to view their jobs as a type of investment—something into which they put more than the required number of hours of effort per day and from which they expect more than the mere satisfaction of lower-level needs.

Some of the reasons these programs are catching on in business should become clear in the following discussion of the human dimension of organization.

THE HUMAN DIMENSION OF ORGANIZATION

hierarchy of needs

No two people are exactly alike in terms of needs, wants, beliefs, values, and attitudes. **Nevertheless, we all have certain basic needs. Abraham H. Maslow arranged these needs in a hierarchy of needs. (See Figure 5.8.) The hierarchy is based on the prepotency (superiority) of needs. They emerge in the following order:**

- **physiological needs**
- **safety needs**

Figure 5.8
Maslow's hierarchy of human needs (adapted from A.H. Maslow, "A Theory of Human Motivation," Psychological Review, 50 (1953), pp. 370–396)

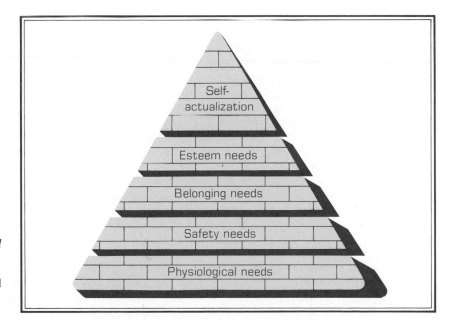

- **belonging needs**
- **esteem needs**
- **self-actualization needs**

The physiological needs (food, clothing, shelter, and sex) are the most prepotent of all needs. This means they must be satisfied before any of the higher-level needs can emerge and serve as motivators of behaviour. If you totally lack satisfaction of all needs in the hierarchy, your behaviour will be motivated by the physiological needs. When the physiological needs are satisfied, they cease to be motivators of behaviour and higher-level needs emerge. Only unsatisfied needs can motivate behaviour. Need satisfaction, however, need not be 100 percent. As lower-level needs become relatively satisfied, we are motivated mainly by the next higher level of unsatisfied needs. The degree of need satisfaction required depends on the individual.

The safety needs are the next to emerge. These include the need to feel that you will survive and that your physiological needs will continue to be met. A cave dweller made a spear for protection against wild animals and other enemies. Our highly stable political and economic system helps to make most of us feel relatively safe from dangers such as starvation and tyrannical government. The safety needs, for most adult Canadians, are not active motivators of behaviour. But there are other examples of the security needs. Job security, for example, is a major issue in many contracts negotiated by labour unions and employers. Nevertheless, we probably can consider physiological and safety needs as basic survival needs.

The belonging needs are more social in nature. They include social belonging, love, affection, affiliation, and membership needs. The family provides much of this but a business firm also can satisfy them by making the worker feel "needed." Co-workers can also satisfy these needs.

The esteem needs are of two basic types—social esteem and self-esteem. Social esteem needs (esteem from others) include prestige, status, and appreciation. They are your needs for relating to other people effectively. Self-esteem needs include competence and self-respect. These needs are very important because success in life leads us to undertake new challenges, whereas repeated failures tend to reduce our willingness to undertake new challenges. Self-esteem and self-actualization needs are our needs for personal growth.

Self-actualization includes the drive for achievement, creativity, and developing your attributes and capabilities. It is your need to achieve your potential in life, to become what you are capable of becoming. People who are seeking self-actualization are very concerned about using their time in an effective manner to accomplish tasks that they believe are worthwhile and challenging.

As we mature, we tend to move up in the hierarchy of needs. The behaviour of infants, for example, is dominated by the physiological and safety needs. Older children and adolescents are more aware of others and their behaviour usually is dominated by social needs. Their primary concern is "fitting in" and "belonging"—being like others with whom they associate instead of "being different." Normally, we tend to be motivated more by ego needs as we mature more fully. At some point in our teenage years, therefore, we become more motivated by self-esteem and self-actualization needs. We want to assert our independence.

The challenge for business is to provide jobs for employees that offer rewards beyond those that satisfy only physiological and safety needs. Money, by itself, loses some of its power to motivate as we move up the need hierarchy, which is not to say that money is not a motivator. Money can help in satisfying higher-level needs just as it can help in satisfying physiological and safety needs. Many people, for example, judge themselves in terms of how much money they earn. For them, money is related to the need for self-esteem. Likewise, money can give social esteem to the person who likes to brag about being a $175,000-a-year executive.

Money, however, is basically an *extrinsic* reward for work, which means that the reward does not come from the work itself. But there are other rewards that are part of the work itself. These are called *intrinsic* rewards. Social esteem can come from job titles and status symbols such as carpeting on the office floor and a key to the executive washroom. Self-esteem comes from competent performance on the job.

In our society the need to achieve one's potential in life (self-actualization) very often involves one's work. Top-level executives and owner-managers, for example, often say that their work is their life. Work can satisfy a wide range of needs for these people. But this view of work is not shared by all people. Some people consider their work to be a sort of necessary evil that must be performed in order to satisfy their basic physiological and safety needs. They tend to look away from the job to satisfy their higher-level needs. As we saw in Chapter 4, managers use different approaches in leading their subordinates. One reason is that they know that work does not have the same meaning to all people.

THE INFORMAL ORGANIZATION

informal groups

People on the job work and live together. They develop habits, customs, and patterns of behaviour and beliefs. This leads to the formation of informal groups. **Informal groups are small, face-to-face groups which spring up naturally as a result of human interaction on the job. They are created by their members to satisfy wants which are not being satisfied on the job by management.**

Workers are influenced in their attitudes and behaviour by the social groups they create to meet their personal needs. These interpersonal relationships cannot always be controlled by management. Employees interact in ways which are not always prescribed in the employee handbook. A business firm, therefore, is a social as well as an economic organization.

informal organization

Within every formal organization there is an informal organization. **The informal organization is the entire complex of informal groups which exists within the framework of the formal organization.** It exists within the formal organization but is separate from it. Human interaction in the formal organization is structured by management. It arises naturally in the informal organization as a result of our social nature.

CAREERS IN MANAGEMENT

CAREER OPPORTUNITIES EXIST FOR MANAGERS IN ALL ORGANIZATIONS. Entry-level positions are generally referred to as management-trainee positions. Senior management positions are held by people with years of proven performance as lower-level managers. The discussion that follows focuses on four careers that involve managerial/administrative responsibilities.

Blue-collar worker supervisors are lower-level managers who direct the activities of their subordinates. Roughly half of these jobs exist in manufacturing. The majority of the others are in the construction, transportation, and public utility industries and in wholesale and retail trade. Their work includes preparing work schedules, teaching workers safe work habits, enforcing safety rules, keeping production and employee records, training new workers, informing workers of company plans and policies, recommending good workers for pay increases and promotion, and disciplining workers whose job performance is inadequate. In unionized firms, these supervisors meet with union representatives to discuss worker problems and grievances. Among the major qualifications for such jobs are experience, skill, and leadership ability. One or two years of college or technical school is a plus, especially in industries with highly technical production processes, such as the chemical and electronics industries.

Hotel managers manage housekeeping, accounting, security, and maintenance departments; direct the operation of food service operations; and set room rates and credit policy. Roughly one-third of these people are self-employed. As in the case of blue-collar worker supervisors, the majority of hotel managers are promoted to their positions from lower-level jobs within the organization. Nevertheless, a bachelor's degree in hotel and restaurant administration or business administration provides strong preparation for a career in hotel management. A growing number of employers are hiring college-educated trainees.

Health service administrators manage hospitals, nursing homes, and clinics. Roughly half of them work for hospitals. These managers direct the various functions and activities of a health organization. If the organization is small, the administrator may do the directing personally. In large organizations, the administrator directs a staff of assistant administrators. Job responsibilities include diverse activities like promoting public participation in health programs, directing fund-raising drives, overseeing food services, records control, and in-service training programs, and reviewing budget proposals. Educational requirements vary according to the position's level of responsibility and size of the organization. A bachelor's degree in public health or hospital or business administration, however, is important.

City managers are usually appointed by elected officials to cope with the problems that population growth and industrial expansion create for housing, transportation, and crime and pollution control. City managers are directly responsible to the elected officials who appoint them. Their duties include coordinating the day-to-day operations of cities — tax collection and disbursement, law enforcement, and public works. They hire department heads and their staffs and prepare annual budgets to be approved by elected officials. They also try to attract new industry and act as liaisons between the town and existing industry. A master's degree, preferably in public or business administration, is rapidly becoming a requirement for city managers. ■

How and with whom a worker chooses to interact can affect that worker's job performance. Some interactions may harm a person's job performance. Others may improve it. An employee may learn good work habits by associating with more experienced employees. Another employee may learn bad habits by associating with careless workers.

The Nature of Informal Groups

Harry Thompson is a new management trainee at Brigdon Corporation. This is his first job after graduating from a community college. As a new employee, Harry was introduced to his immediate boss and several co-workers. He was given information about the company, its objectives, and how he fits into the picture. After touring the plant, meeting a lot of people, and completing numerous personnel forms, Harry returned to his new office. His formal introduction to the job was over.

Suppose that Harry met two old friends who were former students at his college. They graduated one year before him and have been in the management trainee program at Brigdon since then. Harry will probably ask them questions. Now that he knows all the rules and what he's supposed to do, he asks his friends about "how things really are." If Harry had no old friends at Brigdon, he would try to talk to others who have been hired only recently. They, too, want to "talk it over" with people "on the same level."

Because of his need for information, Harry begins to interact with other people in ways which are not dictated by management. Although he was required to attend the formal orientation sessions, no one told him to seek out the advice of co-workers. No one told him to let those other employees influence his behaviour.

Informal Groups in the Firm

Workers learn customs and develop habits through their job experiences. Doing things "according to the book" is often abandoned in favour of short-cuts they learn on the job. The many informal, interpersonal relationships which exist in a firm lead to the formation of social groups. They are relatively small, and their members stick together because they share common values and goals. You become a group member when the group decides that you are a member. A young college graduate assigned to the production department may find it harder to be accepted than another person closer to the educational level of the group.

Work-group leaders are selected from their membership. Thus, even though Shannon Arnold may be the foreman appointed by management, Joe Smith is the person to whom the employees under Shannon go to "air their gripes." Joe has the "inside track" with Shannon's superiors. Joe has been around for a long time and knows "what's happening." He understands the workers' problems and knows how to "take care of them."

Table 5.2 Characteristics of Informal Groups

1. small in size
2. created by their members
3. arise naturally and spontaneously
4. have leaders
5. often resist change
6. cohesive
7. close contact among members
8. develop norms of behaviour
9. enjoy emotional commitment of members
10. rapid communication of facts and rumours through the communications grapevine

Groups develop norms or standards of behaviour, and they pressure their members to conform to them. Members who go against those standards are punished. Thus, a worker who produces "too much" may be rejected by the group.

Since informal groups are based on interpersonal relationships, any changes which threaten to disrupt them are resisted. When changes in work assignments break up the coffee group, resistance will develop. It may take the form of workers asking why the change was made. It may even lead to a slow-down. (See Table 5.2.)

Table 5.3 Informal and Formal Characteristics of an Organization

Characteristic	Informal	Formal
1. Nature of the organization is	social	economic
2. Central concern is	human interaction	profit
3. Members seek to satisfy	social needs	economic needs
4. Structure is	informal, determined by voluntary patterns of interaction	formal, determined by management
5. Communication is	face-to-face, employee grapevine	through the chain of command
6. Leaders are	chosen by members	appointed by management
7. Commitment of members is	emotional	limited, little personal involvement
8. Organization is composed of	small, social groups	departments
9. Contact among members is	close, personal, face-to-face	impersonal, often indirect contact through the chain of command
10. Human interaction is	spontaneous and natural	determined by management

CAREER PROFILE

MY NAME IS JACK REIMER AND I AM currently a Marketing Manager with IBM Canada Ltd. in Vancouver. I joined IBM in 1966 as a programmer trainee after my university training in California, and have held, over the last sixteen years, a variety of professional positions with IBM. I have always been interested in marketing to our accounts, and the position I held prior to my present job was that of an Account Marketing Representative.

My major responsibility as a Marketing Manager is to manage a team of Marketing Representatives and Systems Engineers in one of the Vancouver branches. The Marketing and Systems professionals have a large responsibility in that the business and technical relationship between IBM and its customers depends primarily on their activities. As the manager of this unit, I must work with them in setting their objectives and evaluating the results of their efforts. The guiding technique used by IBM in this process is Management by Objectives. Career counselling and assistance in personal skills development of the employee is also the responsibility of each IBM manager,

Member Benefits from Informal Groups

A worker usually belongs to several informal groups. Each satisfies different needs. Tom belongs to one group whose members work together in the receiving department. Their physical closeness on the job provides a basis for grouping.

On Friday afternoons, Tom goes to the pub where he and several workers from other departments talk over their professional football and hockey clubs. They also talk over the "goings on" in their different departments.

Suppose Tom's boss recently hired someone with new ideas on running the department. If Tom and the older employees see this as a threat to their usual ways of doing things, they might form an informal group to "keep the new boss in line."

Informal groups help their members relate to the formal organization. (See Table 5.3.) Sometimes overspecialization of labour places workers in boring jobs. Membership in informal groups provides relief from such boredom. It enables members to feel human on the job even though they perform mechanical tasks. Beth Welles works on an automobile assembly

since at IBM we want to ensure that the employee is building a career, not simply doing a job. The Marketing Manager must also develop branch (unit) plans and report on whether business targets have been achieved. I am also responsible for ensuring that operating expenses are within the desired range.

There are several rewards that I have experienced in this job. First, I manage professionals who are striving to maximize their career potential. They are very cooperative, and it is very satisfying to work with these highly motivated people. Second, it is very satisfying to accept a challenging job and to do it successfully. This benefits both IBM and its customers. Third, in my work I meet a wide variety of managers in both the public and private sector. Discussions with these people give me a greater awareness of the kinds of problems IBM can potentially solve for its customers. These discussions also sharpen my managerial skills. Finally, I have enjoyed considerable personal growth through my involvement in the rapidly changing data processing industry.

There are, of course, some difficult challenges. A major one is deciding how to allocate personnel resources in such a way that our people are assigned in the most effective manner. At IBM we have a "contention" system for allocating resources to various marketing units and business functions. Basically, those individuals who are most effective and efficient at achieving their objectives have the best opportunity to obtain the resources necessary to do their job. This is a healthy system which encourages people to work effectively, thus enhancing their careers. It also benefits the company as a whole. It does, however, require constant monitoring by management to ensure that resources are balanced against the potential offered by business opportunities. A second challenge concerns time management. In any company as large and complex as IBM, managers are always faced with the temptation to spend time on activities that are really not crucial to their job. For example, if I do not manage my time properly, I can become excessively involved in internal staff work. I must continually put a high priority on marketing activities so that my customers and sales representatives are given the time they need from me.

The IBM Company has become a leader in its field because of its dedicated and energetic employees. Management in such an environment is a constant challenge and, at the same time, extremely rewarding.

line in southern Ontario. She may not feel that she is a real part of the company. Her contacts and experiences in informal groups, however, help her to feel like somebody.

For some workers, the only needs satisfied by the company are physiological and safety needs. The pay cheque buys groceries. The union contract gives some job security. But the higher-level needs are often overlooked. The need to belong is an example.

Beth Welles may know that she is an important part of the lunch group. She is included in their plans. On the other hand, she may feel that the company would hardly miss her, even if she were to die. Nor does the job itself give her much self-esteem. She is "Beth" only to her immediate boss and close friends. The payroll clerk, the timekeeper, the plant superintendent, and others know her only as badge number 121. She feels unimportant to them. This is not true when she bowls with several co-workers. Thus, Beth needs to feel important to herself, and she wants others to look upon her as "somebody."

As individuals mature, they become increasingly conscious of their "selves." They want more independence. A worker who has to punch in, punch out, eat, rest, and wash up at a certain time is, in many respects, being treated like a child. That worker seeks an outlet for developing some degree of independence on the job.

Workers also want to feel that they are doing something "worthwhile" and that they are important for what they do. Workers who perform similar tasks recognize their particular contributions. An informal group may develop to help maintain a feeling of achievement. All the workers know and respect Jerry as the best person in the plant with an acetylene torch even though Jerry may receive no formal recognition from management. The realities of the informal organization are a vital part of the way a firm works — or doesn't work.

SUMMARY AND LOOK AHEAD

An organization is a logical combination of human, financial, and physical resources put together by management so that certain goals can be accomplished. Both company and personal goals must be integrated so that employees will strive to accomplish company goals as well as personal goals. Because perfect integration is impossible, firms must suboptimize objectives.

Activities are the connecting link between the structure and objectives of a firm. Activities are determined by breaking down broad company goals into specific ones for each worker. Departmentation means these activities are grouped and assigned to various departments.

How many subordinates a manager can manage depends on many factors. Upper-level managers, however, usually manage fewer subordinates (a narrow span of management) than do lower-level managers.

Delegation means a superior entrusts part of his or her activities to a subordinate. It involves: (1) assigning responsibility, (2) granting authority, and (3) establishing accountability. There is little delegation in highly centralized organizations because the decision-making power is concentrated at the top.

There are three basic types of organization structures: (1) line, (2) line and staff, and (3) committee. Line authority (the chain of command) is the right to direct subordinates' work. Line functions contribute directly to reaching primary firm goals; staff functions help the line to perform line functions. Staff people advise and serve line managers. The authority of staff people to issue orders to line personnel is called functional authority.

Some of the newer approaches to organization focus on wider spans of management, greater decentralization, less rigid chains of command, and authority based on knowledge instead of position. Examples are the matrix organization and quality-of-work-life programs.

A firm has a social dimension that is not shown on its organization chart. Maslow's hierarchy of needs helps in understanding that workers have needs that must be satisfied on the job. Many of these needs are social needs. If not met by the formal organization itself, these needs lead to the formation of informal groups. The collection of small informal groups in a firm is the informal organization.

Because the topic of management is so complex and important, it is useful to consult detailed texts on the subject. Some of these are as follows:

D. Hellriegel and J. Slocum, Jr., *Management* (Reading, Mass.: Addison-Wesley, 1982).

J. Gray and F. Starke, *Organizational Behavior* (Columbus, Ohio: Merrill, 1984).

R. Mondy, R. Holmes, and E. Flippo, *Management: Concepts and Practices* (Boston: Allyn and Bacon, 1983).

A. Szilagyi, *Management and Performance* (Santa Monica, Calif.: Goodyear, 1981).

H. Smith, A. Carroll, A. Kefalas, and H. Watson, *Management* (New York: Macmillan, 1980).

L. Schlesinger, R. Eccles, and J. Gabarro, *Managing Behavior in Organizations* (New York: McGraw-Hill, 1983).

E. Huse, *Management* (2nd ed.) (St. Paul, Minn.: West, 1982).

In the next section we look at human resources and production management. We will study human resources first from the perspective of personnel management and then focus on labour relations. We will apply what we have learned about management and organization in this section to the discussion of production management. ■

QUESTIONS FOR REVIEW AND DISCUSSION

1. Discuss the similarities and differences between the formal and informal organizations. Why is formal structure necessary in a business organization?
2. What is meant by the "hierarchy" of organizational objectives?
3. Are there any organizational objectives that are common to organizations in general (such as charitable, educational, religious, business, or fraternal organizations)? Are there any objectives that are common to all business organizations? Discuss.
4. Why are business organizations departmentalized? How far should departmentation be carried?
5. For years many provincial legislatures have talked about the need to "consolidate" many of the activities which are currently spread out over various departments. Why is this? Does this have any implications for business organizations? Explain.
6. How are the concepts of delegation, span of management, departmentation, and decentralization related?
7. What is meant by "line and staff"?
8. "Staff positions are generally dead-end jobs in most business organizations." Do you agree? Why or why not?
9. What is an organization chart?
10. Do informal groups exist only in large corporations? Discuss.
11. Discuss the characteristics of informal groups which spring up on the job.

12. What is the informal organization?
13. What "values" does an employee learn from his or her membership in informal groups?
14. How does a person become accepted as a member of an informal group?
15. Why is it typical for informal groups to resist change?
16. How might the informal group put pressure on its members to get them to conform to group standards?

INCIDENTS

Babson Homes

Babson Homes was founded 20 years ago in Calgary, Alberta, by Charles Babson. He foresaw tremendous future population growth in the province because of its vast natural resources.

Babson Homes enjoys a fine reputation as a builder of quality homes in the $75,000 to $125,000 price range. Although company headquarters are still in Calgary, the company builds homes within a 400-mile radius. Most of these homes are built for real estate developers.

From the beginning Mr. Babson has held a tight reign on his company. He makes on-site inspections of potential developments, negotiates contracts directly with the developers and sub-contractors, and personally supervises construction.

Mr. Babson usually works seven days a week. He takes great pride in the fact that he runs the company from the ground up, and he attributes his company's excellent reputation to the fact that he is personally involved in every aspect of its operations.

Babson's employees are non-unionized. They are skilled workers who take great personal pride in their work. They all believe in Babson's philosophy: "If we can't do it right, let's not do it at all." Babson is very proud of their loyalty to the company and their great skill.

Mr. Babson recently negotiated contracts with several large, nationally known real estate developers. Babson now finds himself constantly on the go and never having enough time to do "what needs to be done."

Questions:
1. Why is Mr. Babson in the position of not having enough time to do "what needs to be done"?
2. Would you recommend that Mr. Babson change his way of doing things? Discuss.
3. Do you think "the company" today is comparable to what it was twenty years ago? Explain.

Work Organization on the Assembly Line

Traditional assembly lines do not permit workers much opportunity to interact on the job. A worker performs one routine task as the product moves past. The work cycle, or the amount of time a worker has to perform his or her task, may be only a few seconds. But this task may be repeated hundreds or thousands of times per day. The routine and repetitive nature of the work often creates boredom.

Some firms, therefore, are modifying their work organization by, for example, giving the worker a greater variety of tasks to perform, lengthening the work cycle, and rotating jobs among workers in work groups. Many managers believe that such changes in work organization help make work groups more productive and give the members more opportunity for socializing on the job.

Questions:
1. Why do assembly-line jobs typically focus on highly specialized tasks? (Hint: You may want to refer to the discussion of specialization in Chapter 1 in answering this question.)
2. Is socializing among members of work groups desirable? Why or why not?

A Plague of Job Hoppers

How could anyone expect good teamwork, group loyalty, or a common interest in raising firm productivity when almost half of the work force will either quit or be laid off within twelve months? Neither worker nor company has any interest in the economic success of the other. Workers, including managers, are not willing to sacrifice to help build the future prosperity of the company since they know that they will not be around to share in that future prosperity. Conversely the company is not willing to invest in the future success of the individual since that person is apt to be somewhere else when the investment that goes into training him pays off.

The result is gross underinvestment in creating the on-the-job skills necessary for industrial success. Blue-collar workers are traditionally trained on the job, but with today's high turnover rates no firm wants to invest in training its work force since there is a very high probability that the workers will soon leave for other jobs. For each firm it is cheaper to bid, with higher wages, a skilled worker away from other firms, but this obviously does not work for the economy as a whole. The result is a perpetual shortage of skilled blue-collar workers whenever the economy begins to approach anything remotely resembling full employment.

The problem is visible in foreign trade. To be a successful exporter it is necessary to speak the languages of the countries to which you wish to sell your products. Foreign firms are willing to pay to teach their employees the languages that they need to be salespersons abroad. Canadian firms often are not. The differences show how long they expect their employees to remain on the payroll.

The corporation is accused of having a short-run time horizon. But if everyone, workers and managers, is basically on his or her own when it comes to economic success, how could anyone expect the corporation to have a long time horizon? If each individual foresees that he or she will be with the firm for only a brief period, then it should come as no surprise that the corporation has an equally short time horizon in its planning.

To increase training, strengthen teamwork, and lengthen time horizons, corporations are going to have to adopt management practices that dramatically cut turnover rates. If Canadians want a loyal labour force interested in raising productivity, layoffs have to become the last, rather than the first, resort when a firm is facing difficult economic times. Incentives will have to be structured to give the biggest economic prizes to those who do not job hop. "Every man for himself" is not the route to economic success.

Questions:
1. In Chapter 4 we said that effective managers view their subordinates as human assets and strive to create a work environment in which subordinates will put forth their best efforts to reach the firm's goals. How does excessive employee turnover affect the effort to create such a work environment?
2. How does excessive job hopping affect a firm's strategic planning? What are the implications for the firm's future?
3. How might excessive job hopping among a firm's workers affect its effort to practice management by objectives (MBO)?
4. Do you believe that the quality of its managers and workers is a firm's single most important asset? Explain.
5. Is it possible to achieve a workable integration of personal and organizational objectives in a firm with a high employee turnover? Explain.

Section Three

By now we know what a business firm is. We also know that it must be managed. In this section we discuss the management of personnel, labour relations, and production.

Because a firm's most important resource is its human resource, we devote two chapters to it. Chapter 6 focuses on personnel management tasks. Chapter 7 looks at labour relations. It examines the nature of labour unions and the impact unions have on human resource management.

The nature and management of production is explained in Chapter 8. Production activities create goods and services and those activities require careful management. How well those activities are performed and managed determines to a large extent the productivity of business firms.

HUMAN RESOURCES AND PRODUCTION MANAGEMENT

After reading this chapter, you should be able to:

1. Compare a firm's human asset with its non-human assets.
2. Explain the meaning of human resource management.
3. List and discuss the tasks of personnel management and the personnel department.
4. Differentiate among the three types of interviews used in the selection process.
5. Identify two important controversies regarding the use of selection tests.
6. Draw a chart which shows how a job applicant becomes an employee.
7. Compare job-skill training with management development.
8. Compare the merit rating system with the management by objectives approach to appraising employee performance.
9. Discuss the importance of compensation to a firm, its employees, and its publics.
10. List and discuss three ways by which a worker's pay can be determined.
11. Give three examples of employers' compensation philosophies.
12. List and discuss three ways by which employees can be terminated.

In reading the chapter, look for and understand these terms:

human resource	management development
personnel management	organization development
personnel department	performance appraisal system
job analysis	merit rating system
job description	seniority
job specification	wage and salary administration
recruiting	piece rate
job application form	incentive pay
preliminary employment interview	wage
selection tests	salary
in-depth interview	promotion
background investigation	resignation
final selection interview	exit interview
employee orientation	dismissal
job-skill training	discharge

MANPOWER PLANNING HAS BECOME A well-known term in recent years. In turbulent times such as we in Canada have experienced it is critical (and difficult) for organizations to think about and plan for their future manpower requirements. It is just as important for an organization to think ahead about how many and what type of employees it will require as it is for you as a student to think about what type of career

CHAPTER SIX

Personnel Management

you want and to plan how you will prepare yourself for it.

Changes in the environment of business have created real problems in predicting level of business activity and associated manpower requirements. Changes in technology, in which we see a shift to more automation and office-of-the-future technology, have also created problems for manpower planners. The changing role of women in the workplace and changes in government requirements have also created difficulties.

ANY FIRM'S SUCCESS, IN THE FINAL ANALYSIS, DEPENDS MOST ON THE quality of the people who work for it — its personnel or human resource. This includes workers and managers at all levels in the firm — from top to bottom.

Top management, of course, is responsible for staffing the firm with good personnel. Staffing is a vital function of management. Its importance, unfortunately, is sometimes underestimated. Personnel administration is concerned with setting broad company policy regarding the firm's management of its human resource.

Top management delegates to the firm's personnel manager the task of implementing its human resource policies at the firm's "operations" level. Usually, this involves setting up a personnel department. This staff department is accountable for building and keeping a good work force.

In this chapter, we will discuss the firm's approach to human resource management. In practice, all managers participate in managing this vital resource. But most of the activities of human resource management are delegated to the personnel manager. Our main focus, therefore, is on the nature of personnel management activities.

HUMAN RESOURCE MANAGEMENT

human resource

A firm's most important resource, or asset, is its human resource. **The human resource is the personnel who staff the firm — its workers and managers.** It includes maintenance workers, salespeople, assembly-line workers, typists, and managers at all levels.

A firm's workers and managers make its non-human resources, or assets, productive. Without good personnel, the best-equipped plant will not function properly. A well-financed firm will not make a profit if its workers and managers are incompetent.

If you look at a company's balance sheet, you will find cash, accounts receivable, and inventories listed as current assets. Machinery, equipment, furniture, buildings, and land are listed as fixed assets. But there is no specific accounting for the human asset. Yet, a firm does invest money in recruiting and training employees. These employees are "earning assets." Without them, the firm would fold up.

The human resource, of course, must be managed in any type of organization. In most large organizations specialized personnel departments are created to deal with personnel matters. However, this does not mean that managers should ignore personnel management. To make an organization effective, all levels of management must participate in managing the human resource. Assembly-line bosses, for example, help train their subordinates and motivate them to perform well. Production managers, in turn, help train and motivate their assembly-line bosses.

Human resource management, therefore, is concerned with the management of a firm's most important resource—its personnel. Wherever there are managers and workers, human resource management activities are involved. These activities are discussed in this chapter.

A firm's top management sets the tone for the firm's approach to its human resource management. The importance that top management attaches to the human resource plays a large role in determining how it will be managed.

PERSONNEL MANAGEMENT AND THE PERSONNEL DEPARTMENT

Top management's policies regarding human resource management are carried out through the practice of good personnel management. **Personnel management consists of recruiting, selecting, training, developing, compensating, terminating, and motivating employees to good performance.**

personnel management

As we said earlier, the management of personnel is the job of every manager. But as firms grow, they create specific departments to help managers manage their personnel. Such a department is a personnel department. Top management delegates to the personnel manager the task of carrying out its human resource policies at the firm's "operations" level.

personnel department

A personnel department is a staff department which is headed by a

---

A CONTEMPORARY ISSUE

Human Asset Accounting

Although most managers recognize the value of company personnel, very few of them try to put a value on the firm's human asset. Consider a firm whose balance sheet lists a typewriter as an asset. Shouldn't the typist also be listed as an asset? Without a typist, a typewriter is useless.

A major problem, however, is how to value the human asset. What, for example, would be the "acquisition cost" for a firm's personnel? What about the replacement cost? What about "depreciating" the human asset?

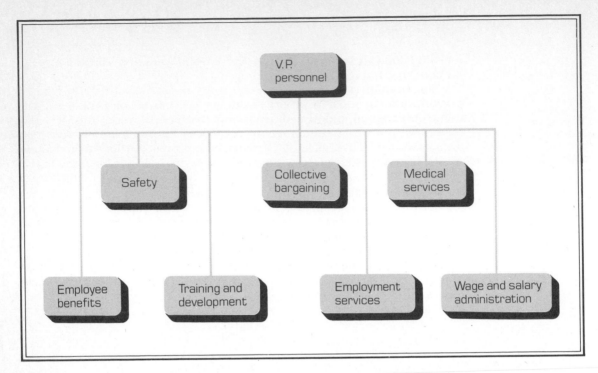

Figure 6.1
Organization of the personnel function

personnel manager. It advises and helps line managers to manage their personnel by performing specialized activities which are assigned to it.

The role played by the personnel department in a firm depends on the authority granted to it by top management. As a staff department, it advises and helps line managers to recruit, select, train, and motivate workers. Thus, final decisions about personnel matters are made by the line managers. But personnel departments in some firms have functional authority. In these firms the personnel department actually makes decisions regarding the hiring of new workers, granting promotions, and so forth.

In large organizations, the personnel function employs many people. Many of these are experts in a certain field such as safety, collective bargaining, or employee testing. Figure 6.1 indicates the functions which are usually performed by a personnel department in a large manufacturing firm.

In the discussion which follows, we look at the work of the personnel manager and the personnel department. This work can be divided as follows:

1. Determining human resource needs
2. Searching for and recruiting applicants to fill those needs
3. Selecting applicants for employment
4. Training and developing personnel

5. Appraising employee performance
6. Compensating employees
7. Promoting employees
8. Providing personnel services
9. Terminating employees

DETERMINING HUMAN RESOURCE NEEDS

For a new firm, the best place to start in order to determine human resource needs is the statement of company objectives. This helps in preparing an organization chart, which provides a skeleton of the firm's needs for workers and managers.

In the case of established firms, some workers and managers are already on the payroll. These firms also must continually study their need for personnel. Old employees retire, leave to take jobs with other employers, and so on. They must be replaced.

Forecasting Human Resource Needs

There are two basic ways to determine a firm's human resource needs. One approach involves no advance planning. The need is recognized as urgent only when a present employee leaves or a new job opening must be filled.

The other approach is to anticipate needs before they become urgent. This involves forecasting the number and types of positions that will be opening up and making a time schedule of when they probably will open up. Ideally the firm should take its sales forecast and "back into" production scheduling and financial forecasting. This helps it to get a better fix on the exact number and types of jobs to be filled.

One indicator of good human resource planning is stability of employment. It is wise to avoid having to hire or lay off a large number of workers on short notice. Well-managed firms try to plan ahead. For example, the forecast of personnel needs may indicate reduced future need for employees. If this is known far enough in advance, attrition (people retiring and people quitting for other reasons) can bring the work force down to an efficient level. This is better than laying off a lot of workers on short notice.

Many firms whose needs for personnel fluctuate often turn to temporary help services for workers. The period of time these temporary helpers are needed may range from a few hours to several months. Firms that use temporary help services are able to build some degree of flexibility into their forecasts of human resource needs.

Specifying Human Resource Needs

job analysis

Job analysis helps a firm to specify its human resource needs. **Job analysis involves defining the jobs that must be done if the firm is to reach its**

```
POSITION DESCRIPTION

POSITION:      Cost Accountant

REPORT TO:     Supervisor, Accounting

DEPARTMENT: Accounting

INCUMBENT:    Linda Ducharme          DATE PREPARED: July 9, 1982


OBJECTIVES

—Ensure the timely input and accuracy of coding of all data entry and accounting entries
  related to Winnipeg plant.
—Review and distribute Winnipeg plant reports.
—Coordinate the preparation and summarization of all inventories.

RESPONSIBILITIES

—Ensure that all data entry for Winnipeg plant is input on a timely basis with due consider-
  ation to accuracy and cut-offs.
—Review all Winnipeg plant purchases for accuracy of coding.
—Review individual orders on completion to determine that costs are complete before
  running job cost reports.
—Coordinate cut-offs and running of plant reports through communications with Rexdale
  plant.
—Receive and distribute plant reports.
—Review all Winnipeg plant reports and report on significant variances.
—Maintain liaison with evening data entry clerks, make sure that time sheets are available
  for keying, and see that schedules are arranged with due consideration to payroll and
  month-end cut-offs.
—Review Winnipeg plant work in process cut-offs and make adjustments to account for
  partially filled material requisitions and partially shipped orders.
—Complete the extension, additions, and summarization of Winnipeg plant inventories with
  such assistance as may be required and report significant changes to the comptroller.
—Complete Edmonton plant inventories, provide missing prices, and summarize.
—Prepare total company inventory summary.
—Check on the existence of "Goods in Transit" and insure proper inventory and accounting
  treatment.
—Prepare journal entries for factory supplies inventories.
—Prepare monthly journal entries for:
      1. Tax on consignment goods
      2. Internal sales
      3. Spoiled work
      4. Transfer sales

DECISIONS

Appropriate coding—GL Codes, Sales Product Codes, Work Centre and Operations codes.

Determine as to completeness of job costs. Determine as to significance of variances to be
reported.
```

Figure 6.2
A job description (Used with permission of Systems Business Forms Limited.)

objectives. Each job is studied to determine what work it involves and what qualifications are needed by the persons who will fill it.

From the job analysis, the job description (or position guide) is prepared. **A job description outlines the nature of a given job—how the job relates to other jobs; the specific duties involved; and the tools, machinery, and supplies needed.** (See Figure 6.2.)

job description

COST ACCOUNTANT   PAGE 2

CONTACTS INTERNAL

Contacts with Junior Accounting clerk to ensure proper completion of accounts payable, timesheets, correctness of entered work.

Rexdale personnel such as Manager, Administration. Winnipeg plant Supervisors and Managers regarding timesheet discrepancies.

Edmonton plant Manager regarding inventories.

Evening data entry clerks—provide instructions and schedule work.

CONTACTS EXTERNAL

None.

SUPERVISION EXERCISED

None. May provide assistance when requested by Supervisor of Accounting in overseeing the work of junior level positions.

SUPERVISION RECEIVED

Directly: Work under general supervision of Supervisor of Accounting, most duties being performed independently. Incumbent is expected to deal with doubtful matters covered by precedent and refer only unusual problems to supervisor.

Indirectly: From Comptroller, Vice-President Administration.

DEMANDS

Month-end deadlines regarding journals, work in process, inventory, weekly deadlines—timesheets information verified and input. Information to be complete for payroll procedures.

DISRUPTIONS

Various questions from different departments, plants, accounting, etc.

QUALIFICATIONS

Minimum of two year's accounting experience, preferably cost accounting experience. Proven ability to work with figures and knowledge of balancing and reconciling techniques.

EDUCATION

High School diploma with some formal accounting training either in High School, technical school, and/or enrollment in a recognized accounting course.

Figure 6.2
A job description (continued)

job specification

From the job description, the job specification is prepared. **A job specification states the personal qualifications needed by the person who is to fill each job—education, skills, experience, etc.** (See Figure 6.3 on page 176.)

Job analysis, job descriptions, and job specifications help make a firm's human resource needs more concrete. They give the firm a clearer idea of

Figure 6.3
Techniques for specifying human resource needs

what types of employees are needed and permit more effective evaluation of people who apply for jobs.

SEARCHING FOR AND RECRUITING APPLICANTS

recruiting

A firm that waits for recruits to come to it has to be satisfied with whoever shows up. This is a poor approach. **Recruiting is the task of attracting potential employees to the firm. It should be a continuous process for most medium- and large-sized firms.** Recruiting for the long range is beneficial because it forces a firm to take stock of its present work force and to plan for future human resource needs, and it helps to eliminate the chance that new employees will be selected from among a small number of applicants.

The nature of the search task depends on the jobs being filled and the general conditions in the job market. The more skills needed, the more complex is the search process. The supply and the demand for people possessing certain skills also affects the search.

Avon Products, Inc. and other firms that sell door-to-door often have annual turnover rates as high as 100 percent among their salespeople. They must recruit new salespeople on a continuous basis. Firms in the microelectronics and robotics industries must do likewise, not so much because of a high employee turnover rate but because people with the needed training and skills are in very limited supply. Consider fast-food restaurants like Burger King. For many years they have relied heavily on part-time teenage workers to fill job openings. However, the number of people in our population between sixteen and nineteen years of age has been falling and some fast-food chains are changing their searching and recruiting practices to find and attract older part-time workers.

Sources of recruits and methods of recruiting vary among employers. Avon's salespeople work in or near their own neighbourhoods. Thus Avon does not have to think about offering free lodging while salespeople are house hunting. But microelectronics firms that recruit microsystems programmers conduct a nationwide search and must often offer this benefit to attract recruits. Firms that are trying to recruit women and minorities will recruit heavily at colleges with large enrollments of women and minorities and place recruitment ads in magazines targeted to them.

Traditional sources of recruits include unemployed workers, present and past employees, their friends and relatives, and workers who are taking their first jobs. Employees who have jobs with other employers but are dissatisfied are also often receptive to job offers.

Among the many methods of recruitment are word-of-mouth, advertisements, government and private employment agencies, vocational, technical, and college recruiting. Word-of-mouth recruiting, however, can be illegal if the "word" finds its way only to white Anglo-Saxon males.

Recruiting Managers

Firms may choose to emphasize internal or external sources of management recruits. Promoting from within boosts employee morale because it demonstrates that a manager can move up the management hierarchy in his or her present firm. Recruiting outsiders, however, may bring needed "new blood" into the firm. Many firms use outside recruitment firms in their search for and recruitment of managers. These firms are sometimes called *headhunters.* It also is not unusual for successful managers to be hired away from other employers. This sometimes is referred to as *pirating* or *raiding.*

SELECTING APPLICANTS FOR EMPLOYMENT

Firms that seek to find the best person for the job will undertake intensive recruiting and be quite careful in selecting applicants. Employers often use job application forms, employment interviews, selection tests, and background investigations in selecting applicants for employment.

The Job Application Form

job application form

The job application form (application blank or biographical inventory) is prepared by an employer and filled in by a job applicant. The applicant provides job-related information that helps the employer to determine if the applicant has the needed education, experience, training, etc., for the job. The care with which an applicant fills out this form can be very revealing. (See Figure 6.4 on pages 178–181.)

Antidiscrimination laws make it illegal to require an applicant to supply data regarding religious preference, colour, race, sex, or nationality. Many firms that formerly required applicants to attach photos to the job application form have dropped the practice. This helps assure the applicants that race will not be considered in the employee selection process. A job application form that asks for "wife's name" instead of "spouse's name" makes it rather obvious that the firm assumes all applicants will be men.

SYSTEMS
SYSTEMS EQUIPMENT LIMITED

CONFIDENTIAL

APPLICATION FOR EMPLOYMENT

PLEASE FILL OUT THIS APPLICATION AS COMPLETELY AS POSSIBLE. WRITE OR PRINT LEGIBLY.

POSITION DESIRED	DATE OF APPLICATION

1 PERSONAL INFORMATION

LAST NAME	FIRST NAME	INITIALS	SOCIAL INSURANCE NUMBER

PRESENT ADDRESS: STREET	CITY	PROVINCE	POSTAL CODE	TELEPHONE RES: BUS:

WHAT PROMPTED THIS APPLICATION?	WHEN COULD YOU BE AVAILABLE TO COMMENCE WORK?	FULL TIME _____ PART TIME _____	HOURS AVAILABLE DAILY BASIS OTHER

CANADA MANPOWER ☐   ONE OF OUR PERSONNEL ☐   ADVERTISEMENT ☐   OWN ACCORD ☐

HAVE YOU PREVIOUSLY APPLIED? ☐ YES ☐ NO

WHEN   INCOME EXPECTED $ _____ PER _____

HAVE YOU EVER APPLIED FOR EMPLOYMENT WITH A JR COMPANY?   YES ☐   NO ☐

IF YES, WHICH COMPANY?	DATES FROM	TO

GIVE BRIEF DETAILS OF PREVIOUS JR EMPLOYMENT IF APPLICABLE

DO YOU KNOW ANYONE WORKING IN THIS COMPANY? WHO?	RELATIONSHIP

WOULD YOU BE WILLING TO RELOCATE? YES ☐ NO ☐ TO WHAT CITY?	DO YOU HOLD A VALID DRIVER'S LICENSE? WHAT PROVINCE?

DO YOU OWN A CAR? WHAT MAKE AND YEAR?	IF REQUIRED, COULD YOU USE YOUR CAR FOR COMPANY PURPOSES? YES ☐ NO ☐

HAVE YOU EVER BEEN BONDED? ☐ YES ☐ NO   WITH WHAT COMPANY?

HAVE YOU EVER BEEN REFUSED A BOND? ☐ YES ☐ NO   IF YES - WHY?

PHYSICAL

PHYSICAL DISABILITIES ☐ YES ☐ NO   WHAT?

HEIGHT	WEIGHT	EYESIGHT	HEARING

CAN YOU DISTINGUISH ALL COLOURS? ☐ YES ☐ NO ☐ DON'T KNOW	WHAT IS YOUR PRESENT STATE OF HEALTH?	HOW MUCH TIME FROM WORK HAVE YOU MISSED IN THE LAST YEAR?

ARE YOU WILLING TO UNDERTAKE PHYSICAL EXAMINATION? ☐ YES ☐ NO

HAVE YOU BEEN UNDER A DOCTOR'S CARE WITHIN THE LAST 3 YEARS. IF YES, WHY? ☐ YES ☐ NO

Figure 6.4
An application form (Used with permission of Systems Business Forms Limited.)

2 EDUCATION

| SCHOOL NAME & LOCATION | AVERAGE STANDING ( ) | | | GRADE COMPLETED |
	ABOVE	AVERAGE	BELOW	
JR. HIGH SCHOOL				
HIGH SCHOOL UNIVERSITY ENTRANCE ☐ COMMERCIAL ☐ HIGH SCHOOL LEAVING ☐ TECHNICAL ☐				
COLLEGE OR UNIVERSITY COURSE(S)				DEGREE OBTAINED
SPECIAL ACADEMIC ACHIEVEMENTS INCLUDING SCHOLARSHIPS				
OTHER EDUCATION OR TRAINING COURSES				

TO BE COMPLETED BY APPLICANTS SEEKING CLERICAL POSITIONS

3 BUSINESS SKILLS

HAVE YOU KNOWLEDGE OF:

TYPING _____ W.P.M. ☐   ACCOUNTS PAYABLE ☐

SHORTHAND _____ W.P.M. ☐   ACCOUNTS RECEIVABLE ☐

DICTA ☐   GENERAL BOOKKEEPING ☐

CALCULATORS ☐   SWITCHBOARD ☐

OTHER SKILLS: TELEX/TELETYPE ☐

TO BE COMPLETED BY APPLICANTS SEEKING FACTORY POSITIONS

4 TECHNICAL SKILLS

WHAT MACHINES ARE YOU QUALIFIED TO OPERATE: (FILL IN THE NAME OF EACH)

PREPARATION   FINISHING

PHOTOTYPESETTER _____   PUNCH UNIT _____

CAMERA _____   STITCHER _____

PLATEMAKER _____   COLLATOR _____

    FOLDER _____

PRESS - SHEET FED   SHINGLER _____

LETTERPRESS _____   CUTTER _____

OFFSET PRESS _____   SHRINK WRAPPER _____

    OTHERS: _____

ROTARY   _____

ROTARY/WEB _____   _____

5 REFERENCES

The following are the names of persons to whom reference may be made concerning myself, in particular with reference to my character and suitability for employment. (References should **NOT** include relatives or former employers).

NAME	ADDRESS	TELEPHONE	OCCUPATION
NAME	ADDRESS	TELEPHONE	OCCUPATION
NAME	ADDRESS	TELEPHONE	OCCUPATION

6 WORK EXPERIENCE

NOTE: IF YOU HAVE A RESUME, PLEASE ATTACH.

COMPANY	ADDRESS				PRODUCT / SERVICE
DATE	STARTED	FINISHED	SALARY AT TERMINATION	REASON FOR LEAVING	
DEPARTMENT					
POSITION					
SALARY (MONTHLY)				ASPECT OF JOB LIKED BEST	
SUPERVISOR S NAME AND TITLE					
NO. OF EMPLOYEES YOU SUPERVISED				ASPECT OF JOB LIKED LEAST	

COMPANY	ADDRESS				PRODUCT / SERVICE
DATE	STARTED	FINISHED	SALARY AT TERMINATION	REASON FOR LEAVING	
DEPARTMENT					
POSITION					
SALARY (MONTHLY)				ASPECT OF JOB LIKED BEST	
SUPERVISOR S NAME AND TITLE					
NO. OF EMPLOYEES YOU SUPERVISED				ASPECT OF JOB LIKED LEAST	

COMPANY	ADDRESS				PRODUCT / SERVICE
DATE	STARTED	FINISHED	SALARY AT TERMINATION	REASON FOR LEAVING	
DEPARTMENT					
POSITION					
SALARY (MONTHLY)				ASPECT OF JOB LIKED BEST	
SUPERVISOR S NAME AND TITLE					
NO. OF EMPLOYEES YOU SUPERVISED				ASPECT OF JOB LIKED LEAST	

I understand that the information given in this application may be verified, for which I authorize and request any and all of my former employers and any other person to furnish information they may have concerning my character, ability, business activities and reputation, history of employment and reasons for termination thereof.

Date _____   City _____   Signature of Applicant _____

Figure 6.4
An application form (continued)

7 OTHER INTERESTS.

LIST INTERESTS, SPORTS, HOBBIES, CLUBS AND ASSOCIATIONS (TO WHICH YOU BELONG OR BELONGED - OMITTING RELIGIOUS, ETHNIC OR RACIAL ORGANIZATIONS): POSITIONS OF LEADERSHIP.

ADD ANY ADDITIONAL COMMENTS THAT YOU FEEL MIGHT HELP US IN EVALUATING YOUR APPLICATION.

I understand that any misrepresentation or omission of facts called for on this application or rejection of bonding or health insurance applications, or any other subsequent forms pursuant to my employment with this company is cause for rejection prior to employment or discharge after employment. If employed by this company I agree to be governed by such rules, regulations and employment policies as the company shall post or publish. It is further agreed that the first ninety (90) days of my employment shall be considered as a probationary period during which time my employment may be terminated with or without notice by either the company or myself. It is further agreed that when I have fulfilled such conditions of eligibility as may exist I will enroll and maintain my membership in the employee benefit plans in existence at the time, and I authorize the company to make such deductions from my earnings as may be required.

_____   _____
Signature of Applicant   Date

SPACE FOR OFFICE USE ONLY

The Preliminary Employment Interview

**preliminary
employment interview**

The preliminary employment interview is the first time that the employer and the applicant meet face-to-face. The employer is usually represented by an interviewer who informs the applicant of job openings and the applicant has an opportunity to ask questions and to discuss skills, job interests, and so on.

Great care also is needed to avoid discrimination in conducting these interviews. For example, questions such as "Do you plan to have children?" or "What does your husband think of your going to work?" should be avoided. Otherwise, the firm may be subject to lawsuits or to government action.

Selection Tests

selection tests

Selection tests are used to measure an applicant's potential to perform the job for which he or she is being considered. These tests include intelligence tests, aptitude tests, performance tests, interest tests, and personality tests. Of course, not all firms will use all of the selection tests we will discuss. The size of the firm and the type of job, for example, influence the types of selection tests that will be used, if any. Selection tests should supplement (not substitute for) judgment and other information that is available about an applicant.

Intelligence tests measure general verbal ability and specific abilities such as reasoning. Aptitude tests measure ability, such as mechanical aptitude or clerical aptitude. Performance tests measure skill in a given type of work, such as typing. Interest tests (inventories), such as the Kuder Preference Record, are designed to predict whether a person will like performing a particular task. Personality tests (inventories), such as the California Psychological Inventory, measure some aspect (or aspects) of a person's total personality. They are designed to predict whether a person will be able to accept a lot of stress on the job, work well with other people, and so on.

The use of selection tests is controversial. Some people believe that the tests are biased. Intelligence tests, for example, have been attacked because of their alleged white, middle-class cultural bias. To stay within the law, selection tests should be carefully designed to measure ability to do the specific job for which an applicant is being considered.

The In-depth Interview

An applicant who passes the selection tests may be scheduled for an in-depth interview, especially if he or she is applying for a higher-level job. **An in-depth interview is one conducted by trained specialists to shed light on the applicant's motivation, ability to work with others, ability to communicate, etc.**

in-depth interview

The Background Investigation

background
investigation

After in-depth interviewing, an applicant's references are checked. **In a background investigation, the applicant's past employers (if any), neighbours, former teachers, etc., are questioned about their knowledge of the applicant's job performance, character, and background.**

There is a lot of controversy here, also. An employer has the right to look into an applicant's suitability for a job, but it is easy to go overboard and invade the applicant's privacy. Employers often use reference letters to obtain information about job applicants. Because reference letters are now open for review by the person about whom they are written, former employers tend to say only complimentary things in writing. A growing number of employers are refusing to provide reference letters other than those that state the person's period and status of employment. Although job applicants cannot be forced to do so, they sometimes are asked to sign a release stating that they are volunteering to take a polygraph (lie detector) test.

The Final Selection Interview

final selection interview

If the results of the background investigation are satisfactory, the applicant is likely to be called in for the final selection interview. **In the final selection interview, all company personnel who have interviewed the prospect are present, along with the manager under whom the applicant will work. The manager is the person who makes the decision whether or not to hire the applicant.** Any hiring decision, however, is contingent on passing the company's physical (and perhaps, psychological) exam.

In recent years there has been some controversy regarding these exams. As long as the exam pertains to job-related requirements, there is no problem. But when a firm sets standards that are not job-related, trouble arises. There is no excuse for denying a physically handicapped person a job if the handicap does not hurt job performance. The same is true of the mentally retarded.

Recruiting, interviewing, screening, preparing job specifications, and other personnel activities require care to avoid illegal discrimination based on an applicant's race, colour, religion, sex, age, or nationality. An employer who wants to hire a female fashion model would not be breaking the law by screening out a male applicant, since employers are allowed to set "bona fide" occupational qualifications. But these must be related to the job being filled. Thus, an employer cannot refuse to hire a female applicant on the grounds that the job is thought to be too physically demanding or because it involves travel with men.

Selecting Managers

Applicants for management positions are screened in somewhat the same way as other employees. But job requirements and criteria for success are much harder to define for managers and managerial skills are harder to test. This is why many firms rely very heavily on interviews in selecting managers.

In recent years the use of assessment centers has become popular in selecting managers. Graduating students who are applying for a management trainee position may be given the standard personality, interest, and intelligence tests, but these are supplemented by a series of typical management problems to be solved as a group. For example, a group may be set up as a "company" to manufacture and market a product. The members are observed by experienced managers who get together to make an overall evaluation of each candidate's performance. Their judgments are passed on to the persons who are making the selection decision.

TRAINING AND DEVELOPING EMPLOYEES

Up to the point of hiring, the main goal of personnel activities is to accept or reject the applicant. After the employer tells the applicant that he or she is hired, the "point of hire" has been passed. The employer can then ask for additional personal information. Of course, it still is illegal to engage in discriminatory practices after the person is hired.

Employee Orientation

employee orientation

Employee orientation (induction or indoctrination) involves introducing the new employee to the job and to the firm. It is the first, and probably most critical, phase of the employee's training. An applicant gets some orientation to the firm and the job during the selection process, but it only touches the surface. For an employee, the orientation should be much more formal and complete. Serious-minded employees always want to know what is expected of them on the job.

A good orientation program helps to relieve the new employee's feelings of insecurity in a new environment. He or she is told about the firm's history, its products, and its operation. Company policies and rules are explained as are company-sponsored employee services. These often are spelled out in a personnel manual, or employee handbook. To acquaint the new employee with the firm, a tour of the plant often is made, co-workers are introduced, and the new employee's questions are answered.

The personnel department coordinates the orientation program, but the new employee's supervisor plays the major role. Effective supervisors know that the time they devote to orientation can save them "headaches" later in disciplining and answering questions from new employees who received a poor introduction to the job.

Figure 6.5 shows the sequence of steps an applicant may go through in the employee selection process. It is basically a matching process in which the employer seeks to hire applicants whose skills, experience, and so on match the employer's job requirements.

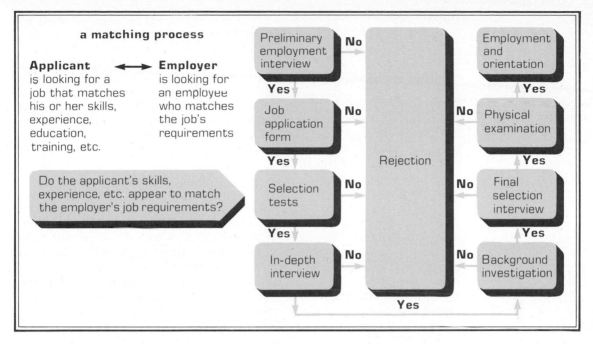

Figure 6.5
The sequence of steps an applicant may go through in the employee selection process

Employee Training

job-skill training

Job-skill training teaches employees specific job skills. It can be done on the job or away from the job.

On-the-job training (OJT) can be used to teach new employees their jobs or to teach new skills to experienced employees. OJT is best suited to teaching simple jobs. The trainee works under the guidance of an experienced worker who advises and shows the trainee how to do the job.

Away-from-the-job training is used when a higher level of skill is required and when OJT is too dangerous, or causes too much interruption of the workflow in the plant. The trainee may go to a company-sponsored training program either at the plant or in the company's training school. He or she is trained on the same machines that are used in the plant, but the training is done in a classroom. This often is called *vestibule training*.

Training is a continuous process because new employees must be trained and those with longer service must be retrained. The rapid pace of technological change means that employee skills become obsolete much faster. Thus techniques of in-company training also are changing. Computers, closed-circuit TV, programmed text materials, videocassettes, and other technical aids are being used. As factories and offices become more automated during the 1980s, firms will be investing huge sums of money to retrain displaced workers for new jobs. This type of investment in the human resource pays off in improved morale and productivity.

Management Development

management
development

Management development refers to efforts to prepare people for managerial positions and to improve the managerial skills of present managers. Among the techniques of management development that are used, especially in larger firms, are lecture, case method, simulation, laboratory training, and transfer.

The *lecture method* is good for presenting facts. It is a good way of informing managers of the meaning of new laws that regulate business activity. In the *case method,* participants are given a problem situation to analyze and solve as if the case situation were real. Examples of *simulation* are management games and role-playing. Simulation techniques force trainees to act out real business behaviour that is supposed to give them practice in decision making. In a management game, for example, several teams compete against each other. Each team is a separate "company." Role-playing emphasizes the human aspects of management. A trainee might play the role of a supervisor who is disciplining a subordinate or evaluating the performance of a subordinate.

In T-group training (also called sensitivity training, *laboratory training,* or encounter groups), small discussion groups become involved with real (not simulated) problems that exist within the training group itself. The purpose is to help trainees learn about their individual weaknesses, how groups work, and how to behave more effectively in interpersonal relations.

Transfers involve rotating a manager among different plants or offices, often in different geographical locations, to broaden their exposure to the firm's operations. Transfers can help both new recruits and more experienced managers to develop their managerial abilities.

Organization Development

organization
development

Management development is concerned mainly with the manager as an individual. **Organization development (OD) is a re-education process that is used to change the values and behaviour of the entire organization in order to improve its effectiveness in reaching its objectives and in solving problems.** OD uses knowledge in the fields of psychology and sociology to improve organizations. OD programs are based on the systems view of management and can lead to organizational changes, such as redesigned jobs and participative work groups.

OD programs can be successful only if the chief executive officer is convinced that change is necessary, is willing to accept it, and can inspire all lower-level managers and workers to want and accept change. The quality-of-work-life programs we discussed in Chapter 5 require a great deal of change in an organization as it moves away from traditional patterns of behaviour. The concept of participative management must be translated into the creation of work teams made up of members who are committed to the belief that it can work and are dedicated to making it work. A major focus is getting supervisors to recognize the need to change their management styles — for example, to become more like Theory Y managers and less like Theory X managers. Personnel departments can help provide the type of training necessary to make an OD program work.

APPRAISING EMPLOYEE PERFORMANCE

performance
appraisal system

The personnel department often helps to develop a formal performance appraisal system to enable supervisors to rate their subordinates' job performance. A good performance appraisal system provides a basis for measuring an employee's contribution to the firm. It reduces employee suspicion that promotions and pay raises are based on favouritism rather than performance. There are several types of performance appraisal systems, and so it is important for supervisors and subordinates to understand which system is being used by the firm.

merit rating system

    Traditional performance appraisal systems require a manager to appraise a subordinate's work habits and personal traits. In the merit rating system, each employee's job performance is appraised every six months or every year. Initiative, ability to work with others, dependability, etc., are appraised. There is, of course, a lot of room for error in rating these personal traits and work habits objectively.

POINT OF VIEW

Employee Evaluation

Supervisor A:

    "As a supervisor, I have to evaluate my subordinates every six months. The people over in the personnel department keep tabs on these evaluations for use when promotions open up and for granting pay raises. Honestly, I think it's a lot of bull. If I rate any of my subordinates low, it's a bad reflection on me. After all, my job is to inspire them to good performance. For example, if I check the box that says 'poor attitude toward job,' in effect I'm admitting that I'm failing as a manager.

    "On the other hand, if I give 'top grades' to my subordinates, I look good to them and to my boss. It sort of reminds me of school and the lousy grading system. You can bet that all of my subordinates always get good marks."

Supervisor B:

    "As a supervisor, I want to evaluate my subordinates every six months. I have an obligation to my subordinates to rate their performances realistically and objectively. They want to know where they stand and how well they are progressing on the job. I also have an obligation to my superiors to make the best use of my subordinates.

    "As a manager, I must work through others. The more that I can help them develop into good employees, the more valuable they are to me, to the company, and to themselves."

seniority

Because of these problems, some firms rely mainly on an employee's seniority as a basis for granting pay raises and promotions. **Seniority refers to an employee's length of service. The longer that service, the more seniority an employee has.** It is a lot easier to be objective in measuring seniority than in measuring initiative or ability to work with others. This is why labour unions favor the seniority system. By and large, however, this approach dodges the issue of appraising employee performance.

As we saw in Chapter 4, the management by objectives (MBO) approach can be used in rating employee performance. It does away with some of the subjective elements in a merit rating system. But it requires mutual trust and respect between boss and subordinate, ability to communicate effectively with each other, and faith in each other's abilities.

COMPENSATING EMPLOYEES

wage and salary administration

Wage and salary administration is the process of developing and implementing a sound and fair method of compensating employees. It involves setting pay ranges for all jobs in the firm and setting a specific amount of pay for each employee.

Compensation is important to employees because pay is the main factor that determines the standard of living for most Canadian families. It is the major source of buying power. Pay is also important in a psychological sense. Many workers, for example, measure their importance to their employers in terms of their pay.

To an employer, employee pay is a cost of doing business. Although wage and salary administrators want to hold this cost down, they know that low pay usually leads to low employee morale. Low pay does not always mean more profit to the firm. We must consider labour productivity. It is better to pay a worker $10 per hour for producing 100 units of output than it is to pay a worker $5 per hour for producing 30 units.

Determining the Basis for Payment

A worker's pay can be based on

- output produced
- time spent on the job
- a combination of output produced and time spent on the job

piece rate

Some workers are paid a piece rate. Each worker is paid a certain rate for each acceptable unit of output produced. A worker who sews together a pair of overalls could be paid a piece rate. This method, of course, can be used only when each worker's labour can be identified with specific units of output.

incentive pay

To encourage greater worker productivity, some firms offer incentive pay. For those units produced by a worker above the normal output per day (the quota), the piece rate is increased. Suppose the quota is 100 pair of overalls per day. A worker gets $.50 for each pair sewed together. Meeting quota means a daily payment of $50. If a bonus (incentive payment) of $.05 were paid for each pair produced above quota, a worker who produced 120 pairs would receive $61 for that day's work (100 pairs × 50 cents + 20 pairs × 55 cents, or $50 + $11 = $61).

wage

A worker paid on the basis of time spent on the job gets paid by the hour, week, or month. **A worker paid on an hourly rated basis receives a wage.** Thus a worker who gets $8 per hour and works 40 hours a week gets $320 in wages for that week. Hourly workers can get overtime pay by working extra hours.

salary

A worker paid a fixed amount on a weekly, biweekly, or monthly basis receives a salary. Salaried workers usually work for a fixed amount of pay per year. Most white-collar jobs are salaried jobs. Salaried workers often do not get overtime pay.

A salesperson might be paid a base salary plus a commission for sales made. This is a combination of time spent on the job and output produced. If a salesperson gets a bonus for selling more than the quota, the pay plan provides incentive.

Features of Wage and Salary Administration

There are four main features of wage and salary administration:

- •wage and salary surveys
- •job evaluation
- •performance rating
- •incentive plans

Wage and salary surveys are conducted to determine the general pay level in the firm's community and industry. The firm can pay above, at, or below the prevailing pay level in the industry or community. If it wants to recruit the best talent available, the firm may pay "above-market" rates. If there are many unemployed people who have the skills the firm needs, the pay level may be set at or below the prevailing level. Of course, other factors, such as minimum wage laws and unions, must be considered. After determining the general pay level, the focus shifts to finding what other firms are paying for comparable jobs.

Job evaluation is a method for determining the relationship between pay rates for particular job classifications. For example, how much pay should typists, accountants, and salespeople receive? Important factors here are the prestige and status attached to different jobs, the desirability of the work, and the amount of skill, experience, or education needed to perform a given job.

A series of rates (steps, or pay ranges) are set for each job. New employees usually start at the base rate for the job, and workers advance to higher rates as they gain experience, proficiency, and seniority. This is called *performance rating.* Some firms set pay ranges on a strictly judgment basis; others develop detailed rating systems, or point systems. Under

WHAT DO YOU THINK?

Should Employee Bonus Plans Be Tied to Profitability?

Some firms pay their employees year-end bonuses tied to profit growth. Thus a firm that increased its profit by a larger percentage in the current year than in the previous year shares some of that profit with its employees. The rationale is that this gives workers an incentive to increase their productivity.

As long as a firm is increasing its profit growth year after year, employees go along with the bonus plan. If a firm's rate of profit growth declines, there may be no bonuses. In recent years many firms have experienced little or no profit improvement and their workers have become upset when there were no bonuses. These workers often say that they have little or no direct impact on a firm's profitability. They prefer bonus plans that are not tied to profitability. Should employee bonus plans be tied to profitability? WHAT DO YOU THINK?

"the relative desirability of the type of work," for example, the firm might set point values for such things as danger and exposure to pollution. Regardless of approach, the goal is to come up with a pay range that is fair for each job in the company.

Finally, wage and salary administrators must decide how much each individual worker should receive. Firms with *incentive plans* pay the base rate only for a "normal amount of production," as determined, for example, through a time study. Employees who produce more than the normal amount get an extra incentive bonus.

The Equity Theory of Compensation

Equity is the *perceived* fairness of what a worker does compared to what he or she receives from the employer. The worker exchanges inputs (such as skills) for outputs (tangible and intangible rewards from the employer) and compares the inputs and outputs to those of other workers doing the same job. Inequity results when there is an imbalance between the inputs and outputs as a result of the comparison process. Pay inequity has been a major issue in the women's movement. Many women argue that they do the same work as men (equivalent inputs) but receive lower pay (unequal outputs).

Workers who feel that their inputs are greater than their outputs might try to get a pay raise, reduce their inputs, quit the job for a more equitable job, or learn to live with dissatisfaction. On the other hand, workers who feel their inputs are less than their outputs may put forth more effort on the job or reevaluate their inputs to "prove" to themselves that they actually are not being overpaid.

Compensating Managers

An owner-manager's compensation is tied to the firm's profit. With professional managers, however, this is not always the case. Many of the same factors that determine a worker's pay affect how much a manager will receive. But there are no union wage scales to serve as guidelines.

Employee benefits in addition to salary are very important to managers in high income-tax brackets. Deferred income plans enable them to receive part of their compensation after retirement. Income deferral shelters some earnings from the high tax rates they pay in their working years. A firm tries to "lock in" good executives by offering many benefits that hinge on their staying with the firm. Liberal retirement benefits are an example.

PROMOTING EMPLOYEES

promotion

A promotion means moving up to a higher position in the firm, usually one that involves more pay and more challenge. It is a way of compensating an employee for good performance in the previous job.

You have probably heard jokes about the employee who got a promotion but no pay increase. "I got promoted, a fancy title, more duties, but no more pay." This underscores the psychological benefit of promotion to an employee. It is a clear form of recognition for good performance. It moves the employee up the firm's job ladder. In most cases, a promotion is much more visible to others than is a salary increase.

Firms set up promotion programs to decide which employees are promotable. The personnel department can help by developing "career ladders" that will encourage promising employees to take the risks involved in being promoted. The important thing is that the system used is fair, is understood by employees, and is consistently and objectively used. Performance in the present job should be the basic factor in determining an employee's promotability to a higher job.

WHAT DO YOU THINK?

Government vs. Private Enterprise: Is There a Difference?

Many people see major differences between the employment practices of government and business. The government uses a system that often results in rigid pay schemes and many levels of bureaucracy. The private sector does not use that system, yet many of the same characteristics are apparent. In both cases, specific qualifications are set out for jobs, and experts in the administration of personnel have developed. Perhaps the only major difference between employment practices in public and private firms is the higher job security evident in government jobs. However, even this is changing as government payrolls are cut due to lack of revenue. WHAT DO YOU THINK?

PROVIDING PERSONNEL SERVICES

Personnel departments are called on to provide a variety of services for the firm and its employees. The personnel manual which we mentioned earlier is usually prepared by the personnel department in conjunction with upper-level managers. Other examples of personnel services include putting together employee benefits packages; establishing employee safety and health programs; and formulating employee discipline policy.

Employee Benefits

Employee benefits are compensation other than wages or salaries — cafeterias, credit unions, group life and medical insurance, paid vacations, and retirement programs. Employee benefits account for about one-third of the typical worker's compensation and their cost is growing about twice as fast as wages and salaries.

A recent innovation is flexible benefit plans, or "cafeteria plans." The employer offers a basic core of benefits to all employees and individual employees are allowed to "buy" additional benefits to suit their own needs. Employees "buy" these benefits with their benefit credits, based on, for example, salary or length of service. Thus, a single male employee fifty years of age might choose to pass up maternity coverage for additional pension contributions.

Employee Safety and Health

Employee safety and health programs help to reduce absenteeism and labour turnover. The personnel department creates and implements the

A CONTEMPORARY ISSUE

Job Safety and Health

Most provinces have passed Industrial Safety Acts which are designed to protect the health and safety of workers. These laws govern such things as sanitation, ventilation, dangerous machinery, plant design, etc. However, there are problems in setting "acceptable standards," and workers, employers, and labour unions

sometimes disagree on how stiff the standards should be.

There are other problems as well. Suppose a steelworker has to be shifted from one job to another job because the present job has exposed the worker to the risk of cancer from breathing oven fumes. Should the worker be guaranteed that he or she will not lose seniority and/or not be transferred to a lower-paying job?

company-wide safety and health program. This program raises productivity and boosts morale by making jobs safer and more healthful.

A good safety and health program helps to reduce job accidents. An accident is an unwanted interruption in work. The safety program helps to eliminate the cause of accidents and the injuries which often result from them. Accidents are caused by unsafe working conditions and/or careless and unsafe activities of employees. Once the causes of accidents are known, measures can be taken to reduce or eliminate them. Likewise, by studying employee activities, steps can be taken to eliminate unsafe ones.

Employee Discipline Policy

The personnel department also plays a major role in formulating employee discipline policy and in explaining it to workers. Although most workers abide by the rules, some workers do break them. Disciplinary action is administered by the worker's supervisor, but usually only when other approaches to correct employee performance problems have failed. For first offenses, employee disciplinary action usually means an oral reprimand in private. The more serious the offense and the greater the number of prior offenses, the stiffer the penalty. After oral warnings, there are written warnings, disciplinary layoffs, and discharge from the company.

Miscellaneous Services

Personnel departments also provide many other types of services, which vary widely among firms. These range from setting up policies to cope with allegations of sexual harassment on the job to helping employees arrange car pools.

Time and circumstances greatly affect the nature of personnel work. For example, a firm may experience a big decrease in one department's work load and a big increase in another department's work load. The personnel department might help the two department managers to shift workers between departments, help in a retraining effort if that is needed, or help to develop a plan for sharing the available work among employees — shorter work weeks for all workers or layoffs in order of seniority.

Personnel departments in many firms help in developing flexible working hours schedules. "Flex time," as opposed to fixed working hours, makes it easier for many workers, especially working mothers, to enter the labour force. The concept of flex time is built around a core of working hours, for example, 10 A.M. to 2 P.M. All employees are required to work between those hours. Each individual employee, however, is given the opportunity to select other hours of work to make up a full work week. Although it presents scheduling problems, flex time also makes it possible for some employees to work full-time instead of having to settle for part-time work.

CAREERS IN PERSONNEL

BOTH IN PRIVATE BUSINESS AND IN GOVERNMENT THERE WILL BE continued growth in demand for people in the field of personnel. Much of this stems from new laws which place stricter requirements on hiring practices and health and safety conditions in firms.

Besides labour relations, which we will discuss in Chapter 7, personnel job areas include training and development, employee benefits, safety and health, records management, and employment processes. A college education is often required to reach the level of manager in any of these personnel areas. Certainly, some college training, preferably in business or public administration, is needed.

Personnel workers do recruiting, interviewing, and testing of applicants, check application forms, contact references, prepare and administer training programs, inspect health and safety conditions, plan and conduct recreational activities, provide personnel counselling, explain company fringe benefits, and keep the many records relating to employee performance.

Nearly all personnel positions require good human relations skills. Safety and health jobs often require technical or professional training in industrial engineering or nursing. Information is available from the Council of Canadian Personnel Associations, 2221 Yonge Street, Toronto, Ontario M4S 2B4. ■

TERMINATING EMPLOYEES

Eventually, every employee will leave the company's service. This may come about by death, retirement, voluntary resignation, or dismissal.

Retirement

Many firms have retirement plans. Employees whose service has been good over their working years get compensation from the firm during their non-working or retirement years. It is a type of deferred compensation. But when is an employee "ready" for retirement?

Some employees are ready much earlier than others. But most retirement plans are based on the employee's age. This forces some workers who should retire earlier to stay on the job. It forces others to leave before they would like to and even though they are still good workers. This is short-sighted. A compromise is to grant year-to-year extensions to productive employees who still want to work but who have reached retirement age. Recently several workers in different locations across Canada have successfully challenged mandatory retirement rules. Their employers must therefore allow them to continue working even though they are past the traditional retirement age.

Some workers want early retirement and their employers grant it. They also help the employee to adjust to this new lifestyle by providing various types of counselling services.

Voluntary Resignation

resignation

Resignation occurs when an employee voluntarily leaves the employer's service. There are many reasons for employee resignation. Some employees want to leave to take a job with another employer. In fact, a lot of firms try to hire away good employees from other firms. Some employees quit in order to dramatize a point of difference with higher-ups.

A wise employer does not want to hold on to an employee who can improve his or her position with another firm because doing so would have a poor effect on the employee's morale. But it is a good practice to conduct exit interview
an exit interview with an employee who is quitting the firm. **The purpose of an exit interview is to determine the reasons why an employee is leaving.** Perhaps the work environment could be changed to discourage others from leaving.

Dismissal

dismissal

Dismissal is an involuntary temporary or permanent type of separation of the employee. Some employees are temporarily laid off when business is slack. Many auto workers are laid off at the end of a model year when plants are being retooled for the new models. Seniority usually deter-

CAREER PROFILE

MY NAME IS GERRY LEWIS AND I AM currently the Education Programs Consultant in the Department of Corporate Human Resources at the Bank of Montreal. My office is located in the Bank of Montreal Institute in Toronto.

I started my career with the Bank of Montreal in British Columbia after graduating from high school. I worked in administration, lending, and as a teller. Over a period of time I gradually began to get involved in training new members of the organization on a one-on-one basis. In 1960 I moved to Winnipeg and took a position as a training coordinator. In that capacity I conducted skill training courses and workshops for management trainees and supervisory personnel. Eventually I got involved in coordinating management development seminars, through the Institute of Canadian Bankers, which were taught by people outside the bank (for example, university professors). In 1975 I was promoted to Training Manager for the Manitoba-Saskatchewan region. In that

mines the order in which they are laid off and the order in which they are called back. Of course, a layoff can become permanent if laid-off workers are not called back.

Discharge

discharge

Discharge is a permanent type of involuntary separation due to a permanent layoff or outright firing of an employee. A firm might permanently lay off workers in a plant when it is closed down. An employee might be fired because of an inability to do the job or serious violations of work rules.

SUMMARY AND LOOK AHEAD

A firm's most important resource is its human resource, its personnel. Top management is responsible for putting together and keeping intact a productive work force that includes managers and workers.

Top management delegates to the personnel manager the task of carrying out its human resource philosophy at the firm's operations level. Usu-

job I coordinated all training activities in the Prairie region.

In 1981 I moved to Toronto to begin my present job. I am now responsible for developing policies, plans, and programs to meet the educational needs of our employees. We are committed, through our tuition refund policy, to giving our people an opportunity for self-development through programs and courses that will benefit both them and the organization. There are, therefore, many areas in which I must be active. The five major functions that I currently perform are: (1) assisting line managers to identify external courses and seminars to meet their specific needs, (2) keeping up to date on continuing education programs that are useful for bankers, (3) coordinating the marketing of these programs to bank personnel, (4) advising people on what continuing education courses they should take, and (5) coordinating in-house university credit courses (in Toronto) for bankers through Ryerson Polytechnical Institute and the University of Toronto.

My present job has several rewarding features. First, it is very satisfying to suggest a course or seminar and then see our people improve both their promotability and their contribution to the bank as a result of having taken it. Second, evaluating and coordinating continuing education programs keeps me up to date on the latest developments in the field of business management and human resources. Third, I like helping people and this job allows me to do just that.

There are, of course, some problems and challenges. When people express an interest in continuing education, I feel it is important they have a clear view of what their career goals are. Some people haven't thought much about these goals and this makes it hard to give them specific advice about what programs or courses they should get involved in. Another problem is corporate red tape. In large organizations like the Bank of Montreal, it is sometimes hard to get approval for a project as fast as I would like. This is true both within the bank and when dealing with outside organizations like universities and the Institute of Canadian Bankers. Committees are often set up to make various decisions, and sometimes considerable time elapses before approval is granted.

Overall, however, I have found management development and personnel work at the Bank of Montreal to be exciting and rewarding.

ally, this means setting up a personnel department headed by a personnel manager. This is a staff position created to advise and assist line managers in managing their personnel.

The main activities of personnel management are (1) determining human resource needs, (2) searching for and recruiting applicants to fill those needs, (3) selecting applicants for employment, (4) training and developing personnel, (5) appraising employee performance, (6) compensating employees, (7) promoting employees, (8) providing personnel services, and (9) terminating employees. (See Table 6.1 on page 198.) All of these activities are interrelated and are vital aspects of human resource management. It is crucial that all these activities be conducted with awareness of antidiscrimination laws.

In the next chapter, we look at labour relations. The viewpoint for personnel management is the employer-individual employee relationship. In labour relations, the viewpoint is the employer-union relationship. The focus is on the employees as a group, as members of one or more labour unions. Labour relations activities often are referred to as "industrial relations." Even when line managers handle negotiations with labour unions, the personnel department is responsible for providing advisory services through its labour relations specialists. ∎

Table 6.1 The Personnel Department's Activities, Objectives, and Procedures

Activities	Objectives	Procedures
1. Determining human resource needs	To specify the firm's need for applicants.	(a) Study company objectives (b) Study organization chart (c) Forecast human resource needs (d) Develop management inventory (e) Perform job analysis (f) Prepare job description (g) Prepare job specification
2. Searching for and recruiting applicants	To attract applicants to the firm.	(a) Specify sources of recruits (b) Recruiting
3. Selecting applicants for employment	To select the most desirable applicants.	(a) Conduct preliminary interview (b) Prepare job application form (c) Administer selection tests (d) Conduct in-depth interview (e) Conduct background investigation (f) Conduct final selection interview (g) Schedule physical examination
4. Training and developing employees	To build and maintain a productive work force.	(a) Handle job orientation (b) Perform job-skill training (c) Aid in management development
5. Appraising employee performance	To rate employee performance objectively.	Develop performance appraisal system
6. Compensating employees	To develop a fair and equitable system for paying employees.	Wage and salary administration
7. Promoting employees	To reward productive employees in order to utilize the human resource more effectively.	Developing promotion policies
8. Providing personnel services	To build and enhance employee morale.	(a) Provide fringe benefits (b) Employee safety and health
9. Performing other personnel activities	To advise and assist line managers in coping with special personnel problems.	(a) Formulate employee discipline policy (b) Retrain employees (c) Share work among employees (d) Counsel employees

QUESTIONS FOR REVIEW AND DISCUSSION

1. When a firm buys a new typewriter, it expects that its value will diminish with the passage of time. It becomes "used up." Is the same true of a new management trainee who recently began working for the firm? Explain.
2. Do you agree that a firm's most important asset is its human resource? Why or why not?
3. Does "personnel administration" mean the same thing as "personnel department"? Explain.
4. Why might a firm create a personnel department?
5. What is a management inventory? What purpose does it serve?
6. Discuss the problems in developing and administering selection tests.
7. What should be covered in an employee orientation program?

8. What are the major similarities and differences between job-skill training and management development?
9. Why is it important to have a good performance appraisal system? Discuss the firm's and the worker's view.
10. What is involved in wage and salary administration?
11. Would it be possible to pay all employees a piece rate? Why or why not?
12. Applicants for managerial positions are usually given more "subjective" tests than are applicants for non-managerial jobs. Why is this? Are there any potential dangers? Explain.
13. Should a firm retrain employees whose skills have become obsolete if it can hire persons already possessing the needed skills? Discuss.
14. Do you think that it is fair for a firm to have a policy of not promoting from within? Explain.
15. Do you think that it is proper for a retailing firm to require job applicants to submit to a polygraph (lie detector) test as a condition of employment? Discuss. Is it fair to require all salespeople to take a polygraph test every six months in order to keep their jobs? Discuss.

INCIDENTS

The Larson Corporation

The Larson Corporation recently began hiring minority group members as part of its efforts to help solve some of society's more pressing problems. Larson management, after many hours of meetings and thoughtful analysis, believed that this would benefit both the firm and the low-income people who would be hired under the program. Larson is a large mining company with operations in Manitoba and Saskatchewan. The new program was launched in one of its northern Manitoba plants because that area is home to many native Indians who did not hold steady jobs.

In the past, Larson hired very few of these people. Many of Larson's jobs require a great deal of skill, and there always were enough trained people to fill job vacancies. As a result, Larson's management lacked experience in dealing with the type of worker this program was designed to help.

But Larson and its employees want to make this new program work. The personnel manager at the plant, Leslie Parks, was instructed to begin actively recruiting minority group members for new job openings. Ms. Parks had to develop a training program for new recruits and integrate them into their new environment.

Initially, the new recruits would be sought for those jobs that required very few skills. In this way, a training program could be developed which would take only a short time to complete. Thus, a new worker could be placed on the job in as short a time as possible. The reasoning here was that this type of employee would become discouraged by a long training program which might take months to complete. Management was afraid that the dropout rate would be too high.

Ms. Parks is now involved in setting up a recruitment and training program.

Questions:
1. Why do you think the firm decided to hire from the ranks of the disadvantaged unemployed?
2. What type of training program would you develop?
3. What kinds of problems might Ms. Parks encounter?
4. What might Ms. Parks do to increase the likelihood that the new program will be successful?

Reliable Motors Company

Adam Cranford is the personnel manager of Reliable Motors Company, a large car dealership in Ontario. Over the years, Reliable has taken pride in the training given to its mechanics. The firm plays this up in its advertising. It claims that most competing dealers hire almost anyone, put them in uniforms, and call them auto mechanics. Mechanics at Reliable, however, must go through a tough training program before they can begin servicing cars. But in recent months, labour turnover at Reliable has been very high.

Mr. Cranford knows that car dealers in the area have been under fire from customers to give better service after the sale. As a result, well-trained mechanics get above-average pay.

After conducting many exit interviews with mechanics leaving Reliable, Mr. Cranford knows that they are going to work at other dealerships in the area. He also learned that very few of the mechanics leaving were dissatisfied at Reliable. Some even said that they had second thoughts about leaving, but they just couldn't pass up the chance to make more money. Mr. Cranford believes that the other dealers can pay more because they do not spend money on training. What their mechanics learn, they learn on the job.

Questions:
1. Do you think that Reliable's mechanics have an obligation to remain with the company after they have gone through the training program? Why or why not?
2. Compare Mr. Cranford's philosophy about the human resource to that of the other car dealers.
3. What should Mr. Cranford do about the situation?

CASE STUDY*

MOVIC MACHINE SHOP

MOVIC IS A MEDIUM-SIZED MACHINE SHOP. IT EMPLOYS AN AVERAGE of eighty-six people of various degrees of skill and a small office clerical group. The shop was started shortly after the Second World War by Joe Kay, who anticipated a strong demand for machine tools and machined metal parts for a world that had had much of its industrial base destroyed during the war. Also, he knew there would be a need to replace worn-out capital equipment and to retool industrial plants now converting from the production of war materials to the production of consumer goods.

After very careful planning Joe was able to rent some space in an old airplane hangar. Here he housed the used equipment he was able to secure. He had little knowledge of the technical side of metal machining, but because of his experience in industrial sales he felt confident enough to launch the new business. His basic approach was to try and secure orders where the parts to be machined were relatively simple and the production run on each part was large. This approach, he believed, would keep both workers and machines busy and would thus make him cost effective. His cost accounting was also simple; he kept most of it "in his head." Aside from the variable costs of raw materials, he knew what his gross average hourly wage rate was and what his basic hourly overhead costs were. To this he simply added a 15 to 30 percent gross margin, depending on the size of the order.

His aggressive approach, combined with his affable manner, made him a natural salesman, and his simple approach to costing allowed him to negotiate orders on the spot. His early success was due in large part to his competitive pricing, but what was really becoming well-known in business circles was his ability to deliver on time and "to come through" when the customer desperately needed a particular machined part.

The business grew rapidly. A three-acre piece of land was purchased, a new building was erected, several additional machines were added, and the number of workers increased proportionately. The plant now operates on a two-shift basis, from 7 A.M. to 4 P.M. and from 4 P.M. to 12 midnight. The shop is departmentalized by grouping similar kinds of machines and by having the auxiliary service departments together. Exhibit 1 on page 202 outlines the basic production scheme employed by Movic.

The company has kept abreast of most of the innovations within the industry, and has added numerically controlled machines and a sophisticated computer system to keep track of the costs assigned to the parts as they move through the various stages of machining, to schedule

*This case was written by Professor Frank Collom of Queen's University.

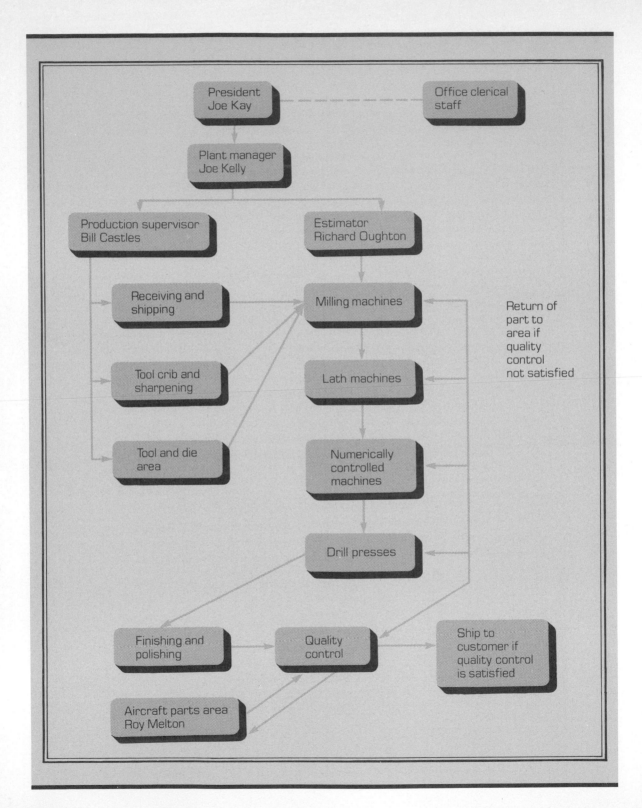

President
Joe Kay

Office clerical
staff

Plant manager
Joe Kelly

Production supervisor
Bill Castles

Estimator
Richard Oughton

Receiving and
shipping

Milling machines

Return of
part to
area if
quality
control
not satisfied

Tool crib and
sharpening

Lath machines

Tool and die
area

Numerically
controlled
machines

Drill presses

Finishing and
polishing

Quality
control

Ship to
customer if
quality control
is satisfied

Aircraft parts area
Roy Melton

the work, and for inventory control. Still, much of the work is highly skilled and is performed by hand by the tradespeople, who range in skill from the top trade of tool and die makers down to apprentices just learning their trades.

The company prides itself on performing quality work and on being able to satisfy customers' emergency needs. However, a notable shift has taken place in the last six years when the firm began to secure orders for parts for commercial and fighter aircraft in both Canada and the United States. These parts require the utmost in quality control, since the tolerances for this industry are very strict. The profit margin for these aircraft parts is significantly higher than for most other parts, but the smallest error in the machining of the parts creates only expensive scrap. Thus, Joe Kay, feeling sure that he wanted to move into this growing area of business, decided to assign one highly skilled machinist with sole responsibility for machining aircraft parts.

The company also evolved a middle- to senior-management structure. This was staffed by individuals who had been with the company almost from its inception, through both good and bad times, and who had a strong loyalty to the company. They were proud of the reputation they had built for the company in "doing whatever was needed" to meet the customer's deadline for a particular part.

In spite of this loyalty and dedication on the job, certain problems were beginning to creep into the overall operation. The problems were not those associated with production, because most of those problems were relatively easily handled by the highly skilled tradespeople. The problems were due to a lack of proper training and development within the staff to produce effective managers at all levels within the company. The company had always operated by a "seat of the pants" management, and Joe Kay realized that a major adjustment had to be made with his personnel if Movic was to continue to be successful.

The growing international aspects of the business required Joe to be away from the plant more frequently and for longer periods of time. In this absence a litany of problems would arise: jobs were not being completed on time; costs were often much higher than had been estimated; scrap was increasing. Often parts were pulled off machines and other parts started in order to get a job through in a hurry, and this greatly affected costs and quality. Bids on prospective jobs were lost because the estimated time of completion was greater than the customer was willing to wait. The quality control section was exercising its power to reject parts as unacceptable, even though "in the old days those parts would have been acceptable," complained many of the old-timers. Conflicts between the day shift and the night shift were a source of increasing friction. And finally, many employees did not like working in certain areas within the plant.

Joe pulled out his organization chart and began to ponder the moves and changes in personnel that would have to be made. He knew that

Exhibit 1   The Movic production scheme

many of the workers would be upset by any proposed changes, and he realized that a great deal of tact would be required in handling any proposal he might come up with. He also felt that he might have to hire one or two new people to the management hierarchy, demote a few, promote others, and shift some to the side. He drafted a brief outline of each man's strengths and weaknesses.

Joe Kelly   Joe was the top tradesman and most senior of all Movic employees. As plant manager he knew every aspect of every job. He was loyal to the company, often worked long hours to make sure jobs were handled properly, and was well-liked, constantly "putting out fires" around the plant. He could never see the "whole picture," but viewed each problem as a distinct and separate item that had to be solved on the spot.

Bill Castles   Bill was the production supervisor, second in seniority to Joe Kelly. He was responsible for scheduling all production on each group of machines in the plant, conferring with Joe as to the best sequence of steps needed to complete the job. After their discussion, he would schedule the required number of hours on each machine and pass the work order on to his foreman. Bill seems to have a chip on his shoulder, and quite often complained that the headaches in the plant were not worth the money he made as supervisor. He often wished he was back on the floor as a tool and die maker. It was not uncommon for him to schedule so much work for certain machines that the work piled up while other machines sat idle.

Richard Oughton   Richard was the chief estimator and responsible for taking the customer's blueprints. From these he would create a bid or estimated cost to submit to the customer. A bid that was too high would mean a lost order. Richard was younger than Joe or Bill but was a long-time employee and equal in skill to the other two. He had risen to the senior position because of his intimate knowledge of machines and machine parts, and his fondness for detail. However, he did not like too much responsibility, was not prepared to work much overtime because of his family, and did not want to return to night school to "learn all that management stuff." He had lots of potential to manage the whole shop but he showed a decided lack of interest in doing so. He was good with customers and was often consulted by them to help them solve their problems.

Roy Melton   Roy was about forty-two years of age and had only been with the company for four years although he was a highly qualified machinist. He was the one who had been assigned the responsibility for the aircraft parts and had done a "brilliant" job in every respect. He was quiet, thoughtful of others, and had extensive knowledge of all machines and production procedures. One of his drawbacks was that he had difficulty "bossing" other people and was uncomfortable with customers. Although he was well-liked by the others, he was considered a loner.

Other top tradespeople   The other top tradespeople in the plant held no management responsibilities.

Art Kruger   Senior milling machine operator. Art was older than most, independent, and "a little hard to handle."

Bill Kendall   Senior tool and die maker. Bill "knew it all" and liked to be left alone. He was not too eager to share his knowledge.

Robert Wuben   Senior numerically controlled machine operator. Robert was a good programmer for the machines and worked closely with the men who managed the N.C. machines. He was quick tempered when things did not happen as he expected and prone to blame the others rather than the programmed machines. He hated the night shift.

Paul Wuben   Paul was Robert's brother, and although he was not the senior lathe operator, he was considered to be the best of all the lathe operators. Younger than the others, he was often not treated with the respect he felt he had earned. He complained about not being paid the senior lathe operator's rate. ∎

After reading this chapter, you should be able to:

1. Explain how the Industrial Revolution changed the "world of work" for workers and led to efforts among workers to form unions.
2. Illustrate the general nature of labour-management relations prior to the 1930s.
3. Give examples of how the legal environment prior to the 1930s was hostile to unionization.
4. List the major federal labour laws and discuss the major provisions of each.
5. Discuss the provincial labour board's role in certifying a union as the exclusive bargaining agent for a firm's employees.
6. Show how a local union and a national union are related to each other.
7. Distinguish between craft and industrial unions.
8. Give examples of political, social, and economic objectives of unions.
9. List several important reasons why workers join unions.
10. Explain how employees and employers collectively bargain through union and management representatives.
11. Cite specific issues which might lead to labour-management conflict.
12. List and discuss labour and management's "weapons" in dealing with conflict.
13. Appraise the future prospects for the union movement in Canada.

In reading the chapter, look for and understand these terms:

labour union
collective bargaining
labour contract
blacklists
unfair lists
Conciliation Act
Industrial Disputes
   Investigation Act
Privy Council Order 1003
British North America Act
Canada Labour Code
craft unions
industrial unions
local union
national union
international union
independent local union
closed shop

union shop
agency shop
open shop
guaranteed annual wage
bargainable issues
COLA clause
conciliation
mediation
voluntary arbitration
compulsory arbitration
grievance procedures
strike
picketing
boycott
work-to-rule
lockout
injunction

CHAPTER SEVEN

Labour Relations

IN RECENT YEARS CANADA HAS HAD one of the worst records for strikes in the Western world. In various places around the country labour-management relations are not very smooth. In British Columbia, for example, the government has laid off workers. In Quebec, wage increases have been rescinded by the provincial government. The federal government's "6 and 5" guidelines for wage increases have caused much bad feeling among workers.

Although provincial and federal government employees can belong to unions, there is often a feeling on the part of the general public that strikes by these workers are not "right." When services provided by these workers are withdrawn (e.g., transit drivers, police officers, postal workers) considerable inconvenience can result for the public.

THE RELATIONSHIP BETWEEN EMPLOYER AND EMPLOYEES IS CRUCIAL in a firm. When the relationship is between the employer and the employees as individuals, it is called employee relations or personnel relations. In many firms, however, the employees belong to labour unions. The relationship between the employer and the employees' union(s) is called labour relations. In this relationship, a third party, the union, comes between the employer and the employees. No longer does the employer deal with an employee solely as an individual.

In labour relations, management representatives bargain with union representatives over wages and working conditions for unionized employees. In some firms, the personnel manager does the bargaining for the employer. But as unions have become more powerful, labour relations specialists are increasingly found in unionized firms.

We begin this chapter with a brief look at the history of the union movement in Canada and the major laws that deal with unions. We will also look at why workers join unions, the organization and objectives of unions, the nature of labour-management relations, and the future of unions in Canada.

WHY UNIONS BEGAN

labour union

Individualism is a basic characteristic of capitalism. When we talk about labour unions, however, we imply collective action. **A labour union is an organization of employees formed for the purpose of dealing collectively with their employers in order to further the interests of those employees.**

collective bargaining

The dealing which occurs between the employer and the union is called collective bargaining. **Collective bargaining is the process of negotiating a labour agreement between union representatives and employer representatives.**

labour contract

The agreement negotiated between employer and union representatives is called a labour contract. **A labour contract sets forth the terms and conditions under which union members will offer their labour services to an employer.**

To explain the apparent conflict between capitalism's emphasis on individualism and unionism's emphasis on collective action, let's briefly study the history of unionism in Canada.

The Work Environment

Before the Industrial Revolution, many workers were skilled artisans. Production was organized around the domestic system. Shoemakers, for example, worked in small shops located in their homes. They bought materials needed for making shoes, made the shoes, and sold them. They were more like independent business owners than workers. They worked for themselves.

The Industrial Revolution changed this. The domestic system was largely replaced by production in factories. Many formerly independent artisans became employees who worked for firms owned by others. Workers lost control over buying, producing, and selling activities. These became activities of organized businesses. The only thing over which workers could have any control was in offering their services to employers. Thus, workers began to organize in order to control that supply collectively.

Furthermore, many skilled artisans became machine operators in big factories. Mechanization (substituting machines for human labour) was also seen as a threat by many workers. To deal with this threat to their security, workers began to organize unions. The "fear" of being replaced by machines still is a fact of life for many workers in our highly mechanized and automated production system.

Because wages paid to employees are a cost of doing business, employers want to hold down both the number of employees they hire and the wages they pay to them. This gives rise to the workers' concern about job scarcity, low wages, and poor working conditions. Labour responded to these concerns by organizing unions for collective action.

Thus, the Industrial Revolution brought rapid changes in the "world of work." But the human problems of this revolution, especially for workers, were not quickly solved. Although organization was a way for workers to deal with their changed world, workers were going to have an uphill battle to have their right to form labour unions recognized.

blacklists

Employers and workers sympathetic to unions battled with each other for many years. For example, employers circulated blacklists among themselves. **Blacklists contained the names of workers who were known to be in favour of unions.** These blacklisted workers were refused employment.

unfair lists

Labour unions circulated their lists also—"unfair lists." **Unfair lists contained the names of employers whom unions considered unfair to workers because these employers would not hire union members.**

The Development of Canadian Labour Unions

The earliest evidence of labour unions comes from the Maritime provinces early in the nineteenth century. Generally, these unions were composed of individuals with a specific craft (e.g., printers, shoemakers, barrelmakers). Most of these unions were small and had only limited success. However, they laid the foundation for the rapid increase in union activity which occurred during the late nineteenth and early twentieth centuries.

A succession of labour organizations sprang up and just as quickly faded away during the years 1840–70. In 1873 the first national labour organization was formed — the Canadian Labour Union. By 1886 the Knights of Labour (a United States-based union) had over 10,000 members in Canada. The Canadian Labour movement began to mature with the formation of the Trades and Labour Congress in 1886. The TLC's purpose was to unite all labour organizations and to work for the passage of laws which would ensure the well-being of the working class.

The growth of labour unions began in earnest early in the twentieth century as the concept of organized labour gradually came to be accepted. Within the ranks of labour, various disputes arose which resulted in numerous splits in labour's ranks. For example, there was concern that United States-based unions would have a detrimental effect on Canadian unions. The Canadian Federation of Labour was formed in 1908 to promote national (Canadian) unions instead of U.S. unions. These and other disputes (such as how communists in the movement should be handled) often led to the creation of rival union organizations which competed for membership.

THEN AND NOW

Child Labour

During the nineteenth century young children were hired to work in factories at very low wages and under extremely poor working conditions. Because most of them were denied the chance to attend school, they remained unskilled. Improvements came slowly.

The founding conference of the Canadian Labour Union in 1873 supported a resolution to prohibit the employment of children under ten in manufacturing establishments where machinery was used. In 1886 the Ontario Factory Act was passed. It prohibited the employment of boys under twelve and girls under fourteen, and set a limit of sixty hours of work per week for women and children.

During the twentieth century major advances were made. At present, the federal government and all provinces have passed child labour laws. The Canada Labour Code allows the employment of individuals under the age of seventeen only if (a) they are not required to be in attendance at school under the laws of their province of residence, and (b) the work is unlikely to endanger their health or safety. In addition, no one under seventeen is permitted to work during the hours from 11:00 P.M. to 6:00 A.M.

THEN AND NOW

Equal Pay for Equal Work for Women

Women, like children, worked for a fraction of men's wages and held only unskilled jobs during the Industrial Revolution. For example, in 1882 male members of the Brotherhood of Telegraphers of the United States and Canada were paid approximately $35 per month, while female operators earned about one-seventh that amount. During a strike of the brotherhood, one of the union's proposals was equal pay for men and women.

Other unions were also seeking equal pay for women. In 1882 the Toronto Trades and Labour Council proposed labour legislation which included an "equal pay for equal work, regardless of sex" provision.

Although gradual improvements in working conditions and opportunities for women have occurred during the twentieth century, it was not until the mid-1950s that serious efforts were made to ensure equal pay for equal work.

The Canada Labour Code prohibits an employer from maintaining different wages for men and women employed in the same industrial establishment and who are doing the same or similar work. Differences in pay between men and women *can* be maintained if they are based on factors other than sex.

By 1956 these disputes had been largely resolved, and the two largest unions — the Trades and Labour Congress and the Canadian Congress of Labour — merged to form the Canadian Labour Congress. This brought approximately 80 percent of all unionized workers into one organization.

The Legal Environment

There were political and legal barriers to collective bargaining until well into the twentieth century. Courts held that unions were conspiracies in restraint of trade. Employers viewed their employees' efforts to unionize as an attempt to deprive the employers of their private property. The employment contract was between the individual worker and the employer — not between the employer and employees as a group. The balance of bargaining power was in favour of the employer.

The employer-employee relationship became much less direct as firms grew in size. Managers were, themselves, employees. Hired managers dealt with other employees. Communication among owners, managers, and workers became more formalized. Big business had the upper hand. Because of mounting public concern, laws were passed to place the worker on a more even footing with the employer.

Conciliation Act

Industrial Disputes Investigation Act

In 1900 government concern for labour disputes resulted in the passage of the Conciliation Act. **The act was designed to assist in the settlement of labour disputes through voluntary conciliation and was a first step in creating an environment more favourable to labour. A more comprehensive law, the 1907 Industrial Disputes Investigation Act, provided for compulsory investigation of labour disputes by a** government-appointed board before a strike was allowed.** However, this act was later found to violate a fundamental provision of the British North America Act (see below).

Privy Council Order 1003

The current positive environment for labour did not come into being until 1943 when Privy Council Order 1003 was issued which (1) recognized the right of employees to collectively bargain, (2) prohibited unfair labour practices on the part of management, (3) established a labour board to certify bargaining authority, and (4) prohibited strikes and lockouts except in the course of negotiating collective agreements. Thus, approximately forty-five years of dealings between labour, management, and government were required before the labour movement achieved its fundamental goal of having the right to collectively bargain.

British North America Act

The British North America Act, passed in 1867, has also affected labour legislation. **This act allocated certain activities to the federal government (e.g., labour legislation for certain companies operating inter-provincially) and others to individual provinces (labour relations regulations in general).** Thus, labour legislation emanates from both the federal and the provincial governments.

FEDERAL LEGISLATION — THE CANADA LABOUR CODE

Canada Labour Code

The Canada Labour Code is a comprehensive piece of legislation which applies to the personnel practices of firms operating under the legislative authority of parliament. The Code is composed of four major sections as follows:

Fair Employment Practices

This section prohibits an employer from either refusing employment on the basis of a person's race or religion or using an employment agency that discriminates against people on the basis of their race or religion. These prohibitions apply to trade unions as well, but not to nonprofit charitable and philanthropic organizations. Any individual who feels a violation has occurred may make a complaint in writing to the Department of Labour. The allegation will then be investigated and, if necessary, an Industrial Inquiry Commission will be appointed to make a recommendation in the case. (Since 1982, Fair Employment Practices have been covered by the Canadian Human Rights Act; beyond this they are covered by the Canadian Charter of Rights and Freedoms.)

Standard Hours, Wages, Vacations, and Holidays

This section deals with a wide variety of "mechanical" issues such as standard hours of work (8-hour day and 40-hour week), maximum hours of work per week (48), overtime pay (at least 1½ times regular pay), minimum wages, equal wages for men and women doing the same jobs, vacations, general holidays, and maternity leave. The specific provisions are changed frequently to take into account changes in the economic and social structure of Canada, but their basic goal is to have consistent treatment of employees in these areas.

SOME IMPORTANT DATES IN CANADIAN LABOUR HISTORY

1827 First union formed; shoemakers in Quebec City

1840–1870 Many new unions formed; influence of U.S. and British unions felt

1871 Formation of Toronto Trades Assembly; composed of five craft unions; went out of existence a few years later

1873 Canadian Labour Union formed; objective was to unite unions across Canada

1879 First coal miners' union in North America formed in Nova Scotia

1881 The U.S.-based Knights of Labour enter Canada

1883 Canadian Labour Congress formed; lasted until 1886

1886 Canadian Trades and Labour Congress formed; later became known as the Trades and Labour Congress of Canada (TLC)

1902 Knights of Labour expelled from TLC

1902 Expelled unions form the National Trades and Labour Congress (became the Canadian Federation of Labour [CFL] in 1908); purpose was to promote national unions instead of international ones

1902–1920 Rapid growth of union membership in both major unions (TLC and CFL)

1919 One Big Union formed; organized in opposition to the TLC

1919 Winnipeg General Strike

1921 Canadian Brotherhood of Railway Employees (CBRE) expelled from TLC

1921 Confédération des Travailleurs Catholiques du Canada (CTCC) organized by the Roman Catholic clergy in Quebec; goal was to keep French-Canadian workers from being unduly influenced by English-speaking and American trade unions

1927 All-Canadian Congress of Labour (ACCL) formed; objective was to achieve independence of the Canadian labour movement from foreign control; made up of One Big Union, the CFL, and the CBRE

1939 TLC expels industrial unions; Canadian Congress of Industrial Organization (CIO) committee formed

1940 ACCL and the Canadian CIO Committee unite to form the Canadian Congress of Labour

1956 TLC and CCL merge to form the Canadian Labour Congress; remnants of One Big Union joined new organization

1960 CTCC dropped association with Roman Catholic Church and chose a new name — Confédération des Syndicate Nationaux (CSN); in English, was called the Confederation of National Trade Unions (CNTU)

1960–1969 Rapid growth of CNTU in Quebec

1971 Center for Democratic Unions formed as a result of secession from the CNTU by dissident members

1981 International building trades unions suspended from CLC

1982 Founding convention of Canadian Federation of Labour (CFL)

Safety of Employees

This section requires that every person carrying on a federal work project do so in a way which will not endanger the health or safety of any employee. It also requires that safety procedures and techniques be implemented to reduce the risk of employment injury. This section requires employees to exercise care to ensure their own safety; however, even if it can be shown that the employee did not do this, compensation must still be paid. This section also makes provisions for a safety officer whose overall duty it is to assure that the provisions of the act are being fulfilled. The safety officer has the right to enter any federal project "at any reasonable time."

Canada Industrial Relations Regulations

This is the final major section of the Canada Labour Code and deals with all matters related to collective bargaining. It is subdivided into seven divisions, as follows:

- •Division I — gives employees the right to join a trade union and gives employers the right to join an employers' association.
- •Division II — establishes the Canada Labour Relations Board whose role is to make decisions on a number of important issues (e.g., certification of trade unions).
- •Division III — stipulates the procedures required to acquire or terminate bargaining rights.
- •Division IV — indicates the rules and regulations which must be adhered to during bargaining; also presents guidelines for the content and interpretation of collective agreements.
- •Division V — states the requirement that a conciliation officer must be appointed by the Minister of Labour if the parties in the dispute cannot reach a collective agreement.
- •Division VI — stipulates the conditions under which strikes and lockouts are permitted.
- •Division VII — a general conclusion indicating methods which might be used to promote "industrial peace."

PROVINCIAL LABOUR LEGISLATION

Each province has also enacted legislation to deal with the personnel practices covered in the Canada Labour Code. These laws vary across provinces and are frequently revised; however, their basic approach and substance is the same as that in the Canada Labour Code. Certain provinces may exceed the minimum Code requirements on some issues (e.g., minimum wage).

Each province also has a labour relations act. To give an indication of what these acts cover, the Manitoba Labour Relations Act is briefly described below.

The Manitoba Labour Relations Act

The Manitoba Labour Relations Act is a comprehensive document dealing with the conduct of labour relations in the province. It is divided into six sections as follows:

Part I — Labour Practices and Rights

This section states some fundamental rights of labour and management (e.g., every employee has the right to be a member of a union, and every employer has the right to be a member of an employers' organization). Neither employers nor unions may discriminate against union members simply because they are union members. Other basic union-management issues are also addressed in this section. Overall, the section is designed to show what unfair labour practices are.

Part II — Certification and Bargaining Rights

This section describes the detailed procedures which must be followed before a union can be certified as a bargaining agent. Included are activities such as who has the right to apply for certification, how the appropriateness of the unit is determined, the certification vote, and the effect of certification.

Part III — Collective Bargaining and Collective Agreements

The actual practice of collective bargaining is described in this section. The major points are as follows:

1. The union can require management to commence bargaining within ten days of its being certified.
2. Conciliation and mediation are available if labour or management request it to help in the development of a contract.
3. Management is required to deduct union dues from employees' wages and remit these dues to the union.
4. Employees who oppose unions on religious grounds may stipulate that their union dues be given to charitable organizations.
5. Management must notify the union at least ninety days in advance if it plans to implement technological changes which will affect the security of a significant number of employees.

Part IV — Lockouts and Strikes

Unauthorized lockouts and strikes are prohibited in this section. Both management and labour are expected to exert a reasonable effort to reach an agreement before engaging in these tactics (at least ninety days must pass after the union has been certified before a strike is allowed).

Part V — Conciliation, Mediation, and Arbitration Boards

The three basic forms of third-party intervention and the administrative structure in which they operate are discussed in this section. The purpose of these boards is to help labour and management settle differences they encounter in developing a new contract or interpreting an existing one. Each person serving on one of these boards must take an oath of impartiality and confidentiality. The boards must write reports of their activities, and these reports must be made available to labour and management. For conciliation and mediation, the expense of the proceedings is paid by the province; for arbitration, the expenses are split by labour and management.

Part VI — General

The concluding section considers a number of other labour relations issues not treated in earlier sections. These include the function and powers of industrial commissions, prosecution of employers or unions for offences under the act, penalties for offences, liability for damages, and the date of commencement of the act.

WHY DO WORKERS JOIN UNIONS?

The answers to this question are as varied as the people who are members of labour unions. For example, maintenance crew workers at a big sports arena might join the International Brotherhood of Teamsters or some other union mainly because they think that membership will bring higher pay. A professional baseball player, on the other hand, may join the Major League Baseball Players Association for other reasons. That union does not negotiate players' salaries, but it did represent them in their 1981 strike against club owners. The union demanded increased compensation for players lost to a rival team as free agents. Let's consider a few general reasons workers join unions.

First, there is strength in numbers. The individual worker's threat to strike would cause little interruption of the workflow. A collective strike, however, could easily cripple the workflow.

Second, union members are represented in collective bargaining by professional negotiators. The employer is also represented by professional negotiators. The outcome is likely to be better for each worker than if each negotiated individually.

A third reason is the feeling of power that workers get from union membership. Although the employer-employee negotiations are handled by professionals, the workers at least have a chance to vote for union officers and also have veto power over any "settlement" that is reached regarding wages, fringe benefits, and working conditions.

Finally, many workers believe that union membership is necessary to keep employers interested in and concerned with their well-being. We will discuss this in greater detail later in the chapter.

THE ORGANIZING DRIVE

A union might try to organize a firm's workers when it is trying to break into new geographical areas, when some workers in a firm are members and it wants to cover other workers, or when it is attempting to outdo a rival union. Thus, in some cases, a union might try to organize workers for purposes other than helping a group of employees to help themselves.

Management often becomes aware of a union organizing effort through the grapevine. These "rumblings" may set off a counter-effort by management to slow the drive. Management must know, however, what it can legally do. A do-nothing approach is rare today. Employers can exercise the right of free speech to present their side of the story to the workers.

Suppose that a union is trying to organize employees of a Manitoba company. If it can show that at least 50 percent of the employees are members of the union, it can apply to the Manitoba Labour Board (MLB) for certification as the bargaining agent for the employees.

A problem may arise regarding the right of different types of workers to join or not join the union. For example, supervisors may or may not be included in a bargaining unit along with non-management workers. The MLB has final authority in determining the appropriateness of the bargaining unit. Professional and non-professional employees are generally not included in the same bargaining unit unless a majority of the professional employees wish to be included.

Once the MLB has determined that the unit is appropriate, it may order a certification vote. If a majority of those voting are in favour of the union, it is certified as the sole bargaining agent for the unit.

HOW ARE UNIONS ORGANIZED?

Like business firms, unions have organized structures. The two basic types of union are craft and industrial unions.

craft unions

Craft unions are organized by crafts or trades — plumbers, barbers, airline pilots, etc. Craft unions restrict membership to workers with specific skills. In many cases members of craft unions work for several different employers during the course of a year. For example, many construction workers are hired by their employers at union hiring halls. When the particular job for which they are hired is finished, these workers return to the hall to be hired by another employer.

Craft unions have a lot of power over the supply of skilled workers. This is because they have apprenticeship programs. A person who wants to become a member of a plumber's union, for example, will have to go through a training program. He or she starts out as an apprentice. After the training, the person is qualified as a "journeyman" plumber.

industrial unions

Industrial unions are organized according to industries — steel, auto, clothing, etc. Industrial unions include semiskilled and unskilled workers. Industrial union members typically work for a particular employer for a much longer period of time than craft union members. But an industrial union does have a lot of say regarding pay and personnel practices within unionized firms.

local union

The local union (or local) is the basic unit of union organization. A local of a craft union is made up of artisans in the same craft in a relatively small geographical area. A local of an industrial union is made up of workers in a given industry in a relatively small geographical area. Thus, plumbers in a local labour market may be members of the local plumbers' union. Truckdrivers and warehouse workers in that same area may be members of a teamsters' local.

Table 7.1   The Ten Largest Unions in Canada (1982)

	Number of Members
Canadian Union of Public Employees (CLC)	274,742
Nat. Union of Prov. Gov't. Employees (CLC)	230,000
United Steelworkers of America (AFL/CIO/CLC)	197,000
Public Service Alliance of Canada (CLC)	157,633
United Food and Commercial Workers (AFL/CIO/CLC)	135,000
United Automobile, Aerospace and Agricultural Implement Workers of America (CLC)	121,829
International Brotherhood of Teamsters, Chauffeurs, Warehousemen and Helpers of America (Independent)	93,000
United Brotherhood of Carpenters and Joiners of America (AFL/CIO)	89,210
Social Affairs Federation (CNTU)	84,000
Quebec Teaching Congress (Independent)	82,122

Source: Labour Canada, Labour Organizations in Canada, 1982, p. 16. Reproduced by permission of the Minister of Supply and Services Canada.

national union

A national union is one which has members across Canada. These members belong to locals which are affiliated with the national union. There are many national unions in Canada, including the Canadian Union of Public Employees, the National Railway Union, and the Canadian Airline Pilots Union.

international union

A union which has members in more than one country is called an international union. The prime example is the United Automobile Workers, made up of locals in the United States and Canada.

independent
local union

An independent local union is one which is not formally affiliated with any labour organization. It conducts negotiations with management at a local level, and the collective agreement is binding at that location only. The University of Manitoba Faculty Association is an independent local union. Membership in local unions in 1977 was 2.7 percent of total union membership.

Table 7.1 shows the ten largest unions in Canada. Figure 7.1 indicates the trend to increasing unionization, and Figure 7.2 on page 220 shows the proportion of the work force in each province that is unionized.

FACTORS AFFECTING UNIONIZATION

Why are some industries more unionized than others and why are unions stronger in some areas than in others? Industries in which a few firms dominate are easier to organize because the workers are more concentrated than when many firms exist. Thus, the auto industry is more unionized than the retailing industry. Furthermore, industry-wide bargaining is more likely where there are few firms.

Another factor is the nature of the production process. It is not as profitable to organize highly automated industries which employ only a few workers as it is to organize industries which employ many workers. To make organizations a paying proposition, a union must expect the dues from new members to more than offset the costs of organizing them. This is generally the case, except when a union is trying to break into an area or industry where unions are weak. Thus, the organizing effort in unorganized industries, such as banks, is progressing.

Workers hired out of union halls identify very little with their employers. Collective bargaining here is quite different from that in which a union represents workers who work for one employer over a long period. Management knows the workers' needs better in the latter case. Union and management can work together to build a healthy relationship. This also explains why different unions seek different goals. A worker hired out of a hiring hall is more concerned with job security than one who has a long record of employment with one firm.

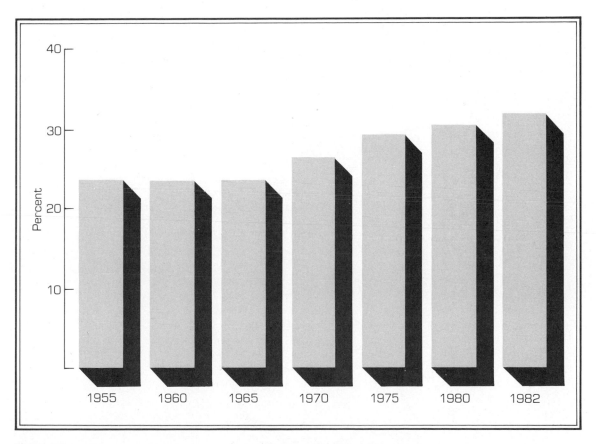

Figure 7.1
Union members as proportion of the total work force. (Source: *Labour Organization in Canada*, 1982, p. 16. Used with permission of the Minister of Supply and Services Canada.)

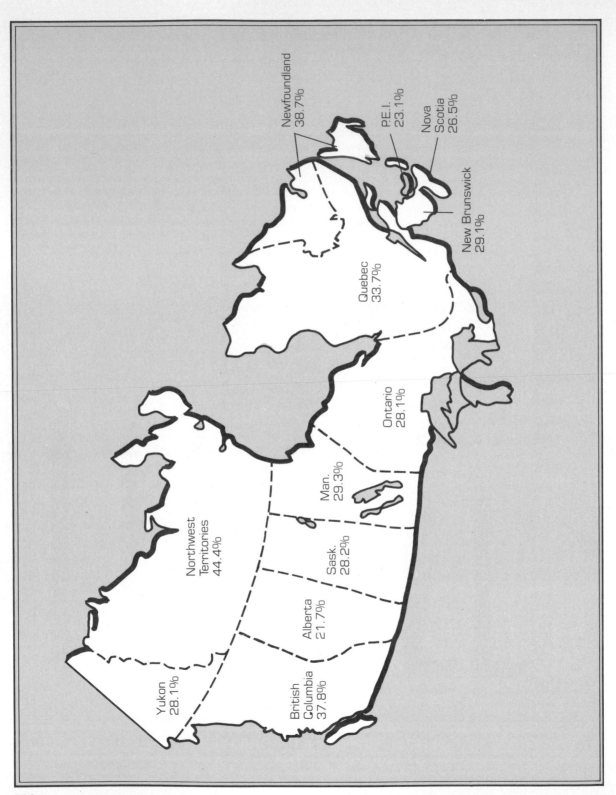

Newfoundland
38.7%

P.E.I.
23.1%

Nova
Scotia
26.5%

New Brunswick
29.1%

Quebec
33.7%

Ontario
28.1%

Man.
29.3%

Sask.
28.2%

Alberta
21.7%

British
Columbia
37.8%

Northwest
Territories
44.4%

Yukon
28.1%

Table 7.2   Characteristics of National and International
Union Membership, 1982

Total union membership	3,617,000
Percentage in CLC/CTC	57.6
Percentage in AFL/CIO/CLC	26.6
Percentage in CNTU	6.0
Percentage in international unions	44.2
Percentage in national unions	51.9
Percentage in independent local unions	2.7
Percentage in directly chartered local unions	1.2
Percentage of total labour force in unions	31.4
Percentage of non-agricultural work force in unions	39.0

Source: Labour Canada, Labour Organizations in Canada, 1982, p. 19. Reproduced by
permission of the Minister of Supply and Services Canada.

In general, the more skilled workers are, the greater their bargaining
strength. Thus, workers in the building trades earn high wages. They are
skilled and their skills have not become obsolete. Many other skilled workers,
such as typesetters, have found their skills outmoded by machines.

UNION OBJECTIVES

The long struggle by unions to be recognized in their right to exist has
resulted in their general acceptance today—at least in acceptance of the
idea that workers have a right to form unions. Union objectives are political,
economic, and social.

Political Objectives

During the nineteenth century union objectives were basically political,
since unions were fighting for recognition of their right to exist. This involved them in the political process. Once this right was recognized, unions
shifted their emphasis to that of advancing the economic interests of their
members. But unions do have political goals.

Unlike most Western European nations, the union movement in
Canada is a minority movement. Only 31.4 percent of all workers are unionized. (See Table 7.2.) Nevertheless, politicians speak of the "labour vote."
There are two dimensions here: (1) the organized (unionized) and (2) the
unorganized (non-unionized). The ability of labour leaders, however, to
deliver the labour vote is questionable. Most Canadians probably vote on
issues other than the candidates' pro- or anti-labour views.

Figure 7.2
Percent of work force that is unionized in each province. (Source: Statistics
Canada publications 71-001 and 71-205. Used by permission of Minister of Supply
and Services Canada.)

But organized labour does try to speak for the labour force. Although there is no party called the "Labour party" in Canada, the NDP is very supportive of labour's goals. Union leaders attempt, with varying degrees of success, to have legislation passed which is favourable to workers. This is particularly true for the minimum wage and hours of work issues.

Economic Objectives

Union leaders are elected by union members. Thus, those leaders seek to satisfy their members' economic needs.

Improved Standard of Living

Unions seek to improve their members' standard of living. In the past this meant getting higher wages. The pay envelope, however, is no longer the only concern of union members. Many want more leisure time. They want to work fewer hours but make more pay per hour. The entire package of fringe benefits is part of the improved standard of living which unions seek. Working conditions, pensions, paid vacations, and so on are important bargaining issues. Inflation in recent years has led union members to demand that labour contracts protect their standard of living. We will discuss this later in the chapter.

Security Objectives

The growing security consciousness of Canadian workers is reflected in union goals. The seniority provision in most contracts spells out the worker's rights when layoffs, transfers, and promotions occur. Employees are ranked in terms of length of service. Those with longer service get better treatment.

Much conflict exists regarding seniority. Two specific examples of conflict relate to women and minority groups. They typically have less seniority and are the first to be laid off and the last to move up to higher jobs. These workers tend to oppose the tradition of seniority.

Union security is another issue. The greatest security is found in the closed shop. **In a closed shop an employer can hire only union members.** For example, a plumbing or electrical contractor who hires workers through a union hiring hall can hire only union members.

In a union shop, an employer may hire non-union workers even if the employer's present employees are unionized. New workers, however, must join the union within a stipulated period of time (usually thirty days).

In an agency shop, all employees for whom the union bargains must pay dues, but they need not join the union. This is a compromise between the union shop and the open shop, and is called the Rand Formula after the individual who proposed it.

In an open shop, an employer may hire union and/or non-union labour. Employees need not join or pay dues to a union in an open shop.

Another security issue is job security, especially in highly automated industries. The guaranteed annual wage reflects the worker's concern

Margin terms:
closed shop

union shop

agency shop

open shop

WHAT DO YOU THINK?

Do Unions Benefit Society?

Some Canadians still feel uneasy about labour unions. Much of this is probably because a lot of the publicity unions get is bad. Strikes are discussed in terms of lost production time; unions often are blamed for inflation; and cases of union corruption get a lot of news coverage.

Some people, even some union members, think that unions are too powerful. They want tighter government control of unions. Many of them want to deny unemployment benefits to workers who are on strike.

Emotions run high when we talk about unions. But unions have played a major role in improving our society. Few people would want a return to the conditions of labour during the nineteenth century. Unions help make democracy work. Labour has a voice in the political process without dividing society into warring classes. Unions have helped create our large middle-income group of consumers without which many firms would have a lot fewer customers. Do unions benefit society? WHAT DO YOU THINK?

guaranteed
annual wage

about job security. **The guaranteed annual wage is a provision in a labour contract which maintains the workers' income level during a year.** Most labour contracts which provide for this guarantee the worker a minimum amount of work during the contract period. This lends stability to the worker's employment. Some contracts provide for early retirement, lengthy vacations, and sabbatical leaves for employees.

The security of unions themselves is also in question. Our most organized industries — steel, auto, transportation, etc. — are almost totally unionized and are rapidly automating. Prospects for new members are not attractive. Furthermore, the stronghold of unions — blue collar labour — is diminishing as a percentage of our labour force. Thus, unions have sought new areas for growth, such as government workers and white-collar workers.

Working Conditions

Suppose that a long strike has been settled. Nevertheless, some locals of the national union remain on strike. The national contract covers major issues such as wage rates and fringe benefits. But specific provisions on rest periods, sanitary facilities, washup periods, and so on vary from plant to plant. These disputes over working conditions are worked out by the local union and the specific plant.

Social Objectives

In the past, much of the emphasis of collective bargaining was on economic issues such as those discussed above. Recently, however, more and more unions have been stressing improvements in the non-economic aspects of workers' jobs. The most popular issue here appears to be the "quality of working life," which we discussed in Chapter 5. This term denotes the

TWO POINTS OF VIEW

The Right to Work

Labour:

"Sure, a worker in a union plant has to belong to the union. The majority rules, and the majority of the workers who voted did vote to organize our union. Under the law, two persons doing the same job must be paid the same wage and receive the same fringe benefits. It would be unfair for a person who doesn't pay union dues to enjoy the same benefits won by a union which is supported by members' dues. Freeloaders should have to pay their fair share.

"To say that unions are unnecessary is plain hogwash. Do away with the union and see how employee-oriented most employers are. Business firms exist to make a profit. The less they pay to their workers, the more they keep as profit. The claim that union leaders have no incentive to do a good job is a lot of XXX! No law requires any firm's employees to form a union. If they weren't benefitting from the union, the members could have it decertified as their exclusive bargaining agent."

Management:

"A worker should not be forced to join a union in order to hold a job in my company. Granted, employees do have a right to form a union, but an employee should have a right *not* to join. Yet, if a union is certified as the exclusive bargaining agent for my production workers, even though not all of them voted to unionize, all of them have to pay dues or else be fired. They don't have freedom of choice.

"Unions have done a lot for the worker in the past, but they are not needed today. Social insurance, workmen's compensation, minimum wage laws, job safety laws, and enlightened management take away the need for unions.

"When you think about it, a customer who isn't satisfied with our product can stop buying it. But if one of our unionized workers isn't satisfied with the union, he or she must still pay dues. What reason do union leaders have to do a good job?

"Finally, when bargaining time rolls around for one of our suppliers and its union, we often build up our inventory of that supplier's product. This is done in case there is a strike at that plant. A strike would cut off our supply source. The end result, of course, is higher prices to consumers to make up for the cost of carrying extra inventory."

---

concern that many jobs (particularly blue-collar ones) are boring and depressing to those who perform them. Improvements in these jobs are being experimented with by a number of companies.

SOURCES OF LABOUR-MANAGEMENT CONFLICT

In Canada, labour and management bargain within a framework in which they share certain basic common beliefs. This is unlike negotiations in some other countries in which the bargaining takes on an air of class warfare — the "working class" is pitted against the "capitalists." In Canada today the vast majority of unions accept the capitalist system. It is within that framework that labour and management bargain.

There are, of course, some basic differences in outlook between labour and management. We will look at several sources of conflict and discuss each from a "labour viewpoint" and a "management viewpoint."

The Profit Issue

Both labour and management accept the idea that a firm must make a profit to stay in business. But there is some difference of opinion as to how profits should be distributed. Unions, for example, keep a keen eye on company profits. High profits, to some, mean that workers are not getting enough pay and benefits. This leads to bigger wage and benefit demands in collective bargaining.

The Loyalty Issue

Some employers think that the presence of a union reduces employee loyalty to the firm. When the collective bargaining process results in a pay raise, for example, the employees may think that the union "won" the raise — it was not "granted" by management. Union people, of course, question whether the raise would have been granted in the absence of the union.

The Jobs Issue

Due to recent widespread unemployment in such industries as auto, airline, and steel, unions have focused more on job security than on big pay hikes and more fringe benefits. In some cases, employers and unions in those industries have made concessions to existing contracts. The conces-

POINT OF VIEW

Employee Loyalty

Roughly one-third of Japanese workers enjoy lifetime employment with their employers — typically the largest firms in Japan. These workers ordinarily start working for their employers as soon as they finish trade school or graduate from college. When they reach the typical retirement age of fifty-five, they receive a handsome bonus payment for their years of service. Many of these retirees are then rehired by smaller firms. These are often the firms that supply the products the larger firms need in their operations. In the case of workers whose skills have become obsolete, employers and the government sponsor retraining programs. This type of employer-employee relationship helps to build strong worker loyalty.

Many employers and unions in Canada think this type of employer-employee relationship is too paternalistic. They tend to view unions and management as adversaries. Furthermore, most unions in Japan are organized along company lines. Thus there is closer cooperation between unions and management than in Canada, where most unions are organized by crafts and along industry lines — not company lines. In general, therefore, Canadian workers do not have as strong feelings of loyalty to their employers as Japanese workers.

sions employers sought involved such elements as wage and benefit cuts, wage freezes, and work rule changes that would help increase productivity. In return for those "givebacks" unions sought greater job security for their members.

Union people's fear that automation will reduce jobs has also been addressed in contract negotiations. Automation has made some jobs obsolete, and unions often try to protect the members whose jobs have been replaced by machines. Some employers, in order to maintain labour peace, have been willing to keep these people on the payroll even if their services are not needed. The result, of course, is higher costs for the firm and higher costs to consumers for its products. Competitive inroads into Canadian markets by foreign-based firms are making this practice distasteful to employers.

Our federal government looks to private firms as the major source of jobs. It is committed to a policy of full employment. When jobs in private industry cannot absorb all those people who are willing and able to work, many want government to step in as the "employer of last resort." In other words, many workers believe they have a right to a job.

In some countries (e.g., Japan) many workers enter into a sort of long-term unwritten contract with their employers. In return for good service, workers are more or less guaranteed lifetime employment. Some Canadian workers would like to have a similar guarantee. The strategy most evident in Canada, however, is for workers to bargain for shorter work weeks and extended vacations. The purpose is to spread the available work around to more workers. But workers want more pay per hour to keep their same take-home pay. Some managers argue that pushed-up wages lead to higher costs, which are passed on to consumers in the form of higher prices.

The "Right to Manage" Issue

An employer must bargain with a union that is certified by a provincial labour relations board. The employer does not have to grant the union everything it wants, but both parties must bargain in good faith on bargainable issues. **Bargainable issues are aspects of the work or job environment that are subject to collective bargaining between union and management representatives.** Examples include vacations, holidays, rest periods, wages, seniority regulations, transfers, promotions, layoffs, and size of work crews.

bargainable issues

Some unionized companies favour including a very specific statement of management rights in their contracts with unions. An example is a statement that management retains the right to institute technological changes. Other firms believe that a specific listing of management rights can become too restrictive. The union could contend that anything that is omitted from the list is outside the exclusive domain of management. These companies tend to include only a very general statement of management rights in their contracts.

When employees are unionized, personnel policies on pay, job transfers, promotions, discipline, fringe benefits, etc., are written into the collective bargaining agreement. Unionization also often results in more centralization of decision-making authority over personnel matters. Decisions on discipline, job transfers, etc., may be removed from lower-level managers in order to exercise more control over these aspects of the collective bargaining agreement.

The quality-of-work-life programs we discussed in Chapter 5 can produce desirable results in unionized plants only if the unions support the programs. Involving workers in plant-floor level decisions about redesigning jobs to make them more satisfying and productive will lead to changes—new job classifications, modified work rules, changes in job assignments, and so on. These are already issues for collective bargaining in most unionized firms. Thus the management rights clause in some labour contracts may have to be narrowed to gain union support of these programs.

The Seniority Issue

Unions often are critical of wage and salary plans that are not based on seniority. Labor argues that any other system is subjective and/or interferes with the collective bargaining process. Union work rules, for example, may limit the use of the MBO method of employee performance appraisal. But management resists basing all pay and promotion decisions on seniority alone, on the grounds that it ignores employee productivity.

The Productivity Issue

Productivity has become a major issue in recent years. Canadian labour's productivity has not been increasing as rapidly as that of workers in some other countries. This is a serious problem when Canadian firms must compete for customers with foreign-based firms whose workers are increasing their productivity at a higher rate.

Management often blames declining productivity on restrictive union work rules, a decline of the work ethic, taxes and inflation that reduce their incentive to invest in new machines, and government regulations, such as pollution laws which require firms to invest in financially nonproductive areas.

Unions, however, argue that management too often is unwilling to invest in training programs to upgrade labour skills. Other criticisms include underspending on research and development, poor product engineering, poor communication between workers and managers, too much red tape in big firms, a dehumanized work environment, and lack of effective cooperation with unions in trying to improve workers' standard of living.

When increases in productivity do occur, management and labour often disagree over how much of the increase in output is due to labour and how much is due to capital. Workers who double their output per hour will want more pay. Management argues that at least part of the increase is due to the fact that workers work with newer and better machines. At any rate, if all the increase in output is paid to the worker in higher wages, management would have little or no incentive to invest money in new plants and equipment. The result, according to management, is rising costs, less profit, and eventually, a business failure because of inability to compete.

The Inflation Issue

COLA clause

Many recent labour contracts have included cost-of-living escalator clauses. **A COLA, or escalator, clause means that, during the period of time covered by a labour contract, wage hikes will be granted on the basis of changes in the cost of living. These hikes are called cost-of-living adjustments (COLA).**

Management has tended to accept COLA on the grounds that it helps to avoid demands for big "catch up wage hikes" when a current contract expires and a new one is negotiated. It also makes unions less likely to want to bargain for shorter pacts and to reopen negotiations when their contracts do not have COLA provisions. A major conflict issue, however, has been whether there should be an upper limit on the COLA employers might have to pay during a contract period—whether COLA should be capped or uncapped. In fact, bargaining over the formula to be used for making the adjustments can be tough. The COLA provision has been one of the items many employers have sought as a "giveback" in negotiating contract concessions with unions during recent years.

WHAT SHOULD MANAGEMENT DO?

Job Enlargement and Job Enrichment

The installation of high technology machinery improves employee productivity. But there are problems. This progress, for example, makes some jobs repetitive and boring due to overspecialization of labour. Many workers today are not satisfied with these types of jobs. Management wants to improve jobs in order to increase employee productivity, and workers and their unions want more satisfying jobs.

One approach is job enlargement—adding more tasks to a job. This makes the job less routine and less boring.

Another approach is job enrichment—improving the quality of the job by providing opportunities for advancement and recognizing employees who do good work.

In some cases, these efforts have raised employee productivity. This benefits management. In many cases, however, these efforts lead to increases in production costs. Unions often criticize these efforts on the grounds that they are merely attempts to get more work out of workers without really improving their job satisfaction.

Managers, therefore, often are caught in a dilemma. They want to achieve efficient production from a cost and quality standpoint, but they also want to provide jobs which satisfy the demands of modern employees and their unions. WHAT SHOULD MANAGEMENT DO?

THE NATURE OF COLLECTIVE BARGAINING

In preparing to bargain on a new contract, the union sets up a negotiating team long before the current contract will expire. This team develops a list of demands that will satisfy the union membership. It also is common for the union members to vote a strike authorization that will go into effect if the current contract expires and a new one has not been negotiated.

The management negotiating team tries to anticipate the union's demands and prepares for them. For example, if management expects the union to bargain for a large wage hike, management negotiators will enter the bargaining sessions armed with forecasts concerning the impact of the higher wages on the firm's ability to compete against other firms in the industry.

During the early bargaining sessions, the union presents its demands first and the management proposes changes in the old contract that it would like to include in the new contract. Any issues brought up for discussion can be objected to by either labour or management, but as we have seen, the law requires both to bargain in good faith on bargainable issues.

By now, both sides have their demands on the table and it may look as if there is little chance of coming to an agreement. The bargaining process then focuses on concessions. Each team is authorized to make concessions in order to narrow the gap between labour's demands and management's offers.

The closer the bargainers get to the expiration date of the current contract, the harder they work to hammer out a new contract. Around-the-clock bargaining sessions may be held to come up with a contract. The union negotiators, however, are not authorized to accept the contract they eventually work out with management. They can recommend it to the membership but rank-and-file union members must vote on it before it can be binding. If they ratify (accept) it, a formal and binding contract is prepared and signed by labour and management.

A national contract covers major issues like wage rates and fringe benefits. But while the national contract is being negotiated, local unions and plant managements work out specific provisions on rest periods, sanitary facilities, washup periods, and so on. These can vary from plant to plant but local negotiations are, in general, consistent with the national contract. If an agreement cannot be worked out on an issue at the local level, the plant may be struck by the local union.

During the collective bargaining process, labour and management sometimes get deadlocked in their negotiations. They can call in a neutral third party to help break the deadlock. **In conciliation the neutral third party's task is to prevent negotiations from breaking down. If negotiations break off, the conciliator tries to get the two parties back to the bargaining table.** The conciliator, however, has no authority over either party.

Mediation goes a step further. **In mediation, the neutral third party's task is to suggest a possible compromise.** The mediator tries to persuade the parties to settle the dispute. Like the conciliator, the mediator has no authority over either party.

conciliation

mediation

voluntary arbitration

In voluntary arbitration the neutral third party hears both sides of the dispute and settles the issue. The two parties decide voluntarily to submit the dispute to arbitration. Both parties are bound by the settlement.

compulsory arbitration

Finally, compulsory arbitration may be compelled by federal or provincial law in certain cases. If labour and management cannot reach an agreement during contract negotiations, they must submit their dispute to an arbitrator. The arbitrator's decision is binding on both parties. An example of compulsory arbitration is the Ontario Hospital Disputes Arbitration Act, under which hospital workers are not allowed to strike. Compulsory arbitration is rare and is used only when essential public services are involved.

Grievance Machinery

If given a choice, most employers probably would prefer that their workers be non-unionized. But a firm may, in fact, benefit from the presence of a union. Unions can help manage employee discontent by bringing problems to the surface where they can be dealt with through collective bargaining. Workers may express their individual discontent through work slowdowns or quitting. A union, however, provides a mechanism for channelling this discontent to management while, at the same time, keeping the work force intact. Thus employer-employee communication improves. Supervisors who want to initiate changes in work procedures will often discuss it with union representatives before they "announce" the changes. This gives the supervisor the chance to "sell" the proposed changes to the union representative who, in turn, may help "sell" them to the union members.

The collective bargaining agreement enables management and labour to coexist. The rights of each are stated. But no such contract could cover every situation in which trouble might occur. Also, problems sometimes arise over the interpretation of the contract.

grievance procedures

A grievance is something that causes a worker to complain. Not all complaints, however, are grievances — only those complaints that relate to alleged violations of the labour contract or the law are grievances. To deal with grievances, labour contracts include grievance procedures. **Grievance procedures spell out the sequence of steps a grieved employee should follow in seeking to correct the cause of the grievance.** These procedures are set up to reduce the chance that employee gripes will cause a breakdown in labour-management relations.

A worker who is told by a supervisor to do a task the worker does not think is part of his or her job may want to file a grievance. The worker might discuss this with the shop steward (a union representative in the plant) who might then take it to the worker's boss. If the issue is not settled at this stage, the grievance may be presented in writing to the union grievance committee and the plant manager. If the issue is still unresolved, it may be presented in writing to still higher union and company officials. Ultimately, the issue may be submitted to binding arbitration. Although, as we said earlier, contract arbitration is very rare, grievance arbitration is common in administering a collective bargaining agreement. It helps reduce the chances that grievances will lead to work stoppages.

WEAPONS OF LABOUR AND MANAGEMENT

Most grievances are settled through grievance procedures. Sometimes, however, issues divide labour and management so much that they resort to certain weapons. This is likely to happen when employee discontent is widespread, the parties are unable to agree on a new contract, or there is a dispute over terms of an existing contract.

Labour's Weapons

Labour's main weapons are

- the strike
- the picket
- the boycott
- work-to-rule

strike
    A strike is a temporary withdrawal of all or some employees from the employer's service. The presumption is that they will return when their demands are met or a compromise is worked out. The strike is the union's ultimate weapon. It ordinarily will not be used, however, unless the union has the financial resources to ride it out.

There are legal and illegal strikes. A strike is legal if the union has bargained in good faith with management and has adhered to all of the provisions of the provincial labour relations act, but has still not been able to reach an agreement with management. A strike is illegal if these things have not been done, *or* if the strikers have been ordered back to work. For example, in 1978 postal workers were ordered back to work by an act of Parliament because their services were considered essential.

picketing
    Picketing means that people (pickets) form a picket line and walk around a plant or office building with placards (signs) informing other workers and the general public that the employer is held unfair to labour. Strikes are usually accompanied by picketing, but picketing may take place without a strike.

In general, picketing is protected under the right of free speech as long as it does not include any fraud, violence, and/or intimidation. An effective picket may keep other employees who belong to different unions from entering a plant. If a picket line around a plant is honored by truck drivers, the picketed firm finds itself without deliveries.

boycott
    In a boycott a union tries to get people to refuse to deal with the boycotted firm. There are *primary* and *secondary boycotts.* Suppose that the employees of Company Y are involved in a dispute. They might send circulars to Y's customers and suppliers asking them not to do business with Y. This is a secondary boycott.

Table 7.3   Types of Strikes, Pickets, and Boycotts

Strikes

1. Primary strike	The employer's workers withdraw from their jobs for their direct and immediate benefit.
2. Secondary strike	*B* Company's union strikes to force *B* to bring pressure on *C* Company because the union has a gripe with *C*.
3. Sympathy strike	A strike called by one union primarily for the benefit of another union.
4. National general strike	All the workers in the nation strike.
5. General strike	All or most of the workers in a particular industry go out.
6. Sitdown strike	The workers cease working but do not leave their place of employment.
7. Slow-down strike	The workers "slow down" rather than cease working altogether. This type of strike is most effective in mass production industries.
8. Partial strike	Only part of the work force strikes, but those who go out are strategically selected to place the employer in a difficult position.
9. Wildcat strike	Some union members go out even though the union did not authorize a strike.

Pickets

1. Primary picket	The employer's workers walk around the building or place of employment with placards informing other workers and the public that the company is unfair to labour.
2. Secondary picket	Several employees of *X* Company (with whom the union has a gripe) picket *Y* Company, a customer of *X* Company, in order to induce *Y* to cease buying from *X* Company.

Boycotts

1. Primary boycott	The workers refuse to do business with (buy from) their employer.
2. Secondary boycott	The boycotters cause third parties to the labour dispute to refrain from dealing with the employer of the boycotters.

Table 7.3 summarizes the various types of strikes, pickets, and boycotts.

The "corporate campaign" is a new and controversial approach to organizing workers whose employers strongly resist unionization. It involves the use of picketing to inform the target firm's customers and others that the firm is non-unionized. It also involves an attempt to induce the target firm's workers and customers to stop buying the firm's products — a boycott. A third element is directed at the outside directors on the target firm's board of directors. These board members are not officers of the corporation, but they are often executives of firms that buy from the target firm or executives of banks that lend money to it. The goal is to encourage them to pressure the target firm's management to cease its interference or resistance to the organizing effort. Otherwise, the outside directors' firms might be targeted for picketing and/or boycotting.

work-to-rule

When workers meticulously follow all rules and regulations in the collective agreement, they are using a work-to-rule strategy to get management's attention. The collective agreement cannot anticipate all the situations which will arise at the workplace. If management and workers are on pretty good terms, workers will often do things that they are not specifically required to do in the collective agreement. Management in turn may not enforce certain provisions of the collective agreement very closely. Overall, this give-and-take creates a reasonable work situation where interpersonal relations are good and productivity is improved.

However, if labour and management have a disagreement (perhaps during negotiations) and labour feels that management is being unreasonable, it may begin working-to-rule. This results in substantially reduced output and is designed to show management that they are very dependent on the goodwill of labour. Work-to-rule tactics are particularly effective in high volume mass production industries because they reduce output levels to a point where the company has difficulty covering its fixed costs. Management therefore has a great financial incentive to resolve the problems as quickly as possible.

Management's Weapons

lockout

For many years management used the lockout to counter labour's threat to strike or to organize. **In a lockout employees are denied access to the plant until they accept the employer's terms of employment.** This weapon is now used mainly as a defensive weapon once a strike is called.

Today the layoff is more effective. A general strike against steel-makers that lasts long enough to deplete their inventories leads to layoffs in steel-using industries. Although auto workers who are laid off claim they are "behind" the steelworkers, a lengthy steel strike brings hardship to the auto workers. This may lead to indirect pressure on the steelworkers to reach an agreement.

injunction

The injunction is a court order forbidding union members from carrying on certain activities such as intimidating workers or impeding other operations of the company. Injunctions have been used frequently in the past, but recently they appear to be used only in extreme cases (such as when workers are actually damaging plant and equipment).

Employers' associations are important in industries with many small firms and one large union which represents all workers. Member firms in an industry might contribute to a strike insurance fund which is used to help members who are struck. They are similar in purpose to strike insurance funds built up by unions.

Firms or industries with labour problems often publicize their side in newspapers and other media to gain public support. Unions also do this. The strength of public opinion sometimes leads to new laws.

THE FUTURE OF UNIONISM

The union movement began in a period when the excesses of early capitalism placed the average worker at the mercy of the employer. For decades unions sought to bargain at arm's length with employers. This goal was met through legislation and the collective-bargaining process. But what is in store for unions in the future?

Public Attitude

Many people considered unionism to be a worthwhile cause up through the 1930s. But some people became critical of some unions toward the end of the 1940s and have continued to be critical up to now. These people argue that some unions have become too powerful and disrupt the economic system when they do go on strike. Nevertheless, white-collar unions continue to grow rapidly as individuals join them in an attempt to get improved economic benefits.

Youth Looks at Unions

Some young people view unions the same way that they view big businesses. They believe that big union organizations are just as impersonal and "distant" as some big businesses. These young people, even if they are union members, do not get deeply involved in union affairs. This difference is apparent in the contrast between the dedicated, older union members who regularly attend union meetings and some of their young counterparts who pay their dues and do not attend.

THEN AND NOW

University Professors and Collective Bargaining

For many years, university professors resisted unionization on the grounds that the "adversary system" of labour-management relations was inconsistent with the "community of scholars" concept at the university.

Recently, however, professors in a number of Canadian universities have unionized, and others are likely to follow suit. The increased sympathy for unions has come from a number of areas, including inflation and faculty perception that university administrators are not responsive to faculty wishes.

CAREERS IN LABOUR RELATIONS

THERE ARE THREE SEPARATE APPROACHES TO CAREERS IN LABOUR relations. One is through the business firm, one through the labour union itself, and the third through independent organizations (sometimes government) serving as mediators between the two. In any case, labour relations careers focus primarily on the interface between a union and a firm. Basically this means negotiating, living with, and interpreting the provisions of a labour contract.

From the union side, a career may start when a union member is nominated as shop steward by his or her co-workers. The *shop steward* deals with day-to-day employee problems on behalf of the union. In larger problems, including contract negotiation, the union *business agent* assumes responsibility. The business agent also promotes the union and recruits new members.

On the management side, *supervisors* deal with shop stewards. The *industrial relations manager* deals with the business agent. The industrial relations manager usually has a college degree in labour economics or management and often is promoted from lower positions in the personnel department.

Qualifications for labour relations work include a good knowledge of labour law, human relations skills, and unusual strength of personality. Information is available from the Canadian Labour Congress, 2841 Riverside Drive, Ottawa, Ontario K1V 8X7, and from the federal Department of Labour in Ottawa. ■

White-collar and Service Workers Look at Unions

White-collar workers now account for more than half of our labour force. In the past some union leaders assumed that these workers were hard to unionize because of their tendency to identify more closely with their employers than with unions and blue-collar workers. But during recent years many white-collar workers have been experiencing many of the same problems blue-collar workers have faced. Mechanization and automation in factories gave rise to fears about job scarcity and stimulated unionization. More recently the effects of automation are being felt in white-collar occupations. Some clerical workers, for example, are facing loss of jobs and rapidly changing job requirements as employers use computers to auto-

235

CAREER PROFILE

MY NAME IS DICK MARTIN AND I AM President of the Manitoba Federation of Labour (M.F.L.). President of the M.F.L. is an elected position. I am in my fifth year in this office.

The M.F.L. is the union of unions in the Province of Manitoba. Approximately 300 local unions belong to the Federation and these represent approximately 72,000 workers in the province. The M.F.L. is essentially formed to speak with a united voice to government and business on issues that organized labour is concerned about.

I was raised in a rural area of southern Ontario. After high school I moved about the country from Montreal to Vancouver to Prince George. In all these cities I was employed in a variety of sales jobs, from furniture sales to electrical equipment, construction equipment, and insurance sales. In 1968 I changed vocations and moved to Thompson, Manitoba, where I was employed as a hard rock miner. After four years in the mine I took up the industrial electrical trade, and in 1976 I received my Interprovincial Electrical Licence.

Throughout my years in Thompson I was active with the United Steelworkers Union, becoming the President of the Local Union in 1976. In 1978 I was elected President of the Manitoba Federation of Labour with which the United Steelworkers are affiliated.

As president my job is to coordinate, lead, and communicate the activities and views of

the affiliated unions to the provincial government and to business. The views of the members are gathered as resolutions at the biannual

mate office operations. Unions are appealing to these and other white-collar workers, including professionals such as librarians, teachers, nurses, and interns in hospitals. We can expect even greater effort by unions in the future to organize these workers.

In Chapter 1 we said that our service industries are growing more rapidly than manufacturing industries. Workers in the service industries traditionally have not been highly unionized. Many work part-time and the typical firm is small. This makes it harder and more costly for unions to organize these workers than it is to organize full-time workers in large factories. Unions will have to intensify their organizational efforts in the service industries.

conventions of the M.F.L. and also through the executive officers of the M.F.L. These views are then formally presented to the government in the form of briefs to the appropriate minister or the Premier and Cabinet.

I have considerable contact with the members of the M.F.L. by attending local union meetings and affiliate conventions, and by individuals just calling me. I also have a great deal of contact with union membership through educational programs offered by the M.F.L. or through meetings of committees such as Occupational Health and Safety, Workers' Compensation, Pension, or Equal Rights and Opportunities Committees.

Similarly, I have regular contact with various departments of government as I must monitor ongoing legislative developments. In addition, I participate in numerous discussions with government or business representatives.

The major problem in my job is being made aware of and then formulating responsive action to anti-labour legislation being proposed by business, government, or other groups. At the same time I must continually promote, in a number of ways, legislation that we think is in the best interest of our members and the general working public. This includes minimum wage laws, pension reform, universal medicare, occupational health and safety, workers' compensation, and of course the labour laws.

In order to properly represent the workers, I must continually strive to assist our affiliated unions in organizing and in obtaining good contracts, and bring all possible assistance to them in case of a strike.

All union leaders are elected. My position is no different and I must stand for reelection every two years. This assures that you are truly representing the workers, their views and aspirations.

The rewards of the job come from the feeling you get when good contracts are negotiated or when a good piece of legislation is passed. Examples of good legislative changes are the establishment of Workers' Advisors' Offices under the Workers' Compensation Act and the awarding of complete compensation benefits to workers who are suffering from occupationally induced cancer.

Other rewards of my job include the personal development one obtains through meeting many interesting people, reading extensively, and studying both the different systems of labour-management relations and patterns of economic development in countries such as Japan and Israel.

For a career as staff member with a union, you usually first need to have considerable experience in the workplace, hold various local union offices, and take part in many labour courses. There are about one hundred professional staff members for all unions in Manitoba. However, unions also employ economists, accountants, lawyers, medical doctors, social workers, and industrial engineers, all with, of course, a pro-labour view. For a career in labour relations you usually need a good understanding of labour history and labour economics, plus many years of experience on the job.

International Unions

During the period 1940–1970, international unions were very prominent in Canada. Much concern was expressed that, because these unions were headquartered in foreign countries (generally the U.S.), they did not have a real concern for the Canadian worker or the Canadian labour scene. In various locations across Canada, workers therefore voted out the international union that represented them and chose a Canadian union to do the job instead. Approximately 52 percent of unionized workers now belong to national (Canadian) unions. This proportion will probably increase since many more white-collar workers are joining unions, and these tend to be national unions.

Women Look at Unions

For years the working woman worked to supplement her family's income. Today many more women are career-oriented. They do not take jobs only between children. In fact, a growing percentage of the female work force is made up of working mothers. In the decade 1966–1976 alone, the female participation rate in the labour force increased from 32 to 45 percent. Career-oriented women view work differently from the way their earlier counterparts did. Along with the sexual revolution there are new ideas about marriage and family. For many women a career rather than the family has become their primary concern in life. As a result, organized labour is making strong efforts to appeal to women.

The overall health of the economy will play a major role in the future of unionism. If labour and management negotiators continue to focus heavily on "givebacks," more employers may find themselves setting up profit-sharing plans so that unions will feel they are getting something in return. "Givebacks" may also reduce the impact of national contracts as they are amended by concessions at local levels. Greater worker participation in quality-of-work-life programs also may mean that unions will push for greater participation in the sharing of profit and a narrowing of management rights clauses in labour contracts.

SUMMARY AND LOOK AHEAD

The modern labour union in Canada evolved from the early craft unions. This was not a smooth evolution. The earliest attempts of workers to form unions were frustrated by court rulings. Labour unions were considered conspiracies in restraint of trade.

Gradually, public sympathy shifted in favour of unions, and laws were passed to guarantee the worker the right to join the union. Once a union is certified, union and management must bargain in "good faith" on bargainable issues. The broadening scope of bargainable issues has narrowed the area of managerial discretion over the years.

Unlike unions in the days prior to World War II, today's unions do not have to fight for the right to exist. Their goals reflect this. Modern unions seek a broad variety of economic, political, and social goals.

We looked at the reasons why workers join unions and the sources of labour-management conflict. Then we discussed how labour and management bargain collectively to negotiate a labour contract and how the parties "live" with the contract. Grievance procedures are important here.

Labour's main weapons are the strike, the picket, the boycott, and work-to-rule. Management also has its weapons—the lockout, the layoff, the injunction, and appeals to the public.

The union movement has always been a minority movement in Canada. In recent years, unions have sought to increase their membership by growing in new directions, such as organizing government employees and other white-collar workers. This is necessary because of the declining percentage of the labour force in blue-collar jobs.

In the next chapter, we look at how firms produce goods and services and how this production effort is managed. ∎

1. Discuss the Industrial Revolution from the viewpoint of the typical worker during that period.
2. Prior to the 1930s, how did employers resist their employees' efforts to form unions?
3. Discuss the provisions of the Canada Labour Code.
4. Is the scope of "managerial discretion" narrowed when a firm's workers form a union? Explain.
5. Distinguish between a craft union and an industrial union.
6. Define (a) local union; (b) national union.
7. Does a union have any responsibility to persons or groups other than the members of that union? Discuss.
8. Do the employees of a firm whose management is "employee-oriented" have a need for a union? Why or why not?
9. How would you explain the fact that the majority of Canadian workers do not belong to a union?
10. List and discuss two major economic objectives of modern unions.
11. In the light of the declining proportion of our labour force engaged in blue-collar jobs, what are unions doing to increase their membership?
12. List and discuss four issues that might lead to labour-management conflict.
13. List and discuss the "weapons" of labour and mangement.

Labour and Management — Adversaries or What?

News reports from Poland in 1981 and 1982 said that in Poland, one of Solidarity's goals was to win the right for Polish workers to choose their own managers instead of having them appointed by the government. Germany's "co-determination" law enables workers to sit on boards of directors as well as on work councils at the plant level.

In the United States and Canada, labour and management have traditionally had an adversarial relationship in collective bargaining. Many people believe that boards of directors, composed of management people, should decide major policy issues, and that unions should be in a position to criticize those decisions from the worker's point of view.

There have been some exceptions, however. For example, in the United States the president of the United Auto Workers sits on Chrysler's board, and unions at Pan American World Airways nominated a director to sit on its board. In both cases, this was largely in return for union givebacks in collective bargaining.

Questions:
1. What are the relative advantages and disadvantages of an adversarial relationship between labour and management in collective bargaining?
2. As we saw in this chapter, givebacks and contract concessions have become more common in recent years. What are the implications of that as far as corporate governance is concerned?
3. Do you think it is possible for labour and management to remain adversaries at the bargaining table while also working together in quality-of-work-life programs at the plant-floor level? Explain.

Gordon McGhee

Thirty years ago, Gordon McGhee establishes the McGhee Manufacturing Company. Mr. McGhee has always been "anti-union." According to him, unions only cause trouble. He once told a friend, "A union cannot raise the worker's pay; only the employer can do that. All the union can do is take some of the worker's pay away in the form of dues on the promise that he or she will receive something in return."

Until recently, Mr. McGhee has had little "trouble" with unions. However, there is now quite an effort being made at his plant to unionize the workers. Mr. McGhee knows those employees who want the union and he called them in for a "talk." He told them, "I'll go out of business before I'll let you ruin the company by bringing in a union."

Questions:
1. Do you agree with Mr. McGhee's statement in the first paragraph? Why or why not?
2. Reread Mr. McGhee's last statement. Describe the nature of the "talk" you would recommend he have with his employees.

CASE STUDY

LAKEVIEW PRODUCTS, LTD.

LAKEVIEW PRODUCTS, LTD. HAD A WORK FORCE OF 500. IN
spite of its size, management had been able to preserve the good
employer-employee relationship which had existed ever since the
company had been founded. Furthermore, Lakeview had a profit-sharing
plan; according to the president, John Rath, the plan gave each worker a
real stake in the company. He believes this is crucial in getting them to
put forth their best efforts.

Recently, however, Rath had noticed some "people problems"
between the plant manager, Brian Swallow, and ten young production
workers who had recently been hired. Rath asked these workers to
come to his office to discuss the situation. He wanted to take steps to
solve the problem between the workers and Swallow before it got out
of hand.

When the workers showed up in Rath's office, it became clear that
the "people problems" were a lot more serious than Rath had thought.
The workers accused Swallow of treating his subordinates like children.

Beth Parasiuk was the most outspoken. She accused Swallow
of playing the "father role." She cited an example. Two months ago a
promotion opened up. The former supervisor of the loading dock
retired and the obvious choice for the job was Mary Friesen. She had
the most seniority in the entire production department, and she wanted
the job. Mary was a good worker and had never had any trouble with
Swallow or anyone else at the plant.

But Swallow passed over Mary and gave the promotion to Grant
Baker. Grant had less seniority than Mary, but Swallow believed he would
be a better choice for the job because "the loading dock supervisor
sometimes has to be tough to keep things moving."

After the meeting Rath thought the situation over. He knew Swallow
was not ready to retire. Rath also felt that he owed him a lot. Without
his help, Lakeview might never have gotten started.

But Rath did understand the sources of the workers' complaints.
He recalled Swallow's discussing with him the reasons he promoted
Baker over Friesen. "John, I know I'm out of step with some of the
newer thinking. If Mary were a man, I'd have given her the promotion.
She really deserves it. But she is a twenty-eight-year-old woman. Can
you imagine the problems I'd have with her as supervisor on the
loading dock?"

At first Rath decided to let Swallow run his department as he
saw fit. But during the next three months Beth stirred up several of
the production workers. At first it was mainly Beth and the other nine

workers who had visited Rath's office. But it soon spread. Complaints about Swallow began to multiply rapidly.

Before long union organizers were trying to unionize Lakeview workers. The "Friesen incident" was a big issue. And Lakeview's workers were the only ones in the industrial park who were not unionized.

Questions:
1. Discuss the meaning of a "good employer-employee relationship."
2. Do you think that a profit-sharing plan for employees helps to make employees feel that they have an ownership interest in the company for which they work? Explain.
3. Do you think that John Rath should have called the ten workers in for a talk? Explain.
4. Could Rath have done anything to prevent the problem as outlined by Beth Parasiuk? Explain.
5. Once the problem involving Mary Friesen was out in the open, what should Rath have done about it? Explain.
6. How successful do you think the union organizers were in unionizing Lakeview's production workers? Discuss.
7. If you were Rath, what would you have done to try to keep Lakeview a non-union company? Explain. ■

CASE STUDY*

HARRY GARDNER

"HEY, HARRY, THE REPAIRMAN IS HERE TO COLLECT FOR REPLACING that broken window in your house," shouted Joe.

"Take the money out of the petty cash box and put the receipt with the other bills," Harry shouted back. "As soon as I've finished unloading this truck I'll slip up to the bank and replace the money in the petty cash."

One thing led to another and Harry did not get ten minutes to go to the bank. At the end of the day Harry reconciled all the day's receipts, the pay-outs from cash, and balanced them against his petty cash "float." Naturally he was out the $42.40 that was paid to the repairman for the broken window replacement. Harry paused for a few seconds, then decided to include the repairman's bill in the "pay-out" column in his reconciliation statement. Everything balanced and, Harry thought to himself, "I'll get the money tomorrow and replace it in the petty cash box, withdraw the bill for the broken window and no one will be any the wiser. At least it lets me balance the day's books."

Harry Gardner worked in a chain store as the manager's assistant and was in the bargaining unit of the union representing all store clerks up to and including assistant store manager. Earlier that day his wife had called to say that their window had been broken by one of their children. Harry told her to phone the local glass repair shop, have the window repaired, and, since she did not have enough money in the house to pay for it, he would pay for it if the repairman would stop by the store.

The next three days passed and Harry did not make his promised substitution of cash for the window repair receipt. The week ended and, since Harry was replacing his manager who was on four-weeks' vacation, Harry was expected to reconcile the whole week's sales, cash, pay-outs, and petty cash float. Harry took the books home with him and felt that it was an hour's work that he could do on Sunday afternoon. During the exercise of reconciling Harry came across his window repair receipt. This time he simply wrote across the receipt, "Paid for broken window. Cash payment from petty cash." He then entered this transaction in the cash disbursements column. The books now balanced with this entry matched against the earlier entry in the "pay-out" column. The repair bill was filed as a receipt against the transaction. Finally, at the end of the four-week period, the monthly reconciliation had to be completed by taking the closing balances from each week's closing and transposing the figures to the monthly ledger. Copies of both the week's ledger

*This case was written by Professor Frank Collom of Queen's University.

and the monthly ledger were sent to the head office along with other financial statements.

On Monday morning the manager returned from his vacation and was pleased with Harry's work in operating the store during the four-week period. Toward the end of the week the manager was going over the books and noticed the entry for the broken window. He queried Harry about it and accepted Harry's story that one of the store windows had been broken and that he had to have it replaced. The story, however, did not quite sit with the manager the more he thought about how inexpensive it was to replace a large window for less than $43.00. The manager picked up the phone and called the glass repair shop. The answer he received was that it was not a store window but a window in Harry's home that had been replaced. Without saying anything, the manager checked the monthly reconciliation statement to see if the transaction had gone through in the "store repair" account. To his disappointment he found it and had no other recourse but to call Harry in for an explanation. Harry confessed and said that he had only made the entries until he could replace the money. The excuse sounded too implausible to the manager who then confronted Harry with a charge of stealing. The manager gave Harry a three-day suspension and told him that he would have to contact head office to see what action they felt was warranted. Harry wrote a cheque for the $42.40, apologized to the manager for the oversight, and expressed a sincere hope that this would not embarrass the manager and that the three-day suspension would be severe enough penalty.

The manager phoned the head office and relayed the events as outlined, explained his action of giving Harry a three-day suspension, and wondered if any further disciplinary measures should be taken. The head office phoned him back the next day and said that the personnel department was issuing a dismissal notice effective immediately. The manager was instructed to phone Harry at his home and notify him that he was not to return to work, since he had been dismissed "for misappropriation of company funds for personal use."

Harry was stunned when he received the call and physically shaken that his improper action should lead to loss of employment and the taint of "being a thief." He called his union steward and repeated the series of events and the action taken by the company. The union immediately filed a grievance for wrongful dismissal. A series of meetings were held between the union and the company as the grievance progressed through the grievance procedure, but the company refused to alter its earlier decision. The union, after exhausting all steps in the grievance procedure, applied for arbitration. During this time, Harry wrote a personal letter to the head office and said that he had "never done anything like that before," and promised that, "if given another chance, I will be a model employee for a company where I have worked without incident for fourteen years."

The arbitration hearing took place almost eleven months after the dismissal. During this time Harry had not been able to secure any other job. The company's lawyer outlined the events as they occurred and no argument was raised by the union over the accuracy of the details. When the union's lawyer took over, he admitted that the company had laid out the facts and events quite accurately, but there was a good argument to be made that the action of dismissal was too severe given the previous good record of his client and certain mitigating circumstances leading up to and subsequent to the event. He argued that the following points should be considered by the arbitrator:

1. The grievor had worked fourteen years for the company.
2. There was not one single incident on his records prior to the incident.
3. His semiannual performance appraisals over the past years had always indicated that he was an above-average employee.
4. He had been promoted three times since joining the company, rising from a clerk to assistant store manager.
5. The event was a momentary aberration in his work career and did not indicate any previous pattern, nor could it be construed as an indication of any future behaviour.
6. He had made restitution and had apologized to his manager and had written to the head office with his apologies.
7. He was fifty years of age and, at that age, would have difficulty in securing other employment. In fact, he had tried to get employment during the period since his dismissal, but with no success.
8. He had lost three fingers in an accident two months prior to the incident and was under heavy medication for what is known as "phantom" pain. (A letter from his personal physician was entered as evidence both to the recurring pain and the medication prescribed.) These pain killers had affected his short-term memory and he was probably acting out of character because of his dulled senses.

In concluding, the lawyer argued that the incident did warrant some form of disciplinary measure of perhaps two-months' suspension, but certainly did not warrant dismissal in light of the above circumstances. He closed by asking for reinstatement with full back pay for all time lost minus the two-months' suspension that, at maximum, this incident warranted. ■

After reading this chapter, you should be able to:

1. Explain the nature of production.
2. Draw a chart illustrating the inputs, processes, and outputs of production.
3. Illustrate the several ways of classifying production processes.
4. Review the management functions and give an example of each as applied to production.
5. Develop a checklist for plant location decisions.
6. Evaluate the dangers of loss of human motivation in a big factory.
7. Explain the process of control as it applies to product quality.
8. Distinguish between value analysis and vendor analysis.

In reading the chapter, look for and understand these terms:

production	control chart
combination	PERT
breaking down	CPM
treatment	quality control
intermittent production	preventive maintenance
continuous production	obsolescence
automation	Materials Requirements Planning (MRP)
labour-intensive	
capital-intensive	reciprocity
make-or-buy decision	value analysis
plant capacity	vendor analysis
plant layout	

IT IS VERY DIFFICULT FOR manufacturing firms in the automobile, steel, and chemical businesses to turn their production activity on and off like a faucet. Companies in these industries have large investments in people and capital equipment, and rapid changes in demand cause great difficulty.

Precisely these kinds of problems were plaguing many Canadian firms in 1981–83. Many workers were laid off, and the problems faced by plant managers because of the recession were substantial.

Cutbacks may save money, but they can also mean laying off trained employees, postponing research and development, and halting recruiting efforts. The cuts not only affect a company's current profitability and its ability to survive a downturn, but they may also affect its ability to compete and grow when the economy recovers. Managers must try to make the cuts that will be most feasible and most effective, while causing the least damage.

CHAPTER EIGHT

Producing Goods and Services

WE BEGIN OUR STUDY OF THE FUNCTIONAL AREAS OF MANAGEMENT with a look at production. The management functions of planning, organizing, staffing, directing, and controlling are used as a framework for studying production management. Special emphasis is given to modern planning and control devices.

Production has a special place in Canadian business history. By doing good production work, and combining new technology with modern organizational techniques, Canadian firms have helped deliver a very high standard of living. Although the earliest application of production techniques was in factories, their use was soon extended to retailing, services, and other forms of business.

There has been considerable growth in production employment. (See Table 8.1.) Using the year 1961 as typical (the index value for that year equals 100), we can compare the growth of various sectors of the economy from 1965 to 1980. Notice that some industries have grown faster than others.

WHAT IS PRODUCTION?

production

Production activity results in the creation of goods and services. Someone or something is "better off" because of production. Production can be viewed as a sequence. It starts with the input of resources. These are fed into one of several kinds of production processes. Finally there results an output of goods or services for use or sale. Figure 8.1

Table 8.1 Employment Indexes in Leading Industries, 1965–1980

	1965	1970	1975	1980
Total	114.3	127.1	141.1	152.4
Forestry	105.4	84.3	76.0	79.3
Mining	105.1	115.3	114.1	142.8
Manufacturing	117.2	122.8	126.3	129.0
Durables	126.0	132.7	139.8	141.2
Nondurables	110.1	115.5	115.5	119.1
Construction	119.8	113.7	117.1	93.5
Transportation	103.9	112.6	125.8	139.3
Wholesale and retail trade	114.2	139.3	168.5	182.4
Financial, insurance, and real estate	116.6	143.6	175.0	208.7
Service	125.8	178.5	231.9	283.7

Source: The Financial Post Canadian Markets, selected years.

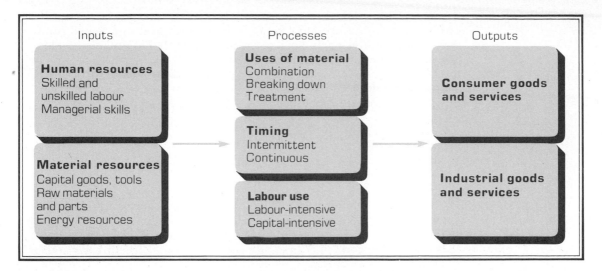

Figure 8.1
The production process

illustrates this view and makes it easier for us to explain the elements of production management.

The ideas presented in Figure 8.1 are relevant for all types of organizations. For example, a manufacturing firm uses human and material resources to produce a physical product like an automobile or a television set. A management consulting firm also uses human and material resources to produce a service (advice on management problems). On the surface, these two organizations may appear to be quite different, but each uses certain human and material inputs and converts them into goods and/or services.

Many business firms sell both products and services. Most people see IBM's main activity as building and selling computers, but it is also very involved with servicing the computers it sells. In addition, IBM markets various kinds of computer-related services to companies. Many other firms which are predominantly service organizations also sell physical products. For example, the major activity of beauty parlours and barber shops is the provision of a hairstyling service, but they also sell some physical products that are related to their main service.

The Inputs to Production

To produce something, the following set of resources is usually needed as input:

- materials
- capital goods
- the human input

Materials include raw materials such as raw cotton, corn, and crude oil; semimanufactured products such as sheet steel and unfinished lumber; and manufactured parts such as spark plugs, bolts, and tires. Electric power and other energy sources are usually included. Capital goods include the plant investment, which can range from a huge refinery to a barber shop, and equipment such as a lathe or a typewriter.

The human input includes

- unskilled labour
- skilled labour
- supervisory skills
- managerial skills

The main distinction between skilled and unskilled labour is ability to perform a special task that cannot be performed by all employees. Examples of skilled workers include carpenters, pipefitters, and technicians. Supervisors and managers, of course, are responsible for directing the activities of others.

One important problem facing producers today is that these inputs are often expensive or in short supply. For human resources, it may be difficult to find skilled workers, technicians, supervisors, and managers at a price the company can afford. For material resources, capital may be hard to get because of high interest rates, or raw materials may be either too expensive or simply not available. If any one of these situations occurs, obviously the processing aspect of production is negatively affected.

Processes

There are several ways of classifying production processes. The first depends on the way that material inputs are dealt with. The second relates to the timing of the process. The third depends on the degree of use of labour.

Uses of Material Inputs

A process may combine two or more material inputs, break down an input, or treat an input.

combination

Combination means putting parts together. It is the most common process. Cars, pumps, and pencils must go through the process of combination. For example, side panels on new cars are traditionally made by combining six or more pieces of steel. This, of course, requires welding to combine the pieces.

breaking down

Breaking down means removing or at least separating some of the original input, usually a raw material. When a log is cut into two-by-fours or when juice is taken from oranges, the process, which is also very common, is one of breaking down.

treatment

Treatment is doing something to an input without adding to it or subtracting from it. It may involve hardening or softening or cooling or reshaping an input. Smoking a ham or moulding a plastic toothbrush handle is a treatment process. Forming a part out of a basic material is often called *fabrication*.

Timing

We can also classify production processes according to a time dimension. They can be intermittent or continuous, and also either for stock or to order.

intermittent production

An intermittent production process starts and stops and starts again, maybe several times. Intermittent production may occur only when stocks fall below a critical level. It may also occur to build up stocks when machines and workers would otherwise be idle. A specialty toolmaker, for example, may nickel-plate certain batches of output and not others. Some products may require special heat treatments. The nickel plating and heat treating departments of the firm are used intermittently.

continuous production

automation

A continuous production process, as the name implies, goes on and on. A cola bottling plant repeats the same process countless thousands of times without interruption. The demand for this product is large and easy to predict. **The process, as in the case of most continuous processes, is highly automated. This means that little human supervision is needed because computers and machines can deal with nearly everything that could happen to interrupt operation.** Automation is discussed more fully in Chapter 17.

Most continuous processes produce products *for stock*. This means that output is kept in inventory in anticipation of demand. This could not be done without losing money if the firm did not have good reason to expect a fairly steady demand. The reason is that keeping inventories costs money in several ways. They take up valuable space, they require financing, and they may be damaged or stolen or become obsolete. Manufacturers of cigarettes and beer use a continuous production process. Demand is fairly predictable and manufacturers can afford to produce in anticipation of actual demand. Electric generating plants and oil refineries also engage in continuous production. Their operations go on around the clock because demand is even more predictable.

The alternative to producing for stock is producing *to order*. This means that the firm waits until there is a specific order in hand before starting to produce. Such production is also called *jobbing*. This kind of production usually uses general-purpose machines and tools—those that can do a variety of jobs. Often production to order is "custom" production in which a specific design or feature is provided for the customer. Boeing and McDonnell Douglas, for example, produce airplanes only upon receipt of orders.

An extreme example of intermittent production to order is a customized stereo-system producer. Such a firm waits for orders, produces a variety of outputs, and tends to be labour-intensive. Some parts of the shop may be idle for extended periods. The size of its labour force may vary. A similar situation exists in producing heavy machinery, ships, and high-fashion dresses.

A manufacturer of soap powder is at the other extreme. This firm has a heavy investment in special-purpose equipment and operates on a

POINT OF VIEW

How Will Modern Technology Affect the World of Work?

An Optimistic View:

"As far as I'm concerned, I can't wait to work less. They say that the thirty-hour week is just around the corner. The computers and robots that are taking over much of the busywork of offices and factories will enable us to produce all our nation needs with fewer hours of work. Certainly the physical effort part of work will be all but eliminated. We'll spend more of our work time planning and making sure that things are done right. And don't forget the leisure time we'll have. I'm already getting into continuing education courses and I've put a down payment on a fishing boat."

A Pessimistic View:

"I look at it differently. It seems to me that those guys who own the plants and big businesses are out to protect themselves, period! They want to install more and more labour-saving machines and computers so that they can avoid the trouble of dealing with workers and unions. These machines make us less important and that means less power for the worker. They talk about retraining programs and higher-skill jobs for us, but you can't fool me. New machines mean less work and less work means lower income for the average person."

---

continuous "assembly-line" basis. It keeps a large inventory of finished goods. Other examples are producers of ball-point pens, paper towels, and gasoline.

Labour Use

labour-intensive

Processes also vary in the amount of human input they need. **Labour-intensive processes depend more on people than on machines.** Some parts of the apparel trade are like this. Labour-intensive processes are most likely to be used when labour is cheap or when there is an artistic element in the work. There are some kinds of jobs, too, in which it is really hard to apply machines because the process varies a lot. Many kinds of farming are still highly labour-intensive as is the making of high-quality jewelry. Today many items of clothing for U.S. markets are made or are partly made by U.S. firms with low-cost labour in less-developed nations.

capital-intensive

The opposite situation exists when machines can do the job better than people. **This calls for capital-intensive processes in which people may have little to do with production. Instead, investment in machinery is great.** The huge petroleum refinery is a classic example of a capital-intensive process. A refinery that may cost hundreds of millions of dollars to build and equip may operate with fewer than one hundred employees.

Coal mining used to be highly labour-intensive. Since the energy crisis began, however, oil, steel, and utility companies have been investing in the coal industry. They are buying expensive equipment to mechanize and automate coal-mining operations. Thus their operations are becoming more capital-intensive. To make such heavy investment in equipment pay

Programmable industrial robots are becoming a familiar sight along the production line.

off, the equipment has to be operated nonstop. Thus their operations more closely resemble continuous production than intermittent production.

Likewise, computers used to be custom-built and their manufacturing processes were highly labour-intensive. In recent years computer manufacturers have turned to high-volume, mass production operations, and manufacturing processes have become more capital-intensive. Strong price competition has driven computer prices down and computer makers have had to focus on lower-cost production. Thus they too have invested millions of dollars to automate their manufacturing operations.

Shortages of skilled workers can also be a problem. For example, some machine tool makers in recent years have been advising their customers that they will experience increasing difficulty in hiring skilled machinists to operate the machines. Thus the machine tool makers are moving into electronic technology and are offering computer-controlled machines that require less-skilled machine operators.

Outputs of Production

The outputs of production are divided into consumer goods and services — those things that are purchased and used by individuals and households — and industrial goods and services — those things purchased and used by businesses and institutions. A full explanation of this classification scheme is provided in the following chapter. At this point, we will offer a few examples of each.

Consumer Goods

Consumer goods surround us. They are produced by every kind of process. If you had Kellogg's Corn Flakes for breakfast this morning you were consuming a consumer good that was produced by a process that included mixing ingredients (assembly) and cooking (treatment). This process is also continuous and capital-intensive. All of the inputs shown in Figure 8.1 were used, including various forms of human input and material input.

Consumer Services

Consumer services also abound. A good example is hairstyling. The process in this case is primarily treatment with perhaps a bit of assembly and/or breaking down. The process is intermittent and labour-intensive. Services are by their nature labour-intensive. The inputs are primarily the skilled labour of the stylist, accompanied by some materials.

Industrial Goods

Industrial goods production can be demonstrated by the case of building construction. To erect a skyscraper in a major city requires a variety of processes, but it is predominantly assembly. It has become more and more capital-intensive, but still requires substantial skilled and unskilled labour input. Construction could also be characterized as intermittent processing, although some parts of the process are continuous, particularly when deadlines for completion are approaching. The material inputs of steel, glass, and insulating materials are assembled by skilled and unskilled workers and supervised by skilled managerial people.

Industrial Services

A good example of an industrial service output might be security services offered to a bank by a firm specializing in protecting people and property. Bank security services might, for example, include some assembly of alarm components and locks, but it is also a labour-intensive service involving the human input of around-the-clock security guards (continuous process).

MANAGING PRODUCTION ACTIVITY

Traditionally, the term *production management* has been used to describe the application of managerial functions (planning, organizing, staffing, directing, and controlling) to the process of converting inputs to output. This is understandable, since the production of physical goods dominated our economy in the early part of the twentieth century. Because of the rapid growth of the service sector since World War II, it is important to broaden our perspective to include goods *and* services. *Operations management* is

GUIDELINES

**An Operations Management View
of Key Decisions in the Life of a
Productive System***

BIRTH of the System	What are the goals of the firm? What products or service will be offered?
PRODUCT DESIGN and PROCESS SELECTION	What are the form and appearance of the product? Technologically, how should the product be made?
DESIGN of the System	Where should the facility be located? What physical arrangement is best to use? How do you maintain desired quality? How do you determine demand for the product or service?
MANNING the System	What job is each worker to perform? How will the job be performed, measured; how will the workers be compensated?
STARTUP of the System	How do you get the system into operation? How long will it take to reach desired rate of output?
The System in STEADY STATE	How do you run the system? How can you improve the system? How do you deal with day-to-day problems?
REVISION of the System	How do you revise the system in light of external changes?
TERMINATION of the System	How does a system die? What can be done to salvage resources?

*Adapted from Richard Chase and Nicholas Aquilano, *Production and Operations Management*, 3rd Edition 1981 (Richard D. Irwin, Homewood, Ill. © 1981).

the application of management functions to the inputs, processes, and output of business organizations, whether they are producing physical goods or services.

An operations management view conceives of a business as a productive system. Within this system several key decisions must be made, as indicated in the boxed insert. To demonstrate the operations management perspective, consider the cleaning and maintenance functions that are necessary in a thirty-story office building.

As you might suspect, cleaning such a building is a massive job. It requires a well-designed system to direct the efforts of hundreds of cleaning people on many different floors. Thousands of wastebaskets need to be emptied, desks dusted, and toilets checked and cleaned. The workers must know and understand their tasks. They must perform them in a coordinated way so that, for example, the elevators are used efficiently, energy is not wasted, and the predetermined time schedule is adhered to.

For all of this to happen there must be a central control post. The superintendent of operations usually has an office in the basement. The building is divided into cleaning zones, each with a supervisor who keeps in regular touch with the superintendent, perhaps by walkie-talkie. Each zone supervisor must know the specific cleaning task assigned to each of the workers under his or her control and must see to it that it is done on time and in the manner specified by the cleaning standards. If modern operations management techniques were not employed, and if the best concepts of organization, planning, staffing, directing, and controlling were not employed, it would be impossible to keep the building clean.

Operations management techniques also played a role in the decision by big retailers like Sears to adopt area cashiering. Studies indicated that management could reduce the number of salesclerks by placing cash registers in a few locations in a store rather than placing them in each department.

Operations management ideas are also relevant for diverse problems like controlling the billing process for a large dental practice, designing the physical layout of a restaurant, or locating a new supermarket for a large chain. Let's look briefly at how we might apply operations management techniques to each of these.

Dr. Jenny Wilson opened her office in a western city soon after completing her internship. The practice grew very quickly. It was a great success after a few years, but she wasn't doing too well when it came to collecting her fees. A management consultant could have pointed out several specific problems. First, she was not regularly recording and filing fees for the oral hygienist. Second, her office assistant was often absent, and his replacement made a lot of billing errors. Finally, there was no routine for following up on slow or nonpaying accounts.

The practice of good operations management methods would have resulted in the design of a routine for recording oral hygiene charges; the hiring of a regular replacement for the office assistant; and the establishment of a past-due bill follow-up procedure and use of a collection agent for extreme cases.

A restaurant needed to bring its fifty-year-old building up to date. An operations management approach to the problem might have started by asking the question, "what has changed between 1930 and 1980 concerning the needs of our customers?" Solutions might have included providing a warmer atmosphere, improved parking, and drive-in facilities.

A systems approach often requires that human inputs be modified along with the plant itself. Good operations management would have recommended such things only after interviewing customers and employees and checking the timing and flow path of patrons inside the building as well as their modes of transportation to the restaurant.

Similar analysis and application of operations management techniques could work for the Safeway supermarket chain in choosing a new retail location. Management might have already started by checking census data and other sources to find those areas of population growth in the city. They might also check the location of competition, the cost of land, traffic flows, zoning information, and the availability of the right kind of land and/or building for lease. The final decision would be made in much the same way as the plant location example discussed later in this chapter.

Management of Safeway would consider factors likely to draw customers and factors affecting costs. The motivation, as in the case of all business management, is mostly profit. The methods of estimating profit found in operations management are quite similar to those a large factory might use.

The above examples clearly show how the concept of operations management is relevant for firms producing both goods and services. Let's now look in more detail at how the basic management functions (planning, organizing, staffing, directing, and controlling) are carried out in an operations management context.

Production Planning

Planning is concerned with the future. It is a mapping out of how things are going to be done. It has short-run and long-run dimensions and requires a forecast of demand.

Planning for production is no exception. It includes planning the product or service (outputs) and planning for capital, labour, and material needs (inputs). We will emphasize strategic, long-run planning with an emphasis on capital goods planning and planning for the product itself.

Product Planning

The logical time to start planning for production is when planning the product. This planning really overlaps the production and marketing functions of the firm and is discussed more fully in our chapters on marketing. At this point we will describe just a few features of the product-planning process.

Product planning amounts to answering the following questions:

•What kind of products or services can be sold at a profit?
•How much can be sold?
•What styles, sizes, and variations should be produced?
•What special features should the product or service have?

The answers to these questions require study to determine the best combination of human and material resources. In many firms these questions are considered on a continuous basis by a product development committee. To be most effective, this committee should have representatives from both marketing and production. This increases the coordination between these two important areas.

In both product and service firms, the product development committee would consider the four questions with respect to new products or variations in existing products. The most basic questions in this type of analysis are "will it sell?" and "can it be sold at a profit?".

The product mix of a firm—that is, the combination of products or services that it produces—has both market and cost effects. Producing a line of related products has certain advantages from the selling standpoint. Producing several products, whether they are related or not, may affect the unit cost. A local Coca-Cola bottling company could begin to bottle other soft drinks in the Coca-Cola Company's line. This would probably increase its total production volume without adding much cost for plant or equipment. Thus fixed costs (such as plant and equipment) would be spread over more units, and the cost per bottle would be reduced.

This general strategy can also be used by service firms. Royal Trust, for example, could use its human and material resources to expand the line of financial services it offers.

make-or-buy decision   **One question that often arises in planning the product is the decision whether to make a product or a component part or to buy it—the "make-or-buy" decision.** If we are talking about a firm that makes only one product, buying it rather than making it would take the firm out of the production business entirely. This could be the right decision if the firm could make more money by buying a product and reselling it than by making it and then selling it.

Other factors are involved in the "make-or-buy" question. If it is to be a question at all, there must be a reliable source from which to buy the product or part. There must be a supplier who is willing to meet the buyer's needs in terms of quality, quantity, and delivery schedules. A decision to buy rather than to make is often made for the component parts of an assembled product. The major auto makers, for example, buy many of the component parts of the cars they make. In the construction industry, a contractor often uses one or more subcontractors to produce various parts of the project.

Once a firm reaches a certain size, it might stop buying one or more component parts and begin to make them. This may reduce total costs of production and make the producer more secure about sources of inputs. However, it may also make the firm less flexible. In recent years, for example, some brewing companies have stopped buying cans from can makers and have started making their own. This, of course, means that the "buyer" has one supplier—itself.

The make-or-buy decision is also relevant for service organizations. A large travel agency like Marlin or Cook Tours develops and sells its own vacation packages. Crocus Tours, a division of Mackie Travel Ltd., develops its own ski tours and trips to Hawaii for professional groups. A small travel agency, however, does not normally "produce" its own vacation packages. Instead, it sells packages that specialized tour companies have developed.

Planning the Plant

There are several important questions which relate to planning for the plant itself. These include the decisions of where to locate the plant (plant location), how large a plant to build (plant capacity), and how to arrange the plant once it is built (plant layout).

Plant location

Plant location can affect overall cost, employee morale, and many other elements of a firm's operation. A manager should weigh carefully any

Producing Goods and Services

Table 8.2 Plant Location Checklist

Area Selection

1. Cost of materials and parts transportation
2. Cost of transportation of finished products or services to customers
3. Location inducements and deterrents by city and provincial governments
4. Quality and quantity of appropriate labour supply
5. Adequacy of power and water supply
6. Attractiveness as a place to live—climate, schools, safety, etc.

Specific Site Selection

1. Sufficient size
2. Accessibility to highways, railways, or water transport
3. Restrictions on land use
4. Land costs
5. Availability of leased facilities such as public warehouses, retail, space, etc.

location decision. A checklist such as the one in Table 8.2 could be a great help. The first question is, "in what area do we wish to locate?" This refers to a city or, perhaps, metropolitan area—but an even broader geographic location decision may be needed first. The factors to consider in selecting an area include input transportation, output transportation, and city and provincial inducements (such as tax exemptions) and deterrents (such as high real property taxes). These should be estimated well in advance of making a decision.

Local labour, water, and power supplies are sometimes crucial. Southern Ontario, with its large supply of skilled workers, would have to be a major contender for a new automobile production plant. Chemical plants, which require large water supplies for processing, cannot ignore sites along rivers or near gas and oil production facilities. Especially in times of tight energy supplies, any plant that will use large amounts of energy must consider if there is enough natural gas, petroleum, or coal at the proposed site.

Input transportation cost depends on the distance of raw material and parts suppliers from the proposed area and the kind of transportation facilities connecting them. Output transportation cost depends on the expected location and density of customers as related to the proposed area. Sometimes these cost factors make it hard to meet competitors' prices.

A less tangible factor is the attractiveness of the area as a place to live. Important considerations here are climate, schools, housing, public parks, police protection, and taxes. A firm trying to decide between two possible locations might make estimates of their comparative profitability, taking into account the expected effects on sales and on the various cost components—especially taxes, transportation, and labour.

Once an area is selected, the next problem is to choose a specific site. The firm makes a survey of available parcels of land which are suitable in terms of size; zoning restrictions; and access by highway, railway, and water. If several sites are satisfactory, the decision might depend on cost.

There is the added possibility of finding a suitable existing plant available for sale or lease. This could mean earlier availability for operations.

Specific site selection calls for compromise among the items on its checklist. A specific firm's choice may be determined by placing emphasis on access to a river or on distance from population centers. It may be selected because it is close to a large university or to a major industrial customer. Plant location decisions are becoming more difficult as land in and near major population centres becomes scarce.

Planning for plant capacity and plant layout

Once a site is chosen, the next step in planning is to design the building itself. With the help of production experts and architects, the firm must plan plant capacity. **Plant capacity is the production output limit of the facility.** A pocket calculator assembly plant, for example, may require 10,000 square feet of space to produce an expected maximum output of 2,000 units a day. A doctor's office might require three examination rooms and a reception area in order to process thirty-five patients a day.

Plant layout describes the relative location of the different parts of the production process in the building or buildings. The planner must answer questions such as those in Table 8.3. The correct answers depend on the kind of production process involved — whether it is labour-intensive or capital-intensive — and on the size and perishability of the units of output. The calculator assembly plant is a continuous, for-stock, labour-intensive process. It might well be laid out on one floor in a straight line. The parts could be stocked at one end; the several-step assembly process could occur in the centre; and the inspection, testing, packaging, and shipping could be done at the other end.

In a manufacturing plant there are two basic types of plant layout — product and process. In product layout a mass production orientation exists, while in process layout a made-to-order (custom) orientation exists. Table 8.4 shows how these two alternatives compare on several important dimensions.

Some people ask, "which of these two production systems is better?". The answer is neither. Each system is useful for satisfying certain consumer needs and hence each is useful for certain things. If consumers want a customized product that fits certain very specific needs, it will probably

plant capacity

plant layout

Table 8.3   Questions for Planning a New Plant

What are output expectations?
Can we operate around the clock with a smaller plant?
Will we operate year-round?
Is inventory storage easy?
What are our financing limitations?
Do we arrange machines by product or by process?
How many storeys are practical?
How much space must be allowed for expansion?

Table 8.4 Product and Process Layout

Characteristics	Product	Process
1. Volume of production	High	Low
2. Nature of production	For inventory	For special order
3. Machine investment/worker	High	Low
4. Type of machines	Special purpose (e.g., sensing devices, robots relevant to a single product, etc.)	General purpose (e.g., welders, sanders, drill presses, etc.)
5. Production flexibility	Low	High
6. Cost/unit of output	Low	High
7. Impact of machine breakdowns	High	Low
8. Size of plant	Large	Small
9. Product flow	Once through each machine	Possibly several times through each machine, *or* a machine may be skipped entirely
10. Type of worker required	Unskilled or semiskilled	Semiskilled or skilled
11. Examples	Mass production of toothpaste, freezers, automobiles, nuts and bolts, soda pop, etc.	Custom production of furniture, car repairs, Eskimo carvings, etc.

have to be manufactured using a process layout because demand will be very low. On the other hand, if consumers are willing to purchase a product that is much like the version their neighbour has, manufacturers will be able to use a product layout because of the high volume production that will be possible. The now defunct De Lorean custom automobile appealed to a completely different market than a mass-produced Chevrolet.

It is important to remember that decisions on plant location, capacity, and layout may not be as complex as they seem, particularly when a company is expanding. Each time a new plant is built, procedures that were used in previous new plant construction can be referred to. For a smaller or slower growing firm, however, new plant construction can take up considerable time and energy. In either case, it must be done carefully.

Organizing for Production

Some of the departmentalization process in manufacturing depends on the type of layout. A plant may be arranged according to process or according to product, depending on the number of products being pro-

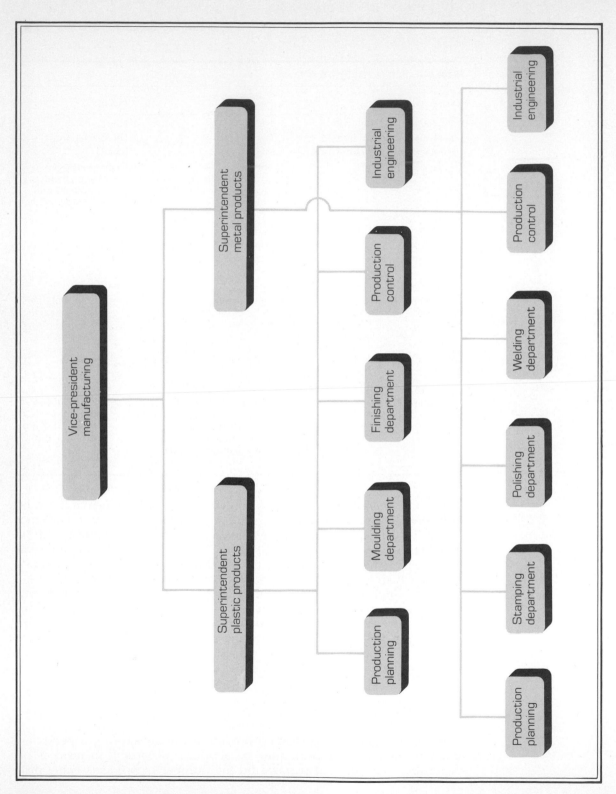

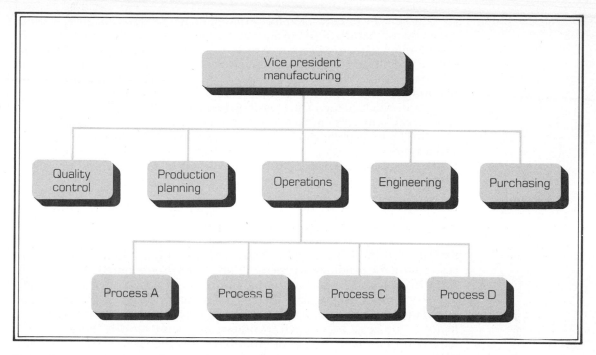

Figure 8.3
Switzer Company—organization for production

duced and the volume of production. A process-organized plant might have a grinding department, buffing department, stamping department, and so on. A product-organized plant might have a ball-point pen department and a mechanical pencil department, each of which is arranged on an assembly-line basis. How machines are related to each other often determines the organizational structure, including the number of persons in each department.

Production Organization Structure

The organization as it relates to production may be on product or on process lines. Sometimes it is a combination of the two. The organization chart for the Dunn-Products Corporation in Figure 8.2 shows such a case in which there are two products, each run by a superintendent. Each product group has two or more processes, each of which is in a separate department. This firm is decentralized in that each product organization has production planning, production control, and industrial engineering departments.

Figure 8.2
Dunn-Products Corporation—organization for production

The specific organization for production in a firm may be heavily influenced by the nature of the production process, as we discussed earlier in this chapter. The number and variety of products will also have a major effect. The Switzer Company produces small amounts of twenty different products at different times of the year. This is the reason that production planning, control, and engineering will be centralized. If the twenty products go through many of the same processes, A, B, C, and D, the organization may appear as in Figure 8.3 on page 263.

Other special organization problems are forced on a firm when it grows and acquires competing or unrelated manufacturing firms. Deciding what can be combined, whether to remain decentralized, and solving related problems may require experimentation.

Staffing and Directing for Production

Staffing and directing together represent the application of the human resource to the production process. Staffing for production is often complicated by the need for highly specialized personnel. More extensive searching processes must be used than in many other kinds of business. The alternative is a long and expensive training program. Another complicating factor is the large role played by unions in manufacturing industries. Labour contracts often restrict or limit personnel managers in the processes of hiring, transferring, and promotion, as well as in job assignments and in setting up working conditions.

A production manager must cope with the fact that machines, their timing, their coordination, and their very high costs determine how the production process is carried out. This includes determining the relationship between jobs, the span of control of supervisors, and other factors which must influence the kind of direction a supervisor can give.

The Human Dimension in Production

A classic problem in organizing a factory is that of combining the human resource with huge capital investments without losing human enthusiasm for work, as the following situation shows. John Bivona's job is to press the green button every time the red light lights up in the boiler room. It is hard for John to see his role in the productive process. This kind of job presents a real challenge to the production manager to make full use of John's ability. Machines can reduce the "humanity" of an organization when they seem to "tell a person what to do."

A related problem is conflict in the assignment of activities among work groups. Introduction of new technology in the plant may cause work to be distributed in a new way. What the machines "dictate" is not necessarily accepted by workers or by their unions. In organizing a factory, traditional labour union definitions of job responsibility—what kind of work a worker can or cannot do in the production process—cannot be overlooked. Nor can a manager ignore provincial health and safety regulations.

It is easier to motivate workers to outproduce co-workers than to motivate them to operate at the pace dictated by a machine. How does a manager set a wage rate which all the workers think is fair when the principal contributor to productivity is a machine? Also, many production workers fear that automation will put them out of work. This makes it hard to motivate them, especially when their unions oppose automation.

In such situations, harmony is hard to achieve. It may be done by means of cooperation between labour and management. Both sides can agree that greater productivity is good for all. If automation can bring about greater productivity and management can assure the labour unions and their members that workers will share fairly in this increased productivity, a good working relationship can be built. It takes planning to prepare for the period of change to automation. This planning includes worker retraining and relocation and other guarantees of security for those workers most affected. Wage rates will rise because workers expect to share in the benefits of increased productivity.

Controlling Production

Controlling production involves setting production standards and developing systems for comparing production performance to those standards. These are several different types of production control. They include

- order control
- product quality control
- plant maintenance control
- inventory control

Order Control and Scheduling

When a plant is engaged in continuous, high-volume production of standard products, close control of individual orders is not very important. But in those plants using intermittent production, it is vital to create systems to control the flow of orders. New orders that have never been processed before must be checked to see what operations must be performed. They must be checked for correct sequence and to see that the right tools are on hand. This may require use of a control chart. **A control chart is a device which shows the standard set of steps to be taken in the performance of a procedure.** It ensures that things will be done as planned. Control charts were first conceived by Henry Gantt in the early 1900s, and today a wide variety of commercial variations of Gantt charts are available. (See Figure 8.4.)

Plants that produce a variety of products on an intermittent basis establish a system of *decision rules* to guide the movement of orders through various manufacturing processes. Suppose there is a question: Which of two orders should be processed first by a given machine? It is not always logical to say that the order with the earliest due date should be processed first. Some firms use a simple "first-come, first-served" rule; others use a "first-come, first-served within priority class" rule for making decisions. Which rule is best depends on the kind of processing going on in the plant. Regardless, some form of decision rule is necessary in intermittent-process

control chart

266

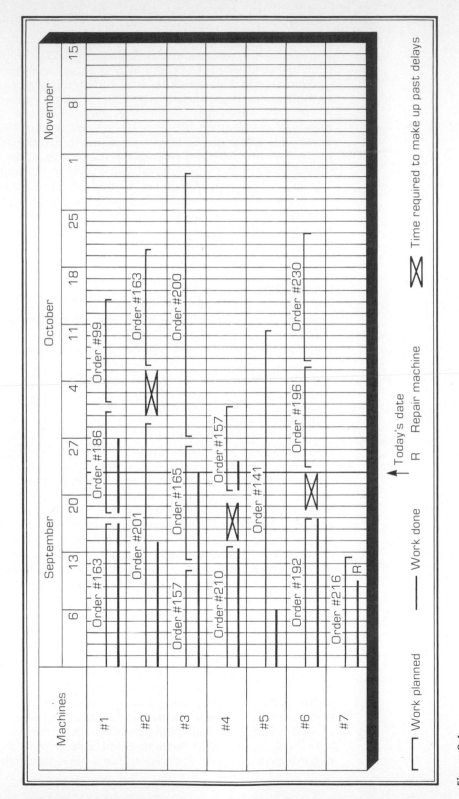

Figure 8.4
A Gantt chart

Figure 8.5
A CPM diagram for constructing a small warehouse

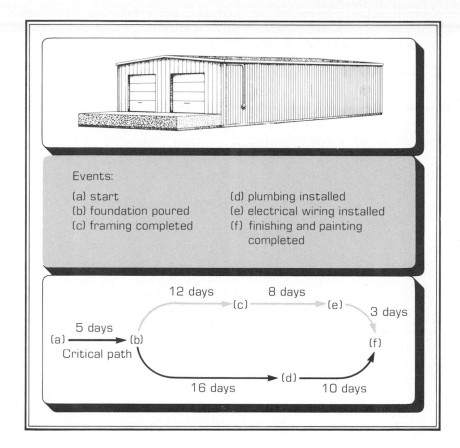

Events:

(a) start
(b) foundation poured
(c) framing completed

(d) plumbing installed
(e) electrical wiring installed
(f) finishing and painting completed

production to guarantee a smooth flow. In recent years, computer simulation techniques have been used to speed up production.

Important tools used in order to assure a smooth scheduling of operations include PERT (Program Evaluation and Review Technique) and CPM (Critical Path Method). **PERT is a planning and control tool focusing on the timing of the occurrence of many operations included in a project.** It helps identify and remove bottlenecks. This tool was first applied by the government to speed up completion of vital weapons systems.

A CPM diagram is illustrated in Figure 8.5. **CPM is much like PERT except that specific estimates rather than variable estimates of elapsed time in operations are used.** Wetherall Utility Buildings plans construction of a standard 20,000-square-foot warehouse by listing the major stages of construction, the time needed for each, and the sequence in which they occur. The letters in parentheses are events. The order of events is indicated by arrows. *Branching* occurs whenever two events can be worked on at the same time. The numbers next to arrow-segments show how many days are needed. A manager can follow a "path" to completion and can tell which chain of events is the longest or "critical" path (ABDF in our example). It is this chain of events that the manager must focus on to cut production time or to avoid delays. This is because if any activity on the critical path exceeds

PERT

CPM

the estimated time, the whole project will be delayed by that amount of time. In addition, if activities not on the critical path are extended beyond the slack time, they may cause the critical path to change.

Order control systems must include rapid communication systems, such as special mail service or teletypes or even direct feedback to a central computer. They help management to take action quickly enough to correct flaws in the operation. This is the essence of control.

Product Quality Control

quality control

Clearly, there is a need to control the movements of orders through a production process. There is also a need for quality control. **A quality control system sets up a standard for an input or output and makes comparisons against this standard to prevent nonstandard items from going into or coming out of the production process.** This, however, does not necessarily mean that quality must be kept high. It means that the level of quality must be known and checked so that it can be kept within a certain range of acceptable quality standards. Obviously, a manufacturer does not always seek to avoid high quality. Lower quality, however, may be acceptable when higher quality control would be too costly. A firm may seek a quality level far below what could be achieved.

The Good Time Corporation makes children's outdoor play products. It produces a backyard slide selling for $19.95. The production manager has specified an inexpensive rust-resistant galvanized nut-and-bolt for fastening the slide's major parts. These nuts-and-bolts sell for one cent apiece in large quantities. The manager could have specified chrome-plated nuts-and-bolts costing eight cents apiece and have been able to guarantee against rust. But customers paying $19.95 for a backyard slide just don't expect chrome-plated parts, so the added cost is unjustified. This does not mean, however, that the production manager would accept even cheaper, lower-quality bolts than the ones selected just to reduce costs by a fraction of a cent. They might cause the slide to fall apart, and the firm would lose its reputation as a maker of good, low-priced play equipment.

What constitutes an acceptable range of quality standards? The range is very narrow for firms in the pharmaceutical, nuclear, aircraft, and genetic engineering industries, but it is much broader for firms that make nails, garbage cans, and household furniture. Determining the proper quality levels in service firms can be very difficult. How does a customer know whether a lawyer, doctor, accountant, or architect has rendered a service where the quality is equal to the price? While there are professional groups in each province that deal with issues like this, many consumers have the perception that these groups simply protect their members, not consumers.

Some firms traditionally insist on buying the highest quality materials available and telling about it in their advertising. For example, some firms advertise that they could reduce their costs by using cheaper ingredients but say that that would hurt their reputation for quality. There is little doubt that a lot of the success of Japanese car makers is due to the image they have created for using strict quality control standards.

Quality standards may also vary within a firm. A manufacturer of canned foods is likely to exercise great care to ensure the highest quality for products it sells under its own brand. For those it sells as unbranded or generic products, meeting the minimum government standards for quality may be enough. Kitchenaid sets higher standards for its top-of-the-line dishwasher than for its bottom-of-the-line model.

It is almost impossible to guarantee 100 percent quality of all inputs and finished products. Ordinarily, this would be too expensive. Most manufacturers, therefore, use sampling in quality control inspection. Thus a bicycle manufacturer's purchasing department may require that a sample of fifty 20-foot sections be examined whenever a shipment of steel tubing arrives. Instructions might require that a shipment be accepted if no more than one defective section is found in the sample. This is called acceptance sampling. In certain types of production, of course, a 100 percent inspection is necessary because the sale of even one faulty unit could have very serious results.

The basis for classifying a unit as defective depends on what features of the unit are "critical." For steel tubing, perhaps hardness and strength are important. Applying these standards may require mechanical assistance or perhaps it can be done visually. Welds, for example, may be examined visually or by using X rays, as was done for the Alaskan pipeline. A variety of measuring and testing machines exist in industry today. Often, however, a simple visual inspection is sufficient. A balance is needed between the cost of inspection and the cost of failure to meet standards.

Quality control applies to the inputs, processes, and output of manufacturing and service firms. A bicycle company, for example, buys tires, tubes, and handle grips from a rubber supply company in large lots. These inputs are inspected upon arrival to see if they meet specifications (standards of quality). During the process of manufacture, welded joints of

WHAT DO YOU THINK?

How Much Quality Should Be Built into a Product?

You have probably heard some people complain about the "low quality" of the products they have bought. Perhaps you have made the same complaint. These complaints mean that customers are not really satisfied with their purchases.

Take a car muffler, for example. If Midas Muffler can make a muffler that is guaranteed to last as long as you own your car, why don't the car manufacturers install them as original equipment on new cars?

What about an electric percolator for making coffee? The top-of-the-line models usually last longer than the cheaper versions. The manufacturers know this, but they still make cheap versions. They defend this by saying that a lot of consumers want the cheap model—"and they get what they pay for."

Decisions about product quality are not easy decisions to make. But they are very important decisions, and they are becoming even more crucial in the age of consumerism. This means that production and marketing activities must be closely coordinated because the consumer's image of the company is very much affected by the quality of the company's product. How much quality should be built into a product? WHAT DO YOU THINK?

the bicycle frame are inspected and the braking assembly is tested. After the entire bicycle is assembled, it is lubricated and "test-driven" for a quarter of a mile. These tests cost money, but they help build the company's reputation for quality. In a management consulting firm, the personnel department screens applicants (inputs) based on corporate policies. During the preparation of consulting reports, several individuals read them to give a balanced view. Once completed, the reports are given to the client and are discussed.

Maintenance and the Control of Plant and Equipment

In a manufacturing plant—particularly a continuous-process, assembly-line plant—one critical machine breakdown means high costs. During this "downtime" most of the other machinery is idled, and all the workers on the line are being paid even though their machines are idle.

preventive maintenance

This points up the need for maintenance. **Many firms practise preventive maintenance. This means that they inspect and/or replace certain critical machines and parts on a regular basis to avoid downtime.** Not all firms practise preventive maintenance, however. It may cost more than a firm is willing to pay. The units may be very expensive to replace. Also, the cost of interrupting the production process for maintenance work may be too high. Some production managers prefer to "leave well enough alone." They install the highest-quality equipment to start with. This decision is a matter of balancing costs.

Control of Inventory Levels

A fourth area of production control is the control of inventory levels. This includes inventories of raw materials, parts, and finished and partly finished goods.

There are some good reasons for keeping high levels of inventory. A firm is less likely to "run out" of parts and partly finished goods where assembly-line production is employed. Running out of inventory can mean expensive downtime. This also applies to finished goods. Big orders (and possibly big customers) can be lost if deliveries cannot be promised. Large stocks protect against this.

There are some equally good reasons for keeping inventories low, however. First, inventories require an investment of funds. A factory which operates with a lower inventory is operating more efficiently—that is, it is producing profits with a smaller investment than a factory with large inventories. Second, inventories take up scarce space. Third, goods in inventory may decrease in value because of deterioration, theft, or damage.

obsolescence

Inventory goods also may be subject to obsolescence. This is what happens when something is out-of-date or not as efficient as newer products. New inputs or new finished goods may be invented or found which would make inventories obsolete. Many firms are now keeping as little inventory as possible. This has been partly caused by the impact of the Japanese "just-in-time" inventory philosophy. As the name suggests, inventory is scheduled to arrive just-in-time to be used in the production process. This cuts inventory storage costs and therefore the total cost of the product declines.

Some firms use mathematical formulas to determine the best inventory levels to maintain. These formulas include such things as order loss risks, storage costs, interest, expected delivery time, and other factors. They also aid in determining the best quantity to order and the time interval between orders.

As we will see in our discussion of accounting in Chapter 11, there are other important control devices relating to production costs. These include cost systems and various budgeting devices.

PRODUCTION AND ECOLOGY

Many production processes cause problems of ecological balance in the areas where a product is produced and consumed. Extracting coal by strip mining has sometimes caused long-lasting environmental damage. The use of aluminum and glass containers for certain consumer products has created a solid waste disposal problem. This has brought unsightly litter to our cities and countryside. The manufacturing process itself has poured smoke into our air and poisonous wastes into our waters. A certain type of aerosol may pose a threat to the ozone belt, which protects us from deadly rays. Our most modern nuclear power plants are viewed by significant numbers of people as dangerous.

For years our factories have made only limited use of waste materials and by-products. They have used these materials only where there was obvious profit in it. There are many recyclable inputs which have little dollar value but which should be recycled for the sake of our ecological balance. The government is setting new standards, and it is up to production management to do its work within the new limits at a cost which will permit the sale of products at competitive prices.

A growing number of firms are burning trash like pallets, crates, sawdust, and waste paper to heat buildings. After labour and raw materials, energy is the third largest cost of doing business for many firms, and energy costs have been rising much faster than labour and raw materials costs. Firms that burn waste products to generate energy not only reduce their energy costs — they also reduce their disposal costs.

The effect of business on the environment is discussed in detail in Chapter 17.

MATERIALS MANAGEMENT

All of the variety of materials purchased by a firm — including raw materials, partly finished products, finished products, supplies, and capital goods — require a special managerial effort. These products must be purchased (or made), physically handled, and stored. Capital goods also need to be maintained in working order.

In a business organization it is important that materials are available in the right quantity at the right time and place. **A Materials Requirements** Materials Requirements **Planning (MRP) system shows which parts and materials will be**
Planning (MRP)

needed in a finished product and then calculates when the orders for these parts should be placed. Because many detailed calculations are needed in MRP, the system is generally computerized, especially for companies that have a large number of different products.

MRP is designed to improve the materials management aspect of production management. It is most useful for companies using mass production methods with high volume output. Companies that have installed MRP systems usually find that inventory levels can be reduced, parts and materials are ordered more accurately, and customer demands are better served. Overall, MRP helps companies keep track of the large number of parts that are needed to build products that customers want.

The most highly developed managerial activity in dealing with materials — one which often requires setting up a special department — is purchasing.

THE PURCHASING TASK

The purchasing task can have a critical effect on profitability for manufacturers, retailers, and wholesalers. In manufacturing, this is especially true when materials and parts are a major part of total manufacturing cost. Many firms establish a separate purchasing department with its own manager. Many large purchasing departments have divisions which specialize in specific types of purchases and divisions for records management and follow-up.

A typical large manufacturing firm must buy fuels, cleaning supplies, lumber, sheet steel, dyes, handtools, nails, electronic calculators, stationery, electrical equipment, paint, food for the company canteen trucks, and many other items. They must stay ahead of these needs by locating adequate sources of supply and actually buying the products.

Sources must be adequate in terms of volume, delivery schedules, and quality levels. The purchasing department must be in constant contact with their suppliers' sales offices to keep up with their pricing policies, new product features, and delivery schedules.

Many firms, especially large ones, practise centralized purchasing rather than allowing individual departments and divisions to make their own purchases. This can result in cost savings from large-volume buying, greater coordination of purchasing and receiving functions, and a more uniform application of standard purchase specifications.

Depending on the nature of the good or service, the purchasing department may provide different types of advice and perform different types of services. When specialized and expensive machinery is needed, the purchasing department must work closely with the production manager whose department will use it.

Often, finance, purchasing, production, and engineering people work together to develop a list of specifications for the equipment and to plan for its financing and procurement. This team approach is helpful in make-or-buy decisions, and it ensures that the right machine will be bought. The production manager alone might specify higher quality than is actually

CAREERS IN OPERATIONS MANAGEMENT

IF YOU LIKE THE IDEA OF WORKING IN OPERATIONS, THERE ARE A WIDE variety of jobs available. They require a wide range of skills and education. We will describe a few.

Purchasing agents, also called industrial buyers, are responsible for maintaining an adequate supply of materials, supplies, or equipment. Their work includes buying goods and services, market forecasting, production planning, and inventory control. In a large firm or government agency, purchasing agents usually specialize in one or more specific commodities. There are no universal educational requirements for entry-level purchasing jobs. Most big organizations, however, require a college degree, especially for promotion into a managerial position. Information is available from the Purchasing Management Association of Canada, 80 Richmond Street, W., Toronto, Ontario M5H 2A4.

Inspectors are needed in every manufacturing operation. They can enter with little technical training and learn on the job. Persons who work well with numbers and measurement, who value accuracy, and who are not afraid of performing repetitive tasks may want such a career. Those who perform well may be promoted to jobs as skilled inspectors or quality control technicians. Opportunities exist in this type of job despite increasing use of automated inspection systems. For further information you might contact the Society for Quality Control, 161 West Wisconsin Avenue, Milwaukee, Wisconsin 53202.

Traffic managers are also needed in manufacturing and wholesaling. They are responsible for physical movement of goods to their destination. They are experts on rates, schedules, and availability of alternative modes of transportation. University graduates make up an increasing proportion of traffic managers. Skills needed are similar to those of purchasing agents. For additional information contact the Canadian Institute of Traffic and Transportation, 44 Victoria Street, Suite 2120, Toronto, Ontario M5C 1Y2.

Industrial engineers determine the most effective ways for an organization to use the basic factors of production—people, machines, and materials. They are more concerned with people and methods of business organization than are engineers in other specialties. To solve organizational, production, and related problems, industrial engineers design data processing systems and apply mathematical concepts (operations research techniques). They develop and conduct plant location surveys; design production planning and control systems; and design or improve systems for the physical distribution of goods and services. Automation is one factor operating to increase the demand for industrial engineers. ∎

needed. If the finance department were to make the decision on its own, perhaps quality would be compromised in order to save money. The team objective is to get the level of quality needed by the using department at the best price. This requires a systems approach to decision making in which the overall welfare of the firm is the guiding principle.

For less expensive items the purchasing department assumes a larger role. For items such as paper clips, the purchasing department makes its own price and quality decisions. Most routine purchases are handled in this way.

Purchasing Policies

Over time, firms usually develop standard purchasing policies. For example, some follow a policy of building up inventories when prices are right. The purchasing agent is a "professional purchaser" who generally has a very good idea of when prices are right. For example, the purchasing agent for an art supply company is in constant contact with several suppliers of quality natural bristle for artists' paintbrushes. He or she buys only when prices are down because storage costs and product deterioration are not a problem. If this purchasing agent received notice and samples of a large shipment available immediately from South Korea at a 20 percent price reduction, he or she might order a one- or two-year supply, particularly if the agent had previously had satisfactory dealings with the selling firm.

Some purchasing agents follow a policy of concentrating all their purchases for a specific good or service with one supplier. This is often because that supplier's past performance has been excellent. Other purchasing agents avoid this for fear of "being taken for granted" or "putting all their eggs in one basket." A strike, for example, at a supplier's plant may place the buyer firm in a bad position.

Other policies deal with such matters as taking discounts offered by suppliers. If a supplier offers a cumulative quantity discount, all purchases made during a certain period are subject to a discount based on the total volume purchased during that period. This builds buyer loyalty but probably reduces the average size of orders. A noncumulative discount probably leads to larger orders but may not do much to develop customer loyalty.

Some firms follow a policy of leasing equipment rather than purchasing it whenever possible. Leasing often offers a tax advantage because lease payments are deductible business expenses. It also shifts part of the risk of equipment obsolescence to the lessor and ties up less of the lessee's capital. Just as firms face "make-or-buy" decisions, they also face "buy-or-lease" decisions. You could lease a truck from Ryder Truck Rental, for example, rather than buy it.

reciprocity **A common purchasing policy involves reciprocity — "you buy from me and I'll buy from you."** Reciprocity is widely practised by industrial marketers and buyers. It makes buyer and seller interdependent and it guarantees the seller a customer but limits the sources of supply. It may also cause buyers to become too lazy in their search for "the best quality at the lowest price."

The purchasing function is being handled increasingly by professionals. Two tools that are receiving growing attention are value analysis and vendor analysis.

Value Analysis

value analysis

Value analysis starts by reviewing existing product specifications as set by user departments. Attention then focuses on identifying and eliminating nonessential cost factors. This review may involve a committee including engineers, cost accountants, production representatives, and others. They review the specifications set by the user department. Wherever a specification is thought to add unnecessary cost, the function of that "spec" is examined to see if it can be eliminated or if a cheaper way of doing it can be found. Such a review requires close contact with potential vendors to verify cost.

Value analysis has played a big role in the auto industry, especially after it showed that parts made from fibreglass-reinforced plastic could be substituted for steel parts in many cases. This helped to reduce a car's weight and decreased fuel consumption.

Careful investigation of the costs of alternative input components can lead to significant savings. However, a value-analysis decision of this type cannot omit consideration of whether the product will significantly lose quality.

Vendor Analysis

vendor analysis

Vendor analysis evaluates and rates the technical, financial, and managerial abilities of potential suppliers in terms of their past performance. It is a method of substituting facts for feelings in the selection of suppliers.

When a purchasing department has made its analysis of possible suppliers, it is in a position to sign a contract. It makes a decision and sends a purchase order to the supplier. Some purchasing departments, however, invite sellers to submit bids. In some cases, the buyer elects to award the purchase contract to the lowest bidder. This competitive bidding requires that the buyer specify in detail what it is which he or she wants to purchase.

WHAT DO YOU THINK?

Should Purchasing Agents Accept Favours?

The purchasing agent is the firm's professional buyer. He or she is a very important person as far as salespeople are concerned. That is why purchasing agents often receive "special favours" from salespeople who want to sell to them. Christmas gifts, free "samples" for the purchasing agent's personal use, and other "favours" are not uncommon.

Is it unethical for purchasing agents to accept "favours" and for salespersons to offer them? WHAT DO YOU THINK?

CAREER PROFILE

MY NAME IS DAVID RABB AND I AM secretary-treasurer of Washtronics, Ltd. We are a custom manufacturer of maintenance and service equipment for transit buses. This includes equipment for washing public transit vehicles, bus interior cleaning equipment, water reclaiming systems, and portable bus hoists.

Our company originally started in the car-wash business. Because we experienced considerable equipment breakdown, we started to manufacture some of our own car-wash equipment. Gradually we expanded this activity until we were selling equipment to other car-washing companies. This continued for several years, but increased competition in that field made us look into other areas.

We decided to begin manufacturing bus-washing equipment, and we applied the basic principles we had learned in manufacturing car-washing equipment. There was, however, considerable experimentation necessary, because car-wash equipment cannot be used for buses without considerable modification. As a result of this experimentation we were the first manufacturer to develop a system that could wash the front, back, and sides of a bus automatically, and we were also the first to develop an automatic, conveyorized bus-washing system.

In other cases, specifications are not so exact, and bids received are subject to further buyer-seller negotiation over price and quality. Bids, however, are not used in all cases. The buyer might contact and deal with only one supplier.

A purchasing department is also accountable for following up purchases already made. Elaborate file systems are used to ensure that deliveries are made on time. This includes the follow-up on transportation details and expected delivery dates. A final responsibility is for the physical receipt of goods. This involves checking contents against invoices before giving approval to the accounting department to make payment.

The production cycle in our business is as follows: First, city transit systems across North America send out specifications on jobs, and we bid on them. If we win the bid, the materials requirements for the job are given to the purchasing agent. The purchasing agent consults with the shop foreman and checks our stock to see if we can use the materials we have on hand. Next, a job number is assigned and then the actual building of the parts is done. To do this work, our machine shop is organized into various sections with lathes, drill presses, painting equipment, metal-cutting machines, and so on, each having its own area. In most cases, we wait until an order comes in before we begin manufacturing, so we do not store very much in inventory.

There are several aspects of our business that cause problems. The major problem is caused by the custom nature of our work. When a city decides to build a transit bus garage, it will hire an engineering firm to design a building that will accommodate the various maintenance and service functions that need to be done on buses. These engineering groups often ask us for advice on how to set up a building so that the maintenance and service work will be done efficiently. We often spend six months to a year doing background work like this. Unfortunately, when the city chooses which bus-washing equipment it will buy, it often does not feel obliged to buy from us, even though we have lent them considerable expertise in terms of helping to design their buildings. This is very frustrating. We can't charge for our advice because the organizations who buy from us would simply go to someone else who would do it for free. Nor can we refuse to give advice because then we couldn't get the contract.

Another problem is the difficulty in keeping good staff. In a custom business like ours there are many ups and down in production. If no orders come in, nothing is produced. It is at these low points when it is difficult to keep good staff. To try to counteract this, we are always on the alert for products that will have steady demand and that can be mass produced. Recently we began manufacturing portable bus-lifting equipment; the demand for this is much more like the demand for automobiles.

There are many rewards in this business. Even though there is intense competition in the industry, opportunities still exist for creative, innovative firms that keep alert for the kinds of equipment that transit companies need. Satisfying these needs creates profit opportunities for our company.

Perhaps the major reward is the feeling of satisfaction I get from having done something efficiently. In a custom business like ours, it is important to keep control of accounts receivable, inventory, the price of raw materials, and so forth. If these are watched closely, a very effective business will be the result. Generally our percentage return on gross sales is much higher than most manufacturing firms; we are able to do this because we are so efficient.

SUMMARY AND LOOK AHEAD

Production creates goods and services by a variety of processes out of human and material inputs. The management of such a process begins with the planning of the product, the plant, and its location. Production includes special organizational and staffing problems related to the impact of technology. It requires the application of a variety of control devices to assure uniformity of quality of output and efficient production scheduling.

Purchasing, we have seen, has evolved into a science in itself. Centralized purchasing departments develop purchasing policies and procedures to help assure that the firm gets goods and services of required quality at a minimum price.

The mountain of products and services generated by a giant production system demand an ingenious marketing effort to move them into Canadian markets. Financing a manufacturing plant and its related facilities is also a complex undertaking which requires up-to-date accounting methods. Computers are needed to support the production, finance, accounting, and marketing. All of these will be examined in the next few chapters. Marketing is the first to be examined. It is such a large subject that we will devote two chapters to it. The first chapter is an overview of the marketing task. ∎

QUESTIONS FOR REVIEW AND DISCUSSION

1. Who was Frederick W. Taylor? Check an encyclopaedia. Do you agree with his philosophy of management and work?
2. Distinguish between production management and operations management.
3. Does continuous production or intermittent production justify larger capital expenditure? Why?
4. To locate a plant near suppliers but far away from customers would imply what about the nature of inputs and outputs and their transportation costs?
5. Give one example of how a Gantt chart may be used.
6. Distinguish between production organization along product lines and along process lines.
7. Does production management have human relations problems not found in financial or marketing management? Explain.
8. Consult Fraser's *Canadian Trade Directory* and give a brief description of its contents.
9. What is reciprocity? Is it a sound basis for purchase decisions? Why or why not?
10. What are the pros and cons of centralized purchasing?
11. What is the essential idea of value analysis?
12. Give an example of the use of operations management in the control of the quality of hamburgers at a McDonald's restaurant.
13. Develop a detailed example of the inputs, process(es), and output(s) of a plant in your town. What would happen to the process and output if one input were not available?
14. Draw a simple CPM chart, modifying the example in your text. Identify the critical path. In what sense is it critical?
15. Find a real-life example of buying on a bidding basis and discuss the advantages of this to the buyer.

INCIDENTS

The Bake-Loc Company

The Bake-Loc Company is about to choose a location for its new factory. With help from the accounting, production, and marketing experts, Don Kaczmarek, head of the expansion committee, has come up with cost comparisons. They have narrowed the choice down to the cities of

Saskatoon and Winnipeg because they are nearest to the market not presently being served. The sales and cost estimates are shown below.

	Saskatoon	Winnipeg
Estimated annual sales in units	80,000	120,000
Selling price	$ 5.00	$ 5.00
Cost of materials	1.10	1.20
Labour	1.20	1.40
Average transportation to market	1.30	1.10
Taxes	.60	.80
Other costs	.20	.20
Total costs per unit	$ 4.40	$ 4.70
Net profit per unit	.60	.30
Expected total annual profit	$48,000	$ 36,000

Questions:
1. Which city is the better choice? Why?
2. What assumptions are necessary to reach a conclusion in Question 1?
3. How would you answer if estimated sales in Saskatoon were 60,000 units? How would you answer if taxes in Winnipeg were 30 cents per unit?

The Parkins Corporation

The offer came from Lister Industrial Supplies and was being discussed by top management at the Parkins Corporation. Lister's offer was as follows: To provide the requirements of Parkins' plant for tools, cleaning supplies, and lubricants. (These represented 6 percent of Parkins' total annual costs.) They offered a 10 percent discount for an exclusive one-year arrangement.

With costs in general rising rapidly, and profits slipping, Parkins' management is seriously considering the offer. Recent purchasing history showed that the service and quality of products provided by five suppliers (including Lister) to Parkins was quite satisfactory.

Questions:
1. What are the principal advantages and disadvantages of the Lister offer?
2. How would you advise Parkins' management in this case? Should they make a counter-offer to Lister? Discuss.

CASE STUDY

KELVIN FURNITURE

KELVIN FURNITURE, LTD. BEGAN OPERATIONS IN 1971 AS A CUSTOM manufacturer of office furniture. The company manufactured wood, plastic, and steel furniture in a one-storey, 10,000-square-foot plant located in Edmonton. Production activity did not start until an order was received; once an order was received, the materials necessary were assembled, and the relevant machinery (welders, metal cutters, sanders, drill presses, etc.) was scheduled.

The company quickly developed a reputation for high-quality work, and by the early 1980s demand was increasing substantially in spite of the sharp downturn in the economy. John Kelvin, the president, began to realize that success and growth can create serious problems. Both the production equipment and the plant size were clearly inadequate to cope with the firm's increasing business. Production workers (now numbering about thirty) complained that the cramped space in the factory did not allow them to do their job safely and properly. In addition, the number and variety of orders were so large that the firm was two weeks behind schedule on deliveries. Equipment was rapidly "falling apart," despite good maintenance and supervision by Mark Sherrell, the assistant production manager. Sherrell argued that a new plant was essential, and after some discussion with Kelvin, they agreed to call in a consulting architect to design it.

Looking ahead at what Kelvin expected to be the future production level of various products, the seasonal factors, and the chances of obsolescence, the architects and Kelvin agreed on a one-level, 60,000-square-foot plant with nine "shops," or processing areas, as well as office, inspection, packaging, shipping, and receiving areas. The nine processing areas included painting, wood assembly, plastic moulding, metal stamping, and five other areas. Each was capable of performing one of the major production processes for one or more of the three types of furniture produced—wood, metal, and plastic.

A site was selected near Calgary with access to major highways. The site was also close to suppliers of some of Kelvin's parts and raw materials. When this became known, some differences of opinion arose among Kelvin's managers about the move. Some argued that moving the plant to Calgary would create great morale problems among their loyal production workers who disliked moving. Finding replacements in Calgary would, at least in the short run, cause lots of problems, and further inhibit the company's attempt to reduce the order backlog. Both workers and managers expressed concern about how their work might be different in the new facility.

Questions:

1. Classify some of the production processes at Kelvin according to the process classifications discussed in the text.
2. Do you agree with the kind of plant arrangement worked out by the architects? Why or why not?
3. Can you think of any alternatives to building a new plant? Explain.
4. What are the criteria for site selection that were not mentioned in the case?
5. How should John Kelvin deal with the concerns being expressed by managers and employees? How could problems like this have been prevented? ■

CASE STUDY*

KRISTIANSEN CYCLE ENGINES LTD. (A)

IN JULY, 1981, HAAKON (PRONOUNCED HOKEN) KRISTIANSEN, the founder of Kristiansen Cycle Engines Ltd. (K-Cycle Ltd.), faced an interesting situation. In June, 1981, an arrangement was about to be completed which raised $8 million (U.S.). The money was to be used to finance a research and development program aimed at bringing an agricultural and industrial application of the K-Cycle engine to the stage of commercialization by 1985. The challenge was to select and successfully implement the most appropriate means to move toward commercialization.

THE K-CYCLE ENGINE

The K-Cycle engine is based upon a new thermodynamic cycle. The Engine's power stroke is longer than its intake stroke. It theoretically allows for a significant improvement in brake thermal efficiency (B.T.E.). B.T.E. is defined as the ratio of the useful work output of an engine to the heat value of the fuel supplied. It was felt that the improvement in thermal efficiency should enable a 40 to 50 percent improvement in fuel economy (see Exhibit 1).

The K-Cycle engine is an orbital cylinder, fixed-cam engine whose primary parts are the cylinder rotor and pistons. The rotor resembles the cartridge chamber of a revolver in that the cylinders are arranged parallel to one another so that they orbit the engine axis as the rotor and shaft revolve (see Exhibit 2 on pages 284–285).

This mechanism has secondary benefits in that there is one common combustion zone, utilizing one ignition source rather than the multiple sources in conventional engines. There is a single fuel intake port, dramatically simplifying the manifold and, with fuel injection, the fuel distribution system required. The exhaust manifold is similarly simplified, with only one exhaust port and no need for the complicated branching system in other designs. Internally, the engine does not require a valve train, with the associated cam shafts, lifters, push rods, rocker arms, springs, and valves all incurring wear and mechanical inefficiency.

*This case was prepared by Dr. Brian E. Owen, Professor, Faculty of Administrative Studies, the University of Manitoba. This case was prepared as a basis for classroom discussion only, not to illustrate effective or ineffective handling of an administrative situation. Copyright © 1981, The Faculty of Administrative Studies, The University of Manitoba.

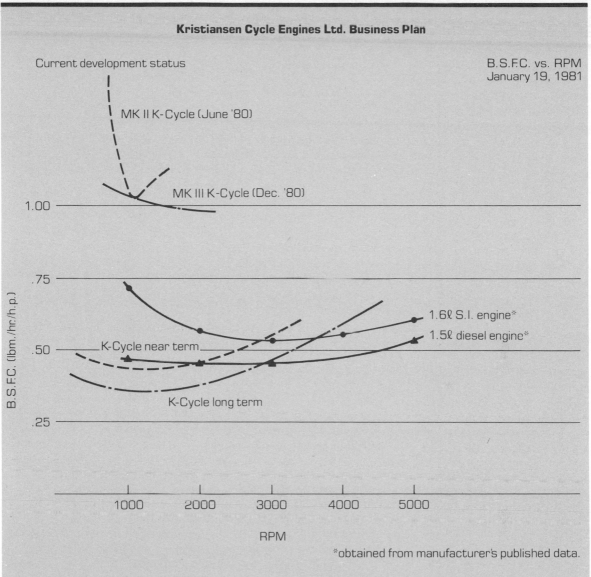

Exhibit 1 Brake specific fuel consumption compared to revolution per minute:
K-Cycle vs. conventional cycles.

   The company believed that, when fully developed, the K-Cycle engine should have the following major benefits when compared to conventional internal combustion Otto and Diesel engines (the Otto cycle is the conventional gasoline internal combustion cycle engine):

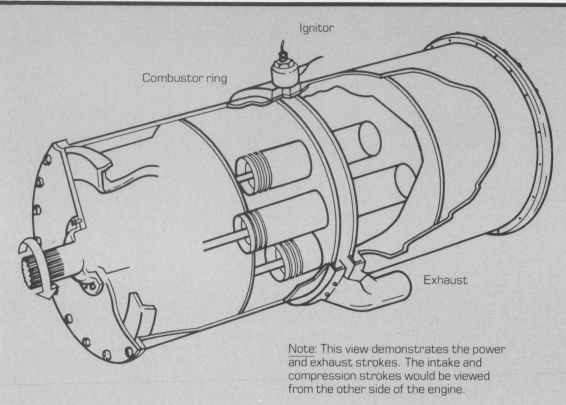

Ignitor

Combustor ring

Exhaust

Note: This view demonstrates the power and exhaust strokes. The intake and compression strokes would be viewed from the other side of the engine.

Exhibit 2   K-Cycle cut-away drawing.

1. Fuel economy—the result of significantly greater thermal efficiency which is achieved by the power stroke being longer than the intake stroke (in conventional engines both strokes are of the same length, so that more of the fuel energy is dissipated into the exhaust rather than converted into useful horsepower). The theoretical efficiency of the K-Cycle engine is 41 percent, compared to 27 percent for the conventional Otto cycle, and 33 percent for the diesel engine.
2. Reduced complexity, size, and weight—the result of using fixed cams instead of a crankshaft system, sliding seals instead of a valve train, and a single ignition location instead of multiple locations.
3. Smooth, quiet operation—the result of one power stroke per cylinder for every revolution, as compared to one power stroke per cylinder for every second revolution in a conventional four-stroke engine.
4. Multi-fuel capability and reduced emissions—the result of continuous combustion made possible by the single ignition location and of controlled combustion made possible by the fixed-cam system.
5. Simplicity of manufacture and servicing—the result of a reduced number of components and interchangeability of parts.

Comparison of thermodynamic cycles

Conventional cycle using a crankshaft

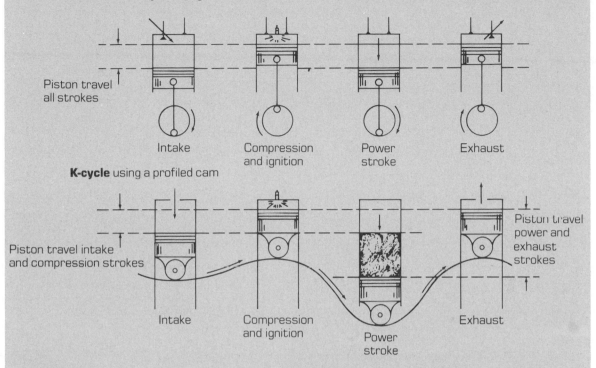

Piston travel
all strokes

| Intake | Compression and ignition | Power stroke | Exhaust |

K-cycle using a profiled cam

Piston travel intake
and compression strokes

Piston travel
power and
exhaust
strokes

| Intake | Compression and ignition | Power stroke | Exhaust |

Exhibit 2 (continued)

BACKGROUND

Haakon Kristiansen first conceived the concept of the K-Cycle in 1959. At the time Mr. Kristiansen, a Canadian engineer of Norwegian origin, was working in Manitoba as a Design and Development Engineer for Bristol Aerospace Ltd. In 1968 he became Director of Engineering and Quality Control at Midwest Airlines (later Transair Ltd.). In 1974 Mr. Kristiansen obtained the capital from several Manitoba individuals with which to found Kristiansen Cycle Engines Ltd. Since then, he had devoted himself to building a development team and the actual development of the K-Cycle engine and its related technology.

With the completion of the first prototype K-Cycle engine, the MK I, in 1977, the company made its initial public offering of common stock. By December 31, 1980, two further stock issues had been made, and the company had constructed four K-Cycle engines. Two of the engines had been installed in a contemporary automobile for road evaluation.

DEVELOPMENT HISTORY OF THE K-CYCLE ENGINE

The following is a brief history of the K-Cycle engine's prototype development:

April 1975	Detailed design work on MK I, K-Cycle engine commenced.
May 1977	MK I first run on own power.
April 1978	MK II operational for testing purposes.
September 1979	MK II installed in automobile.
March 1980	Second MK II operational for assessment of design alternatives.
September 1980	MK III operational for incorporation of design improvements.
November 1980	Second MK II installed in automobile.
December 1980	Single bank engine* operational for testing purposes.

*This engine was built solely for the purpose of research into the combustion dynamics involved in the single combustion chamber feature of the K-Cycle engine.

Testing to July 1981 had brought the engine power to within 20 percent of the near term performance estimate. This was primarily achieved with improvements in combustion and mechanical efficiency. Fuel consumption was expected to be improved with the incorporation of improved combustion chamber configurations using up-to-date combustion technology. Some improvements were in process, and it was felt the near term goal should be reached within two to four months. The near term performance goal was expected to fall short of the ideal or long-term performance, due to the refinements still required in the combustion chamber design and the mechanical efficiency of the mechanism. Although further improvements could be achieved in the short term, it was felt it could take at least six to twenty months to develop optimum designs, manufacture the corresponding hardware, and demonstrate it in the test bed.

Patents Under agreements dated December 17, 1974, and November 12, 1977, the company acquired from Haakon Kristiansen all rights, title, and interests in and to the K-Cycle engine and the patent rights related thereto. In exchange, Hakkon Kristiansen received stock in the company.

The company had been issued internal combustion engine and operating cycle patents in the United States, Canada, The United Kingdom, Iran, Australia, Italy, Japan, and France, which covered the physical configuration of the K-Cycle engine and the thermodynamic cycle of the K-Cycle. Applications were pending for similar patents in Germany, Sweden, the Union of Soviet Socialist Republics, Mexico, Brazil, and Argentina. While the company was also applying for other patents relating to other features of the K-Cycle engine, it was of the opinion that the patents already issued protected the essential features of the K-Cycle engine in those countries where application had been made. It was the opinion of the company's patent counsel, Breneman, Kane and Georges of Washington, D.C., that all fundamental engine designs of the K-Cycle engine were fully protected by broad generic patents issued in the United States, and that the United States patent position had been coordinated with Canadian Patent Counsel and numerous foreign law firms to obtain the best possible protection throughout the world for the engine.

PLANNED TECHNICAL WORK

It was the intention of the company to use the proceeds of the underwriting to finance a research and development program aimed at bringing an agricultural and industrial application of the K-Cycle engine to the stage of commercialization by 1985.

Significant technological advances had already occurred in a number of specific areas related to the projects. These included work in the following areas:

1. the cam and cam follower (piston) mechanisms
2. the cooling system
3. the lubrication system
4. the sliding seal function
5. the single ignition source

In the summer of 1981, development was being directed toward the refinement of the combustion process and in-depth study of the prototype's mechanical efficiency. A three-phase development program was intended (see Exhibit 3 on page 288).

PHASE I Performance Parameter Optimization— Development of full function, including superior fuel economy, but with potentially short-life components. To be accomplished through the use of existing prototypes and simplified one- or two-cylinder test devices to optimize all performance parameters. Combustion technology improvements were being sought. A concern was to ensure that as much of the fuel as possible would combust at the proper time. Work was progressing on this front.

Toward the end of this eighteen-month phase, which was expected to be completed by December 1982 (depending upon the attainment of satisfactory performance levels with the test devices), design a market-oriented engine (MK IV) for reliability testing.

PHASE II Reliability Testing—Development of test-bed reliability for a period of not less than 1,000 operating hours. To be accomplished through test-bed evaluation and development of three MK IV engines. A goal was to at least double the durability of the engine. Durability improvement efforts were to focus on two areas. Experimentation with different materials such as case-hardened steel and aluminum would be undertaken to develop a reciprocating cam mechanism that would work trouble-free. Durability of the sliding seal also had to be improved. Here again, tests with different

K-cycle engines

Description	1981	1982	1983	1984	1985
	J J A S O N D J F M A M J J A S O N D J F M A M J J A S O N D J F M A M J J A S O N D J F M A M				

Month

Phase I

Optimize comb. param.
(existing and new hardware)

Optimize mech. effic.
(existing and new hardware)

Develop fuel injection
and compression ignition

Phase II

Design and manufacture
MK IV engine (qty. 3)

Reliability testing and
development of MK IV

Phase III

Design and manufacture
MK V engine (qty. 6)

Field testing and
product development

Exhibit 3   Project planning schedule.

materials such as refined grain cast-iron running against a steel- or chrome-plated surface were to be undertaken.

Toward the end of this eighteen-month program, which was expected to be completed by December 1983, design would be completed on six field-trial engines (MK V) with all necessary accessories built in.

PHASE III Field Testing—Field testing in target market-related application to a level of reliability of not less than 2,000 operating hours. To be accomplished through testing of the six MK V engines.

During the final year of this twenty-two-month phase, which would complete the research and development, it was anticipated that the company would be working with an engine manufacturer for the production engineering phase of development.

The final production design and testing of individual production components would follow the prototype design and testing stage. At this stage of going from prototype to production the emphasis would be upon reducing component cost, producing the lightest engine possible, and appropriate simplified design for mass production. Mr. Kristiansen noted, "It is possible to have conflicts between the research engineers and production engineers at this stage because their goals are different. It is our intention, however, to have our research engineers form the nucleus of the production engineering team. They will work with engineers from the company or companies licensing our engine. They can also be supplemented by part-time or consulting engineers with necessary specializations."

EXPENDITURES

The estimated costs of the various development phases are indicated below:

	Phase I (June '81–Dec. '82)	Phase II (June '82–Dec. '83)	Phase III (Sept. '83–June '85)	Total
Design	$ 430,000	$ 200,000	$ 200,000	$ 830,000
Engineering	900,000	500,000	500,000	1,900,000
Manufacturing	500,000	600,000	1,600,000	2,700,000
Consulting services	100,000	150,000	300,000	550,000
Testing	800,000	500,000	720,000	2,020,000
Total	$2,730,000	$1,950,000	$3,320,000	$8,000,000

The company believed that $8 million was a realistic budget for the research and development program described above. However, there was provision for an additional $1 million if necessary. The additional $1 million would be available, it was anticipated, because the money raised was in U.S. funds. ■

Section Four

Section 3 described human resources and the production process. Firms are guided in their production activities by what they perceive to be the demands of the marketplace. The process of marketing matches these demands with the firm's production capabilities. The use of resources to produce goods and services depends greatly on marketing.

In Chapter 9 we show how production and marketing are interdependent and how rising income levels affect marketing. We introduce the marketing concept and some basic marketing strategies, and also examine the role of marketing research and the challenge of consumerism.

In Chapter 10 attention is turned to the marketing mix, with special emphasis on the role of the product and its distribution. The different means of bringing products to their point of consumption are described. Promotion and price are also examined. We discuss the complementary relationship between advertising and personal selling. We also examine basic price-setting and its place in the marketing mix. Special attention is given to the marketing of services.

MARKETING MANAGEMENT

1. Illustrate the fact that marketing is a matching process.
2. Explain the role of the consumer in the marketing process.
3. Distinguish among four kinds of utility in a product.
4. Give an example of a marketing mix for a specific product or a service.
5. Show what justifies the existence of middlemen.
6. Describe the principal characteristics of the industrial goods market.
7. Draw up a list of consumer goods and tell which are convenience, shopping, and specialty goods.
8. Compare the strategies of differentiation and market segmentation.
9. Name and explain two different approaches to market research.
10. Describe a case of conspicuous consumption.
11. Find an example in the newspaper of consumerist activity and criticize it from the consumer's and the firm's points of view.

KEY CONCEPTS

In reading the chapter, look for and understand these terms:

marketing	shopping goods
managerial approach to marketing	specialty goods
marketing concept	product differentiation
marketing mix	market segmentation
product	marketing research
price	secondary research
promotion	primary research
distribution	focus group interview
target market	conspicuous consumption
industrial goods	form utility
consumer goods	place utility
middlemen	time utility
convenience goods	ownership utility
	consumerism

CONSIDER THE CAR RENTAL BUSINESS. Hertz dominated the market when Avis entered, but Avis differentiated itself through its advertising slogan—We're number two. We try harder.

Hertz, Avis, and National are major companies in the car rental business. Other firms have managed to make a profit in this business by catering to selected market segments. Budget Rent-A-Car's market research helped it target a segment of customers—the professional core segment—that these three companies had not identified. This segment consists of people who consider travel directions an important part of the service they are buying. Budget, therefore, developed a program to supply its customers with specific preprinted travel directions.

Rent-A-Wreck went into business by appealing to specific market segments with special products. They rent and lease used cars to people who want to pay much lower rates than those charged by firms renting and leasing new cars.

CHAPTER NINE

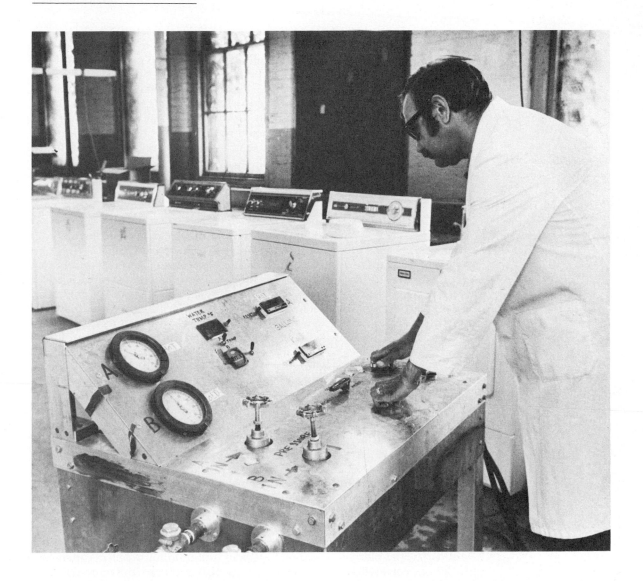

The Marketing Concept

THIS CHAPTER INTRODUCES THE SECOND IMPORTANT AREA OF decision making for firms — marketing. It builds on concepts developed in earlier chapters on economics and management. It also prepares us for the detailed discussion of marketing activities which will be presented in the next chapter. We'll see why a "marketing" orientation has been adopted by many firms and how this is reflected in their approach to the customer. We'll also see the difference between utility creation in production and in marketing and learn about the special interdependence of production and marketing in a high-level economy. At the outset, it will prove helpful to define what is meant by "marketing."

WHAT IS MARKETING?

marketing

Marketing is the set of activities needed to find, build, and serve markets for products and services. It is the performance of activities that are necessary to get goods and services from producer to consumer, and that result in satisfaction to consumers and profit for the company. It often involves finding out what products and services people already need or want and then designing, promoting, and distributing them. Sometimes it involves stimulating new wants, and other times it tries to satisfy established wants. Marketing activities include such things as marketing research, retailing, sales force management, advertising, and transportation.

In order for the marketing function to make a positive contribution to the firm, activities must be well coordinated. The primary formal coordination device is the organization chart (see Figure 9.1). Each specific aspect of the total marketing function must be integrated with others to insure that a coherent set of marketing activities is performed.

If we look at the marketing function from a society-wide perspective, we find that the greater the production ability of a nation or a firm, the more important it becomes to improve its marketing ability. The benefits of production technology are wasted in a free economy if the wrong things are produced or if people don't know about the product or service. It is vital that every firm design a good marketing program to sell what it makes.

Should Marie, a hairdresser from Halifax, open a shop in Vancouver, she would face a serious problem despite her ten years experience in Halifax. The problem is essentially a lack of understanding of the Vancouver market for hairstyling. She could overcome this problem, however, with the right kind of marketing. To succeed in Vancouver, Marie would certainly have to learn a lot about her new market. She would have to find out as

Figure 9.1
Marketing organization for a typical manufacturing firm

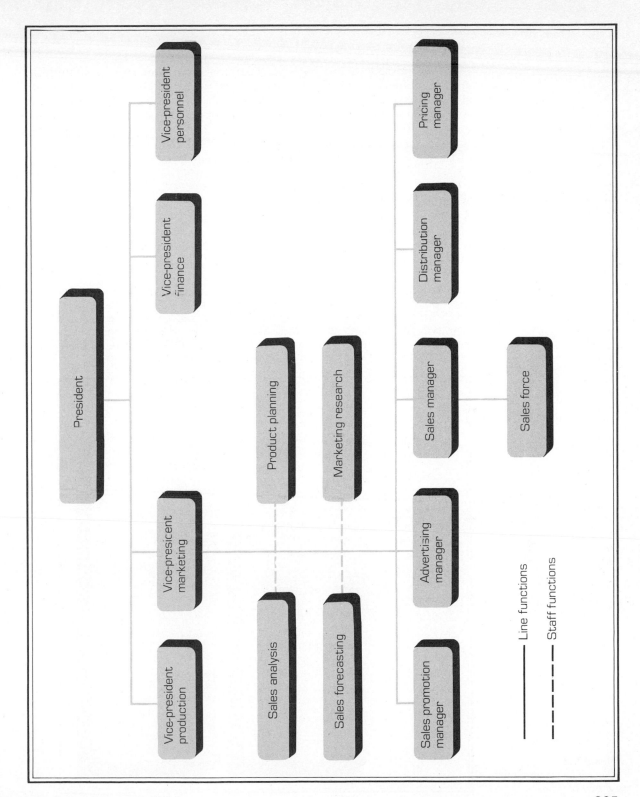

President

Vice-president personnel
Vice-president finance
Vice-president marketing
Vice-president production

Product planning
Marketing research
Sales analysis
Sales forecasting

Pricing manager
Distribution manager
Sales manager
Advertising manager
Sales promotion manager

Sales force

——— Line functions
----- Staff functions

much as possible about hairstyle fashions in Vancouver and something about techniques and supplies used there which might differ from what she had used in Halifax. This might require a period of apprenticeship under a Vancouver-area stylist. When she opens her shop she will have to look carefully at the competition to decide such things as the right location, hours of operation, shop atmosphere, and promotion techniques. All of these have to be considered in a complete marketing plan.

MARKETING AND DISCRETIONARY INCOME IN ADVANCED ECONOMIES

In a rich nation like Canada, there are many choices available to consumers. The more income a family or individual has, the smaller is the proportion

The Browns and the Collinses are each four-member families of two adults and two children. The Brown's income after taxes is $30,000. After spending $28,000 on necessities, they have only $2,000 to spend or save as they like. The Collinses, with $40,000 income, spend $34,000 on necessities and have three times as much as the Browns ($6,000) left over. As income increases, discretionary income increases at a greater rate.

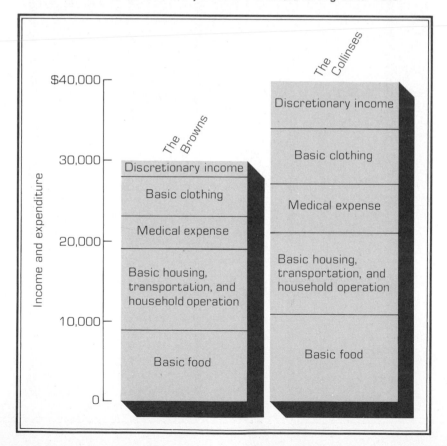

Figure 9.2
Discretionary income of two families

of income required for absolute necessities. Wealthy buyers can shift their spending patterns around. As we have seen in Chapter 2, what a buyer has to spend on things other than necessities is called *discretionary income*. Figure 9.2 shows that one family, the Collinses, has 33 percent more after-tax income ($40,000 versus $30,000) than another family, the Browns. However, it also demonstrates that the discretionary part of the Collins's income is 200 percent greater than that of the Browns ($6,000 versus $2,000). Rising income, then, means businesses find it harder to predict what will be bought. This complicates the marketing task and makes it even more important to watch the consumer closely. The consumer's tastes and preferences can change quickly.

In recent years there has been a big increase in the number of *multi-earner families*—families with more than one earner. The rise in job opportunities for women together with the rising number of working wives means a big jump in discretionary income for many families. These multiearner families are reputed to spend more on household help and dining out and less on child-related goods and services. They represent a market for luxury goods and services.

The marketing process must also cope with risks related to technology. A firm never really knows when a competitor will devise a new product that outdates the firm's present product or that makes its present product unnecessary. The invention of the versatile food processor, for example, has led to a decline in the demand for many single-purpose kitchen tools.

THE MARKETING CONCEPT AND THE MANAGERIAL APPROACH

The broad field of marketing has been analyzed in many ways. Some people study the major institutions (wholesalers, retailers, etc.) involved in the marketing process. Others study how different commodities vary in the way they are marketed (marketing of grain, meat, hardware, etc.). Still another method is to divide the total marketing task into its separate functions (buying, selling, pricing, etc.).

managerial approach to marketing

Today the most common way of studying the subject is called the managerial approach to marketing. This approach takes the point of view of a firm which must make a variety of marketing decisions, each of which may affect the profit of that firm. We'll use this approach because it is the most popular one today and because it fits the scheme of this book.

The Marketing Concept

We have seen in Chapter 8 that Canada has a long history of advances in production. In recent decades this has been matched by equally impressive advances in marketing. With the growth of discretionary income, stiffer competition, and the maze of government regulation, a new concept has been adopted by most of the leading firms in the country. **This new concept is called the marketing concept. It means that the whole firm is coordinated to achieve one goal—to serve its present and potential**

marketing concept

customers and to do so at a profit. This means getting to understand what customers really want and to follow closely the changes in tastes that occur. If the firm is to follow up on this awareness of customer wants in a profitable way it must operate as a system, well-coordinated and unified in the pursuit of the common goal—customer satisfaction.

Adopting the marketing concept means that financial, production, and marketing components of the firm must *all* be guided by the common goal. The need for such an orientation throughout the firm has led many businesses to select their leadership from their marketing departments.

The Marketing Mix

marketing mix

To apply the marketing concept effectively, a firm must understand the major factors or tools it may use to meet (and to influence) consumers' wants. These factors are called the marketing mix. The marketing mix includes four elements: product, price, promotion, and distribution. (See Figure 9.3.)

product

The product element is concerned with the firm's product or service offering. **The product, however, includes much more than a physical**

Figure 9.3
The marketing mix

product. It includes the guarantee, service, brand, package, installation, alteration, etc., which go with it. The product can best be thought of as a bundle of utilities. A person who buys a car is not only buying steel, glass, and nuts and bolts. That person is buying satisfaction such as transportation or prestige.

price

The price element of the marketing mix is also important. **Price is the amount of money for which the product sells.** How a firm sets this price is discussed in our next chapter. It involves setting a basic price and then adjusting it through discounts and markups to arrive at a price target customers are willing and able to pay.

promotion

The third element in the mix is promotion. **Promotion is concerned with persuading people to buy the firm's products — turning people into customers.** It includes advertising, personal selling, publicity, public relations, and sales promotion. As we will see, promotion is basically concerned with a firm's efforts to communicate with its customers.

distribution

The final element in the mix is distribution. **Distribution (place) means getting things from where they are made to where they are used.** Distribution requires transportation, warehousing, and, in many cases, middlemen.

All four elements of the marketing mix are focused on the consumer and are influenced by factors in the environment such as the society, technology, the economy, and the law.

There are many possible combinations of those four major elements. Price, for instance, might play a big role in the mix for selling fresh meat but a very small role in selling perfume. Distribution might be very important in marketing gasoline and not so important for lumber. Promotion could be vital in toy marketing and yet be of little importance in marketing nails. The product is important in every case but probably less so for toothpaste than for cars. We'll discuss the four parts of the marketing mix in detail in our next chapter.

THINK ABOUT IT!

The Marketing Functions

The process of marketing can be divided into many separate "marketing functions." These are identifiable tasks which must be performed before the complete marketing task — bringing goods or services from the producer to the consumer — can be done.

The marketing functions have often been divided into those relating to buying and selling and those relating to physical movement and storage. In the first group are such functions as creating demand, determining needs, negotiating prices, transferring title, advising buyers, and finding buyers and sellers. In the second group are transporting, storing, classifying, packaging, assembling, and dividing.

Think of a particular product with which you are familiar. How does it get from the producer to the consumer? Who performs the function of creating demand? the function of transportation? of negotiating prices? THINK ABOUT IT!

THE TARGET MARKET

target market

If a firm is to adopt the marketing concept, it must define the characteristics of its customers. This set of customers is called the target market. Aiming at this target guides the firm in designing its marketing program. Often there are certain factors, such as existing investment in production facilities or experience of personnel, that restrict the kind of target at which the firm "aims." In other words, there may be a compromise between the resources already available for marketing and the selection of target markets. Thus RCA, after having started marketing computers, decided to withdraw from that line of business. It discovered that its resources and capabilities were better suited to marketing other products.

When choosing a target, one thing is usually easy — deciding whether the item produced will be used for its own sake or whether it will be used to make something else or to help provide a service. This is an important distinction.

industrial goods

Industrial goods are goods or services that will be used by a firm or an institution to make another product or to provide a service. For example, tractor tires sold to Caterpillar Tractor or an examining table sold to a doctor is an industrial good. Manufacturers, hospitals, and lawyers buy goods and services for reasons that are different from those of ordinary consumers. These buyers are *industrial buyers.*

consumer goods

Consumer goods are goods and services that people buy for their own use — to wear, to eat, to look at, or to live in. We usually call these buyers *ultimate consumers.* Their motives and buying behaviour are quite different from those of industrial buyers.

middlemen

Besides industrial buyers and ultimate consumers, firms must also consider a third kind of customer. These are called middlemen because they usually hold products briefly during the process of bringing them from their producer to their user. Retailers and wholesalers are examples of middlemen.

Let's clarify the importance of defining the target market by comparing the industrial goods market with the consumer goods market and with other distinctive markets.

The Industrial Market

What are the features of industrial goods markets? First of all, the target market is generally smaller than it is for consumer goods. A maker of shoemaking machines has fewer customers than a candymaker or a tuna canner or a TV manufacturer.

Industrial customers are often more concentrated geographically than are household or individual customers. Many industries which are the sole users of certain products are centered in one or a few areas. The manufacture of agricultural implements, for example, is concentrated in Winnipeg, Saskatoon, Regina, and Yorkton.

Industrial buyers are also different from ultimate consumers because industrial buyers have more formal systems for buying (see Table 9.1). They

Table 9.1 Sweeny Ltd. Buys an Air-Conditioning System

1. In early May workers began to complain that it was too hot in the main assembly plant.
2. In mid-May the production manager noted a decrease in productivity and further complaints about the inadequacy of the old air-conditioning system.
3. At a conference between the executive vice-president, the production manager, the comptroller, and the plant engineer on June 1, it was decided to replace the system immediately.
4. The plant engineer prepared a description of the system Sweeny Ltd. needs and a time schedule for installation. These specifications were sent to five local industrial air-conditioning contractors on June 14, with a request for installation bids and proposals.
5. Four proposals were received by July 4. Each was checked by the plant engineer, the purchasing agent, and the production manager. These three conferred with the comptroller and the executive vice-president and awarded the contract to the Acme Company. Their bid was somewhat higher than one of the others, but their reputation for quality was very high and their service and warranty were at least equal to those of all other bidders.
6. On July 10 contracts were prepared by the purchasing agent and signed both by him and by Acme Company representative. Work was begun the same day.

set up purchasing departments to handle procurement. Purchasing departments in large firms may buy thousands of products from hundreds of sellers.

A firm also has *more clearly defined* and *profit-oriented purchase motives.* Industrial markets can be especially risky because of the dynamic nature of technology. One change in technology can cause the sudden death of many industrial products (parts, supplies, etc.) that go into the production of one newly obsolete major product. Conversion from the older type of electron tube to solid state parts in TVs and radios hurt many small producers of the older tubes.

Industrial goods include:

- *installations,* such as plants, office buildings, land, and very expensive assets like cranes
- *raw materials,* such as cotton, iron ore, and lumber
- *accessory equipment,* such as typewriters, accounting machines, and small fork lift trucks
- *supplies,* such as maintenance items (brooms and light bulbs); repair items (nuts and bolts to repair equipment); and operating supplies (lubricating oil and typewriter ribbons)
- *component parts and materials,* such as tires, batteries, and steel beams
- *business services,* such as uniform rental, security services, and cargo transportation

These goods and services have either narrow or broad target markets. The target depends on how widely the goods or services are used in industry. Many types of supplies (stationery and fuel), accessory equipment (typewriters), and services (legal assistance) are used by nearly all firms. On the other hand, most types of major equipment or installations, raw materials, and parts have a much narrower market.

The breadth of a market for an industrial product is limited by the product's nature. Who the customers of a given firm are also depends on its location, its experience and good name, its financial strength, and the size and the strength of its distribution system.

Governmental and Institutional Markets

Goods sold to nonprofit institutions such as federal, provincial, and municipal governments, hospitals, and schools are also industrial goods. Many of the same products sold to businesses are also sold to nonprofit institutions. These are often like industrial firms because they use a formal, usually professional purchasing system. They draw product specifications and request bids from several suppliers.

Marketing to the federal government is a special case because of the complex purchasing system it uses. Some firms sell exclusively to the government. Large defence purchases may involve years of parliamentary debate and lobbying. Marketing for such products is in a class by itself.

The purchase of the CF-18 jet fighter is an example. Each plane costs $33 million, and the total price is expected to be about $4 billion. There was great political controversy about the plane because of its limited range (800 kilometres) and high price. McDonnell Douglas eventually beat out four other manufacturers for the contract; in the process, they promised that more than $1 billion of related work would be done in Canada.

The Consumer Market

Manufacturers which produce goods for ultimate consumers often face a huge, tricky target market. The "household" buyer is not as professional or formal as the industrial firm. However, the high level of income among Canadian consumers leads to a fantastic number of different products and services being bought. This affluence makes possible frequent changes in taste. These changes, together with the amazing rate of technological progress, cause a rapid "turnover" of consumer products. New products and new brands of products appear daily on retail shelves. Nearly as many soon disappear. This tougher competition for the consumer dollar represents the main challenge in marketing consumer goods. A number of different marketing strategies are used to meet the challenge.

Consider a few examples from recent years. Per capita beef consumption has been decreasing while per capita chicken consumption has been increasing. A major reason for these changes is that people want to reduce their cholesterol and fat intake. Another change results from the aging of the "baby boom" generation. This has meant reduced sales of soft drinks and increased sales of wine, a fact that may help explain why the Coca-Cola company acquired Taylor Wine Company.

Perhaps the most obvious adaptation to taste and technological change has been the abandonment of traditional full-size cars in favour of sub-compacts. Not many years ago owners of imported sub-compacts were considered a little offbeat.

Tougher competition for the consumer dollar represents the main challenge in marketing consumer goods and services. A number of different marketing strategies are used to meet the challenge, as we will see later in this chapter and in the following chapter.

Classes of Consumer Goods

Although many specific products are hard to classify, it is useful to distinguish three kinds:

- •convenience goods
- •shopping goods
- •specialty goods

This classification depends on frequency of purchase, the product's significance to the buyer, and the buyer's preselection of a specific product brand.

convenience goods

Convenience goods are items bought frequently, demanded on short notice, and often purchased by habit. Cigarettes and many foods and drugs are examples. These are usually low-priced products that people don't think much about when buying. They don't make very careful price and quality comparisons.

shopping goods

Shopping goods are items which are taken seriously enough to require comparison and study. Most clothing, appliances, and cars fall into this category. Gifts are almost always shopping goods. Stores that sell shopping goods are frequently grouped together, often in planned shopping centers, to help customers make price and quality comparisons.

specialty goods

Specialty goods are those for which strong conviction as to brand, style, or type already exists in the buyer's mind. The buyer will make a great effort to locate and purchase the specific brand. Usually, such products are high in value and aren't purchased frequently. Examples are Leica cameras and Steinway pianos. For some customers, however, a can

Selling convenience goods

Selling shopping goods

of soup could be a specialty product. The class depends on the individual consumer's buying behaviour. A certain item (a shirt, for example) could be classed in three different ways by three different people. However, there is enough agreement among consumers on most products to make this product-class scheme useful to firms in decision making. Marketers judge the way that most customers will behave toward the product and classify it accordingly.

How a firm classifies a product greatly influences the way it is sold. A manufacturer who considers a product a convenience good will want it to be sold in as many places as possible. Coke, Wrigley's gum, and Export A cigarettes are available in countless supermarkets, drugstores, and vending machines. If, however, the product is viewed as a shopping good, it is likely to be placed in stores that are near stores selling similar shopping items. A typical consumer shopping for a new TV wants to be able to compare Zenith, Sony, RCA, and so on. A specialty good manufacturer needs to worry less about retail location. There are relatively few Rolls Royce dealerships. A consumer who wants to buy one is willing to make a special effort to find a dealer — even if the dealer is a few hundred miles away. Since such buyers will go out of their way to locate the product, the firm's distribution channel problem is simplified. These are only a few examples of how the way that consumers classify products may affect the way that they are marketed. Table 9.2 summarizes the features of the three classes of goods.

In summary, consumer goods producers must put themselves in the shoes of the buyer to figure out the probable class in which most buyers will place a given product. This is an application of the marketing concept and makes it more likely that the marketing effort will be truly matched to what consumers want.

Table 9.2 Classes of Consumer Goods

	Convenience	Shopping	Specialty
How far will a buyer travel?	short distance	reasonable distance	long distance
How much does it cost?	usually low price	usually middle to high price	usually high price
How often purchased?	frequently	occasionally	infrequently
Emphasis on comparison?	no	yes	no
Purchased habitually?	often	never	not usually
Which advertising media?	television, news-papers, and general magazines	television, news-papers, and general magazines	special-interest magazines and catalogues
Time spent in purchasing	short	moderate	long
Distribution policy	intensive	selective	selective or exclusive

---

CAN YOU EXPLAIN THIS?

Why Are There So Many Brands of Bath Soap?

On your next trip to the supermarket, pass by the shelf which displays bath soaps. You'll see many different brands. Some are packaged in fancy foil wrappers. Notice how many different sizes there are. Some soaps are deodorant soaps, some are mild enough for babies, and some have ingredients that promise to give you youthful-looking skin.

But don't we all buy bath soap for the same reason? Isn't the reason we buy soap to wash ourselves? Why are there so many brands of bath soap? CAN YOU EXPLAIN THIS?

PRODUCT DIFFERENTIATION

The way in which a firm approaches and defines its target market or markets may include a strategy of product differentiation. This strategy requires a good understanding of the target customer, whether that customer be a household, an individual, or a business firm.

product differentiation

Product differentiation is a process of convincing target customers that one brand is different from, and better than, the competition's. It can be done by stressing distinctive product features or the product's guarantee, service, or availability. Peugeot cars have silver-tipped spark plugs that last longer than ordinary spark plugs. Curtis-Mathes televisions come with a four-year limited warranty, and Sears' Craftsman hand tools are replaced free if they break.

Product differentiation can also be achieved by an advertising campaign that emphasizes product features or creates the impression of special product advantages. When Procter & Gamble introduced Crest in 1960, ads stressed the fact that it contained Fluoristan. When Advanced Formula Crest was introduced in 1981, the ads stressed that it contained Fluoristat. No other brands claim to have that ingredient because Fluoristat is a trademark registered by Procter & Gamble.

MARKET SEGMENTATION

market segmentation

A strategy of product differentiation may treat customers as one general target group to be aimed at with one common marketing mix. **A strategy of market segmentation, however, calls for making a special marketing mix for a special segment of the market or several different mixes for several different segments.** The idea is that there is really more than one set of needs to be satisfied within the general market for a product. If a firm believes it will improve its market position, it might make a different version of the product to satisfy the special needs of each group, or market segment. In some cases, market planners focus on only one segment of a

Figure 9.4
Selecting two market segments for sportswear

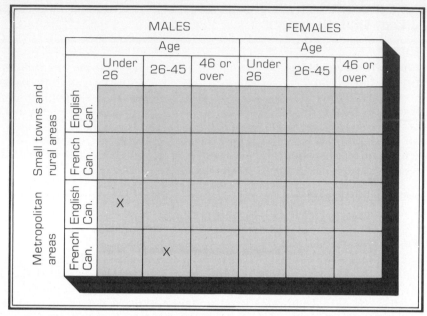

market. For example, Pennington's sells only the larger sizes of women's clothing. Mr. Big-and-Tall sells clothing for men who are taller and/or heavier than the average man. Certain copier companies stress certain segments of the copier market.

A marketer's success in serving one segment may lead it to expand its marketing effort to other segments. For example, Volkswagen used to focus only on economy-minded car buyers with its Beetle. Recently it has been marketing several models, including the Rabbit which is targeted to a more affluent buyer. When it first started in the 1950s, McDonald's sold hamburgers, fries, and shakes from walk-up windows and did most of its business during the evening hours. Now, McDonald's provides extensive seating, an expanded menu, and does business morning, noon, and night.

A firm might use the demographic characteristics of its customers to construct a grid such as Figure 9.4 to decide on two profitable segments toward which to focus its efforts in marketing sportswear.

Consider the case of a producer of wristwatches. Such a firm might design one marketing mix to satisfy the "jewelry" watch market and another to satisfy the "time-telling" watch market. There might be important differences in product design, perhaps gold cases with gems for one and waterproof steel cases for the other. Advertising themes for one would emphasize romance or prestige, while the other might emphasize accuracy, durability, and price. They might even use two different sets of retail stores. The expensive ones might be sold in jewelry stores and the cheaper ones in drug and variety stores. Deciding which of these means of segmentation to use requires a study of the market and the cost of segmenting.

AUTHORS' COMMENTARY

The Ultimate Segmentation

Rapid development in computer-controlled factories will permit easier gratification of the individual tastes of every buyer of cars and appliances. These kinds of products were among the first to benefit from cost-cutting mass production of assembly lines. At that time, however, the consumer had to pay a large price in the form of a very standardized product. Henry Ford said, "Give them any colour they want as long as it is black." Today, the firm that bears his name is able to produce such an astounding combination of features, styles, colours, and accessories that it is possible to produce a unique car for every car buyer in Canada.

There may be some exaggeration in this kind of claim, but with the advent of computer-based rapid communication, and the robot precision of the assembly plant, the day may have arrived when car dealers will be able to order and deliver such customized cars on very short notice. The computer will have successfully combined the advantages of mass production with the ultimate capacity to segment the market — a unique car for every buyer.

Other bases of segmenting markets for certain products might be age, sex, income, educational level, or personality traits. At the broadest level, segmentation can be done on a cultural or language level. In Canada, for example, there are significant differences in consumer attitudes and behaviour between English- and French-speaking Canadians, and prudent marketers must take these differences into account in order to be effective. Segmentation by culture or language is also practised by many businesses with respect to certain regions of the country and to geographic concentrations of various ethnic groups.

At the other extreme, segmentation would provide a "custom" design for each buyer. In this case, each individual customer is a "segment." Profitable segmentation requires good consumer knowledge on the part of the seller.

MARKETING RESEARCH

marketing research

Intelligent decisions about marketing strategies — whether they relate to product, price, promotion, or channel of distribution — require a clear understanding of those who are or might become customers. This kind of decision calls for marketing research. **Marketing research means applying methods of science to marketing problems. These techniques are largely directed at the people who make up the market.**

Two general approaches to the study of the market are the "demographic" approach and the "behavioural" approach. The former collects facts about people, families, or firms who are thought likely to be customers. It concentrates on counting and tabulating. The demographic features of a market of ultimate customers are such things as the age, sex, race, and income of its members. Often, a firm makes assumptions about the relationship between these characteristics and the likelihood of a person buying a product. These assumptions may be based on past knowledge about customers. For example, we might assume that only persons over age sixty are interested in a certain health tonic. We might also assume that only persons with incomes of $40,000 or more will be interested in a trip around the world.

secondary research

Assume that a firm decided which characteristics are related to consumption of its product. Now it seeks information about the number of such prospects in the area to be served. A firm may find this additional demographic information on consumers in Canadian census publications or other government or private sources. This is called secondary research.

primary research

The firm might also do some primary research. **Primary research is getting new facts for a specific purpose.** For example, the Swiss Clock Company may include in each package of its product a "registration" card. They request the buyer to fill in facts about herself or himself and mail it in to the company. These cards tell the firm about the people who buy their clocks.

Primary research can be much more involved than this. Some firms, for example, set up consumer panels made up of people who normally use the product. These people give opinions on the product's strengths and weaknesses. This helps the company in making decisions about possible product changes. A company can also gather data about a product or service by using questionnaires. Detailed questions are developed on the topic of interest to the company. The responses are usually analyzed by computers and any trends are noted. These trends help marketing executives make logical decisions about the product or service. The Career Profile near the end of this chapter gives some insights into how this process works.

Instead of finding out who the customers are, what they buy, when they buy, and so on, the behavioural approach asks the question, "why do they buy?" This approach assumes that what people buy often depends on complex motives which can be understood only by psychological probing. Experts in human motivation test a sample of people to find out the basis for their product choice. The researcher might try to find, for example, what a particular brand name "means" to certain people. These researchers often use techniques borrowed from psychologists to discover motives and/or attitudes which customers might ordinarily try to hide.

focus group interview

Another important marketing research technique that helps firms to understand consumer attitudes and behaviour toward their products and services is called focus group interviewing. **A focus group interview entails listening to eight to twelve people at one time with very little formal questioning by the interviewer. The idea is to provide a natural conversational setting in which a group of similar people frankly exchange opinions and attitudes toward a product, store, or idea.** Focus groups provide stimulating ideas for further research. For example, a firm that developed a new filter for air-conditioning systems used a focus group to help identify target markets for the product. It singled out families in

---

THINK ABOUT IT!

The Quebec Market

During the last fifteen years a number of studies have compared the behaviour and attitudes of French and English Canadians. Some of the interesting findings are as follows:

1. Quebec has the highest per capita sales of sweets in Canada — soft drinks, syrup, etc.
2. French Canadians drink very little lager, whereas English Canadians drink both ale and lager.
3. The French-Canadian woman is more involved with home and family than is her English-Canadian counterpart.
4. Quebec leads all provinces in per capita expenditures on clothing and cosmetics.
5. French Canadians drink three times more fresh orange juice than the rest of Canada, and eat less frozen food.
6. The French-Canadian woman is less oriented toward convenience food than her English counterpart.

What implications do these differences have for marketing? THINK ABOUT IT!

---

which one or more members had allergies or respiratory problems and persons seriously concerned about air pollution as good potential targets (Keith K. Cox, James B. Higginbotham, and John Burton, "Applications of Focus Group Interviews in Marketing," *Journal of Marketing*, Jan. 1976, pp. 78–79).

Regardless of the approach, marketing research must be undertaken on a continuous basis. You need only look at the changes in products for sale in the last few years to see how dynamic the market is. How long ago was it that we had never heard of home smoke detectors, food processors, video games, and household computers? Consumer tastes and values change so fast that a firm must keep its eyes open to the future. This requires marketing research.

PATTERNS OF CONSUMPTION

conspicuous consumption

In the last thirty years in Canada we have witnessed wide swings in attitudes toward discretionary spending (spending beyond basic needs). **For some people there has been a lot of conspicuous consumption. This means spending in a visible way so that your neighbours will be aware of your wealth and "good taste."** This kind of "show-off" buying often has been widespread among people when they first have extra buying power. They're trying to tell others that they have "made it."

A large number of our younger adults in the late 1960s reacted strongly to "conspicuous consumption." Many rejected the "middle-class" consumption pattern. Of course, this rejection was not limited to the kinds of products purchased. It included the entire lifestyle, the politics, the religion, and most of the values of their parents. This rejection caused many people of all ages to question the values of the majority, including the value of high-level consumption. These doubts are still alive.

Even stronger doubts about high-level consumption and the accompanying waste were caused by the oil crisis. It began to make people wonder about the good sense of "gas-guzzling" cars and other wasteful practices we have accepted because of wealth. If oil is running out, what about our other scarce resources? Does our "throw-away" mentality make sense? Will Canadians really have to reduce their scale of living? Some believe that businesses may have to engage in demarketing—marketing activities aimed at making adjustments to shorter supplies of certain materials.

A further complication is the emergence of many new kinds of stores and new products that didn't exist even a few years ago. Many clothing stores now carry great depth in one or two lines (for example, jeans), but they have very little breadth. Microcomputers are sold in numerous retail outlets, and many people are now buying generic products (those that have no brand name) because the price is cheaper. The rental of movies to be played at home on video cassette recorders is rapidly expanding. These and other developments in consumption patterns present both problems and opportunities for marketing people. Marketing research helps in predicting patterns of consumption and it suggests how a company can capitalize on these patterns.

MARKETING AND UTILITY

The utility of goods and services is at the heart of the marketing problem. We can distinguish the following kinds of utility: form utility, place utility, time utility, and ownership utility. We will show how these four aspects of utility relate to the household purchase of sugar.

form utility **Form utility is utility resulting from a change in form.** It is produced by treatment or breaking-down processes such as those we described in Chapter 8. Sugar, for example, becomes more useful after the juice is extracted from the sugar cane or sugar beets and is cooked and refined. Sugar refineries are in the business of creating form utility.

Form utility, unfortunately, is not enough to satisfy the millions of people who want this sugar for use in their homes. Place utility is place utility needed, too. **Place utility is that aspect of usefulness determined by location.** Raw sugar on a loading dock in New Orleans must be moved to Toronto before its usefulness to a Toronto family can be realized. The ship, train, or truck that transports the sugar creates place utility for the people in Toronto.

time utility **Time utility is somewhat harder to explain. It is that aspect of utility determined by the passage of time as it relates to consumption.** It depends on an idea we explored in the early chapters, the principle of diminishing marginal utility. Let's take the case of the Jones family in Vancouver. They have a pound of sugar in a bowl on the kitchen table. A five-pound bag on the shelf of the supermarket down the street is not yet fully useful to the Joneses for several reasons. One, as we have seen, is that it needs more place utility. Another is that more time must pass until the present stock of sugar is used up and they "need" more sugar — enough to go to the store to buy it. That bag on the supermarket shelf is gaining time utility as the bowl of sugar at home is used up.

Finally, full usefulness of the five-pound bag on the supermarket shelf, as far as the Jones family is concerned, can't be reached until they own it. Because of the concept of private property, this sugar must be bought. **Ownership utility is that aspect of the usefulness of a product related to the passage of legal title to the final user.** When Mr. or Mrs. Jones goes to the store, pays for the sugar, and brings it home to fill the sugar bowl, the full utility of the sugar is realized. Marketing activities have been directly involved in the creation of place, time, and ownership utility. How firms do this is the main topic of this chapter and the following one.

ownership utility

CONSUMERISM

consumerism

Consumerism is a movement to strengthen the power of product users in relation to the power of product makers and sellers. This movement is still strong and centers around the idea of certain basic consumer rights — the right to choose, the right to be informed, the right to be heard, and the right to safety. (See Figure 9.5.)

Throughout the 1960s and into the 1970s, the consumer movement grew and began to include an ever-larger list of objectives. Leadership in the

TWO POINTS OF VIEW

Consumer Protection

The Firm:

"This consumer movement is going to ruin us! We just get our new model on the market and bang! The self-appointed guardians of the people are starting a campaign against us. They're writing to Consumer and Corporate Affairs, and they're even giving TV interviews saying that the ZINGER is a death trap and that it has a faulty braking system.

"We market-researched that car and know we've built in the features which customers said they wanted — super styling, bucket seats, stereo system — the works. It's got all the latest accessories, too. I call that real consumer responsiveness! We have been pioneers in applying the marketing concept."

The Consumer Advocate:

"The marketplace does not provide consumers with guarantees to protect them from unscrupulous manufacturers like the ZINGER Company. Most consumers don't know enough about technical products like cars to know if they are getting gypped. All it takes is a high-pressure ad campaign and a lot of superficial gadgets to convince them to buy.

"Consumers need protection. They need product safety codes with heavy penalties for those firms who don't follow them. At present, only the consumer movement is around to prevent consumers from making dumb mistakes. Without us they are almost helpless against the marketing skills of the giant corporations. Corporations don't care who gets hurt as long as they make their profit."

The right to choose from an adequate number of products and brands

The right to be informed of all the important facts about the product or service (price, durability, health, and safety hazards, etc.)

The right to be heard by producers and government when treated unfairly or when a question or complaint arises

The right to safety in the use of all products and services

CAN YOU EXPLAIN THIS?

Private Organizations and Consumerism

The Consumers Association of Canada (CAC) is a private consumer organization. Its bimonthly magazine, *Canadian Consumer,* gives information on product tests which are conducted by the CAC. The organization originally received a $415,000 federal grant in 1966 to finance its operations. However, it has experienced a chronic shortage of funds, and is currently appealing for funds to the general public, on whose behalf it has been working for many years. Why has this happened? CAN YOU EXPLAIN THIS?

U.S. movement has been provided primarily by Ralph Nader, who first became well-known when he wrote a book critical of General Motors and the Corvair in 1966. By pointing out the defects in the Corvair, Nader succeeded in gathering support for the consumerism movement throughout the United States and Canada. The news media have been an important aid in making the consumerism movement well-known.

In Canada, the consumerism movement has resulted in many laws being passed to protect consumers. The Consumers Association of Canada (CAC) has been a leader in espousing consumer issues (see box later in this chapter on private organizations and consumerism).

Since the appearance of the energy crisis and economic difficulties of the mid-1970s, there has been some weakening, or at least a shift in emphasis, in the consumerism movement. Certainly auto emission control has taken a backseat to better mileage. More emphasis has also been given to protection of consumers from prices which are higher than they should be.

In any case, the consumerism movement is still alive and well. It still has some very important meaning to marketers of products and services. Reaction to the movement by firms has varied a lot. Some view it as a threat to free enterprise. Some see it as a passing annoyance which can be solved by an extra effort in public relations and lobbying. Many, however, see it as a true reflection of customer anger over abuses of market power by firms. Such firms have taken steps to correct the problem and to bring greater credibility to the marketing concept.

The Gillette Company, for example, has a vice-president for product integrity. This officer, who is directly responsible for the safety and quality of Gillette's more than 800 products, has the power to (1) remove them from the market any time they fail to meet quality standards, (2) modify advertising claims, or (3) prevent new product introduction. In 1973 this executive

Figure 9.5
The basic rights of consumers

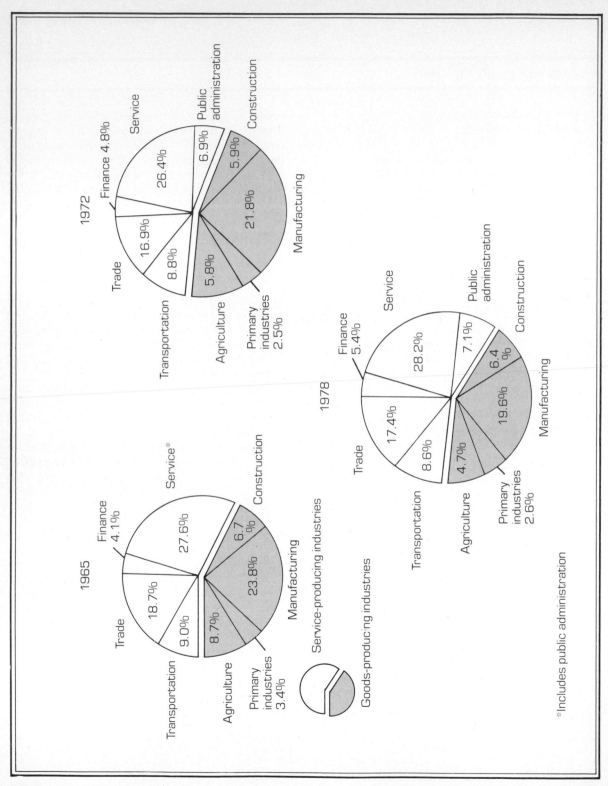

1972

Finance 4.8%
Service 26.4%
Public administration 6.9%
Construction 5.9%
Manufacturing 21.8%
Trade 16.9%
Transportation 8.8%
Agriculture 5.8%
Primary industries 2.5%

1978

Finance 5.4%
Service 28.2%
Public administration 7.1%
Construction 6.4%
Manufacturing 19.6%
Trade 17.4%
Transportation 8.6%
Agriculture 4.7%
Primary industries 2.6%

1965

Finance 4.1%
Service* 27.6%
Construction 6.7%
Manufacturing 23.8%
Trade 18.7%
Transportation 9.0%
Agriculture 8.7%
Primary industries 3.4%

Service-producing industries

Goods-producing industries

*Includes public administration

314

caused the recall of more than $1 million of antiperspirants because there was a question about the safety of one of the ingredients.

Many firms have taken similar steps which do much more than pay lip service to consumerism. This, they believe, does not hurt the long-run profit of their firms. Rather, they wonder about the survival of firms which do not react positively to public complaints and thereby bring on oppressive government controls.

MARKETING OF SERVICES

Employment in services has been growing at a rapid rate in recent years. (See Figure 9.6.) A service is like a product in that it provides a benefit, but it is unlike a product in that it is not a concrete, physical object. Services represent a big part of what consumers and business firms buy. A service may be quite personal, such as the service provided by a physician or beautician. It can be impersonal as well. Banks, insurance agents, and people who do repair work provide impersonal services in the sense that the human tie between the producer and consumer is not close. In any case, it is usually hard to separate the service from the person who provides it. It almost always requires that the producer be a specialist. Wayne Gretzky and Dieter Brock provide the service of entertainment in their respective sports. They are highly paid because they are specialists. The same is true of a heart surgeon or an actress. Insurance agents are specialists, too, as are plumbers and electricians.

Since we have defined the product part of a marketing mix in terms of the "bundle" of services it provides, it follows that marketing of services is not very different from marketing a product. There are a few differences, though. Perhaps the biggest difference is the simple fact that most service producers have not paid as much attention to marketing as they should. Only recently have bankers, for example, realized the importance of the marketing concept. They have begun to think in terms of attracting and pleasing customers and of differentiating their services.

Legal services are limited in the use of promotion by their ethical codes. However, there is often a need for developing the marketing mix by improving the human dimension of the service (product) and by improving access to lawyer offices and the courts (distribution). Pricing, in the competitive sense, has been discouraged by ethical codes in law and other professions. However, for some specialists, high fees are viewed as a positive marketing factor. The whole question of lack of price competition in the professions is hotly debated these days and may be changing.

For most services all four parts of the marketing mix—product, distribution, promotion, and price—should be developed. Success in marketing services, even more than in marketing tangible products, depends upon

Figure 9.6
Employment by industrial group, selected years (Source: Canada Year Book. Reproduced by permission of the Minister of Supply and Services Canada)

CAREERS IN MARKETING

CAREERS IN MARKETING ARE ABOUT AS VARIED AS ARE TO BE FOUND IN any field. However, the nature of this field is such that it depends heavily on people who are creative and who have communications skills. Two of the largest areas of opportunity are advertising and personal selling.

In advertising there are jobs in ad agencies, in magazines, newspapers, and television as well as in the marketing or advertising departments of manufacturing and service firms. Some of the most interesting jobs are with ad agencies, including jobs as account executives, media buyers, graphic artists, and copywriters. Besides creativity, an *account executive* needs business training and understanding of accounting and statistics in order to provide the client with an effective advertising program. Usually, this job requires a college degree, either in business or in communications. *Media buyers* need business training too, so they can purchase the "best" time and space in the media within the budget agreed to by the advertiser. A college degree (four years) is preferred, but not always necessary. *Graphic artists* and *copywriters* need training in their respective crafts so they can design attractive layouts and filmstrips and write exciting copy. Usually, these workers have some college training, although a four-year degree is not always required. Except for the account executive, who may do a fair amount of travelling to confer with clients and prospective clients, these are desk jobs. Pay is high for account executives, especially in large agencies. Those representing major national accounts often earn between $50,000 and $100,000 a year. Account executives in smaller agencies have a less stable income, which depends on the success of their ad programs. The other agency-related jobs usually pay somewhat less.

Jobs related to selling are also many and varied. *Retail selling* usually requires the least education and training and pays less than jobs in industrial or wholesale selling or specialized selling such as insurance or real estate. Retail selling is mostly in-store and often amounts to little more than "finding what the customer wants." The exception here is in the case of shopping goods retailing which often requires skills in customer relations and detailed knowledge of the product. Higher level retailing careers, however, such as *merchandising manager* and *buyer,* often require college degrees.

Personal selling of technical products such as computers or pharmaceuticals often requires a business degree in addition to courses and training in, for example, engineering or biological sciences. Personal selling of simpler products, such as some types of building materials or office supplies, does not usually require a college degree, although some college work is helpful. *Outside selling* jobs require exceptional human relations skills and great self confidence. Often, much travel is involved. Pay is usually at least partly on commission and can range very widely, depending on the competitive position of the product or service and on the energy and skill of the salesperson. Some salespeople earn well over $100,000 in a year.

Marketing jobs are also available in retail and wholesale activities. *Sales management* and *purchasing* are closely related fields which may interest you. ■

CAREER PROFILE

MY NAME IS CATHY DRAPER AND I AM A market research analyst for Western Opinion Research, Inc. Our company offers customized market research to the Manitoba and Western Canadian market. This involves gathering and analyzing market data for a variety of clients.

I received my B. Comm. degree in 1982. Prior to graduation, I held several different jobs, ranging from Administrative Secretary to manager of a tourist resort in Ontario. For two summers while attending university I also managed the office of a company that sold swimming pools.

My present job with Western Opinion Research, Inc. involves doing all the activities necessary to develop a report which analyzes market opinion data. The process works as follows: A company approaches us about a market-related problem they would like analyzed. (For example, a telecommunications company was providing an experimental communication service to a small town and wanted to know the townspeople's reaction to the service.) We meet with a representative of the company to discuss the problem and ways in which the data could be gathered to resolve it. The next step is the design of the instrument(s) which will be used to get the required information. This is usually done in consultation with the client. The actual gathering of the data is the next step; this may involve administering a questionnaire or interviewing certain people. Once the data have been gathered, I analyze the data using a variety of relevant statistical techniques (we are now using a micro-computer to assist us in the data analysis). The last step is writing the market research report. This report includes a statement of the problem or the objective(s) of the research, the instrument(s) that were used to develop the data and, most importantly, the conclusions we reached as a result of the data analysis. My job also involves

knowing the buyer well and serving his or her needs. This is especially true for personal services where success means treating each client as an individual market segment.

For many services the distribution or "place" part of marketing is a little different. Usually the producer and distributor are the same. In most cases there is not "channel" of distribution as we normally think of it. Yet, the location of the bank branch or the watch repair shop or even the doctor's office must be considered carefully. A successful TV repair shop often provides home pickup and delivery. A marketer of rented apartments in a distant suburb might offer private commuter bus service to tenants. This is just another way of "distributing a product."

the development of promotion for our company, i.e., writing advertising copy which is designed to attract clients to our firm.

There are several rewards associated with my job. First, I am very independent. Usually I oversee all the daily marketing research on a particular project, and can therefore exercise considerable discretion in that regard. On these projects I am responsible for my own work, for meeting deadlines, and for interacting with the clients. However, as I am relatively new in this position, I consult regularly with other members of the firm to get their opinions, insights, and the benefit of their expertise. Second, I meet a diverse group of people who are important decision makers in their own firms. It is very gratifying to work with individuals who can make decisions which allow me to go ahead with my work. It is also very informative to get involved in all these projects and to learn what other businesses are doing. Third, there is a great sense of accomplishment in my work. Doing the entire job from start to finish gives me a real sense of having completed something worthwhile. I can also see the entire picture that is relevant for a particular client. Finally, I have a considerable amount of responsibility even though I joined the firm only recently. As well, there is a great deal of potential for even more responsibility in the future.

There are also some challenges in this kind of work. First, I have found myself involved in projects which require data analysis on the leading edge of new technologies. This requires me to spend time learning about the technology before gathering and analyzing data on

it. This can be time-consuming and sometimes frustrating when you would like to get on with the actual data gathering and analysis. Second, after having gone through a B. Comm. program and being exposed to many theoretical ideas, I now find that there must be some bridging of the gap between theory and practice. For example, the consequences of a recommendation or recommendations made by myself or by the company are very real in terms of their effects on my professional reputation, the reputation of Western Opinion Research, and the company for whom we are conducting the research. To coin a phrase, "in the real world," research decisions are usually the foundation for further decisions about a firm, a product or service, or a new technology, and while a certain learning process occurs as a result of the uniqueness of each project, the "trial and error" flexibility of a classroom does not exist. A third challenge involves writing advertising copy. Together with another member of the company, I am currently developing an advertising brochure which indicates the services our company offers. Actually using the brochure to interest clients will be a challenge. However, I am looking forward to this challenge because I don't feel that I can continue to spend 100 percent of my time analyzing data and writing market research reports; rather, I must become competent in some other areas of the business.

Overall, this is a very interesting and rewarding job and much of the material I learned at university and the experience gained in the work force have been very useful as background for the work that I am currently doing.

The marketing of services has a long way to go, however. The sooner service producers realize that the marketing concept applies to their "product," the better off the consumer will be.

SUMMARY AND LOOK AHEAD

Marketing is a very large part of the economic activity in Canada. Its role is becoming central to business planning as firms adopt "the marketing concept." The reason for this is that business profit and the national rate of economic growth depend on the growth of consumption. Businesses must learn more about their customers and concentrate on satisfying them if they are to succeed.

It is convenient to think of a set of customers as a "target market." This target might consist of an industrial market or of a market of ultimate consumers. Consumer goods can be classed as convenience goods, shopping goods, and specialty goods.

The kind of good and the consumer help to define the "marketing mix" or combination of product, distribution, promotion, and price a firm will use. A successful marketing mix depends on consumer knowledge gained from market research.

Successful marketing also requires that firms pay attention to spending behaviour such as "conspicuous consumption." This includes a positive response to the spirit of consumerism. If firms reject consumerism, it could possibly trigger widespread attacks on our marketing system.

In the next chapter, we'll show how business firms can approach the problem of designing a marketing mix and the policies which accompany such a mix. ∎

QUESTIONS FOR REVIEW AND DISCUSSION

1. Why is the marketing task more complex in an economy where there are high levels of discretionary income than in one where the people live at the subsistence level?
2. Do you think that high mass consumption is desirable? Why or why not?
3. How is the marketing concept related to the economic problem we discussed in Section One?
4. If a firm adopts and implements the marketing concept, all of its actions are oriented to the satisfaction of its target market. Is that desirable? Discuss.
5. If a product possesses only form utility, is it useful to a customer? Why or why not?
6. Why is there a demand for industrial goods?
7. What is product differentiation? Give an example.
8. Why is market research necessary?
9. Does marketing activity induce or persuade people to want things they do not really need? Explain.
10. Two divergent views of the proper relationship between buyer and seller are "let the buyer beware" and "let the seller beware." Which is the "proper" view? Why?
11. Why is a consumerism movement under way in Canada when consumer sovereignty is a basic characteristic of capitalism?

INCIDENT

Will Snyder

Will Snyder, a marketing research professor at an eastern university, was approached by the local Chamber of Commerce to find out why the area was not attracting new industry. Snyder had been observing the economic conditions of the area for ten years. He was provided with a substantial budget and had the services of five experienced student workers.

The city in question had a population of 150,000 and, besides the university, its major source of employment was a steel fabrication plant specializing in trailer bodies and a variety of specialty vehicle bodies. The newest major industrial plant had arrived six years before the study. It was a fruit and vegetable canning operation servicing area growers. The Chamber of Commerce knew very little about the cause of the problem of attracting new industry. They wanted Snyder to make no easy assumptions in getting at the answer.

Questions:
1. If you were Snyder, would you start with primary or with secondary sources of information? Explain.
2. Would you recommend using focus group interviews at any point in this study? Why or why not?

CASE STUDY*

KETTLE CREEK CANVAS COMPANY

IN MAY 1980 MELANIE STEVENS, MANAGER AND HALF-OWNER OF the Kettle Creek Canvas Company, reflected on the firm's first year of operation. Located in Port Stanley, Ontario, the firm manufactured brightly coloured canvas garments and accessories. These were retailed by a company-owned store in London, as well as a seasonal showroom at the Port Stanley Head Office. First year retail sales were modest, but above budget, at approximately $90,000. Melanie's partner, Jim Sorenti, estimated that with adding two more outlets, retail sales could exceed $600,000 in the second year. The partners had enjoyed enthusiastic consumer reactions and had been approached by various individuals and groups regarding possible franchising or partnership opportunities. Melanie was not sure what to do, but since the technology was simple and since none of the firm's designs were patented or trademarked, she felt that she must act soon.

COMPANY HISTORY

The firm began manufacturing its products in Port Stanley in April 1979, and opened its seasonal retail showroom in May. In November 1979 a small retail store was opened on the main street of London. The product line consisted of men's and women's casual clothing (Exhibit 1), tote bags, purses, stuffed animals, and an assortment of odd items such as canvas file holders.

Production of these items was quite straightforward. Melanie simply ordered canvas, from stock, from a Toronto-based wholesaler. The canvas was laid out and cut in the cutting room. The parts were matched and tagged as to the name and the size of the item. The parts were then picked up by one of twenty-five local housewives who took them home and sewed them at her convenience. When the batch was completed, the sewer returned them to be checked for quality. If the garments passed, an invoice from the sewer to Kettle Creek was filled out and paid on the spot.

Melanie and Jim were pleased with this arrangement and felt that they could support wholesale sales of $1,000,000 ($2,000,000 retail) without any changes. When expansion came, it would be the enlargement of the cutting facilities. Good sewers seemed to be in ample supply.

*This case was written by Gerald Higgins during the 1981 Case Writing Workshop. Case material of the School of Business Administration is prepared as a basis for classroom discussion. Copyright © 1981, School of Business Administration, The University of Western Ontario.

Exhibit 1　Kettle Creek Canvas Company

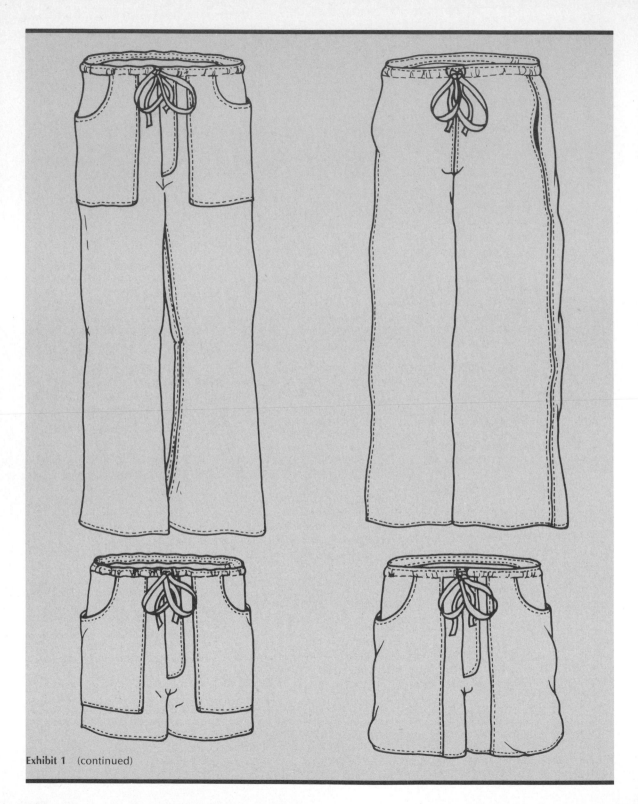

Exhibit 1 (continued)

Exhibit 2 Kettle Creek Canvas Company (Wholesale Division)
Statement of Income for the Year Ended April 30, 1980

Sales	$ 69,000
Cost of goods sold	61,800
Gross profit	$ 7,200
Less expenses	19,000
Net profit (loss) for the period	$(11,800)

Exhibit 3 Kettle Creek Canvas Company (Retail Division)
Statement of Income for the Year Ended April 30, 1980

	London (six months of operation)	Port Stanley (three months of operation)
Sales	$70,000	$20,000
Cost of goods sold	35,000	10,000
Gross profit	35,000	10,000
Less expenses	23,400	6,600
Net profit (loss)	$11,600	$ 3,400

Financial data for the first year of operation can be found in Exhibit 2 (wholesale) and Exhibit 3 (retail).

THE CONSUMER

In May of 1980, the partners still knew very little about their consumers. Prior to the opening of the London store, a local marketing consultant was brought in in an attempt to predict sales volumes. He soon gave up, saying, because of the odd product mix, the firm could not be compared to any data on existing consumer groups or existing store groupings. The consultant did, however, state that he had never seen products or a product mix quite like those at Kettle Creek. This confirmed the partners' suspicions that they were at the bottom of a product life cycle and that they would have to act decisively.

OPPORTUNITIES FOR EXPANSION

Jim and Melanie felt that they had hit upon a new concept but that it could easily be copied. Since they looked at their partnership as a business, they were anxious to exploit the situation as much as possible. Melanie also expressed the idea that they might even be able to sell the firm in a few years and move on to something completely different.

EXPANSION OPTIONS

A. As Is

Both of the partners were young and energetic. They felt that to remain as is would first bore them and second not take full advantage of the situation.

B. Manufacture and Wholesale Only

Melanie felt that this was a viable alternative. It would certainly cause less strain on their limited resources. She wondered, however, about control of how and where the products would be sold. Was this important? Also the partners were not sure how important it was to establish the Kettle Creek name prior to the inevitable entry of competition.

C. More Retail Outlets

This alternative could actually take at least three forms:

1. More company-owned stores
2. Partnerships
3. Franchised outlets

Exhibit 4 Kettle Creek Canvas Company Balance Sheet, April 30, 1980

Assets	
Current:	
Cash	$ 100
Accounts Receivable	11,100
Notes Receivable	700
Inventory	54,000
	65,900
Fixed:	
Machinery (Net)	3,400
Leasehold Improvement (Net)	3,000
	6,400
Other:	
Note Receivable	4,100
Total assets:	$76,400

Liabilities and Proprietory Capital	
Current:	
Bank—Overdraft	$ 7,300
Bank—Demand Loan	24,100
Accounts Payable	47,900
	79,300
Proprietors Capital (Deficiency)	(2,900)
Total liabilities and proprietory capital	$76,400

Estimated retail sales for the first full year in London were $160,000 and for a downtown Toronto store were $225,000. The cost of leasehold improvements for new stores were estimated at $10,000 each. Annual rent, wages, and miscellaneous expenses were projected to be $35,000 and $75,000 in London and Toronto respectively. Melanie also felt that a store could be started in Vancouver with much the same costs and sales as the proposed Toronto location.

D. Some Combination of the Above

Regarding costs, the manufacturing department took their direct costs and doubled them to arrive at a wholesale price. Wholesale administrative expenses were relatively fixed, as in Exhibit 2. The retail stores simply doubled the wholesale price to arrive at a retail price. All wholesale prices would be F.O.B. Port Stanley. Melanie estimates shipping costs to average 5 percent of the wholesale selling price.

For the franchise alternative, Melanie felt a one-time $20,000 set-up fee was fair. The franchisee would then pay 3 percent of retail sales to Kettle Creek on an ongoing basis.

A young, well-to-do couple had also approached the partners, with the idea of a partnership. These new partners were prepared to pay Jim and Melanie $40,000 for 49 percent of the equity of the proposed new store in downtown Toronto. The new partners would then manage and staff the new store.

CONCLUSION

As Melanie Stevens considered her next step, she kept in mind the firm's present financial position (Exhibits 2, 3, and 4) and what seemed to be a chronic cash squeeze. ■

After reading this chapter, you should be able to:

1. Identify the bundle of services offered by a product to its user.
2. Draw a chart illustrating the life cycle of a product.
3. Present arguments for and against a broad product mix.
4. Explain the functions which a package performs.
5. Draw a chart which illustrates how a middleman may bring about economies in distribution.
6. Distinguish between an integrated and a non-integrated channel of distribution.
7. Provide an illustration of the total cost concept.
8. Describe ideal distribution task conditions for each of the major modes of transport.
9. Describe how an advertising agency serves a large seller of consumer goods.
10. Compare the advantages of the various media.
11. Act out with another student an example of personal selling as it should be done.
12. Show the difference between the cost and the demand approaches to pricing in a small dress shop.
13. Describe two possible strategies for introducing a new product.

In reading the chapter, look for and understand these terms:

product life cycle

planned obsolescence

new product committee

product mix

brand

patent

trademark

information labelling

place (or distribution)

channel of distribution

manufacturers' agent

franchised retailer

physical distribution

total cost concept

common carrier

contract carrier

private carrier

containerization

promotion

advertising

advertising agency

account executive

advertising media

AIDA process

personal selling

publicity

public relations

sales promotion

oligopoly

price leadership

monopolistic competition

markup

pricing model

cash discount

trade position discount

functional discount

quantity discount

market penetration pricing

market skimming pricing

inventory turnover rate

price lining

CHAPTER TEN

Marketing Decisions

VIDEOTEX — IS IT A BIGGER phenomenon than printing and TV? Press a button and watch your TV screen for any of the following:

- all types of news and feature stories
- detailed weather reports
- sports scores and other statistics
- price and product information
- restaurant menus
- stock market and other financial information
- your bank statement
- games and quizzes
- TV and radio program schedules
- telephone directories
- movie theatre and other entertainment listings
- road conditions
- real estate, classified, and help wanted advertising
- educational materials and curriculum lists

If you wanted a printed copy and your set has facsimile capability, press another button. This viewer-controlled information revolution is a reality. Like TV itself forty years earlier, it is viewed by some as just a toy. Yet others predict that by the end of this century it is possible that videotex will be so enmeshed in our everyday living that we will wonder how we ever did without it.

IN THIS CHAPTER WE WILL EXPAND OUR DISCUSSION OF THE FOUR elements in the marketing mix. In its broadest sense, the product is the basis of any marketing program. The flow of products to customers requires a distribution system which is often complex, and relationships between participants in the channel of distribution are of critical importance to that system. Promotion stimulates this flow, and price often interacts with promotion, distribution, and product in determining marketing success.

PRODUCT

Decisions about what and how much to produce represent the first step in the product-planning process. Good product planning requires coordination with other marketing mix elements and strong customer orientation. The relationship between a firm and its customers focuses mainly on the product (or service). A product is a "bundle of services," which might include a variety of things. For example, when a mother buys a sweater for her baby at a department store, she buys warmth and comfort. She is also buying assurance that the product will last and the right to return it if it does not fit. When a man buys a cartridge of razor blades, he is buying comfortable shaves and convenient blade replacement. Buyers of ice cream think of the good taste and nutrition they are buying. This is the product.

It is very important for a firm to know what "bundle of services" customers expect from its product offering.

For example, what is the buyer of a new trash compactor buying? The product item consists of a motor and other component parts enclosed in a steel casing. This product item will perform the function of compacting trash, but the total product is much more than the product item. What about the benefits and satisfactions the buyer is getting? The product will reduce the number of trips the buyer must make to take out the trash, thereby providing convenience and more time to spend on more enjoyable activities. The retailer who sells the compactor is also a critical factor in the "bundle of satisfactions" the buyer receives. This includes such aspects as the convenience of the location, the parking facilities, credit, assortment, skill of the salespeople, returned merchandise policy, and all those things that may attract customers. The enjoyment of shopping itself is for many customers a very important part of the "bundle of satisfactions."

The Product Life Cycle

product life cycle

The life history of a product is called the product life cycle. The cycle has four phases: introduction, growth, maturity, and decline. Figure 10.1 shows a typical life cycle for a product. Both product classes and individual brands of products have life cycles. The brand's lifetime is shorter than that of the product class. People still drive cars (product class) but they no longer can buy Edsels, DeSotos, and Packards (brands).

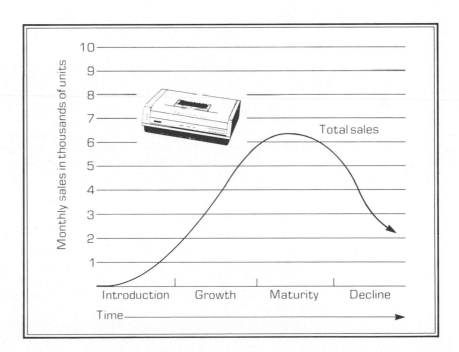

Figure 10.1
The product life cycle

Introduction

A new product is introduced to the market during the introduction stage of its life cycle. Because the marketer's basic goals are to gain initial acceptance and distribution of the new product, he or she will invest heavily in promotion to create awareness and interest among potential customers. Nevertheless, sales volume is very low during the introductory stage.

One of the most critical and delicate marketing tasks occurs when a firm introduces a new product. Because only one out of perhaps twenty new products is successful, most firms try to avoid expensive failures by using marketing research. This reduces, but doesn't by any means prevent, the chance of loss. Success depends on the new product's ability to perform a service customers will buy at a price that more than covers the firm's cost of making and selling it. It also depends on good introductory promotion and strong distribution.

Services also require innovation to succeed. Examples from recent years include automated bank tellers, pay TV, drive-in claims adjustments by auto insurance companies, rental clubs for movies to be shown on videotape cassettes, and the addition of breakfast to McDonald's menu.

Growth

A new product that has been introduced successfully will experience rapidly growing sales in the growth stage. Many of the customers who first bought the product in the introduction stage are making repeat purchases, and new customers are buying for the first time. Notice in Figure 10.1 the steep increase in the sales curve.

Maturity

Sales volume begins to level off and decline in the maturity stage, the longest part of the cycle. By the time the product enters this stage of its life cycle, many rival brands are on the market. Because rivals tend to copy features of successful brands, the various brands tend to become very similar. Once the market for a product becomes saturated, the profit potential for marketers of brands in that product class declines.

Many marketers try to extend the lives of their profitable brands. For example, baking soda sales started to decline when homemakers decreased their use of the product for baking. The brand's life cycle was extended, however, by developing new uses for the product. These include using the product as a deodorant for kitty litter boxes, refrigerators, and kitchen drains.

Decline

Marketers usually cut back on promoting their brands near the end of the maturity phase. This phase ends when a better product appears or a need disappears and the old product enters the decline stage. Examples of products that have entered the decline stage of the life cycle include CB radios, eight-track tape players, four-barrel carburetors, and black-and-white TVs.

Some companies simply stop marketing their brands when they reach the decline stage, but others try to recycle them to extend their life. Wood-

POINT OF VIEW

Are There Too Many Products on the Supermarket Shelf?

Shopper A:

"After my recent trip to several Soviet Bloc countries and to several of the less affluent Western European nations, I realized what an incredible selection Canadian supermarkets provide for their patrons. It really was a treat after my return from abroad to wander slowly through the endless rows of products. There must have been over a hundred choices of brands, types, and sizes of cleaning products alone. And the variety of meats, fruits, vege-tables, and frozen foods was astounding. There was nothing like it in East Germany or in Bulgaria."

Shopper B:

"It really drives me crazy to find my way through the maze of aisles and displays past the needless duplication of brands and minor product variations in the supermarket. I wish the government would *do* something about this waste. If advertising were reduced and the markets required to stock no more than three brands and two sizes of each basic product, we'd all save time and money."

burning stoves, for example, were well into the decline stage by the 1950s because of the advent of central heating. However, the manufacturers that stayed in that business now find that the demand has increased because of energy conservation and the use of wood as an alternate fuel. The convertible was a very popular car model in the 1950s, but by the early 1970s hardly any were being produced. Now some manufacturers are starting to make them again.

planned obsolescence

When a firm intends to replace a product, it is called planned obsolescence. Business has been criticized for this practice on the grounds that it is wasteful and somewhat deceptive. Many people feel that they are not getting a full lifetime out of the appliances and other durable goods they buy. When obsolescence occurs because of new technical features, it is called *technological obsolescence.* Invention of the electric type-writer made the manual typewriter technologically obsolete. The word processor now has begun to make the electric typewriter technologically obsolete. We will discuss the technological environment of business in more detail in Chapter 17. When only appearance or style is changed, it is called *fashion obsolescence.* Promotional activities help to create this type of obsolescence by making customers dissatisfied with the "old" product.

Regardless of the type of obsolescence—technological or fashion—a product that is no longer purchased is obsolete. As we have seen, a firm spends money on research and development (R&D) to improve its product so that it won't become obsolete. Sometimes R&D leads to an entirely new product that takes the place of the old product, making the old product obsolete. Polaroid spent many years and millions of dollars to develop Polavision—a product that enabled people to take home movies and show them without having to send the film away for processing. It extended the idea of instant photography to home movies. The product was on the

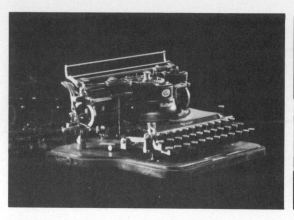 

*The change from mechanical technology to electronics has revolutionized the
business machine market. These units, spanning almost a century of progress,
suggest the importance of research, engineering and market analysis in avoiding
product obsolescence.* (Courtesy of CPT Corporation.)

market only a short time when it was made obsolete by the introduction of
video cassette recorders. Polaroid, therefore, dropped the product.

New Product Committee

new product committee

**In many larger firms the task of developing new products is performed
by a new product committee. This committee, an example of the matrix
form of organization which we discussed in Chapter 5, consists of
personnel from several different departments, such as production,
marketing, finance, and R&D.** Such a committee brings together different
kinds of expertise to review and act on new product ideas generated by
the firm.

The Product Mix — Broad or Narrow?

product mix

**A manufacturer's or a retailer's product mix is the combination of
products it produces or sells.** General Mills produces hundreds, while
Coca-Cola produces a much smaller number. The size of the product mix
affects marketing policy.

First of all, there is safety in numbers. A firm with a broad product mix
has a kind of insurance against the dangers of obsolescence. Also, economies of scale (lower costs per unit as volume rises) often make the difference between success and failure. A firm with many products can spread
its overhead cost over the entire product mix. This means savings in production costs if the products are manufactured in the same factory. It also
cuts unit distribution cost. A firm can save on distribution costs by using the
same salespeople or transportation system for all the products in its mix.
Thus General Mills' salespersons can represent many products when they
call on customers, and can ship in larger, more economical quantities.

At the retail level and, to some extent, at the wholesale level, firms with many products (a broad product mix) have an advantage in the form of product exposure. When a shopper goes to Eaton's to buy toys, he or she will also see children's clothing and may buy some along with the planned purchases. This couldn't happen in a single-product store like Hans Christian Toy Stores. A single-product store has some advantages, however. A firm that has a narrow product mix also tends to have a lot of depth to its product mix. Although a shopper can only buy toys at Hans Christian, there is a much greater variety of toys than at Eaton's. Hans Christian can promote itself as a specialist in toys. This projects an image of knowledge-ability and credibility to customers. A department store, on the other hand, is a generalist.

Packaging

All the elements that constitute the broad concept of "product" must be considered in developing the product mix. Among these is the *package.* In recent years, packaging has become a more important part of product policy. Packaging does several things:

- protects the product
- divides the product into convenient units
- becomes part of the product
- helps with promotion

Think of what polyethylene packaging has done to protect thousands of food and clothing items sold in self-service stores! The egg carton and the plastic or cardboard six-pack or twelve-pack beverage container illustrate the importance of convenient unitizing. For many cleaning and polishing products, the can or bottle also serves as the dispenser or applicator for the product. In countless consumer products advertised on TV the package and the brand are displayed together prominently so that they will be remembered when the shopper sees them on the supermarket or other self-service store shelf. Brands are an important part of marketing all by themselves.

Branding

brand

A brand is "a name, term, symbol, or design, or a combination of them, which is intended to identify the goods or services of one seller or group of sellers and to differentiate them from those of competitors" (from Committee on Definitions, Ralph S. Alexander, Chairperson, "Marketing Definitions: A Glossary of Marketing Terms," p. 8. Chicago: American Marketing Association, 1960). Brands usually include both a *name* and a *symbol.* The key to successful branding is making a lasting impression in customers' minds. A good brand name such as Bic or Seven-Up is distinctive and easy to remember.

Brand names like Coke, Jell-O, Jeep, Scotch tape, Styrofoam, Vaseline, Formica, and Xerox are so widely known that many people think they are

YOU MAKE THE DECISION!

Convenience vs. Ecology

Fairchild Bottling Company is a leading soft drink bottler in a Western province. You are the president and a major stockholder. Until 1965 you used exclusively returnable bottles in three sizes. At that time there were loud complaints by large supermarket chains and slight indication of consumer concern over the inconvenience of returning bottles. Along with many bottlers, Fairchild switched to "one-way" bottles and increased average prices by 10 percent. Sales were unaffected except that one large grocery chain, which had dropped the product earlier, picked it up again.

The ecology movement in the province has made many people, especially the young, very conscious of litter in the streets and the parks

and beaches. Environmental groups have made many public demonstrations against "one-way" bottles. They have succeeded to the extent that Fairchild still receives about 100 letters a week complaining about the problem. Also, for the last five years a private member's bill to ban nonreturnable bottles has been introduced in the legislature, and there is concern that the party in power may support the bill this year.

Assuming that Fairchild's cost of converting back to returnables would be about the same as the long-run savings in bottle cost, what would you do? Is the possible loss of some retail outlets outweighed by the expected gain of public support and the threat of government-enforced conversion later on? As president, you make the decision.

---

dictionary words that describe a product category. They are actually brand names whose owners go to great lengths to protect them from becoming dictionary words. Thus we see Xerox ads reminding us that Xerox is not a synonym for photocopying.

Brands also play a role in the marketing strategy of wholesalers and retailers. Brands developed by such middlemen are called distributor's brands or private brands. Sears' Kenmore appliances and Craftsman tools are examples. They are produced by other firms for Sears. Large grocery chains do the same thing. They generally make a larger profit per unit on private brands.

Many major retailers of grocery and related products have begun to sell unbranded products, sometimes called "generics." These products, such as paper towels, dog food, green beans, and laundry detergents, are priced even below private brands and may have some features which make them less attractive than manufacturer's or private brand items. String beans may be uneven or peas may not be uniform in generic packages, although the nutrition is equal to that of branded items.

patent

Legal protection is available for products and brands. This is especially important for small firms which cannot spend a lot on advertising. **A patent protects an invention, a chemical formula, or a new way of doing something from imitation.** The item the inventor wants to patent must be *novel* (it must not have been publicly available previously), *useful* (it must do what the inventor claims it will do), and *inventive* (it must be an improvement that would not have been developed by someone with average skills who works in the area).

If the inventor wants patent protection, he or she must file an application with the Canadian Patent Office (which is part of Consumer and Corporate Affairs). The application must contain drawings showing the features of the invention and a statement on how the invention is useful, how it works, and how it is new. If the application is successful, a patent is granted; this gives the inventor the exclusive right to the patented product or idea for a period of seventeen years. If anyone else tries to use the idea for their own financial gain, the patent holder can sue that person for damages (patent infringement).

trademark

The patent office also protects a name or symbol which, when registered, is called a trademark. Brut cologne and Dream Whip are examples of trademarks. They are also, of course, brands.

information labelling

One of consumerism's goals is the informative labelling of products. This would help a buyer to make a more informed choice among products — particularly when self-service is involved. The label could describe in simple terms the content, nutrition, durability, precautions, and other special features of a product. It might also indicate the grade or standard of quality of the item as established by industry-wide agreement or by law.

Informative labelling can lead to better purchase decisions only if the labels are read. For example, how many consumers bother to read the list of ingredients found on boxes of breakfast food? For those who do read them, how do the items listed affect their purchasing behaviour? Some consumers want a massive consumer education program to teach buyers the benefits of using label information.

Much of a firm's product policy is governed by its decision to segment or not to segment the market. As explained earlier, it is often wise to design special marketing mixes for each segment. The product is usually at the centre of a segmentation strategy.

PLACE

Both time and space separate a manufacturer from its customers, as we have seen in the previous chapter's discussion of the various forms of utility. Such time and space "gaps" occur as a result of differences between the production rate and the consumption rate and because the final users of products are more widely scattered than the producers.

place (or distribution)

Place (or distribution) is an element of the marketing mix concerned with the movement of products through a channel from producer to consumer or industrial user. This movement is accompanied by the performance of a wide range of functions which are essential to marketing, including storage, breaking bulk, and creating new assortments. Marketers set up channels of distribution to perform these functions.

Channels of Distribution

channel of distribution

A channel of distribution is the firm, or usually the set of firms, directly involved in selling a product. Channels also make up for the difference between one manufacturer's product mix and the product mix a consumer wants. Since these two mixes rarely match, other firms are often needed to complete the marketing process. For example, General Foods and Robin Hood each produce many consumer products. But a grocery shopper wants their products *and* the products of other firms such as Procter & Gamble, Campbell, Kraft, Borden, and so on. Wholesalers bring these products together and make them available to retailers, such as grocery stores.

Figure 10.2
Typical channels of distribution

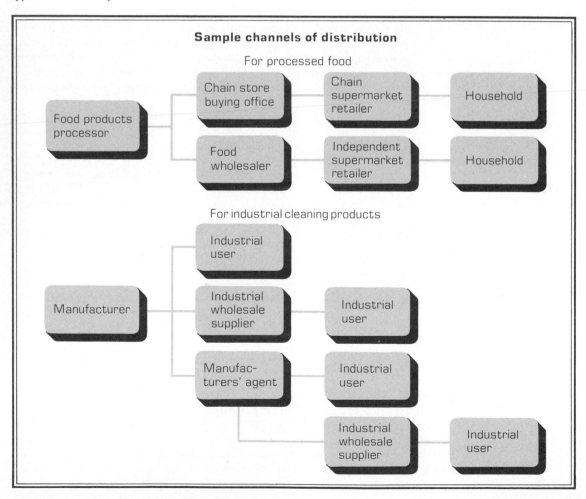

This enables the grocery shopper to buy, in one place, a broad assortment of products. These firms, except for the producer, are usually called *middlemen.* The type and number of such middlemen describe the distribution channel (see Figure 10.2).

Some consumer products manufacturers sell directly to consumers. Examples of products that are distributed this way are Avon cosmetics and World Book Encyclopedias. This type of direct distribution is much more common in industrial marketing because a typical manufacturer of industrial product sells to a much smaller number of customers than a typical consumer products manufacturer. Thus Xerox can afford to send salespersons directly to its customers. This would be too costly for Procter & Gamble because its customers number in the millions. The final decision about how to get products to customers requires a compromise between cost control and providing the best service and convenience. This means that the final development of a channel depends on

- the number of customers
- the functions which the channel is expected to perform
- the costs of alternative channels
- the importance of controlling the marketing process

Thus a maker of lathes selling to a handful of industrial firms may sell directly to customers. A maker of toothbrushes selling to millions of customers, by contrast, will need a long (several levels of middlemen) channel. A firm making several different appliances with high unit profit margins, like Singer, can operate its own retail stores because the overhead cost is spread over several products. A manufacturer of blankets could never afford to do so.

It is important to understand that marketers are always trying to develop new and better channels to reach their customers. Xerox, for example, decided recently to begin producing and marketing copiers for small-volume users to compete with copiers by Savin and other rival firms. Xerox knew that to call on small users, such as doctors, lawyers, accountants, and small business firms, would require too large a sales force so it began opening its own retail stores to reach them. Meanwhile, Xerox continued to use its direct sales force to call individually on large-volume users. This is an example of the use of multiple channels to reach a firm's customers.

The Principal Middlemen

There are three basic types of middlemen:

- merchant middlemen
- agent middlemen
- facilitating middlemen

Merchant middlemen actually take title to the products they offer for sale, while *agent middlemen* do not. *Facilitating middlemen,* like transportation firms, participate in the transportation and storage of the product, without actually buying and selling it.

Examples of merchant middlemen include *wholesalers* and *retailers.* These firms regularly buy stocks of products and resell them. Retailers are involved in selling a wide variety of consumer products. Food, for example, is sold mostly through food and grocery retailers known as supermarkets, some of which are parts of large chains (Dominion, Loblaws, Safeway) and some of which are independent. Independent supermarkets usually buy from independent wholesalers, while chain stores receive products from their own firm's central distribution points, which perform the wholesaling function.

The top part of Figure 10.2 shows a typical channel of distribution used by a processor of a food product. This firm sells to a central buying office of a large food chain which, in turn, distributes to its retail stores. These, of course, sell to households. Other important retailer types include department stores, drug stores, variety stores, discount houses, and vending machine operators.

Agent middlemen include manufacturers' agents, brokers, and selling agents. These firms are involved in selling a wide variety of products, including consumer products and industrial products. **Manufacturers' agents are paid a commission to represent manufacturers of several non-competitive lines in a limited geographic territory. Without taking possession of products, such agents aggressively seek to establish these products in this territory,**

A manufacturer's agent may help a producer of industrial cleaning products to introduce the line in British Columbia. Since the agent gets paid a commission only for the actual sales made, this can be a more efficient way of distributing in a new territory, rather than dealing directly or through wholesale industrial suppliers. The bottom part of Figure 10.2 shows the "set" of channels which a manufacturer of industrial cleaners might use. In some cases, this firm sells directly to large industrial users, using its own sales force. In other cases, the producer sells to industrial suppliers (wholesalers) who sell to industrial users (usually the smaller customers). Another method is to use the manufacturer's agent to reach either users or wholesale industrial suppliers. It is common for a national manufacturer to use different channels of distribution in different parts of the country.

The more direct a channel is, the more control a manufacturer has over its distribution. Control is improved by means of franchising. **A franchised retailer is tied closely by contract to a manufacturer, and its operations are strictly supervised. Examples of franchised outlets include McDonald's and other fast-food firms, as well as auto dealers and many gasoline stations.** Franchising is discussed in detail in Chapter 15.

Facilitating middlemen are not pictured in Figure 10.2, although they may be involved in each case. These are railroads, warehouse companies, insurers, and other firms which facilitate or help in distribution but are not directly engaged in buying or selling.

manufacturers' agent

franchised retailer

CAREERS IN RETAILING AND WHOLESALING

LIKE MOST CAREER AREAS, RETAILING OFFERS OPPORTUNITY AT MANY levels and in a variety of jobs. Most people enter retailing as a floor salesperson or as a worker in the stockroom. Usually this does not require college work or even a high school diploma. As a matter of fact, distributive education programs in many cities allow high school students to work in retailing while they study related courses. Similar programs also exist in community colleges where students train more specifically for higher positions. A person from a community college may become a suburban sales manager, an assistant buyer, a buyer, or a credit manager. Many four-year university graduates begin their retail careers in selling. They often spend short periods in several different sales departments and store branches during their time as trainees.

Retail selling requires skills in customer relations, simple mathematics, an eye for merchandise and display, and a good memory for inventory information. It also requires physical endurance to stand for long periods and to cope with hectic "sales."

Branch suburban managers require supervisory skills and a willingness to work long hours. They usually do not have buying responsibilities but must be skilled in customer relations. Assistant buyers and buyers must understand merchandising and be able to spot changes in customer tastes. They must be skillful negotiators.

Higher education is not essential for promotion to buyer or executive positions, but competition for such positions is great and the more education you have, the better your chances are. A university graduate with a marketing or retailing specialty is especially likely to be promoted. For information, write the Retail Council of Canada, Ste. 525, 74 Victoria Street, Toronto, Ontario M5C 2A5.

Wholesaling also offers opportunities in selling. A high school diploma is usually required, although a community college or university background is extremely helpful for success and promotion, especially where the product is technical in nature. Without some college training a person will not begin in wholesaling as a salesperson, but rather as a clerk, a stockperson, or a driver.

Wholesale selling involves learning the product line, the competitors' lines, and the needs of potential customers in your territory. You will spend a lot of time in the field, working alone. It can be physically and emotionally demanding. Often the wholesale salesperson spends many hours driving, trying to make contacts, entertaining clients, and making out reports.

A wholesale salesperson may be "promoted" by being assigned to territories with less travel requirement or higher sales potential. Successful salespersons may become local, regional, or general sales managers or may move into buying, credit work, or public relations for their firms. ■

Selling without a middleman usually takes place in special circumstances.

Are Middlemen Necessary?

At some time you might have heard a friend say that she got a great bargain from a store because she bought it "direct from the factory" or "eliminated the middleman." Your friend assumed that the price was reduced by the profit which would have gone to the middleman. Such a claim would lead you to believe that middlemen are unnecessary and expensive and should be abolished. Let's examine this claim.

The Glammer Company is a hardware wholesaler. Glammer buys saws, nails, electrical fixtures, adhesives, and camping equipment from five different manufacturers. Glammer buys a rail carload of each product each month. It sells most of these five products to fifty retail hardware stores in southern Ontario. The retailers each make small purchases of some of the five products every week or two from Glammer. The hardware retailers also buy from three to six other wholesalers in order to keep a complete inventory.

Why don't the retailers buy all the items they carry direct from the manufacturers? The answer is clear — they save money by buying through the wholesaler. The Glammer Company simplifies the number of purchases and sales and reduces unit shopping costs and record keeping. It provides quicker delivery to the retailers than they could get by dealing directly with the manufacturers. Figure 10.3 illustrates this principle. Each connecting line represents a transaction. Without the wholesaler, each retailer would have to deal with all four manufacturers. Each manufacturer would also have to deal with all four retailers. With the wholesaler, each retailer and each manufacturer need deal only with one intermediary — the

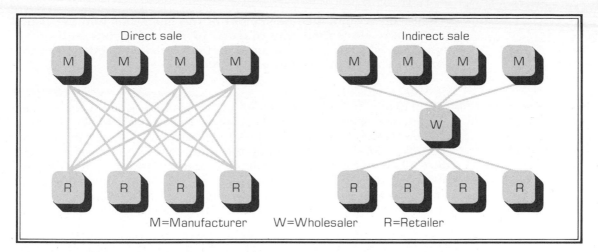

Figure 10.3
Direct versus indirect sale

wholesaler. Thus, the wholesaler reduces the number of transactions and makes it possible to increase the average size of transactions. This increase brings about economics of scale and thereby justifies the existence and the profit margin of the middleman. Clearly, shipping in carload lots is much cheaper than the many small shipments which would be needed for direct sales from manufacturers to retailers.

There are great economic advantages in a system of distribution which uses a wholesaler. This middleman (1) buys in large quantities and sells in small quantities; (2) makes it possible for the retailer to simplify its buying process by carrying a broad line of hardware items; (3) often takes credit risks which manufacturers might not accept; and (4) guarantees delivery on short notice so that retailers need not keep large stocks. In most cases, wholesalers and their margins (the difference between the costs of goods to them and what they sell them for) are justified.

If your friend got a real bargain from the retailer who "eliminated the middleman," she probably made the purchase under very special circumstances. Maybe the retailer is practising "leader" pricing with this one product. Practising leader pricing means setting a price low on a widely bought item to attract buyers to a store. The retailer also could be part of a chain operation with a very high volume of sales. In any case, the functions usually performed by the wholesaler have to be performed by someone. This costs money.

Physical Distribution

physical distribution

The growth in volume and variety of goods sold, together with new transport technology, has turned the attention of manufacturers toward the problem of physical distribution or logistics. **Physical distribution is con-**

cerned with the physical movement of raw materials into the plant, the in-plant movement and storage of raw materials and semi-manufactured goods, and the movement of finished goods out of the plant to the ultimate consumer or industrial user.

The Total Cost Concept

total cost concept

At one time physical distribution management was mainly concerned with minimizing the cost of transportation. This is a narrow view because the transportation cost may be less than half the total cost of physical distribution. **Modern firms apply the total cost concept, which considers all costs related to a particular means of physical distribution. Their goal is to minimize their total costs without sacrificing their desired level of customer service.** In addition to transportation, there are storage costs and "out-of-stock" costs. Concentrating only on transportation rates is shortsighted.

Many firms have developed distribution systems that depend on computers to schedule the flow of products from manufacturer to consumer or industrial user. They select the best location for intermediate storage points and the best means of transportation. These computer-based systems take into account the costs of transporting and storing as well as the cost of "running out" of merchandise. Such accurate cost systems are common where the channel is under the control of a retailer or manufacturer. The objective of modern physical distribution management is to achieve a *balance* between costs and service.

The Modes of Transportation

Firms have a choice among railroads, motor trucks, air freight, and, in some cases, ships and barges or pipelines to move their products. Decisions like this are in the hands of the *traffic manager.* This important decision maker keeps track of the in-and-out flow of materials, delivery dates, and storage space with the goal of coordinating all aspects of physical distribution and thereby ensuring customer satisfaction at the lowest cost. Recent history, as can be seen in Figure 10.4, has seen some dramatic shifts in the relative importance of the various modes of transportation.

There is a legal relationship between a firm that wants to move freight (the shipper) and the transportation firm (the carrier) that will handle the actual transport. Carriers (railroads, truckers, shipping companies, etc.) can be

- common carriers
- contract carriers
- private carriers

common carrier

A common carrier offers its services to the general public at uniform, published rates. These carriers' rates and services are supervised by public agencies.

contract carrier

When a firm needs to move goods which can't be moved by common carrier, it may call on a contract carrier. **A contract carrier is a firm, such as a trucking company, that negotiates long- or short-term contracts with shippers to handle their freight.** It is a private contract. The shipper

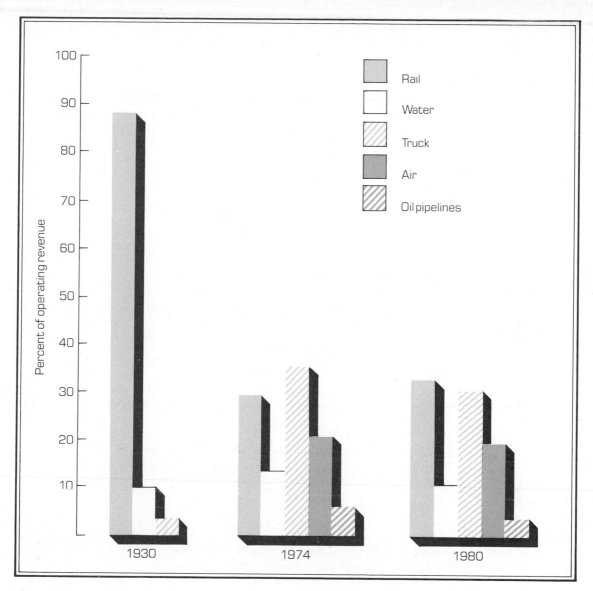

Figure 10.4
*Per cent distribution of operating revenues by mode of transportation: 1930,
1974, and 1980.* (Canada Yearbook, 1976-77, p. 731. Also publications 52-208,
54-205, 55-201, 53-222, and 51-002, 1980. Used by permission of the Minister
of Supply and Services Canada.)

may want customized service and may want a guarantee of availability
without investing in its own truck or barge fleet.

private carrier   **If a manufacturer or middleman owns and operates its own transportation, it is called a private carrier.** This kind of operation is justified

when a large, predictable volume exists and common carriers are not as economical or can't do exactly what the shipper needs.

Railroads.

Each of the major modes of transportation has its good and bad points. The railroad's major advantage has alway been low cost, long haul transportation for heavy and bulky commodities that have a low value in relation to weight. Coal, sand, gravel, steel, lumber, and grain are examples of products hauled by railroads. The railroad also provides reliable service, because varying weather conditions do not often affect it. Economies of scale are evident in railroading because one diesel engine can pull one or many loaded cars. This enables the railroad to spread the cost of the motive power over a large number of shipments.

The major limitations, however, also relate to *economies of scale.* Less-than-carload lots (l.c.l.) are not well-suited to rail movement. Modern railroads use mechanized loading and unloading equipment that is designed to handle single, large units. Small shipments require very costly manual handling. Furthermore, the more cars that can be moved with one engine, the lower the cost to move each car. Therefore, the small shipper may find its shipment waiting on the siding while a large train is being made up.

New types of equipment and operating procedures are helping railroads to increase their traffic in farm products other than grain, manufactured products, as well as bulk commodities. Snowy freight cars, for example, have a two-inch coating of foam insulation to keep pre-cooled perishable products like fruits and vegetables at the desired temperature enroute without ice or mechanical refrigeration devices. Aerated cars haul dry bulk cargoes like flour and cement. They operate on the vacuum cleaner principle and "inhale" their cargo when loading and "exhale" it when unloading. This reduces the need for packaging. Hot slab gondola cars haul hot slabs of steel from steel plants to rolling mills. This, in effect, makes rail service a part of the steel industry's production line.

Trucking.

The major advantage of motor truck transport is flexibility. Trucks can go anywhere there is a road. Thus by truck the shipper can reach many more potential customers than by other modes.

As in the case of the rails, there are many different types of trucks, some of which are highly specialized. Because the required investment is rather small, many shippers own and operate their own trucks. Door-to-door service is possible with trucks, and service is speedy.

A major problem facing highway carriers today is the high cost of fuel. In their efforts to reduce fuel consumption, many truck lines are placing air deflector shields on top of their long-haul tractors, switching to more fuel efficient radial tires, and installing devices that disconnect the cooling fans on big truck engines when not needed. Studies have shown that such fans are needed only 5 percent of the time the motor is running.

Waterways.

Water transport is important in both domestic and foreign commerce. The major advantage is low cost transport for low-value, bulky products. As bulk goes up and value goes down, the advantage of water transport increases. On the other hand, as delivery time becomes more important, barges become less attractive. Accessibility to waterways and ports is, of course, necessary.

Pipelines.

Pipelines are the most "invisible" of the modes, although they move many millions of tonnes of goods over many miles. Thousands of miles of pipelines move crude and refined petroleum, chemicals, and natural gas from major production points and ports of entry to cities all over Canada. A process called batch processing permits several different products to be moved at the same time. Lines are also now built for the movement of pulverized coal in slurry form (suspended in water) but, as the demand for coal rises, problems arise due to the increasing water shortage in major coal-producing areas.

Pipelines are almost completely unaffected by weather and, once they are installed, the cost of operation is very low. Very little labour is involved in operating them.

Airlines.

In the not too distant past, airplanes were considered basically "people carriers." At best, they could move only very high-value, low-bulk cargo. The arrival of the jet age and jumbo jets, the increased number of airports, and sophisticated materials-handling techniques have changed many of these ideas. Air transport is speedy, safe, and can help the shipper in reducing other elements of total distribution costs. Many airlines appeal to the shipper on the basis that if it is willing to spend a little more money on transportation, its other distribution costs can be reduced. One major problem is that higher fuel costs have led some airlines to discontinue service to smaller cities.

Containerization

containerization

Our discussion of physical distribution would be incomplete without some discussion of containerization. **Containerization is the practice of using standard large containers, preloaded by the seller, to move freight.**

Modern containers move many types of freight. They are loaded at the shipper's plant, sealed, and moved to the receiver's plant. Instead of many individual items being individually handled, the entire container is mechanically handled. They move with great efficiency from truck to train (piggyback), from train to ship (fishyback), and from truck to plane (birdyback). This is called *intermodal transportation*. The savings in distribution cost can be great because of reduced theft and damage as well as lower transportation rates on intermodal movements.

AUTHORS' COMMENTARY

Containerization Will Continue to Change Water Transport

Containerization on a giant scale is changing the face of ocean-going commerce. One variety of containerization is RO/RO, or roll-on, roll-off. Loaded trailers are trucked to a port where they are wheeled aboard the ship for the ocean voyage. When the ship arrives at the overseas port, the trailers are wheeled off and trucked to their final destinations.

On an even greater scale, an increasing variety of industrial and consumer products are being loaded aboard barges that serve as containers. These barges are then loaded aboard specially designed ocean-going ships. Thus a ship may carry seventy barges loaded with cargo across the Atlantic Ocean. At Rotterdam they are off-loaded and pushed or pulled by tugboats on the inland waterways to their final destinations. The time needed to unload these vessels is only a fraction of the time conventional ships require to load and unload one pallet at a time by crane. This means the vessels can spend more time at sea and less time in port. Quick, and therefore economical, use of capital equipment, together with less pilferage and wear-and-tear, are the reasons that containers will continue to change the decisions physical distribution managers make.

PROMOTION

promotion

Promotion is probably the most dynamic, aggressive, and persuasive element of the marketing mix. Promotion includes all communication by a firm with its customers or potential customers for the purpose of expanding sales, directly or indirectly. Promotion is communication that

- gains attention
- teaches
- reminds
- persuades
- reassures

At any point in a product's life cycle, promotional communication can be used to do any of these things. The major goal of most promotional effort, however, is to *persuade* target customers to do something. Usually, of course, this means persuading target customers to buy the product. Quite often target customers are persuaded to respond very quickly. Ads on TV that feature record albums and tapes, for example, often include a toll-free number that viewers can call to place their orders immediately after seeing the ad.

Promotional effort is also devoted to *reassuring* present customers that they made the right decision in buying the firm's product. Auto dealers and auto manufacturers, for example, often send letters to their new car buyers congratulating them on their purchase decision. The purpose is to help reassure these buyers that they made the right decision — they bought the

Figure 10.5
*The communication
process in promotion*

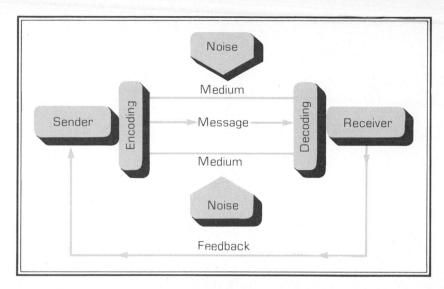

"right" car. This can help to dispel any second thoughts they may be having about the new car they just bought.

Because of the dynamic nature of competition, promotion must be viewed as a communication process. It is the process of sending messages through a variety of media. Figure 10.5 illustrates the communication process. It shows that a message must be encoded (expressed in a particular way), sent through a particular medium (such as television, word-of-mouth, or billboards), and decoded (interpreted by the target market). This must occur despite noise (distractions) which might interfere with the communication such as competing commercials, traffic sounds, or rock music. A complete communication process also involves some kind of feedback. This is another way of saying that when a message is sent out there is usually a response of some kind. In most cases, the desired response is purchase of the product or service by target customers. The choice of a medium can influence the way that the message is received. For example, it would be a mistake to promote burial insurance during a TV situation comedy program.

The principal methods of promotion are advertising and personal selling. Of somewhat less importance are sales promotion, publicity, and public relations. Let's discuss these methods and how they relate to one another.

Advertising

advertising

Modern Canadians are familiar with the process of advertising. They are subjected to it during a large part of every day of their lives, much of it through TV. **Advertising includes all nonpersonal promotional activity for which a fee is paid.** The special feature of advertising is its ability to reach large numbers of people at the same time and at a moderate cost per

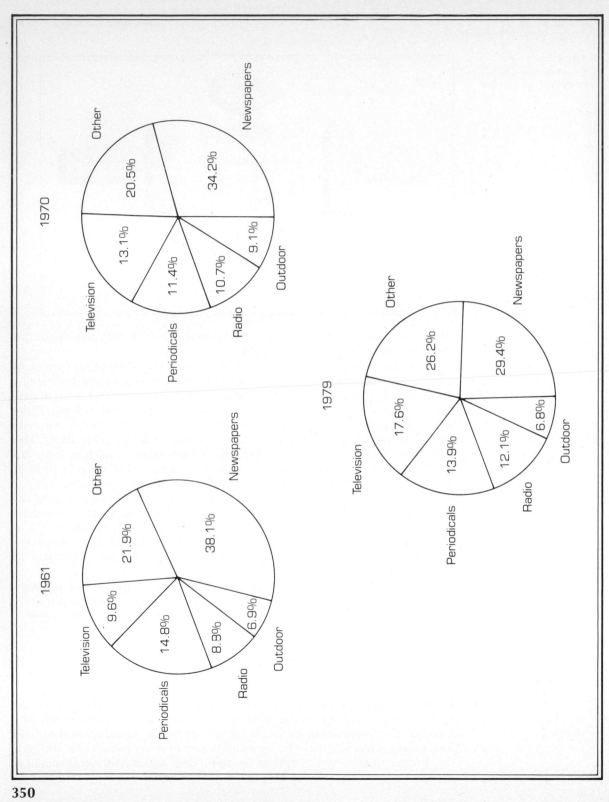

contact. It is done through the principal advertising media of television, consumer magazines, newspapers, business publications, radio, direct mail, and billboards. It is carried on by such institutions as advertising departments of firms or advertising agencies.

The volume of advertising in each of the major media is shown in Figure 10.6. The use of TV continues to grow at the expense of newspapers and magazines.

Individual firms spend most of their advertising budgets on *brand, or selective, advertising.* This means that the purpose is to promote the particular brand of product sold by that firm. Sometimes firms also engage in *institutional advertising,* which promotes the good name of the firm as a whole. When a group of firms advertise a general class of product without mentioning brands, this is called *primary demand advertising.* You have probably seen ads urging you to drink more milk or eat more beef. Let's turn now to a discussion of the principal institutions that are involved in advertising and examine the functions of each institution.

Advertising Institutions

The principal institutions involved in making advertising decisions are

- advertising departments of firms
- advertising agencies
- advertising media — newspapers, television stations, magazines, and so on

Advertising Departments.

Most large- and medium-sized firms have a separate department to oversee advertising activities. If a firm has adopted the marketing concept, its advertising department is under the authority of the top marketing executive. This provides for coordination of advertising with other promotional activities and with the rest of the marketing mix. Advertising departments serve as communicators between the firm and the advertising agency.

Small firms, on the other hand, generally do not have an advertising department. One or two people usually handle the firm's advertising. When they have ideas for an ad campaign they go to the local newspaper, radio, or TV station and present those ideas. If the small firm buys a certain minimum amount of newspaper space or radio or TV time, the medium will handle the production of the ad at no cost to the client. The client pays only for the space or time. Local, independent grocery stores often take this approach in running their weekly ads.

Advertising Agencies.

advertising agency

The principal creative centres for advertising for most medium-sized and large firms are their advertising agencies. An advertising

---

Figure 10.6
Net advertising revenues by media (in $000's) (Used by permission of McLean-Hunter Research Bureau)

agency specializes in performing advertising functions for other firms.
It serves its clients by planning advertising campaigns, by buying time
and space in the broadcast (radio and TV) and print (newspapers and
magazines) media, and by checking that ads appear as agreed. Sometimes
ad agencies perform additional marketing functions, such as marketing
research and public relations. Agencies are normally paid a 15 percent
commission based on the dollar amount of advertising placed in the media.
They also charge additional fees if they perform marketing research or
other special services for their clients.

A key role in the advertising agency is played by the account executive.
**An account executive is in charge of the entire relationship between
the agency and a particular client (account) and coordinates the work
of the group of professionals involved in the client's ad program.**

account executive

Advertising Media.

advertising media

**The advertising media carry the message designed by firms and
their agencies to many receivers (customers or potential customers).
The most important media are newspapers, television, direct mail, and
magazines, in that order.** As we have seen in Figure 10.6, since 1968, the
largest gain in the share of total advertising volume has been made by TV.
The other major media have lost share except for radio. Newspapers and
magazines were the big losers.

An advertiser selects media (often with an agency's help) with a number
of factors in mind. The marketing executive must first ask "Which medium
will reach the people I want to reach?" If a firm is selling turkey breeding
equipment, it might select *Turkey World,* a business paper read mostly by
turkey breeders. If it is selling silverware, it might choose a magazine for
brides. If it is selling toothpaste, the choice might be a general audience
television program or a general audience magazine like *Reader's Digest.*

Another important factor in media choice is the medium's ability to
deliver a message effectively. Some messages need visual communication
and some need the added dimension of colour. Foods are an example of
products that benefit from colour in communication. Selling an electric
organ requires a sound-oriented medium. Some messages need colour,
sound, and motion. This is only available in colour television, the medium
with the greatest set of "communicating tools."

There are other special considerations in media selection. For example,
print media are more permanent. They can communicate several times or
be taken to the store as a shopping aid. Some media (radio, television, and
daily newspaper) provide frequent communication and relatively short
"lag" time before the ad will appear. Finally, there is the cost per contact
with a customer or prospect. This will vary greatly, but the one-dimensional
media, such as radio and newspapers, are usually inexpensive per contact.
TV costs more.

How an Advertisement Works

Much of what advertising can do can be shown by careful examination of
a particular advertisement. **A promotional process can be thought of**

AIDA process

in terms of how it works on a particular receiver or prospective customer, leading him or her through the stages of attention, interest, desire, and action — the AIDA process.

The advertisements at the end of this chapter illustrate how a printed ad may apply to this process. Headlines are usually attention-getters and interest-builders. Sometimes they go a long way toward building desire, too. Copy, in many ads, is the desire-builder or convincer because it gives facts and anticipates objections by the reader. The signature is usually the familiar company trademark or brand name. It says who is sending the message. Sometimes it is accompanied by a coupon or an action-inducing offer.

The ads shown at the end of the chapter display a variety of appeals or themes used to "reach" customers. The advertiser uses the appeal which fits the product and the customer.

The arrangement of parts in a print ad — illustration, headline, and copy — is called the layout. Ideally, the layout makes it easy to "carry the reader through" the phases of attention, interest, desire, and action. A similar AIDA "game plan" can also be used in personal selling.

Advertising Complaints and Regulation

Because advertising is such an obvious part of the lives of Canadians, it is not surprising that it is subject to much criticism and government regulation. Complaints come from consumer groups, conservationists, sociologists, and economists about the effects and some of the methods of advertising.

Some complaints relate to truth in advertising. Some exaggeration about the quality of products has always been permitted, but there are limits to such exaggeration. The Combines Investigation Act has, in recent years, been amended so that false and misleading advertising is more closely controlled. Its ground rules provide that all statements of fact be supported by evidence.

Other questions about advertising that are worth mentioning are (1) are we being brainwashed? (2) is too much advertising wasteful? (3) does advertising lead to monopoly and high prices? and (4) what effect is advertising having on the values of our people? While some of these questions have merit, it is hard to imagine how the great productivity and wealth of our economy could have happened without the stimulating effect of modern advertising.

Personal Selling and Sales Management

In some situations there is no substitute for one-to-one human persuasion. All of us experience it nearly every day. There is a lot one person can do to convince another of a point of view. This could mean one's willingness to try a new brand of beer or change an attitude toward a politician. However, persuasive talent cannot serve a business effectively unless it is properly managed.

CAREERS IN ADVERTISING

IF YOU ARE INTERESTED IN ADVERTISING, YOU SHOULD CONSIDER positions like account executive, copy writer, and media buyer.

Advertising *account executives* work for advertising agencies and co-ordinate the services the agencies provide for their clients. They are planners, bugdet makers, salespersons, and "idea people" all rolled into one. This requires a rare combination of creativity and good "business sense." It usually takes a university degree and at least a few years working in related advertising jobs. As a career it can have drastic ups and downs, depending on the gain and loss of large accounts by the agencies. Levels of pay vary widely, depending on the size of the agency and the success of ad campaigns created under the account executive's control.

Among those persons who work with account executives in advertising agencies are copy writers and media buyers. *Copy writers* are creative people who have a way with words. They are often, but not always, college graduates with backgrounds in English or journalism. Pay depends on the degree of success of their creations. Copy writers also often work for the advertisers or the medium (newspaper or TV stations) instead of the agency, but they do the same type of work.

Media buyers work for ad agencies or for advertisers themselves. They are experts in finding space and time in the media for their employers. They analyze rates and availability of media to maximize the advertising dollar. A B.Comm. helps but is not essential. Information is available from the Canadian Advertising and Sales Association, Suite 369, Hotel Queen Elizabeth, Montreal, Quebec H3B 1X8. ■

personal selling

Personal selling includes any direct human communication for the purpose of increasing, directly or indirectly, a firm's sales. The special quality of personal selling is its individuality—the one-to-one relationship between the seller and the buyer—and the fact that the seller may give very special attention to the buyer's needs. The tone of personal selling can vary widely. It can be like that of a sideshow barker or of a skilled computer salesperson. The styles are different, but the goal is the same—to sell. Both hope to guide the receiver through the AIDA process. (See Table 10.1 for a typical example of how a salesperson might follow this process.) Advertising and personal selling are complementary; they work well together. Avon, for example, advertises on TV to stimulate interest in its products. It also has a door-to-door sales force of nearly one million people to make personal calls on its target customers.

The modern view of personal selling is that salespeople are expected to help their prospects identify and solve problems. An Avon salesperson, for

Table 10.1   A Typical Personal Selling Sequence

Salesperson (S)	Prospect (P)
Enters situation with thorough knowledge of product, incomplete knowledge of prospect's needs. Is confident.	Enters situation with a poorly formed idea of need, very little information about salesperson or product. Some distrust and hostility toward salesperson.
1. Attracts attention of *P* by setting up appointment and, perhaps, by indicating some awareness of the needs of *P*.	2. Greets *S*, attitude improved by the pleasant, interested manner of *S*.
3. Begins to show how product can solve a problem *P* has.	4. Becomes more deeply interested but brings up certain objections regarding price and quality.
5. Answers *P*'s objections by describing credit plan and explaining how the service department of *S*'s firm can overcome the problems in (4) by *P*. Asks for the order.	6. Finds another reason to object to signing order, but the objection is mild.
7. Answers last objection and closes with, "If you'll just give me your okay on this, we can make delivery on the first of the month."	8. Agrees to buy on a trial basis.
9. Thanks *P*, checks over details of order. Later, checks on *P*'s satisfaction.	10. May experience some post-sale doubt, but reassures self of wise decision.

example, may demonstrate to a woman with very sensitive skin how a particular type of makeup can help her to deal with the problem. In many cases industrial salespeople require training in engineering, chemistry, data processing, or other scientific and technical areas in order to deal effectively with their prospects' problems. Thus a salesperson who sells oil field equipment must know a lot about petroleum engineering. Many firms staff their sales organizations with sales specialists who call on prospects in particular types of markets. Thus some sales representatives may call on banks, others may call on hospitals, and others may call on schools. Because these prospects' problems often vary, the sales reps who call on them should be trained to handle their specialized problems.

Selling and sales management both require the development of a wide variety of skills and techniques. The nature of the sales task will determine which kinds of skills and techniques are needed. Retail selling, for example, requires quite a different kind of preparation and ability than selling technical equipment, such as computers, to industrial buyers.

Salespeople operate in many different ways, but most of them

• do some "prospecting" and/or "qualifying." This involves developing lists of prospective customers and screening them for likelihood of purchase and profitability as customers

•get to know their products and services in every way possible, including strong points and weak points
•formulate sales strategies that best suit their product and their customer as well as their own personal talents
•learn to answer customers' objections
•learn to be persistent, positive, and confident enough to close the sale
•follow up to ensure customer satisfaction

There are special problems in managing a sales force that are not evident in managing other personnel. To be successful, salespeople must be confident in themselves and in their product. Their morale must be kept high. Sales managers are often handicapped in trying to maintain high morale because they usually lack continuous personal contact with sales personnel.

The sales manager's responsibilities include

•building an effective sales force
•directing the sales force
•monitoring the sales effort

To build a sales force, the sales manager must develop recruiting sources and techniques, devise methods of selecting from the recruits, and maintain an effective sales training program for those selected. Directing the salespeople includes developing workable pay plans, which might include salaries, commissions, and/or bonuses, and programs for appealing to higher-order motivations such as those discussed in Chapter 5. The third task, that of monitoring sales effort, is a special form of control. The sales manager must, therefore, set up standards — such as sales quotas and sales expense budgets for sales territories, products, and individual salespersons — and make regular comparisons of actual sales results to such standards and make the necessary corrections. Corrective action may range from redefining sales territories to additional sales training to dismissal of ineffective sales employees.

Thus, in order to be effective, the sales manager must perform the functions of management — planning, organizing, staffing, directing, and controlling. Within the context of personal selling, this means doing activities like manpower planning, recruitment, selection, training, and evaluating salespeople. It also requires the sales manager to develop policies and procedures, establish territories and quotas, analyze sales and costs, and work closely with salespeople so that they reach their potential.

Other Promotional Methods

Promotional activities other than advertising and personal selling sometimes play a major role in the marketing mix of business firms. These include publicity, public relations, and sales promotion.

Publicity

publicity

Publicity is a communication through the news media as a legitimate part of the news. It is usually an inexpensive means of promotion, because its only cost is preparing the news story or press release. But only items considered "newsworthy" by the press are used and, very often, carefully prepared items are never printed or broadcast. Often, news stories (like the announcement of the new models of Ford Motor Company) may be cut down by newspapers for lack of space. Thus publicity is a promotional method over which the firm has little control. Also it is limited to reporting facts.

Firms sometimes receive negative publicity. The marketer of a product that is recalled from the market will receive some negative publicity. Firms, of course, try to avoid this by, for example, following quality control procedures in manufacturing their products. But sometimes things go wrong. The question is how to deal with this negative publicity? The consensus appears to favour cooperating with regulatory agencies and the news media in providing relevant facts rather than attempting to cover them up. Thus a firm that is either ordered to recall a product or that does so voluntarily would want to provide the media with information for consumers concerning how to get the product repaired or replaced.

Public Relations

public relations

Public relations is harder to define. **Public relations includes any personal communication with the public or with government (lobbying) that seeks to create goodwill for the firm. Its effect on sales is usually indirect and long-run.** Recently, for example, some people have been strongly critical of the use of nuclear reactors to generate electricity. To help dispel this criticism and to give the public an opportunity to see the safety features built into such plants, some companies conduct guided tours of their facilities. Your college or university probably also has a public relations department. One of its activities might include sending representatives to talk to students at nearby high schools to point out the advantages of attending the college or university.

Sales Promotion

sales promotion

Sales promotion includes special events directed at increasing sales. Special sales, coupon offers, contests, games, entertainment features, and trading stamps are examples. Some would include specialty advertising devices such as matches, calendars, and ballpoint pens. Others might add "spiffs," which are cash payments to retailers and their employees to promote a manufacturer's products.

Sales promotion is often directed at consumers. Marketers of food products are major users of cents-off coupons. *Reader's Digest* sponsors frequent consumer sweepstakes. Sales promotions can also be directed to a manufacturer's sales force, middlemen, and middlemen's sales forces. For example, various companies give their top salesperson a trip to the Caribbean in January or February. Other firms supply retailers with point-of-purchase displays to help increase sales.

WHAT DO YOU THINK?

Are Sweepstakes an Effective Sales Promotion Tool?

During the late 1970s and early '80s many firms like McDonald's, Sweet Caporal, *Reader's Digest,* and General Motors ran well-publicized sweepstakes programs. Obviously these firms feel that these contests will positively affect sales, but it is very difficult to measure the impact of sweepstakes. Critics argue that while there may be a positive short-run effect on sales, sweepstakes do not have much influence in the long run. WHAT DO YOU THINK?

The four promotion activities (advertising, personal selling, publicity, and sales promotion) together constitute the firm's promotional strategy. The overall promotional strategy is designed to effectively reach the target market the company has identified (see Figure 10.7).

PRICE

In a competitive world dominated by promotion and product differentiation, price still plays a part. Most firms still concentrate much of their effort on the problem of setting price. How this process fits into the firm's planning is a different story for almost every firm. The role of price in the mix is not as great as it once was. However, the importance of careful pricing cannot be ignored.

Market Conditions and Pricing

The key concepts of price, market, supply, and demand were introduced in Chapter 2. These explanations were limited to a rather narrow range of market conditions (a large number of buyers and sellers, a homogeneous product, easy entry into the market, and market information in the hands of buyers and sellers). A homogeneous product means that the buyers do not make any distinction between the products for sale. Easy market entry occurs when no large capital investment is needed for new sellers to emerge. The necessary market information includes facts about the numbers of competitors and supply and demand conditions.

As consumers, we know that all these conditions rarely exist. The more common kinds of market conditions are oligopoly and monopolistic competition. **An oligopoly means there are only a few sellers of the same or slightly different products.** The market for automatic washing machines, for example, might be classified as oligopolistic. There are few sellers and prices are generally stable.

oligopoly

price leadership

monopolistic
competition

In oligopoly, one of the stronger competitors may sometimes
raise price, and it is likely that others will follow suit. This is called
price leadership.

**Monopolistic competition is a market in which many somewhat
differentiated products or servces are sold.** This is most common in
retail and service firms. Location and quality of service are the differentiating factors. New competitors can easily enter the market. This prevents the typical competitor from making large profits.

There is such a great array of markets and products in the developed
Western nations that labels such as "oligopoly" and "monopolistic
competition" are not enough. They help us understand some of the price
behaviour, but they are not enough to guide price decisions. Such theoretical market concepts don't account for the use of the marketing mix
elements other than price. Price is only one of the competitive tools.

The issue of pricing is further complicated by government involvement
in pricing in both the private and the public sector. For example, provincial

Figure 10.7
The elements in promotional strategy

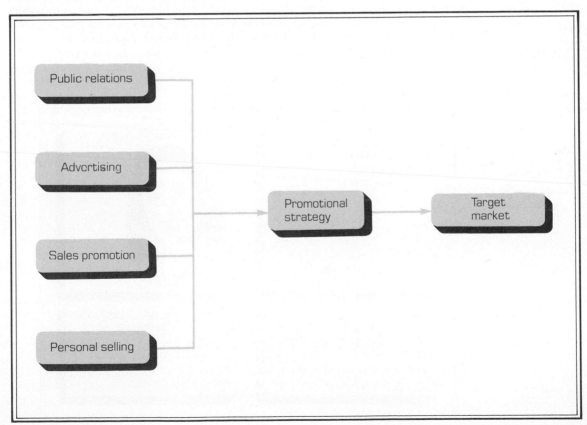

utilities must get approval for rate increases from a provincial board. Government also affects price by subsidizing activities like public transportation. Marketing boards establish prices for agricultural products, and this further influences prices consumers have to pay.

Setting Basic Price

Under the guidelines of pricing objectives, firms must set basic prices. We will examine two different approaches to the problem of setting basic price: the cost approach and the demand approach (see Figure 10.8) and then we will see how some firms combine these two approaches. First, let's look at the cost approach.

The Cost Approach

markup

The cost approach to setting basic price involves "building" unit selling prices on the basis of cost. This approach is simple when the cost of one unit is easy to identify. **A markup is an addition to cost to reach a selling price.** It is usually expressed as a percentage. Mr. Schultz, who operates a men's clothing store, uses a percentage markup applied to his unit costs for an item or group of items. Thus he might buy 100 suits at $80 apiece and apply a 50 percent markup on cost, resulting in prices of $120 per item for his customers (150 percent of $80). Schultz might use this same percentage markup on all items in his store. If so, his basic price policy is a very simple one with a cost basis. He probably has allowed demand factors to influence his markups only in an indirect way.

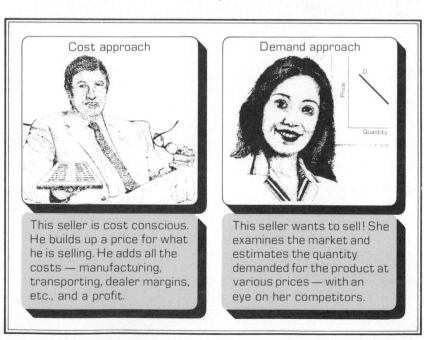

Cost approach

Demand approach

This seller is cost conscious. He builds up a price for what he is selling. He adds all the costs — manufacturing, transporting, dealer margins, etc., and a profit.

This seller wants to sell! She examines the market and estimates the quantity demanded for the product at various prices — with an eye on her competitors.

Figure 10.8
Two approaches to price

Mr. Schultz probably knows from past experience about how much his customers are willing to pay. But he does not look at consumer price attitudes very closely because cost-plus pricing is so easy for him. He also knows that, over the years, the policy has allowed him enough gross margin (the difference between total dollar sales and costs of goods sold) to pay his rent, his clerk's salary, and other costs of operation, and to leave him a fair profit. These calculations will be covered more completely in the next chapter when we discuss the income statement in accounting.

Manufacturers may also use a cost approach to pricing. However, it is not always easy for them to identify costs attached to a given unit of output. It becomes more difficult as the number of units produced increases. Cost accounting systems have been developed to aid in this task. Manufacturers who sell to governments often use cost-based pricing because government buyers frequently specify such pricing, sometimes called *cost-plus*. In some cases the federal government is a firm's *only* customer. The government often requires cost-plus pricing which allows the contractor to cover cost and to make a certain profit.

The Demand Approach

In its most extreme form, the demand approach to pricing neglects the cost side. It is more in tune with the marketing concept than the extreme cost approach because it considers possible customer reaction. More precisely, it estimates the amounts which are likely to be sold at different prices (the slope of the demand curve). The most extreme form of demand-approach pricing would set prices very low to sell the greatest number of units.

The Sayles Company, for example, is owned by a former salesperson whose past experience (remote from production cost considerations) leads him to accept the demand approach, giving only some thought to costs. Mr. Sayles realizes that costs, in the long run, must be covered if he is to stay in business. He is, however, more likely to accept lower prices than a cost-oriented firm would, because he is accustomed to thinking in terms of sales growth. He knows that customers and competition must be considered in order to build sales.

The concept of a *customary price* is important in understanding the demand approach to pricing. The classic example of a customary price was the nickel candy bar. Candy makers resisted raising the price for many years despite increases in their production costs. Of course, the cost increases eventually became too great and the nickel price had to be increased.

Combined Approaches

Many firms set prices by making both cost and demand estimates. These are translated into profit estimates at various unit price and sales levels. Breakeven charts, which are explained in Chapter 12, may be used to help in such analysis. Some firms use a technique borrowed from economic theory called *marginal analysis* which helps to estimate the "best" price and quantity produced in terms of greatest profit.

Pricing models might be developed in firms that have trained economists and computers at their disposal. **A pricing model is an equation or**

pricing model

set of equations that represents all the important things in a pricing situation to help decide on the "best" price. Past experience in pricing and knowledge of the market conditions help to determine the equation that best predicts pricing results. This process is known as *model building.* No matter how carefully it is done, it still requires judgment about what other human beings will do and what their tastes and needs will be.

Discounts

Specific prices actually charged by a manufacturing firm often vary from the basic price. Such variations generally result from an established discount policy. Discounts from "list" prices are granted for a number of

cash discount

reasons. **For instance, it is common for a firm to offer small discounts for prompt payment of bills. These are called *cash discounts.*** Another typical discount is the *trade position discount.* A wholesaler who normally sells to retailers, for example, may make a special sale to another whole-

trade position discount

saler at a discount from the regular price to retailers. **Any discount granted because of a difference of position in the distribution channel is called a trade position discount.**

functional discount

Sometimes a functional discount is granted to a customer in return for services rendered. A retail grocer, for example, may receive a discount or allowance from a detergent manufacturer if the grocer features the manufacturer's brand in local newspaper ads. Some would argue that this practice is not really a discount but rather a simple purchase of a service. Such a discount could also be called a promotional allowance.

quantity discount

Still another common discount is the *quantity discount* which involves reduced unit prices as the size of the order increases. A firm's discount policy makes its pricing more flexible in special competitive situations. However, it is often also the cause of serious legal problems concerning price discrimination laws. Figure 10.9 shows how some of these discounts are computed.

Pricing New Products

Some special considerations arise in pricing a new product. There are two opposite approaches: market penetration pricing and skimming pricing.

market penetration pricing

To feature low price when introducing a new product is called market penetration pricing. The firm's goal is to build a large initial market share and to build brand loyalty before competitors can enter the market. The initial low price discourages some competitors who foresee smaller profit at such a low price.

market skimming pricing

To feature a high price when introducing a new product is called market skimming pricing. The goal is to get the greatest early revenue from sales to recover product development costs before competitors enter the market. This approach is often used by small firms, by firms with large development costs, and by firms that are not well protected by

Cash discount	The Smith Insurance Agency receives a bill for $1,000 from Walter Stationery Supplies with payment terms of 2/10, net /30. A cash discount of 2/10, net /30 means that the full price is due within 30 days of the invoice date. But Smith Insurance is entitled to a 2 percent discount if payment is received within 10 days, which is 20 days earlier than the due date. If Smith pays the bill in 30 days, it is like paying 36 percent interest per year, because there are 18 twenty day periods in a year. (18 × 2 percent = 36 percent). Even if Smith has to borrow money at 20%, it will pay them to take the cash discount.
Quantity discount	A quantity discount is based on the quantity of merchandise a buyer buys from a seller. There are two types: noncumulative and cumulative.
Noncumulative quantity discount	Suppose a bottler offers the following discounts on cases of pop:

Cases purchased on individual order	*Discount percentage*
1–100	0.0
101–250	2.0
251–500	3.5
over 500	5.0

	If Johnny's Pop Shop ordered 450 cases at a base price of $3 a case, the store would pay the bottler $1,350 less 2 percent, or $1,323.
Cumulative quantity discount	When purchases are totaled during a year and the discount percentage depends on the total volume of purchases made during that year, this is a cumulative quantity discount. If Johnny purchases 810 cases during the year and the bottler's discount schedule is as shown below, Johnny will get a check for $315 from the bottler at the end of the year. (810 × $3) × 4 percent = $97.20

Total cases purchased	*Discount percentage*
1–100	2.0
101–500	3.0
over 500	4.0

Trade position discount	A manufacturer receives two orders for small appliances. One comes from a wholesaler and the other from a retailer. The wholesaler gets a discount of 50 percent off the suggested price to ultimate consumers. The retailer gets a discount of 30 percent from the same suggested price to ultimate consumers.
Functional discount	A processor of frozen turkeys grants a special discount of 2 percent to a supermarket chain in return for featuring the product in the chain's weekly ad in Regina papers the week before Thanksgiving.

Figure 10.9
Examples of discounts

patents and good reputations. This policy amounts to "getting it while the getting's good." For example, SmithKline Corporation, a pharmaceutical firm that is research and development oriented, invested millions of dollars to develop Tagamet, a drug used in the treatment of ulcers. The

"...Second tire at half-price when you buy the first tire at double price....!!"

(Source: *Wall Street Journal*)

firm practised skimming pricing in this case in order to recoup its development costs as soon as possible.

Retail Pricing

Most prices charged in retail stores are determined by a markup mechanism. Ms. Jill Gladney runs a jewelry store. She knows that, on the average, her costs of doing business—including salaries, rent, and desired profit—have amounted to about 50 percent of sales revenue. She also knows that the cost of goods she buys for resale accounts for the other 50 percent. She might plan prices so that, considering special "sales" to sell slow-moving items, she would realize a 50 percent gross margin (difference between gross sales and cost of goods). Thus, her average initial prices might need to be more than double the cost of goods. A shipment of rings costing her $100 apiece might be marked up to $250 and finally sold at $200—just enough to provide a gross margin of 50 percent of sales.

Jill Gladney's initial "markup" could be expressed two ways. It represents $150/$250 or 60 percent of the originally established sales price and $150/$100 or 150 percent of the original cost price. It should always be made clear whether a percentage markup is expressed in terms of cost or in terms of expected selling price. Of course, Ms. Gladney may assign different markups to different classes of items in her inventory, depending on competitors' practice and her experience with the "turnover" rate of various items.

inventory turnover rate   **The inventory turnover rate in a particular period of time is determined by dividing cost of goods sold by the average inventory value.** It can be expressed in units or in dollars. Thus, if inventory is worth $20 on January 1 and $30 on December 31 and if the cost of goods sold in that year amounted to $250, the average inventory is $25 and the turnover rate is 10.

If Ms. Gladney uses different markups on different items, she will try to average them out to provide her desired "gross margin." Sometimes

---

WHAT DO YOU THINK?

Consumer Credit — Curse or Blessing?

If the typical Canadian household were denied credit, its standard of living likely would be lowered. Ours is a credit economy. Consumers can enjoy goods during the time they are paying for them. This runs the gamut from houses to cars to clothing — to practically anything. But some people believe that some of us go overboard with credit. In some cases, this leads to personal bankruptcy.

To reduce this possibility, each province has enacted legislation to protect consumers. Two types of laws are most prominent — those which require lenders and sellers to state the annual interest rate which is being charged, and those which forbid credit reporting agencies to include certain kinds of information about consumers on their credit reports.

Is consumer credit a curse or a blessing to the consumer? What about sellers? What about our economy? WHAT DO YOU THINK?

---

retailers use very low markups on certain items to attract customers. This is known as a "leader" item. The goal is to increase sales of items carrying higher margins. Such practices may be illegal if it is shown that the item is sold below cost. Some firms use illegal "bait-and-switch" schemes. This means advertising one inexpensive item which is really not available and then convincing people to buy a more expensive substitute when they arrive.

Many retailers use price lining. An apparel retailer may make ten purchases of men's sportcoats in a season. Marking up each of these by the

price lining

same percentage might result in ten different prices for sportcoats. **Partly to simplify choices for customers and partly to simplify the job of the salespeople, the retailer may use price lining — grouping the costs at three or four sales price levels.** Thus, Bill's Men's Wear might make ten purchases of coats in a cost range of from $11.50 to $38.50 per unit and present them to customers in the $29.95, $39.95, and $69.95 price lines. This makes it easier for the salesperson to get the customer to "trade up." He comes into the store expecting to buy the $29.95 sportcoat he saw in the newspaper ad and finally buys the $39.95 or $69.95 coat, after comparing quality and listening to the salesperson's advice.

The prices selected by Bill's Men's Wear are "odd" amounts, and they were close to the next $10 break." Partly out of tradition and partly because of a slight psychological effect, retailers tend to set prices at $39.95 rather than $40. A price starting with thirty "sounds" like more of a bargain than one starting with forty.

Special promotions such as "one-cent sales" and "two-for-one sales" also are a part of the art of pricing. They require careful estimation and experience in order to result in overall profits for the retailer.

CAREER PROFILE

MY NAME IS ELIZABETH BALLANTYNE, AND I am the Media Director for one of the regional offices of McKim Advertising, Ltd. McKim is a full-service advertising agency offering expertise in a wide variety of marketing communication services.

I received my B.A. in English in 1969; I also attended graduate school and studied history. After graduating I went to work for a small advertising agency where I coordinated a public relations program for a group of manufacturing firms that were trying to improve their corporate image. I also worked as communications manager for a trust company. In that position I was responsible for coordinating internal communication as well as communication between the company and its external environment. I have also worked for various government agencies and Crown corporations as a communications consultant. I took my present position in 1978.

My current job has two major dimensions. First, I am responsible for developing a media strategy for a client's product or service that they want to tell consumers about. The first step in dealing with problems like these is to find out as much as possible about the product or service. This often requires considerable background research. The next step is to look at sales projections and to develop the advertising objectives for the product or service. This is done in close consultation with the client. Next, we must answer several specific questions. For example, what are the creative requirements for the message (do we need to show people a picture, does the product or service look good only on television, etc.)? Overall, in this step we must ask, "what arc we trying to do?". Some clients have as their goal the sale of a product or service, while other clients simply wish to create a better image for their company. The final step in this process is my recommendation on a media budget. This decision is made after much consideration of

the issues noted above and extensive conversation with the client. I also recommend a certain media mix (the proportion of the total budget that will be allocated to each medium).

The other major dimension of my job is putting into practice the decisions that have been made. This involves actually buying media time and space. Data bases like Starch and the Bureau of Broadcast Measurements are used to determine which advertising mix is most appropriate and whether or not our target audience is actually being reached. We also are making increasing use of computers to assist in buying media time and in assessing the effectiveness of our advertising program.

The major reward associated with my job is knowing that a company has reached the objectives that were stated for the advertising campaign. This is very important to me, because I can see the results of all the work that went into the campaign. When the objective evidence, such as sales figures, attitude surveys, and image data, show that a campaign has been a success, it is very gratifying. A good example of a successful campaign is the advertising program we developed for Canadian Life and Health Insurance Association. Consumer research revealed that the public perceived the insurance industry as inaccessible and unresponsive to consumers' needs. The Association organized a Life Insurance Information Centre, and we developed a television and newspaper campaign designed to inform the public about (1) the Centre and its toll-free number, (2) the new easy-to-understand policies, and (3) other actions taken by the industry to improve relations with its policyholders. Ongoing research was conducted to monitor the effectiveness of the advertising, which, after two years, showed a significant improvement in public attitudes. As well, the campaign continued to build momentum, with the number of calls to the Information Centre nearly doubling from the first to the second year.

There are several challenges associated with working in this business. First, clients sometimes do not have a clear idea in their own mind about what they want advertising to accomplish. We must often spend a considerable amount of time clarifying just exactly what it is the client wants to do. Second, it is sometimes difficult to get the client to think about what the criteria of success are. Some clients may not be clear on whether they are trying to sell a product or a service or are simply trying to improve the image of their firm. Third, some clients have an unreasonable view of what advertising can do. For example, one client reported substantially increased traffic in his store but not substantially increased sales. This client concluded that it was the advertising that had not been successful. In this case, however, advertising had succeeded, because the purpose of the campaign was to increase store traffic. Some other aspect of the marketing mix (product, price, or distribution) clearly had not been "right." So, part of my work must involve educating clients to the fact that advertising is only one element in the total marketing mix. These challenges are actually beneficial, because they sharpen my own views about my job and about the role of advertising in our society generally.

Examples of different advertisements appear on pages 368–372. Consider the format of each advertisement. What different appeals does each use to attract its particular audience? Are they effective?

Anatomy of a Puma:
Basketball Winner
Official Shoe of the Canadian National College Champions

SKY HIGH

TWIN VELCRO FASTENERS FOR POSITIVE ANKLE SUPPORT AND EASY ADJUSTMENT

JUMBO ASYMETRIC POLYURETHANE TONGUE FOR MAXIMUM COMFORT, PROTECTION — WILL NOT SLIP

FULL GRAIN LEATHER UPPERS WITH VENTILATED BUCKSKIN TOE FOR MAXIMUM HEAT DISPERSAL COMBINED WITH LIGHTNESS AND COMFORT

HEAVY DUTY TEXON MIDSOLE FOR LATERAL STRENGTH AND SHOCK DISPERSAL

STITCHED DUAL DUROMETER AIR CELL UNIT SOLE FOR SHOCK PROTECTION, LIGHTNESS, DURABILITY AND STRENGTH

OUTSIDE HEEL COUNTER FOR FIT, STABILITY AND COMFORT

This is an example of a "soft-sell" advertisement. The ad stresses the unique features of the product but does not even mention price. Nor does it urge the consumer to buy the product. An advertisement like this would normally appear in national trade publications like *Canadian Runner*.

Competition Design for Top Performance

CANADIAN DISTRIBUTOR
fma

PUMA
Strong. Sleek. Supple.

NEW HORIZONS

With the creation of Richardson Greenshields of Canada Limited, two of this country's most prominent investment firms have joined forces. This development offers exciting prospects for our clients.

We now provide access to markets for both the buying and selling of securities from over 74 offices world-wide.

More than 800 Richardson Greenshields Representatives armed with the findings of Canada's largest investment Research Department, provide counsel on financial matters at both the personal and corporate levels. These Representatives offer the widest selection of investment instruments possible for a Canadian Investment Dealer.

Most important, our continuing commitment is to excellence in the provision of investment services to our clients at home and abroad.

RICHARDSON GREENSHIELDS OF CANADA LIMITED

AFFILIATE OF
JAMES RICHARDSON & SONS, LIMITED
ESTABLISHED 1857

At Richardson Greenshields ~ every investor is a preferred client.

This is a brand advertisement. It is designed to promote the services of a specific company, not the entire industry. The advertisement gives the characteristics of the firm providing the service and indicates how these characteristics will benefit the customer. The ad argues that the customer will benefit most by patronizing this company rather than some other investment company.

NATURE'S NEARLY PERFECT DRINK

Delicious, wholesome milk. It's an excellent dietary source of protein, calcium, riboflavin and vitamins. It's relatively low in carbohydrates unlike many other drinks, including unsweetened fruit juices. And even smooth, rich-tasting whole milk is 96.5% fat-free!

Milk~it's got what's good for you.

Amounts shown for 250 ml (8.8 oz.) glasses	Protein (grams)	Carbohydrate (grams)	Fat (grams)	Calories
WHOLE MILK	8	12	9	157
2% MILK	9	12	5	129
SKIM MILK	9	13	0.5	90
ORANGE JUICE unsweetened, from frozen concentrate	2	31	trace	127

Milk is one of the good things in life. Cold, it will refresh you and chase away your hungry thirst. Hot, it will help relax you and lull you to sleep. Drink it any time as part of a balanced diet. Drink in the goodness of milk.

A message from the Manitoba Milk Producers Marketing Board.

GOOD STUFF~BEAUTIFUL MILK.

This is a generic advertisement. It is designed to promote a basic product (milk) but not a particular brand of that product. A comparison is made with another generic product (orange juice) in an attempt to convince consumers to decide in favour of increased milk consumption.

Ben's Unbeatable!

30% off

Seiko Watches

That's every Seiko watch in every Ben Moss store!

Save a big 30% on Seiko watches right now at Ben Moss. And not just a selection of watches, but every Seiko, Seiko Quartz and Seiko Lassale watch we have!

It's a fabulous assortment of styles — with a guarantee of quality that you can count on.

Our regular $110 to $995. Sale $77 to $696.50.

For a limited time only!

Ben Moss Jewellers

—is a girl's (and guy's) best friend—

Visa·MasterCard·American Express

Layaway now for Christmas!

This is an example of a "hard-sell" advertisement. The ad places strong emphasis on price and reminds the consumer to purchase now because the price is for a limited time only. An advertisement like this would normally appear in a daily newspaper.

THERE'S MORE TO LIFE THAN MEETS THE EYE

Life Insurance companies in Canada do more than simply conduct business in our province. Their contributions touch nearly all of us.

Unless you're one of the 3,520 people who are employed directly by insurance companies in Manitoba, you have probably never stopped to think about how these firms may be contributing to your life. Not in the obvious ways—by providing life insurance protection, health care plans, and pension savings services to more than 600 thousand Manitobans—but in other, more indirect ways.

Investing in your future

In 1981, Manitobans paid $361 million in premiums for life insurance and annuities. Of that total, $239 million went to insurers based outside of the province. However, nearly $539 million paid by residents of other provinces flowed back to Manitoba-based insurers, providing a very attractive "balance of trade" for our province.

What becomes of these premiums? They're channelled into carefully planned investments so that the costs to the consumer can be kept down and future benefits paid. For example, in 1981 benefits paid to Manitobans by life insurance companies totalled $281 million. Thanks to these wise investments and competition within the industry, the cost per thousand dollars of life insurance coverage is twenty percent less today than it was twenty years ago.

Investing in Manitoba's future

Life insurance companies currently have more than $2 billion invested in Manitoba, and every year, they invest an additional $250 million in this province. These investments help to create places for Manitobans to live, work and shop, and generate much-needed employment in the process. For example, by 1980, Manitoba life insurance companies

had invested an accumulated $440 million in government bonds. These millions have contributed toward the building and improvement of schools, roads, sewers and other public works in this province.

Over $650 million has been invested in Manitoba mortgages and real estate. $285 million of this is in housing, while the balance is helping Manitoba businesses to establish or grow, and assisting institutions such as hospitals and senior citizens homes.

In addition to investment dollars placed in the province, insurance companies pay Manitoba taxes—corporate taxes, premium taxes, payroll taxes, municipal taxes and licence fees. These, also, contribute to the well-being of all Manitobans.

Investing in your quality of life.

Four major life insurance companies have their head offices in Manitoba. These firms have a deep commitment to this province and to the quality of life here, because they and their employees are actively involved citizens, contributing to and benefiting from our communities.

In addition to their yearly payroll expenditures of more than $45 million, these companies pay over $2.5 million annually in realty and business taxes alone, millions of dollars to Manitoba utilities, and tens of millions to Manitoba suppliers. Each year, their charitable contributions to community and cultural organizations total more than $500,000.

Employment for Manitobans.

There are over 100 private life insurers who are licenced to do business in Manitoba, in addition to the four locally-based firms and four other firms with Canadian head offices in this province. These companies employ 3,520 Manitobans—including underwriters, agents, branch managers,

researchers, analysts, and office management and staff. Like insurance company investments, the salaries of these people work to stimulate Manitoba's economy as they go to buy homes, to feed families, and to purchase goods and services from other Manitobans.

The spin-off effect—indirect jobs.

A healthy life insurance industry creates employment throughout the province's economy. According to figures commonly used by government bodies, there are three indirect "spin-off" jobs for every one in the industry. That means nearly 11,000 Manitobans owe their livelihood indirectly to the insurance industry—jobs in food services, office supplies, computer and communications services, and many more.

Helping Manitobans Prosper

Life and health insurance companies have a commitment to Manitoba, and to the quality of life here. We want to see Manitobans prosper, because we want to share in that prosperity. Our goal is to contribute to more jobs, more investment, and a better quality of life for all of us.

If you would like to have more detailed information on life insurance investments or activities in Manitoba, please contact the Manitoba Life and Health Insurance Information Committee at Box 1946, Winnipeg, Manitoba R3C 3R2.

Yes, please send me more information

Name _____

Address _____

Canadian Life and Health Insurance Association Inc.

A message from the Manitoba Life and Health Insurance Information Committee.

This is an advocacy ad. Its purpose is to convince readers to develop a favourable attitude and to contribute money to the cause that is mentioned. The ad gives a variety of information designed to convince the reader of the value of the cause.

SUMMARY AND LOOK AHEAD

The full meaning of the idea of a marketing mix is now apparent. A firm adds a promotion program to its product offering and distribution system and decides upon a basic pricing system. These four components of a marketing mix together describe a firm's marketing policies and strategy. They cannot be developed independently of each other, however.

Product policy is the focal point of the marketing mix of many firms. They watch the sales trends of products in their product mix to determine how far along each is in its "life cycle." This permits them to take corrective action to prolong product life if possible or to replace old products with new products. Research and development make it possible to postpone failure of a product or to replace a dying one.

Another key marketing mix element is the selection of distribution channels. These channels are made up of middlemen who assist in bringing goods to customers. Where possible, manufacturers select channels that bring the necessary elements of service and convenience to customers without raising costs so high as to bring prices above competitive levels.

Promotion is primarily composed of advertising and personal selling activities which complement one another. Advertising reaches a large number of people, while personal selling is more aggressive and personally tailored to the customer. Both seek to convince the potential customer that a product or service is worth buying. They use a wide variety of appeals to do so.

Price, we have seen, is capable of administration. Firms emphasize a cost approach, a demand approach, or a combination approach in setting basic price. They may offer a variety of discounts and try to control prices at the retail level. There are special pricing problems related to new products and to retail stores.

In the next two chapters we will turn to the subjects of accounting and computers. We will describe the use of accounting techniques as well as the fantastic capabilities of computers. These topics will give us yet another perspective of the dynamic world of business management. ■

QUESTIONS FOR REVIEW AND DISCUSSION

1. When you purchase a new toaster, what "bundle of services" are you buying? How about a tube of toothpaste?
2. How long does a product "live"? Why does a fashion product "live" a shorter time than a hardware item like a wrench? Explain the concept of "life cycle" as applied to these two types of products.
3. Has packaging become more important or less important in selling consumer goods in recent years? Discuss.
4. Name six brand names which you think have good "memory value." Name six which you think are poor. What makes the difference?
5. Why does the distribution channel for an industrial good usually differ from a convenience consumer good channel? How does it differ?
6. How is it that "middlemen" exist even though they must cover their cost of operation and make a profit? Are their functions necessary? Why or why not?

7. Draw a chart illustrating four different channels of distribution which a manufacturer of toys might employ.
8. What are advertising media? Which ones are most important to a department store? Why?
9. Write a brief piece of copy for a television commercial announcing a new chain of sandwich shops called "Margy's" to be introduced in your city next month.
10. Write a paragraph giving advice to a salesperson for a hardware wholesaler going out on his or her route for the first time.
11. How can a sales manager tell if Tom Raincheck is a good salesperson before hiring him and six months after hiring him?
12. What is basic price? Give an example in which cost-plus basic pricing is a sensible alternative.
13. If you want a gross margin on sales of 40 percent, would your average initial markup (as a percentage of selling price) have to be more or less than 40 percent? Why? If the markup on selling price is 40 percent, what is the equivalent markup expressed as a percentage of cost?
14. Is price as important a part of the marketing mix today as it was fifty years ago? Discuss.
15. What is the AIDA process? How does it apply to personal selling?
16. What are the broad responsibilities of a sales manager?
17. Compare the two approaches to setting basic price.
18. What is the difference between cash discounts and trade position discounts?
19. What are the various functions of promotion?

INCIDENT

Pricing Used Sub-compact Cars

Sandy's Used Cars used to follow a simple pricing strategy. If a used car cost them $800 they would advertise it for twice that amount. Faced with a recession and a general upheaval in public attitudes toward Canadian and foreign cars, Sandy's manager is considering using different markups for domestic and foreign cars.

Questions:
1. Should Sandy's use two different markups for domestic and foreign cars? For full-sized and sub-compact cars?
2. Describe the markup policy you would like to see employed.

CASE STUDY

CARSON TOYS, LTD.

CARSON TOYS, LTD. PRODUCES A LINE OF CHILDREN'S TOYS. THE company had always been successful, but recent reports showed that sales of two of Carson's most successful nonseasonal toys were down substantially. If allowed to continue, this would have a negative effect on profits, so Jonathan Carson, President of Carson Toys, called in Martha Bucyk, the vice-president of marketing, for an explanation. She gave several possible reasons for the decline.

First, she said that she had been told by several of Carson's salespersons that some customers were placing trial orders with a toy manufacturer in Taiwan. This manufacturer produced two high-quality toys which were very similar to two of Carson's toys. The major difference was the price. In Canada the imported toys sold at retail for 75 percent of the retail price of Carson's two toys. Martha suggested that retail toy buyers were growing more price conscious, because the uncertain economic environment in Canada was causing customers to demand more for their money.

She also suggested that the recent increase in the cost of plastic had led to a reduction in the thickness of the plastic used to make several Carson products, including the two problem products. She thought that this had hurt the company's reputation for making quality toys. In fact, Carson had received 150 letters from retail customers complaining about "shoddy" toys, and three customers said they were reporting the problem to the Department of Consumer and Corporate Affairs. They claimed that their children had received cuts on their hands from jagged pieces of plastic, which became exposed when the toys broke during normal play. Martha and Jonathan worried about this. They knew that three competitors had removed several unsafe toys from the market. Martha suggested, however, that this was a production problem and not her concern.

Her third reason for decreased sales was the declining birth rate in Canada. The two problem toys appeal to children between the ages of two and four, she pointed out, and so, with the number of potential users declining, Carson toys cannot be surprised if sales also decline.

She suggested, too, that many parents were complaining about the tremendous volume of advertising aimed at children and that the constant bombardment of TV commercials was "bad" for them. Carson had concentrated its advertising on Saturday-morning children's television shows and several parents had written to Carson and accused the company of "taking advantage" of children. Martha also knew that the government was investigating these complaints from parents and that restrictive legislation was possible. As a result, the company had decided several months ago to reduce its advertising. However, they may have been too late and these complaints may have caused the decline in sales.

Finally, Martha reminded Jonathan that more and more toys were now being sold through "price-cutting" discount stores. Carson had always refused to sell through discount stores because many toy store owners said they would stop buying their products if they did. This had become a big problem, Martha said, and something had to be done about it.

Questions:
1. What action, if any, should Carson take regarding the new competition from Taiwan?
2. Who is Carson's target market, children or their parents? Discuss. Are there any other target markets?
3. With respect to the marketing mix, Carson has problems with product, place, price, and promotion. Discuss the nature of these problems and how you would deal with each of them for each element in the marketing mix. ■

CASE STUDY*

KRISTIANSEN CYCLE ENGINES LTD. (B)

IN JULY, 1980, HAAKEN KRISTIANSEN, PRESIDENT AND CHAIRMAN of Kristiansen Cycle Engines Ltd., was giving consideration to how marketing activities of the company should be handled. The $8 million underwriting offer had created a need to reassess the marketing approach.

Traditionally the company had viewed marketing as consisting of three different activities:

1. licensing of the right to manufacture and sell the K-Cycle engine
2. sales of treasury shares and securing of grants from governments to permit research to continue
3. sale of internal combustion engine testing services

Activity to sell treasury shares and secure government grants was not seen as necessary following the underwriting. Prior to this time it was estimated that one-third of the organization's time had been devoted to this activity.

INTERNAL COMBUSTION ENGINE TESTING SERVICES

The company offered an engine testing service using their test bed facilities. This service was made available as a condition of a grant of $300,000 from the Government of Manitoba in March, 1980, which permitted the construction of the company's own 5,000-square-foot research and testing laboratory on land made available by the City of Winnipeg. The completed laboratory, costing approximately $500,000, was immediately adjacent to the company's head office, which occupied 5,500 square feet of leased space in Winnipeg's Fort Garry Industrial Park.

The laboratory was supplied with testing devices which made it one of the better-equipped engine research facilities in Canada. Previously the company had used test facilities provided by the University of Manitoba. Once fully operational, it was felt this "fee-for-service" engine and fuel testing service effort would have several benefits:

*This case was prepared by Dr. Brian E. Owen, Professor, Faculty of Administrative Studies, the University of Manitoba. This case was prepared as a basis for classroom discussion only, not to illustrate effective or ineffective handling of an administrative situation. Copyright © 1981, The Faculty of Administrative Studies, The University of Manitoba.

1. to generate some revenue
2. to create greater awareness of the company and to build its credibility in areas of engine research and testing
3. to provide experience with the use of alternative fuels and their handling and performance characteristics

The fee-for-service program was the company's first digression from total involvement with the K-Cycle engine. It was, however, believed to be complementary to the engine development program and consistent with the objective of being a research and development company rather than a manufacturing company.

The involvement of the company in the conduct of fee-for-service work in the engine-testing field was new and, as a result, it was difficult to assess the amount of work available, the speed with which it could be generated, or the profits it would create. An example of the type of work performed was a recently approved program whereby the company would conduct studies for a government agency and a local fleet on the use of a range of alternate fuels. The program was for about $25,000 and would be spread over a six-month period.

MARKETING LICENCE RIGHTS TO MANUFACTURE AND SELL THE K-CYCLE ENGINE

The company's primary projected future source of revenue was from the licence fees for the commercially developed K-Cycle engine. The licensing policy of the company was designed to take into account short- and long-term requirements of the company. In the short term, the company required cooperative development (i.e., the $8 million underwriting). In the mid-term, advance royalty payments were required to provide ongoing funds before production by third parties commenced. In the long term, the broadest base of distribution and thereby volume would be required to generate maximum revenue for the company and its shareholders.

It was company policy that licensing was defined as "the creation of a non-exclusive right or privilege to develop, manufacture, use or sell internal combustion engines operating on the Kristiansen thermodynamic cycle. This is to include all patents, trademarks, designs, know-how (all intelligence personally conveyed by word of mouth or in written form), and technical data (all physical matter conveyed to the licencee, such as blueprints, specifications, drawings and manuals)." It was also policy that licensing was to be non-exclusive on a long-term basis in that others would be permitted to obtain a licence to manufacture a K-Cycle engine to satisfy the power requirements of a similar product. Exclusivity of use for a period of time would be considered when substantial investment and effort were required, and it was conducive to the generation of long-term volume to provide such exclusivity. It would be possible, with the approval of the company, for a licencee to become a party to a sub-licensing agreement to another party within his or her geographic area. If this situation arose and it was of benefit to all concerned, a sub-licensing agreement would be executed between the company and the sub-licencee providing the licencee with a portion of the royalty payments obtained from such an agreement.

Further, it was policy that royalty payments under the agreement would be based on engines manufactured, assembled, or sold from the country of manufacture, not in the country where wholesale or retail sale took place. It was intended that royalty payments should equal 5 percent of the wholesale selling price of the engine. This would take the form of royalty on sales revenue, a percentage of selling price per unit, or a fixed price per unit. Flexibility would be used to reach agreements which worked toward early commercialization of the engine and generation of the greatest long-term production volume.

Italian Licensing Agreement

An agreement had been reached in April, 1978, with an Italian manufacturer of gears, axles, and small engines. The agreement called for the two parties to participate in the development of the K-Cycle engine. The licencee was to contribute his expertise in the manufacturing side, and K-Cycle was to contribute the research assistance to achieve full performance. In exchange for the development work they completed, the licencee was to be entitled to certain specified royalty rights with respect to European production of K-Cycle engines. The agreement also provided that any improvements in the K-Cycle engine developed by the licencee would become the property of Kristiansen Cycle Ltd. The relationship with this manufacturer was being reevaluated. A conclusion was to be reached in the near future.

As of July, 1981, the company had no other royalty or licensing agreements with any outside corporations, entities, or individuals, except for agreements dated December 17, 1974, and November 12, 1977, under which the company would pay the inventor a royalty of 1 percent of the total monies received from the licence, royalty, lease, or sale of K-Cycle engines.

Marketing Licenses

The process by which any engine is brought to market was broken down into the following areas by the company:

1. concept research and development
2. production engineering
3. manufacturing
4. distribution and marketing
5. service

In some small-volume applications, where distribution and marketing were not necessary and after-sale service would be the

Exhibit 1 1977 World Engine Production Estimates (1,000 Units)

	Commercial Vehicles	Motor Cycles	Marine	Agriculture	Industrial	Construction	Automobiles	Total
North America	4,086	5,406	546	Tractors: 219 Combines: 25	12,382	128	10,381	33,173
Western Europe	1,516	4,400*	N/A	Tractors: 560 Combines: 48	1,538*	N/A	12,534	20,596
Balance of World	3,928	4,805	N/A	1,078	3,560	N/A	7,136	20,507
Total	9,530	14,611	546	1,930	17,480	128	30,051	74,276

N.B. No relevent statistics for aircraft engine production have been obtainable.

* These statistics include some data for 1970, where 1977 data was unobtainable.

Source: Company records.

responsibility of the purchaser (e.g., military applications), it was felt it would be possible for the company to become the manufacturer. In all other situations, however, where broad distribution was necessary to obtain volume, it was felt that the engine should be manufactured and distributed by organizations which had the capital, expertise, and organization to production engineer, produce, and sell the engine.

Although the company was focusing primarily upon the licensing of rights, it had not completely excluded the possibility of larger-scale manufacturing. In fact, a proposal was being considered to enter into an agreement with a Saskatchewan government agency for a joint venture to design and manufacture a K-Cycle engine in Saskatchewan.

A major challenge was seen to be the selection of the appropriate target groups and individual companies for contact and follow up. Engine production estimates were subdivided into categories by industry (see Exhibit 1).

The automotive market was by far the largest single sector. However, the likelihood of an automobile manufacturer being the first to manufacture a new engine was extremely remote. The automobile industry, while strongly motivated to move toward fuel efficient engines by market forces and legislation, probably would require a substantial operating history before any commitment was made to the K-Cycle.

The same situation applied to the aircraft engine industry, although in this case the volume was low enough and the resulting unit price high enough that custom building and an earlier introduction could in theory be possible.

POSSIBLE INITIAL TARGET MARKET

Based on contacts with industrial and agricultural equipment manufacturers, Mr. Kristiansen believed that these market sectors may be most attractive in terms of their potential for early introduction of a K-Cycle. There were no government standards for emissions or fuel economy and, therefore, no requirement for certification by the F.A.A.

(Federal Aviation Administration) or E.P.A. (Environmental Protection Agency) as in the case of the aircraft or automobile industries. The K-Cycle's potential advantages of high fuel efficiency, high torque at low speeds, and smooth, quiet operation made the engine suitable for industrial and agricultural applications. Specific items of equipment which could be investigated were:

1. farm tractors
2. front-end loaders
3. generators
4. compressors

In each category of equipment a compression ignition (diesel fuel) engine operating in the 1,800 to 2,000 R.P.M. speed range would fulfill the power plant requirements. The four categories were therefore believed to represent a market segment for which one design of the K-Cycle engine would be able to compete. Information from all manufacturers of these types of equipment had been collected and a contact program established. As a next step, a marketing effort could distill this information down into a series of personal visits to assess interest and begin the process of establishing licensing agreements (Exhibit 2).

Exhibit 2 Manufacturers and Suppliers in Potential
K-Cycle Market Segments

	Equipment Manufacturer	Engine Supplier
Farm tractors	Versatile	Perkins, Cummins
	Massey-Ferguson	Perkins, Cummins
	John Deere	John Deere, Kohler
	White	White, Perkins
	International Harvester	Caterpillar, I.H., Toyo Kogyo
Front-end loaders	Clark	G.M., Perkins, Cummins
	Case	Case, Renault
	Caterpillar	Caterpillar, Ford
	Ford	Onan, Wisconsin
	New Holland	Ford, Kohler, Wisconsin
Generators	Kohler	Kohler
	Onan	John Deere, Onan
	Flygt	Ford, Lister, Deutz
	Winco	Briggs & Stratton, Cummins, Wisconsin, Hatz
Compressors	Gardner-Denver	Waukesha, Ford, G.M.
	Joy	I.H., John Deere
	Ingersoll-Rand	Caterpillar
	Compair	Ingersoll-Rand
	Le Roi	Ford, G.M., Briggs & Stratton, Wisconsin

Source: Company records.

Exhibit 3 Forecasted K-Cycle Engine Shipments*

Year	K-Cycle unit shipments	Revenue/ engine	Total values	5% Royalty to Kristiansen
1985	100,000	$1,400	$ 140.0	$ 7.0
1986	300,000	1,498	449.4	22.5
1987	600,000	1,603	961.8	48.1
1988	950,000	1,715	1,629.2	81.5
1989	1,300,000	1,835	2,385.5	119.3
1990	1,650,000	1,963	3,239.0	162.0
1991	1,700,000	2,100	3,570.0	178.6
1992	1,750,000	2,247	3,932.2	196.7
1993	1,800,000	2,404	4,327.2	216.4
1994	1,860,000	2,573	4,785.8	239.4
1995	1,910,000	2,753	5,258.2	263.0
1996	1,970,000	2,945	5,801.6	290.3
1997	2,030,000	3,152	6,398.6	320.0
1998	2,090,000	3,372	7,047.5	352.6
1999	2,150,000	3,608	7,757.2	388.1
2000	2,220,000	3,861	8,571.4	428.8

Assumptions: 1. 5% penetration of agricultural and industrial engine market achieved in 1990, and maintained thereafter
2. 3% market growth
3. 7% cost inflation

*No account is taken here of possible future K-Cycle engine applications other than for agricultural and industrial markets.

Source: Company records.

Exhibit 3 presents a company forecast for possible future sales of K-Cycle engines to, and royalty income from, the agricultural and industrial engine market. ■

Section Five

This section introduces you to two fundamental tools for managing business information. One is very old and the other is very new. Chapter 11 describes the rule of accounting—a very old tool of business—in making information available and useful to managers, creditors, and investors. The principal emphasis is on financial accounting and preparing and interpreting a firm's financial statements.

Section 5 also presents an overview of computers—the dynamic new partner of accounting in managing information for decision making. In Chapter 12 we will discuss computer-related concepts, major uses of computers by business, and some of the problems encountered in introducing computers to a firm's operations. Basic concepts of hardware and software are explained.

This section is closely related to the next in that it sets the stage for understanding financial management and the many institutions related to today's world of finance.

ACCOUNTING, COMPUTERS, AND INFORMATION MANAGEMENT

After reading this chapter, you should be able to:

1. Distinguish between financial and managerial accounting processes.
2. Identify the three principal tasks of accounting.
3. Describe what a CA does.
4. Prepare a chart showing the major information flows of accounting.
5. Explain the relationship between transactions and accounts.
6. Complete both of the principal accounting equations.
7. Draw up a simple example of the two principal financial statements.
8. Explain the purpose of the two principal financial statements.
9. Demonstrate how an investor might use the statements of a firm he or she may wish to invest in.
10. Explain and use at least one of the "key" ratios.
11. Show how a budget may be used in internal control.

In reading the chapter, look for and understand these terms:

accounting	current asset
financial accounting	fixed asset
managerial accounting	depreciation
accountants	current liability
account	accrued expense
asset	income statement
equity	gross profit
liability	key ratio
owners' equity	tangible net worth
revenue	current ratio
expense	budget
transaction	sales forecast
basic accounting equations	responsibility accounting
net profit	product cost accounting
balance sheet	

ACCOUNTING IS AN IMPORTANT BUT complex part of modern business operations in Canada. Constantly changing tax laws, inflation, and uncertainty about the responsibility of chartered accounting (CA) firms are all problems that accountants must cope with.

Recently there have been several cases in which some people felt that certain CA firms had not adequately assessed the financial condition of a company, and hence investors had made poor investment decisions. For example, the Winnipeg Mortgage Exchange was placed in receivership in 1982 and many people lost their investment. In July 1983 creditors of the Mortgage Exchange filed a class action suit against the CA firm that had been the Exchange's auditor. The creditors claimed that the CA firm's yearly audits were inaccurate and failed to reveal just how bad the financial condition of the Exchange really was. This false information led investors to loan money to the Exchange, which they later lost when the company became insolvent.

Problems like this are very difficult to resolve. Critics say that when a CA firm comments on the financial condition of a

CHAPTER ELEVEN

Accounting

company, investors are guided by this expert opinion, and, if it is wrong, the CA firm must bear some responsibility for errors. Others point out that information can be distorted or hidden from auditors, and it may be difficult for anyone to get a clear picture of a company's financial condition.

IF YOU WERE ASKED TO DESCRIBE OR EVALUATE YOUR FIRM, HOW would you do it? A lot would depend on why the request was made and who made it. If the request came from a new employee, you might want to describe the wage and promotion policies and the working conditions of the firm. If it came from a new customer, you might want to describe the quality of your product and your delivery, price, and credit policies. But what if you were the executive vice-president of a firm and the president asked you to evaluate the sales growth of the firm over the last five years? Or what if the president asked you to make a report on the firm's financial position for a bank that may lend the firm a million dollars?

The last two requests could not be met completely by the use of words. These two requests are common, however, and they both require the use of accounting.

WHAT IS ACCOUNTING?

accounting

Accounting has been defined in many ways. We will define it as a process of recording, gathering, manipulating, reporting, and interpreting information which describes the status and operation of a firm and aids in decision making.

This process is guided by certain widely accepted principles and rules. These principles are especially important when a manager must report to people outside the firm. They play a smaller role when accounting is for internal use. We call the internal processes managerial accounting and the external processes financial accounting. Both financial and managerial accounting are useful to managers.

financial accounting

Financial accounting helps the manager to "keep score" for the firm. It watches the flow of resources and lets those who have an interest in them know where they stand.

managerial accounting

Managerial accounting calls attention to problems and the need for action. It also aids in planning and decision making. It is aimed more at control and less at valuation than financial accounting. It is also less traditional.

Like any tool, accounting must be designed to do its various jobs (score-keeping, calling attention, and helping in decision making) quickly and at a fair cost. The accounting system must provide clear and efficient estimates of financial facts. What it produces must be, above all, relevant. Accounting is relevant when it is useful to managers, creditors, investors, or government agencies in doing their jobs. Accounting is a much broader term than simple bookkeeping. Bookkeeping is simply the mechanics of accounting—the recording of financial data.

What Is an Accountant?

An accountant is much more than a person who keeps the books. Accountants know basic procedures for recording transactions quickly, accurately, and with maximum security. They know how to summarize data so that all kinds of users can understand it. They know enough about the law to build a system of accounts which reflects those laws—especially tax laws. They know where to find specialized information about law and other tough questions—especially as they relate to the firm they serve. For example, an accountant for a forest products company would keep a library relating to land valuation and the use of natural resources. He or she must also be aware of the history and policies of the firm.

accountants
  Accountants are individuals who have satisfied the knowledge and experience requirements of a professional group and have been admitted as members of the profession. Accountants may be employed by public auditing firms (companies which express an opinion as to the fairness of the financial statements prepared by the accountant of a firm). Auditors are just as expert as the accountants employed by industrial or commercial firms. Often their knowledge must be broader, because they deal with the accounting processes of many different firms.
  Accountants are also employed by individual firms in both the private and the public sector. In these positions, accountants keep track of revenues and expenditures for the company as well as doing many of the functions which are the subject of this chapter. Some accountants serve government directly and develop a much more specialized skill in reporting and checking the spending of public funds. Careers in accounting, then, are available in public, private, or governmental accounting.

Accounting to Whom and for What?

Accounting traces a sequence of information flows. Figure 11.1 indicates something about who is "accounted to." Employees at the operating level use accounting to "account to" managers (*A*) who must use accounting to "account to" owners (*B*). The firm's manager must also "account to" creditors and future creditors (*C*) and to government agencies (*D*).
  The flow of information is quite varied—and some of the bits of information reaching managers do not go any further, but are retained for internal purposes (*E*). Firms have many uses of their own, as we will see when we discuss managerial accounting.

Figure 11.1
The flow of accounting information

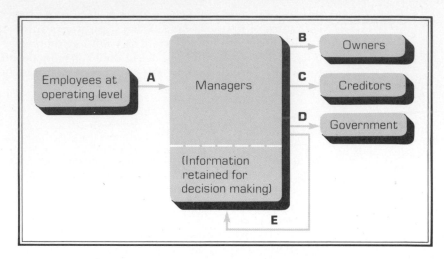

Much of the same information is contained in flows *B, C, D,* and *E,* although it takes different forms and emphasizes different kinds of facts, depending on who is to read it.

What are accounted for are the firm's resources, expressed in dollars and cents (usually cost) terms. In some cases, units other than money are accounted for, but it's usually money.

FINANCIAL ACCOUNTING

Financial accounting is an old and traditional practice designed to "keep tabs" on a firm's assets and to protect its owners' property rights. It also has many built-in safeguards for outsiders who want to know of the firm's financial condition. Financial accounting is a "score-keeping" process.

Financial accounting is a general system because it includes the entire firm (or entity). Managerial accounting, on the other hand, usually focuses on one activity within the firm.

Transactions and Accounts

account

A basic idea in accounting is that of an account. This is a register of financial value. The set of accounts kept by a firm represents all those separate classes of values, both positive and negative, and the changes in value that occur. There are four principal kinds of accounts:

- asset
- equity
- revenue
- expense

THEN AND NOW

Certification Programs in Accounting and Finance

Not too long ago, when you talked about a professional certificate in accounting, you were talking about the CA, or Chartered Accountant. To become a CA, a person must first earn a university degree, then complete an accounting-oriented educational program, and then pass a national exam. About half of all CAs work in public accounting firms (CA firms). These firms give external opinions on their client's financial statements. The other half work in business, government, and other non-profit organizations. The main emphasis in CA work is on financial accounting, auditing, and taxation accounting.

In recent years, accounting and financial skills have become increasingly specialized. In addition to the CA, the following certification programs are now available:

1. *Certified General Accountant (CGA)* — To become a CGA, a person must complete an educational program and pass a national exam. A university degree is not required for admission to the program. To be eligible for the program, a person must have an accounting job with a company. There are fewer CGAs than CAs, and in most provinces they are not allowed to give opinions on financial statements of publicly held companies. Almost all CGAs work in private companies, but there are a few CGA firms. Some CGAs work in CA firms.

2. *Registered Industrial Accountant (RIA)* — The goal of the RIAs is to train accountants for industry. To become an RIA, a person must have an accounting position with a company and must complete an educational program (a university degree is not required for admission). Unlike CAs, RIAs have management accounting as their focus, that is, they are concerned about internal uses of accounting data, not external uses as the CAs are.

3. *Certified Financial Analyst (CFA)* — This program is relevant for people in investment jobs. To earn the CFA designation a person must complete an educational program and pass a national exam dealing with securities regulations, investments, and related topics.

---

asset	**An asset is something of a positive dollar value to a firm.** Asset values are registered in asset accounts. Usually a firm keeps a large number of asset accounts. Examples are Land, Cash, and Accounts Receivable (money owed to the firm by customers).
equity	**An equity account is a register of claims or rights of different groups to a firm's assets.** These include the claims of outsiders and the claims of owners. The sum of all equity accounts, as we shall see, always equals the sum of all asset accounts.
liability	**The claims of outsiders are called a firm's liabilities.** An example of such an account is Notes Payable, which shows what a firm owes in the form of promises or orders to pay. Another example is the account designated Wages Payable, which indicates how much pay is due to the firm's employees.
owners' equity	**The claims of insiders, or owners, are kept in owners' equity or capital accounts.** Examples of these are Retained Earnings and Common

"I can explain my excessive and unexplainable deductions. When I made out the return, I was at the lowest point in my biorhythm chart."

(Source: *Wall Street Journal*)

Stock. Retained Earnings represents additions to the owners' equity attributable to profits.

revenue

A revenue account is a register of gross earnings or inflows of value to a firm during a given time period. The most important revenue account is Sales. It includes the total selling price of all goods or services sold during a given time period.

expense

Expense accounts are measures of the using up of resources in the normal course of business in a given time period. Typical examples are Wages Paid, Utilities Paid, Rent Paid, Interest Expense, and Supplies Used. Expenses are deducted from revenues to calculate profit or loss.

transaction

The term *transaction* **is used to describe any change in an asset or an equity.** If we buy raw material for cash, we must reduce the Cash account balance and increase the Raw Material account balance. If the firm sells an order of merchandise on credit, it must increase the Sales Revenue account and the Accounts Receivable account by the amount of the sale.

For a better idea about how the basic types of accounts are related, we will study some basic accounting equations that underlie the financial statements.

Important Accounting Equations

An equation represents the fact that two expressions are equal. One expression is placed on the left side of the equal sign, and the other expression is

basic accounting
equations

placed on the right. For example, $12 + 4 = 16$. **Basic accounting equations are equations that explain the basic system of relationships in financial accounting.**

The first basic accounting equation represents the fact that the sum of the assets equals the sum of the equities (claims on assets) and that these equities include liabilities and owners' equity. This basic accounting equation, then, is

$$\text{Assets} = \text{Liabilities} + \text{Owners' Equity}$$

or

$$\text{Assets} = \text{Equities}$$

If one side of the equation (assets) is increased or reduced, then the other side must be increased or reduced by exactly the same amount, just as in algebra. Some transactions, of course, affect only two individual assets or only two equity accounts. They do not affect the totals on either side of the equation, as in our earlier example concerning the cash purchase of raw materials.

A second equation reflects current operations. It is as follows:

$$\text{Revenues} - \text{Expenses} = \text{Net Profit}$$

AUTHORS' COMMENTARY

Inflation Will Require Major Changes in Accounting

The method most firms traditionally use to value inventories of raw materials or component parts or goods purchased for resale is known as FIFO (first in-first out). This means, for example, that if a new shipment of 1,000 units of steel plate costing $20 per unit is received by a fabricator who already has 500 units in stock costing $15 per unit, the fabricator will charge out all of the $15 units to the production cost of finished products before charging any of the $20 units.

LIFO (last in-first out) works the opposite way, so that the fabricator would charge the more recently purchased units to production costs first. In this period of rapid inflation there has been a shift from FIFO to LIFO among Canadian firms. This has the effect of in-

creasing costs of production and reducing profit (and income tax) as reported by the firm. There has been no real loss in such a case, but rather an indefinite postponement of profit-reporting and of the accompanying income tax.

Should substantial inflation continue to plague our business environment, the acceptance of LIFO inventory valuation and other methods which distort reported results could make much traditional financial accounting meaningless. The profession is already taking steps to require firms to account for inflation in such a way as to portray a true financial picture to all interested parties.

It is likely that many accepted accounting reporting practices, especially those relating to inventory valuation, will be revised unless inflation is controlled.

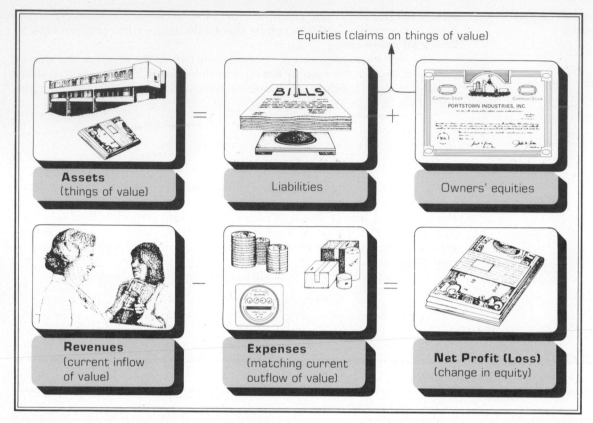

Figure 11.2
Two basic equations that sum up financial accounting

net profit

Current revenue minus the expenses incurred in gaining that revenue equals net profit. Net profit measures the success of the firm's current operations during the period. When expenses exceed revenues, there is a net loss for the period. Net profit is also an index of the change in the owner's equity that occurs during the period. The capital account, Retained Earnings, is increased by profitable operations and reduced by payments to owners. Net profit is added to or net loss is deducted from retained earnings. The basic equations are illustrated in Figure 11.2.

FINANCIAL STATEMENTS

You have probably seen financial statements in a newspaper or in a firm's annual report. Two of them, the balance sheet and the income statement, have been widely used for more than a century. These statements are useful for managers, investors, and creditors. They are central to financial accounting.

Current assets:			Current liabilities:		
Cash	$ 6,000		Accounts payable	$10,000	
Accounts receivable	18,000		Accrued expenses payable	1,000	
Merchandise inventories	10,000		Estimated tax liability	7,000	
Prepaid expenses	2,000		Total current liabilities		$18,000
Total current assets		$36,000			
Fixed assets:			Other liabilities		
Land		4,000	Bonds payable		10,000
Building	$ 8,000		Owners' equity:		
Less depreciation	4,000	4,000	Common stock	$25,000	
			Retained earnings	1,000	26,000
Other assets:					
Goodwill		10,000			
Total assets		$54,000	Total equities		$54,000

Figure 11.3
*Gloria's Dress Shop, Ltd. Balance Sheet (December 31, 19*3)*

The Balance Sheet

balance sheet

A business is a living, functioning entity. **A balance sheet (also known as a statement of financial position) presents a financial picture of a firm at one point in time.** Family albums filled with snapshots of children as they grow represent a record of that growth for their parents. A file of X rays kept by a doctor records the progress a fractured bone makes in healing. Likewise, a set of balance sheets drawn at the end of each year, over a period of years, depicts the rate of growth and nature of the growth of that firm.

Figure 11.3 is a balance sheet for Gloria's Dress Shop as of December 31, 19*3. This is a more detailed way of expressing the first basic accounting equation: Assets = Equities. The firm's assets are divided into three major classes: current assets, fixed assets, and other assets.

Current Assets

current asset

A current asset is one that the firm normally expects to hold no longer than a year. Examples are *cash* (currency and checking account), accounts receivable, merchandise inventories, and prepaid expenses. *Accounts receivable* are amounts owed to the firm from its normal operations. In this case, they are amounts owed by customers for dresses purchased from the firm recently. As of December 31, 19*3, forty-three different customers owed the firm the total sum of $18,000 "on account."

Merchandise inventory consists of all goods purchased for resale but not yet sold. Most retailers must take an inventory of stock at the end of the year to determine the value of their goods for balance sheet purposes. At the end of the year, Gloria's counted $10,000 worth of goods for sale.

Prepaid expenses might include prepaid insurance premiums which have not yet been used by the firm. Gloria's purchased a fire insurance policy on July 1, 19*3, and the premiums were paid one year in advance. Thus the firm now owns something of value — that is, a prepaid insurance policy, only half of which has been "used."

Two current assets not shown in Figure 11.3 are *marketable securities* and *notes receivable.* The former are short-term investments a firm holds, such as stocks and bonds of other firms and government bonds. The latter represent short-term loans to customers or others.

Fixed Assets

fixed asset

A fixed asset is a tangible resource that is expected to remain useful for more than a year. Such an asset is valued at its cost to the firm. When a firm buys a building, it is listed among the firm's fixed asset accounts at a value equal to its purchase price.

depreciation

As an asset loses value, it suffers depreciation. This loss of value is charged off as an expense and the stated value of the fixed asset is reduced on the balance sheet. In Figure 11.3 $4,000 has been deducted from the value of the building because of depreciation. This means that this fixed asset is "half used up."

There are many acceptable methods of figuring depreciation in traditional accounting. The simplest is called *straight line depreciation.* It provides for charging equal parts of the original cost of an asset in each year of its expected life. Thus Gloria's firm is using straight line depreciation on the building which was purchased four years before the date of the balance sheet. This building, the only *depreciable* asset Gloria's has, will be fully depreciated four years after the date of this balance sheet.

One other general class of assets is included in Figure 11.3. It is an intangible asset known as *goodwill,* which results from years of good business reputation. According to accepted accounting principles, goodwill is assigned a dollar value only when it is bought by the firm. In other words, when the corporation bought the assets of the previous sole proprietorship, it was estimated that the corporation paid $10,000 more than the tangible net worth of the proprietorship (the difference between the value of tangible assets and the liabilities).

Current Liabilities

Under the liabilities section of Figure 11.3, the current liabilities total $18,000. This figure includes the $10,000 due to suppliers, $1,000 of accrued

current liability

expenses, and $7,000 in estimated taxes owed. **These are current liabilities because they will be paid off within a year.**

accrued expense

Accrual is a major accounting principle. Expenses are charged against revenue in the period in which the firm benefits from them. An accrued expense is used up but not paid for yet. Gloria's accrued expenses are the result of some work performed by several salesclerks during the Christmas season who had not yet been paid as of the end of the year.

Long-term Liability and Owners' Equity

Gloria's owes bondholders $10,000. This is a long-term liability because it won't be paid off within a year. Owners' equity is listed at $26,000 including the original "stated value" of the stock when it was issued and $1,000 in retained earnings (earnings of previous years which have been put back into the firm). Together these add up to what the owners' claims on assets are — *owners' equity*. If the firm were still a proprietorship, the owners' equity would simply be listed on the balance sheet as "Gloria Smith, Capital." The owners' equity, then, is the owners' claim against the firm's resources.

In any case, the sum of the equities is always equal to the sum of the assets. The basic accounting equation always holds. The $54,000 in current, fixed, and other assets have claims upon them (equities) in the amounts of $18,000 (current liabilities), $10,000 (bondholders), and $26,000 (owners).

The Income Statement

income statement

The balance sheet, or statement of financial position, shows a "cross-section" of a firm's resources and equities at one point in time. **The income statement, on the other hand, shows what actually happened over a period of time to explain some of the differences between successive balance sheets. It summarizes the revenue and expense accounts, just as the balance sheet summarizes the asset and equity accounts.** Figure 11.4 illustrates Gloria's income statement for the period ending December 31, 19*4, one year after the statement in Figure 11.3.

Net sales			$267,000	(100.0%)
Less cost of goods sold			152,000	(56.9%)
Gross profit			$115,000	(43.1%)
Less expenses:				
Wages and salaries paid	$68,200	(25.5%)		
General and administrative expenses	38,000	(14.2%)		
Interest expenses	1,500	(0.6%)	107,700	(40.4%)
Net profit before taxes			$ 7,300	(2.7%)
Taxes (paid and accrued)			2,000	(0.7%)
Net profit after taxes			$ 5,300	(2.0%)

Figure 11.4
*Gloria's Dress Shop, Ltd. Income Statement (year ending December 31, 19*4)*

Revenues

Gloria's sold $267,000 worth of dresses this year. The selling price of the dresses is used in this valuation rather than the original cost. Sales are *net* because any discounts or returns and allowances granted to customers have been subtracted from the gross sales.

From net sales is deducted the actual cost of goods sold. The cost of goods sold is calculated as follows. First, a physical inventory of goods in stock at the end of the year is taken. The cost of these goods is then subtracted from the sum of the cost values of (a) the inventory a year earlier and (b) purchases made during the year. Gloria's had $10,000 in inventory at the beginning of the year, bought $180,000 more during the year, and had $38,000 remaining when the closing inventory was taken ($10,000 + $180,000 − $38,000 = $152,000).

Expenses

gross profit

The difference between net sales and cost of goods sold is gross profit. Figure 11.4 shows a few expense accounts, including wages and salaries, general and administrative expenses, and interest expenses. Wages and salaries include Gloria's salary, wages of a bookkeeper and a janitor, and wages and commissions paid to salespersons. General and Administrative Expense includes depreciation, office expenses, utilities, and insurance. Interest Expense includes interest paid to the Bank of Montreal for a loan made and repaid during the year. The difference between gross profit and expenses is $7,300 — Net Profit Before Taxes. From this amount taxes paid or accrued are deducted in the amount of $2,000. Notice the taxes that apply to this year's operations — whether paid or not — are rightfully deducted from this year's revenue. This is another example of the principle of accrual. Net profit after taxes is $5,300, or 2 percent of sales. Of this, the board of directors can allocate a part to dividends, and the rest goes to owners' equity as retained earnings.

Figure 11.5 shows the new balance sheet one year later.

The usefulness of the income statement, especially for internal purposes, is increased when it includes a "percentage of net sales" column as does Figure 11.4. This feature makes the income statement easier to compare to those of earlier years, to those of other firms, and to industry averages.

Financial Accounting — Users and Uses

Before we begin a discussion of key ratios, we will describe two specific cases tying in accounting processes and their use. These examples will show how financial accounting serves the interests of investors as well as credit users and givers. We will start with the case of Dr. William Franklin.

William Franklin is a retired doctor who has invested a large part of his savings in the common stock of the Marshall Corporation, a producer of steel tubing. He owns 2,000 shares, which represent about 3 percent of Marshall's outstanding stock. Dr. Franklin is interested in getting a reasonable return on his investment in the form of common stock dividends.

Current assets:			Current liabilities:		
Cash	$17,000		Accounts payable	$10,700	
Accounts receivable	22,000		Accrued expenses payable	$1,000	
Merchandise inventories	38,000		Estimated tax liability	1,000	
Total current assets		$77,000	Total current liabilities		$12,700
Fixed assets:			Other liabilities:		
Land		4,000	Bonds payable		10,000
Building	8,000				
Less depreciation	5,000	3,000			
Other assets:			Stockholders equity:		
Goodwill		10,000	Common stock	$69,000	
			Retained earnings	2,300	71,300
Total assets		$94,000	Total equities		$94,000

Figure 11.5
Gloria's Dress Shop, Ltd. statement of financial position (Dec. 31, 19*4)

This investor does not know any of the corporation's officers or managers personally, and he lives in a town in which none of the firm's plants is located. He needs information, so he must rely on the firm's financial statements to judge the quality of his investment.

Let's review how these statements came to be. Dr. Franklin could not have made a wise decision about his investment if someone (probably Marshall's treasurer or comptroller) had not set up an information collecting, processing, and reporting system (see Figure 11.6) that did the following things:

- retained facts about financially significant events on a variety of source documents
- classified these into accounts
- summarized accounts in financial statements
- distributed statements to stockholders

First, the firm's operations were scanned to identify financially significant events (those having a bearing on the firm's profit), and these were

Figure 11.6
How the Marshall Corporation generated its financial statements

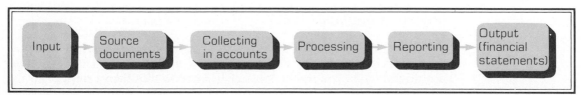

entered on some kind of source document. For example, when the office manager bought an order of stationery, he or she signed a purchase order describing the items to be purchased and the amount to be spent. The purchase order, or perhaps a copy of the invoice (list of items shipped) made out by the stationery store, is a source document for the purchase event.

The second step involved recording the dollar amount and the nature of the event in some form of register (account) set up in advance by the comptroller. This is the classifying function. The basic facts found in the purchase order were entered into the firm's computer and stored for later use.

At the end of the quarter, Marshall's accounting department took all the stored bits of data, such as the stationery purchase record, and processed them. The department also added up all company expenditures by type and constructed Marshall's quarterly financial statements.

The reporting function has also been fulfilled. The statements, first printed by the firm's computer, were checked by the accounting staff and published for distribution to stockholders. This is how Dr. Franklin got the financial statement he needed to evaluate his investment. He can calculate earnings per share (total profit divided by the number of outstanding shares of common stock) and other financial ratios from these statements. He can, of course, get similar earnings-per-share and dividend data about other firms from his stockbroker.

Financial accounting can also help make credit decisions. Suppose Hydraspace Company wishes to sign a long-term contract with the Marshall Corporation that will make Hydraspace the supplier of an important part for Marshall's major product. It's important for Hydraspace to know about Marshall's financial condition so that it can be sure that Marshall can pay on time. Hydraspace will use a number of sources of information for this purpose. They will depend a lot on Marshall's past financial statements, especially those statements that indicate Marshall's ability to pay its current bills.

Marshall's accounting system should be able to provide a summary of its past payment behaviour if the firm wishes to give this information to Hydraspace. In practice, this kind of information is accumulated by independent credit reporting services, such as Dun & Bradstreet, and sold to their customers.

Once the contract is negotiated and the first shipment of parts has been made, Hydraspace becomes a trade creditor of Marshall. For further insight about how a creditor might interpret financial statements, we now turn to the subject of ratio analysis.

Important Financial Ratios

The numbers on the financial statements take on more meaning when they are related to each other. For instance, the net profit of a firm is more meaningful when it is mathematically related to that firm's sales or to the stockholders' equity. Such relationships are usually expressed as financial ratios or "key" ratios.

key ratio

A key ratio is a value obtained by dividing one value on a financial statement by another value. A particular firm's financial condition can be judged by comparing several important key ratios of items from its financial statements with typical key ratios of similar types of firms.

Dun & Bradstreet publishes typical key ratios for a variety of types of firms. Such typical ratios are presented in Table 11.1 on page 400 and explained in Table 11.2 on page 401.

Let's look at several of these ratios and see how Gloria's Dress Shop compares with other women's clothing stores as reported by Dun & Bradstreet. First, let's look at a ratio which measures overall performance — net profit to tangible net worth.

tangible net worth

First of all, tangible net worth is equal to stockholders' equity minus goodwill (goodwill is an intangible asset). From Figure 11.5 we see that Gloria's tangible net worth equals $61,300. From Figure 11.4 we see that net profit after taxes is $5,300. The ratio, then, is 5,300/61,300 = .0865 or 8.65 percent. Now, turn to the "typical ratio" of net profit to tangible net worth in women's ready-to-wear stores as found in Table 11.1. The sixth item in the table pertains to women's clothing stores. The circled figure in the fifth column represents the median or typical net profit/tangible net worth ratio for such stores in that year as reported by Dun & Bradstreet. Gloria's ratio is lower than average. This suggests that Gloria's is not performing as well as the average store of its type.

Gloria's will compute this ratio and others each year to measure its financial strength. Banks or investors will compute such ratios to see whether they should lend money to Gloria's when the firm requests it. Let's look at some other ratios which measure specific things about a firm.

current ratio

A short-term key credit ratio which is widely used is the current ratio. It is computed by dividing current assets by current liabilities. On December 31, 19*4 (Figure 11.5), Gloria's current ratio was 77,000/12,700 = 6.06. This is excellent and it means that Gloria's is quite solvent — it can easily pay off current debt, since it has $6.06 of current assets for every $1.00 of current liabilities. Compare this ratio with the typical one in the third column (circled) of Table 11.1. The average women's ready-to-wear store had a current ratio of only 1.90, that is, only $1.90 of current assets for every dollar of current liabilities.

The sales-to-inventory ratio (also known as stock turnover) is computed from Figures 11.3, 11.4, and 11.5:

$$\frac{\$267,000 \ (\text{sales})}{\frac{1}{2}(\$10,000 + \$38,000) \ (\text{average inventory})} = \frac{267}{24} = 11.1$$

This is better than the average ratio of 5.8 shown in column 8 of Table 11.1.

Dun & Bradstreet has been a pioneer in the development and analysis of key ratios. For many years it has published "industry average" ratios for many kinds of firms. This provides benchmarks by which the financial status of similar firms may be evaluated.

Table 11.1 Key Business Ratios Canada—Corporations

Line of Business (and number of concerns reporting)	Cost of Goods Sold Percent	Gross Margin Percent	Current Assets to Current Debt Times	Profits on Sales Percent	Profits on Tangible Net Worth Percent	Sales to Tangible Net Worth Times	Collection Period Days	Sales to Inventory Times	Fixed Assets to Tangible Net Worth Percent	Current Debt to Tangible Net Worth Percent	Total Debt to Tangible Net Worth Percent
ALL COMPANIES (221,243)	69.4	30.6	1.09	5.64	12.82	2.27	60	6.6	105.5	170.9	280.1
RETAIL TRADE (39,944)	73.9	26.1	1.46	3.94	26.84	6.80	16	7.0	47.1	107.6	135.0
Auto acc. & parts (1,566)	72.0	28.0	1.32	1.90	14.90	7.84	21	5.1	55.3	179.1	248.6
Book & stat. stores (474)	57.0	43.0	2.07	2.58	10.44	4.05	86	4.5	22.3	104.4	162.0
Clothing, men's (1,358)	67.4	32.6	1.65	3.36	11.86	3.53	26	4.0	23.2	84.0	106.2
Clothing, women's (1,812)	62.7	37.3	1.90	3.25	16.32	5.02	20	5.8	36.5	97.2	151.9
Dept. stores (141)	66.4	33.6	1.51	1.60	7.34	4.59	14	6.1	34.7	78.7	111.1
Drug stores (2,339)	69.1	30.9	1.57	2.49	14.35	5.76	11	4.4	35.7	116.2	159.2
Dry goods (1,514)	67.6	32.4	1.67	2.56	10.99	4.30	23	4.3	30.2	90.3	122.1
Elec. appliances (225)	68.7	31.3	1.48	2.17	16.28	7.51	44	5.2	51.2	174.4	253.5
Florists (508)	48.7	51.3	1.12	3.54	18.52	5.24	34	17.2	83.0	101.5	159.3
Food stores (4,070)	82.3	17.7	1.24	1.01	9.10	9.02	4	15.6	58.3	69.7	123.8
Fuel dealers (635)	69.2	30.8	1.28	3.28	8.18	2.50	62	17.7	44.8	62.1	109.9
Furniture (3,633)	69.0	31.0	1.58	2.57	13.92	5.42	43	5.0	31.2	133.2	175.9
Gas serv. stns. (3,554)	74.8	25.2	1.08	2.09	18.42	8.80	24	10.9	95.0	198.3	294.6
General mdse. (1,712)	80.7	19.3	1.69	2.83	15.04	5.28	22	6.7	55.7	80.2	134.3
Hardware (1,452)	66.9	33.1	1.94	3.01	13.81	4.58	31	4.3	28.6	87.6	133.4
Jewelry stores (800)	53.0	47.0	1.99	5.62	15.32	2.73	45	3.0	20.2	73.5	97.9
Motor veh. dealers (4,113)	83.2	16.8	1.19	1.13	16.82	14.91	13	7.4	75.5	243.4	308.6
Motor veh. repairs (2,081)	64.2	35.8	1.25	3.28	19.26	5.87	30	11.6	64.9	112.1	160.6
Shoe stores (832)	61.4	38.6	1.72	2.06	8.08	3.92	14	4.0	31.5	85.9	119.9
Tobacconists (118)	83.4	16.6	1.48	1.42	13.04	9.16	3	9.3	60.9	123.9	330.4
Variety stores (518)	64.9	35.1	2.20	3.34	12.90	3.86	18	4.8	49.4	51.6	82.8

Source: Reprinted by permission of Dun & Bradstreet Ltd.

Table 11.2 How the Ratios are Figured—What They Mean

These ratios are based on analysis of a composite sample of audited financial statements published by Business Finance Division of Statistics Canada. The statements were filed by Corporations with Dept. of National Revenue for income tax purposes for the taxation year 1973. These ratios are averages and include both profitable and unprofitable concerns.

COST OF GOODS SOLD

This includes the cost of inventory which has been sold or used, freight or transportation, customs duties, direct labour and factory overhead. Discounts on purchases are deducted. The ratio is a percentage of sales.

GROSS MARGIN

This ratio is derived by deducting the cost of goods sold from the sales figure. It answers the question "Is the markup on cost to selling price sufficient to show a profit?"

CURRENT ASSETS TO CURRENT DEBT

Current Assets are divided by total Current Debt. Current Assets are the sum of cash, accounts receivable, inventories including supplies, and Government securities. Current Debt is the total of bank loans, accounts payable, tax liabilities and amounts due to shareholders. This ratio is one test of solvency.

CURRENT YEAR PROFITS ON SALES

Obtained by dividing the profit declared by the companies, by total sales. This important yardstick in measuring profitability should be related to the ratio which follows. Profits are shown after taxes.

CURRENT YEAR PROFITS ON
TANGIBLE NET WORTH

Tangible Net Worth is the equity of stockholders in the business, as obtained by adding preferred and common stock plus surplus (less deficits) and then deducting intangibles. The ratio is obtained by dividing Profits by Tangible Net Worth. The tendency is to look increasingly to this ratio as a final criterion of profitability. Generally, a relationship of at least 10% is regarded as a desirable objective for providing dividends plus funds for future growth.

SALES TO TANGIBLE NET WORTH

Sales are divided by Tangible Net Worth. This gives a measure of the relative turnover of invested capital.

COLLECTION PERIOD

Annual sales are divided by 365 days to obtain average daily credit sales and then the average daily credit sales are divided into accounts receivable. This ratio is helpful in analyzing the collectability of receivables. Many feel the collection period should not exceed the net maturity indicated by selling terms by more than 10 to 15 days. When comparing the collection period of one concern with that of another, allowances should be made for possible variations in selling terms.

SALES TO INVENTORY

Dividing annual Sales by Inventories. This quotient does not yield an actual physical turnover. It provides a yardstick for comparing stock-to-sales ratios of one concern with another or with those for the industry.

FIXED ASSETS TO TANGIBLE NET WORTH

Fixed Assets are divided by Tangible Net Worth. Fixed Assets represent depreciated book values of buildings, leasehold improvements, machinery, furniture, fixtures, tools, and other physical equipment, plus land. Ordinarily, this relationship should not exceed 100% for a manufacturer, and 75% for a wholesaler or retailer.

CURRENT DEBT TO TANGIBLE NET WORTH

Derived by dividing Current Debt by Tangible Net Worth. Ordinarily, a business begins to pile up trouble when this relationship exceeds 80%.

TOTAL DEBT TO TANGIBLE NET WORTH

Obtained by dividing total current debt plus mortgage and other funded debt by Tangible Net Worth. When this relationship exceeds 100%, the equity of creditors in the assets of the corporation exceeds that of owners.

Source: Reprinted by permission of Dun & Bradstreet Ltd.

WHAT DO YOU THINK?

Should Auditors Be Responsible for Uncovering Fraud?

Auditors are responsible for checking to see if a client has followed accepted accounting principles in reporting its results of operations. Recent discovery of fraud in the financial reporting of major firms has led to some serious questioning by the government and by the accounting profession itself of the adequacy of present auditing practices. The possibility of suing auditing firms for not uncovering fraud has also been raised.

A large CA firm, Peat, Marwick, Mitchell & Co., has pointed out that traditional auditing practices are not enough to detect management fraud in worldwide businesses tied together by computer. New tools quite different from ordinary auditing are needed. Some believe lawyers should accompany CAs; others recommend that auditors should automatically "blow the whistle" to government when suspicions arise instead of bringing discoveries to the firm's management. Should auditors be responsible for uncovering fraud? WHAT DO YOU THINK?

An overview of modern accounting must also include dicussion of some of the internal management tools. Although financial accounting helps, a good manager needs some managerial accounting tools, too.

MANAGERIAL ACCOUNTING

Managerial accounting provides information for a manager's own use. It helps management to plan, to measure and control performance, to set prices, and to analyze situations. The biggest difference between managerial and financial accounting is the lack of traditional rules and principles in managerial accounting. Management is free to make up its own systems.

Because managerial accounting practices are less rigid, different systems will be found in every firm. The idea is to keep any kind of record or summary of costs and revenues that managers need for planning or control purposes. They might want to evaluate other managers or to judge the success of new products or a new piece of equipment.

Such special accounting is needed because regular financial accounts aren't enough to measure the performance of departments or products or managers within the firm as a whole. They focus, rather, on overall firm profit.

If the Norton Sales Company wishes to evaluate the performance of its sales force, it must maintain adequate records of the sales force's activities. Suppose those records show that the average travel expenditure per salesperson has been 20.2 cents per month per square mile of sales territory. After analysis, the sales manager decides to adopt this average amount as a standard. Any salesperson whose expenses exceed the average would be checked out. This shows how accounting can be used to control selling costs.

Managerial accounting can be used to set minimum order sizes, to decide whether to shut down a production line, to help a manager allocate funds for growth among territories, or to set standards for entertaining customers. Such managerial accounting activities fall under one of two headings: budgeting or cost accounting.

Budgeting

By tradition, financial accounting is not expected to provide predictions of a firm's condition. Predicting is a risky business, but it must be done. Managers use special managerial accounting tools to help them make predictions. One such device is the budget.

budget

A budget is a formal dollar-and-cents statement of expected performance. It is a means of (1) requiring managers to plan carefully for the future; (2) causing managers to examine present and past performance critically; and (3) helping to coordinate the plans made by different parts of the firm. A budget may be very specialized, or it may be general. It may be a short-term (one year or less) or a long-term budget.

The marketing manager, for example, is expected to prepare an advertising budget for the coming year. In consultation with the advertising agency and the comptroller, the marketing manager will specify how the money he or she needs to accomplish advertising objectives will be spent. This includes the amount designated for each product to be marketed, the amounts earmarked for each advertising medium, and a month-by-month schedule for the year's spending.

sales forecast

The sales forecast is the starting point for a general (master) budget. It predicts what sales will be over a certain period of time. This forecast depends on what effect the marketing manager thinks the planned changes in the marketing mix will have on sales. Sometimes the sales forecast is tied to a projection of Gross National Product or to industry sales forecasts. Larger firms, employing a staff of economists and computer facilities, often construct models to predict sales. Whether it be made by such a method or by a simple assumption of a 5 percent increase over the current year, the sales forecast is a keystone for planning.

Cost Accounting

responsibility accounting

Cost accounting includes responsibility accounting and product cost accounting. **Responsibility accounting involves setting up responsibility centres in a firm. These are used to classify cost information so as to evaluate the performance of various parts of the firm and their managers.** The costs of operating the shipping department, for example, may be collected in a shipping department responsibility centre. Figure 11.7 shows how responsibility accounting works.

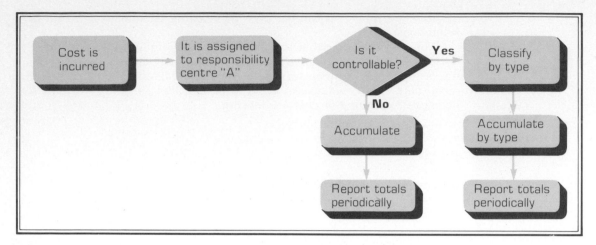

Figure 11.7
The responsibility accounting process

Suppose that a plant has set up responsibility centres to control its costs, and that one such centre is the plant loading dock. The dock superintendent buys an insect fogger to reduce the problem of mosquitoes on the dock. The accounting system assigns this cost to the loading dock responsibility centre. Company accounting policy classifies such an expenditure as *controllable* and further classifies it as a "miscellaneous operating expense." During the month this responsibility centre incurs thirty-seven other cost items. Six of these were required by general company policy and so were determined to be *uncontrollable* by this responsibility centre. The other items, including purchase of paint for the dock floor and parts for the dock scale, are accumulated by type. The paint is classified as a maintenance expense and the scale parts as a mechanical repair cost. At the end of the month all controllable expenses are totaled by type and reported to the plant manager. The manager now has a monthly measure of the controllable costs incurred by this responsibility centre. This helps the manager evaluate the dock's efficiency for the month.

product cost
accounting

Product cost accounting systems also use cost centres to allocate all costs to the various products made by a firm. This gives a firm a better idea about which products are profitable and which are not. Some firms use *standard* product cost accounting systems. Standard costs assigned in such a system are those that should have been incurred, not those actually incurred. Differences between actual and standard costs are called *variances* and are charged to *variance accounts*.

MANUAL VS. COMPUTER-BASED ACCOUNTING SYSTEMS

For many years accounting activities were restricted in what they could do because they were manual. They started with a handwritten record of a

ACCOUNTING AND RELATED CAREERS MAY BE DIVIDED INTO TWO categories according to the amount of formal training required. Some, like bookkeeping jobs, cashiers, credit officials, and bank clerks, do not require college preparation. To do these jobs, you must like to work with numbers and be good at detail work and simple mathematics. In most of these jobs personal dependability ranks above human relations skills. Bookkeepers record financial information, make out invoices, check the accuracy of financial records, and prepare tax reports. Cashiers and bank clerks do a lot of counting, checking, and tracing of financial data. Credit officials interview credit applicants; they also check and evaluate credit records. All of these positions may lead to promotion to higher-paying jobs or supervisory-level positions, such as bank teller, head bookkeeper, or credit manager.

The second category does require a university or community college degree. Private accounting jobs such as internal auditor, tax accountant, budget analyst, or cost accountant require considerable technical skill and knowledge of law and business commercial practices. They require some understanding of computer information systems as well as some appreciation of facts peculiar of the specific type of firm they work for. A cost accountant for a furniture manufacturer, for example, would need to understand its manufacturing processes. An internal auditor for a bank would have to know the clerical and control procedures of that bank. Such positions may lead to financial executive posts or to top management jobs in corporations.

Accounting positions and survey of incomes

Years since professional designation achieved	1	2	3	4	5–6	7–9	10–12	13–15	16–18	19–23	24–30	Over 30
				AVERAGE SALARY OF RESPONDENTS								
Public Practice												
• Employee	26,615	30,016	32,096	36,128	39,780	46,310	°	44,640	40,166	°	°	°
• Owner/ Partner	35,000	30,750	—	47,240	44,033	55,823	61,615	67,629	83,779	81,206	87,243	74,642
Industry	°	36,134	39,623	46,434	47,706	54,372	72,665	81,612	81,379	72,266	80,530	81,826
Government and education	°	°	32,564	°	39,037	43,616	46,313	44,007	51,303	49,880	50,258	50,588

Note: ° = No respondents in these categories

Source: Survey of Income of Members by The Institute of Chartered Accountants of Manitoba, as of November 1982.

Rapidly expanding opportunities exist in private accounting. There is also a great demand for governmental accountants and for public accountants. Government accountants do a variety of jobs similar to private accounting, except that they deal with expenditure and control of public funds. Budget preparation and auditing are major areas of government accounting. Government accountants are also involved in the regulation of private industry and in taxation. Revenue Canada, for example, employs many accountants.

Public accounting firms usually hire graduates of community colleges (CGAs) and universities (CAs and CGAs). Public accountants do auditing work and offer tax and management services. Promotion within these firms often requires that the employee first pass a national exam. A young CA or CGA may progress from junior accountant to auditor to senior accountant and possibly up to manager or partner. Partners are the top positions in firms. In smaller firms the number of steps in promotion is not so great, and travel requirements may not be as great as with large national firms. Earning potential is high for skilled CAs and CGAs. Information is available from the Canadian Institute of Chartered Accountants, 250 Bloor Street East, Toronto, Ontario, Canada M4W 1G5, and from the Certified General Accountants Association of Canada, 535 Thurlow Street, Room 800, Vancouver, British Columbia V6E 3L2. ∎

THINK ABOUT IT!

How Should Oil Companies Evaluate Reserves?

One of the important questions in accounting circles today is how to evaluate oil reserves held by firms which explore for and produce petroleum. The two methods used by the industry traditionally have been the "successful" efforts method and the "full-cost" method. The first method takes the cost of the unsuccessful efforts ("dry holes") and charges off these immediately. The second method lumps in all developmental costs (regardless of success of effort) and assigns this value to oil reserves, to be written off over the life of the reserves. WHICH SYSTEM IS MOST REASONABLE? THINK ABOUT IT!

---

transaction that was later copied by hand into a summary book of some kind for monthly or weekly tallying purposes.

Such simplified manual systems still exist in small businesses, but they are gradually being replaced by machine- or computer-based systems. Some of these systems depend on modern cash register equipment, and some depend on punched cards. Although every accounting system is a data processing system, we now restrict the use of the term *data processing* to machine- or computer-based systems.

A data processing system must do the following:

- select relevant data describing the business transaction and prepare a document containing such a description
- classify and store these input items in appropriate places and summarize them for future use
- convert such information into proper form for use by decision makers
- prepare reports, such as financial statements

A computer-based accounting system requires still another step to convert the source document to a form that can be handled by the system. In the typical case the original document is converted to machine-readable form and stored either in the computer's own memory, as punched cards, or on magnetic disk or tape. In Chapter 12 we will see how such computer storage makes it easier to classify, summarize, and report.

SUMMARY AND LOOK AHEAD

Accounting's task is threefold: (1) to "keep score" of the use of financial resources; (2) to draw attention to problems; and (3) to assist in decision making. Financial accounting does the first task and managerial accounting does the second and third.

Accounting principles guide managers in making and interpreting financial statements. Two principal financial statements represent the

CAREER PROFILE

MY NAME IS MARY LEA McANALLY. I AM AN articling chartered accounting (CA) student in my first year with the Calgary office of Dunwoody & Company, a medium-sized national accounting firm with international affiliation.

Being an articling student is similar to being an apprentice. During my three-year "apprenticeship" I have to take courses offered by the Institute of Chartered Accountants of Alberta and accumulate a certain number of work hours in various disciplines, including auditing, accounting, and taxation. Each province has its own entrance and articling requirements, but every CA student in Canada must write the Uniform Final Examination (UFE). It is a four-part exam that strives to test the student's ability to handle situations a CA may encounter in practice. I will be eligible to write my UFE next year.

A bit of personal history: I was born and raised in Edmonton, Alberta. During my school years I was actively involved in 4–H, a girls' choir, school clubs, and sports. I obtained a Bachelor of Commerce degree from the University of Alberta in 1981. During my university years I became involved in student politics as well as in sports and volunteer work.

I joined Dunwoody in Calgary after investigating and interviewing with most of the larger

firms. I was most impressed with Dunwoody's medium size, its client service mentality, and

focus of the financial accounting process: (1) the balance sheet, and (2) the income statement. Key financial ratios are applied to values reported on the financial statements to help make comparisons of the performance of a single firm over time, or to make comparisons among firms in the same year.

Managerial accounting is internally oriented. Planning for financial (and other) resources can be greatly assisted by a variety of budgeting techniques. Cost accounting is another broad component of managerial accounting. It usually takes the form of responsibility accounting or product cost accounting. In either case, costs must be identified and assigned so as to improve internal managerial control of operations.

What we have learned about financial and managerial accounting also helps to explain the need for computers in business. This is the subject of

the room for advancement it presented.

My first year with the firm has been a hectic one because I am constantly learning. My job involves several aspects including auditing, taxation, and special assignments. An audit involves making sure that the financial statements of a firm fairly present the position and operating results of the firm. The audits I participated in were substantive audits, which means we did most of our work at the end of the firm's fiscal year; we "substantiated" the balance sheet and income statement items. The second part of the audit is writing a letter to the owners or management of the firm detailing problem areas or weaknesses we uncovered during our audit and suggesting means of improvement. The management letter is probably the most useful feature of an audit from the firm's point of view.

This year I was exposed to both corporate and personal taxation. During March and April, as a member of our office tax team, I completed one hundred personal tax returns.

I have done two or three special projects for clients during my first year. This is a very interesting aspect of my job because it requires more imagination than does auditing. One client I worked for in this regard was a landscaping firm that wanted to computerize its accounting system and needed advice regarding software packages available. Another special job I did was to develop an educational package for new Dunwoody articling and technical students.

Taking the CA courses is really another part of my job, since Dunwoody management considers my performance in my courses when they evaluate me as a student. To date I have completed four of the seven required courses.

The challenges I face as an articling student are numerous. Revenue Canada and the provincial tax department create problems with tax reassessments which we often dispute. Another challenge is dealing with clients and their staff, particularly their accounting staff where diplomacy is often required.

Some of our clients have no accounting staff at all, which presents a different kind of challenge; the books must either be written up for the full year or straightened out if someone has made only a half-hearted attempt to write them up.

The challenges are really what make my job worthwhile. My work is varied and exciting; I'm constantly being given more responsibility, which in itself is rewarding. The "C.A." designation is a respected one, and I'm looking forward to passing my UFE and becoming a chartered accountant.

A word of advice to students: Become involved in things in addition to your studies. While scholastics are an integral part of your post-secondary success, extra-curricular activities will round out your education. The people you meet and the experiences you have through your involvement, be it in sports, politics, or volunteer work, will make your university or college years more rewarding.

our next chapter. With a basic knowledge of accounting and computers we will be able to proceed with the next section of the text — financial management. ∎

QUESTIONS FOR REVIEW AND DISCUSSION

1. What kinds of information are communicated by means of accounting? Give two examples.
2. To whom is the accounting process directed? What are its three principal tasks?
3. Must all accountants be CAs? Discuss.
4. What do we mean when we say that financial accounting is relevant?
5. Is it possible for a transaction to occur without affecting the balance of any account? Discuss.

6. What are the basic accounting equations? Show how a change in one side must result in a change in the other.
7. What is the functional relationship between a statement of financial position (balance sheet) and an income statement?
8. Define working capital. In what sense is it "working"?
9. What kind of business is Dun & Bradstreet in? Ask any manager what his or her relationship with this firm is, if any.
10. What is meant by the principle of accrual? Explain by giving an example involving rental expense.
11. Give an example of a simple budget. Your weekly expenses will do.
12. In what way could an accounting system help to control salespeople's entertainment expenses? Explain.
13. Examine a large corporation's financial statements (they are found in the Annual Report of the company). What are the strong and weak points of the financial statements? What suggestions can you make to improve the understandability of these statements?

INCIDENTS

Bell's Hardware Store

The Williams family had inherited a large sum of money and were looking for a good investment. They were approached, through a mutual friend, by Samuel Bell, the owner-manager of Bell's Hardware Store. He suggested they purchase a half-interest in his store.

With the help of an accountant they examined Bell's audited financial statements and computed some of the key ratios. They discovered that the current ratio for the most recent full year of operation was 2.0, and that the return on net worth was 6 percent in that same year. Ratios for the two previous years were very similar.

Despite Bell's assurance that the stable ratios over the three years were evidence of consistent, stable management, the Williams family remained apprehensive.

Questions:
1. How would you advise the Williams family regarding the proposed investment?
2. Is the fact that the statements were audited important to the Williams family? Why or why not?
3. How would you evaluate Bell's Hardware Store's credit standing? Which ratio measures this? What other information would you like to have?

Alma Wintergreen

Alma Wintergreen's husband recently died and left her $40,000. She wishes to invest it in a good small corporation. The Alpha Corporation has assets of $5 million and liabilities of $4.2 million. For the last five years Alpha Corporation's earnings have averaged $10,000. Beta Corporation has assets of $10 million and liabilities of $7 million. Average earnings for the Beta Corporation for the last five years have been $20,000.

Questions:
1. Would you advise Mrs. Wintergreen to invest in either of these corporations? Explain your answer.
2. Which of the critical ratios are you able to compute for Alpha and Beta?
3. What other information do you suggest she get before making a decision?

After reading this chapter, you should be able to:

1. Describe one important way that a computer enters your life.
2. Give some examples of common business applications of computers.
3. Distinguish between automation, data processing, and word processing.
4. Draw a diagram of a computer system.
5. Recognize common input-output devices for computers.
6. Explain the function of software.
7. Explain the impact of microcomputers on business.
8. Contrast several ways that people react to computers.
9. Compute an arithmetic mean and median.
10. Prepare a breakeven chart.

KEY CONCEPTS

In reading the chapter, look for and understand these terms:

computer	COBOL
data processing	BASIC
word processing system	Pascal
computer program	Ada
hardware	documentation
central processing unit (CPU)	quantitative tools
outside data storage systems	statistics
input-output (I-O) devices	arithmetic mean
modem	median
distributed data processing (DDP)	mode
software	frequency distribution
time sharing	histogram
controllers	sample
online real-time system	breakeven analysis
assembly language	operations research (OR)
machine language	linear programming
FORTRAN	

SOME PEOPLE CALL IT THE "PAPERLESS office of the future." With that goal in mind, traditionally noncompetitive organizations, including electronics firms like Nabu Ltd. and IBM and telecommunications companies like provincial telephone utilities, are developing strategies to capture a big piece of the market for desk-top computer terminals. Such terminals are used in many ways by more than 2 million white-collar workers in businesses all over North America in a variety of industries. It has been predicted that this number will exceed 12 million by 1990. Today these terminals, hooked up with computer-stored data inside or outside the firm, are proving to be a mainstay of business communication. They may indeed lead to the "paperless office."

These terminals look like a typewriter with a TV screen attached and they are used by stockbrokers, airline reservation clerks, bank tellers, and typists. The latter, as we will see later in this chapter, are fast becoming known as word-processor operators. The

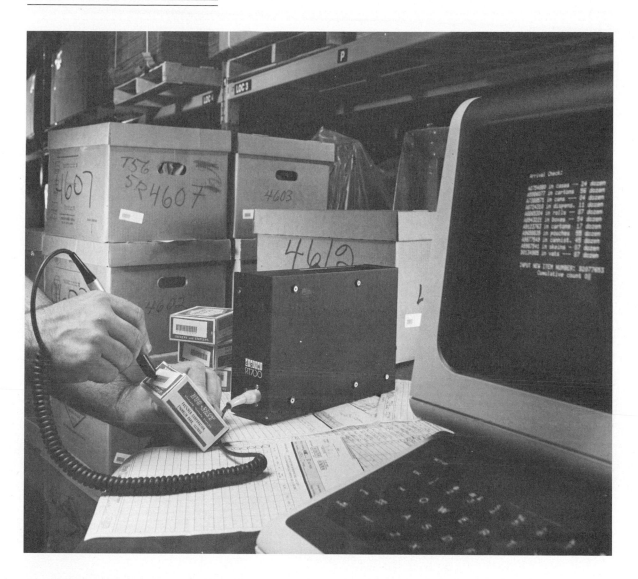

CHAPTER TWELVE

Computers and Basic
Quantitative Tools

terminals are often sold in combination with telephone-connection devices and are used to tie together widespread operations of large corporations.

Although the new terminals, selling for little more than the price of a top-quality electric typewriter, are mainly used to communicate with large centralized sets of information stored in distant computers, they have other uses, too. They can provide intercompany electronic mail service, routing and storing memos and messages electronically.

WHAT WE HAVE JUST DESCRIBED IS ONLY ONE PART OF THE DRAMATIC story of the arrival of the computer age in the business arena. This chapter will explain the basic concepts related to business use of computer systems. We will discuss the components of such a system and the many uses to which they are put. We will also introduce some mathematical tools which, with accounting systems and computers, make up a powerful array of tools for data gathering, analysis, and retrieval for business.

HISTORY OF COMPUTER SYSTEMS

Electronic data processing systems were preceded by mechanical systems developed prior to the twentieth century. For example, in 1642 Blaise Pascal, a young Frenchman, developed a machine for adding numbers. Later in the seventeenth century a German mathematician Gottfried Leibniz, developed a mechanical device that could multiply and divide numbers. A variety of modifications and improvements continued to be made to mechanical machines.

A significant development took place in the 1880s when Herman Hollerith was asked to develop a mechanical device to assist in compilation of 1890 U.S. census data. Hollerith's device, a punched-card mechanical data processing system, formed the basis for the Tabulations Machine Company. Hollerith's company was later to become part of a group of companies which in 1924 became known as the International Business Machines Corporation (IBM).

During World War II the first electronic, as opposed to mechanical, data processing machines were developed. The first, the ENIAC (Electronic Numerical Integrator and Calculator), weighed 30 tons and covered 1,500 square feet. An equivalent amount of computer power today would be placed on a single silicon chip.

WHAT IS A COMPUTER?

computer

A computer or, more exactly, a computer system is an electronic machine capable of storing and retrieving huge amounts of data and

performing mathematical calculations very quickly. It is also called an electronic data processing (EDP) system. Computers are an important part of many thousands of business firms and nonbusiness organizations.

The Wide Range of Computer Uses

Computers play a big role in your everyday life. Stop and think about it! They do some of the little everyday things like figuring your bank balance or the size of your family's bill at the Bay. A computer likely even prepares your grade reports. Computers do thousands of repetitive operations like these. They perform very efficiently for a big institution like a corporation or a university. They store a huge mass of information and make thousands of routine calculations. They allow large or small firms to communicate with all their customers, employees, or suppliers quickly and accurately.

Firms and people at home are finding all kinds of new uses for small computers. Income tax preparers are using them to figure out and print income tax returns. Garages and service stations are using specialized computers to find out what is wrong with your car. In fact, small special-purpose computers called *microprocessors* are being built into cars and

AUTHORS' COMMENTARY

Computer Application to House Design

Feature a potential customer walking into the office of a house building firm with the floor plan of a house sketched on a paper napkin. The customer tells the company's president that he wants the house built as soon as possible. Eight days later the house arrives at the site in numbered sections ready to be assembled.

This situation actually occurred at the offices of Designex Buildings, Ltd. in North Battleford, Saskatchewan. The key to the service was a computer program the company had developed. The program allows the company to do a complete house design or to change a single specification in a design.

The program, which took two and a half years to develop in its initial form, was felt, by company representatives, to be probably the most advanced technology in the industry available on the continent at the time. The development of the program was supervised by Mike Mahar, son of the company co-founder, a company director, and at the time Dean of the College of Commerce at the University of Saskatchewan.

The computer could take any house plan (even a sketch on a napkin), adjust it to required building standards, choose the lumber, calculate all measurements, and print out the final plan and all drawings in less than four hours. Manually, the same work would take at least four days.

Customization of home design by computer provides flexibility, speed, and accuracy. The uses of computers in this and other types of design applications will increase dramatically in the last half of the 1980s.

Source: Canadian Business, February 1980, p. 86.

appliances to improve their performance. High technology firms like Mitel Corporation are pouring millions of dollars into research for new ways to apply these electronic marvels. In recent years there has been a flood of electronic games. Each of these games is controlled by a special purpose computer. Special purpose computers even control those electronic video games you see in amusement centres and other public places.

Suppose you use your VISA card to buy gas at a service station. The attendant uses it to print your account number before you sign the charge slip. This slip ends up being processed by a computer. The amount of your purchase is added to your VISA bill. Because of the great speed and accuracy of computers, thousands of transactions, like your gasoline purchase, can be quickly and accurately processed.

But a computer can do a lot more than routine data processing or controlling an electronic game. Think of its role in the space program! Without computers, space shuttle flights would have been impossible. In fact, much of the progress in science and technology has depended on computers. Computers touch your life in at least these two ways—as a go-between for large institutions and the people they deal with and as an instrument that speeds up technological and economic progress.

Common Business Applications

It is obvious from what we have seen in our earlier chapters about production, marketing, and accounting that much of the success or failure of a firm depends upon its ability to *collect, process, organize,* and *retrieve* information. The accounting department needs to collect data concerning transactions and periodically produce financial statements. The production department needs to keep records of inventories and costs of production and to estimate production schedules. Financial managers need to measure cash flows and construct capital budgets. All of these and many additional jobs in all but the smallest firms require the speed, accuracy, and data-handling capacity of the computer. A successful firm needs to be able to gather, store, combine, and use this mass of data at a cost that is lower than the benefit it brings. If a computer is well designed and well used, it can do this.

Businesses use computers to

- prepare payrolls
- analyze past-due accounts receivable
- prepare and mail out bills
- keep social security and tax records
- keep track of inventories
- simplify reordering of goods
- control production costs

There are thousands of other specific jobs a computer can do for a business. The previous chapter outlined some of the financial and manage-

This NCR ad describes the benefits of a computerized inventory system

rial accounting functions that are often computer-aided. Some more detailed examples follow.

Some Specific Examples

A company that uses a combination of ingredients to make syrups and beverages needs to keep track of all the formulas the company uses. It also needs to print the batch tickets that are sent to the production facility. In addition, the company needs to know the costs of any quantity of the formula for the various container sizes. Such an application is called a *formula costing* system and is ideally suited to a computer. The NCR ad on page 417 illustrates inventory applications.

Professional firms (lawyers, accountants, engineers) need to account for and bill their time and expenses. A *professional time analysis and billing* system on a computer will allow a data entry person to set up a master file containing the names, addresses, and other important information about the professionals and their clients. The system allows timely entry of the time and expenses of the professionals as they relate to their clients. Using this system, the firm can get accurate analysis reports and bill their clients.

An architectural firm needs to know direct labour costs, indirect miscellaneous expenses, and outside consultant costs for each project. The firm must have up-to-date information regarding a project's budget and the actual costs for any given period of time. A *job costing* system allows original entry of personnel and client information as well as constant updating. The system calculates labour costs by multiplying hours worked by the billing rate per hour. Some job costing systems can also be used by the firm to calculate a bid on a contract.

Many businesses need to send out marketing-oriented messages, letters, or perhaps Christmas cards to all their customers. In order to get a cheaper mailing rate, bulk mail must be sorted in postal code order. A computer can perform a sorting job like this in minutes, thereby saving time and money. The business can use the computer to print the sorted customer mailing list.

BASIC TYPES OF COMPUTER APPLICATIONS

Before discussing how a computer works, let's discuss three general types of computer applications in business. These are data processing, word processing, and automation.

Computers and Data Processing

data processing

As we saw in Chapter 11, all businesses need to collect, store, manipulate, interpret, and report data. This is called data processing. It includes financial and nonfinancial data. Governments and other non-business institutions need to process data too. These data processing needs vary a lot because of the great differences in the type and the size of data flows among these institutions. In all cases, however, there is a need to keep accurate tallies of all those numbers that are important to these institutions — counting hospital admissions or adding cash collected by a grocery store or figuring the net profit of an oil company.

The size of the data flow (need) and the financial resources of the institution (ability to pay) determine the scale and complexity of its data processing system. Not all firms need, nor can they afford, computers.

On a very small scale, such as would be found in a small rural gasoline service station, no machines at all may be involved.

Computers and Word Processing

It is midnight and a paper that you were assigned six weeks earlier is due tomorrow morning. As usual, you waited until the last minute to type it. Now, after it is typed and you are reading the copy, you realize that it needs major reorganization and that much of the material must be moved around. Because a good grade is important, you lose some sleep and stay up to retype the whole paper. The next morning, when you are about to turn it in, you notice that you spelled two words incorrectly throughout. There goes your "A"!

word processing system

A word processing system would have greatly simplified your problem. **A word processing system is a computer that is programmed to manipulate letters, words, and paragraphs. It is a text-editing computer.** This means that you can type your paper (text) as you normally would, but instead of the characters appearing on paper as you type, the characters are displayed on a television-like screen (CRT terminal) and at the same time are stored on a floppy disk — a soft plastic disk similar to a record. Once you have typed your text, you can re-display it on the screen at a later date and, with simple key strokes, make changes. You don't have to retype your paper. All you need to do to make changes is to indicate where you want to move the text. The word processor can also be used to correct spelling errors by simply keying in the correct letters in place of the incorrect ones. The word processor will repaginate the text and type the revised paper on a printer that looks like a typewriter. Deleting, adding, or otherwise editing your paper is very easy with a word processor. This makes it one of the most useful applications of computers for the business community. It is one feature of the "office of the future" that is here now!

Computers and Automation

In Chapter 8 on production we used the term *automation*. An activity or process is automated when it is possible to set its controls in advance so that it can work a long time without human attention.

Some automated processes are fairly simple and don't require computers. An example is a household heating and air-conditioning system. The thermostat permits the system to operate automatically, without much human interference.

A petroleum refinery is a more complex system. There are many points in the refining process at which information must be fed continuously into a computer. The information relates to such things as the rate of flow, temperature, and so on. The refinery's central computer has been programmed so that it uses this information to control the refining process.

The computer automatically makes certain computations and relays instructions to machinery in the factory. It does this in accordance with the program fed into it at an earlier time. Thus valves are opened and closed and temperatures are raised and lowered automatically.

Programming, as we will see in greater detail later in this chapter, is the process of telling a computer what to do. **A computer program is a detailed set of instructions in a special computer language.**

computer program

COMPUTER HARDWARE

Any discussion of computers often falls under two headings: the *hardware* and the *software.* Two other important elements of computer systems are communications capability and the data base.

hardware

Computer hardware consists of the machinery and electronic components. Let's examine the various parts of the hardware and what they can do.

The tasks performed by the hardware, in logical order, are

- input
- storage and/or manipulation
- output

The tasks of inputting, storing, manipulating, and outputting are performed by four kinds of parts or components: (1) input devices; (2) central processing units; (3) outside data storage systems; and (4) output devices. (See Figure 12.1.)

central processing unit (CPU)

The heart of any computer is its central processing unit (CPU). The CPU includes an internal memory for storing data, an arithmetic unit for performing calculations, a logic unit for comparing values and helping to "make decisions," and a control unit that actually operates the computer and sends instructions for controlling all of the other components.

outside data storage systems

A computer's internal memory can be added to by means of outside data storage systems. These are separate systems for storing information, such as magnetic disks, floppy disks, cassette tape, magnetic tape, and decks of punched cards. (See Figures 12.1 and 12.2.) Information can be recorded on any of these devices and read into the computer at any time. Internal memory is used when response speed is important, such as during a sorting operation. Outside memory devices are usually used for information that is not in constant use by the computer system.

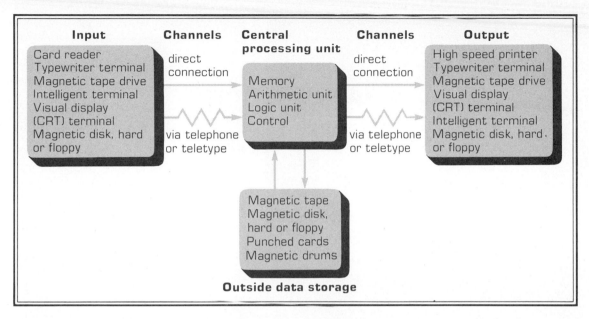

Input	Channels	Central processing unit	Channels	Output
Card reader Typewriter terminal Magnetic tape drive Intelligent terminal Visual display (CRT) terminal Magnetic disk, hard or floppy	direct connection via telephone or teletype	Memory Arithmetic unit Logic unit Control	direct connection via telephone or teletype	High speed printer Typewriter terminal Magnetic tape drive Visual display (CRT) terminal Intelligent terminal Magnetic disk, hard. or floppy

Magnetic tape
Magnetic disk,
hard or floppy
Punched cards
Magnetic drums

Outside data storage

Figure 12.1
Hardware components of a computer system

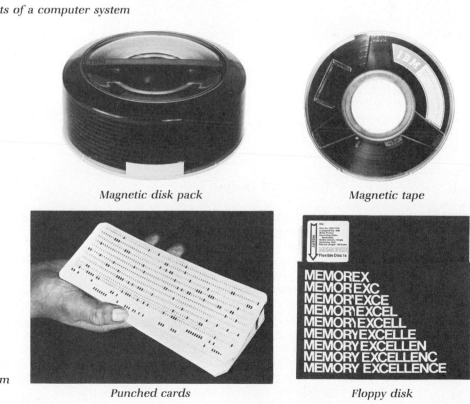

Magnetic disk pack

Magnetic tape

Figure 12.2
Some of the devices used to store, enter, and retrieve data from computer systems

Punched cards

Floppy disk

The Burroughs B7900 mainframe computer system

Input and Output Devices

input-output (I-O)
devices

Input and output (I-O) devices are the hardware used in getting information in and out of the computer. These pieces of hardware, as a group, are also called *peripheral* equipment.

Magnetic disk and magnetic tape units are commonly used as both input and output units. They are usually wired in directly to the central computer. As noted above, the data they contain may be stored outside the system itself. Still in use, but becoming obsolete, are card readers for input and card punch units for output. The punched card, pictured in Figure 12.2, was once the principal medium for data storage in computer systems.

An important output device is the high-speed printer. This unit is especially important for creating long lists of data such as in payrolls, invoices, and summary reports for accounting purposes. Some line printers can produce hundreds of lines of data per minute.

POINT OF VIEW

Composing Tunes by Computer: Bach to Basics

As anyone knows who's gone to a rock concert recently, making music is hardly a simple business any more. In fact, the musicians are apt to be outnumbered by all the engineers they need to keep their equipment running. Now Toronto musician David McLey, 34, has found a better way. After 12 years of tinkering he's come up with a computer-based electronic music system appropriately dubbed the McLeyvier. A unique, versatile instrument that has already caught the interest of such music stars as Stevie Wonder and the Moody Blues' Patrick Morizz, by 1984 the McLeyvier could bring in sales to the tune of $22 million a year for Toronto's Hazelcom Corp.

Electronic synthesizers are already popular both on the stage and in the studio because they can simulate existing sounds and create new ones. This means that advertisement producers, for instance, can create a commercial jingle without a full studio orchestra. But McLey's wonder box goes further than that. The McLeyvier incorporates the buyer's choice of a 61- or traditional 88-key piano-type keyboard, a video display terminal and a "typewriter" keyboard (used to give commands to the system). There's also a pen plotter, which prints on paper, in publishable form, any piece of music composed on the machine. A musician can sit down at his McLeyvier, compose a piece of music for, say, piano and flute, play it back instantly and, if he wants, add harpsichord to the flute line and viola to the piano line just by typing in simple instructions. And an arrangement can be altered at any time by using the piano keyboard. If the user isn't sure of an instruction, he can type in "Help." That activates a self-teaching program that lists and explains the function he's trying to execute. If he doesn't like what he's composed, he can just as easily delete lines. It's a snap, too, to create new sounds, such as breaking glass or howling wind, which can then be stored permanently in the computer's vast memory. And the user can see what he is playing, on the screen or on paper, by pushing a button.

The McLeyvier can duplicate the sound of as many as 128 separate voices or instruments simultaneously. And it will tune itself, or put itself in tune with another instrument, in two minutes. "You can set it up and go out for a coffee, and when you come back, it's in tune," says McLey.

The McLeyvier isn't cheap. At an average cost of $40,000, the setup is beyond the reach of your average high-school rock band (a smaller system without scoring functions, to cost about $12,000, will be available in September). But as the machine finds its way into the right hands — namely people as innovative as McLey — more musicians across North America will be calling their own tunes.

Source: Canadian Business, March 1982 (p. 16).

---

modem

One of the most important input and output units in use today is the typewriter terminal, often accompanied by a visual display screen (cathode ray tube, or CRT). **Such terminals are often connected to the central processing unit by means of telephone lines. The device used to make this possible is called a modem. A modem modulates or converts direct current (DC) signals to tones and demodulates or converts tones back to DC signals.** These remote units may have computing power themselves and perform some data accumulation and processing functions in-

Table 12.1   Special Purpose Input and Output Devices

COM (computer output microfilm)	Displays data on a CRT screen from microfilm. Example: parts specifications at a large warehouse
OMR (optical mark recognition) reader	Device that reads data recorded in pencil on documents. Example: computer-graded test answer sheets
MICR (magnetic ink character recognition) reader	Device that reads characters written on documents with magnetic ink. Example: account number and amount on cheque
UPC (universal product code) reader	Device that reads the special product code identification bars on grocery items as they pass over the checkout counter at the supermarket
Voice digitizer	Device that translates voice input into digital form for processing in the computer

dependent of the central computer as well as feed information to the central computer. These are called *intelligent terminals* and may be programmed to "converse" with the central computer.

Today there are a wide variety of special purpose input and output devices you will come across in your business career. Some of these are described briefly in Table 12.1. The first item listed is an output device and the remainder are input devices.

IBM's new, low-cost, small business microcomputer system

The Boom in Microcomputers

The recent invention of very tiny but powerful electronic components has led to the development of a new set of business and individual "microcomputers." Microcomputers, which cost only one-fiftieth as much as a large computer, can do much more than one-fiftieth of the work. The low cost of models made by many vendors has made the computer available to hundreds of thousands of small firms and private households. More than half a million "home" microcomputers had been sold by the end of 1981. Homemakers all over Canada are now using IBM, APPLE, PET, TRS-80, or other microcomputers for a variety of purposes: to teach math or grammar to their children; to learn to speak German or to play bridge; to balance their chequebooks; to keep an inventory of their household possessions; or to manage their personal finances.

The potential volume of microcomputer sales to small businesses appears to be even greater than the home computer market. (See Table 12.2.)

Table 12.2 Microcomputers and Their Advantages and Disadvantages

Computer Maker	Price	Capacity	Advantages	Disadvantages
Apple II	Basic unit $1,900–$2,300	16–256K	More than 90 outlets in Canada 90-day warranty Software support improving; very good in many cases	Expansion is expensive No numeric key pad on keyboard
Commodore Business Machines	Basic unit $1,500–$3,000	16–96K	More than 80 outlets in Canada 90-day warranties offered by dealers only	Business software lagging Disk drives expensive Fewer vendors catering to business
HP Series 80	$4,250–$6,000	32–56K Expandable to 600K	Worldwide network 90-day warranty Phone-in assistance usually within an hour	Limited HP software Tiny screens
IBM	Basic unit 2 disk drives $3,900	16–256K	Nationwide service network 90-day warranty Well-written manuals IBM name and reputation	Limited software Modular: have to buy separate pieces Limited number of outlets at present
Radio Shack Model II	Basic unit Built-in disk drive $5,400	64–256K	Worldwide network, many vendors More than 50 outlets in Canada 90-day warranty	Very little support for outside software Many users complain sales-people are not knowledgeable Not very portable

Source: Canadian Business, September 1982 (pp. 108–111).

Although many managers of smaller firms might still be skeptical about having their own system, the financial reasons for not doing so are rapidly disappearing. These small systems have been marketed with broad accounting packages and specialized programs tailored for many industries. They can do payroll, general ledger, billing, inventory, and sales analysis; and clerks, secretaries, and floor salespeople can use them after a short training program.

In the larger firm, microcomputers may have a similar impact. Larger firms, in recent years, have felt the pressure of mounting data processing loads and a shortage of trained computer operating staff. This problem has caused them to centralize data processing in larger, more powerful computers. It seems, however, that centralization, in turn, has often led to conflict between those actually using the systems and those controlling them at data centres. The falling cost of microcomputers has started to reverse the trend toward centralized data processing.

COMPUTER COMMUNICATIONS

distributed data
processing (DDP)

Firms that implement distributed data processing (DDP) can avoid the frustration created by large centralized computers. **DDP is a multiple systems approach to information handling. It puts computer power in many different places.** Microcomputers enhance large-scale computers by placing additional computing power throughout an organization. Such linkages are called *networks*. When a firm discovered that the recently installed central computer at its head office was causing some slowdowns in decision making at remote distribution points, management installed microcomputers (Apple IIs) at these points. These low cost systems easily handled the everyday load of inventory and other problems at these locations. Linkage between these units and the main computer also provided the necessary central control and information.

The Air Canada reservations system is an excellent example of a computer system that utilizes a communication network. Many computer service bureaus also utilize communications capability to enter data from all parts of Canada.

The Canadian telephone companies have a great deal of expertise in the transmission of data to, from, and between computers. In the near future it is likely that considerable communication will take place between in-home computers, utilizing the telephone network provided by telephone companies.

COMPUTER SOFTWARE

software

Computer software complements hardware by giving instructions and setting hardware into motion. It includes system software and application software, both of which are written in a computer language and require a kind of interpretation called documentation. All of these topics are discussed below.

Software is just as important as hardware. In fact, it is reported that software now costs more than hardware and that the proportion of computer system dollars spent for software will increase greatly in the future.

System Software

time sharing

System software consists of internal instructions which tell the computer system how to manage the various tasks assigned to it. **System software may enable a computer to permit many users to interact with the computer at the same time. Such a process is called time sharing.** The internal speed of the computer, together with the relative slowness of the several remote input-output devices, makes such time sharing possible. Thus the inventory clerk in a warehouse can be typing in data on a newly arrived shipment of bolts while the payroll department is feeding in a magnetic tape containing information needed to print this week's paycheques. There is no noticeable interruption of either input. **Devices known as controllers regulate the "traffic" of peripheral hardware into the computer's central processing unit.**

controllers

online real-time system

When those using the system are in direct communication with the computer, either by telephone or directly wired in, the system is called an online system. When such a system can respond immediately it is called a real-time system. A large proportion of the computers in use today are online real-time systems. Such a system may, for example, be used for constant energy management.

With such a system, thousands of employees can use a modern building with a minimum of heating, cooling, and lighting. Thermostats and other monitoring devices send information to the computer. The computer is programmed to digest this information and to make a variety of computations and "decisions" that will keep energy consumption to a minimum.

Instead of online real-time systems, some firms use *batch processing.* Batch processing is data processing in which data are collected for a period of time before being entered into the computer system. Batch processing is used where there is a large amount of input, but no need for immediate output. For example, the University of Manitoba library accumulates records of books checked out by students, faculty, and the general public. These records are periodically entered into the university computer and summaries of outstanding books are printed by the computer and sent out at the end of each semester.

System software and, as we will see in the next section, application software require programming. Programming, in turn, requires a computer language.

assembly language

Systems software programs are usually written in assembly language. This is called an intermediate level language because it lies between machine language and the higher-level (English-like) languages used in writing applications programs. These are discussed in the next section. **Machine language consists of binary (1 and 0 digits only) code and relates to a specific computer or set of computers.** It is used because the CPU only understands the fact that its tiny memory cells

machine language

are either on or off. A cell turned on is recognized as a 1 and a cell turned off is recognized as a 0.

Application Software and Programming

Application software means programs that are designed to do a variety of jobs for users, such as the financial accounting functions described in Chapter 11 or market research tabulations discussed in Chapter 9. These programs are likely to be written in one of the major languages described below—FORTRAN, COBOL, BASIC, Pascal, and Ada.

FORTRAN

FORTRAN has for years been the most widely used language for scientific and engineering programming applications. FORTRAN is short for FORmula TRANslator.

COBOL

COBOL (Common Business Oriented Language) is specially designed for conventional commercial applications. COBOL is especially good for handling large files of alphabetic and numerical data such as payrolls.

BASIC

BASIC was originally designed to teach students how to program. Because it is easy to use, it has become the most widely implemented language for microcomputers. Recent enhancements have made it useful in both business and scientific applications.

Pascal

Pascal is a relatively new language that uses most of the modern techniques of good programming design. It features an important software design technique called *structured programming.* **It is powerful in its data description and in its ability to process that data.** It is also used in microcomputers.

Ada

Ada is a programming language recently developed by the U.S. military in an attempt to design a more efficient language than any of the above. It is suited to both scientific and business applications.

The BASIC program in Figure 12.3 is explained as follows: The computer responds to input from the operator. It performs a series of steps in the order of the program line number at the left of each line. Lines 10 and 20

```
10   PRINT ''EACH TIME YOU SEE '?'TYPE IN A
     NUMBER. WHEN YOU HAVE NO MORE NUMBERS TYPE
     -99.99 AS YOUR FINAL NUMBER.''
20   PRINT ''I WILL TELL YOU THE SUM OF THE
     NUMBERS THAT YOU TYPED.''
30   LET T = 0
40   INPUT X
50   IF X = -99.99 THEN 80
60   LET T = T + X
70   GO TO 40
80   PRINT ''THE SUM IS '';T
90   END
```

Figure 12.3
A BASIC program for finding a sum

are directions to the operator. Line 30 sets the counter for the sum, T, at zero. Line 40 allows the operator to enter a number. Line 50, in effect, tells the program when to stop adding. It does this by checking for a "dummy" number, -99.99. Line 50 says: "When you come to the dummy number (-99.99), skip to line 80." Line 60 is the actual adding process. It tells the computer to set up a counter, T, and to add the next value of X to the counter, T. Line 70 says to start the cycle at line 40 again. The computer continues the cycle of lines 40 to 70 until the dummy number, -99.99, is typed in. Line 80 says to print the words "The sum is" and the value of T. Line 90 tells the computer to stop the program.

This may seem like an awful lot of trouble for a simple addition. It is. But if there were hundreds of numbers and much more complex mathematics than addition, it would be worth the trouble.

Documentation

documentation

An important part of software is known as documentation. This means an explanation either in English (or other spoken languages) or in diagram form of what a program does, how it is used, and how it works.

Documentation is important to both those who write and those who use programs. Programmers are interested in the documentation that concerns the design, logic, function, and utility of the program. Users are interested in the purpose of the program, when to use it, and what preparations are necessary to run it successfully. Documentation for the user is written in the ordinary spoken language of the nation in which it is used, and is usually given to the user in the form of operator instructions.

In developing programs for most businesses today, the traditional method of flowcharting is used as documentation for programmers. Flowcharts, or block diagrams, such as the one shown in Figure 12.4, give the nontechnical person a graphic illustration of the logical steps in a program. This particular illustration describes the steps taken to produce a weekly payroll for a sales force whose income depends on their commission on sales. The flowchart shows that the computer: (1) searches files for all salespeople who have made sales during the last weekly payroll period; (2) arranges these in alphabetical order by sales region; (3) reads from sales records the amount sold and the commission rate; (4) multiplies units sold times commission rate; (5) prints the cheque; (6) goes to the next sales record, etc. until all cheques are written; and (7) stops processing. This is a bit simpler than a real-life computation which might include different commission rates on different products and various tax deductions from the total pay due.

Flowcharts are still widely used for both whole system design and individual program design, but there is a big change in documentation taking place today. The change stems from the rise in the use of structured programming, mentioned earlier in the description of Pascal. The concept is a complex one and would take a chapter of its own to explain fully. The general idea, however, is to simplify the process of program development and then, at a later time, to simplify program modification.

Figure 12.4
A flowchart (block diagram) for a payroll

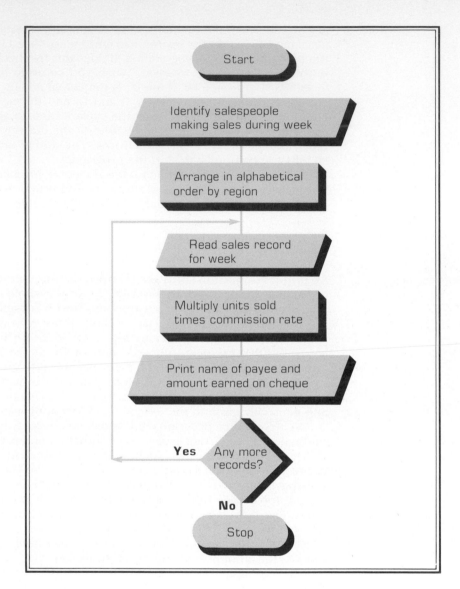

HOW ARE COMPUTER SYSTEMS SELECTED AND INSTALLED IN A FIRM?

A sad fact about the typical use of computers in businesses is the poor planning that often occurs. This is caused by a variety of things. Consider this typical sequence of events leading up to the installation of a computer system at the Ajax Bolt Company.

Selecting a System

Ajax is a middle-sized manufacturer which once had an outdated, partially manual system of processing data. The information systems in the production, marketing, and finance departments were all somewhat different. There was a serious need for a modern computer-based information system.

The subject of computers came up at a board of directors meeting after Ajax's president, Sam Black, visited a competitor's plant. He saw the fancy computer room there, with all the blinking lights and spinning reels of tape. Sam also noticed the lower volume of paperwork and learned that the competitor's profits had improved since the system was installed.

The next time the computer firm's sales representative visited Ajax, Sam listened carefully to the sales pitch. The salesperson outlined what seemed to be a very good application of the computer company's hardware and software to Ajax's needs.

The proposed system provided for more integration of all the marketing, production, and financial data gathering, sorting, analysis, and reporting. It seemed to provide an improved basis for making decisions in these three functional areas and for top management planning.

Being a smart businessman, Sam arranged for three computer firms to make presentations to his staff. After study and comparison of the proposals (which were all similar), Ajax picked a medium-priced computer made by the firm with the best service reputation of the three.

Ajax's need for a computer system was clear, but Sam Black did not take the best approach. Ideally, Ajax should have started by hiring an independent systems consultant or a permanent systems analyst. This person would have talked to all department heads to develop a complete set of concepts of the firm's needs. Next, with the analyst's help, Ajax would have examined the computers made by several manufacturers, including a variety of components that best fitted Ajax's needs. Finally, the necessary programming, testing, and installation would have been done.

Under this plan, Ajax would have had a better understanding of its needs. This understanding would not have been limited by the ready-made systems of a given manufacturer and by such a firm's "outsider's view" of Ajax's problems and operations. In other words, it's wise to define your true computer needs first. The following guidelines can help a lot.

Hardware evaluation:

- •What are the costs involved? The rent, lease, or purchase price as well as the costs of operation and maintenance must be considered.
- •Can it perform to your satisfaction? This includes adequate work volume capacity and speed.
- •Is it compatible with the system already in operation?
- •Is it expandable to meet your growth expectations?
- •Can your staff be trained to run it?

Software evaluation:

•Do packaged programs fit your needs and staff expertise?
•Are programs documented adequately?
•Are the operating system, compilers, etc., reliable?

Vendor evaluation:

•What are the maintenance capabilities of the vendor?
•Does the local office of the vendor provide programming and systems support?
•What support will the vendor provide during conversion?
•What is the record of the vendor as to past performance, consistency during negotiations, and so forth?

Other Options

Firms that are thinking about a new computer, of course, have other options open to them besides the choice from among hardware manufacturers. First of all, they now have the choice of leasing from manufacturers or of leasing from computer leasing firms. The latter are independent middlemen who can often provide combinations of various manufacturers' hardware components which might more closely meet the user's needs than can the products of one manufacturer. Often, a user can save money by using a middleman's services.

Another option available is to lease a line connected into an existing large system with time-sharing capabilities. Such an arrangement can be made with a large user such as a bank or with a leasing firm. This option, of course, is not feasible for a firm that needs a large, complex data processing capacity. Another option for the small firm is to let a computer service firm take over its data processing needs entirely.

How People React to Computers

Human reactions to the computer range from worship to outright fear. Most people who know computers reject these extremes. Rather, they learn that the computer is a marvellous tool. They find that people and computers can bring their different abilities together and that this combined power can be used very effectively.

Fear of the computer takes different forms. Some fear that people will become so dependent on complex control systems that a small human error in programming or data entry could produce chaos. The Three Mile Island near-disaster in the United States is a reminder of the basis for such fears. Some people fear the computer because they feel it can bring about mass unemployment. Others fear it because it brings change in the firm — new ways of doing things. Still others fear the computer for another reason. They know that the government and many private agencies have stored huge quantities of personal data about private citizens and feel that this is a violation of their right to privacy. This is a special problem because of the prevalence of electronic spying.

Closely related to the question of privacy is the fear or loss through "computer crime." Clever thieves have, in many cases, discovered ways to abuse computer systems, often in bank accounts or in payroll systems, for their personal gain. This is a growing problem which computer system designers are working on. Naturally, there's not much publicity about techniques being used to combat such theft. Space-age thieves are too clever.

Computer "pranksters" have also gained access to computer data banks. For example, in 1980 four thirteen-year-olds from a private school in New York, using their school's computer, gained access to several corporations' data. Among other "pranks," the teenagers erased 10 million bits of data from a Canadian cement company's computers.

One measure being tested that specifically avoids the theft of private information is coding, not unlike the coding used in military communications. Such codes are being developed by specialized computer consulting firms for use by all kinds of businesses. All messages on SWIFT, for example, a computer network linking 500 international banks, are being sent in coded form. And banks are issuing "secret passwords" to their customers who use automatic tellers to transact business.

Some people (even managers) believe that computers will magically solve all their problems. This belief is as wrong as is fear of the computer and can cause many problems for a firm. The truth is that managers must plan very carefully. They must get accurate data and a "debugged" program (one in which all the problems have been worked out) before they can count on using a computer's output. Someone invented the phrase GIGO (garbage in–garbage out) to describe how much the computer depends on reliable human input. It's unlikely that a chimpanzee will ever be able to count its toes, even with a computer's help!

WHAT FUTURE APPLICATIONS ARE POSSIBLE FOR BUSINESS?

If you hate the thought of data entry on a keyboard, perhaps by the time you graduate, you will not need to know how to type. Research is already well under way on designing electronic hearing devices to decode human speech, regardless of accent. At the same time, work is continuing on electronic voice output. Texas Instruments' *Speak and Spell* toy has already demonstrated low cost electronic speech.

Alvin Toffler, in his book, *The Third Wave*, introduced the concept of the "electronic cottage." By the time you graduate, you may not need to commute to work daily. With the use of a microcomputer, a phone, and a modem at home, and a large-scale or minicomputer at work, you may be able to work at home. Only an occasional visit to your employer's office will be necessary. The electronic cottage will be made possible by the explosion in data communications—with distributed data processing and advanced telecommunications.

WHAT DO YOU THINK?

What Do You Think about SINs?

There has been considerable controversy over how the federal government should use Canadians' Social Insurance Numbers (SINs). Some administrators would like to collate all the information on specific individuals according to their SINs. If this were done, all the information about an individual collected by the government could be accessed by knowing that person's SIN. This would be useful for a variety of applications including things related to police work, immigration and emigration, health care, sociological research, financial checks, and so on.

Others argue, however, that so much organized information in the hands of one agency could be dangerous. They say that information about individuals should not be organized by SINs. WHAT DO YOU THINK?

As the designers of computers become more sensitive to human needs, the distinction between data processing and word processing will decrease. We will also see extensive use of colour graphics in both business and scientific applications. A picture is worth a thousand words!

Eventually, programming that you may have seen in offices will become obsolete. Computer systems themselves will be able to write the programs for particular office needs.

quantitative tools

While computers have grown to be a vital part of business activity, a parallel growth has occurred in the use of mathematics and statistical tools. That these two things have grown at the same time is not coincidence. **Many of the mathematical and statistical tools depend on computers for their practical application. We refer to this whole set of mathematical and statistical applications to business as quantitative tools.**

SOME QUANTITATIVE TOOLS FOR MANAGEMENT DECISIONS

The use of quantitative tools by managers is increasing. Whereas managers in the past often relied only on their own judgment, modern managers strengthen their judgment by collecting and organizing data to support it. We will examine some basic statistical concepts and some examples of quantitative tools used today.

Statistics for Business

statistics

Managers have dealt with numerical data in their decision making for many years. These numerical data and methods of summarizing them are called statistics. Data may represent internal facts, such as number of units sold, or external facts, such as the population of the provinces in which a firm does business.

It is often helpful to summarize numerical data by using special kinds of averages. For example, we may wish to refer to average family income in Canada or to the average number of years of school completed. An average is a summary figure that describes the facts we are studying. There are three principal types of averages:

- the arithmetic mean
- the median
- the mode

arithmetic mean

The arithmetic mean is an average computed by first adding numbers, finding the total, and then dividing that total by the number of numbers that were added together. Look at Table 12.3. It is a list, or array, of the ages of seven employees in the receiving department of a factory. It also shows that the sum of their ages is 210 years. We can compute the arithmetic mean of their ages, their average age, by simply dividing 210 years by 7. The answer, of course, is 30 years. This is the most common form of average.

median

Another measure of an average is called a median. It means the middle number when numbers are listed in rank — from smallest to largest or vice versa. To find the median of the ages of the employees in Table 12.3 we first rank ages in an array, starting with the youngest. The list becomes 26, 27, 27, 28, 30, 34, 38. The middle number is 28 years (Janet's age). There are three people older than Janet and three who are younger.

To find a median of an even number of numbers, we still rank the numbers and then take an arithmetic mean of the two "middle" numbers only. If we added Paul, aged 29, to our list the median would be 28.5, which is the arithmetic mean of the two middle numbers, 28 and 29.

mode

A third average is called a mode. It is the most common or frequent number in a list. In our example, only two people are the same age. Clyde and Susan are both 27, so this is the mode. Their age, 27, is the modal age.

These types of "averages" are different ways of making a summary measurement of a characteristic of a group. Which one is best depends on the use to which the measurement is put and how the raw data are distributed.

Table 12.3   Ages of Employees in the Receiving Department

Employee	Age
Harold	30
Janet	28
Gordon	38
Clyde	27
Susan	27
Richard	34
Thomas	26
Total	210

Table 12.4 Frequency Distribution of Family Incomes

Annual Family Income	Number of Families
$ 0– 5,999.99	180
6,000–11,999.99	752
12,000–18,999.99	957
19,000–25,999.99	702
26,000 and over	140
Total	2,731

Suppose we collected statistics on family incomes in your home town and organized them into five groups. The statistics might appear in grouped form as shown in Table 12.4. This is called a frequency distribution.

frequency distribution

A frequency distribution is a table that shows how many members of a larger group fall within various classes or subgroups. In this case it shows how family incomes are distributed among five income intervals or ranges. There are, for example, 180 families who received less than $6,000, and 752 who received at least $6,000 but less than $12,000. Of course, the same information could have been provided by giving a whole list or array of all families and their incomes. The frequency distribution gives a clear summary of what family incomes are in the town without the extreme detail of such a list. It also tells us more than a single average of incomes could tell. It shows something about how incomes are dispersed or scattered around the average income. Figure 12.5 shows the same information in the form of a histogram. **The histogram, or bar chart, portrays a frequency distribution in vertical or horizontal columns whose length, measured on an accompanying scale, indicates the number or percent in each class.** The average, frequency distribution, and histogram are

histogram

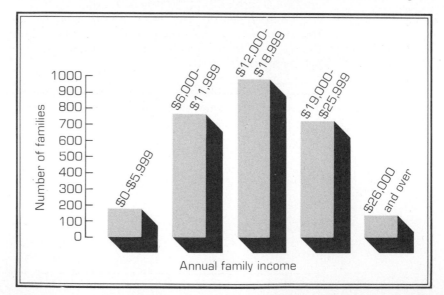

Figure 12.5
Histogram of data in Table 12.4

examples of *descriptive statistics.* Managers use them in preparing reports that describe their business operations or marketing data.

Sampling

sample

Another widely used tool is the *statistics of sampling.* **A sample is a part of a larger group called a universe or population. It is intended to take the place of the larger group and to convey some information about that larger group.** Political analysts, for example, project winners in elections by studying a relatively small number of voters (the sample). The time, costs, and effort involved in interviewing every voter (the universe) would be too great. By interviewing a sample of voters, a pollster can make a good estimate of the election results.

Businesses also use sampling. Suppose a manufacturer of light bulbs wishes to guarantee that its bulbs will last a certain number of hours. The company might find, based on a study of a sample, that the average bulb life is 200 hours. It would be unrealistic to base the guarantee on a study of all the light bulbs it produces. Its entire inventory would have to be "burned out." So it tests a sample of these bulbs.

A TV program sponsor uses a rating to decide whether to keep a particular program. A TV rating firm such as A.C. Nielsen cannot check all viewers in the country. Think of the cost! Nielsen conducts a sample drawn from all viewers and then estimates the national audience from the sample.

Some samples are selected in such a way that certain things can be estimated about the larger group with a given degree of confidence. Other samples are not drawn according to strict mathematical rules but still try to approximate the characteristics of the larger groups. They don't provide a measurable degree of confidence in their accuracy, but they are cheaper to get and are more often used than the other (random) kind because of the lower cost.

Breakeven Analysis

breakeven analysis

A useful management tool in both production planning and pricing of products is breakeven analysis. Breakeven analysis demonstrates the profitability of various levels of production. The breakeven point shows at which level total costs are exactly equal to total sales revenue. As you can see in Figure 12.6, the number of units produced is measured on the horizontal scale and dollar costs and revenues are measured on the vertical scale. The sales revenue line starts at the zero point (lower left corner). Because the product sells for $100, this line moves up $1,000 each time it moves to the right by 10 units. If we make and sell 20 units, we get $2,000 in revenue.

Costs are of two kinds: fixed and variable. *Fixed costs* occur whether we produce zero or 20 or 1,000 units. These costs are often called *overhead costs.* They include depreciation on plant, insurance, and other costs that do not vary with the level of production. In this case fixed costs are $1,000.

Figure 12.6
A breakeven chart

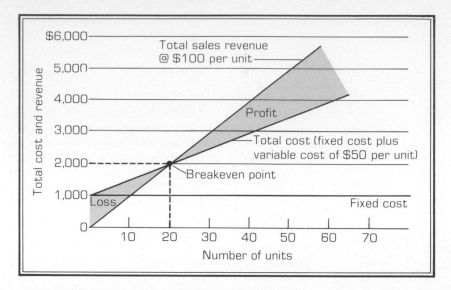

Variable costs depend on the number of units produced and sold. These might include raw materials, labour, and other costs that go into each unit produced. For each unit we produce and sell, it costs us $50 more—in addition to fixed costs. The effect of variable cost is represented by another line sloping up from the $1,000 mark on the left vertical axis. This line, because it starts from the $1,000 fixed-cost level, also measures total cost at various levels of production. If 20 units are made, the total cost is $2,000, consisting of $1,000 in fixed costs and $1,000 (20 × $50) in variable costs. If 25 are made, the total cost is $2,250.

At the level of 20 units of production, the cost and revenue lines cross. This is the *breakeven point,* the production level beyond which the firm begins to make a profit. For each additional unit made and sold the firm realizes an increase of $50 in profits. This is so because unit revenue minus unit variable cost ($100 − $50) equals $50.

A breakeven chart can help a plant manager decide several things. It can help a manager decide whether to install expensive new machines that would change the production cost structure. It can help to set prices or help to decide whether to buy or to lease a plant. A retailer could also use a breakeven chart to make similar decisions. Without the use of a breakeven chart the breakeven point (BP) can be computed by dividing total fixed cost (TFC) by the difference between unit revenue or price (P) and unit variable cost (VC):

$$BP = \frac{TFC}{(P - VC)}$$

Operations Research

Many new mathematical tools have been developed to solve business problems. For example, determining how many units of a product to keep in its

IF YOU ARE CONSIDERING A CAREER IN EITHER ACCOUNTING OR computers, there is good news and bad news. The good news is that there are more opportunities in these fields than almost any other. The bad news is that you'd better get down to serious business if you want to succeed in them. These are among the most challenging of all occupational paths.

Most accounting-related jobs — auditing, tax accounting, budgeting, managerial accounting, and public accounting — emphasize the need for university or community college accounting courses. About the only accounting-related jobs that don't require a university or college course are simple bookkeeping and personal tax preparation jobs. If you want to be a CA, of course, you must also pass a very difficult national examination. The rewards are great, however.

In computers, opportunities are also quite attractive, and the educational requirements are great for most of these jobs. Data entry position — keypunch and peripheral equipment operators — are the exception in that they require relatively short training periods and do not call for a college degree. Programmers usually require some college training, sometimes two-year college diplomas. Computer operators require similar training and education. If you are thinking of a position as a systems analyst, a four-year degree is necessary, usually with a major in computer science or mathematics. Such higher-level jobs require attention to detail and the application of logic and mathematical concepts.

Nearly all of the computer and accounting jobs are "inside" — office-bound jobs with regular hours. When auditing or systems analysis is performed for clients, travel is required for such consultation. Working conditions for all of these jobs, which are found wherever large- to medium-sized businesses are found, are quite comfortable. ■

operations research (OR)

warehouses is a tough problem for a firm selling hundreds of products around the world. Mathematical tools are available to help solve this and other problems. **The various quantitative techniques used to solve problems of scheduling or allocation are called operations research (OR).** Without computers, however, the mathematical calculations needed to apply these techniques could take years to perform. Linear programming is one of the techniques of operations research.

linear programming

Linear programming is a mathematical tool used to allocate resources in the "best way" so as to maximize or minimize a desired objective. This desired objective may be the greatest profit, the least cost, or another "best" result for the firm. For example, this technique could allow a firm that is selecting a location for a new plant to minimize the total cost of getting raw materials into the plant, getting finished goods to ware-

CAREER PROFILE

MY NAME IS CARMEN PICHE, AND I AM A Financial Management Trainee for the City of Calgary. I have been in this job for one year.

My educational background is high school, followed by a Bachelor of Commerce (Honours).

The Financial Management Trainee program is a new one for the City of Calgary. Four other people started on it with me. The training program is designed to last for a two-year period. Over this time I will work in four of the six major finance areas of the city. Over the period I will gain an overview of the City of Calgary financial system. This will include an understanding of what the different types of departments are; how they relate to the central city administration; and how they each handle the different elements of financial administration such as payroll, accounts payable, accounts receivable, budgeting, and reporting.

My first assignment was to the police department. I am currently working in the Accounting and Management Reporting System (AMRS) division of the Central Finance Department. I am working with and testing a new computer software package — an online journal entry and edit system — that will allow various city departments to enter data on financial transactions remotely rather then having to send them all to the central department for

houses, and moving them to customers. It would consider these and the many other variables that influence plant location and determine the "best" location. Linear programming is widely used in situations in which there are limited resources (time and money) and a value (profit or cost) that is to be maximized or minimized. The limitations are called constraints.

SUMMARY AND LOOK AHEAD

How the special talents of computers fit in with unique human talents is gradually being learned as people and computers work together solving business problems. Computer hardware and software together comprise a computer system that can serve a firm in many ways.

Computers are used in information storage and retrieval tasks. They simplify the manipulation and organization of data. Computers, together with people who know how to use mathematical tools, expand the power of managers and help them solve problems quicker and with less chance

entry. I am learning and testing the software package, developing procedures, writing a procedural manual, and developing control and security policies. After completing these tasks I will probably be teaching departments how to use the system.

The first major problem I encountered on my job resulted from the fact that we five trainees had been recruited from outside. Because of this we had to deal with a certain amount of resentment from some individuals who had been with the city for some time. Another problem area relates to the difficulty of communication in a large bureaucracy such as the City of Calgary. For example, I have seen the situation where memos go out from one department asking for input for a budget to be prepared by another department, but the information is requested in a format different from what is required by the department preparing the budget. When this happens you have to scramble after-the-fact to make things right.

The major rewards I have found come from doing a good job. Completing a task and knowing it is well done is very satisfying. When I started with the police department there were four large accounts, each with six months of backlog that required reconciliation. I reconciled them after some others had been unable to. This was rewarding.

I also feel rewarded when I am complimented for my work. At the police department they were very generous with their praise. I had several letters of recommendation written to my superiors by inspectors and others when I completed my work with the department.

I find that feedback, whether positive or negative, is very important to me. Though it is always nice to be told you are doing a good job, your performance will not greatly improve unless you are also informed as to which aspects of your work can be improved.

My advice to students is that they go into their first job with their eyes open. Too many students go out with the attitude that they will walk into a senior position right off the bat. In fact, graduates are not as well prepared as they think they are. They are familiar with some of the language and concepts which are useful on the job; however, working nine to five and taking your favourite subjects are two different things. I think that a primary benefit of school is that it prepares your mind so that you are open to new things.

I am toying with the idea of going back to school for an MBA, but I don't want to do this before I get at least a couple of years' experience.

---

for error. The mathematical tools include statistics, sampling, and break-even analysis.

In the next chapter we begin our survey of the world of finance. A major subject is banking, but we will look at many other financial institutions, too. We will see how they fit in the scheme of business decision making. ∎

QUESTIONS FOR REVIEW AND DISCUSSION

1. Name the three major hardware components of a computer. How are they interrelated?
2. What is a computer language? Name and describe two common ones.
3. What kinds of business processes make good use of the rapid repetitive capabilities of a computer?
4. What is a computer program?
5. Explain what is meant by documentation. Draw a simple block diagram.
6. Contrast the alternatives of computer leasing and time sharing.

7. Fixed costs are $100 and variable costs are $1 per unit. How many units must be sold at $2 to break even?
8. Identify two probable future applications of computers to business.
9. Besides the space shuttle, what startling modern accomplishments do you think never could have happened without computers?
10. Review the experiences you had yesterday and try to determine which of these were in some way influenced by the existence of computers.
11. Will the growth of microcomputers in small business widen the use of various quantitative tools?
12. What happens to the breakeven point when the sales price goes up?

INCIDENTS

Office Automation

In the late 1970s office costs represented 20 to 30 percent of a company's total operating costs. Some feel this will increase to 40 to 50 percent in the 1980s. Until recently the office was the least examined segment of most businesses. A commonly cited example is that in the last ten years an average investment of $25,000 per blue-collar worker has been made, resulting in a 90 percent increase in productivity per blue-collar worker. In contrast, the average investment per white-collar worker was only $2,000 with a resulting 4 percent increase in productivity.

Some feel this will change. With investment in word processing and other office automation the average investment per office worker could be $10,000 by 1985. Another estimate is that the word processing market will grow at about 30 percent a year through the mid-1980s.

Questions:
1. How can you explain the tremendous growth in the number of white-collar and service workers in Canada?
2. What incentives can you cite for firms to automate their clerical tasks?
3. What are the problems and opportunities that firms will face as they seek to automate their clerical tasks?

Hardware or Service — Which to Buy?

In a recent magazine ad, Automated Data Processing, Inc. (ADP) stated, "A computer, expertly used, will eventually pay for itself. But certainly not the first week. Computing, on the other hand, pays for itself almost at once. Mainly because you buy only what you need.... With computing you avoid not only the cost of the hardware, but also the inevitable add-ons: installation, programming, maintenance, re-programming, maintenance, re-programming and re-programming."

An ad for a computer hardware manufacturer would make a different argument. It might say that its product, once installed and doing a high volume of work, would be more efficient than the services of a firm like ADP.

Questions:

1. How can you tell whether it is wiser for you to hire a computer service company or to buy a computer?
2. In what way might you use a breakeven chart to make this decision?

CASE STUDY

CA FIRM GROWS PROSPEROUS BY HEEDING ITS OWN ADVICE

ACCOUNTANTS ARE IN A POSITION TO SEE THE RESULTS OF GOOD AND bad management. Many advise clients how to improve their businesses. So it's ironic that some of them don't manage their own practices very well.

Any accountant worth his or her certification would caution a small business owner to set aside time for managing and planning. Yet accountants often don't take their own advice.

"It's difficult to properly manage your practice when you haven't allocated time for it," says Jake L. Netterville, chairman of a professional association committee on management of an accounting practice. The fortunes of small practices tend to be limited by the amount of work the principals can do. Most small-practice CAs, Mr. Netterville says, "are always overworked." They're busy doing financial statements, tax forms and other client work, but seldom managing their own practices.

When Harold Carter and Edward Mauro formed a partnership in 1974, they were concerned with survival, not managing a practice. "We didn't know if we were going to make a living," says Mr. Carter who concentrates on client and banking relations for Carter & Mauro. But the Ottawa CA firm has prospered because its principals realized they needed to devote time to building the practice.

They resigned from another firm because it wasn't growing. "We did a lot of one-shot things," recalls Mr. Mauro, a tax specialist. "We weren't building clients."

Although they had been in accounting more than ten years at that point, it was like starting over. "We did everything ourselves," Mr. Carter says. Even so, they took in $138,000 in fees the first year. Clients referred them to prospective clients, and Mr. Carter's extensive social and political activities brought in business, too. Soon they had too much work to do themselves.

A decision to hire help started them toward a prosperous practice. "Profits are made from those who work for you," Mr. Netterville notes. Many CAs practising alone ignore this obvious business tenet because they are accustomed to "working and not managing other people."

The first year of their partnership Messrs. Carter and Mauro made more than in the second year, when they had 30 percent more revenue and four employees. It was four years until they earned as much as in their first year together. But they continued to add staff, which they value.

"We do everything we can to make them happy," Mr. Carter says. "We don't want them to leave. We give raises every six months." Most have stayed. In 1975 they lured a friend, Paul Rich, from a large CA firm A year later, he became an actual partner.

The partners decided about three years ago that their own firm had to be put in order. "We were growing too rapidly and were scattered all over the field" in types of clients, Mr. Rich says. They dropped clients who weren't worth keeping. Some had marginal businesses, others were so demanding that "we knew they wouldn't let us make any money from them," Mr. Carter says.

They also raised their fees. "Those were scary days," Mr. Carter says, "We didn't know how our clients would react. But the first few said 'Yes,' and we got the courage to ask the others. I don't know what we would have done if they'd said, 'No.'" After dropping 15 percent of its clients and raising fees, the partnership increased its revenue 30 percent.

The firm has about 150 clients today and revenues that exceed $1 million, which suggests that each partner earns more than $133,000 a year. The partners could make more by adding new clients, though they're selective nowadays. Says Mr. Mauro, "Implicit in a good client is someone with a financial awareness and a desire to get good advice."

Finding good staff has slowed expansion, not a lack of prospective clients. "Our biggest problem is getting people with good solid accounting knowledge," says Mr. Rich, who oversees personnel. "We advertise almost every week for accountants." Starting pay for an experienced person is $30,000 to $40,000 a year.

Questions:
1. Explain why "accountants are in a position to see the results of good and bad management."
2. Is a CA firm a business? Explain.
3. Are Carter & Mauro engaged in financial accounting or managerial accounting? Discuss.
4. In addition to auditing accounting records, what else might a CA do for a client firm?
5. If you were in charge of personnel at a big CA firm, how would you go about recruiting new accountants?
6. Is the firm of Carter & Mauro more likely to use computers today than they might have when they first started? Why or why not? ■

Section Six

This section surveys the major financial institutions and their use by business managers in pursuit of profit objectives. Chapter 13 concentrates on chartered banks and the Canadian banking system. Chapter 13 also includes a discussion of the securities (stocks and bonds) market and the major institutions involved in it.

Chapter 14 turns to the role of the financial manager. It explains the general sources of funds for business and the criteria for their selection. The uses and sources of short-term financing are then discussed, including various forms of loans and the use of commercial paper. Risk management is the second major topic of Chapter 14. The basic concepts of risk and risk-shifting by means of insurance are discussed. The underlying principles of insurance and the major types of insurance are described.

Chapter 14 closes with a discussion of extraordinary financial arrangements, with special emphasis on mergers and acquisitions.

FINANCIAL MANAGEMENT

After reading this chapter, you should be able to:

1. Compare the services offered to business and nonbusiness customers by chartered banks, life insurance companies, trust companies, credit unions or caisses populaires, factoring companies, sales finance companies, consumer finance companies, government financial institutions, venture capital funds, and pension funds.
2. Explain why the chartered banks are important to business firms.
3. List the different types of money in Canada.
4. Develop an example showing how the banking system creates money.
5. Demonstrate how the Bank of Canada controls the money supply.
6. List and identify the major types of credit instruments used by business firms.
7. Tell the difference between common stock and preferred stock.
8. Identify three concepts of value with respect to common stock.
9. Give examples of value with respect to common stock.
10. Give examples of several types of preferred stock.
11. Compare the underwriting and brokerage function of investment dealers.
12. Tell the difference between listed and unlisted securities.
13. Compare the workings of the over-the-counter market with the workings of the securities exchange.
14. Translate a quote for a stock or bond as reported on the financial pages of newspapers into dollar-and-cents terms.
15. Compare speculating with investing.
16. Compare the workings of commodity exchanges with the workings of securities exchanges.

KEY CONCEPTS

In reading the chapter, look for and understand these terms:

money	public market
chartered bank	common stock
demand deposit	preferred stock
time deposit	bond
prime rate of interest	over-the-counter market
bank rate	underwriting
reserve requirement	brokerage function
trust company	securities exchanges
credit union	speculative trading
life insurance company	margin trading
factoring company	short selling
sales finance company	mutual fund
consumer finance company	prospectus
venture capital firm	commodity exchanges
pension funds	cash trading
Industrial Development Bank	futures markets

CHAPTER THIRTEEN

Financial Institutions

OUR CANADIAN BUSINESS SYSTEM could not function without financial institutions to facilitate the flow of money. Money has been referred to as the "life-blood" of the business system. If this is so, then financial institutions must be the "circulatory system" that keeps money flowing to and from business firms.

Canada has a highly developed set of financial institutions that are among the most respected in the world. However, in recent years Canadian financial institutions have had to cope with major changes in economic environments. Interest rates have fluctuated widely creating problems for many financial institutions. Many borrowers found it difficult to meet the very high interest rates of the early 1980s and lenders had to make hard decisions about whether to continue to support them or force them into bankruptcy.

The world oil price situation has created a number of problems for Canadian financial institutions. They participated in recirculation of money paid to OPEC oil exporters. They also had to decide whether to make loans to petroleum industry companies. A major example, with implications for the entire banking system, was the Dome Petroleum financial package.

Federal government legislative changes created new competition for traditional financial institutions. More foreign competitors entered the Canadian market, and traditional financial institutions such as banks and trust companies broadened their services and came into more direct competition with each other.

ALL FIRMS NEED MONEY TO BEGIN A BUSINESS AND TO REMAIN IN IT. Money is the life-blood of a firm—it enables a firm to buy buildings, equipment, inventories, and pay its employees. Money flows into a firm as sales revenues and flows out as the expense of doing business and as a return to the owners.

But where does a firm get money? Some of it comes from the owner's (or owners') original investment in the firm. Some of it comes from profits which are reinvested in the firm. Often, however, that is not enough. Most firms need the services of financial institutions to provide them with the money they need.

We examine these financial institutions in this chapter, starting with financial intermediaries. There are many different types of financial intermediaries, each of which serves business firms and individuals in different ways. Two of the most important financial intermediaries are banks and life insurance companies.

We also examine the workings of investment dealers and securities exchanges to see how they help business firms get the money they need. These financial institutions facilitate the growth of corporations. In fact, most firms would stay very small if they could not get money from people who are willing to lend it as bondholders and/or from people who are willing to invest their money to become owners or stockholders.

THE FINANCIAL SYSTEM

The financial system is very important to business firms in Canada. A financial system is composed of organizations and individuals who are sources of funds, users of funds, and/or who facilitate the flow of funds from sources to users. (See Figure 13.1.) People or organizations with surplus funds will want to earn a return on them. An individual may put his or her money into a savings deposit, buy a bond or a life insurance policy, or invest in the stock market. A business firm, depending upon how long the money will be available, may deposit its money in a bank on a short-term basis, buy treasury bills, or buy long-term securities. Charitable organizations and governments may also have surplus funds they wish to invest for certain periods of time.

Without money, business as we know it could not exist. Money enables us to progress beyond barter (exchanging goods for goods) because it permits specialization and exchange.

Money is anything people will generally accept in payment of debts. Paper currency and coins issued by a recognized government are legal

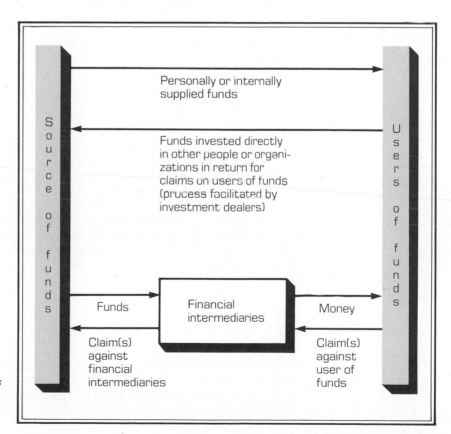

Figure 13.1
Sources of funds, users of funds, financial intermediaries, and investment dealers.

tender in that nation. If you owe a debt which is stated in money terms, your creditor must accept your payment in legal tender.

But that is not all there is to money. Most Canadian workers, for example, are paid with cheques. Many workers deposit their cheques in their chequing accounts and pay their bills with cheques. This is possible because of our modern banking system. **Money, therefore, means paper currency, coins, and chequing account balances.**

money

All people and organizations are users of funds. Sometimes they are unable to raise all the funds they require from personal or internal sources. In this situation, money must be raised from other people or institutions who have surplus funds. Individuals borrow money for certain purposes. Business firms raise money to finance projects. Governments also borrow money.

Financial institutions facilitate the flow of funds from sources to users. There are many different types of financial institutions. It is important to understand them if you are in an organization which either has surplus funds to invest or is in a deficit position and must raise funds. It is also important to understand the institutions if you are interested in a career in one of them.

There are two basic types of financial institutions. One type is the financial intermediary. Financial intermediaries issue claims against their assets to sources of funds and in return provide funds to users in exchange for claims against them. For example, a bank will accept funds (deposits) from people and organizations. The depositor has a claim against the bank for the value of the money he or she has deposited. The bank will then make loans to individuals and organizations in return for claims against these borrowers. Life insurance companies offer a different type of claim against their assets to the public, and they in turn also invest the money they have accumulated.

The other basic type of financial institution facilitates the direct transfer of funds from sources of funds to users. The source, or supplier of funds, receives a claim against the user. A common example is Canada Savings Bonds. The sources of funds (individuals who buy bonds) receive claims against the Government of Canada (Savings Bonds). Similarly, if a corporation wanted to raise money, it could issue stocks or bonds (claims) which would be purchased by individuals and organizations (sources of funds). The process of transferring funds directly from sources to users is facilitated by investment dealers through their brokerage and underwriting functions.

FINANCIAL INTERMEDIARIES

There are a variety of financial intermediaries in Canada. They vary in size, in importance, in the types of sources they appeal to, in the form of the claim they give to sources of funds, in the users they supply credit to, and in the type of claim they make against these users of funds.

Chartered Banks

chartered bank

A chartered bank is a privately owned, profit-seeking firm which serves individuals, nonbusiness organizations, and businesses. Chartered banks offer chequing accounts, make loans, and offer many other services to their customers. They are the main source of short-term loans for business firms.

Chartered banks are the largest and most important financial institution in Canada. They offer a unique service. Their liability instruments, or claims against their assets, are generally accepted by the public and by business as money or as legal tender. Initially these liability instruments took the form of bank notes issued by individual banks. The Bank Act changes of 1944 removed the right to issue bank notes.

Canada has a branch banking system. Unlike the United States, where there are hundreds of banks, each having a few branches, in Canada there are only eleven banks, each with many branches. Of these, five account for about 90 percent of total bank assets. (See Table 13.1.) Some of them also

Table 13.1   Characteristics of Chartered Banks in Canada

Chartered Bank	Total Cash Resources	Total Securities	Total Loans	Acceptance and Other Fixed Assets	Total Assets Dec. 1982	Total Assets Dec. 1981
The Royal Bank of Canada	14,377.4	7,496.4	60,790.4	6,598.7	89,262.9	87,469.5
Canadian Imperial Bank of Commerce	4,967.8	5,101.0	52,817.8	4,568.1	67,454.6	66,475.6
Bank of Montreal	9,114.4	5,492.7	44,375.0	4,915.0	63,897.3	62,099.3
The Bank of Nova Scotia	12,785.9	3,329.4	34,625.2	3,613.4	54,353.9	51,143.8
Toronto Dominion Bank	4,909.9	3,885.5	32,578.0	3,387.6	44,761.1	44,097.5
National Bank of Canada	816.0	1,325.7	14,248.5	966.9	17,357.3	19,297.2
Continental Bank of Canada	276.0	361.9	3,558.7	139.7	4,336.3	3,559.5
The Mercantile Bank of Canada	299.2	368.9	3,375.9	279.0	4,323.1	4,279.9
Bank of British Columbia	178.7	292.4	2,535.9	93.9	3,100.8	3,085.5
Canadian Commercial Bank	109.1	100.7	1,616.4	95.4	1,921.6	1,610.9
Northland Bank	25.0	75.5	529.3	47.5	677.2	534.5

Note: All amounts are in millions of dollars, and figures may not add because of rounding.

Source: Compiled from the Canadian Bankers Association, *Chartered Banks of Canada.* Statement of assets as of: December 31, 1982.

have branches in other countries. There are more than 7,300 branch bank offices in Canada, or about one for every 3,300 people.

Services Offered by Banks

Table 13.2 lists several types of services offered by chartered banks. Banks are chartered by the federal government and are closely regulated when they provide these services.

Chartered banks provide a financial intermediary service by accepting deposits and making loans with this money. Banks make various types of loans to businesses. When applying for a business loan, it is wise for the manager to remember that the banker is interested in making the loan because it will make money for the bank. The banker is also interested, however, in how the loan will be repaid and how it will be secured. When making an application, it is important to indicate what the money is required for and how it will be repaid. A brief written statement accompanied by a cash-flow analysis is a useful approach when applying for a loan.

Bank Deposits

demand deposit

One type of deposit a customer can make in a bank is a demand deposit. A demand deposit is a chequing account. Customers who deposit coins, paper currency, or other cheques in their chequing accounts can write cheques against the balance in their accounts. Their banks must honor these cheques immediately. That is why chequing accounts are called demand deposits.

time deposit

The other type of deposit a customer can make in a chartered bank is a time deposit. **A time deposit is one which is to remain with the bank for a period of time. Interest is paid to depositors for the use of their funds.**

Table 13.2   Some Important Services Provided by Banks to Business Firms

1. Offer chequing accounts.
2. Offer savings deposits.
3. Offer safe-deposit boxes.
4. Offer personal term deposits.
5. Store idle cash in certificates of deposit.
6. Make short-term loans (1–16 months).
7. Make long-term loans.
8. Make loans to a firm's customers.
9. Exchange Canadian dollars for foreign currencies.
10. Exchange foreign currencies for Canadian dollars.
11. Finance export operations.
12. Give advice to businesspeople on financial matters.
13. Handle details of registration of corporations' stocks.
14. Buy and sell securities.
15. Safeguard property entrusted to them.

There are two types of time deposits. The most popular is the regular passbook account. Although a bank can require notice before withdrawals can be made, this is seldom done. These accounts are intended primarily for small individual savers and nonprofit organizations.

Another type of time deposit is the savings certificate. This is a deposit which is made for a certain period of time. It can range from twenty-eight days to several years. Savings certificates are available to all savers. The interest rate paid on a savings certificate is higher than that paid on a regular passbook account, but a saver must give up interest if a savings certificate is cashed in before its maturity date.

Bank Loans

Banks are the major source of short-term loans for business. Although banks make long-term loans to some firms, they prefer to specialize in providing short-term funds to finance inventories and accounts receivable. Many loans made to businesses are secured by inventory under section 83 of the Bank Act. Section 86 of the Bank Act allows banks to make loans against the security of bills of lading and warehouse receipts. Section 82 allows banks to take as security hydrocarbons in store or under the ground.

prime rate of interest

Borrowers pay interest on their loans. Large firms with excellent credit records pay the prime rate of interest. **The prime rate of interest is the lowest rate charged to borrowers.** This rate changes from time to time owing to changes in the demand for and supply of loanable funds and also to policies of the Bank of Canada.

A secured loan is backed by collateral such as accounts receivable or a life insurance policy. If the borrower cannot repay the loan, the bank sells the collateral. An unsecured loan is backed only by the borrower's promise to repay it. Only the most credit-worthy borrowers can get unsecured loans.

THEN AND NOW

Banking and Credit

Because people used to believe more strongly in thrift and staying out of debt and because people were not generally as affluent, most purchases were made for cash. Most people, even in the early twentieth century, believed that you should "save up" enough money to "pay cash" for your purchases — even the purchase of a house.

Today, many Canadian households use Master Charge and/or VISA cards to pay for purchases. Most households have chequing accounts. The "cashless" society is getting closer.

The age of electronic banking is in its growth stage. Currently, many people use Automated Teller Machines to deposit or withdraw cash, transfer funds among accounts, and borrow money. Computer terminals located in retail stores and shopping centres can serve as branch banks of financial institutions. The "chequeless" society is arriving. These and other developments will revolutionize banking in the near future.

TWO POINTS OF VIEW

What a Bank Should Be

McDonald Stevenson:

McDonald Stevenson is the manager of a large bank branch in the Maritimes. He believes that a bank's main job is to protect the funds entrusted to it by its depositors. Loans should be granted only to firms with proven profit records and ability to pay. Mr. Stevenson is very skeptical of trying to market bank services in the same way that some of the consumer goods firms like Procter & Gamble do.

"We're a different breed of business firm. Our depositors expect us to be cautious with their money. After all, it is their money. We can't take the risks that other firms can take. For us, slow growth is the best type of growth. Swinger-type bankers will sooner or later wind up in trouble — writing off hundreds of thousands of dollars in bad debts and damaging their chances for promotion within the bank."

Rosalie Hedgerow:

Rosalie Hedgerow is the manager of a bank branch in Ontario. She believes that a bank's main mission is to serve the financial needs of borrowers and savers. To her, a bank is a sort of middleman operation between people who have money to lend (depositors) and people who need loans (borrowers). The greater the variety of services a bank can offer, the better it is fulfilling its mission, according to Ms. Hedgerow.

"We're not all that different from other firms. We need to offer new services that meet our customers' needs. The days of bars on teller cages are gone forever. We have a responsibility to serve the financial needs of new firms as well as those of older firms. The trouble with some bankers is that they are so conservative about lending they are willing to lend only to firms which really don't need loans. At my bank, we are heavily involved in consumer finance, lending to new firms with good ideas, and many other types of programs to better serve our business and nonbusiness customers. Bankers who crow about the virtues of slow growth are really making excuses for their own failures as executives."

Deposit Expansion

Suppose you saved $100, took it to a bank, and opened a chequing account. Some portion of your $100 is likely to stay in your account. Your bank can earn interest by lending some of it to borrowers.

Banks must keep some portion of their demand deposits in vault cash or as deposits with the Bank of Canada. These are legal reserves. Let's assume that the reserve requirement is 10 percent. Your bank then must keep $10 of your $100 deposit in legal reserves. It therefore has $90 to lend.

Now, suppose Tom Powers borrows that $90 from your bank. Tom has $90 added to his chequing account. Assume that Tom writes a cheque for $90 payable to the Acme Stores. Acme's bank ends up with a $90 deposit. But Acme's bank has to keep only 10 percent of $90 ($9.00) in legal reserves. Acme's bank, therefore, can lend out $81.00.

This is the process of deposit expansion. It can continue as shown in Table 13.3. The banking system creates money in the form of demand deposits. Of course, the process of deposit expansion is much more complex in practice. General economic conditions, for example, influence

Table 13.3   How the Banking System Creates Money*

Bank	New Deposit	New Loan	Legal Reserve
Your bank	$ 100.00	$ 90.00	$ 10.00
Bank 2	90.00	81.00	9.00
Bank 3	81.00	72.90	8.10
Bank 4	72.90	65.61	7.29
Bank 5	65.61	59.05	6.56
Bank 6	59.05	53.14	5.91
Bank 7	53.14	47.83	5.31
Bank 8	47.83	43.05	4.78
Bank 9	43.05	38.74	4.31
Total for first nine banks	$ 612.58	$551.32	$ 61.26
Total for entire banking system	$1,000.00	$900.00	$100.00

*Assuming a reserve requirement of 10 percent.

the willingness of bankers to make loans and the willingness of borrowers to borrow.

As you can see from Table 13.3, your original deposit of $100 could result in an increase of $1,000 in new deposits for all banks in the commercial banking system. Remember, we are assuming a reserve requirement of 10 percent. Thus, your original deposit of $100 could expand by 10 times (the reciprocal of the reserve requirement, 100/10), or to $1,000. Our example assumes that no borrower takes part of his or her loan in cash and that the banks want to lend as much as they legally can. Otherwise, the increase would be less than $1,000.

The Bank of Canada

The Bank of Canada was formed in 1935 and is Canada's central bank. It has an important role to play in management of the Canadian economy and in regulation of certain aspects of chartered bank operations.

The Bank of Canada is managed by a Board of Governors composed of a governor, a deputy governor, and twelve directors who are appointed from different regions of Canada. The directors, with Cabinet approval, appoint the governor and deputy governor. The deputy minister of finance is also a non-voting member of the board. Between meetings of the board, which are normally held eight times a year, an executive committee acts for the board. This committee is composed of the governor, the deputy governor, two directors, and the deputy minister of finance. The executive committee meets at least once a week.

Operation of the Bank of Canada

The Bank of Canada plays a very important role in management of the money supply in Canada (see Table 13.4).

Table 13.4 Bank of Canada Actions and Business Activity

To stimulate the economy, the Bank of Canada:
1. Buys government securities.
2. Lowers the bank rate.
3. Lowers the reserve requirement.

To slow down the economy, the Bank of Canada:
1. Sells government securities.
2. Raises the bank rate.
3. Raises the reserve requirement.

If the Bank of Canada wants to increase the money supply, it purchases government securities. People will sell their bonds for money, which they deposit in their banks. This increases bank reserves and their ability to make loans.

If the Bank of Canada wants to decrease the money supply, it sells government securities. People spend money to buy bonds. This draws down bank reserves and reduces their ability to make loans.

Member Bank Borrowing from the Bank of Canada

bank rate

The Bank of Canada is the lender of last resort for chartered banks. **The rate at which chartered banks can borrow from the Bank of Canada is called the rediscount, or bank rate.** It serves as the basis for establishing the chartered banks' prime interest rate. By raising the rediscount rate the Bank of Canada can depress the demand for money, and by lowering it the demand for money can be increased. In practice, chartered banks seldom have to borrow from the Bank of Canada; however, the bank rate is an important instrument of monetary policy as a determinant of interest rates.

Setting the Reserve Requirement

reserve requirement

The Board of Governors sets the reserve requirement. **The reserve requirement is the percentage of its deposits member banks have to keep in vault cash or as deposits with the Bank of Canada.** Lowering the reserve requirement increases the money supply. Raising it decreases the money supply.

The reserve requirement differs for demand and time deposits. For demand deposits it is 4 percent and for time deposits it is 12 percent.

Trust Companies

trust company

Another financial intermediary which serves individuals and businesses is the trust company. **A trust company safeguards property—funds and estates—entrusted to it. It also may serve as trustee, transfer agent, and registrar for corporations and provide other services.**

A corporation selling bonds to many investors appoints a trustee, usually a trust company, to protect the bondholders' interests. A trust company can also serve as a transfer agent and registrar for corporations. A transfer agent records changes in ownership of a corporation's stock. A registrar certifies to the investing public that stock issues are correctly stated and in compliance with the corporate charter. Other services include preparing and issuing dividend cheques to stockholders and serving as trustee for employee profit-sharing funds. Trust companies also accept deposits and pay interest on them.

Caisses Populaires and Credit Unions

credit union

Credit unions are important to business because they lend money to consumers to buy durable goods like cars and furniture. They also lend money to businesses. **A caisse populaire, or a credit union, is a cooperative savings and lending association formed by a group with common interests.** Members (owners) can add to their savings accounts by authorizing deductions from their pay cheques or by making direct deposits. Members can also borrow short-term, long-term, or mortgage funds from the credit union. Credit unions also invest substantial amounts of money in corporate and government securities.

Life Insurance Companies

life insurance company

An important source of funds for individuals, nonbusiness organizations, and businesses is the life insurance company. **A life insurance company is a mutual or stock company which shares risk with its policyholders for payment of a premium.** Some of the money it collects as premiums is loaned to borrowers. Life insurance companies are substantial investors in real estate mortgages and in corporate and government bonds. Next to chartered banks, they are the largest financial intermediaries in Canada.

Factoring Companies

factoring company

An important source of short-term funds for many firms is the factoring company. **A factoring company (or factor) buys accounts receivable (amounts due from credit customers) from a firm.** It pays less than the face value of the accounts but collects the face value of the accounts. The difference, minus the cost of doing business, is the factor's profit.

A firm which sells its accounts receivable to a factor "without recourse" shifts the risk of credit loss to the factor. If an account turns out to be uncollectable, the factor suffers the loss. However, a factor is a specialist in credit and collection activities. Using a factor may enable a client to expand sales beyond what would be practical without the factor. The client trades accounts receivable for cash. The factor notifies the client's customers to make their payments to the factor.

Financial Corporations

There are two types of financial intermediaries referred to as financial corporations. These are sales finance companies and consumer loan companies.

Sales Finance Companies

sales finance company

A major source of credit for many firms and their customers is the sales finance company. **A sales finance company specializes in financing instalment purchases made by individuals and firms.**

When you buy a durable good from a retailer on an instalment plan with a sales finance company, the loan is made directly to you. The item bought serves as security for the loan. Sales finance companies enable many firms to sell on credit, even though the firms could not afford to finance credit sales on their own.

General Motors Acceptance Corporation (GMAC) is a sales finance company. It is a "captive" company because it exists to finance instalment contracts resulting from sales made by General Motors. Industrial Acceptance Corporation is a large Canadian sales finance company.

Sales finance companies also finance instalment sales to business firms. Many banks also have instalment loan departments.

Consumer Finance Companies

consumer finance company

An important source of credit for many consumers is the consumer finance company. **A consumer finance company makes personal loans to consumers.** Often these loans are made on a "signature basis," and the borrower pledges no security (collateral) for the loan. For larger loans, collateral may be required, such as a car or furniture.

These companies do not make loans to businesses. But they do provide the financing which turns many would-be customers into actual paying customers. Household Finance Corporation is an example of a consumer finance company.

Venture Capital or Development Firms

venture capital firm

A venture capital, or development firm will provide funds for new or expanding firms which are thought to have significant potential. Venture capital firms obtain their funds from initial capital subscriptions, from loans from other financial intermediaries, and from retained earnings.

Venture capital firms may provide either equity or debt funds to firms. Financing new, untested businesses is risky, so venture capital firms want to earn a higher-than-normal return on their investment. The ideal situation would be an equity investment in a company which became very successful and experienced substantial appreciation in its stock value.

Pension Funds

pension funds

Pension plans accumulate money which will be paid out to plan subscribers at some time in the future. The money collected is then invested in corporate stocks and bonds, government bonds, or mortgages.

Government Financial Institutions and Granting Agencies

In Canada there are a number of government suppliers of funds which can be important to business. In general, they supply funds to new and/or growing companies. However, established firms can also use some of them.

Industrial Development Bank

The Industrial Development Bank (IDB), a subsidiary of the Bank of Canada, makes loans to business firms. The Federal Business Development Bank (FBDB) took over operation of the IDB in 1975. The IDB was set up to make term loans, primarily to smaller firms which are judged to have growth potential but are unable to secure funds at reasonable terms from traditional sources. It also expanded IDB services by providing proportionally more equity financing and more management counselling services.

There are also a variety of provincial industrial development corporations which provide funds to developing business firms in the hope that they will provide jobs in the province. These are discussed in Chapter 15.

The federal government's Export Development Corporation can finance and insure export sales of Canadian companies. The Canadian Mortgage and Housing Corporation (CMHC) is involved in providing mortgages and in guaranteeing them. The CMHC is, therefore, very important to the construction industry.

There are a number of federal and provincial programs specifically designed to provide loans to agricultural operators. Most of these, with the exception of farm improvement loans which guarantee bank loans to farmers, are long-term loans for land purchase.

In addition to these activities, governments are also involved in providing grants to business operations. For example, the federal government provides grants for certain types of business expansion in designated areas of the country. Other federal government grants are available for activities such as new product development.

International Sources of Funds

It should be noted that not all of the financing requirements of Canadian businesses and governments are met from within Canada. Foreign sources of funds are very important. The financial institutions of Canada — financial intermediaries and investment dealers — play a role in facilitating the flow of funds into the country.

The Canadian capital market is one part of the international capital market. Canadian provinces borrow extensively in foreign markets such as in New York. Canadian corporations likewise find it attractive to borrow in foreign markets.

Foreign sources of funds have been important to the economic development of Canada. We are now at a stage where we are concerned about foreign ownership of Canadian firms. However, projections of Canada's future capital requirements indicate that we will continue to need foreign sources of funds. Canadian financial institutions will continue to play a large role in making these funds available.

THE PUBLIC MARKET

Banks are the major source of short-term funds for businesses. Insurance companies, pension funds, and other financial institutions discussed previously are important sources of long-term funds for some firms. In the discussion that follows we look at stocks and bonds and the workings of securities exchanges.

public market

With very few exceptions, most large- and medium-size corporations use the public market as a source of long-term funds. **The public market is made up of millions of people who buy stocks and bonds and the business and nonbusiness organizations which also invest in corporate securities.** Also included in the public market are the various securities "middlemen" who bring buyers and sellers of securities together.

INVESTMENT DEALERS

Two very important financial functions are performed by investment dealers. They are crucial to both the purchase and sale of stocks and bonds. One function is the primary distribution of new stock and bond issues (underwriting). The second function is facilitating secondary trading of stocks and bonds both on stock exchanges and on "over-the-counter" stock and bond markets (the brokerage function).

STOCKS AND BONDS

The two major financial instruments by which a firm gains access to the public market are stocks and bonds. As we saw in Chapter 3, only corporations issue stock. While a firm need not be a corporation to issue bonds, a form of long-term debt, it usually must be a well-financed and sound firm if it is to attract any buyers of its bonds.

Stocks

All corporations in the private sector issue shares of stock. Stock represents ownership of a corporation. There are two basic types—common and preferred.

Common Stock

common stock

Common stock is a certificate showing ownership in a corporation. All shares of common stock are equal in value, and all common stockholders enjoy the same rights. Common stock is voting stock. Common stockholders are the residual owners of a corporation. They own what is "left over" after all debts have been paid.

Three different concepts of value associated with common stock are

- book value — the difference between the dollar values of what a company owns (its assets) and what it owes (its debts, or liabilities) divided by the number of shares of common stock.
- market value — the price the shares of stock are selling for on the market. This changes daily in response to supply and demand.
- par value — the value the corporation that originally issued the stock certificate may have printed on it. This is called par value stock. If no value is placed on the stock certificate, it is called no-par stock.

In most cases, the book value, market value, and par value of a corporation's stock are three different amounts.

Consider, for example, the giant corporate takeovers of recent years. Part of the explanation for them is that the stock market was depressed — the market value of many companies' stock was way down. Now consider the book value of the stock. Inflation drives up the cost of replacing assets like plant and equipment. As we saw in Chapter 11, these assets are carried on a firm's books at acquisition cost — not replacement cost. Thus many of the companies that are buying up other companies are, in effect, getting tremendous bargains.

Three other terms are also important:

- stock split
- cash dividend
- stock dividend

A stock split gives stockholders a greater number of shares but does not change the individual's proportionate ownership in the corporation. Sue Adams, for example, owns 100 shares of IBM common, which is selling at $100 per share. The market value of her shares is $10,000. If the directors vote for a 4-for-1 stock split, Sue will have 400 shares valued at $25 per share. The total market value of her shares right after the split is still $10,000. The purpose of the split is to reduce the selling price per share. This may make the stock attractive to more buyers, increase the demand for it, and raise its selling price.

A cash dividend is a payment of cash to stockholders. It rewards them for their investment in the corporation.

If a corporation wants to keep its cash, it might declare a stock dividend. This is a payment to stockholders in additional shares of stock rather than payment of cash. A 20 percent stock dividend means that each stockholder gets two new shares for each ten he or she already owns. A stock dividend is a way to reward stockholders when a firm wants to reinvest its earnings

WHAT DO YOU THINK?

How Do You Go About Raising a Lot of Money?

Dome Canada raised $400,000,000 in one stock sale in 1981. At that time this was the largest sale of stock ever made in the history of Canadian business. Dome sold 40.0 million shares through underwriters. They were offered to the public at $10 a share.

Dome Canada's management and board of directors, of course, had several options which might have been examined to meet the capital needs of this new company. Had they floated debenture bonds, for example, $400,000,000 worth of bonds might have required an annual interest payment of more than $50,000,000 to bondholders. Bonds would eventually have to be paid off, too, whereas the common stock offering does not. Why did Dome decide to sell the stock? WHAT DO YOU THINK?

in the business. It conserves cash. Like a stock split, a stock dividend does not increase the stockholder's share of ownership in a corporation.

preferred stock

Preferred Stock

Preferred stock is a certificate showing ownership in a corporation. Preferred stockholders, however, usually cannot vote their shares. But they do enjoy certain preferences.

Preferred stockholders have a right to receive a stated dividend (indicated on the stock certificate) before common stockholders receive any

Table 13.5 Types and Characteristics of Preferred Stock

Types	Characteristics
1. Cumulative preferred	1. Dividends not paid in one or more years cumulate and must be paid before common stockholders receive any dividends.
2. Non-cumulative preferred	2. Dividends not paid in one or more years need not be paid in future years but, in a given year, must be paid before common stockholders receive any dividends.
3. Fully participating preferred	3. Once the dividend stated on the stock certificate is paid and the common stockholders receive the same sum, preferred shareholders share in any remaining dividends.
4. Non-participating preferred	4. Shareholders are entitled only to the dividend stated on the stock certificate.
5. Convertible preferred	5. Preferred shareholders can convert their preferred stock to common stock at their option.
6. Redeemable preferred	6. Preferred stock issued with a call price, at which price the issuing corporation can legally require the holder to sell his or her shares back to the corporation.

dividends. This dividend, however, is not owed until declared by the board of directors. If a corporation goes out of business and sells its assets, the preferred stockholders share in these proceeds before common stockholders. Table 13.5 discusses several important types of preferred stock.

Bonds

Although all private sector corporations issue common stock, not all issue bonds. Stockholders provide equity (ownership) capital, while bondholders are lenders. Stock certificates indicate ownership, while bond certificates indicate indebtedness.

bond   All levels of government issue bonds, as do many nonbusinesses. **A bond is a written promise to pay. It indicates that the borrower will pay the lender, at some stated future date, a sum of money (the**

Table 13.6 Types and Characteristics of Bonds

Types	Characteristics
1. Secured bonds	1. Backed by security pledged by the issuing corporation. This can be sold by the trustee and the proceeds used to pay off the bondholders if the corporation fails to pay principal and/or interest.
(a) Real estate mortgage bonds	(a) Secured by real property.
(b) Chattel mortgage bonds	(b) Secured by movable property.
(c) Collateral trust bonds	(c) Secured by stocks and bonds in other corporations which are owned by the issuing corporation.
2. Unsecured bonds (debentures)	2. Not secured or backed by specific assets but by the general credit and strength of the issuing corporation.
3. Registered bonds	3. Owner's name is registered with the issuing corporation and is printed on the certificate. Interest is mailed to him or her by the corporation or its trustee.
4. Coupon bonds	4. Owner's name is not registered and does not appear on the certificate. Owner must clip coupons from the bond and present them to the corporation's bank.
5. Convertible bonds	5. Can be converted to common stock at the bondholder's option.
6. Serial bonds	6. The issuing corporation issues a large block of bonds which mature at different dates.
7. Sinking-fund bonds	7. The issuing corporation makes annual deposits with the trustee so that those deposits, along with earned interest, will be available to redeem the bonds upon maturity.
8. Redeemable or callable bonds	8. Can be called in or redeemed prior to maturity.

principal) and a stated rate of interest. Bondholders have a claim on a corporation's assets and earnings which comes before that of common and preferred stockholders.

Most bond issues are sold to individuals. The agreement under which they are issued (the indenture) names a trustee to represent the bondholders' interests. This trustee is usually a large bank or trust company. Table 13.6 describes several important types of bonds.

Listed Securities

Securities traded on organized stock exchanges such as the Toronto Stock Exchange (TSE) and the Montreal Stock Exchange (MSE) are called listed securities.

The TSE is made up of about one hundred individual members who hold seats on the exchange. Owning a seat enables a brokerage firm to buy and sell on the TSE floor. The securities of most major corporations are listed here. A fee must be paid before a security can be listed on an exchange.

Buying a Listed Security

Suppose you want to buy a listed security. If you have never "dabbled" in the market, your first step is to go to a branch office of an investment dealer and open an account. A corporation has only a certain number of outstanding shares (issued by the corporation and owned by investors). If you want to buy some of those shares, you must deal with people who own them. The investment dealer brings you (the buyer) and someone else (the seller) together.

When you go to the investment dealer, you will be introduced to an account executive. This person is often called a stockbroker, because he or she is involved in the brokerage function. If you are serious about becoming an investor, take the time to get acquainted with your account executive. Be truthful about your investment goals and your financial situation. Because all of your dealings with the investment dealers will be handled by and through your account executive, you must know and understand each other.

After talking with your account executive, Ms. Perkins, you decide to buy some Imperial Oil common stock. You ask her what the selling price is. Ms. Perkins uses an electronic device on her desk to tell her the last price at which the stock sold. Now you must make a decision. If you tell her to buy "at market," she will buy the number of shares you want at the lowest price offered. If that price is $30 per share, you would pay $3,000 plus commission, if you buy one hundred shares.

But suppose you want to pay no more than $29 per share. You can place a "limit order" with Ms. Perkins. Your order would not be filled unless she could find someone willing to sell for $29 or less per share.

If you placed an "at-market" order, Ms. Perkins contacts her firm's Toronto office. That office contacts its representative on the Toronto Stock Exchange floor who goes to the "post" where Imperial Oil stock is traded. That floorperson buys the shares at the offering price. No delay is involved, since someone is always willing to sell if a buyer is willing to pay the seller's asking price.

Within minutes, Ms. Perkins will get an electronic message direct from the exchange floor telling her that the transaction is complete. Meanwhile, the seller's account executive sends his or her client's stock certificate to Imperial Oil's transfer agent, who cancels it and issues a new certificate in your name. This may be held by your account executive for safekeeping or sent to you.

THE OVER-THE-COUNTER (OTC) MARKET

over-the-counter market

Many securities are not listed on any of the organized securities exchanges. Making a market in these securities is the third most important function of investment dealers. They are traded in the over-the-counter (OTC) market. In reality this is an over-the-telephone market. **The over-the-counter market is a complex of dealers who are in constant touch with one another.** Stocks and bonds of some smaller corporations are traded on the OTC market. All fixed-income securities including bonds and debentures are traded in this manner.

Security dealers in the OTC market often buy securities in their own name. They must maintain an inventory of securities in order to make a market in them. They hope to sell them to their clients at a higher price. These dealers also buy shares at the request of their clients. Dealers receive a commission for this. Dealers selling to one another charge a wholesale price and sell to their customers at a retail price.

STOCK AND BOND PRICES

Stocks and bonds traded on the exchanges and the OTC market are listed and reported in the financial section of many daily newspapers. Major newspapers all give daily detailed coverage of stock price changes and trading volumes.

Stock Prices

Table 13.7 indicates the type of information newspapers give about daily market transactions of individual stocks. The corporation's name is shown along with the number of shares sold (expressed in round lots of 100 shares). Prices are quoted in dollars and fractions of a dollar ranging from ⅛ to ⅞. A quote of 50⅝ means that the price per share is $50.63.

Table 13.7 How to Read a Stock Quotation

1. STOCK
   INCO Ltd.
2. SALES
   62,701
   Total number of shares traded this date. There were 62,701 shares sold
3. HIGH LOW
   16⅛ 15⅝
   During the trading day the highest price was $16.125 and the lowest, $15.625
4. CLOSE
   16
   At the close of trading on this date the last price paid per share was $16.00
5. NET CHANGE
   −⅜
   Difference between today's closing price and previous day's closing price. Price decreased by $0.375

Stock	*Sales*	*High*	*Low*	*Close*	*Net Change*
H Bay Mng	1557	$ 21	20¾	21	+½
H Bay Co	1440	$ 21⅞	21½	21⅞	+⅜
HBC pr	5386	$ 15½	15¼	15½	
Hu-Pam o	1600	55	52	52	−10
Husky Oil	17520	$ 8⅞	8⅝	8¾	+⅛
Husky 13p	9605	$ 40½	39	40¼	+1
Hydra Ex o	4000	80	74	80	+10
ITL Ind	2000	60	60	60	+5
IU Intl	622	$ 22¾	22	22¾	+½
Imasco	26511	$ 37	36	36⅞	+34
Imasco A p	200	350	350	350	+25
Imasco B p	350	$ 74	73	74	+1⅜
Imp Life p	400	$ 27¾	27¾	27¾	
Imp Oil A	18390	$ 28⅜	27¾	28¼	+⅜
Imp Oil B	z6	$ 27½	27½	27½	
Inca o	46285	$ 6⅜	5⅞	6⅜	+¾
Inca w	28100	275	246	255	+25
Inco	*62701*	*$ 16⅛*	*15⅝*	*16*	*−⅜*
Inco 7.85	400	$ 18	17½	17½	−½
Inco wt	14600	$ 6¼	6⅛	6¼	−⅛
Indal	z75	$ 17½	17¼	17½	
Inland Gas	5580	$ 13⅜	13	13	−⅜
Inland G p	z17	$ 9	9	9	
Inter-City	24500	$ 11	10⅝	11	+⅜
IBM	908	$124⅝	123⅜	124⅝	+2⅛

Bond Prices

Bond prices also change from day to day. These changes provide information for firms about the cost of borrowing funds.

Prices of domestic corporation bonds, Canadian government bonds, and foreign bonds are reported separately. Bond prices are expressed in terms of 100 even though most have a face value of $1,000. Thus, a quote of 85 means that the bond's price is 85 percent of par, or $850.

A corporation bond selling at 155¼ would cost a buyer $1,552.50 ($1,000 par value times 1.5525) plus commission. The interest rate on bonds is also quoted as a percentage of par. Thus, "6½s" pay 6.5 percent of par value per year.

The market value (selling price) of a bond at any given time depends on (1) its stated interest rate; (2) the "going rate" of interest in the market; and (3) its redemption or maturity date.

If a bond carries a higher stated interest rate than the "going rate" on similar quality bonds, it will probably sell at a premium above its face value—its selling price will be above its redemption price. If a bond carries a lower stated interest rate than the "going rate" on similar quality bonds,

Table 13.8   How to Read a Bond Quotation

	Price	Yield	Change
GOVERNMENT OF CANADA			
Canada 4½ Sept 1–83	97.90	8.93	+0.10
Canada 16 Oct 15–83	103.60	9.78	⋯
Canada 16¼ Apr 1–84	106.10	10.11	+0.10
Canada 15 Aug 1–84	106.00	10.30	⋯
Canada 15¼ Jun 1–86–93	119.25	11.94	⋯
Canada 15 Mar 15–87	112.00	11.22	⋯
Canada 13 May 1–01	100.62	12.22	+¼
Canada 9½ Oct 15–01	86.00	11.33	+¼
Canada 15½ Mar 15–02	122.75	12.35	+½
Canada 11¼ Dec 15–02	94.87	11.93	+¼
Canada 11¾ Feb 1–03	98.75	11.92	+¼
Canada 10¼ Feb 1–04	89.75	11.56	+⅛
PROVINCIALS AND GUARANTEED			
Alta 12¼ Dec 15–02	99.00	12.38	+¼
BC Hy 14½ Apr 14–06	109.25	13.21	+¼
NB 13¾ Apr 8–86	105.00	11.76	⋯
Nfld 13⅜ May 15–86	103.50	12.00	⋯
NS 15½ Apr 15–87–97	117.25	12.82	⋯
Ont Hy 15½ May 12–87	112.00	11.78	⋯
Ont Hy 17 Mar 3–02	123.25	13.56	+¼
Ont Hy 14¼ Apr 21–06	109.50	12.94	⋯
Que Hy 17½ Nov 24–86–91	124.50	12.75	+½
Que 16¼–½ Mar 22–87–97	119.00	13.40	⋯
CORPORATES			
Bel 11 Oct 15–04	90.50	12.26	+½
BC Tel 16⅜ Apr 1–87–92	117.00	13.11	⋯
CIL 14½ Apr 15–96	105.75	13.45	+¼
Cdn Util 17½ Mar 15–97	119.00	14.32	+¼
Dofasco 17 May 1–97	*117.00*	*14.17*	+¼
Nova 17½ Feb 15–87	115.00	12.57	⋯
Nova 17¾ Feb 15–97	118.00	14.68	⋯

1. Dofasco
   Company name is Dofasco Ltd.
2. 17
   Annual rate of interest at face value is 17 percent
3. May 1–97
   Maturity date. In this case, May 1, 1997
4. 117.00
   On this date this was the price of the last transaction
5. 14.17
   Annual interest paid divided by current market price
6. +¼
   The closing price on this day was up $0.25 from the closing price on the previous day

it will probably sell at a discount — its selling price will be below its redemption price. How much the premium or discount is depends largely on how far off in the future the maturity date is. The maturity date is indicated after the interest rate.

Table 13.8 illustrates the type of information daily newspapers give about bond transactions.

Bond Yield

Suppose you bought a $1,000 par value bond in 1977 for $650. Its stated interest rate is 6 percent, and its maturity or redemption date is 1997.

You paid $650 for the bond and its interest rate is 6 percent per year of par value. You get $60 per year in interest. Based on your actual investment of $650, your yield is 9.2 percent. If you hold it to maturity, you get $1,000 for a bond that originally cost you only $650. This "extra" $350, of course, increases your true, or effective, yield.

Stock and Bond Averages

To give investors an overall idea of the behaviour of security prices, several types of stock and bond averages are reported. The TSE index gives an average for stocks. Common stocks on the TSE are averaged so that an investor can tell in dollars and cents how much an average share changed in price on a given day.

Underwriting

underwriting

Underwriting is quite different from banking and the other financial institutions we discussed earlier. **Underwriting involves helping corporations and governments to sell new issues of stocks and bonds.**

Suppose the Jaron Corporation decides to expand its plant and wants to sell $10 million worth of bonds to finance the expansion. It might contact an investment dealer to help with the sale. If its study of Jaron's financial condition is favourable, the underwriter would offer, in effect, to buy Jaron's bonds. If Jaron accepts, the cash is made available to it. The investment dealer then sells the bonds. The underwriter earns a profit by charging a commission for its services or by selling the securities at a higher price than it paid for them.

If the risk of selling a large issue of stocks and bonds is too great for one underwriter, several may combine in a syndicate to underwrite the issue. Each agrees to take a portion of the securities offered for sale. In other instances, the underwriter may arrange to sell the entire issue to a financial intermediary such as an insurance company. This is called a "private placement." In this case, the firm is acting as an agent rather than an underwriter, because no financial risk is assumed.

brokerage function

The Brokerage Function

The brokerage function involves buying and selling securities which previously have been issued by business and governments.

Large investment dealers perform many brokerage-related functions for corporations and investors in addition to underwriting. They perform a brokerage function when they buy and sell previously issued securities on behalf of their investor-clients. Secondly, they perform a credit function when they finance purchases made on credit by securities buyers (margin purchases). Thirdly, they perform a research function when they compile information about firms. Fourthly, they perform an advisory function when they use the information gathered through research to advise their corporate clients on issuing new securities and when they advise their investor-clients on buying and selling securities.

SECURITIES EXCHANGES

securities exchanges

Many stocks are traded on securities exchanges. **Securities exchanges are places where buyers and sellers deal with each other through members of the exchanges.** The exchanges are set up by investment dealers to reduce the cost and increase the efficiency of the brokerage function. Members of an exchange own "seats" on that exchange. Only members can trade on an exchange.

Most large brokerage firms hold seats on all of the exchanges in Canada and some in the United States. Of course, there are securities exchanges in other countries also.

A corporation does not receive any money from the sale of its securities on stock exchanges. If Joe Smith buys 100 shares of Bell Telephone common on an exchange, the money goes to the party who sold the shares, not to Bell.

SPECULATING AND INVESTING

Speculating

Some people think that buying stocks and bonds is a way to get rich quick. They buy on the basis of "hot tips." This is called speculative trading.

speculative trading

Speculative trading means buying or selling securities in the hope of profiting from near-term future changes in their selling prices.

Sometimes, amateur speculators do "strike it rich," but the losers far outnumber the winners. Speculating is most popular during a bull market, when stock prices as a whole are rising and there is a great deal of optimism among speculators. Speculating is less popular in a bear market, when stock prices as a whole are falling and there is a great deal of pessimism among speculators. Some people are successful speculators. Successful speculation requires courage, persistence, judgment, and the analysis of all available facts.

Margin Trading

A speculator has to pay cash for securities bought only when the margin requirement is 100 percent. Otherwise, the speculator buys partly on credit.

margin trading

Margin trading enables speculators to buy more shares for a given amount of money because they are buying partly on credit. Brokers put up the shares they sell on margin as collateral for the loans they make to finance their clients' margin purchases. As long as the price of a stock bought on margin rises, there is no problem. The banker's collateral increases in value. But if its price falls, the banker wants more cash from the broker or wants to sell the shares.

In the 1920s, many speculators were buying on 10 percent margin. When stock prices began falling, bankers started selling, in large volume, the stocks they held as collateral. This helped to bring on the eventual collapse of the stock market.

Short Selling

Speculators may also make a profit from selling stocks when prices are falling. Martha Todd, an established client of Broker *B*, believes that the selling price of ABC common stock will fall in the next few weeks. It is now selling at 65. Martha does not own any ABC stock but "borrows" several shares from her broker. Many investors do not take possession of the stock certificates they own. They let their brokers keep them for them. Thus, brokers can "lend" some of this stock to their other clients.

short selling

Martha tells her broker to sell 500 of these borrowed shares at 65. If the price subsequently falls, Martha buys the shares to "cover" her earlier sale. She buys in, say, at 55. She thus makes a $10 profit on each of the 500 shares (less commission). But if the price went up instead of down, Martha would have incurred a loss. This practice is called short selling. **Short selling means selling a security which you do not own by borrowing it from your broker.** At some time in the future, you must buy the security to "cover" the short sale.

Investing

Unlike a speculator, an investor invests in securities for the longer haul. Before even considering investing, much less speculating, you should have a cushion of cash reserves and adequate insurance. You should be able to choose when you want to sell your shares and not be forced to sell them because you need cash for an emergency.

Your approach to buying and selling securities should be logical. Your investment goals should guide your buying and selling decisions. The kinds of goals may vary among investors, but each investor should have definite goals.

An important goal for investors is to protect their invested dollars. You could do this by putting your money in a safe-deposit box. But this earns nothing; because of inflation the buying power of these dollars declines. You would be wiser to put your money in an insured savings account. You might also buy government bonds. All those are highly liquid investments which can be quickly converted into cash. Furthermore, they are very safe investments. In fact, they involve almost no risk at all. But to increase your earning potential, you will have to make riskier investments.

How Much Risk?

Of course, different investment strategies involve different degrees of risk. Investing in preferred stocks of established and profitable corporations is less risky, for example, than investing in common stocks of new and risky ventures. But in terms of return, the new venture might prove to be the better investment. In other words, risk and return are directly related.

There is no one answer to the question of how much risk you should assume in your investment program. You have to consider your financial situation, age, investment goals, patience, self-discipline, and so on. To put it simply, if your goal is to get rich quick, you will have to take a lot more risk than someone else whose goal is to get rich more slowly.

Balancing Objectives

The typical investor wants a safe investment which will return regular earnings and has a lot of potential for future growth. But it's hard to satisfy all three objectives.

Investing in securities involves keeping up with developments in the economy and in the industries and firms in which you invest. If you don't have the time or "knowhow" to do this, you might invest in a mutual fund. **The owners of a mutual fund pool their investment dollars and buy securities in other businesses. Buying one share in a mutual fund makes you part owner of all the securities owned by the fund.** You spread your risk over a broad range of securities. Mutual funds are professionally managed. Before they were created, only people with large sums to invest could afford to hire professional managers to oversee their portfolios (the stocks and bonds they own).

mutual fund

Figure 13.2 lists various types of mutual funds and explains how they work.

SECURITIES REGULATION

Canada, unlike the United States with its Securities and Exchange commission (SEC), does not have comprehensive federal securities legislation or a federal regulatory body. Government regulation is primarily provincial. There is also self-regulation through the various securities exchanges.

In 1912 the Manitoba government pioneered in Canada with "blue sky" laws applying mainly to the sale of new securities. Issuing corporations must back up securities with something more than just the "blue sky." Similar laws were passed in other provinces of Canada. Provincial laws also generally require the licensing of stockbrokers and the registration of securities before they can be sold. In each province, issuers of proposed new securities must file a prospectus with the provincial securities exchange. **A prospectus is a detailed registration statement which includes information about the firm, its operation, its management, the purpose of the proposed issue, and any other things which would be helpful to a potential buyer of these securities.** The prospectus must be made available to prospective investors.

prospectus

In recent times, Ontario is regarded as having the most progressive securities legislation in Canada. The Ontario Securities Act contains disclosure provisions for new and existing issues, prevention of fraud, regulation of the Toronto Stock Exchange, insider trading, takeover bids, and others.

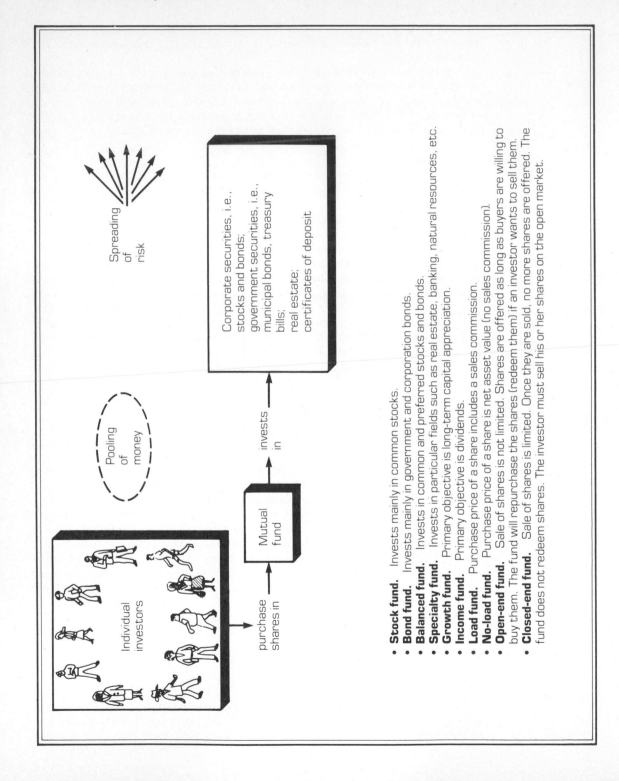

Individual investors

purchase shares in

Mutual fund

invests in

Corporate securities, i.e., stocks and bonds; government securities, i.e., municipal bonds, treasury bills; real estate; certificates of deposit

Pooling of money

Spreading of risk

- **Stock fund.** Invests mainly in common stocks.
- **Bond fund.** Invests mainly in government and corporation bonds.
- **Balanced fund.** Invests in common and preferred stocks and bonds.
- **Specialty fund.** Invests in particular fields such as real estate, banking, natural resources, etc.
- **Growth fund.** Primary objective is long-term capital appreciation.
- **Income fund.** Primary objective is dividends.
- **Load fund.** Purchase price of a share includes a sales commission.
- **No-load fund.** Purchase price of a share is net asset value (no sales commission).
- **Open-end fund.** Sale of shares is not limited. Shares are offered as long as buyers are willing to buy them. The fund will repurchase the shares (redeem them) if an investor wants to sell them.
- **Closed-end fund.** Sale of shares is limited. Once they are sold, no more shares are offered. The fund does not redeem shares. The investor must sell his or her shares on the open market.

CAREERS IN SECURITIES AND INSURANCE

SECURITIES SALESPERSONS OR BROKERS WORK FOR INVESTMENT dealers. They study the investment potential of stocks and bonds and analyze the investment or speculative goals of their clients. They recommend purchases and sales of securities, place orders, and keep their clients informed of opportunities.

Their income depends primarily upon commissions earned from trading securities for their clients. Technical skills in interpreting financial statements and comparing financial performance of firms are required. Human relations skills are also needed.

Large investment dealers provide training programs for new salespersons. The demand for such people is expected to grow moderately. Income potential depends greatly on personal skill and market conditions. Information is available from the personnel department of any large investment dealer, or from the Investment Dealers Association of Canada, P. O. Box 217, Commerce Court South, Toronto, Ontario, Canada M5G 1E8.

Insurance-related careers include those of agent, broker, underwriter, claims adjuster, claims examiner, and actuary. *Agents* sell insurance for one firm or for several firms. *Brokers* serve their clients by selecting and buying insurance for them. *Underwriters* evaluate and select risks the insurance firm will take on. *Claims adjusters* check and settle claims against insurance companies. *Claims examiners* investigate large or suspicious claims. College degrees are helpful for agents and brokers and are highly desirable for underwriters, adjusters, and examiners.

Actuarial jobs involve the assembling and analysis of statistics on expected losses. This is done in order to fix premiums for policyholders so that costs and profit are covered. Tough exams are given for certification as an actuary.

All the insurance-related careers we have described require human relations skills, particularly the agent-broker careers.

All require computational skills, factual observation, and reporting skills. Of the jobs discussed here, actuaries earn the highest average incomes. The most successful of agents can earn even more. Perhaps the greatest financial rewards result from operation of an insurance agency. Agency owners, of course, assume the same risks as any business owner. Information is available from the Insurance Institute of Canada, 220 Bay Street, Toronto, Ontario, Canada M5J 1P3. ∎

Figure 13.2
How a mutual fund works. Investors in a mutual fund send their money to the trustee for the mutual fund, and the trustee is told which securities to buy or sell by the fund's investment advisor. A management firm performs the recordkeeping for the fund.

CAREER PROFILE

MY NAME IS MARK CULLEN. I AM A VICE-President and Director of Pitfield Mackay Ross Limited. As Resident Director of the company for British Columbia, I am responsible for all of the firm's activities in the province.

Pitfield Mackay Ross Limited is one of Canada's major investment dealers. Our company's principal function is to bring together people who want investment capital and people with capital to invest. We also provide a market for outstanding unlisted securities, including bonds, treasury bills, finance paper, corporate paper, and unlisted stocks. Our activities include underwriting new corporate and government securities, stock brokerage, trading outstanding securities for our own account, investment research, portfolio management, and money market operations. We operate forty-eight offices in Canada located from St. John's to Victoria and also have international operations in New York, Geneva, and London, England.

I was born and raised in Ottawa, Ontario. I obtained a B.Com. from the University of Ottawa in 1963 and an MBA from the University of Western Ontario in 1971. Throughout my working career I have been employed by a large insurance company in the computer programming and systems field, by a small university as manager of its computer operations, and by one of Canada's largest retailing organizations as a corporate planner. I joined Pitfield Mackay Ross in late 1972, and since that time I have been involved in the corporate finance and investment marketing functions.

I was appointed to my present position as the senior Pitfield Mackay Ross representative in British Columbia in May 1982. Currently we operate five branch offices (Vancouver, Victoria, Nanaimo, Vernon, and Salmon Arm) and employ 110 people in the province. Our prime activity in these offices is stock brokerage. We also have underwriting, institutional investment sales, and money market functions in our Vancouver office.

My principal responsibility and activity on a day-to-day basis is the company's corporate finance function in the province. Currently we have four major corporate clients in British Columbia. They are British Columbia Telephone Company, British Columbia Forest Products Limited, Westcoast Transmission

Company Limited, and Genstar Corporation. We provide them with financial advice on an ongoing basis and assistance in raising their investment capital when the need arises. I maintain working relationships with their senior management and must keep up-to-date with their operations, plans, and capital requirements, and also developments in their industries. When new capital is required, I am fully involved in the structuring, preparation, pricing, and marketing of the new security offering, which will not only meet the corporation's capital requirements but will also be sold successfully to investors. The financing process, on average, takes three months to complete.

One of Pitfield's corporate objectives is to gain more corporate clients in British Columbia. Therefore, an important part of my job is corporate development. This involves meeting with key senior management of potential corporate clients, making them aware of our firm's strengths in corporate finance and distribution of securities, and presenting our financing ideas. This is an ongoing activity. I should also add that there is intense competition in our industry for new corporate clients.

I am also involved in investment industry and community-related activities. Currently I am Vice-Chairman of the Pacific District of the Investment Dealers Association, and in this position my prime function is to liaise with the provincial government on industry matters. I am also working in the major corporations division of the Greater Vancouver United Way.

The main problem I face on a daily basis is to be able to manage my time. It is a myth that as one progresses in a company the work load is reduced. In fact, the opposite is true. In addition to providing services to existing clients and corporate development activities, I must spend time each day on management of our operation. As well, I must keep current on financing methods. I achieve this through reading prospectuses and financial journals and by daily conversation with my corporate finance colleagues in other parts of the country. I also read a wide variety of general and business publications.

The major rewards of my position are both self-satisfaction and financial. There is a high degree of satisfaction when I present a $50 or $100 million cheque to a client upon completion of a successful offering of securities and three months of sustained effort. I also get satisfaction from the growth of new employees whom I recruited and helped train. There are also financial rewards. My company is owned by our employees. Although my personal investment is subject to a high degree of risk, the returns over the years have been commensurate with the risk.

In summary, from my experience, I would observe that a successful career requires knowledge and the ability to apply that knowledge in the workplace. Hard work is a must. Being in the right place at the right time can also be an important factor. First, one needs a sound education, whether of a general nature or related to a specific discipline. Once employed, the individual must be able to build on his or her education by gaining in-depth knowledge and the skills related to his or her employer's specific activity. By and large, this is an "on the job" learning experience and continues throughout one's career.

For those contemplating a career in business, I would strongly recommend participation in activities such as debating and public speaking in order to develop oral and written presentation skills. It is important to note that almost all jobs have a sales element, whether they involve the selling of ideas or direct sales of products. Such skills are invaluable to those wishing to progress up the corporate ladder. In view of the rapidly changing business environment, I would also recommend that university students have as much exposure as possible to computers and their applications.

The Toronto Stock Exchange provides an example of self-regulation by the industry. The TSE has regulations concerning listing and delisting of securities, disclosure requirements, and issuing of prospectuses for new securities, among others.

commodity exchanges

Commodity exchanges provide a market for commodities much as securities exchanges provide a market for stocks and bonds. They are voluntary trade associations whose members must follow specified trading rules. The Winnipeg Commodity Exchange is the largest commodity exchange in Canada. The Chicago Board of Trade is the world's largest commodity exchange.

cash trading

Commodity exchanges deal in cash trading. **Cash trading involves the actual buying and selling of commodities for delivery.** A sales contract may call for immediate delivery or delivery at a specified date in the future. The contract is fulfilled upon delivery.

futures markets

The larger commodity exchanges also have futures markets. **In futures markets, traders buy and sell contracts to receive or deliver a certain quantity and grade of commodity at a specified future date.** Prices are set on the exchange floor by traders. Most futures trading does not result in the physical exchange of goods.

Suppose you expect the price of flax to go down. You sell a futures contract for flax you don't actually have. You sell at $8.00 per bushel. The price goes down to $7.90, and you buy to "cover" your sale. You make 10 cents per bushel in profit (less commission). But if the price had gone up instead of down, you would have incurred a loss.

Suppose instead that you expect the price to go up. You buy a futures contract in June at $8.00 per bushel for delivery in October. In July, October futures are selling at $8.25 per bushel. You sell in July at $8.25. Your purchase and sales contracts cancel each other. But you make 25 cents per bushel in profit (less commission). If, however, the price had gone down instead of up, you would have incurred a loss.

Although many people have made fortunes on the commodities exchanges, they are no place for amateurs.

SUMMARY AND LOOK AHEAD

The financial institutions we discussed are vital to modern businesses. Ours is a modern banking system. The chartered bank, which is at the heart of this system, is the most important source of short-term funds for business firms. Our chartered banking system creates money in the form of demand deposits. The Bank of Canada is the central bank of Canada. Its main job is to control the nation's money supply.

In addition to chartered banks, other financial intermediaries include trust companies, caisses populaires and credit unions, life insurance companies, sales and consumer finance companies, venture capital funds, government financial intermediaries, and pension funds. While the others are not as important to businesses as the chartered bank, they play an important role in providing services to their business and non-business customers.

The public market is made up of the millions of people who invest in corporate securities and the "middlemen" who bring them together for buying and selling. A corporation which issues new stock may use the services of an investment dealer underwriting department to help sell the securities. Through their brokerage function, investment dealers buy and sell previously issued securities for their clients.

A corporation's common stockholders are its residual owners. Common and preferred stock indicate ownership in a firm. Bonds indicate indebtedness.

A speculator looks mainly for short-term profits from buying and selling securities — in some cases (short selling) by selling something he or she does not own. An investor takes a longer-run view. Speculating is very popular during bull markets and much less popular in bear markets.

Commodities such as grain and copper are traded on commodity exchanges such as the Winnipeg Commodity Exchange. The cash market involves the actual buying and selling of commodities, whereas most futures trading does not result in the physical exchange of goods.

Just as banks and the commodity exchanges are regulated, so are the securities exchanges, brokerage houses, and stockbrokers.

In our next chapter, we will see how businesses use these financial institutions. Our topic there is financial management. ■

QUESTIONS FOR REVIEW AND DISCUSSION

1. What are the major sources and uses of funds from a chartered bank's point of view?
2. Explain what an Electronic Funds Transfer (EFT) system can do for a bank customer.
3. Contrast: (a) a factoring company and a commercial finance company and (b) a sales finance company and a consumer finance company.
4. Explain how the chartered banking system creates money.
5. Why might a small retailer sell its accounts receivable to a factoring company?
6. List and define three different concepts of "value" for common stock.
7. What is the purpose of (a) a stock split; (b) a stock dividend; and (c) a cash dividend?
8. What is the purpose of a stock exchange?
9. How do listed securities differ from unlisted securities?
10. What is a mutual fund? Explain how it works.
11. Does the securities exchange guarantee the value of a corporation's stocks and bonds to investors? Explain.
12. Give several examples of uses of long-term financing.
13. Contrast the use of bonds and stocks for acquiring long-term funds.

INCIDENTS

The Madisons

Russ Madison is a forty-three-year-old, middle-level manager of a medium-size corporation. He currently earns $45,000 a year and expects that he will be promoted to higher management because of his good work record. Russ and Ann Madison have a daughter who is in grade ten and a son who is in his first year at a university. They have no other children.

The Madisons have $20,000 in savings certificates. They have a joint savings account with a balance of $4,500. They also have $5,000 in Government of Canada bonds, and the mortgage on their home will be paid off in ten years. Russ has a $100,000 life insurance policy on his life. Finally, ten years ago, Russ and Ann began buying shares in a no-load mutual fund which emphasizes capital appreciation. The current market value of those shares is $15,000.

The major financial obligation the Madisons face in the future is the expense of putting their son and daughter through college. Russ and Ann began planning for this at the birth of their children by opening savings accounts for each of them. The balances in those accounts are now adequate to pay their children's tuition and expenses. Obviously, the Madisons are in good financial shape — in fact, quite enviable shape!

Russ and Ann believe that they can assume a little more risk in their approach to investing.

Questions:
1. Why do the Madisons believe they can assume greater risk in their investment program now than when their children were born?
2. Why do you think that Russ and Ann chose a no-load mutual fund whose objective is capital appreciation?
3. What investment advice would you offer the Madisons at this time? Explain your reasoning.

Gorgeous Day Boutique

The Gorgeous Day Boutique is a small partnership owned by Doris Gammel and Gloria Hyde. The partners have been in business for nine months. They carry a medium-priced line of women's sportswear and casual wear. Sales are running about $30,000 a month.

Doris and Gloria invested all their personal savings in the firm when they started out. Business has been better than they expected, but they believe that it could be better still.

The partners started out selling on a "cash-only" basis. But they are now reconsidering their decision not to sell on credit. They estimate that one in three persons who come into the store does not buy when he or she learns that Gorgeous Day does not offer credit.

Doris and Gloria are now trying to decide how they should go about offering credit to their customers. They both lack experience in dealing with credit, but each has her own ideas on the matter.

Questions:
1. Why do you think that the partners originally decided not to sell on credit?
2. Why do you think the lack of charge privileges caused some shoppers not to buy from Gorgeous Day?
3. What advice would you give to Doris and Gloria with respect to offering credit? Justify your advice.

CASE STUDY*

CENTRAL DECAL, LTD.

LATE IN THE EVENING OF JANUARY 20, 1981, ROGER McINTYRE SAT IN his hotel room in Calgary thinking about one of the most significant and difficult business decisions he had ever been faced with. During the last several months McIntyre and his business partner, John Altman, owners of Central Decal, Ltd., had been having problems with their business. McIntyre attributed some of these to Altman. At dinner earlier in the evening McIntyre told Altman that either Altman had to leave the firm or he would. Altman expressed shock and surprise at this comment and asked why McIntyre felt this way. McIntyre replied that Altman's work in the finance area of the firm was completely unsatisfactory, and that, unless this problem was resolved, the company could not survive.

As he sat in his hotel room, McIntyre wondered if he had done the right thing in giving Altman such an ultimatum.

COMPANY BACKGROUND

In June, 1978, Roger McIntyre and Bill Merrill formed Central Decal, Ltd., a private corporation with McIntyre and Merrill as the shareholders. Each man had put $15,000 into the business. As well, they had received a $40,000 DREE grant after they promised to create eleven new jobs with the money.

The company manufactured four products: (1) decals, (2) point-of-purchase displays for retailers, (3) displays for trade shows, and (4) plastic forming products. Most of the sales of the firm were to retailers and manufacturers in the Prairie provinces, Eastern Canada, and the Upper Midwest in the United States.

Production

The major production activity is screen printing. This is a process in which a piece of polyester or similar fabric (the screen) is stretched over a frame. The screen is then coated with a chemical called an emulsion and put on a vacuum table. An air pump sucks all the air out of the table, forcing a negative piece of artwork tightly against the screen. The vacuum table is then moved to a vertical position and exposed to a high intensity arc lamp which burns the image of the artwork into the screen. The screen is then taken out of the vacuum table and put into a wash tank with a pressure washer. Where the image of the art work has been burned into the screen, the emulsion has not hardened; where there is

*This case was written by Professor Frederick A. Starke.

481

no image the emulsion has hardened and sealed the holes in the screen. When the screen is spray washed, the image of the art work is left.

There are few restrictions regarding the type of material that can be printed on. The finished screen is either printed by hand (for low volume jobs) or by machine (for high volume jobs). Ink is poured on top of the mesh frame and then a squeegee is used to spread the ink across the mesh. The ink is then forced through the mesh to yield the finished product.

Central uses ultraviolet screen printing (UVSP), which is a specific type of screen printing that uses solid-based ink, whereas traditional screen printing uses solvent-based ink. Since solvents evaporate during printing, they can be a health hazard. These problems do not exist in UVSP.

The company has $200,000 worth of machinery (book value) in the plant. The equipment is as modern as any in Western Canada. In fact, there is only one other firm in Canada that can compete with the UVSP process used at Central.

Exhibit 1 Central Decal, Ltd. Balance Sheet (as of April 30, 1981)

Assets	1981	1980	1979
CURRENT ASSETS			
Cash	$ 100	$ ···	$ ···
Accounts receivable	235,407	160,943	62,719
Inventories	134,032	81,239	25,057
Prepaid expenses	1	626	978
	$369,540	$242,808	$ 88,754
OTHER ASSETS			
Shareholder loans receivable	$ ···	$ ···	$ 6,015
Development incentives grant receivable (DREE)	5,352	5,352	5,352
Deposits	$ ···	3,521	6,868
	$ 5,352	$ 8,873	$ 18,235
FIXED ASSETS			
Equipment and leasehold improvements	$210,070	$175,761	$ 88,874
Less accumulated depreciation & amortization	57,702	31,549	7,950
	$152,368	$144,212	$ 80,924
TOTAL ASSETS	$527,260	$395,893	$187,913
Liabilities			
CURRENT LIABILITIES			
Bank advances, secured by demand debenture over all assets	$198,949	$155,440	$ 76,160
Bank loan	···	58,946	···
Accounts payable and accrued liabilities	135,514	119,276	67,409

Marketing

The basic marketing problem is to avoid getting into contracts that consume significant amounts of production time but don't give much financial return. Since screen printing can be done on almost any material, there is a temptation to accept a wide diversity of jobs. Specialization and high volume in a few areas are the key to both production and marketing success. McIntyre doesn't know what the total market potential is, but the company has never had any trouble generating sales.

The marketing strategy involves both personal and mass selling. The company employs five industrial salespeople (including McIntyre and Altman) who are paid a salary plus bonus. The company also spends approximately $600 per month on advertising in the Yellow Pages and elsewhere. The company does extensive direct mail advertising and regularly attends trade shows. Sales are often made to other exhibitors at trade shows. The emphasis in all these areas is on what Central can do for the customer. To implement this, the company is actively involved in making up samples of their work that are relevant to a potential

Exhibit 1 *(continued)*

Liabilities	1981	1980	1979
CURRENT LIABILITIES *(continued)*			
Taxes payable	$ 13,366	$ 10,658	$ 4,425
Principal due within one year on long-term debt	8,002	8,002	8,002
Cheques in excess of cash on hand	45,966	...	...
	$401,797	$352,322	$155,996
LONG-TERM DEBT			
GMAC loans, payable $867 monthly including principal, interest, secured by chattel mortgages	$ 17,194	$ 24,262	$ 31,598
Less principal included in current liabilities	8,002	8,002	8,002
	$ 9,192	$ 16,260	$ 23,596
SHAREHOLDERS' LOAN	$151,334	$108,484	$ ...
DEFERRED DEVELOPMENT INCENTIVES GRANT	$ 1,784	$ 10,706	$ 21,413
TOTAL LIABILITIES	$564,107	$487,772	$201,005

Capital Stock & Deficit			
CAPITAL STOCK	$ 63,000	$ 31,000	$ 46,000
DEFICIT	(99,847)	(122,879)	(59,092)
Excess of deficit over capital stock	$ (36,847)	$ (91,879)	$ (13,092)
	$ 527,260	$ 395,893	$ 187,913

Exhibit 2 Central Decal, Ltd. Statement of Income and Deficit
(Year Ending April 30, 1981)

	1981	1980	1979
Sales	$855,653	$581,605	$192,992
Cost of goods sold	556,174	416,032	145,781
Gross profit	$299,479	$165,573	$ 47,211
Expenses	276,447	229,360	106,303
Net profit (loss)	$ 23,032	$ (63,787)	$ (59,092)

customer. Sales contracts are often signed after the customer sees these samples.

Finance

The relevant financial information for the company is contained in Exhibits 1 and 2.

Personnel

Employees are hired if they are experienced in screen printing and if their personal interview is successful. There is no union at the company. No formalized personnel testing is done. Performance appraisal is also informal. Wage rates for production workers are based on their performance and aggressiveness as determined by Roger McIntyre. Thus, workers with more seniority may make less than workers with less seniority. McIntyre feels that there will be no need to hire any production or administrative staff (excluding replacements for resignations) for at least one year.

RECENT DEVELOPMENTS

In December, 1979, Bill Merrill left the business for personal reasons. Roger McIntyre was left as the only shareholder, so he began looking for someone who wanted to join the firm and share the management responsibilities. After some searching, John Altman was brought into the firm as one of the shareholders because he was both a Chartered Accountant and a management consultant for small business. Central was growing very rapidly, and McIntyre felt that some financial control was necessary. Altman came into the company on the understanding that he would produce the firm's financial statements, conduct the financial dealings with the bank, and share the management responsibilities with McIntyre. Shortly after Altman joined the firm, however, two problems arose. First, Altman had difficulty delegating authority. As a result, many jobs were not being completed on time because Altman would not delegate the work, nor could he do it all himself. There was also some uncertainty among the workers in the company concerning whom they should report to—McIntyre or Altman.

Second, it became clear that Altman was actually more interested in production and marketing than he was in finance and accounting. The cash flow projections and financial statements which Altman was supposed to produce rarely got done. Relations with the bank were also less than satisfactory. In May, 1980, several of Central's cheques were returned because of insufficient funds. McIntyre felt certain that Altman knew a cash flow crunch was imminent, but Altman had made no plans to cope with it. Promises had been made to the bank that they would get monthly financial reports on the firm's condition, but this had not been done either. When the crunch came, Altman put about $50,000 of his own money into the business to resolve the crisis. (He was able to do this because he came from a wealthy family.) After this incident, McIntyre and Altman had a meeting and agreed that Altman would not let this happen again. However, after about two months it became clear that things were returning to their former disorganized state. A second meeting was held where McIntyre basically demanded that Altman either do the job properly or get someone who could.

When the second crunch came in September, 1980, Altman put in another $50,000 to resolve the problem. McIntyre felt that this behavior on Altman's part merely hid the real financial problems the firm was facing. McIntyre discovered, for example, that Altman had not increased the firm's line of credit, even though monthly sales volume had nearly tripled. Altman had not pursued further DREE grants either, even though these were likely to be approved because the company had more than fulfilled its obligation to create a certain number of jobs with its first grant. On top of all this, the bank had sent a very critical report to McIntyre detailing many other shortcomings in the financial affairs of the company.

After the second incident, McIntyre had reached the end of his rope. He knew that Altman would be financially solvent even if the business folded because he was wealthy; Altman also had a CA degree which was very marketable. McIntyre, on the other hand, had nothing to fall back on. He felt that he had several alternatives: (1) buy out Altman's shares, (2) drop out of the business and sell Altman his shares, or (3) start a new screen printing company. With regard to the first alternative, McIntyre had approached several individuals about financing and they had agreed to put up $250,000 each in return for being made shareholders. McIntyre could then use this money to buy Altman's shares and to put the firm on a more solid financial footing. McIntyre believed this to be a desirable alternative, except that Altman probably would resist selling his shares.

With regard to (2), McIntyre felt that Altman could not keep the business going by himself because (a) during the last few months Altman had been showing signs of extreme anxiety and emotional stress, and (b) McIntyre decided that Altman, in spite of his management consulting background, couldn't manage the firm. McIntyre was uncomfortable about leaving the company because he felt he had a moral obligation not to put Altman in a position that would cause Altman even more stress than he had been experiencing.

With regard to (3), McIntyre was confident that he could start a new business and sure that many of Central's customers would bring their work to his new firm, once it got started. However, he still felt something of a moral obligation to Altman; the increased competition of another screen printing company would make it even harder for Altman to keep Central going alone.

As he considered these alternatives, McIntyre had a hard time deciding what to do. He wondered if there were other alternatives to be considered, or if he should just make a decision and get it over with.

Questions:
1. How has Central Decal, Ltd. been financed to this point in time?
2. What type of financial institution, if any, might help the company?
3. What problems does Roger McIntyre face?
4. What should McIntyre do? ■

After reading this chapter, you should be able to:

1. Identify the three principal duties of a financial manager.
2. Demonstrate a case in which a manager balances the twin objectives of liquidity and profit in the use of working capital.
3. Draw a chart showing the normal flows of working capital in a manufacturing firm.
4. Explain the relationship between technology and fixed capital needs.
5. Illustrate the use of two major sources of short-term credit/trade credit and bank loans.
6. Contrast the advantages of issuing bonds with the advantages of issuing preferred stock for getting long-term funds.
7. List four kinds of risks that can be reduced by good management techniques.
8. Distinguish between pure and speculative risk.
9. Show how the law of large numbers is used to figure insurance premiums.
10. Contrast the procedures of voluntary and involuntary bankruptcy.

In reading the chapter, look for and understand these terms:

working (short-term) capital	intermediate-term financing
liquidity	equipment trust certificates
opportunity costs	rolling over
long-term capital	sinking-fund
capital budget	self-insurance
lease	pure risk
debt financing	speculative risk
equity financing	law of large numbers
maturity	merger
trade credit	amalgamation
line of credit	holding company
revolving credit	recapitalization
secured loans	bankruptcy
floor planning	

SIR FREDDIE LAKER STARTED LAKER Airways in 1978, when his standby fare, no-frills budget Skytrain service made air travel between Europe and North America suddenly affordable for thousands of tourists Early in 1982, however, Laker Airways collapsed because of both long- and short-term financing problems.

The company had millions of dollars of outstanding long-term loans that were made to finance its purchases of planes. It also had millions of dollars of outstanding short-term debts to suppliers of fuel and other items.

What had started as a unique no-frills airline in 1978 had become only one of several airlines offering this type of service in the early 1980s. Laker's success led other airlines to offer similar service and the competition for passengers heated up. In a last-ditch effort to avoid collapse and to raise cash,

CHAPTER FOURTEEN

Financial Decisions
and Risk Management

Laker attempted to sell several of its planes in early 1982. The company intended to use the proceeds to help offset its negative cash flow, which was caused by the company spending more cash than it was taking in. But it could not find buyers for the planes in what, at the time, was a depressed aircraft market.

IN TWO PREVIOUS CHAPTERS WE STUDIED THE COMMUNICATIONS devices of accounting and the financial institutions available to financial managers. In this chapter, we'll see how a manager uses the services of chartered banks, stockbrokers, and insurance companies in managing the firm's financial affairs. Accounting systems provide the basis for most of these financial decisions.

THE FINANCIAL MANAGER AND FINANCIAL PLANNING

Financial decisions are the task of the financial manager (who may be called the comptroller or the vice-president for finance). This executive projects the firm's long- and short-term financial needs and meets them with the help of banks and others. He or she is the chief guardian of the owners' equity. The financial manager's job is to get the best return on the owners' investment without taking unnecessary risks.

Company presidents may include non-economic or social objectives in their decision making, but financial managers must think of dollars and profit. Financial managers specialize in funds and their allocation. They help to provide the president of a firm with a purely economic, profit-maximizing point of view.

A financial manager must do three things. The first duty is to meet the firm's short-term (working) capital and long-term capital needs in the face of uncertainty. A second duty is to evaluate and select from several sources of funds. Finally, it is the financial manager's duty to protect the owners' resources while helping to maximize their return.

The financial manager's first task is financial planning. This means identifying the firm's basic financial needs for working capital and for long-term capital. Let's begin by checking the uses for these funds. Then we'll discuss the sources of funds.

Uses of Funds

As we have seen, the two basic financial needs are working capital and long-term capital needs. Each has its special characteristics.

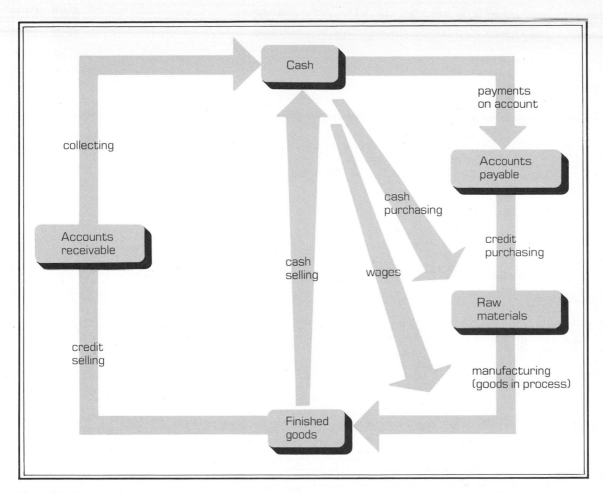

Figure 14.1
Day-to-day operations of a firm

Working Capital

working (short-term) capital

    Working capital is a term applied to a firm's investment in short-term assets — the current assets we discussed in Chapter 11. It includes those assets which flow regularly in the day-to-day operations of a firm — cash, accounts receivable, and inventories. (See Figure 14.1.) If we deduct the amount owed as current liabilities from the gross working capital (the sum of current assets), we are left with net working capital.

liquidity

    Working capital must be handled carefully by the financial manager so as not to interrupt or slow the regular operations of the business. **The firm needs to have enough cash coming in to meet bills, wages, and other current payments. This ability to make payments which are due is the**

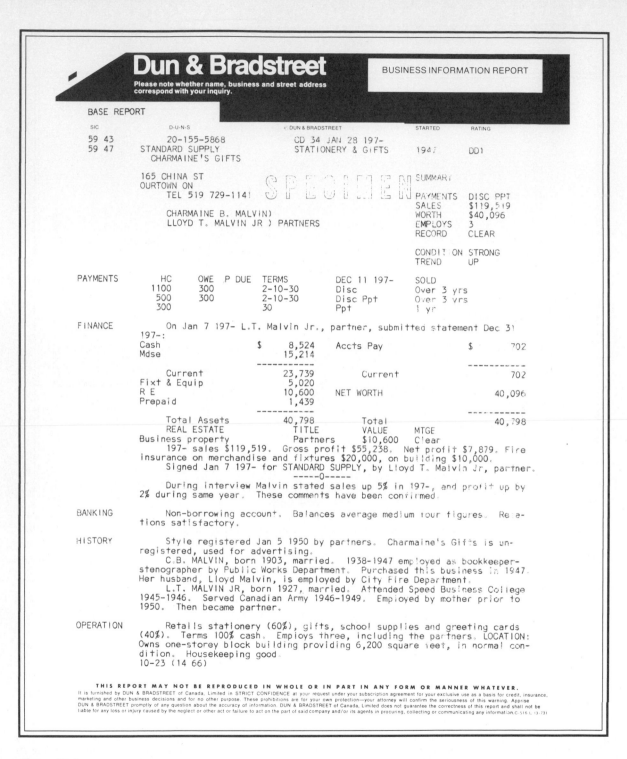

Figure 14.2

A credit report (Reprinted by permission of Dun & Bradstreet, Canada, Ltd.)

test of a firm's liquidity. If the Mangham Feed Store has a payroll of $800 due next Monday as well as a repair bill of $500 due on the same day, the manager must examine Mangham's liquidity. If the firm has only $200 in its chequing account and expects no significant cash inflow before Monday, some borrowing may be in order — maybe from the bank. If Mangham borrows $1,500 from the bank, the firm increases its gross working capital — but its net working capital stays the same because it has created a new current debt — a note payable to the bank. The firm could have found some temporary cash in other ways, as we will see.

The financial manager seeks to balance liquidity with profit. The goal is to minimize the idle cash balances by keeping "near cash" on hand. This means money which would otherwise earn no return is invested and becomes an earning asset. A manager seeks stable short-term investments which are readily convertible into cash. Examples are certificates of deposit (CDs) in banks or short-term government securities such as treasury bills. Tying up cash in long-term investments such as bonds of another firm does not meet the goal of balancing liquidity with profit. Long-term investments of cash do not qualify as "near cash," because they might not be convertible into cash quickly or they might involve some loss due to changes in their market value.

Credit sales represent another use of short-term funds. A firm which sells "on credit" uses its funds to finance its customers' operations. The credit manager and the sales manager often disagree on credit policies. The sales manager sees this as a means of increasing sales. The credit manager sees it as leading to more bad debts.

The financial manager seeks to achieve a balance. The firm wants profits to increase if more working capital must be tied up in accounts receivable. If the increase in receivables results from purchases by proven paying customers, profits will increase. The Mangham Feed Store may be wise to avoid selling on credit to a young farmer whose farm is poorly managed. Even if the debt will be repaid, it might take a long time to collect — tying up valuable working capital. The financial manager uses Dun & Bradstreet, Canada, Ltd. or other credit reporting services to judge possible credit customers. An example of a credit report is presented in Figure 14.2.

Other current assets shown in Figure 14.1 are inventories of raw materials and finished goods. Raw materials are changed into finished goods through the production process. Between these two stages, they are called goods in process. (See Figure 14.1 again.) The financial manager seeks to reduce excess inventories at all three stages. There may be a conflict with the production manager because production may be simplified by keeping large inventories of inputs.

Suppose that the sales manager of the Wonder Mattress Corporation forecasts a 10 percent increase in sales during the next year. The production manager bases estimates of raw materials needs on this sales forecast. Now, suppose further that the purchasing agent can receive a 12 percent discount if the order of raw materials is increased by 20 percent rather than by 10 percent. Should the financial manager approve this use of funds to earn the additional discount?

This depends on whether the Wonder Mattress Corporation could use the additional funds tied up in raw materials more profitably elsewhere. If the raw material is perishable or if storing it would be costly, the larger order would probably not be approved. On the other hand, if the price of raw materials is expected to rise, the manager would probably approve the larger order. The value of a systems approach to decision making is clear here. Better decisions are made when finance, marketing, and production are viewed in terms of their overall goal of helping to increase the firm's profit.

Still another use of working capital involves the current asset "prepaid expenses." You can buy a three-year insurance policy on your home, for example. Paying the three-year premium in one lump sum means that you are prepaying your insurance coverage. The same is true for a firm.

opportunity costs

A financial manager carefully evaluates the option to pay insurance premiums "in advance." The choice depends on the other uses which could be made of those funds. Prepaying expenses is wise when the savings exceed the opportunity costs. **Opportunity costs are costs of losing the option to use the funds in another way.** Let's assume that for the Sanford Ice Cream Company the savings from paying a lump sum for three years of fire insurance coverage, rather than paying on a year-to-year basis, amounts to $100. Assume further that Sanford's comptroller could have earned $150 of interest on the prepaid part of the expense during the last two years of the policy life. Clearly, the comptroller would not prepay in this case. The current (and expected) interest rate is a major factor in making all such financial decisions because it determines what unused dollars can "earn."

A manager should have an overview of the flow of working capital such as we saw in Figure 14.1. He or she must understand this flow and the timing of it from one use to another. If the firm has a good sales forecast and a good collection policy, it can achieve the goal of providing enough working capital but not too much.

Long-term Capital

long-term capital

Long-term capital is the firm's investment in fixed assets. Such capital is committed for at least one year (usually much longer), and it requires a different perspective. The amounts are larger and the risk is greater. A bad mistake could cause the firm to fail.

Long-term capital is invested in land, buildings, heavy machinery, and other fixed assets which, to a large extent, determine the direction in which the firm is going. When RCA went into the computer business, it directed a large part of its long-term capital into assets that could not be sold without loss. RCA management assumed that such an investment would be profitable. This decision proved to be wrong, and RCA later sold its computer holdings at a loss of millions of dollars. Ford had a similar experience with the Edsel. Auto makers in the mid-1970s had to decide how much production capacity to convert to compact and sub-compact cars. Decisions like these involve many millions of dollars in long-term investments.

capital budget

Financial managers must take a long-run view of the firm's operations. They use some of the accounting devices referred to in Chapter 11. **One is the capital budget. This projects the expected need for fixed assets**

for a period of five to ten years. This long planning period means that budget makers must use every scrap of information about the long-range plans and expectations of the firm. They must take the environment into account, too. This includes technological events outside the firm and changes in consumer needs and tastes which might require changes in plant machinery and equipment.

Technology is especially hard to predict. It is difficult to say when a competitor might come up with a product or a process that makes your own obsolete. For firms that sell a standard product such planning may depend only on a forecast of sales. The Rustic Nail Company (see Figure 14.3) prepared its sales forecast primarily from government projections for the home construction industry in its market area.

Some steel producers have plants that are nearly obsolete because of recent developments in production technology. Yet these firms compete with foreign steel producers whose plants, in many cases, are newer and

Figure 14.3
A sales forecast for the Rustic Nail Company

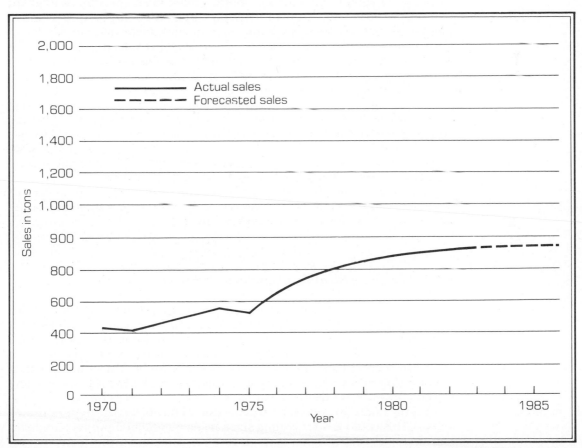

use the latest equipment and techniques. The capital budgeting problem in this case is to find sources of funds to enable the firm to update plant and equipment.

Consider the great technological changes that have occurred in the airline industry. The propeller-driven airplane has been replaced by jets; airlines are now opting for more fuel-efficient, less noisy aircraft in making fleet additions. An airline must face the possibility that even recently bought planes will soon become obsolete. If they do, a decision must be made whether or not to replace them and, if so, with what. Some airlines did not place orders for the Boeing 747 for some time after it was introduced. Fuel costs have since caused some airlines to reduce or stop their use.

Each decision depends on the expected payoff from this type of capital investment. Such decisions call for expert planning in the use of long-term capital. In some cases, firms will avoid the risk of long-term asset purchase by resorting to leasing.

The Alternative of Leasing

lease

One way of avoiding the need for long-term financing for land, buildings, or equipment is to lease them. **A lease is an agreement to grant use of an asset for a period of time in return for stated regular payments.** Leasing such assets has several advantages over the choice of borrowing funds for their purchase. First, it reduces the outstanding debt of the firm. Secondly, leased equipment may be replaced with more modern equipment without the losses which result from replacement of owned equipment. Thirdly, it is often a tax advantage to lease. The entire lease payment is tax deductible.

The decision to lease, however, is not always so obvious. There are advantages to outright ownership. Often the cash payments on a lease are considerably higher than the equivalent financed purchase payments. Also, there are often restrictions on the way a firm might use or modify leased assets. Such restrictions don't apply to owned equipment.

A bank or a manufacturer often leases computer equipment instead of buying it. Such leasing can be viewed as a "source of long-term funds" rather than as an alternative to borrowing.

Evaluating and Selecting Sources of Funds

Once a financial manager determines the needs for short- and long-term funds, the question is, "who will provide them?" For some firms there is little choice. For most, however, there is some choice of sources of funds. The basic choice is between debt financing and equity financing.

debt financing

Debt financing is the use of borrowed funds. This could mean a major corporation issuing bonds or it could mean a barber shop borrowing $1,000 for sixty days from a local bank.

equity financing

Equity financing means the provision of funds by the owners themselves. This could involve issuing stock or using retained profits. Canadian non-financial corporations since 1970 have used somewhat more equity financing than debt financing. Less than one-fourth of the equity capital was gained through stock issues.

Criteria for Evaluation

maturity

There are several important features of financing which help a firm decide between the use of debt and equity. These are shown in Table 14.1. **Maturity is the factor of time of repayment. When a debt matures, it must be paid.** If funds are internal, they need not be repaid at all. If they are borrowed, the date of maturity (due date) may vary.

Equity and debt financing also differ in the way they affect the claims on assets and earnings. To issue bonds means that the new bondholders will get the designated interest payment before stockholders get any dividends. They have a prior claim on income. Bondholders also come first in the event the firm goes out of business. They are paid off out of the proceeds of the sale of the firm's assets before stockholders receive anything.

Still another factor in the choice of debt or equity capital relates to control of the corporation. If a firm issues more common stock and this stock is bought by newcomers to the firm, the original common stockholders may lose control over the election of the firm's board of directors. They might lose some influence over policy decisions. A bond sale would not run such a risk for the controlling shareholders.

Of course, the main reason businesses borrow in the first place is that they feel they can earn a higher return on borrowed dollars than the cost

Table 14.1   Five Crucial Differences between Debt and Equity Financing

Criterion	Debt	Equity
Maturity	Has a due date.	No due date.
Claim on income	The lender has a prior claim on earnings of the firm over the owners of the firm. This claim is fixed in amount.	The owners have no prior claim on earnings of the firm. They have a residual claim.
Claim on assets	The lender has a prior claim on assets.	Preferred stockholders have a claim prior to the residual (common) stockholders but after those of creditors.
Right to voice in management	Issuance of bonds or borrowing money from other types of lenders does not have any direct effect upon the control of the firm.	Issuance of additional common stock may result in dilution of control.
Income tax effect	Interest on bonds is tax deductible.	Dividends to stockholders are not tax deductible.

WHAT DO YOU THINK?

Should Interest on Home Mortgages Be Deductible for Federal Income Tax Purposes?

The purchase of a home is the single largest investment a typical household will make. Most Canadians want to own their own home; however, unlike homeowners in the United States, Canadians cannot deduct interest paid on a home mortgage from their income. On the other hand, the Canadian government has instituted a Registered Home Ownership Savings Plan under which $1,000 per year can be deducted from income if it is being saved in preparation for buying a home. Which system is most beneficial to the individual? What will happen to interest rates and house prices if a bill goes through the Commons making house payments tax deductible? WHAT DO YOU THINK?

---

or interest they must pay to their lenders. To improve earnings by borrowing is called *leverage.* Financial markets also play a role when a firm seeks new sources of capital. Sometimes there is a lot of money available to lend and sometimes there is not. The final selection is often a compromise between what management would like most and what suppliers of capital are willing to give.

A large firm that pays its bills on time and has a high current ratio is in the best position for selecting from among financing sources. Small firms may overcome the advantage of larger firms by building a good credit record and practising good money management.

Sources of Short-Term Funds

What are the sources of short-term funds? "Short-term" here means a period of one year or less.

Most firms need to borrow short-term funds regularly for many reasons. The most common reason is to meet working capital needs. Of course, the expected level of working capital needs may be largely financed from long-term sources, while temporary liquidity is provided by short-term sources. (See Figure 14.4.) The Klutz Corporation normally uses $10,000 in working capital (divided in equal parts among cash, accounts receivable, and inventory). Suppose there is a seasonal need to expand this to $15,000. This puts the firm in the market for $5,000 of temporary short-term credit. These funds are likely to be obtained either from trade creditors (open-book account), from bank loans, or from secured loans made by a variety of lenders. Let's examine these three sources.

Trade Credit

trade credit
Trade credit or "open-book account" differs from other types of short-term credit because no financial institution is directly involved.

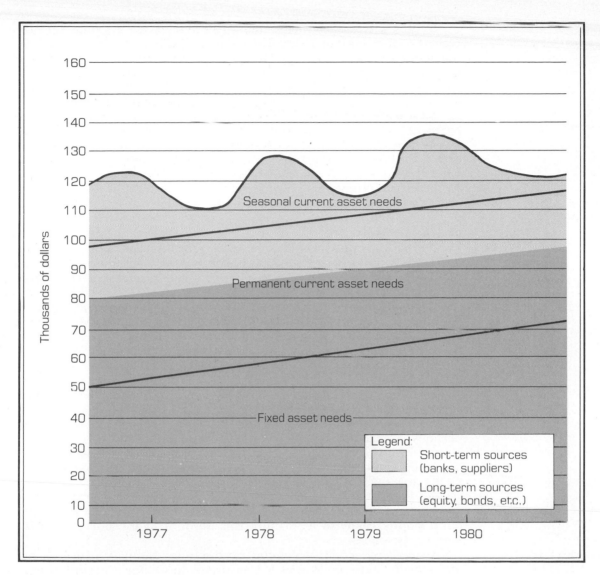

Figure 14.4
Asset needs and their financing by source

It is simply credit extended by sellers to buyers. To the seller trade credit means accounts receivable. To the buyer it means accounts payable. When one firm (manufacturer, wholesaler, retailer) buys materials or merchandise from another, the transaction is handled in open-book accounts. There are no complex credit papers. The buyer records a new account payable. The seller makes an entry showing a new account receivable. Nearly 90 percent of sales are handled this way.

In effect, the seller "lends" the buyer money for the time between receipt of the goods and payment for them. Without this type of credit, many firms could not survive. The same type of credit exists between the consumer and the retailer. When you "charge" the purchase of a TV on your account, the seller is really lending you money for a while. Instead of calling this an open-book account, most people call it a "charge account."

Most trade credit involves cash discounts for early payments. Invoice terms of "2/10, net/30" mean that the buyer can deduct 2 percent of the invoice price if paid within 10 days; otherwise it is due in 30 days. In other words, the buyer is "giving up" the use of the seller's money for 20 days for which the buyer earns a 2 percent discount. This is equal to an annual rate of 36 percent. Thus, many firms will often borrow from their banks in order to take advantage of cash discounts.

Chartered Banks

The bank, as we saw in Chapter 13, accepts time and demand deposits and lends a part of these funds to businesses for their short-term commercial needs. Banks are a popular credit source among smaller business borrowers.

Depending on the current balance between the demand and supply of commercial credit, bankers will adjust standards for lending. When money is short, bankers are likely to become more careful about those to whom they lend money. In any case, a bank will always check a new borrower's past credit record and ability to manage. The banker will screen loan applications also on the basis of the current ratio of the firm as well as on some of the other key credit ratios. The bank loan officer may obtain a credit report such as the one described earlier.

A banker expects that the loan will be repaid normally out of seasonal declines of inventories and accounts receivable held by the borrower. The bank and borrower must agree on four principal terms of a commercial loan: (1) the general nature of the arrangement; (2) the interest rate; (3) the quantity and type of security (if any); and (4) when the loan will be repaid. Firms that have a continuing need for funds from the bank often use a line of credit or revolving loans. **When a line of credit is set, the bank stands ready to lend up to this amount to the borrower with some restrictions.**

line of credit

revolving credit

A revolving credit agreement, on the other hand, is a very formal and specific agreement which guarantees funds for a period of time with strict rules limiting the borrower.

Secured Loans

secured loans

Many commercial loans to smaller firms and to firms with lower credit ratings are "secured" loans. Here, the lender is protected by a pledge of the borrower's assets. This also may be done by firms that have reasonably good credit records and wish to borrow unusually large sums or want favourable interest rates. Items pledged as security for loans may include accounts receivable, inventories, equipment, or stocks.

floor planning

A special kind of secured financing is called floor planning. An auto dealer who gets a shipment of new cars signs a note to a bank or other

THINK ABOUT IT!

Borrowing to Save Money

When a business manager bought supplies from Acme Paper Company, they sent a bill for $1,000 with terms of 2/10, net/30. He had the choice of paying $980 by June 10 or the full amount by July 1.

Since he had no spare cash, he went to the bank and talked to the vice-president. She of-fered him a loan of $980 for 20 days at an annual interest rate of 10 percent. Total interest cost was only $5.44 (20/360 × 10% × $980=$5.44). He saved $14.56 as follows by borrowing from the bank to pay the bill early:

Bill saving:	$20.00
− Bank interest	5.44
Net Saving	$14.56

financing agency for the amount due. **Title passes to the lender who pays the bill.** A trust receipt serves as a substitute for the actual asset. The bank holds the trust receipt for the cars until they are sold and the loans are paid. Chartered banks are also the major institutions involved in the use of the other credit instruments described in Chapter 13— promissory notes, drafts, acceptances, and certified cheques.

Other lending institutions used by firms for short-term financing include factors, commercial finance companies, and sales finance companies.

Sources of Intermediate-Term Funds

intermediate-term financing

Between the short-term borrowing period (one year or less) and the long-term period (usually ten years or more) there is intermediate-term financing. To fill this kind of need firms have begun to turn to a variety of sources. One of the more traditional sources has been the term loan from a chartered bank or an insurance company, usually accompanied by a promissory note and secured by collateral to protect lenders in case of default.

equipment trust certificates

Some firms have issued equipment trust certificates of five- to ten-year maturity. These are like short-term bonds backed by the equipment purchased with revenues from their sale. Such intermediate-term obligations have become a popular means of avoiding long-term bond issues at high fixed interest rates.

Other firms have avoided long-term commitments at high interest rates by turning to the short-term market. They are borrowing by means of short-term commercial paper and "rolling over." **Rolling over means successive renewals of short-term notes as a substitute for longer-term financial commitments.** This kind of "invasion" of the short-term money market by the long-term market stems from unwillingness to obligate firms to high fixed payments. When interest rates are very high, some financial

rolling over

experts feel that this practice if used extensively could bring serious troubles for the entire short-term money market. This added demand would drive up short-term interest rates.

Sources of Long-Term Funds

The sources available to corporations for long-term funds are much more numerous than the sources available to partnerships and sole proprietors. In any case, there is some choice between internal (equity) and external (debt) financing.

Sources for Corporations

Corporate long-term capital is available in the public market by means of stock issues and bond issues. As we have seen, there are several types of stocks and several types of bonds. Issuing preferred stock is a source of growth funds for corporations with stable earnings. Common stock is more likely to be issued when good growth is expected but earnings are considered to be unpredictable. The "new" common stockholder joins the "old" common stockholder on an equal footing. Depending on the relative size of "old" and "new" common stockholdings, the "old" shareholders may risk loss of, or reduction in, their control over the firm's affairs.

A corporation that needs additional debt financing for the long run may issue bonds. Firms have an implied right to borrow as long as it is done for the company's benefit.

sinking-fund

A major decision in a bond issue is selecting a method to pay off bondholders. The most attractive way for a strong, growing firm is by debt replacement—relying on the ability of the firm to exchange maturing bonds for new bonds or for stock. **In other cases, firms set up a sinking-fund to retire maturing bonds. This means putting aside money each year from profits to pay them off.** This is more likely to be done in a firm that is not expanding or that might find this investor protection feature the only way to attract bond investors. Also, using a sinking-fund will bring the interest rate on the bonds down.

A profitable firm has the option of using profits to pay dividends or to "plough back" into operations. This permits fixed asset growth without the use of money markets. It is a form of equity financing.

Common shareholders may or may not favour such financing, depending on their investment goals. Investors who view their shares as "growth stock" expect it to appreciate over the long run. They don't demand immediate dividends. Others invest for immediate income. They prefer to receive regular (and large) dividend cheques rather than have profits stay in the business.

Conflict often exists among shareholders concerning the "dividend vs. retained earnings" policy. Managers and shareholders may conflict on this point, too, unless managers are also shareholders. The availability of large amounts of capital is usually more attractive to managers than it is to shareholders. Retained earnings (a form of equity financing) has no maturity date and does not dilute managerial control as common stock does.

TWO POINTS OF VIEW

Stockholders Often Disagree

Stockholder A:

"Right, we will have to build a new production plant in the Western region in the next couple of years. But, the important thing is to finance it by issuing a new block of common stock. We've already got a pretty heavy load of bonds outstanding, and retained earnings just have not been large enough. Besides, if we put all of our earnings into expansion, we won't be able to pay a decent dividend."

Stockholder B:

"You're all wrong, buddy. Plant expansion should be financed by issuing $5 million worth of debenture bonds. That way, the chances are that common stockholders like you and me will be able to gain greater returns in the long run. The profits from the new plant will far exceed the cost of servicing the debt. This multiplies our earning power. It gives us leverage. Besides, to issue additional stock will dilute our control of the corporation. Let's use somebody else's money to grow. Maybe current dividends will be smaller than usual. I can wait."

Like common stock, retained earnings places no prior claim on income or assets. Financial managers are attracted to retained earnings as a source because they are not subject to the evaluation of the marketplace in their use of such funds.

Another outside source which has been available for long-term funds in recent years is insurance companies. Such companies have huge reserves to invest. They make these funds available, especially to large corporations, for long-term expansion at rates similar to, or somewhat lower than, those paid to bondholders.

Sources for Non-corporate Firms

Sole proprietorships depend on the personal funding of the owner-operator for equity financing. Partnerships have the same kind of limited source of funds except that there are two or more partners who may contribute fixed capital.

All forms of ownership may generate new funds internally if the firm succeeds. The amount available, in part, depends on the amount of retained earnings. In addition, the amount charged for depreciation of assets is "available" for current or long-term financing. Such equity capital is available for an indefinite period of time and has a subordinate (after creditors) claim on the firm's earnings and assets. It can lead to dilution of control of the present owners if a new partner is added.

PROTECTING THE FIRM'S RESOURCES

Owning and using resources leads to risk of many kinds. Risk is the possibility of loss. To protect these resources — to deal with these risks — is the third major task of a financial manager.

1. **Risk assumption:** Self-insurance against fire, theft, etc.

2. **Risk avoidance and/or reduction:** Sound business management enables the firm to avoid unnecessary risk (i.e., credit policies which grant credit only to persons with good credit records) and/or reduce risk (i.e., safety training to teach employees safe work habits).

3. **Shifting risk:** Shifting the risk to another party such as an insurance company.

Figure 14.5
How a business manages risk

Kinds of Risks

There are risks in everything and the degree of risk may vary greatly. In lending money, we risk loss. In buying things, we risk the possibility of defective merchandise. In running a factory, we risk liability for accidents to employees or visitors. In owning buildings and cars, we run risks of fire, vandalism, and theft. We risk that secret processes or designs will be discovered and risk the death of officers. All of these threaten the firm's resources and must be dealt with if the firm is to survive and prosper.

Self-Insurance and Risk Avoidance

There are three basic approaches to dealing with risk (see Figure 14.5). They can be used in combination. One is to assume it yourself. The second is to avoid or reduce it. The third approach is to shift the risk to others.

self-insurance

Many firms practise self-insurance of certain types. This means assuming your own risk and preparing for loss. If, for example, a large chain of shoe stores regularly sets aside a certain amount to cover the possibility of fire in one of its outlets, it is practising self-insurance. The idea is that, with a very large operation, some fire damage is bound to happen. Instead of paying insurance firms, the self-insurer pays itself.

Such a practice, of course, makes a firm very conscious of ways to avoid fires so as not to have to spend its reserved funds. It will install sprinklers, inspect heating systems, prevent unnecessary smoking in the stores, and take other steps to minimize risk. There are many other types of operational precautions a firm can take to reduce or avoid risks in different phases of its business.

Mechanized cash control systems help to protect against theft, as do basic cash audit procedures and regulations for writing cheques and making cash purchases. Related procedures provide for systematic purchasing (sometimes on a sealed-bid basis) to avoid losses because of favouritism in buying or commercial bribery. Usually, more than one signature is required for approval of purchases over a certain amount. Careful inspection of both quantity and quality of goods received also plays an important part in resource control.

Firms which deal in new ideas and processes must maintain secrecy. This includes careful personnel screening and constant development of employee loyalty. Also included are normal security precautions such as checking visitors to plants. Careful patent protection is another means of protecting this kind of resource from being copied by competitors.

There is always a danger that changes in market conditions will hurt a firm. A retailer may find some goods hard to move. To avoid losses, he or she may use one of several legal devices which allow the return of merchandise to the producer or wholesaler. We call this buying on consignment. To protect against sudden rises in the cost of needed supplies, a firm might have a policy of stocking up large quantities when the market is down.

Such protective measures complement the role of insurance, which is our next topic.

Shifting Risk and the Use of Insurance

Insurance companies assume the risks of their policyholders for a price. A firm pays a premium for a policy which pays if it sustains certain types of losses. The policy specifies the types of risks which are covered, the amount of coverage, and the premiums.

pure risk

The insurance company is a professional risk taker, but it takes only certain types of risks. Insurance is available only for pure risks. **Pure risks are those which offer only a chance of loss. There is no chance of gain.** Examples are risk of fire and risk of death.

speculative risk

Speculative risks are "gambles" in which there is possible gain as well as loss. This can happen at the racetrack or when one goes into business, where the quality of a new product or management may lead to profit or loss. Insurance is not available to deal with such speculative risks.

The federal and provincial governments are also in the insurance business. Their involvement is evident in such diverse programs as unemployment insurance, workmen's compensation, social insurance, crop insurance, and automobile insurance.

Firms deal with insurance companies for the same reasons that individuals do. Most homeowners, for example, carry fire insurance rather than bear the entire burden of the risk themselves. The same is true of firms. Insurance companies combine the risks of many policyholders — firms or individuals — into a group.

The Law of Large Numbers

Insurance firms study the past to see how many people die each year at age 50 or age 60 or at any age. They develop mortality tables from these facts. Mortality tables are used to predict the number of policyholders who

law of large numbers

will die in a given year. **This prediction depends on the law of large numbers. In other words, if the insurance firm has a large number of policyholders, it can pretty well predict how many of them will die in a year from the mortality tables.**

The same principle applies to other insured risks such as risks of fire or theft. Past experience and the law of large numbers give insurance firms a fair idea of how much they will have to pay out in claims. They set their premiums at a level which will allow them to cover expected claims as well as to cover operating costs and profit.

Of course, an insurer attempts to avoid writing insurance for a group if the peril (danger) insured against would damage all members in the group at the same time. For example, a fire insurance firm would not concentrate all its coverage in one section of a city. A major fire there could affect too many policyholders and could ruin the insurance firm.

The risk from the insurance firm's point of view relates to how accurately it can predict total losses within a group of policyholders. If the probable range of losses is great, the risk is great.

EXTRAORDINARY FINANCING ARRANGEMENTS

Sometimes, special conditions lead a firm to make extraordinary financing arrangements. These include devices for external expansion as well as the processes of recapitalization and reorganization.

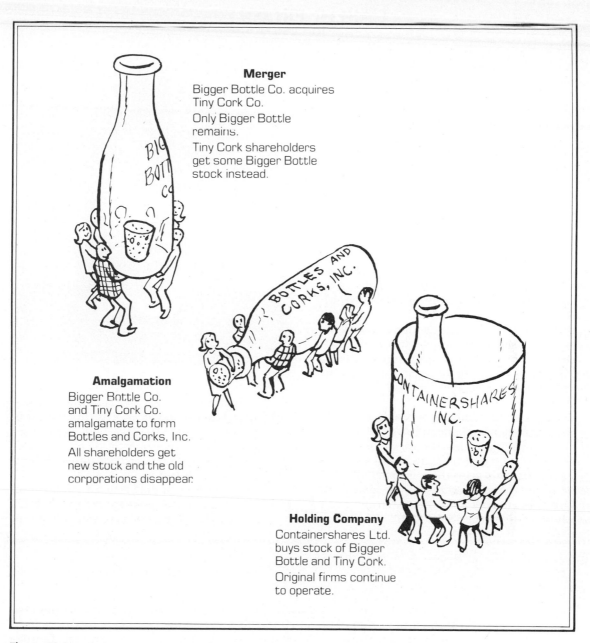

Merger
Bigger Bottle Co. acquires Tiny Cork Co.
Only Bigger Bottle remains.
Tiny Cork shareholders get some Bigger Bottle stock instead.

Amalgamation
Bigger Bottle Co. and Tiny Cork Co. amalgamate to form Bottles and Corks, Inc.
All shareholders get new stock and the old corporations disappear.

Holding Company
Containershares Ltd. buys stock of Bigger Bottle and Tiny Cork.
Original firms continue to operate.

Figure 14.6
Methods of expanding a firm

merger

amalgamation

External expansion can be achieved through merger, amalgamation, or the creation of a holding company. **In a merger one firm (the absorbing firm) keeps its identity, and another firm is absorbed and loses its identity.**

In an amalgamation both firms lose their identity. A new corporation is formed, and shareholders of both former firms receive stock in the new corporation in exchange for their old shares.

CAREER PROFILE

MY NAME IS CATHY CRANSTON. I AM THE Senior Operations Officer in a large branch of the Bank of Nova Scotia in Brandon. The Bank of Nova Scotia is, as you know, one of the five major chartered banks in Canada.

I have been working with the Bank of Nova Scotia for almost two years. Prior to joining the bank I earned a Bachelor of Commerce degree from the University of Manitoba. During university I held a variety of jobs including research assistant to the Premier of Manitoba.

As Senior Operations Officer of my branch I am senior to all employees except the five assistant managers and the manager. My job consists of three primary functions. I run the accounting department, conduct a daily internal audit, and am in charge of all the bank's collateral and safekeeping.

Running the accounting department involves supervision of six people. It also involves, in addition to recordkeeping and ensuring proper processing of daily work, the preparation of numerous reports for our head and regional offices.

Conduct of the daily audit requires that I see every transaction made in the bank the day after it is made. I sample from these thousands of transactions on an imaginative and selective basis to ensure that everything is being handled correctly and that all systems are in balance. To conduct this internal audit I must know what the job of everyone in the branch is, and what

their cash or credit limits are. I am the eyes and ears of the bank manager in this function. It is my job to make sure that the bank's interests are protected and to be constantly on the lookout to see if the ways we are currently handling activities can be improved.

Being in charge of the branch's safekeeping includes keeping the gold inventory and arranging the vault storage of very valuable items

---

holding company

A holding company owns the stock of one or more other corporations and controls the corporations. When the holding company is itself an operating firm, it is known as an operating holding company. Control can be exercised without majority ownership, by means of proxies. (See Figure 14.6 on page 507.)

recapitalization

Recapitalization occurs when a firm changes its capital structure to meet changing conditions. It does not raise more capital. It may involve replacing a high-yield preferred stock with a lower-yield preferred stock or floating a new bond issue to replace a maturing one. Sometimes a stock

for customers. I must also ensure that documentation and records of all negotiable and non-negotiable loan collateral held by the bank is correct. We must be sure that all the necessary forms are properly filled out and signed, because, if the bank ever gets involved in a court case, it is essential that the documentation be complete and correct.

Some types of problems I deal with on a regular basis include internal branch people problems, problems with other branches and regional and general (head) offices, and customer problems.

The most frequent problem involves dealing with people in the branch. We have thirty people in our branch and there are often situations where any one of them may have a problem or complaint. As an example, I deal with such situations as employees' concern about treatment at promotion time. I find that, even when I think I am communicating well to an employee, he or she may not feel that I am. I constantly have to strive to communicate well when answering questions from employees and providing guidance to them.

Dealing with regional and general offices involves a large volume of letters back and forth.

About once a week I get a customer problem to deal with. Often this involves a situation such as, someone has just walked in off the street and wants to cash a cheque, which we cannot cash because it is not drawn on our bank or on our branch. I ask the tellers and side counter staff to refer angry or irritated customers to me, because I believe that seeing a supervisor often calms customers down and

that staff should not have to deal with angry customers. In dealing with this type of situation I take the time to try to explain to the individual why we cannot cash his or her cheque. I also make a concerted effort to point out to them alternatives that will enable them to get their money. In most cases these actions satisfy the individuals. I always try to think of these agitated people as potential customers in our bank.

The most rewarding aspects of my job come from dealing with people and from learning more about my job every day. I love it when the people in the bank come to me with questions or problems and I am able to solve them. Every time I can answer a question that resolves a situation I feel good.

My experiences in the bank in helping my subordinates solve problems make me realize that this is possible because I learned how to learn and be resourceful throughout my university years. It is not because I am necessarily more intelligent than others working for me, but I have the initiative to learn and to do what is necessary to keep learning while some others do not. Because I want a career in banking I feel it is critical for me to keep on learning.

I am going back to school for an MBA. I have always intended to do this but felt I wanted and needed experience first. After I get my MBA I want to stay in finance and go back to the Bank of Nova Scotia. I will probably go back to a regional or general office position after my MBA to get experience in credit. Ultimately my goal is to get into an international banking position.

---

split is used to attract investors. Recapitalization often requires that the corporation amend its charter or receive permission from a provincial securities commission.

Firms go into debt (both long- and short-term) in the hope that they will be able to pay the interest and principal out of earnings. If this doesn't work out over the period of indebtedness, the firm is in trouble. A firm that cannot meet its maturing financial obligations is insolvent. **If, in addition, its liabilities are greater than its assets, the firm is bankrupt. Such a firm is said to be in bankruptcy.**

bankruptcy

PEOPLE WHO HOPE TO RISE TO A POSITION OF PRESIDENT OR CHIEF executive officer of a large corporation might be wise to consider a career in finance. Many chief executives in this country started in financial management.

Positions in finance include credit manager, financial analyst, and chief financial officer (comptroller or treasurer). *Credit managers* supervise the granting of credit to customers and establish criteria and procedures for evaluating credit applicants. *Cash-flow managers* oversee the cash position of the firm to assure liquidity and avoid loss of earnings on idle cash balances. They choose short-term investments. *Financial analysts* or *project analysts* study a firm's major capital investment decisions such as new plants and new ventures so as to maximize return on them. The *chief financial officer* supervises all of these activities and plans for security issues and major long-term borrowing. He or she helps set dividend policy.

All of these positions, with the possible exception of credit manager, usually require a university degree with some specialization in accounting or financial management. Persons who want to advance in the financial field must possess skills and aptitude for mathematical computation. They often start as financial management trainees. These people are shifted around various financial departments of the firm and often to various geographic locations. Information is available from the Canadian Bankers Association, Box 282, Toronto Dominion Centre, Toronto, Ontario M5K 1K2, and from the Financial Executives Institute Canada, Suite 409, 45 Sheppard Avenue East, Willowdale, Ontario M2N 5W9. ∎

Under voluntary bankruptcy, a person or firm files a petition in court claiming inability to pay debts because the debts exceed available assets. This petition asserts willingness to make all assets available to creditors under court supervision.

Under involuntary bankruptcy, a person or firm's creditors seek to have a debtor declared bankrupt by proving that the debtor committed one or more acts of bankruptcy as defined in the law. Once a defendant is declared bankrupt by the court, the procedure is the same as it was in voluntary bankruptcy.

SUMMARY AND LOOK AHEAD

The financial manager's job is complex and requires a variety of talents. One must be aware of present and future needs for working capital and fixed capital. Capital budgeting helps in performing this task. The financial executive must also evaluate and select sources of funds. He or she thinks in terms of maturity, claims against assets and income, and control of the firm when deciding how to get funds. For short-term funds, trade credit and banks are the major sources. Stocks, bonds, and retained earnings are the sources of most long-term funds.

To protect the firm's resources, a financial manager must think of ways to avoid, reduce, or shift risk. Insurance companies play a major role in risk shifting for firms as well as for individuals.

In addition to the ordinary long-term financing sources — retained earnings and stock and bond issues — extraordinary means for long-term financing are sometimes needed. These include external expansion devices and recapitalization.

In the next section we look at small business and international business. In the chapter on small business we will discuss how small businesses are started and some of the problems of small business management. In the chapter on international business we develop an understanding of how important it is for Canadian business to operate internationally. In addition, we discuss some of the details of conducting business internationally. ■

QUESTIONS FOR REVIEW AND DISCUSSION

1. Briefly explain why it is important to distinguish short-term financing from long-term financing.
2. What specific uses are made of working capital?
3. How can short-term notes payable be increased and how can they be decreased?
4. What factors may affect the supply of credit to a small manufacturer?
5. How do debt and equity financing differ in terms of their maturity? Their claims on income?
6. Describe two of the operational precautions that a firm might apply in order to protect its resources.
7. What is the law of large numbers? How does it relate to the size of insurance premiums?
8. Describe two types of property insurance.
9. How do investors' objectives influence their position on the question of adding to debt or equity capital?
10. What capital need is served by "open book account," or trade credit? Compare this source to the chartered bank.
11. Why can some firms use self-insurance while others cannot?

INCIDENTS

Wonder Petroleum, Ltd. Hikes the Credit Charge

Wonder Petroleum recently announced that they would demand of their dealers a 3 percent processing charge on all retail purchases made with Wonder credit cards. Considering the rise in credit card theft, and the growing rate of nonpayment by consumers, this action is not difficult to understand. The typical dealer is faced with the question of whether to pass this added cost on to the customer. The dealer must ask "is the luxury of credit purchasing worth this additional charge to my customers?" The dealer also must consider whether this added charge will go unnoticed in the face of past jumps in gas prices. The cost of credit is as real as the cost of gasoline and both of them are mounting.

Questions:
1. If the average customer can delay paying for gas exactly one month because of the credit card and pays the added 3 percent for that delay, what effective annual rate of interest is the customer paying?
2. Suppose the dealer absorbs the charge instead of passing it on. What effect does this have on his or her short-term capital needs?

Ms. Winthrop Barnes

Ms. Winthrop Barnes has been very successful in her small real estate sales firm. She has been earning a net profit of 20 percent on her investment for the last three years. She sees the opportunity for adding a branch sales office in a nearby smaller city. Profit opportunities there, she believes, are at least as good as in her present operation. She plans to sell $30,000 worth of bonds paying 14 percent interest to finance the expansion.

Questions:
1. Would you advise Ms. Barnes to sell the bonds?
2. What are the main reasons for and against the sale?
3. What are her alternatives?

CASE STUDY

CONVENIENCE AUTOMOTIVE

ONE FRIDAY IN EARLY JANUARY, 1979, MR. JIM TREVOR, vice-president of finance at the Convenience Automotive Company in Toronto, had to make a decision. The lease agreement for their warehouse was to end in three months, and the group vice-president

---

Exhibit 1

Reese's Offer to Sell:
Selling price: $3,650,000 (includes the land valued at $215,000). With one 20-year mortgage, the payments would be as follows:

Year	Interest $(000)	Principal $(000)	Total $(000)
1979	393.4	54.4	447.8
1980	387.2	60.6	447.8
1981	380.4	67.4	447.8
1982	372.8	75.0	447.8
1983	364.2	83.6	447.8
1984	354.6	93.2	447.8
1985	344.0	103.8	447.8
1986	332.2	115.6	447.8
1987	319.0	128.8	447.8
1988	304.5	143.3	447.8
1989	288.1	159.7	447.8
1990	269.8	178.0	447.8
1991	249.6	198.2	447.8
1992	226.9	220.9	447.8
1993	201.8	246.0	447.8
1994	173.6	274.2	447.8
1995	142.4	305.4	447.8
1996	107.6	340.2	447.8
1997	68.6	379.2	447.8
1998	25.3	422.5	447.8
	5.306.0	3.650.0	8.956.0

The mortgage agreement would also include:

a. An agreement that Reese will have the first choice to design and build any future additions to the existing warehouse.
b. An agreement that Convenience will buy from Reese, at cost, three other pieces of property across the road, valued approximately at $300,000.
c. Permission to use the mortgage for collateral security against other loans Reese might want to use.

Exhibit 2

Reese's Offer to Lease:

Yearly rent (as of 1979) — $344,200.

Term: 30 years

Escalation clause: An increase in yearly rent, every five years, equal to 25% of the overall five-year increase in the consumer price index. If, for example, over a certain five-year period, the CPI increases by 40%, then the increase in rent would be 10%. (The new rental rate would then remain fixed for 5 years.)

---

had asked Jim to come up with a suggestion as to whether they should continue to lease the warehouse or purchase it.

Convenience Automotive was a leading distributor of automotive hardware, sporting goods, building materials, and electrical supplies. The company had won acclaim and recognition throughout North America as a progressive and innovative organization, and in 1979 stood as a national distributor serving consumers and retailers from coast to coast in Canada. The company attempted to reach the consumer through more than 1,200 selected retailers, such as franchised automotive stores, building supply stores, and sporting goods retail specialists.

To effectively organize the flow of a vast variety and quantity of merchandise from the manufacturer to the consumer, Convenience Automotive operated two modern well-designed warehouse facilities. One of these was a 155,000-square-foot company-owned distribution centre. With growing sales and an increasing volume of merchandise handled, the company expanded its storage and distributing capacity in 1976 by leasing a second centre two miles away from the existing one. By the end of 1978, the total warehouse space had reached some 400,000 square feet, including the additional construction made on the leased facilities since 1976.

The rapid growth of the company and the need to secure a permanent warehouse location prompted Mr. Roscoe Brenton, group vice-president of Convenience Automotive, to explore the possibility of purchasing the leased warehouse. With this purpose in mind, in the autumn of 1978 he asked Mr. Peter Reese, owner and also architect of

---

Exhibit 3

Financial Highlights of Convenience Automotive for 1978:

Gross sales	$65,000,000.
Net income	1,170,000.
Per common share	2.00
Inventories	10,000,000.
Working capital	11,000,000.
Return on net worth	18%

---

the facilities, whether he would sell the premises, and if so, under what conditions. Reese's sales proposal is given in Exhibit 1. Reese was also agreeable to signing a long-term lease (see Exhibit 2).

Upon receipt of the proposals, Mr. Brenton asked Jim for an evaluation of the two alternatives. Knowing that the tax rate applicable to depreciation, interest, and lease payments was 50 percent, and that Convenience used straight-line depreciation with a warehouse useful life of twenty years, Jim was now faced with the task of evaluating the two alternatives and coming up with suggestions by Monday morning. ■

Section Seven

You can lose your perspective by thinking of business firms only as large corporations. Firms come in all sizes and dimensions. For many firms there is a need to "think small" and for others a need to "think international."

We will adjust our sight in Chapter 15 to take a look at businesses that are quite small and that have many problems peculiar to small business. We will also see that many opportunities exist for small business.

In Chapter 16 we will look at businesses that have an international perspective. There we examine the special challenges and opportunities involved in conducting business across national borders.

PERSPECTIVES ON THE SCOPE OF BUSINESS

After reading this chapter, you should be able to:

1. Explain, in your own words, the meaning of a "small-business firm."
2. List and discuss three ways a person might become a small-business owner.
3. Give two or more reasons why small firms can compete effectively with larger competitors.
4. Develop a "self-test" to find out whether you have the basic requirements to be a small-business owner.
5. Compare the benefits and burdens of entrepreneurship.
6. List and discuss the first steps in starting your own business.
7. Explain, in your own words, the nature of a franchise operation.
8. List and discuss the benefits of franchising to the two parties to a franchising agreement.
9. Develop criteria by which a person can assess the potential franchising offers as a method of doing business.
10. Compare the views of critics and supporters of government aid to small business.
11. Describe the kinds of government assistance which are available to small business in Canada.
12. Identify the challenges to survival faced by small firms.
13. Explain, in your own words, why a small firm's owner may want to seek growth of his or her firm.
14. Identify two or more ways by which a small firm might grow in size.

In reading the chapter, look for and understand these terms:

venture capitalists
Better Business Bureau (BBB)
Chamber of Commerce
economic development council
franchiser
franchisee

franchising agreement
Small Business Loans Act
Federal Business Development Bank
Counselling Assistance to Small Enterprises (CASE)

MURRAY PEZIM, A VANCOUVER financier, built up an equity of many millions of dollars by promoting and investing in junior mining stocks. His principal investment in the Hemlo mining operation was very lucrative. Nelson Skalbania and Peter Pocklington are other high-profile Canadian entrepreneurs who come to mind. Both have had periods of great financial success and have suffered some setbacks. Their activities, however, have provided inspiration for other entrepreneurs.

Each year thousands of new businesses are started by people who want to go into business for themselves. Only a relatively small percentage of them turn out to be successful and profitable, however. Despite this fact, the challenge and potential rewards of starting one's own business attract many Canadians.

CHAPTER FIFTEEN

Small Business

ALTHOUGH OUR DISCUSSION ON PRODUCTION, MARKETING, FINANCE, and so on in earlier chapters applies to all firms regardless of size, there are several aspects of small business that require separate treatment. If you have ever considered going into business for yourself, or if you already have done so, you will be especially interested in this chapter.

Most people who go into business for themselves start out in small businesses. A small business is a firm that is small in relation to its competitors. "Smallness" relates to such things as number of employees, dollar sales volume, funds invested in the firm, and so on. As we will see, it's hard to provide a definition of "small business" that would be meaningful and satisfactory in all cases.

We also discuss how and why a person might start a small business. Then we look at the pros and cons of going into business for yourself. After that, we take a close look at franchising, a way of doing business which has enabled many people to go into business for themselves. Finally, we examine the various ways that provincial and federal government agencies have become involved with small business.

In the end, a small-business owner's success (or lack of it) is the result of good (or poor) management. As you will see, it's still possible to make "big money" by going into business for yourself. On the other hand, it's just as possible to lose everything you have invested.

WHAT IS A SMALL BUSINESS?

In Chapter 3 we saw that there are thousands of sole proprietorships, partnerships, and corporations in Canada. Many of these firms are small businesses, but "small" is a relative term. For example, you might consider Home Oil to be a "small" company in comparison with Imperial Oil, but compared with many other business firms, Home Oil is very large.

At present, the federal government defines a small business as one where taxable income does not exceed $1 million for any fiscal year. However, there is no single definition of small business that is entirely satisfactory. Let's say, then, that a small business is one that can be started with a relatively modest investment of funds by the owner or owners. Of course, what is "relatively modest" is just that—it is relative to the industry in which the firm exists. Some industries, however, are made up almost entirely of small firms. Examples are barber shops, beauty parlours, sandwich shops, and so on. The concept of relative size in its industry has little real meaning in these cases. One simple way to resolve problems like these is to define small businesses as those having fewer than a certain number of employees, but so far there is no agreement on what this number is.

WHAT DO YOU THINK?

Would You Like To Be Your Own Boss?

To listen to a lot of people these days—and that includes some business teachers and textbook writers—you'd think everybody works for a big corporation. Of course, a lot of people do. But a lot find it much better working for themselves—running their own businesses.

Why not ask yourself this question: "am I better equipped to work for somebody else or to be my own boss?" Weigh the points on each side. Can you handle a lot of uncertainty? Can you come up with enough money to start a business? Do you have something to sell? If the answer is yes to all of these, then maybe you should start out on your own. If you value security, if you have a small bank account and no one to back you financially, if you don't have a strong, clearly defined service or product to offer, then go to work for an established firm.

Maybe you have only some of the things you need. In that case it might be a good idea to go to work for a small business. In this way you may learn a lot and earn enough to overcome your handicaps. Later you can start your own business—older, wiser, and richer. As somebody with a lot of sense once said, "making mistakes with somebody else's money is much easier to take than making mistakes with your own money!"

In addition to being small in size, a small business is usually localized in its operations. Its owner(s), employees, and customers often live in the same town in which the firm is located, although this is not always the case.

A small business is most likely to be a sole proprietorship, a partnership, or a family-owned corporation. Ownership and management are seldom separated; the owners usually run the business directly.

Becoming a Small-Business Owner

A person becomes a small-business owner in one of three ways:

•by taking over the family's business
•by buying out an existing firm
•by starting a new firm

Each way has its own set of problems and opportunities.

Taking Over the Family Business

Not too long ago, it was common for a father to train his son to take over the family's business someday. Usually, these firms were very small and employed only family members. The oldest son was expected to keep the business going after the father stepped down. This meant the father made the choice of occupation for his son. A grocer's son would become a grocer. A barber's son would become a barber.

During the twentieth century, this method of becoming one's own boss lost much of its appeal. Apprenticeship under the father generally has been replaced by formalized education.

Nevertheless, every year many firms are taken over by relatives of the former owners. In many cases the person taking over a firm is the spouse or one of the children. But this often is not planned in advance and makes it very hard for the person taking over, especially when the former owner is not there to help the new owner.

Buying Out an Existing Firm

Many people go into business by buying out an existing firm. In many cases an agreement can be reached whereby the seller helps the new owner learn the business from the ground up. It is good practice to have a written contract outlining the duties of ownership for the new owner.

Sometimes buying out an existing firm means buying it from a surviving spouse. This presents a different problem, since the original owner is not there to help the new owner get oriented to the firm. In many of these cases the surviving spouse has neither the desire nor the ability to continue the firm. This points out the need for a plan to continue the firm after the owner's death. However, many small-business owners never prepare such a plan.

A person might go into business with the intention of selling out after the firm becomes a going concern. Some companies are formed to buy out small firms which have good growth potential. Often, these firms give financial and managerial help to promising new firms and offer to buy them out. In some cases they "go public." This means that they become corporations and sell shares of stock to the public. Many investors want to buy stock in new ventures.

Starting a New Firm

In the previous examples the business owner takes over an existing business. It has an established customer base and is a going concern. A person who starts a new firm, however, must build a going concern.

A new firm is not troubled with many of the problems that accompany the takeover of a firm that has been in business for some time. There are no dissatisfied customers, no fixed plant or store location and layout, and no bad debts for a new firm. The owner has the opportunity to build the firm from the ground up.

Many young people today are turned off by the thought of working for somebody else. They want the personal direct involvement that is best achieved by being their own boss. Going into business may reflect a search for identity. In cities where universities are located there are small firms which were started by students who recognized profit opportunities. Examples are small clothing stores that cater to young adults, swimming pool maintenance firms, and home or apartment maintenance services.

Some universities now offer courses in entrepreneurship or in starting a new business firm. While some students don't have the money to start a business right after graduation, many want to do it after they gain the necessary funds and experience.

OPPORTUNITIES IN SMALL BUSINESS

There are countless opportunities for small firms to serve ultimate consumers and industrial users. Opportunity exists in manufacturing, agriculture, retailing, wholesaling, and even in the extractive industries. Each year many new firms are opened to exploit opportunity in those fields. Many start out as small firms.

The big question is: "how does a would-be entrepreneur learn how to spot opportunity?" It is partly a matter of being sensitive to the environment. One of your authors recalls a success story of a former student. This was just before the widespread popularity of pre-washed denim jeans. As a part-time salesclerk in a "jeans shop," the student recognized a growing preference for pre-washed jeans among young people. He wanted to try "something on his own," so he bought one hundred pairs of jeans from his employer. He had them washed by a commercial laundry so that they "looked old." He gave ten pairs free to college students to wear. They were asked to take orders from people who wanted the "new look" in jeans. The cost of the jeans that were given away, the laundering cost for one hundred pairs, and the commissions he paid to his "sales force" amounted to $845. His revenue on the whole deal was $1500, leaving a profit of $655. He now owns a very successful clothing store which caters to young men and women.

We could discuss many such "success" stories. What they teach is that opportunity always exists but hardly ever "knocks at your door." In a competitive economy you can be sure that it never knocks twice! Opportunity does not come to you. You must discover it!

Some people say that opportunity has all but dried up for small businesses. They argue that only large corporations can afford to hire the talent needed to spot trends and to capitalize on them. But "bigger" does not necessarily mean "better" as far as business is concerned. A large discount chain store can't give its customers the personal attention a small clothing

---

Table 15.1   Examples of Situations That Tend to Favour Small Firms

1. When a product does not lend itself to large-scale mass production, such as custom-tailored clothing and custom-made kitchen cabinets.
2. When customer convenience is more important than price and selection, such as in the case of small convenience food stores that offer late-night shopping and fast checkout to hurried shoppers.
3. When demand and/or supply fluctuates with seasons of the year, such as fresh produce that is harvested locally and sold at roadside markets by truck farmers.
4. When potential sales in a market are not large enough to attract a large firm, such as small communities that have many small retail shops rather than a major department store.
5. When large firms compete with each other for the big market segment and ignore one or more smaller segments, such as commuter airlines, which escape competition from major airlines.
6. When the product or service being offered requires a lot of personal attention to the customer by the seller, such as hair styling and funeral direction.

store can give. A big manufacturer with many products can't give any one of them the attention a small firm can give to its one or two products. A small firm is usually more adaptable than a large firm. It often can react to change a lot faster. Table 15.1 identifies several situations that tend to favour small business.

SHOULD YOU GO INTO BUSINESS FOR YOURSELF?

Let's assume for a minute that you want to become your own boss. You have a rich uncle who will lend you the money to get started. If that's not enough to tempt you, you also can assume that you have a product or service that will definitely lead to a good profit if you can succeed as a manager. Should you go into business for yourself?

Given these assumptions (and they may be very unrealistic), you still must evaluate a third vital input — you, the entrepreneur. Before you make your decision, you must consider your goals in life. Then you must determine whether you have what it takes to reach those goals.

The Basic Requirements

Ask yourself the following questions to see whether you have the basic requirements for starting your own business:

1. Are you afraid of risk?
2. Are you unable to put off enjoying the "good life" today because you are afraid you won't be here tomorrow?
3. Are you overly security conscious?
4. Do you have trouble getting along with people?
5. Do you lose interest in things that don't work out as quickly or as well as you thought they would?
6. Are you a thinker but not a "doer"?
7. Are you a "doer" but not a thinker?
8. Are you easily frustrated?
9. Do you have trouble coping in situations that require quick judgments?
10. Do you "cave in" under stress?
11. Does your family make heavy demands on your time?
12. Are you emotionally unstable?
13. Are you unable to learn from your mistakes?
14. Are you "too good" to do manual labour?

If you answered "yes" to several of these questions, you probably are not ready to start your own business. In any case, this sort of thinking is very important in deciding whether you have what it takes to be your own boss. If you do "measure up," then you can begin to weigh the benefits and the burdens of starting your own firm.

The Benefits of Entrepreneurship

Perhaps the best thing about being your own boss is the sense of independence you feel. You get a great deal of personal satisfaction from being directly involved in guiding your firm's growth. It is also possible to make a sizeable personal fortune. You not only draw a salary, but you also own the firm, the value of which may increase manyfold over the years.

Owning your business is also good for your ego. You are respected by others because you are not a "cog in a wheel." You *are* "the wheel"! For many people, achieving their true potential is being their own boss. Clearly there are personal, economic, and social benefits.

The Burdens of Entrepreneurship

Being in business for yourself, however, requires your full attention. You usually will not leave the office or shop at 5:00 P.M. Nor do you leave "job problems" at the office or shop. They follow you home as "business problems" and "business homework." This means you have less time for your family.

A person with very limited abilities may be able to hold a job in a large company by doing just enough to get by. Maybe others will cover up for his or her shortcomings. There is, however, no one to "carry" you when you are in business for yourself.

While you may not have to report to a boss, you often have to bend over backward for your customers. You have to contend with creditors, employees, suppliers, government, and others. In short, you are never completely independent.

When you work for somebody else, you may be paid a salary based on a normal work week of forty hours. If you work fifty hours, your pay will be greater (if you get paid on the basis of the number of hours worked). If you are a manager, your salary is based on a "normal work week," even if it is usually more than forty hours. As your own boss, however, you might work for many months and not be able to take a penny out of the business. Your profits may have to be reinvested to meet short-term demands for cash or for long-term growth. Thus, you may not be able to draw a salary during the period it takes to establish a truly "going concern." Many small-business owners fail to anticipate this when they start out. It is a major cause of new business failures.

STARTING A SMALL BUSINESS — THE PRELIMINARIES

It's a sad fact that many people who want to start their own firms do not do so because they just don't know how to do it. Some people think that there is so much red tape involved that you need a team of lawyers to start a firm. At the other extreme, some people open shops without even checking to see if they need permits or licences. Both views are wrong.

Starting a business always requires careful planning. In the following discussion, we will outline some of the steps in getting started.

Financing

Perhaps the most important step in starting a new business is estimating the amount of money needed to get started. Underestimating can result in failure to get the business off the ground. Start off with a ball-park estimate and refine it as you learn more about the business you are considering.

Projecting Your Financing Needs

A good starting place in estimating the amount of money needed is to draw up an overall business plan, setting your overall objectives and plans for accomplishing them. Focus on formulating specific plans for production, marketing, and personnel. For example, you should state the quantity and type of equipment you will need to manufacture your product, how the product will be sold, and how many employees you will need to get started.

The business plan is the basis for setting up a capital budget, which we mentioned in Chapter 14. This will give you a good idea of how much money you will need to acquire buildings, equipment, and other fixed assets.

You should also prepare a month-by-month projected income statement in which you forecast your sales revenues and operating expenses during the start-up phase of your business. A review of Chapter 11 will help in preparing these projected income statements.

Next, you should focus on the need for cash in your month-by-month projected cash flow statements. This may help you spot potential cash-flow problems.

As we saw in Chapter 13, money will flow into and out of your business as you carry on your business activities. Cash inflow comes mainly from selling your product or service. Cash outflows are necessary to pay for supplies, salaries, telephone, etc. Some of these expenses are start-up expenses that have to be paid only once. For example, you do not have to pay a deposit to the telephone and electric company every month. Other expenses, such as wages and supplies, are recurring sources of cash outflows.

The main element in estimating cash inflows and cash outflows is timing. You must meet your bills as they come due. It's a good idea to seek help from an experienced accountant. He or she can help you learn to use leverage to maximum advantage. Your accountant can show you that buying the equipment you need on time allows you to pay off the purchase price with cash inflow from your operations. Skillful use of trade credit also can help. If you are in a retail business, you may be able to buy merchandise from a wholesaler on credit and pay off the wholesaler with money you receive from sales of that merchandise to your customers. Your accountant will also point out the pros and cons of leasing equipment rather than buying it.

As a final planning tool, you should prepare a projected balance sheet to determine the projected net worth of your business at, for example, the end of the first year of operations. As we saw in Chapter 11, this will tell you what your firm owns and what it owes.

These projections of your financing needs will result in a ball-park estimate of the amount of money you will need to get started and survive the critical early years in business. It will also stimulate some serious thinking about the form of ownership your business should have.

Planning the Form of Ownership

We discussed forms of ownership in Chapter 3. Given the projected amount of money you will need to get started, can you realistically expect to be a sole proprietor, or should you consider taking in a partner or partners? If you decide on a partnership, for example, you should set the minimum percentage of ownership in the firm that you are willing to settle for. What about incorporating?

In most cases it is not wise to put all your personal assets into the business. Financial reserves, such as a personal savings account, are needed to help you get your firm off to a good start. Don't count on quick profits to help finance operations in the beginning. The firm may be in operation for one or more years before it shows a profit. And even then you may be taking out little or no salary from the business. Beginning entrepreneurs tend to *over*estimate sales revenues and *under*estimate costs.

Planning for Debt vs. Equity Capital

If you need more money to start up than you either have available or can borrow, you will probably decide to form a partnership or a corporation. In other words, you will seek equity capital. We discussed the relative advantages and disadvantages of equity versus debt financing in Chapter 14.

Venture capitalists can be an important source of equity capital for many new firms. **Venture capitalists are individuals or businesses that are willing to provide equity capital to entrepreneurs who have new products or new product ideas that are as yet unproven on the market but that have a good chance of becoming successful.** Some venture capitalists will help to finance the start-up of a new firm, while others are interested only in firms that have been set up and need additional financing for rapid growth. Venture capitalists often acquire a controlling interest in the firms they help to finance.

venture capitalists

Debt financing may be available to you from the various types of financial institutions we discussed in Chapter 13. In general, you will find that chartered banks are more conservative about making loans to new businesses than are some other sources.

If you cannot get a bank loan, you may be able to get a personal loan from a consumer finance company. Or you might turn to the growing number of small-business money brokers who arrange loans for their clients through various types of financial institutions, such as commercial finance companies.

Licences and Permits

Before you start operations, you must have the required licences and permits. Which ones you will need depends on provincial and city laws.

In many cities you will need a certificate of occupancy which certifies that your type of business is permitted in your location. For example, you could not operate a pet shop in a location zoned exclusively for single-family residences, nor could you set up a steel foundry in a location zoned "light commercial."

In most provinces you must get an occupational licence to engage in business or professional activity. These licences are usually available from the city in which the business is carried on. The cost depends on the type of business activity which is engaged in.

If your business deals with food, you will probably need a local food permit. These are usually issued by city health departments. If you plan to sell liquor or tobacco, you will also need a special permit. Requirements in this area vary considerably across provinces. If you wish to go into business for yourself selling door to door, you will have to have a local vendor's permit.

The best advice on licences and permits is to check with the local chamber of commerce or the provincial or city government. You may need more licences than you expect!

Sales Taxes

Most provinces collect retail sales taxes. In these provinces you must register with the department of finance in order to comply with the law. This permits you to collect the tax for the province.

Employer Taxes

If you hire employees, you must withhold federal and provincial income taxes as well as Canada Pension Plan (CPP) and unemployment insurance (UI) deductions from your employees' wages. You must also pay your own share of their CPP and UI.

Workers Compensation Insurance

If you hire employees you must carry workers compensation insurance. This covers employees who are injured or killed on the job. The premium is a percentage of your estimated payroll.

Information Sources

In starting your new firm, you may need more information on many aspects of your business. Of course, if you are in a large city, you will have access to more sources than if you are in a rural area or a small town. The following discussion covers some of the basic sources.

**Better Business
Bureau (BBB)**

Many cities have a Better Business Bureau (BBB). **A BBB is a nonprofit organization of business firms which join together to help protect consumers and businesses from unfair business practices. Businesses "police" themselves through the workings of the BBB.** Suppose you have doubts about buying from a particular supplier. You can call the local BBB to ask if any complaints have been filed against that supplier. If you have trouble with a supplier, you can file a complaint against that firm. It's a good idea to join the BBB.

Chamber of Commerce

Many cities also have a chamber of commerce. **The Chamber of Commerce is a national organization of local chambers of commerce in cities and provinces throughout Canada. Its purpose is to improve and protect the free-enterprise system.** A local chamber of commerce is a useful source of data on business conditions in that area. Active involvement in the local chamber can put you in contact with potential customers and suppliers.

**economic development
council**

Some cities have an economic development council. **An economic development council is an organization of business firms and local government officials. It seeks to further the economic development of the area in which it is located.** It is a good source of data on the local economy. In many areas local governments cooperate with local action groups to aid small businesses. A check of local libraries may help you find other information you may need in starting your business.

Business Insurance

Before you start operations you should have business insurance. Your selection of an insurance agent is an important step. The agent can give advice on the types of coverage you'll need in your line of business. But be sure to shop around for the best combination of price and coverage.

THINK ABOUT IT!

Cultivating Outside Expertise

Starting your own business takes a lot of planning. Running your business also takes a lot of know-how. Unlike most larger firms, however, your firm will not have a staff of experts for you to turn to on tax problems, insurance problems, legal problems, and financial problems. In fact, lack of expertise in these areas is one of the major reasons why some entrepreneurs fail.

Remember, you are not out "to do it all yourself" without any outside help. Often, whether you can get that outside help will be the main factor in your success as an entrepreneur. At the minimum, you should know an accountant, a banker, an insurance agent, and a lawyer you can turn to for advice in setting up your firm and guiding it through its early life. Take the time to cultivate this type of assistance from "outsiders." It can make the difference between success and failure. THINK ABOUT IT!

FRANCHISING

Franchising is not a form of ownership like a sole proprietorship or a partnership. It is a method of doing business. During the 1960s franchising became a very popular way of going into business for many people. Familiar examples are Holiday Inn, Pizza Hut, McDonald's, Midas Muffler, Radio Shack, and Canadian Tire.

franchiser

There are two parties in franchising. Each has certain duties or obligations and each receives certain benefits. **The franchiser is the firm that licenses other firms to sell its products or services.** The McDonald's Corporation is a franchiser.

franchisee

The party that is licensed by the franchiser is called the franchisee. **A franchisee has an exclusive right to sell the franchiser's product or service in his or her specified territory. Each franchisee is an independent business owner.** The McDonald's Corporation licenses independent franchisees to make and sell McDonald's hamburgers. Each franchisee pays an initial fee and yearly payments to the McDonald's Corporation for the right to use the McDonald's trade name and to receive financial and managerial assistance from the franchiser.

franchising agreement

The franchiser and the franchisees are related to each other through the franchising agreement. **A franchising agreement is a contract between a franchiser and its franchisees which spells out the rights and obligations of each party.**

Many fast-food franchisers are owned by parent firms in the food and beverage industries. For example, PepsiCo owns Pizza Hut; Pillsbury owns Burger King; and Heublein owns Kentucky Fried Chicken.

Franchising and the Franchisee

Among the potential benefits of franchising to franchisees are:

•franchisee recognition
•standardized appearance and operation
•management training and assistance
•economies in buying
•financial assistance
•promotional assistance

Recognition

A person who wants to go into business in the fast-growing services industry (such as the fast-food industry) will run into many obstacles. Perhaps the most important one is becoming known. A new Joe's Hamburger Joint just doesn't have the instant recognition that Joe Jones would get as a McDonald's franchisee.

Standardized Appearance and Operation

A franchiser enjoys widespread consumer recognition because the units are all basically alike. A Midas Muffler shop in Winnipeg is very similar in appearance and operation to one in Toronto. The franchiser usually provides the franchisee with a blueprint for constructing a building which will be just like all other franchised outlets.

The franchiser also insists on standardized operation of all outlets. These are spelled out in the franchiser's operations manual and are backed up with standardized forms and control procedures so that all outlets look and operate alike. This is important in a society where people are highly mobile. A newcomer to a town feels a lot safer about buying a McDonald's hamburger than he or she might feel about eating one at Joe's Hamburger Joint. A traveller is more relaxed about staying at a Holiday Inn than he or she might be about staying at the Three Pines Motel.

Management Training and Assistance

A major reason why many small firms fail is the owner's lack of management skills. Many franchisers operate training schools where franchisees learn business skills like record keeping, buying, selling, and how to build good customer relations. Ongoing training is also important. Many franchisers send representatives to give their franchisees advice and assistance. Franchisees with special problems can turn to the franchiser for help. Thus, franchisees are not left entirely on their own in managing their businesses.

Economies in Buying

A franchiser either makes or buys ingredients, supplies, parts, and so on in large volume. These are resold to franchisees at lower prices than they would pay if each of them made or bought them on their own. In the past some franchisers required franchisees to buy their supplies from them. Even if a franchisee could get a better deal from another supplier, he or she had to buy from the franchiser to keep the franchise. This is no longer legal. A franchisee who can get a better price without sacrificing quality can buy from any supplier.

Financial Assistance

A franchisee can get financial assistance from the franchiser to go into business. Usually, a franchisee puts up a certain percentage of the cost of land, building, equipment, and initial promotion. The rest is financed by the franchiser, who is paid back out of revenues earned by the franchisee. The franchising agreement spells out the amount of financing the franchiser will provide and the terms of repayment. The franchiser also provides working capital by selling to franchisees on account.

In some cases the two parties agree on a joint-venture arrangement. The franchisee does not pay back the money put up by the franchiser. Instead, the franchiser becomes a part owner of the franchisee's business.

Finally, a franchisee may find local banks more willing to grant loans than if he or she were completely on their own. Bankers know that a reputable franchiser will license only dependable franchisees and will help them to be successful.

Promotional Assistance

Franchisers usually supply their franchisees with various types of promotional aids. These include in-store displays, advertising mats for use in

CAN YOU SETTLE THE ISSUE HERE?

How Independent Is a Franchisee?

David Darren has been a franchisee of a large franchiser in the fast-food field for the past three years. David's business has been very successful. He has had a good working relationship with the district representative of the franchiser, Rachel Petersen. David always consulted Rachel on important business matters and followed her advice on running his business.

Last week, David had lunch with his nephew, Sam. Sam is a college student majoring in business. He wants to go into business for himself after he finishes school.

When David told Sam about the terrific opportunities in franchising, Sam reacted rather negatively. "But, Dave, you're not your own boss. You're pretty much the same as a store manager—just like the person who manages a Loblaws or a Safeway. The only differences are that franchisers make you think you're boss and make you risk your own money. You really work for them—you're an employee, not an independent businessperson." David was somewhat upset by Sam's assessment. CAN YOU SETTLE THE ISSUE HERE?

---

local newspaper advertising, radio scripts, publicity releases, and many others. Franchisers also help them develop their promotional programs.

Franchising and the Franchiser

Among the potential benefits of franchising to franchisers are:

- franchiser recognition
- promotion
- franchisee payments
- motivation
- attention to detail

Recognition

A franchisee benefits from being able to use the franchiser's name and products at his or her location. The franchiser benefits by expanding the area over which the trade name is known. A franchiser can achieve national, and perhaps international, recognition much faster than if he or she were to do it alone. This increases the value of the franchise to both parties.

Promotion

A local franchisee pays a lower rate for newspaper advertising than a national franchiser. By sharing the cost of advertising, the franchiser and the franchisee both benefit. This is called cooperative advertising. Also, by using local radio and TV advertising in his or her franchise areas rather than blanket network coverage, the franchiser may avoid wasted coverage—

advertising in areas that don't have a franchisee. There are benefits from "localizing" promotion to suit customer tastes in a given area or to tie in with local events. Furthermore, a franchisee can promote the business as being locally owned. This may give the franchisee a competitive advantage over chain-store operations in some areas.

Franchisee Payments

The franchising agreement sets out the amount and type of payments which the franchisee will make to the franchiser. Sometimes the franchisee pays a royalty based on monthly or annual sales. In some cases the fee is fixed at a certain amount and is payable monthly or annually. Often the fee is determined on the basis of the market size in the franchisee's territory. In still other cases a combination of these methods is used. Less frequently, the franchiser gets only a one-time payment from the franchisee. Also, keep in mind that franchisees increase the funds available to a franchiser for expansion purposes through their payments of fees.

Motivation

Some large chain stores have trouble recruiting and developing well-motivated store managers. These hired managers are not independent business owners. Franchisees are their own bosses. Their profits belong to them. A franchisee is, therefore, more likely to accept long hours and hard work than a hired manager.

Attention to Detail

The headquarters of a chain-store operation must keep payroll, tax, and other records on all its units. It must be concerned with local laws regarding sales taxes, licences, permits, and so on. In a franchise operation, keeping records and complying with local laws are the job of local, independent franchisees.

Franchising and You

Do you have a future in franchising? The answer depends on your willingness to work, your ability to find a good franchise opportunity, and your ability to buy into the operation. Many independent business owners have been very successful as franchisees.

There are, however, some possible drawbacks. Franchising has become a "get-rich-quick" scheme for some "fast" operators. These fast-talking promoters will try to develop a franchise operation around practically anything. If you are thinking of becoming a franchisee, check into the franchiser's reputation for honesty and record of past performance.

Also, carefully read and take time to understand any proposed franchising agreement. Some make promises which the franchiser cannot fulfill. Don't be in a rush to "sign up before someone else does." Look for clauses that might permit the franchiser to buy you out at his or her discretion. If necessary, consult a lawyer to help you understand the proposed agreement.

Look out for oversaturation (too many firms) in that particular type of operation in your area. This is why location is so important. Show-business people and gimmicky promotions are poor substitutes for facts about market potential in a given location. Some of the best-promoted franchises have failed because they were poorly conceived.

Fortunately, the "franchising fever" of the 1960s has died down. But, as in any type of investment, franchising has its risks and rewards. On balance, however, it still offers a lot of promise to would-be-entrepreneurs. But don't be sold on the rewards without considering the risks. Be careful! Ask for the names and addresses of current franchisees. Talk to them. They can give you more objective insight. But don't be all-trusting here, either. They might be looking for someone to sell out to!

GOVERNMENT AND SMALL BUSINESS

Throughout our history the small-business owner has been admired and respected. The entrepreneurial spirit is most closely associated with the small-business owner's dedication to thrift and hard work. The owner realizes the dream that anybody can become their own boss if they can get enough money to start a firm and keep it going through hard work and know-how.

During this century, however, several basic changes took place in our economy, and many Canadians lost sight of the dream of going into business for themselves. For many, "making a living" meant going to work for someone else. Growing aversion to risk and the high failure rate among small businesses led many Canadians to reject the role of the entrepreneur.

Recently governments at both the federal and provincial levels have become more involved in programs to assist small business. These programs and agencies have given substance to the belief that small business should be encouraged. They are also partly intended to ensure that the economy is not exclusively controlled by large firms.

Critics of government assistance to small business say that the government should not equate preserving competition with preserving the number of competitors. They suggest that if a small firm cannot survive without the government's help, it should fail. They say that, although everyone has a right to go into business, no one has a right to expect the government to

WHAT DO YOU THINK?

Is the Entrepreneurial Spirit Declining in Canada?

A lot has been said during recent decades about the decline of the entrepreneurial spirit in Canada. Some people believe that it has not only declined but is "deathly ill." Others see a revival of the entrepreneurial spirit during very recent years. They argue that it is "alive and well. WHAT DO YOU THINK?

help him or her to start a business or to stay in business. The Canadian taxpayer has little to gain, they argue, by subsidizing business.

The argument that preserving competition does not mean preserving the number of competitors is rejected by most small-business owners. They believe that big firms want to reduce the number of competitors by setting their prices so low that small firms cannot make a profit. A firm that sells one hundred different products can sell one of them at a price that only covers cost. It can make its profits on the other ninety-nine. A small firm that sells only one product can't do this. Yet, when the small firms are run out of business, the large firm can raise its price back to a high level. In other words, small businesses feel that competition laws are not enough.

Government Financial Assistance

Unlike the United States where small-business assistance is federally coordinated through the Small Business Administration, in Canada separate federal and provincial organizations exist to help small-business owners. These are examined below. (Additional information is provided in Chapter 19 in the section on incentive programs.)

Federal Government Assistance

Federal assistance is available in both the financial and management areas. **The Small Business Loans Act helps proprietors get loans to purchase and/or update fixed assets and to improve facilities in general.** The government places a ceiling on the amount which will be loaned ($50,000) as well as a time limit on the loan (ten years maximum). **The Federal Business Development Bank also encourages loans to small business by charging increasingly higher interest rates as the amount borrowed increases.** This encourages small businesses, because, with their relatively small needs, they receive the lowest interest rates. The Income Tax Act allows all Canadian-controlled private corporations (many of which are small) to pay a low tax rate on the first $150,000 income per year.

As far as management aid is concerned, firms with less than seventy-five employees are eligible to use the Counselling Assistance to Small Enterprises (CASE) services. The CASE program is designed to help owner-managers more effectively manage their business in all areas, not simply the financial end of the organization.

Provincial Assistance

In addition to federal aid, each province has passed legislation or formed agencies to aid small business. This aid varies widely from province to province, but the aim is always to encourage small-business activity. Some examples of provincial aid are as follows:

1. *The Enterprise Development Group of Manitoba* is designed to specifically assist the 83 percent of all firms in the province that have fewer than fifty employees. Help is provided in areas such as

**Small Business
Loans Act**

**Federal Business
Development Bank**

**Counselling Assistance
to Small Enterprises
(CASE)**

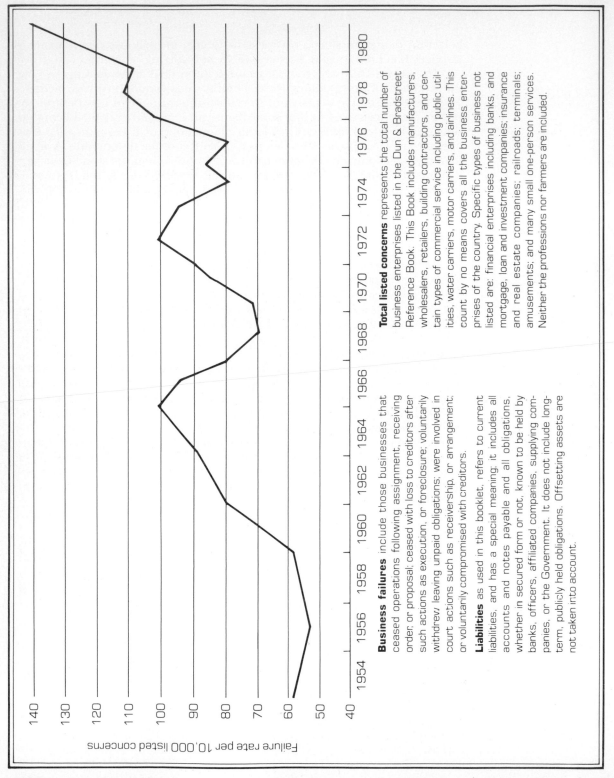

Failure rate per 10,000 listed concerns

140 130 120 110 100 90 80 70 60 50 40

1954 1956 1958 1960 1962 1964 1966 1968 1970 1972 1974 1976 1978 1980

Business failures include those businesses that ceased operations following assignment, receiving order; or proposal; ceased with loss to creditors after such actions as execution, or foreclosure; voluntarily withdrew leaving unpaid obligations; were involved in court actions such as receivership, or arrangement; or voluntarily compromised with creditors.

Liabilities as used in this booklet, refers to current liabilities, and has a special meaning; it includes all accounts and notes payable and all obligations, whether in secured form or not, known to be held by banks, officers, affiliated companies, supplying companies, or the Government. It does not include long-term, publicly held obligations. Offsetting assets are not taken into account.

Total listed concerns represents the total number of business enterprises listed in the Dun & Bradstreet Reference Book. This Book includes manufacturers, wholesalers, retailers, building contractors, and certain types of commercial service including public utilities, water carriers, motor carriers, and airlines. This count by no means covers all the business enterprises of the country. Specific types of business not listed are: financial enterprises including banks, and mortgage, loan and investment companies; insurance and real estate companies; railroads; terminals; amusements; and many small one-person services. Neither the professions nor farmers are included.

536

small-enterprise development, existing enterprise improvement, human resource management, and marketing.
2. *The Alberta Opportunity Company* is designed to facilitate economic growth by establishing new businesses in the province. A wide variety of profit-oriented businesses are eligible for both financial and management counselling assistance.
3. *The Industry Development Branch of Saskatchewan* encourages new business formation in the manufacturing, service, distribution, and processing industries. The Development Branch does this by locating and evaluating development opportunities and providing information on the province's economic climate.

SURVIVAL OF THE SMALL FIRM

Each year many new and old firms go out of business because they cannot meet the competition. Most of these failures are small businesses. (See Figure 15.1.)

The Struggle to Survive

Small firms are often thought to be at a disadvantage in the struggle to survive. Larger firms use banks as a source of short-term funds. These firms usually make ninety-day loans. They can borrow from other lenders, such as insurance companies, for longer-term capital needs. They also can issue more stocks and bonds. Small firms, for the most part, depend mainly on their local bankers for borrowed capital.

A small firm's loan may take as long as ten years to repay. This, by itself, makes the small firm's loan risky. Thus, small firms pay higher interest rates than larger firms. Their loan requests are more closely checked to see if they can meet monthly loan payments. Whereas a larger firm can shop around for a low interest rate, a small firm usually has to deal with a local banker. This is why the small business owner's relationship with his or her banker is so important.

Government loans are vital to small firms' survival. But some small-business owners argue that these have a negative side. Because they are easier to get than loans from banks, some business owners tend to borrow too much. This may overburden the firm with loan repayments and lead to a strain on working capital.

Challenges to Survival

Clearly, a small firm faces many challenges to its survival. A major one is lack of funds. Too many firms are started on a shoestring. Often, the owner realizes too late that more funds are needed to stay in business.

Figure 15.1
Business failures. (Reprinted by permission from the Canadian Business Failure Record, 1982, Copyright 1982 by Dun & Bradstreet Canada Ltd.)

A firm which starts off with too much money tied up in fixed assets runs into a shortage of working capital. Too much money tied up in plant and equipment leaves little working capital to finance accounts receivable, pay off trade creditors, and maintain adequate inventories. But if a firm can't manage these, it will go out of business.

Small firms also find it hard to estimate and control expenses because they lack the advanced cost control methods and accounting procedures of larger firms. Also, small firms ordinarily don't have dependable data on the market potential for their products and services. Too often a "sure thing" turns into a disaster in terms of sales. In other cases the owner may be content with a sales volume that is well below potential.

Sometimes the owner pays himself or herself too much salary. Living too high on the firm's profits robs it of funds needed for growth. This is why self-discipline and a proper outlook are so vital to small-business success.

GROWTH OF THE SMALL FIRM

Owners of many small firms tend to "think small." This is especially true when an entrepreneur goes into business "to escape" from having to work for someone else. Many small firms are started by people whose primary motivation is to escape the "rat race." Many of them don't really want their own firms to go through "growing pains." After all, they had enough of working for growth-oriented larger firms. This is especially the case when entrepreneurs are past middle age when they start out in their own firms.

TWO POINTS OF VIEW

The Fear of Failure

Some people believe that business failures represent a tremendous waste of resources. Buildings and stores become vacant, bank loans are not paid off, employees are laid off, tax collections go down, and the entrepreneurial spirit dies. Some of these people believe that government should control the entry of entrepreneurs into business. For example, before a person could open a clothing store, he or she would have to apply for and receive permission from the local government. This permission would be granted only if there is a demonstrated need for this proposed business firm in the community. This, they say, would at least increase the chances of success and reduce the social and personal costs due to business failures.

On the other hand, some people believe that government control of entry into business would destroy the free-enterprise system. These people are especially upset with the notion that a business failure is a disgrace. Sure, nobody goes into business to fail. But a failure, according to them, is not totally bad. Entrepreneurs can and do learn from their failures. A business failure is not necessarily a personal failure. If everybody were afraid to fail, we would not enjoy the high standard of living we have in Canada.

To many, starting and running their own firms amounts to little more than a hobby or something they "have to do" to prove that they can do it.

There is nothing wrong with wanting to remain small. But there are many reasons why small-business owners should consider the benefits of a planned strategy of growth.

Why Seek Growth?

A firm which offers only one service or product is in deep trouble if demand for its product or service falls off sharply. It may have to close down. All its eggs are in one basket.

Growth may enable a firm to achieve the benefits of specialization and economies of scale. There are always fixed costs connected with operating a firm, and by expanding production and sales these fixed costs may be spread out over a greater volume of output. Putting on two shifts of workers, for example, may enable the plant to operate more efficiently. This may help the small firm to be more competitive with larger firms. But the wisdom of any approach to growth depends mainly on the owner's skill and vision.

A small firm that seeks to grow may provide greater motivation to its employees. New chances for promotion arise. This may reduce labour turnover. Aggressive and growth-oriented employees don't want to work for a firm that is not growing.

Of course, there is the chance for greater profits from growth. Because business opportunity is dynamic, a firm should also strive to be dynamic.

Many small firms are started by people who want to sell out to someone else eventually, maybe to a larger, growth-oriented corporation. An aggressive strategy of growth may make this possible at an earlier date. The owner may also realize a big profit from selling such a firm.

A firm which doesn't grow may also find it harder to borrow money. The greater the competition among borrowers for loanable funds, the greater the disadvantage in being a "standstill" operator.

Growth Strategies

A small firm can grow in many ways. It can expand its present business. A small gift shop in a downtown location, for example, might expand by opening a branch in a suburban shopping centre.

Some small firms don't grow simply because they lack direction. Maybe the owner spends too much time running the firm and not enough time thinking about growth. Many small firms have been launched into aggressive growth strategies, including new lines of business, by bringing in some "new blood."

Merger is another way to grow. By joining together, two small firms might enjoy economic benefits and be able to exploit opportunity which neither could by itself.

CAREER PROFILE

MY NAME IS KEN ENNS AND I AM ONE OF THE two majority shareholders in Mycroft Business Computers, Inc. We sell Apple computers to individuals, small businesses, and corporations. We are ourselves a small business with a professional staff of five full-time and six part-time people.

After receiving my Bachelor of Science in Mathematics and Economics, I went to work for NCR as a junior programmer. I later worked as a data processing manager with a trust company and as a systems analyst for Computer Sciences of Canada. After analyzing the sales data for computers, my associate and I concluded that the retailing of small computers was the most rapidly expanding approach to selling microcomputers, so we set about registering a corporate name, choosing office space, and negotiating supplier agreements. Our target market is business firms because all of our experience was in that area.

While my main function in our company is that of systems analyst (the evaluation of customer requirements and the matching of those

Seeking new customers is always a way to grow. Two often overlooked sources of customers for small firms are government contracts and export sales.

Of course, there are other avenues to growth. The approach that is best for a firm depends on its resource strengths and weaknesses and on its environment.

Survival of the Fittest

Even with government help most small firms find it hard to survive. "Survival of the fittest" is the rule of the game. Unfortunately, not all entrepreneurs realize the need for good management or possess enough management skills. To survive, an entrepreneur must constantly be alert to new opportunities and be careful about spending. Creativity, determination, careful planning, and a willingness to work are the keys to survival.

needs to a system of hardware and software), I wear several hats: secretary, shipper, salesman, janitor, payroll clerk, etc. Needless to say, these duties do not fit into a nine-to-five day. A venture of this kind requires the patience and understanding of one's spouse and banker. In the absence of ready cash, a friendly banker is a definite asset. However, as friendly as one's banker may be, he or she will still demand collateral before loaning any money!

We have experienced several typical problems during the first few years of operation. These include maintaining just the right amount of inventory (not too much or too little), keeping our cash flow going in the right direction, and keeping our sales up. We must also deal with a constantly changing product. Advancing technology and the rapid growth in our market ensures that what sells today will be obsolete in several months. Maintaining enough knowledge of our product in order to support it is a full-time job in itself. In a company the size of ours, this places considerable strain on our staff, who are required to exercise almost the same amount of flexibility that we as owners demand of ourselves. Coupled with the above is what I see as our most unique challenge: maintaining our separate identity in the middle of a growing number of small computer stores. We do not want to be seen as just another "hamburger restaurant." While computer awareness is fast increasing among the general public (to the point where people will shortly be able to select the right program to go with the right hardware for themselves), we supply what amounts to a free consulting service to our clients in an effort to ensure their long-term satisfaction and our good reputation.

This brings me to the "plus" side of our business: the rewards from and satisfaction in owning my own company. Having a good reputation in the business community is also extremely gratifying. This has taken us some years to develop and has cost us in terms of lost sales and foregone short-term opportunities, but a long-term benefit is the steadily increasing customer base. Any monies I earn beyond what I need for my living I look at as an indication of my ability to compete in a tough market. In summary, I would say that a reputation for competence, a positive financial picture, and being relative master of my own destiny more than offsets the work and risk of establishing one's own "small" business.

SUMMARY AND LOOK AHEAD

The entrepreneurial spirit is "alive and well" in modern Canada. Many Canadians, including a growing number of young people, want to start their own firms. The opportunities are there for those who can spot opportunity and exploit it.

But it takes work, know-how, and a determination to succeed in the face of chilling statistics on failures of new, small firms. Lack of funds and management know-how are the most often cited causes of failure.

There are possible benefits and definite headaches involved in going into business for yourself. The best approach is to be realistic in assessing them. Don't let the "dream" of becoming your own boss turn into a "nightmare."

We presented a summary of the first steps in starting a firm. Local requirements may differ, so you must study them carefully.

Franchising is still a growth industry. It provides good opportunities for those who want to start their own businesses, but it does not guarantee success.

The government helps small business in many ways by giving financial and managerial help. These agencies can help you to get started and to stay in business.

Small firms must face the challenges of survival and growth. Recognizing the challenges to survival is an important first step in developing the ability to survive. The same is true about growth.

In our next chapter we will look at international business. Here, too, there are challenges and opportunities for small, medium-size, and large firms. ∎

QUESTIONS FOR REVIEW AND DISCUSSION

1. What are some of the problems in defining "small business"?
2. What are the three ways a person might become a small-business owner? Discuss each.
3. What are the basic requirements for becoming a successful entrepreneur?
4. What are the benefits and burdens of entrepreneurship? Discuss each.
5. Briefly list and discuss the preliminaries of starting a small business.
6. Explain how a franchising agreement works.
7. List and discuss the advantages of franchising to an entrepreneur.
8. How does a franchiser benefit from a franchising agreement?
9. Discuss the types of federal and provincial assistance that are available to small business.
10. List five key reasons why a small business may have trouble surviving.
11. What are the potential benefits of a planned strategy of growth for a small business?

INCIDENT

Roger Bond

Roger Bond has always been very interested in business. In university now, Roger is an active member of several business and professional organizations.

In his third year at university Roger and two other student entrepreneurs (Kay Dobbs and Randy Pitts) formed a small business. They recognized an opportunity for a firm which could perform household cleaning chores for working couples who lived in apartment complexes.

The firm is called Janitoil. The advertising slogan is "Don't Toil. Call Janitoil." From a rather modest beginning, the firm now employs fifteen part-time student employees. Business is booming!

Roger, Kay, and Randy are now in their fourth year at university. They are thinking about making this a full-time business after graduation. They are considering franchising. They want to license entrepreneurs on other college campuses in Canada to offer the same service.

Questions:
1. Why do you think franchising is appealing to Roger, Kay, and Randy?
2. What advice would you give them at this point in time with respect to the attractiveness of the franchising opportunity they see for Janitoil?
3. What kinds of "problems" will the three entrepreneurs face if they decide to go into franchising?
4. Would you be willing to become a Janitoil franchisee? Why or why not?

CASE STUDY

WHITE WATER WATER SLIDE

YOU HAVE JUST RECEIVED THE FOLLOWING PROMOTIONAL MATERIAL from the White Water Group, a Vancouver-based firm which designs, manufactures, and constructs water slides. You are interested in undertaking a business venture in your home town, and intend to carefully evaluate the potential for a water slide park.

PROPOSED WATER SLIDE

Definition

A water slide is a recreational device which incorporates a flume of fibreglass construction. The flume is elevated at one end with a fall of approximately one in ten. The flume can vary in length to whatever the designer or owner desires. It can be straight or curved to fit the landscape. The flume is flooded with water at the top end to a depth of approximately 3 inches; the water cascades down the flume and carries with it the patron wanting to participate in a thrill ride.

At the top end of the flume is a receiving tub approximately $4' \times 8' \times 2'$ deep with steps at one end. The patron enters the tub down the steps and sits at the overflow of the tub where it enters the flume.

At the lower end of the flume is a receiving pool approximately 3½ feet deep where the ride terminates.

A cross-section of the flume is a U-shape approximately 3 feet deep and 3 feet wide with a semicircular bottom similar to an old-fashioned cast-iron bathtub, but elongated and without ends.

Function

The water is pumped to the top end of the flume from the receiving pool and circulated on a continuous basis. A portion of this is bypassed through filters and heaters to insure a clean and warm content.

Participants of this recreation pay a fee for the privilege of sliding down the flume.

Scope

An economic water slide could incorporate four flumes starting at a common platform and all terminating at a pool approximately $30 \times 30 \times 3½$ feet deep.

The location of such an enterprise should be in or near a centre that caters to tourism and/or in a location with a large population base. The entrance fee for those willing to participate is generally set on a daily or partial-day basis so that the participant can have many slides (e.g., $7.50 per day and $5.00 after 5:00 P.M.).

Requirements

Land: Approximately four to five acres, where climatic conditions are warm and favourable for ninety to one hundred days per year. This land could be hillside or flat and should have access by road and be serviced by water, sewer, electricity, and, if possible, natural gas.

The land will be divided for parking lot, building area, and water slide area.

If the land is flat, an elevated area will have to be created by either earth fill or timber and/or steel construction to support the raised end of the flume. Each flume will be approximately 450 feet in length. The support under these is a major consideration.

Service buildings include ticket booth, concession stand, changing rooms, shower area, plus accommodation to house the necessary pumps, water heaters, and filtration equipment.

Other optional property expenditures will include fences, blacktop parking lot, sidewalks, spectators' grandstand, landscaping, and the general beautification of premises. The complex may also feature a souvenir shop, arcade, mini-slides/pools, whirlpool, surfpool, sun garden, mini-golf, or other recreational devices.

MECHANICAL EQUIPMENT

1. Pump, preferably a vertical turbine design, capable of delivering 1000 gpm to each flume plus bypass water for heater filter. (4 flumes × 1000 gpm = 4000 gpm + 1000 gpm to filters and heaters total 5000 gpms.) Total lift of pump will be 55 feet to top platform plus pipe friction and valve losses, say, 65 feet T.D.H.

$$\frac{5000 \times 65}{3960 \times 82\%} = \text{Bhp.}$$

2. Driver for above pump can be:
   (a) single internal combustion engine of the heavy-duty low-speed type
   (b) double internal combustion engine of the heavy-duty low-speed type (smaller than (a) but with back-up possibilities)
   (c) single electric pump
   (d) double electric pump (smaller than (c) but with back-up possibilities)
   (c) multiple electric pump (i.e., one pump for each slide)

   The combustion engine alternative would be heat exchanger cooled with or without a clutch. Desired fuel would be natural gas, size up to 1000 C.I.D.
3. Boiler for pool heating. The boiler will be designed and built to be compatible to the engine. The exhaust gas from the engine will fire

the boiler and heat the shower water, mini-pools, and large receiving pool at no cost. With an electrically driven pump the water would be heated by natural gas, propane, or electricity.

4. Filter and chlorination equipment. Three swimming pool type filters will be required, each with reserve flow cleaning feature and adequately sized to filter the pool in less than two hours. A variable feed type hypo-chlorinator will insure the ultimate in keeping the local Department of Health satisfied with water quality.

COST

Assumption:	A four-slide site with approximately 1800 feet of flumes on 4 to 5 acres.	
Land:	Cost not included below. Values vary as to location; leasing may be considered.	
Complex:	Flumes and completed support system installed including earth	$ 425,000.00*
	Platform and walkways	30,000.00
	Main receiving pool	75,000.00
	Whirlpools (2)	60,000.00
	Mini complex (flumes included above)	50,000.00
	Mechanical including pumping, filtration, and heating installed	120,000.00
	Utilities, miscellaneous piping	25,000.00
	Service buildings +/−6000 sq. ft.	270,000.00
	Paving and grading	120,000.00
	Mechanical equipment for concessions	40,000.00
	Furniture and fixtures	40,000.00
	Landscaping and fencing	55,000.00
	Design, architectural, engineering, layout, and site supervision	100,000.00
	Signage	10,000.00
	Exterior lighting	10,000.00
	Miscellaneous contingencies	70,000.00
		$1,500,000.00

*Deduct $75,000.00 if hillside method used.

RETURN ON INVESTMENT

The foregoing described water park is capable of handling 2,500 patrons with 12 employees.

Income

Slide average per day attendance of—		
1000 patrons:	750 @ $7.50 day pass	$ 5,625.00
	250 @ $5.00 p.m. pass	1,250.00
Souvenirs and concession—$2.00 per patron		2,000.00
		8,875.00

Expenses

Advertising	600.00
Cost of sales — souvenirs and concession	1,000.00
Insurance (1.0% of gross)	69.00
Maintenance	100.00
Manager's salary	200.00
Supplies including chlorine	95.00
Utilities, water, gas, and electricity	200.00
Wages, 13 hours × 12 employees × $4.00/hr	624.00
Miscellaneous (business licence, garbage, telephone)	40.00
	2,928.00
Income before debt service	$ 5,947.00
Income for 100 days season	$594,700.00

The foregoing prospectus is predicated on four existing water slides; costs are current for 1982. Profits are also current. Return to shareholders, interest, and principal repayments were not considered. Income from lockers, arcade, and other features have been excluded.

In Canada, by using waste heat, as with the natural gas engine heat recovery boiler, a 50 percent write-off can be realized. In B.C., Provincial Tax is exempted on all waste heat recovery equipment.

CONCLUSION

Should land be available in the type of area suggested and at a feasible price, this type of project is a winner.

Questions:
1. What is your assessment of the potential market for a water slide park in your home town?
2. What is your assessment of the potential profitability of a water slide park?
3. How could you raise the money necessary to establish a water slide park?
4. Would you go ahead with this project?
5. Would you recommend to someone else that they go ahead with this project? ∎

After reading this chapter, you should be able to:

1. Give an example of why two nations would trade because of the principle of absolute advantage.
2. Give an example of why two nations would trade because of the principle of comparative advantage.
3. Differentiate between natural and human-made barriers to international trade.
4. List and discuss the human-made barriers to international trade.
5. List and discuss the arguments used to justify tariffs and present counter-arguments to those justifications.
6. Distinguish between a country's balance of trade and its balance of payments.
7. Explain how Canada's balance of payments could be unfavourable while its balance of trade is favourable.
8. Give examples of how the Canadian government aids Canadian firms in conducting international business.
9. Give reasons why firms import and export goods.
10. Understand some of the specifics required for getting involved in exporting.
11. Compare the different degrees of commitment a firm might have to international business.
12. Compare a multinational firm's view of opportunity with that of a purely domestic firm.
13. Discuss the extent of foreign ownership of Canadian business and the steps which are being taken in response to this situation.

In reading the chapter, look for and understand these terms:

international trade
absolute advantage
comparative advantage
state trading company
private trading company
trade barriers
tariffs
embargoes
non-tariff barriers
countervailing duties
exchange control
isolationism
regional trading bloc
tax control
expropriation
nationalization
confiscation

balance of trade
balance of payments
devaluation
shipper's export declaration
combination export manager
piggyback exporting
foreign assembly
contract manufacturing
licensing
joint venture
multinational company
cartel
foreign direct investment
portfolio investment
extraterritoriality
FIRA

CHAPTER SIXTEEN

International Business

AFTER HAVING BEEN ALMOST completely devastated by World War II, Japan is today a major industrialized nation. Its economic rebirth has been described as a miracle by many people. But this miracle could not have occurred if Japan had been unable to trade with other nations. Japan has very few natural resources available domestically. If it could not obtain the oil, coal, iron ore, bauxite, and other raw materials it must import to supply its industries, Japan could not have become a major industrialized nation. Because of international trade, Japan can buy these resources from other nations and manufacture them into products. Some of these manufactured goods are consumed in Japan. Many, however, are exported to other nations, including many of the nations from which Japan imports raw materials.

UP TO NOW WE'VE DISCUSSED BUSINESS MAINLY IN TERMS OF Canadian firms operating in Canada. In this chapter we look at international business. Business activity is becoming more international in character. Some of our large corporations sell more abroad than they sell in the "home" market. Many of them have set up manufacturing operations overseas.

The days of political and economic non-involvement with other nations are gone. Canadian-made goods are exported to almost every nation in the world. They are even found in many of the communist countries. Canadian-owned manufacturing plants are also located in many foreign countries.

But foreign firms also export goods to us. Familiar examples are Japanese television sets, Colombian coffee, West German cars, and French perfumes. A less familiar example is Russian tractors.

Foreign firms also have manufacturing plants in Canada and invest heavily in "Canadian" business. There are many examples of foreign ownership of Canadian businesses.

International business creates new types of business opportunity, stimulates international contact, and leads to new business practices and new business challenges. Ours is truly an exciting age of international business. Let's begin with a discussion of the reasons why nations trade with each other.

WHY NATIONS TRADE

As we saw in Chapter 1, within rather broad limits greater specialization makes possible greater output. But specialization requires exchange, or trade. These processes do not have to be limited to the people within a country. Broadening the scope of the market makes greater exchange and specialization possible. This is one reason nations buy from and sell to each international trade other. **International trade involves the exchange of goods and services** between one country and other countries. Let's examine some basic principles of trade that explain why nations specialize in certain kinds of products.

The Principle of Absolute Advantage

absolute advantage

A country enjoys an absolute advantage in producing a good when either (1) it is the only country which can provide it, or (2) it can produce it at lower cost than any other country. If a good can be produced only in Switzerland, any other countries which want it must trade with Switzerland. Lake Winnipeg goldeye is produced only in Canada, so other countries who want this product must buy it from us. If a good can be produced at a lower cost in France than in any other country, the other countries must either trade with France to get it or pay the higher cost of producing it themselves.

If all nations followed this principle, each would specialize in producing the goods in which it enjoyed an absolute advantage. Each would import all others it wished to have. Let's assume that Japan and Canada are the only countries in the world. If Japan can produce steel more cheaply than Canada, Japan has an absolute advantage in steel production. We would import steel from Japan. Suppose Canada has an absolute advantage in producing grain. According to the theory, we should specialize in producing grain and import Japanese steel. The Japanese should specialize in producing steel and import our grain. Both countries would be better off.

The Principle of Comparative Advantage

Suppose the president of a large firm can type faster than his or her secretary. The president, therefore, enjoys an absolute advantage over the

---

WHAT DO YOU THINK?

Textile Industry Assistance

The textile industry in Canada, located primarily in Quebec, employs many workers. The costs of production of the Canadian textile industry are higher than in some other countries of the world. Some people argue that because the textile industry is important to Canada, and because it employs so many people, tariff barriers should be maintained to keep cheaper foreign imports out and to protect the Canadian industry.

Other people say that if the industry is not competitive internationally it should not be protected by artificial measures. They argue that if protective measures were removed and adjustment assistance given to the companies and workers, the country would be better off in the long run. WHAT DO YOU THINK? Should textile tariffs be raised, or should we buy more from others who can produce textiles at lower cost?

secretary in typing ability. But should the president spend time typing? Although he or she is a better typist than the secretary, the president is, more importantly, a much better decision maker than the secretary. The president is wiser to attend to the duties of president rather than to type. The choice here should not be based only on "absolute advantage."

The same is true of countries. Suppose a country can produce everything its people consume more efficiently than all other countries. It can still benefit from trade. Decisions made to cope with the economic problem are made on the basis of the best use of our resources. While the company president may be making "good" use of limited time by typing, he or she is not making the "best" use of that time. "Comparative advantage" rather than "absolute advantage" should guide decision making here. **Comparative advantage means that a country should specialize in producing those goods in which it has the greatest comparative advantage or the least comparative disadvantage in relation to other countries.**

comparative advantage

STATE AND PRIVATE TRADING COMPANIES

Although our main concern in this chapter is the international operations of business firms, we cannot ignore the fact that some foreign trading is handled by government agencies.

Because state-controlled economies like the Soviet bloc countries view their foreign trade largely as an instrument of foreign policy, politics plays a large role in their trade with the noncommunist world. These countries conduct their international trade through state trading companies. **A state trading company is a government-owned operation that handles a country's trade with other governments or firms in other countries.** For example, a Canadian firm selling to the People's Republic of China sells to one of seven state trading companies. These companies do the actual buying for the Chinese. The firm does not deal directly with the people who will finally use the product.

state trading company

In Canada we have some state trading companies, like the Canadian Wheat Board.

On the other hand, most international trade of noncommunist countries is carried out by private individuals and business firms. You should not confuse state trading companies with private trading companies. **A private trading company is a privately owned business that buys and sells goods in many different countries, either in its own name or as an agent for its buyer-seller clients.**

private trading company

Perhaps the best known private trading companies in the world today are based in Japan. Such a company might buy iron ore and coal in Canada and Australia as an agent for a Japanese steel mill and also sell the mill's steel products to buyers in other countries. Private trading companies provide many services for their clients. These services may include financing their sales, providing service on their products, storing and transporting their products, and getting the products distributed through retailers and wholesalers in many countries.

There are big obstacles to trade between communist and non-communist nations. There also are many types of barriers to trade between noncommunist nations. Let's look at these barriers.

BARRIERS TO INTERNATIONAL TRADE

Even though international trade among people in free economies is carried out mainly by private business firms, government actions and policies can affect the willingness of firms to trade. So can natural things like the distance between countries. For example, even if a good can be produced more cheaply in Country *X* than in Country *Y*, the cost of shipping the good to *Y* might wipe out the cost advantage.

trade barriers

Trade barriers are natural and "created" obstacles which restrict trade among countries. Technology has helped us to reduce many of the natural barriers. Because of the jet airplane, distance between countries is measured in hours of flying time. This is very important for products that spoil rapidly. It is also important for products that are expensive to transport. The big problems, however, are the "created" barriers. Let's discuss these.

THINK ABOUT IT!

The Principle of Comparative Advantage

Assume that skilled labour is the only scarce factor of production in Canada and Japan. A Japanese worker can make 16 radios or 4 TVs per day. A Canadian worker can make 4 radios or 2 TVs per day. Thus, the Japanese worker is 4 times as efficient in making radios and 2 times as efficient in making TVs as the Canadian worker.

Without trade the Japanese have to give up 4 radios to get 1 more TV. The Canadians have to give up 1 TV to get 2 more radios.

Trade can take place and be profitable for both Japanese and Canadian consumers at any ratio of exchange between 4:1 and 2:1. The

	Radio	TV	Radio-TV Ratio of Advantage
Japanese worker	16	4	4:1
Canadian worker	4	2	2:1

ratio of exchange is determined largely by the relative bargaining strength of the trading partners. Suppose, therefore, that Japan specializes in radios and Canada specializes in TVs. They settle on a radio-TV ratio of 3:1. Thus, the Japanese give up 3 radios to get a TV. The Canadians give up 1 TV to get 3 radios. This is the principle of comparative advantage. THINK ABOUT IT!

Tariffs

tariffs

Tariffs are duties or taxes which a government puts on goods imported into or exported from a country. Governments rarely impose tariffs on exports, because they generally favour exporting goods to other countries. However, Canada does have a duty on oil exported to the United States.

Purposes of Tariffs

Tariffs serve two main purposes—revenue and/or protection. A revenue tariff raises money for the government which imposes it. The purpose is not primarily to reduce imports of the good on which the tariff is imposed. Revenue tariffs were important during our early history when we had very little domestic industry. By taxing goods coming in from abroad, our government raised revenue. Of course, the final effect is that people pay more for the goods they import since the foreign sellers add the tariff to their selling prices.

The purpose of a protective tariff is to discourage imports rather than to raise revenue. Our government has a comprehensive set of tariffs designed to protect manufacturers and encourage their establishment in Canada. Tariffs have been an important instrument of government economic policy since Confederation. A protective tariff also leads to higher prices of the imported good. Table 16.1 summarizes the major arguments used to "justify" tariffs.

Table 16.1 Arguments for Tariff and Non-Tariff Barriers

Argument	Reasoning
1. The infant industry argument	1. Tariffs are needed to protect new domestic industries from established foreign competitors. Once imposed, they are hard to remove. The industry which "grows up" under such a tariff tends to need it in adulthood.
2. The home industry argument	2. Canadian markets should be reserved for Canadian industries regardless of their maturity levels. Canadian consumers pay higher prices, and these tariffs are easily matched by other nations. The principle of comparative advantage is completely overlooked.
3. The cheap wage argument	3. Keep "cheap foreign labour" from taking Canadian jobs. When labour is a large cost of producing a product, firms in low-wage countries can sell it in Canada at lower prices than Canadian manufacturers. In periods of high domestic unemployment, this argument influences policy. Keeping such products out of Canada denies potential foreign buyers the Canadian dollars with which to buy our products.
4. The national security argument	4. Certain skills, natural resources, and industries are judged to be vital to national security. Many such industries are protected. Examples of protected industries in Canada include airlines, railroads, banking, radio and television, and others.

POINT OF VIEW

Japan's "Voluntary" Export Quota

Because of the large and growing volume of Japanese-made cars imported by Canada, there was a lot of talk in 1980 and 1981 about the need for the federal government to impose an import quota on these cars.

Our federal government wanted the Japanese to restrict automobile exports to Canada.

In the summer of 1982 a program was put in place that required an individual customs check on every Japanese car entering Canada through the port of Vancouver. This tactic delayed the entry of Japanese cars. The objective was to get the Japanese to agree to a voluntary export restraint order on cars to protect auto industry jobs in Canada.

Eventually the Japanese agreed to this "voluntary" restraint. DO YOU THINK THAT THESE TYPES OF TACTICS ARE APPROPRIATE?

Types of Tariffs

There are three ways of setting tariffs: (1) ad valorem; (2) specific duty; and (3) combination ad valorem and specific duty.

An ad valorem tariff is one levied as a percentage of the imported good's value. It is used mainly for manufactured goods. A specific duty is one levied on an imported good based on its weight and its volume. It is used mainly for raw materials and bulk commodities. The duty is figured on the basis of pounds, gallons, tons, and so on. In a combination ad valorem and specific duty, both types of tariffs are imposed on an imported good.

Embargoes

embargoes

Embargoes prohibit the import and/or export of certain goods into or out of a country. This may be done for health purposes (the embargo on the import of certain kinds of animals), for military purposes (the embargo on the export of Candu nuclear reactors to certain countries), for moral purposes (the embargo on the import of heroin), or for economic reasons. Embargoes are also used for political purposes such as trade embargoes against Rhodesia in the mid and late 1970s. In 1971 the United States lifted its 21-year embargo on trade with the People's Republic of China. Many countries also have embargoes on trade with South Africa because they disapprove of its racial policies.

Non-Tariff Barriers (NTBs)

non-tariff barriers

There are a variety of measures which a government can take to restrict imports into a country. **The measures to restrict trade, other than tariffs, are referred to as non-tariff barriers. These can include things such as**

bilingual labelling requirements, package size or characteristics, product safety requirements, requirements for import licences, inspection of perishable products and emission standards, to name a few.

If a nation introduces tariff or non-tariff barriers which effectively reduce imports, or give it an export advantage, other affected trading nations are likely to retaliate by introducing their own countervailing measures. **Countervailing duties are tariffs or non-tariff barriers introduced by a nation to offset an artificial advantage gained by another nation as a result of trade barriers.**

countervailing duties

Exchange Control

A Canadian firm which opens a branch overseas wants the branch's profits to go to its Canadian owners. If the branch is in West Germany, West Germans pay for the goods in marks. But the Canadian owners want dollars. If West Germany is short on dollars, it might stop the branch from sending the profit to Canada. This is done by limiting the amount of marks which can be converted to dollars. It is called exchange control. **Exchange control means government control over access to its country's currency by foreigners.**

exchange control

Isolationism

isolationism

Isolationism is the tendency of a country (or a group of countries) to limit social and economic contact with other countries. Isolationism decreases the amount of foreign trade that occurs. Because foreign trade is so important, we are opposed to any tendencies toward isolationism.

regional trading bloc

In some areas, isolationism has given way to regionalism. **A regional trading bloc is a group of countries which agree to eliminate restrictions which limit trade among member nations.** Often, this is at the expense of "outsider" countries. The members want to trade with each other, not with nonmembers.

In 1968 the European Economic Community (EEC), or the European "Common Market," was formed by Belgium, France, Italy, Luxembourg, the Netherlands, and West Germany. Since then, several other countries have joined. The member countries have moved toward closer economic, and limited political, integration. They strive to eliminate trade barriers for their mutual advantage. Other regional trading blocs are the European Free Trade Area (EFTA), the Latin American Free Trade Association (LAFTA), and the Central American Common Market (CACM).

Canada, as a member of the British Commonwealth, had the commonwealth preferential tariff. When Britain entered the European Economic Community we lost our preferential status in trade with her. Canada is very dependent upon the United States as a trading partner. More than half of our trade is with the United States. We have been actively trying to increase trade with Western Europe to offset this situation. We sought a "special trading status" with the EEC.

Tax Control

tax control

Foreign-based firms are reluctant to invest in countries which practise tax control. **A country practises tax control when it uses its tax authority to control foreign investments in that country.** Underdeveloped countries, for example, need revenues but have no tax base at home. Taxing foreign-owned firms is an easy out. In extreme cases tax control can lead to virtual control of these firms by a country's government.

Expropriation

expropriation

Perhaps the biggest political risk of setting up a plant in some countries is the risk of expropriation. **Expropriation means that the government of a country takes over ownership of a foreign-owned firm located in its country.** The firm that is taken over may then be sold to private citizens of the expropriating country.

nationalization

    Nationalization, however, means that the expropriating government keeps ownership and runs the firm. When Salvador Allende came to power in Chile, the copper mines in that country were nationalized. Some potash mines in Saskatchewan have been nationalized.

    A government which expropriates property may or may not compensate the owner. In some cases the owner is paid part or all of the market value of that property. **Confiscation, however, means that the government does not compensate the owner for the expropriated property.**

confiscation

In Saskatchewan the owners were compensated for their mines. In Chile they were not.

REMOVING TRADE BARRIERS

Governments can help to promote trade. Many seek to attract foreign investment by giving informational, financial, and promotional assistance to foreign firms.

    Foreign investment is needed to help newly emerging nations to develop. It helps to raise their standard of living.

    Many economically advanced countries lack sufficient domestic supplies of certain resources. Japan's domestic growth, for example, is due largely to its government's encouragement, rather than restriction, of international business.

    But what about the home government of a firm which invests overseas? A government's attitude toward its country's firms which invest abroad depends largely on the situation and the time. It can involve foreign policy and the national interest.

    Political differences with some nations may cause a government to discourage firms from investing in them. Balance of payments problems can lead a government to restrict foreign investment by its country's firms. On balance, the Canadian government encourages and helps Canadian firms to do business overseas.

Table 16.2   Some Examples of Governmental Assistance to
International Business

Institution	Purpose
The Export Development Corporation (EDC)	This agency was created by the federal government in 1969 after a study indicated that export insurance and financing facilities were more adequate in other countries than in Canada. The EDC finances export credits as well as insuring and guaranteeing such credits provided by suppliers, bonds, or other institutions.
Provincial Export Development Agencies	A number of provinces have export promotion programs. They will work with firms to develop export opportunities.
Trade Commissioner Service	The Trade Commissioner Service of the federal Department of External Affairs will work with firms to identify and develop potential trade opportunities.
The International Bank for Reconstruction and Development (World Bank)	The World Bank began operations in 1946 to advance the economic development of member nations by making loans to them. These loans are made either directly by the World Bank using its own funds, or indirectly by the World Bank borrowing from member countries.
The International Monetary Fund (IMF)	The IMF began operations in 1947 to promote trade among member countries by eliminating trade barriers and promoting financial cooperation among them. It enables members to cope better with balance of payments problems. Thus, if firms in Peru wish to buy from Canadian firms but lack enough Canadian dollars, Peru can borrow Canadian dollars from the IMF. It pays back the loan in gold or the currency it receives through its dealing with other countries.
The General Agreement on Tariffs and Trade (GATT)	GATT was negotiated in 1947 by member nations to improve trade relations through reductions and elimination of tariffs. GATT has resulted in tariff reductions on thousands of products. The latest round of GATT negotiations was completed in 1979.
The International Development Association (IDA)	The IDA began operations in 1960 and is affiliated with the World Bank. It makes loans to private businesses and to member countries of the World Bank. In addition to the IDA, there are similar organizations which make loans to governments and firms in certain country groupings. The Inter-American Development Association, for example, is for countries belonging to the Organization of American States.
The International Finance Corporation (IFC)	The IFC began operations in 1956 and is also affiliated with the World Bank. It makes loans to private businesses when they cannot obtain loans from more conventional sources.

The federal government's Department of External Affairs organizes trade missions and operates permanent trade centres in many foreign countries. The department provides information and promotion services to Canadian firms interested in overseas business. Table 16.2 discusses several ways governments aid international business.

Many agencies and groups promote international business. Many provincial and municipal government programs seek to boost exports. Provincial industrial development commissions and mayors often go to the United States and overseas to lure foreign firms to their areas.

Private efforts are also important. The Canadian Chamber of Commerce provides information and advice to firms interested in selling overseas. Private firms and organizations also participate in and sponsor trade shows. When banks, insurance firms, transportation firms, ad agencies, accounting firms, and marketing research firms help and promote international business, they bring new business to themselves.

INTERNATIONAL TRADE

The Balance of Trade Problem

An export from one nation is an import to another nation. International trade is a two-way street. Some governments, however, see it as a means

WHAT DO YOU THINK?

Government Subsidization of Export Activity — Tannereye Ltd. of Charlottetown, P.E.I.

Tannereye Ltd. manufactures high-fashion leather optical frames and sunglasses and exports approximately 98 percent of its finished products. When the company needed more working capital to expand, it approached the federal government for assistance. It received:

1. a research grant of $79,000 which covered 75 percent of the cost of its new product design program;
2. a 90 percent loan guarantee on $130,000 from the Enterprise Development Program; and

3. an export credit insurance policy from the Export Development Corp. (This policy covers a large percentage of any losses on foreign accounts due to economic or political reasons.)

According to President Peter Leunes, "we would have survived without help, but because of the three government programs, we've actually been able to expand."

Should the Canadian government directly subsidize Canadian-based firms to help them compete in world markets? WHAT DO YOU THINK?

Source: Adapted from *Canadian Business* 55 (10), October 1982, p. 113.

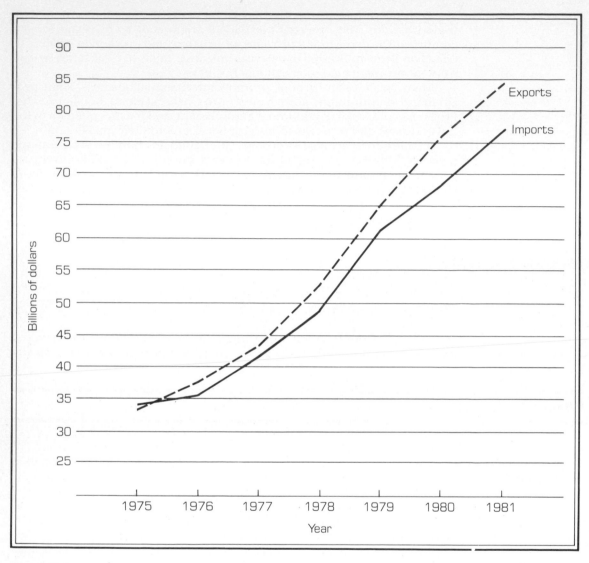

Figure 16.1
Canadian imports and exports of merchandise. (Source: *Bank of Canada Review,*
December 1982 pp. S140–S141.)

of gaining an economic "edge" over other countries. National pride and
mutual distrust cause many nations to view trade as desirable only if their
exports are greater than their imports.

balance of trade   **A nation's balance of trade is the difference between the money
values of its exports and its imports.** If it exports more than it imports,

Table 16.3 Selected Major Export and Import Commodities of Canada for 1981

Merchandise Exports	Millions	Merchandise Imports	Millions
Total motor vehicles	$13,084	Total motor vehicles	$15,996
Natural gas	4,370	Crude petroleum	7,861
Newsprint paper	4,326	Communication and related equipment	2,770
Wood pulp	3,820	Office machines	2,582
Wheat	3,728	Total farm machines	2,396
Lumber	2,989	Aircraft and parts	2,347
Crude petroleum	2,505	Nonferrous metals	2,194
Chemicals	2,394	Drilling and excavating machines	1,567
Total aircraft (includes engines and parts)	1,797	Total chemicals (inorganic and organic)	1,489
Iron	1,540	Apparel and accessories	1,423
Fish and shellfish	1,484	Measurement control and scientific	1,408
Aluminium	1,467	Primary other iron and steel	1,313
Other cereals	1,418	Metal fabrication	1,269
Communication and related equipment	1,373	Plastics and synthetic rubber	1,164
Fertilizers and materials	1,343	Photography goods	929

Source: Statistics Canada, Canadian Statistical Review, No. 11–003E, January 1983, pp. 110–113.

Table 16.4 Major Trading Partners of Canada for 1981

Merchandise Exports to Major Countries	Millions	Merchandise Imports from Major Countries	Millions
United States	$55,378	United States	$54,350
Other Asia	7,513	Other Asia	6,881
Japan	4,521	Japan	4,038
United Kingdom	3,347	South America	3,249
South America	2,270	Venezuela	2,385
U.S.S.R.	1,867	United Kingdom	2,377
Middle East	1,558	Saudi Arabia	2,273
West Germany	1,321	Central America	1,843
Other Africa	1,273	West Germany	1,612
Netherlands	1,209	Other Africa	1,047
China	1,007	France	879
France	1,004	Italy	702
Oceania	994	Oceania	661
Italy	928	Australia	499
Belgium and Luxembourg	856	Brazil	431
Venezuela	829	Belgium and Luxembourg	297
Australia	828	Netherlands	296
Mexico	734	India	107
Norway	428	Jamaica	98
India	348	Iran	3

Source: Statistics Canada, Canadian Statistical Review, No. 11–003E, January 1983, pp. 108–109.

its balance of trade is considered favourable. If it imports more than it exports, its balance of trade is unfavourable.

At one time nations used gold for settling trade imbalances. A country which imported more than it exported (an unfavourable balance of trade) paid for its excess imports by shipping gold to the creditor nations. Because a nation's gold supply was considered a measure of its "strength," a government would restrict imports and grant tax breaks to firms that exported goods. This enabled it to hold its gold.

Canada has enjoyed a favourable balance of trade since 1975 (see Figure 16.1 on page 560). Our major merchandise imports and exports indicate that we have tended to export raw materials and import manufactured products (see Table 16.3 on page 561). The United States is by far our largest trading partner (see Table 16.4 on page 561).

The Balance of Payments Problem

balance of payments

A nation with a favourable balance of trade can have an unfavourable balance of payments. **A country's balance of payments is the difference between its receipts of foreign money and the outflows of its own money due to imports, exports, investments, government grants and aid, and military and tourist spending abroad.** For Canada to have a favourable balance of payments for a given year, the following would have to be true. The total of our exports, foreign tourist spending in Canada, and foreign investments in Canada must be greater than the total of our imports, Canadian tourist spending overseas, payments on foreign debt, and the investments made by Canadians abroad.

The Rate of Exchange

Assume that a French importer buys goods from a Canadian firm. If the Canadian firm wants payment in Canadian dollars, the French importer has to exchange francs for dollars at a bank in France. How many francs are needed to buy a dollar (or vice versa) depends on the rate of exchange between francs and dollars. Even if the Canadian firm accepted payment in francs, it could exchange the francs for dollars. Our exchange rate is important to our imports and exports. If the exchange rate decreases, the value of our dollar falls in relation to other currencies—our exports will become less expensive to other countries, and their products (our imports) will become more expensive for us to buy. If the exchange rate rises, the reverse situation occurs.

If a country has a persistent balance of payments deficit there will be downward pressure on its exchange rate. This will eventually bring about a devaluation on its currency in relation to that of other countries.

The Role of Gold

Until 1971 gold played an important role in settlement of the international balance of payments. The price of gold was established at $35 per ounce (U.S.), and foreign countries could settle any accounts with the

United States in gold if they chose. This situation provided the base for international exchange transactions.

In 1971, however, the United States had a $6.3 billion deficit in its balance of trade. This resulted from the long-term increasing productivity of foreign firms and their greater ability to compete with U.S. firms for customers. Furthermore, in the United States people were buying lower-priced foreign goods in record volume.

Because of the United States' shrinking gold supply, some foreigners began to question its ability to continue to convert foreign-held dollars into gold. Many of them tried to convert their dollar holdings into gold. These "runs on the dollar" got so severe that, in 1971, the United States stopped paying gold in exchange for dollars held by foreigners. An embargo was placed on the shipment of gold.

devaluation

The U.S. dollar was officially devalued in 1972 from $35.00 per ounce of gold to $38.00 per ounce, and in 1973, from $38.00 to $42.22 per ounce. Before the 1972 devaluation, the U.S. dollar was worth 1/35 of an ounce of gold. The 1973 devaluation meant that the dollar was worth 1/42 of an ounce of gold. **Devaluation, therefore, means reducing the value of a currency in relation to gold or in relation to some other standard.**

EXPORTING AND IMPORTING

We've used the terms "exports" and "imports" in our discussion of trade. Imports are goods that are shipped into a country from other countries. Exports are goods that are shipped out of a country to other countries.

Why Firms Export Goods

Exporting is a special kind of "selling." Exported goods cross over national borders. But these borders are political borders. They are not related to the nature of business activity. Some mass production industries have to produce in large volumes to get the cost per unit down to a low level. If the home market is too small to absorb this output, these firms look to other countries for additional customers. Many Canadian firms do not have sufficiently large-scale plants to produce at a competitive cost relative to other industries, because the Canadian domestic market is too small. This is particularly true in relation to the United States, our largest trading partner. The United States has a domestic market roughly ten times as large as Canada's.

In other industries, such as mining, the majority of our products are exported. These companies must export because the markets in Canada cannot absorb their level of production. Often exporting is undertaken only after domestic markets are satisfied and overhead costs have already been met. Japan, although a very large exporter, exports only a percentage of the goods which are domestically consumed. This means that margins can be higher in export markets. If the product and the selling approach have been

THEN AND NOW

The Soviet Union and Consumer Goods

For many years the Soviet Union showed a general lack of interest in consumer goods production. They concentrated on building heavy industry and a first-rate military establishment. Some Soviet citizens complained about the lack of attention to consumer goods and the poor quality of what was available.

The Soviet Union is now eager to expand its exports of consumer goods. Soviet-made watches, television sets, cameras, cars, radios, camping equipment, pianos, and other types of consumer goods are sold in the Western European nations, Canada, and the United States.

The incentive for this is the Soviet desire to bolster its prestige in the world and to earn foreign exchange.

developed and tested in the home market, moving into another country may require little additional preparation expense.

The demand for many products is seasonal. Some firms shift their off-season production into foreign markets where the product is in season. This may lower production cost due to better production scheduling.

Finally, a firm might find it more profitable to expand its market coverage to foreign countries than to develop new products for sale at home. Its skills may be put to best use by producing and selling its traditional product rather than by risking the development of new products.

Why Firms Import Goods

Importing is buying. Canadian firms import bananas and coffee because they are not available in Canada. Sometimes domestic sources must be supplemented by foreign sources. Thus, Canada imports large quantities of crude petroleum for use in the Eastern provinces.

Prices of foreign goods are often lower than like goods produced at home. This may be due to lower labour costs overseas. Some cars, steel, textiles, and electronics equipment are imported into Canada. Remember, however, that low-cost labour is a bargain only when it is productive. A Canadian worker who can produce two units of output per hour is more productive than a foreign worker who produces only one unit of output per hour. As long as the Canadian worker's wage is less than double that of the foreign worker, the Canadian worker is more productive in real terms.

Importing goods from foreign producers may lead to exporting goods to them. This accounts for a lot of foreign commerce. This is the type of trading the Soviet Union prefers.

In other cases imported goods have prestige value. Some Canadians, for example, are willing to pay extra for imported wines or perfumes.

Getting Involved in Exporting

Let's assume that you have uncovered an opportunity to make a profit by exporting goods to an overseas buyer. You are ready to begin exporting and must familiarize yourself with export and import permit requirements, shipping documents, international finance, collection documents, methods of payment, and export services and middlemen.

Export and Import Permits

In most cases you will not require an export permit to export goods. There are some exceptions. The Export Control Section of the Export and Import Act provides for a published list of countries which require export permits. The list changes from time to time as the international political situation changes. Also specified are the products that require an export permit. These products are usually ones defined to be of strategic or military importance.

Shipping Documents

shipper's export declaration

A Canada customs export declaration is required for all goods exported from Canada. (See Figure 16.2 on page 566.) **This document declares the quantity and dollar value of the goods and must be filed with the collector of customs at the port of exportation.**

Other important shipping documents include dock receipts, bills of lading, packing lists, and insurance certificates.

A dock receipt shows that your goods have been received in good condition by the carrier (ship or plane) and in the stipulated quantity. It transfers accountability for the goods from the domestic carrier to the international carrier.

A bill of lading is: (1) a document of title that can be transferred after endorsement; (2) a contract between the shipper and the transportation company; and (3) a receipt for the goods the shipper has placed on the carrier.

A packing list is a complete, itemized description of your goods' weight, size, type of packing, and so on. An insurance certificate is a form certifying that freight insurance was obtained, the value insured, and the type of insurance coverage.

International Financing

The first thing to do when arranging for payment from the importer is to talk with the international department of your local bank. If your bank branch does not have one, it can put you in touch with a branch that does.

International banking departments of Canadian chartered banks offer their exporter-clients many services. These include securing credit information about specific importers, collecting overseas accounts, providing information, giving assistance in planning trips overseas, exchanging currencies, and arranging for letters of credit.

An international banking department's overseas correspondent banks can also help you. They can be one source of information on the importer's

B 13 CANADA CUSTOMS EXPORT DECLARATION

SEE CUSTOMS MEMORANDUM D22-1 AND STATISTICS CANADA EXPORT COMMODITY CLASSIFICATION

| 1 EXPORTER | 2 REPORT NO. | 3 SHIPPER'S REF. NO. |
| | | 4 PAGE OF PAGES |

| 5 CONSIGNEE | 6 STAMP OF CHIEF PORT |

RE-EXPORTS – INDICATE COUNTRY OF ORIGIN INDIVIDU- ALLY IN LEFT HAND MARGIN | 7 CTRY. OF FINAL DESTINATION

11 TERMS OF DELIVERY AND PAYMENT

12 IF FOREIGN GOODS IN SAME CONDITION AS IMPORTED, GIVE COUNTRY OF ORIGIN

| 8 LOCAL CARRIER | 9 FROM |
| 10 EXPORTING CARRIER | (LOCAL POINT OF LADING) |

13   14
MARKS AND NUMBERS   NUMBER AND TYPE OF PACKAGES: DESCRIPTION OF GOODS, GIVE SUFFICIENT DETAIL TO PERMIT CODING ACCORDING TO STATISTICS CANADA EXPORT COMMODITY CLASSIFICATION.

15 QUANTITY IN UNIT REQUIRED FOR EXPORT COMMODITY CLASSIFICATION

16 CURRENCY OF VALUE

17 SHIPPING WEIGHT

20 (IF APPLICABLE) ARE/WERE THE GOODS   SUBJECT TO DRAWBACK ☐   IMPORTED ON 1/60TH BASIS ☐   IMPORTED UNDER LICENCE ☐ | 21 EXPORT PERMIT NO.

22 ESTIMATED FREIGHT CHARGES TO PORT OF EXIT $ .... OR ....TO DESTINATION $ ....

25 IF GOODS NOT SOLD STATE REASON FOR EXPORT, (LOAN, REPAIR, PROCESSING ETC.)

23 MODE OF TRANSPORTATION FROM POINT OF EXIT
ROAD ☐   RAIL ☐   WATER ☐   AIR ☐   OTHER ☐ | 24 CONTAINERIZED YES ☐   NO ☐

I HEREBY CERTIFY THAT THE INFORMATION GIVEN ABOVE AND ON THE CONTINUATION SHEET(S), IF ANY, IS TRUE AND COMPLETE IN EVERY RESPECT

27 GIVE FIRM NAME AND ADDRESS IF .... DIFFERENT FROM EXPORTER BOX ABOVE ....

B 13 4/78

26 RETURN ADDRESS

28 DATE ....
29 SIGNATURE

30 STATUS
☐ OWNER   ☐ AGENT

Figure 16.2
Canadian customs export declaration

566

creditworthiness, and can help you collect payment and schedule trips to foreign markets to search out potential customers.

The Trade Commissioner Service and the Export Development Corporation may also assist you in scheduling trips to foreign markets to search out potential customers.

Collection Documents

In order to receive payment for your exported products, you must complete several types of documents in addition to the very important shipping documents indicated above. These include commercial invoices, certificates of origin, and inspection certificates.

A commercial invoice is a bill for the goods from you to the buyer. It shows all the facts associated with the sale—descriptions, costs, measurements, delivery date, payment terms, and so on. A certificate of origin certifies that the goods were produced in Canada. An inspection certificate is a document importers often require. It states that the goods were inspected by a third party to ensure that they are as described by the exporter to the importer.

Method of Payment

The most common methods of handling payment by the importer to the exporter are cash in advance, cash on delivery, open account, letter of credit, and drafts.

Cash in advance eliminates both the risk that the buyer will not pay and any problems that could be created by exchange controls or political changes. However, the buyer may interpret it to mean that you suspect his or her creditworthiness. Furthermore, if payment must be made before the receipt of goods, it ties up the buyer's working capital.

With an *open account* arrangement, the seller ships the goods to the buyer and the seller's commercial invoice indicates the buyer's liability to pay. Open account is used primarily when the seller is sure of the buyer's willingness and ability to pay. The Export Development Corporation performs a valuable service in insuring open account transactions.

By far the most common method of payment is a *letter of credit*, which is a document from the bank to you. It guarantees that the buyer's bank will pay you, or your bank, for the goods if you meet the conditions set out in the letter. Usually, the exporter and the importer agree on the terms of sale in advance and incorporate these terms in the letter of credit. If a letter of credit is confirmed by a Canadian bank and is irrevocable, it is considered the safest method of payment for international transactions.

A *draft*, or bill of exchange, is a written demand for payment. You could, for example, draw a draft instructing the buyer to pay the invoice to the buyer's bank. Your bank would send the draft to the buyer's bank for collection. A sight draft requires the buyer to pay before taking possession of the documents for the goods. A time draft allows the buyer a period of time, usually 30 to 180 days, to pay the invoice. The buyer takes possession of the documents for the goods before paying for them, but only after accepting the time draft.

Most exporters are paid in U.S. dollars, although in a very small number of cases payment may be in the importer's currency. Thus, a German importer will pay you in U.S. dollars, or in marks, and you will have to convert them to Canadian dollars. The number of Canadian dollars the U.S. dollars or marks will buy can change from day to day, depending on the foreign exchange rate. Your banker can give you information about foreign exchange rates and help you protect yourself from extreme fluctuations. Most manufacturers who export would probably keep permanent U.S. dollar accounts and use them to pay for supplies imported from other countries.

Federal Export Services

There are a variety of valuable export services available from the government of Canada. The Department of External Affairs has regional offices all across Canada that provide export advice and assistance.

The Export Development Corporation provides export insurance such as in the open account transactions discussed above. The EDC also becomes involved in some cases in providing financing to buyers from Canadian exporters. This improves the Canadian exporter's competitive position in competing against suppliers from other countries.

The Trade Commissioner Service maintains offices in numerous foreign countries. Many who use it believe it provides an excellent service. It is viewed as one of the best trade commissioner services in the world—even better than the U.S. service. The Trade Commissioner Service will research a foreign market for you; provide you with lists of potential contacts; provide introductions for you; and even schedule meetings for you in foreign countries.

Export Middlemen

Export middlemen include freight forwarders and export trading houses. Freight forwarders provide a number of services, including preparation of shipping documents.

Export trading houses operate in a variety of different ways. These include:

- Export merchants, who buy goods from Canadian manufacturers and export them.
- Commission agents, who charge a revenue-based fee for helping Canadian sellers to export.
- Buying houses, which help foreign buyers locate and purchase products in Canada.
- Export management companies, which act as organizations' export departments for a fee or a commission.
- Bartering houses, which arrange for two suppliers of different types of merchandise to trade with each other. The company will arrange both ends of the transaction and assume the risk.
- Consortia management, which is a group of companies—mostly engineering—each with different skills, that bid collectively on overseas projects.

TYPES OF INTERNATIONAL BUSINESS

Involvement in international business can range all the way from un-intentional exporting to setting up complete branch operations in one or more foreign countries. Let's examine these various degrees of commitment to international business.

Unintentional Exporting

Many firms' products are exported without their knowledge. For example, a supplier of a part used by Versatile Manufacturing in making farm tractors might be unaware that the part ends up on a tractor used by a farmer in the United States.

Many firms have resident buyers in foreign countries. These buyers buy goods in those countries and send them to their employers. Thus, a Canadian firm might be selling to a resident buyer for an Italian firm without knowing it.

Unsolicited Exporting

Sometimes, a firm might get an unsolicited order from an overseas buyer. Unlike the examples above, the firm is aware that the customer is overseas. Often, however, the firm may not be interested in selling overseas. Many firms, especially small ones, have a mistaken notion that selling overseas involves too much "red tape." Various Canadian government agencies and programs, as we have seen, help these firms do business overseas. Canadian federal and provincial governments help small firms get involved in exporting.

Intentional Exporting

Intentional exporting means that the exporter is committed to selling abroad. But there are degrees of commitment. At one extreme are firms that consider their export business to be secondary to their domestic sales. Such a firm might accept orders from overseas buyers but not seek them. It might have a small department which accepts orders from foreign buyers. At the other extreme, a firm might have a large, well-staffed, well-financed division which seeks export sales.

An intentional exporter must decide how to handle its export business. In direct exporting the firm handles the export task for itself. In indirect exporting, outside specialists handle the export task for the firm. Which approach is best depends on such factors as the company's size, its export volume, the number of foreign countries involved, the investment required to support the operation, the profit potential, the risk present, and the desires of the overseas buyers. If the firm exports many products, it may go direct with some and indirect with others.

combination
export manager

Some firms are afraid to get involved in exporting because they don't know how to do it. **The combination export manager can help. This middleman represents several exporters and handles all the work involved in moving their goods overseas.**

Many firms, especially small and medium-size ones, cooperate with each other in their exporting. Several firms and the federal government have brought small producers together to form export consortia to bid on large-scale international contracts.

piggyback exporting

Another type of cooperation is piggyback exporting. **In piggyback exporting, one firm (the carrier) uses its overseas distribution network to sell noncompetitive products of one or more other firms (riders).**

Overseas Manufacturing

Overseas manufacturing involves a greater commitment to international business than exporting does. Let's discuss several types of overseas manufacturing.

Foreign Assembly

foreign assembly

One example of overseas manufacturing is foreign assembly. **In foreign assembly the parent firm exports parts overseas where they are assembled into a finished product by its overseas subsidiary or a licencee.** A Canadian tractor manufacturer, for example, might export parts overseas for assembly into a finished tractor. This may be wise when the tariff on the parts is much lower than the tariff on an assembled tractor. The overseas assembler might be a subsidiary of the Canadian firm. Usually, the Canadian firm would also have a sales subsidiary in that country. Perhaps the overseas assembler is a foreign-owned firm which is licensed to assemble the tractor. The sales task here is handled by the licencee. Sony televisions and Honda motorcycles are "foreign goods" which are assembled in the United States for sale there.

Contract Manufacturing

contract manufacturing

Another example of overseas manufacturing is contract manufacturing. **In contract manufacturing the firm that wants to do business in a foreign country enters into a contract with a firm there to produce the product.** The overseas company, however, does not handle the sales task. This arrangement is popular with big consumer goods firms such as Procter & Gamble. Procter & Gamble might contract out the production work to a foreign firm, but the company takes on the marketing task.

Licensing

licensing

The main difference between contract manufacturing and licensing is that a licencor-licencee relationship usually extends over a longer period of time. **In a licensing arrangement, licencees are licensed to manufacture and market products in their countries. The licencor gets an agreed-upon percentage of the licencee's sales revenues.** Many Canadian firms have licensing agreements with firms in the United States.

Joint Venture

joint venture

A joint venture is similar to the licensing arrangement. **But a joint venture involves some ownership and control of the foreign firm by the firm wanting to do business there.** Suppose a Canadian firm forms a joint venture with a Japanese firm. The Canadian firm would have a partial ownership in the Japanese firm and would also have some say in managing it. Because of this, some governments discourage joint ventures between domestic and foreign firms.

Foreign Manufacturing and Marketing

Foreign manufacturing and foreign marketing represent the greatest commitment to international business. The firm owns and controls the overseas plant and the marketing of its products. It may build the plant from the ground up or buy out a firm already in business there. This brings us to the multinational company.

THE MULTINATIONAL COMPANY

multinational company

A multinational company is a firm that is based in one country (the parent country) and has production and marketing activities spread in one or more foreign (host) countries. The greater the number of these host countries, the more "multinational" it is. Such a firm truly becomes a global enterprise.

We tend to think of the United States as the home country of most international corporations. Firms such as International Business Machines (IBM), Procter & Gamble, Coca-Cola, and F.W. Woolworth Company are U.S.-owned firms. In fact, they are global firms. They look at the world as their base of operations. Many such firms sell more overseas than they sell in the United States.

The United States is not the parent country for all multinational firms. For example, Switzerland's Nestlé does more than 90 percent of its business outside of Switzerland. Royal Dutch Shell and Unilever Corporation do more than 80 percent of their business in host countries. France's Michelin Tire Company and Canada's Massey Ferguson Ltd. and INCO Ltd. are other examples of multinational corporations.

The multinational company has become more visible and controversial since the end of World War II. Some people believe they are not subject to enough social control. These people question the "allegiance" of a firm headquartered in one country but having operations in scores of other countries. Some people think they have too much economic and political power.

THE "WHY" OF MULTINATIONAL BUSINESS

Modern communications and transportation have shrunk the world's size. Satellites in space can bring us live televised news from foreign nations. Jet travel means we are only hours away from foreign cities. Within seconds you can place a telephone call to someone on the other side of the globe. People of different nations know more about each other and each other's wants than anyone could have known at any other time in history. It is not strange, therefore, that many firms consider the whole world when they think about market opportunity.

One key fact helps to explain why firms engage in multinational business — the world's resources are unequally distributed among the nations. Some have lower standards of living and an abundance of labour. This tends to make labour less costly than in other countries where labour is scarce. If those workers have the skills needed by a global firm, or if they can be taught those skills, the firm has an incentive to locate a plant there. Of course, the productivity of labour must always be considered.

Raw materials-producing nations have been at a trading disadvantage with the industrialized nations for a long time. They argue that foreign-based firms come in and "take" their natural resources. These are exported to the industrialized nations and manufactured into goods. The "foreigners" get the high-paying manufacturing jobs; their governments get taxes from the firms; and the workers spend their money at home. They also believe that they are in a poor bargaining position against the big firms.

This is why some raw materials-producing nations have formed cartels.
cartel   **A cartel is a group of business firms or nations which agree to operate as a monopoly.** Thus, they regulate prices and production.

Raw materials-producing nations want a better deal in trading. Multinational firms are aware of this. Many firms, rather than transporting raw materials home from a foreign country, build plants to process these materials at the source. Sometimes the nation providing the raw material insists on this arrangement. In Canada, where there is a heavy emphasis on export of primary goods, we see some evidence of discussion about cartels. The potential wheat cartel mentioned previously is one example. The Canadian government also arranged for a cartel of uranium producers in the early 1970s.

FOREIGN INVESTMENT IN CANADA

Canada's manufacturing economy has developed behind a protective tariff barrier. This has made it attractive for foreign firms to establish or acquire subsidiaries in Canada to supply the Canadian market. In this manner foreign firms supply goods to the Canadian market less expensively than by exporting to Canada and paying the tariff on the product. Canada's rich natural resources — minerals and petroleum — also attracted money from abroad. (See Table 16.5.)

Foreign firms which invest in Canada because of the tariff barriers often build small, inefficient plants to serve only the Canadian market. The Canadian market is much smaller (approximately 24 million) than the over 200 million people in the United States or in Western Europe. This cost of production, in addition to the tariff barriers erected by other countries, and the fact that most export allocations are made by head offices of

Table 16.5 Degree of Foreign Ownership by the United States and
Others in Canada, As Measured by Assets, 1977–1980

Industry	Assets of U.S. and Other Foreign-Controlled Corporations, As a Percentage of Total Industry Assets			
	1977	1978	1979	1980
Agriculture, forestry, and fishing	7.4	6.4	4.8	4.3
Mining:				
Metal mining	37.7	36.7	34.7	31.3
Mineral fuels	60.2	52.9	58.6	53.3
Other mining	55.0	48.1	48.3	40.4
Total mining	51.1	46.9	49.9	45.1
Manufacturing:				
Food	39.2	38.6	36.6	29.4
Beverages	31.1	31.2	31.4	31.7
Tobacco products	99.8	99.5	99.8	99.7
Rubber products	94.1	93.1	90.6	91.0
Leather products	20.3	19.1	23.6	22.8
Textile mills	58.1	57.6	55.2	54.1
Knitting mills	17.7	15.8	15.4	14.8
Clothing	16.2	15.3	13.9	14.1
Wood industries	21.0	21.2	20.5	19.0
Furniture industries	16.2	14.8	10.7	12.0
Paper and allied industries	41.5	39.5	38.3	35.3
Printing, publishing, and allied industries	11.2	11.3	11.8	11.5
Primary metals	14.0	13.9	14.4	13.4
Metal fabricating	40.1	39.6	36.6	34.5
Machinery	64.0	60.9	55.4	51.7
Transport equipment	76.9	74.7	73.2	70.7
Electrical products	69.0	66.2	58.5	53.9
Non-metallic mineral products	70.0	71.8	71.9	70.4
Petroleum and coal products	92.3	83.9	69.2	69.8
Chemicals and chemical products	67.2	67.8	77.2	77.4
Miscellaneous manufacturing	48.0	47.8	44.4	42.9
Total manufacturing	53.8	52.0	49.4	47.6
Construction	11.7	10.4	11.1	10.0
Utilities:				
Transportation	12.2	8.2	7.8	7.3
Storage	6.4	4.7	5.8	5.2
Communication	14.3	13.2	13.2	13.0
Public utilities	2.1	2.0	2.2	0.3
Total utilities	7.3	5.8	5.8	4.5
Wholesale trade	26.1	26.7	25.8	24.0
Retail trade	15.6	15.2	13.0	13.0
Services	17.4	18.4	14.9	14.6
Total non-financial industries	30.4	29.0	28.9	27.3

Source: Statistics Canada, Corporations and Labour Returns Act, Annual Report, 1978,
p. 147; 1980, p. 149.

foreign countries, makes it difficult for these firms to compete actively as exporters.

The market size and the tendency for much technological development work done by foreign-owned companies to be conducted outside Canada means that Canadian subsidiaries do not conduct autonomous new process or product development work. This, it has been argued, is another major disadvantage of the high degree of foreign ownership of Canadian corporations. The other side of the argument, of course, is that Canadian firms would have less access to technological developments if it were not for these foreign subsidiaries. (This subject is discussed further in the section on "The Technological Environment" in Chapter 17.)

Government Studies

foreign direct investment

There has been concern about the level of foreign direct investment in Canada since the early 1950s. **Foreign direct investment, defined in the *Report of the Royal Commission on Corporate Concentration*, is the transfer of a package of assets from a foreign-domiciled corporation through corporate channels into an enterprise in Canada, either by acquisition of an existing firm or by the creation of a new enterprise, which thereafter becomes a subsidiary of the foreign corporation and subject to its control.** The assets transferred in the package may include capital, a licence to use a brand name, and preferred access to markets and sources of new materials.

portfolio investment

Another type of foreign investment, portfolio investment, is purchase of the stocks and bonds of Canadian corporations by nonresidents.

Foreign investment in Canada increased dramatically from $8.7 billion in 1950 to $68.6 billion in 1975. Foreign direct investment, measured as the total of equity investments, undistributed retained earnings, and long-term debt owed to the parent firm, has increased from about 45 percent of total foreign investment in 1950 to almost 60 percent in 1975.

There have been several studies of foreign investment in Canada. The first was the Gordon Commission Report in 1957. The report pointed out that there were dangers to foreign investment. A major concern was the possibility that if U.S. subsidiaries in Canada were faced with a conflict between U.S. and Canadian positions they would choose to support the U.S. position. A key recommendation, which was subsequently acted upon, was that financial intermediaries should be in Canadian hands.

extraterritoriality

The Watkins Report in 1968 dealt with extraterritoriality, that is, the application of U.S. laws to the subsidiaries of U.S. companies in other countries. The report examined U.S. government guidelines for U.S. direct investment abroad, the application of U.S. law on subsidiaries trading with communist countries, and the application of U.S. anti-trust law to subsidiaries.

Major recommendations of the Watkins Report were to create a government agency to survey multinational activities in Canada; to compel foreign subsidiaries to disclose more of their activities in Canada; to en-

CAREERS IN INTERNATIONAL BUSINESS

ALMOST ANY BUSINESS-RELATED JOB YOU COULD NAME CAN BE FOUND in a firm engaged in international business. In many cases these jobs are exactly the same as they would be in a firm that sells only in its domestic market. Many others, however, require additional skills, such as knowledge of a foreign language or knowledge of the culture or business practices of a foreign nation.

Some international firms employ *interpreters* to deal with language-related problems.

You might be interested in the opportunities available to you as an *import sales manager* for a firm. This job involves keeping in close contact with overseas suppliers and your domestic sales force. Remember, opportunities are not limited to big corporations. If you like to travel, you will more than likely have the opportunity to visit your suppliers' countries from time to time to negotiate contracts with them.

If you want to go into business for yourself, you might consider becoming an *export agent*. You would handle the export task for your clients, for which you would be paid a commission. This takes a thorough knowledge of the laws and regulations governing exporting. A lot of it is detail work. Thus, you must have a knack for handling details.

Many firms that engage in international business hire people whose main job is to keep in close contact with potential buyers. This person would maintain contact with foreign embassies in Canada and call on foreign visitors and foreign buyers who are in Canada to negotiate supply contracts.

Resident buyers are hired by importers to place orders for them in the country in which the buyer is located.

Because the physical distribution problem in export selling is often complex, many firms turn to the services of *foreign-freight forwarders*. They prepare documents needed to export goods and handle all the details involved in moving the goods to the buyer. The experience you'll get working for a foreign-freight forwarder will be very valuable to your future in international business.

Canadian banks also have departments of international business. If you are interested in a career in finance and international business, you should investigate opportunities with the chartered banks. ∎

CAREER PROFILE

MY NAME IS BARRY HALL, AND I AM MARKET Development Manager for CSP Foods Ltd. CSP Foods purchases canola and sunflower seed from farmers, processes the seed, and sells the processed product. Processing involves crushing the products into oil and meal, which we sell. We further process some sunflower oil into products such as margarine. Our head office is in Saskatoon. We have crushing plants at Altona and Harrowby, Manitoba; and Nipawin, Saskatchewan. We also have a refinery at Dundas, Ontario. Our marketing offices are located in Winnipeg, Toronto, and Vancouver.

I have been with CSP Foods for just over three years. I obtained an undergraduate degree in agriculture in 1965 and a master's degree in plant science in 1967. I worked for Geigy Corporation and the Canada Grains Council prior to joining CSP Foods.

My primary involvement is with export sales of canola oil. Historically, CSP Foods has sold about 100,000 tonnes of canola oil in Canada and 25,000 tonnes in export markets. Our new plant at Harrowby raises our production capacity to 200,000 tonnes annually, which means we will be able to raise our export sales to 100,000 tonnes.

Basically there are two ways to sell a product like canola oil in export markets. One is FOB (free on board) our plant in Canada. In this situation the buyer — either an end user or more typically an international trading company like Bunge or Mitsui — will purchase the product from CSP Foods and arrange for shipping it. Most of our sales to countries like India, Taiwan, Australia, and Chile are made in this manner.

Our large sales to Algeria are made on a different basis. Here we arrange for all the

shipping and insurance requirements. It is called a CIF transaction — Cost, Insurance, and Freight. It is much more involved, requires more work, and has a higher level of risk; but, if successful, it is a more profitable way to sell internationally.

The Algerian sale has been very interesting for me. We are one of a group of three companies involved in a long-term arrangement to supply canola oil to Algeria. Between February and August, 1981, we worked closely with the Canadian Commercial Corporation (CCC), a

courage nationalization of Canadian industry; to subsidize research and development and management education in Canada; to form the Canada Development Corporation; and to forbid the application of foreign laws in Canada.

The 1970 Wahn Committee investigation examined Canada-United States relations. Much of its work was based on that done by the Watkins

federal Crown corporation, in setting up the deal with Algeria. The CCC was involved because Algeria, a socialist state, wanted to deal government to government. During the period when the deal was initially negotiated I was in Algeria four times. The canola supply agreement with Algeria is currently being renegotiated. It will take four to five months to complete the renegotiation.

Different markets have different characteristics. In Algeria and India they know what canola is and have purchased it for many years from various suppliers. Selling in these types of markets is primarily a matter of having the best price.

A country like Venezuela is different. In that country, they are unfamiliar with canola, so market development is required before sales can be made. We would have sold canola to Venezuela on a trial basis in 1983–1984; however, the 1982 Canadian crop was poor and we had an insufficient quantity and quality of canola to supply them that year.

The United States market is blocked to Canadian canola because canola imports are prohibited. Canola is not on the United States' GRAS (i.e., Generally Regarded as Safe) list because of the erucic acid content of a predecessor to canola called rapeseed. Erucic acid can be toxic to livestock. It is likely that the U.S. prohibition will be lifted because canola does not have the erucic acid content that rapeseed had.

Problems that must be dealt with in my job include how to handle shipping products. I am also deeply concerned about the tendency of other countries to subsidize production and export of canola.

First, the shipping problem. In many markets (i.e., buying countries) shipping is so difficult that you almost need to have people in these countries with knowledge of local conditions if you are going to sell CIF. For this reason it is often easier to use international trading companies and sell product FOB the plant in Canada.

Our major problem is one that many Canadian agricultural product exporters must face. It involves a shift in the international competitive environment. The EEC (European Economic Community) has become a huge canola producer and exporter. In addition, the EEC is heavily subsidizing farmers and canola crushers. The U.S. is now beginning to retaliate. I fear a major trade war, which countries like Canada and Australia just could not afford to keep up in. If this happens we would be unable to keep our prices low enough to be competitive.

I find that my job is very rewarding. The canola export business is an exciting business to be in, particularly when you are in the front line of action like I am. I enjoy it when with a phone call I can put together a deal worth millions of dollars, with the only collateral being my word.

Another element of the job I enjoy is the travel, although it can be tedious at times. I have been to parts of the world I would never have been to if I were not in this business, and I would miss the travel if I wasn't doing it.

I often think that with my training as a technical agrologist I have no business being in the job I am in. I'm not certain, however, what the ideal career training would have been. Perhaps economics, perhaps commerce or an MBA. What does strike me is that it is useful to have a broad general knowledge of the world which you can get from courses in world geography, history, and the like. The ability to speak several languages is also useful. French and Spanish in addition to English are probably the most useful. Japanese would also be useful, although it is a difficult language.

Report. One recommendation was that over time all foreign-owned firms in Canada should allow for at least 51 percent of their shares to be owned by Canadians.

The Gray Report in 1976, *Foreign Direct Investment in Canada*, attempted to determine the economic forces that promoted foreign investment and to measure its benefits and costs. The report saw the major benefits of foreign direct investment as access to new technology. It resulted in increased productivity in Canada and the introduction of new and improved products in Canada. The Gray Report recommended a foreign investment review agency to screen new foreign direct investments in Canada to determine their effect.

Foreign Investment Review Agency

FIRA

The government of Canada established the Foreign Investment Review Agency (FIRA) to screen new foreign direct investment in Canada. Its purpose is to ensure that significant benefits accrue to Canada from new foreign direct investment. It screens:

1. Most acquisitions of control of Canadian businesses by non-Canadians.
2. The establishment of new Canadian businesses by non-Canadians, who either do not already have any business in Canada or do not have any business in Canada to which the new business is or would be related.

Five general criteria are used to assess potential investments to determine whether significant benefits would accrue to Canada. These include:

1. The effect of the level and nature of economic activity in Canada, including employment, processing of resources, reduction of imports and increase in exports, purchasing of Canadian goods, and other such "spillovers."
2. The level of participation by Canadians as managers, shareholders, and directors.
3. The effect on industrial efficiency, technological development, and product innovation and variety.
4. The effect on the competitive behaviour of firms already in the industry.
5. The compatibility of the investment or acquisition with government industrial and economic policies.

After its initial review FIRA will bargain with the applicant to increase the net benefit of the project to Canadians.

SUMMARY AND LOOK AHEAD

Trade among countries broadens the market and permits greater exchange and specialization. The principles of absolute and comparative advantage show why there is economic benefit in international trade. National trade enables each country to use its limited resources to the best advantage in raising its people's standard of living.

Despite the advantages of trade there are many "created" barriers such as tariffs, embargoes, exchange control, isolationism, tax control, and balance of trade and payments problems. There are also natural barriers, such as distance. But progress has been made in removing many of the "created" barriers. As governments recognize the mutual benefits from trade, they want more trade.

In free economies, international trade basically means international business — firms and individuals in different countries whose perspective is the world, rather than an isolated regional area, buying from and selling to each other. There are, however, some forms of state trading even in free economies. In state-controlled economies, trading is handled through state trading companies.

There are many reasons why firms export and import goods, and there are different types of international business involvement. An unintentional exporter is much less committed to international business than is a multi-national company. A multinational company is based in a parent country and has production and marketing activities in one or more foreign (host) countries.

In the next three chapters we consider the many environmental factors which can affect business decisions in Canada. These environmental factors have both national and international dimensions. ■

QUESTIONS FOR REVIEW AND DISCUSSION

1. Explain how trade between two countries can benefit their citizens.
2. Do governments engage in international trade? Explain.
3. List the two general types of trade barriers and give an example of each.
4. Are the majority of tariffs on imports into Canada protective tariffs or revenue tariffs? Explain.
5. Does the General Agreement on Tariffs and Trade (GATT) help to restrict or to increase international trade? Explain.
6. Can a nation with a favourable balance of trade have an unfavourable balance of payments? Explain.
7. What effects do fluctuating exchange rates have on international trade?
8. Suppose a country has an unfavourable balance of trade and an unfavourable balance of payments. Will this tend to result in a rise or a decline in the foreign exchange rate of its currency? Explain.
9. Contrast unintentional exporting and intentional exporting.
10. Discuss the licensing requirements for a person or firm planning to export goods from Canada.
11. Identify and discuss the types of shipping documents required to export goods from Canada.
12. Contrast an exporting company and a multinational company in terms of their commitment to international business.
13. To which country does the management of a large multinational company owe its primary allegiance?
14. Is it ethical for a Canadian-based company to open a plant in a low-wage country when unemployment in Canada is at a high level?
15. "Investments made by multinational firms in foreign countries are good for both the host country and the foreign countries." Do you agree?

16. "It is easier for a firm to live up to its social responsibility when its operations are confined to one country than when it engages in international business." Do you agree?

17. Doing business in many countries exposes a firm to many risks that could be avoided by limiting its operations to its home country. What are these risks and how does a firm cope with them?

INCIDENTS

McFarlin Company

The McFarlin Company makes farm machinery. During the past three years McFarlin has marketed heavy equipment in a South American country as part of its effort to develop its export potential more fully. The equipment is produced in Canada and is exported to an independent distributor in that country.

Recently the country passed a law which will go into effect in two years. At that time, all heavy equipment, such as that sold by McFarlin, will have to be produced in that country.

Questions:
1. What does this new law mean for the company?
2. What kinds of information would you want before making a decision as to whether or not to begin production operations in that country?

Forest Products Company

Several years ago the Forest Products Company began exporting timber and timber products to industrial buyers in Japan. The company originally sold through an import agent in Osaka, Japan, but has since opened its own foreign sales office in Osaka. Forest Products has had sales increases each year since it began selling abroad. In fact, its foreign sales are growing much faster than its sales in Canada.

Everything was fine until a few months ago. It seems that legislation being supported by a conservation group in Canada would, if passed, raise timber prices. Forest Products fears it might lose Japanese customers to new competitors in Australia.

Meanwhile, a trade association of home-builders is placing the blame for the rising cost of building materials squarely on the shoulders of "companies like Forest Products which deplete Canadian forests and cause home-builders to pay higher prices, which, in the end, cost the home-owner." The firm has been criticized for exporting "goods needed at home."

Forest has received a lot of unfavourable publicity and criticism. In fact, political candidates on the Pacific coast have picked up on the controversy as a campaign issue.

Questions:
1. Why do you think that Forest Products Company began selling its products in Japan?
2. What types of arguments do you think are being made by the conservation lobby and the home-builders? How should the company react to these arguments?
3. Suppose you were one of the political candidates and you decided it would be "good politics" to side with the conservationists and home-builders. What arguments would you offer the voters to sway them to your side?
4. Develop a strategy for the Forest Products Company in light of these recent developments.

CASE STUDY

NATIONAL SYSTEMS LIMITED

JAMES CARTWRIGHT IS THE MARKETING MANAGER FOR communications products for National Systems Limited. National Systems Limited is a Canadian company based in Brampton with sales in all ten provinces. Sales revenues are in the area of $210 million annually.

National Systems had indicated its intention to expand its marketing efforts to countries other than Canada.

In Canada, the cummunications products division has a 28 percent market share. Their product competes against products imported from other countries. They are regarded as having one of the better products for the Canadian market.

Issues that Mr. Cartwright is considering in determining whether to enter international markets and how to enter them include the product he offers, what markets he should attempt to sell in, what personnel he can utilize to develop these market opportunities, and what arrangements if any he should make with organizations in potential foreign markets.

Regarding the product issue, Mr. Cartwright knew that his product competed well in Canada. He wondered whether the same product features and characteristics would be equally applicable in various foreign markets. He also wondered whether it was necessary to develop new products for each foreign market or whether he should follow an approach of testing and proving his products in Canada and not offering them for sale in other countries until they were proven successful in Canada.

Regarding the market, he was concerned whether he should initially attempt to penetrate the United States market, or whether he should focus on developing the market for his product in developing countries. The concerns he had about the United States were that competition was fierce in that country. Offsetting this concern was the fact that this very large market was geographically and culturally the most similar to the Canadian market which he was intimately familiar with. Regarding markets in developing countries, he felt that the Canadian reputation and the quality of his products were particularly strong points. He would be able to use products which had been tried, tested, and proven in the Canadian market, some of them for a number of years. On the other hand, there were cultural problems and market development problems associated with the sophistication of product use in many of the developing countries.

Another issue was the personnel he had available to develop these markets. He had what he considered to be five key senior marketing management people in Canada, along with fifteen other people at the level immediately below them. They were all fully engaged in their present jobs and none had any international marketing experience. Mr. Cartwright himself had no international marketing expertise other than a two-week seminar he attended on international marketing. One option was to recruit a new graduate from a university program in business administration. His concern in this instance was that the individual would not have sufficient experience or qualifications to be able to handle the area. Another option was to recruit someone from a major consulting firm which specialized in international marketing. His concern with this approach was that this would not lead to long-run development of an international marketing team.

Another issue was to decide how to enter different foreign markets. Should they export from plants in Canada? Should they license people to manufacture the product in foreign markets? Should they enter into a joint venture agreement to market the product in these other countries?

There was also the general issue, raised by the Board of Directors of National Systems Limited, of whether or not expansion from the Canadian market was wise. Some of the attractions for international expansion included increases in sales and potential for profit; the experience and learning that would take place in working in other countries; the fact that many of their domestic competitors were from other countries and international experience would make it easier for National Systems to compete in the Canadian market. Some of the disadvantages to international expansion were the investment that would be required to develop these markets; the fact that other companies had a considerable lead on National Systems in the international market; and the fact that they were already doing well and were profitable in serving only the Canadian market.

Questions:
1. Are there other considerations that James Cartwright should take into account in formulating his recommendation about whether to advise National Systems to go into foreign markets?
2. Are there other issues that are important to James Cartwright if they do decide to enter foreign markets?
3. Considering the issues he faces of products, markets, personnel, and business arrangements, what are the options available and what are the pros and cons of each option? Where can Mr. Cartwright look for information that will be useful to him in addressing these issues? ∎

Up to this point we have shown why economic systems exist and why the business firms within them come into being. We have also discussed the motivations of businesspeople in a capitalistic system and have described the production, marketing, and financial functions of business. All management decision making takes place in an environment that can mean the difference between a firm's success or failure.

In the next three chapters we look at this environment. It includes social, political, physical, economic, ecological, and technological dimensions. All are interconnected and are constantly changing.

Business managers can make better decisions if they know how the environment affects those decisions. Recognizing trends in the environment helps managers to plan business activity and to understand customers and employees. Understanding values in the environment helps managers set standards for their own business behaviour. This is important, because in the long run a firm's management must behave in a way that is acceptable to society. What society expects of business usually ends up in the form of laws. Business executives must understand and comply with the laws.

The economy, its health, and its growth rate have a lot to do with business success; technology often determines the success or failure of an economy and the firms in it. A business must know what is happening in the area of technology as it relates to the firm's products or services.

WHAT IS AN ENVIRONMENT?

The environment of an organization consists of all those outside things that come in contact with it and influence it. The influence can be direct or indirect. A carrot seed planted in a garden has an environment. It includes the soil in which it is planted, the temperature of the air around it, and the moisture which is provided. The growth and development of the seed depend on the environmental conditions and the quality of the seed itself.

The success of a business organization, like that of any living thing, depends on two major things: (1) the quality of the inputs, and (2) the quality of the environment in which it is found. We have examined the inputs of a business—human and material. Business managers cannot be successful as decision makers over the long run if they consider only *internal factors. We now turn to the other major determinant of success—the environment.*

Since a firm is often a large set of people and things, it could be said to have an "internal environment" distinct from those things outside which affect its operation. The internal environment might include the attitude of workers toward the firm and toward their own jobs—their morale. It might also refer to physical working conditions, such as lighting, temperature control, space, and so on. However, in this last section we are referring solely to the external environment of business.

The external environment of business can be studied in different ways. It can be looked at as comprising an almost infinite number of different influences. It is more appropriate, however, to group these influences together into a smaller number of categories. One way of grouping environmental influences is to group them into different institutions. These institutions include government, labour, consumers, environmentalists, professionals, education, religion, technology, the law, customs, ideas and beliefs, and many more. The difficulty with the institutional approach to the study of the environment is the large number of different institutions which must be studied and the complexities of the relationships between them. In our approach, institutions and the relationships between them are discussed as part of the social environment.

We have adopted a "factors" model of the environment. In other words, the environment is viewed as being composed of political, economic, social, technological, physical, and ecological factors.

THE BUSINESS ENVIRONMENT

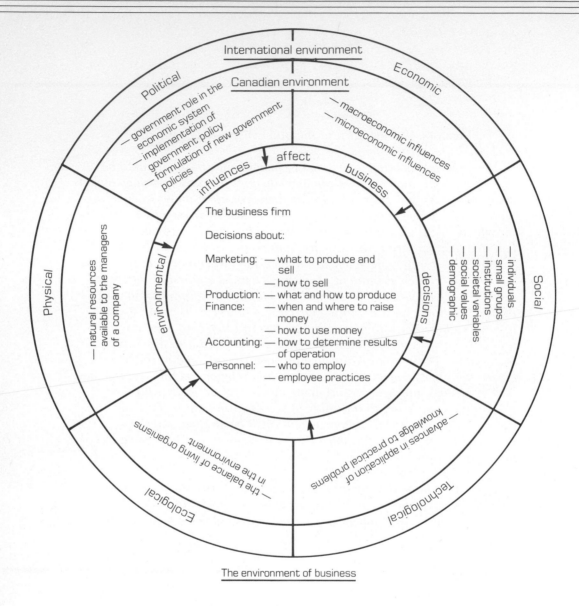

The environment of business

The Environment Is Dynamic

The accompanying diagram suggests that the various aspects of the environment of business are dynamic. They are subject to rapid change.

Something that seemed irrelevant last year might be vitally important this year. For example, a change in an immigration law might make it easier for a firm to hire skilled foreign workers. This could make a big difference in management's decision regarding the kinds of machines to install or the price to charge for the firm's product. A rise in the minimum wage might lead a supermarket chain to reduce the size of its labour force. The growth of the women's movement may cause an advertiser to change the content of a series of TV commercials.

The Environments Are Interdependent

The social, economic, political, and other environments are interdependent. For example, the economic health of a country affects the growth of technology in that country. More money is available for research and development in wealthy countries than in poor countries. Likewise, the ethical and cultural values of a democratic people are reflected in the laws they pass and the kind of government they elect.

Even though the environment is external to a firm, a firm can have some influence on it. For example, business firms work to influence government decisions at federal, provincial, and local levels. A firm's advertising can influence consumers' attitudes toward its products or services.

In the three chapters of this section you will become acquainted with many of the significant environmental factors which business managers must cope with. You will be presented with a framework for understanding and dealing with the various environmental factors. You will also study many important environmental trends and gain an appreciation of their impact on business decision making. In addition, there will be some discussion about predicting future environmental conditions.

Chapter 17 deals with the physical, ecological, and technological environments of business. It discusses our basic resource endowment, its ecological limits, and how the basic resources can be enhanced by technology.

Chapter 18 describes economic and social environmental variables which business managers must consider.

Chapter 19 describes the political environment of business firms and how it affects the decisions of business managers.

MR. YAMAZAKI, SENIOR EXECUTIVE managing director of the Yamazaki Machinery Works, Ltd., points toward a cavernous factory in which giant computerized machines—each with a pair of yellow tool drums which resemble enlarged roulette wheels—are grinding, boring, and fashioning parts for high-technology machines like themselves.

"Robots making robots" is the catch-phrase used to describe the process here. Only a few human workers are involved; they direct cranes that load metal castings onto fixtures which are then wheeled automatically to a storage area.

On the night shift, the machines work unassisted. The place is rather dimly lit. One solitary human sentinel—the night security guard—patrols the factory floor armed with a flashlight as the machines labour on, milling metal castings weighing several tons and moving them about the plant.

The startling leap forward in Japanese robot technology has given North American business leaders reason to reappraise their international competitive position in many markets. Canadian manufacturing technology will have to adapt to these kinds of changes if we are to remain internationally competitive.

CHAPTER SEVENTEEN

The Physical, Ecological, and Technological Environments

THIS CHAPTER DEALS WITH THE PHYSICAL, ECOLOGICAL, AND technological environments of business. Technology is perhaps the most important contributor to our current standard of living. Technological developments can have a great influence on decisions of business managers. Ecological conditions are, in some instances, disrupted by technological and industrial developments. Maintaining balance in the ecological environment can be an important factor in decisions made by business managers. Physical environmental factors such as the weather and natural resource availability can influence the decisions business managers make. They can also affect the outcomes of actions taken by managers.

THE PHYSICAL ENVIRONMENT

physical environment

The physical environment is the base from which all economic activity starts. **The physical environment is our natural resource endowment and includes minerals, vegetation, animal, and water resources. The weather, as part of our natural resource endowment, is also an extremely important part of the physical environment of business.**

At first glance, it may be difficult to grasp the importance of the physical environment to business. This is particularly true for individuals who were reared in cities. However, there are many industries in Canada that are not only influenced by, but dependent upon, the physical environment. These include companies involved in primary industries such as agriculture, fishing, mining, petroleum, and forestry. These industries have been the traditional strength of the Canadian economy, and they still account for considerable employment. Furthermore, they are important exporting industries.

Our dependence upon these industries has led to the observation that Canadians are "hewers of wood and haulers of water." Continued economic prosperity and resolution of problems such as the energy crisis will require that companies continue to develop more efficient ways to utilize the existing resource base. Efforts will also be required to at least maintain and, if possible, expand the size of the resource base. In the case of petroleum and base minerals, this will involve exploration efforts to find new resources. Attempts will be made to bring new agricultural land into production. Efforts must also be made to halt the encroachment of urbanization into highly productive fruit- and vegetable-producing land, such as the Niagara Peninsula and the Okanagan Valley. The forest industries must continue to husband their resources as well.

Other industries are also influenced by another facet of the physical environment—the weather. The classic example is tourism. Hawaii, because of its natural setting and climate, attracts far more Canadian tourists than many parts of Canada. Airline operators are another example of firms that are influenced by the weather. When the weather is bad and prevents flights from taking off or from landing at specified destinations, it interrupts the routine operations of these companies. Farming operations are also influenced by the physical environment. The type of soil will have an effect on what crops can be grown and the yield of these crops. The weather also has an effect on the amount and types of crops that can be grown in an area. For example, fruit crops can be grown in the Niagara Peninsula but not in northern Ontario. Variations in rainfall, temperature, and abnormal conditions such as hail can influence the year-to-year crop yield.

Adverse weather conditions over a wide area can result in significant decreases in world grain production. This can result in increases in grain prices. People interested in the grain trade watch with interest for reports of wheat crop predictions in large producing countries such as the United States and the USSR.

Beverage company sales can be affected by weather conditions. For example, hot sunny weather will result in higher sales of beer and soft drinks than will cool and cloudy weather. There has been some concern in recent years that the long-term trend is toward a cooler climate in Canada. This would have serious implications for agriculture in particular.

Secondary Effects

There are many manufacturing and service industries which are influenced by the relative success of the primary industries in coping with and/or exploiting the physical environment. A new mineral or oil discovery can result in expansion of town sites in the vicinity. Supply and service industries benefit from the existence of companies that cope successfully with the physical environment. For example, there is a tremendous amount of activity associated with development in any major project—whether drilling for oil off Canada's East Coast or developing a major coal project in British Columbia or a major hydroelectric project in Quebec.

The economic potential associated with resource project development is so large that the economic strategy of "mega-project" development was seen at one time to be the key approach to Canada's economic development into the 1990s.

Management and the Physical Environment

In earlier times when people had less understanding of the physical environment, they accepted it as it was and they worshipped various facets of it (e.g., the sun, the wind, and the rain). Phenomena such as solar eclipses, earthquakes, and floods were taken as signs from the gods.

We are now in a position, because of the technology which has developed through the centuries, to better cope with our physical environment. Construction firms are able to divert waterways for electrical generation, flood prevention, and irrigation. By using fertilizers, farmers are able to reduce the adverse effects of low levels of rainfall on crop yields. Chemical herbicides and insecticides make it possible for farmers to cope with pests which threaten their crops.

Weather forecasting techniques also make it possible to anticipate adverse conditions and to prepare for them in advance. Sophisticated exploration techniques for oil and metals make it possible to search farther below the surface of the earth for these resources.

The physical environment is still tremendously important to our economy and, to a greater or lesser degree, to various firms in the economy.

Much economic activity is based on, or influenced by, our natural resource endowment. Changes in the physical environment such as weather conditions can have profound effects on many types of firms. Management cannot control the physical environment. Through use of technology, however, such as in mineral exploration, it is possible to predict certain characteristics of the physical environment that can lead to better management decision making. It is also possible, through technology, to anticipate certain changes, such as in weather conditions, thus allowing for more informed decision making.

THE ECOLOGICAL ENVIRONMENT

ecology
Ecology is the branch of biology that deals with the relations between living organisms and their environment. The ecological environment of business is important, because many people feel that business firms have contributed to pollution of the physical environment. There is particular concern about water and air pollution and about litter and clutter affecting the visual environment.

The activities of some business firms do pollute the environment. Wastes are dumped into inland waters. Examples include the mercury emission controversy in the English-Wabigoon River system in northern Ontario, the discharge of materials by chemical and forest industry companies, and the use of water as a coolant which is returned to its source at a higher-than-normal temperature.

Many examples of air pollution can also be found. One is the emissions in the area surrounding Sudbury. There is also concern in some areas about the aroma of large cattle feed-lot operations. Acid rain is another example of serious air pollution.

Products produced by business firms often can be seen littering the countryside and roadsides. Although soft drink manufacturers did not intend their containers to be left after use, they are often held to blame for the problem.

Pollution in Canada tends to occur in isolated and individual situations, as opposed to being a general problem, but it is still important that these individual situations be seriously assessed and that appropriate action be taken. The heightened interest in North America regarding control of the spread of pollution in the 1960s was a positive step forward. With the oil crisis of the 1970s and economic problems of the 1980s there was some slackening in the move toward pollution control. However, there is still a great need for, interest in, and commitment to a clean environment.

Need for Priorities and Trade-Offs

Decisions about which anti-pollution measures to use must take monetary issues into account. It would be possible to control all emissions from public and private sources so that absolutely no pollution would occur. However, there would be a tremendous cost associated with this level of control. Priorities must be established by governments and business regarding what pollution problems to address and how many resources to allocate to pollution control relative to other things.

At a general level, the dilemma for business, and for governments as well, is that emphasis on pollution control in a single industry will result in that industry's output being noncompetitive internationally if other countries do not have the same pollution standards. A similar situation exists for individual companies in an industry. If one company buys pollution control equipment and other companies do not, then the innovating company will have costs which are uncompetitively high.

In dealing with the pollution questions raised by the ecological environment, business managers must be aware of the increasing emphasis on pollution control. In general, every attempt should be made to maintain the

WHAT DO YOU THINK?

Private and Public Weather Forecasting

The Atmospheric Environment Service (AES) of the government of Canada provides weather service to many companies, as indicated in the following examples:

A small designer of solar-run buildings requests radiation statistics for Toronto, including mean hours of sunlight, by month, since records were first kept in 1938.

Coca-Cola Ltd. wants to know deviation from normal levels for both temperature and precipitation at different spots across the country so sales curves can be related to local weather conditions.

Imperial Oil Ltd. is routinely supplied with specialized forecasts for its drilling operation. The British Columbia Forestry Service receives forecasts and data related to its needs.

Five departmental meteorologists were aboard oil rigs in the Beaufort Sea supplying on-site wind and wave forecasts to a subsidiary of Dome Petroleum Ltd.

There are more than fifty private weather consultants in Canada. Some firms undertake activities which span the full range of meteorological services offered by private industry.

Private companies resent AES activity such as that provided for Dome Petroleum. One comment was that "The government has for years been actively discouraging the growth of the private sector's role in meteorology by increasing the services it offers." WHAT DO YOU THINK? Are weather forecasting services useful to companies? Should this work be done by the private sector or left to the government?

best possible emission standards. However, the costs of pollution control must be carefully assessed. Business managers must also be aware of the prescribed emission levels laid down by governments. Dealing with the ecological environment is a complex problem for business managers.

Increased concern about the ecological environment has also created numerous opportunities for new products. An entire industry has grown up which sells products to reduce air and water pollution. Devices to process smokestack emissions and waste before it is released into water sources are products for which markets have developed since the early 1960s.

THE TECHNOLOGICAL ENVIRONMENT

technological
environment

The technological environment includes all applications of knowledge which have an impact upon a business firm. The high standard of living which today's Canadians enjoy depends on our desire and ability to pursue the benefits of technology. Technology has enabled us to move far beyond the products and the life style available from a primitive physical environ-

technology

ment. **Technology is the application of knowledge so that people can do entirely new things or do old things in a better way.** It is, in other words, the application of knowledge for practical purposes. Technology created a new "trash compacter" for the household and an "atom smasher" which has revolutionized warfare and energy production. Technology makes it possible for firms to develop new products and processes.

What Is Technological Progress?

Technological progress results in improvements in the state of industry, manufacturing, and commerce. But not all such progress leads to the betterment of humanity. This is one of the most serious challenges facing us today. How do we harness our great technological know-how for human welfare?

In the past, business growth depended on technological development. While this is still true, the progress is partly offset by problems created by technology. These include the harmful effects of obsolescence, waste, ecological disturbances, and the threat of atomic war.

The rate of productivity improvement in Japan has been greater than that in Canada or the United States (Figure 17.1). Many people have attributed this to the ability of the Japanese to adapt technologies to the workplace. This ability to use new technologies has also contributed to the great economic growth of Japan.

Some Recent Technological Developments

Since 1940 many fantastic discoveries have been made: nuclear power, space exploration, television, computers, microelectronics, biotechnology,

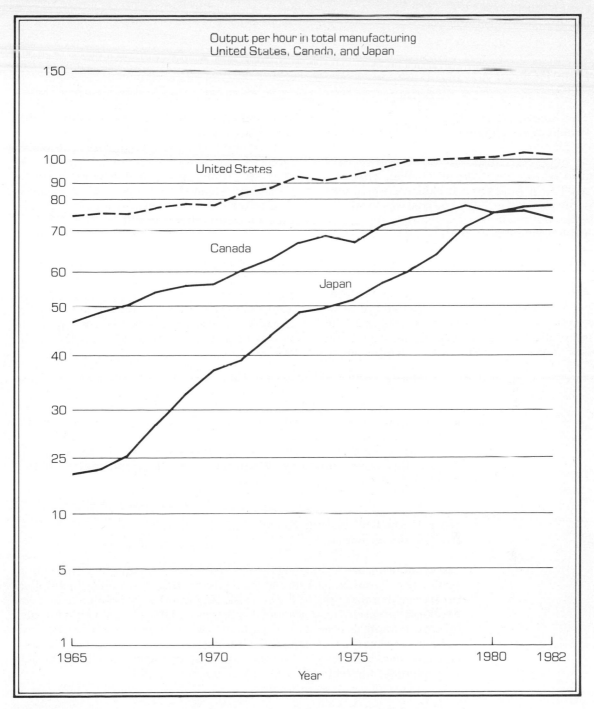

Figure 17.1
Output per hour in total manufacturing (United States, Canada, and Japan)
(Source: Donald J. Daly, *Canada's Comparative Advantage* (Ottawa: Economic
Council of Canada, 1979), pp. 37–38, updated from United States Bureau of
Labor Statistics, *News,* May 26, 1983)

POINT OF VIEW

The Alcohol Car — The Brazilian Experience

In mid–1981, four out of every five cars sold in Brazil were run on alcohol. This was all part of a long-term Brazilian government program started in 1975. The goal was to substitute alcohol made from sugar cane for nearly half the gasoline used in the country. The program included subsidies, experimentation in government-owned fleets, and a huge promotional campaign.

Although alcohol has met the goal of providing at least 75 percent of the efficiency of gasoline, it has caused many serious problems. The worst of these is that it has a corrosive effect on engine parts. In addition, it is much harder to start the engine in the morning with alcohol than with gasoline.

Ford and Volkswagen engineers at Brazilian factories are working on the corrosion and start-up problems and feel that they will be overcome. Meanwhile the average Brazilian is disillusioned and not yet convinced by the industry's claims that it is still "a good deal."

The lesson in all this for Canadian drivers is that technology comes to grips with problems (the fuel shortage) slowly and not without taking some false steps. Will alcohol play a major part in the future of energy consumption? What is your interpretation of the Brazilian experience? What is your point of view concerning a technological solution to the energy shortage?

and means to control major diseases like polio. Less dramatic, but of major importance to human welfare, are developments in statistical techniques, human psychology, crop yields, contraceptive methods, and exploration of the sea. Businesses must know about new technology and contribute to it in order to survive.

How Does Technology Affect Business Decisions?

Nearly all firms are influenced by new technology. It can affect marketing, production, finance, personnel, and accounting decisions. Technology presents either an opportunity or a risk. An opportunity is when a firm can develop a successful new product or process and thereby gain either a sales or cash advantage over its competitors. One risk is when a firm's competitors develop the technological advantage, resulting in negative financial consequences for the firm. Another risk is that management will not be able to implement the technological development profitably.

Technology and Management

There is considerable opportunity for business firms in Canada to improve their economic performance by initiating and using technological improvements. For business firms, technology, or the application of knowledge to practical problems, is utilized either to develop new products, to improve existing products, or to improve the process by which a product is produced.

Two different activities are involved in the commercial introduction of technological improvements. The first is the development of the technological improvement, and the second is its implementation. The two activities require very different abilities. The person or firm good at one may not be good at the other. Success in developing a new product or process does not guarantee commercial success. In this sense, technological improvements are no panacea for owners and operators of firms. The skill to develop technological improvements must go hand-in-hand with the marketing, finance, personnel, and other management skills required to successfully operate a firm.

Technology and the Need to Plan

Another outgrowth of rapid change in technology is the vital need to plan. If a firm is to succeed in the long run, it must not define its objectives too narrowly. Petroleum producers are wise to think of themselves as "energy companies." They must consider substitutes for oil as sources of energy. Most manufacturers of containers used to be specialists in one kind of container (glass, paper, or metal). Now they produce all three types, mostly because of uncertainty about which type of container will prevail in the long run.

Technological obsolescence means the replacement of a technical product or product feature by a newer, better, or cheaper one. This encourages firms to reduce the risk of obsolescence by introducing their own new product. As we have seen, many firms engage in planned obsolescence. In other words, they plan to introduce new versions of products which will encourage previous buyers to replace their older (but still useful) models.

Patents give a legal protection from theft or imitation of technological ideas. They play an important role in this kind of planning. When a firm wants a patent on a new discovery, it registers it with the Canadian Patent Office. A patent protects that discovery from being copied by competitors for a number of years.

Patent law is highly complex. A large number of patents may be needed to protect a new idea fully. Careful development of patents is one way of planning to meet future product competition.

Technology and Social Problems

Ever since machines became important in the production process, there has been concern that they would take over the work done by humans and that massive unemployment would result. Does automation cause unemployment? The best answer to this question is that automation does cause unemployment in the immediate area where it is applied, but overall,

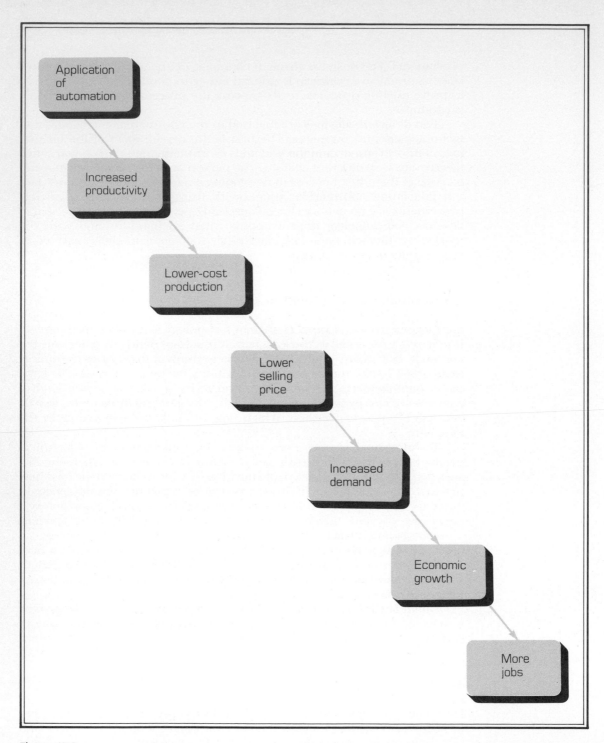

Figure 17.2
Automation and unemployment

598

automation creates far more jobs than it takes away. The reasoning behind this conclusion is shown in Figure 17.2.

The use of automation (e.g., in a factory) will generally result in lower costs in producing the product, and hence in increased productivity. This increase in productivity allows the company to sell the product at a lower price. Generally speaking, the lower the price of a product, the greater the demand; increased demand for goods in general results in economic growth. With economic growth comes an increase in demand for workers and an increase in the number of jobs.

The above analysis is an accurate reflection of how automation affects unemployment on a society-wide level, but it may not be accurate in a specific situation. Consider the case of the Weed Drill Company, which is planning to open a highly automated factory with only twenty-five supervisory and maintenance personnel. The new factory will replace a nearly obsolete factory which presently employs 300 workers. Weed Drill Company must face the problem of the unemployed workers. Economic theory says that improved technology will, in the long run, benefit the whole economy. But this theory gives little comfort to those who will be out of jobs.

The problem is especially tough when a worker in such a case is not easily reemployable. If there is already an oversupply in the worker's specialty, the worker may have to be completely retrained. Sometimes private or government-sponsored retraining programs are available. If the Weed Drill Company has other plants, it may find a place elsewhere for its workers. If it is unionized, the union contracts may have special provisions to protect members who cannot find suitable jobs. In any case, technology can contribute to worker displacement, which, in turn, creates social problems.

We have already discussed another technology-related problem which affects society—pollution. A specific case which relates to energy technology has become a major issue of the day. Rapid depletion of high-grade, low-polluting fuels (natural gas and oil) makes the use of low-grade, high-polluting fuels (coal) more economically feasible. This does not make such a use socially desirable, though. Situations such as these require solutions that are not 100 percent satisfactory in terms of either ecology or profit. We will probably design less-polluting techniques for burning coal. In other words, technology will, we hope, overcome the bad side effects of other technology.

Technological advances such as computers are also used to combat social problems. Computers are used to spread job information among various labour markets. They are also used to improve educational systems and to analyze law-enforcement problems.

Research and Development

Firms must be aware of technological change so that their processes, products, and product features will not become obsolete. They must also be ready to counteract the competitive effect of such technology. If a firm is aggressive, it will be the first to introduce a new, cheaper way to make its "Product X." It might also introduce "Product X–Mark II" with features which make a competitor's Product Y obsolete. Any of these objectives requires substantial investment in research and development (R&D). **R&D is a general name applied to activities that are intended to provide new products and processes.** It usually requires a large investment in laboratories, equipment, and scientific talent.

research and development (R&D)

R&D can lengthen a product's life cycle. It can also lead to the quick end of the life cycle of a firm's product or that of its competitors. R&D, then, is the key to much competition today and represents a major class of business activity. It often results in rapid improvement in the quality of products.

Today there is growing criticism of this kind of economic growth. Because of the perceived waste and pollution it brings, some favour a slowing down of product innovation, particularly as it applies to luxury products. Is it important that we produce endless numbers of "bigger and better" products?

Some firms consider R&D as a substitute for price competition. A few large firms which can afford major research programs use them to strengthen their hold on the market. By means of continuous product improvement and innovation, they can prevent entry of competitors. Improved use of technologies in product and process development is likely to be an important condition for future economic growth in Canada.

A technological advance can be an important competitive weapon for a small firm establishing itself. A small firm that gives its scientists freedom to explore and a modest budget sometimes comes up with a "breakthrough" which puts it on a competitive basis with the giants in its industry. Dr. E. H. Land's photographic genius made "Polaroid" a name to stand beside "Kodak" in an industry that was nearly a monopoly before World War II. Smaller firms are often forced to merge with others to be able to afford R&D. Sometimes they must purchase patent-licensing rights from larger firms.

Research and Development and the National Interest

Technological advances result from research and development work. This work can take a variety of forms. It may be the inspiration of a practising manager about how to perform a particular task more efficiently. It may be heavily funded work over a period of time by a business, government, or university research team.

It is important that research and development contribute to technological advance in Canada so that our industries can remain internationally competitive.

Because wage rates in Canada are higher than in many other countries, technological leadership is a factor which can give us a competitive advantage over other countries. Technologically advanced products can contribute to the export performance of Canada.

Table 17.1   Gross Expenditures for R&D in the Natural Sciences as a Percentage of Gross Domestic Product

| | *Total R&D in All Sectors as a Percent of GDP* | | |
	1973	*1977*	*1979*
Canada	1.1	1.1	1.1
France	1.8	1.8	1.8
Germany	2.1	2.1	2.3
Japan	1.9	1.9	2.1
Netherlands	2.0	2.0	2.0
Sweden	1.6	1.9	1.9
Switzerland	2.3	2.3	2.5
U.S.A.	2.5	2.4	2.4

Source: Statistics Canada, *Service Bulletin, Science Statistics,* Education, Science and Culture Division, Vol. 6, No. 12, November 1982 (p. 3).

In 1979 Canadian expenditures on R&D were only slightly over 1 percent of Gross National Product.

International comparisons show that Canada's R&D effort is below the levels in other industrial economies, as shown in Table 17.1. This table shows that Canada lagged in terms of total R&D.

Since 1963 expenditures on R&D performed in Canada have shifted from government to business to a degree. The percentage distribution of R&D expenditures by performer is shown in Table 17.2.

Within the private sector, R&D spending is highly concentrated in a relatively few companies and in relatively few sectors. This pattern of a small number of large companies doing the largest share of private sector spending on R&D is not unique to Canada. For example, in the United States companies with more than 25,000 employees were reported to have accounted for 75 percent of industrial R&D expenditures.

Table 17.2   Percentage Distribution of Gross Expenditures in Canada on R&D, by Performer

| | *Average (percent)* | | | |
	1963–1967	*1968–1972*	*1973–1977*	*1978–1982*
Government	34.0	31.0	29.0	24.0
Business enterprise	41.0	39.0	41.0	49.0
Universities	21.0	26.0	26.0	23.0
Other	4.0	4.0	4.0	4.0
Total R&D	100.0	100.0	100.0	100.0

Source: Statistics Canada, *Service Bulletin, Science Statistics,* Education, Science and Culture Division, Vol. 6, No. 5, June 1982 (p. 3).

THE INTERNATIONAL TECHNOLOGICAL ENVIRONMENT

Problems and Opportunities

One of the biggest differences between "have" and "have-not" nations is the technology gap. Advanced transportation and communication are taken for granted in Canada. In many underdeveloped nations they are almost non-existent. Managers must evaluate the level of technology in those countries where they expect to operate. This may enable them to adapt their operations to the present technology or attempt to "import" new techniques. But importing these "new ways" sometimes leads to resistance, especially when the local people do not understand them.

The high level of foreign ownership of Canadian industry may account for the low level of R&D spending by the private sector. A study conducted by the federal Ministry of State for Science and Technology indicated that large Canadian-owned firms imported less than half the R&D they required. On the other hand, foreign-owned firms tended to concentrate their R&D activities in their home countries. Subsidiaries which performed a

WHAT DO YOU THINK?

Need for an Industrial Strategy

In a speech to the International Federation of Operational Research Societies in June 1978 (reported in *The Globe and Mail,* Toronto, June 21, 1978), Josef Kates, Chairman of the Science Council of Canada, said that there is a trend toward technological protectionism among industrialized countries because of the growing awareness that technology confers certain competitive trade advantages. "This has reached the level of serious policy discussion in the United States, with proposals being considered for a seven-year moratorium on the export of any technology financed by the Government."

Technology, he saw, was one of the few competitive factors currently favouring Western economies. Unless Canada begins to move toward greater technological independence, it will continue to lose its market share in international trading.

The real problem, according to Mr. Kates, lies in Canada's tariff policy, which has created a "fragmentation of manufacturing plants and inhibited the growth of Canadian companies." Extractive industries and branch plant operations have proliferated, but technology-based manufacturing industries have not been encouraged.

He said: "If we do not seize upon some strategy, and quickly, we will continue to lose control of our economic destiny .... Ten years from now, our area of choice, our capacity for self-determination and our will to resolve the problem will be further and perhaps irretrievably vitiated." WHAT DO YOU THINK? Do you agree that Canada should adopt a national strategy to funnel more resources into industrial research and development?

significant amount of R&D in Canada relied heavily upon their parent's R&D activities.

Subsidiaries of foreign-owned firms (primarily U.S.) obtain much technology from their parent companies. Domestically owned firms often utilize arrangements whereby they get access to foreign-developed technology through licensing agreements. They pay a fee for the licensing agreement, and often the agreement includes a clause about what markets (export) can be served by the Canadian firm. Exports by U.S. subsidiaries and Canadian-owned firms are also often limited by a smaller scale of operation in this country which results in higher costs than in competitive exporting countries. The extent of exports by U.S. subsidiaries is also often determined by decisions made at the U.S. head offices of these companies.

The argument has been made that Canada's reliance on foreign sources of technology may harm us in the future. Because increasing international competitiveness will in the future be tied to technological advantages, we could be harmed if foreign governments began to limit the export of their technology. The conclusion of the argument is that Canada should become more technologically competitive. One other side of the argument, however, is the fact that we would have to sacrifice some other things in order to apply resources to development of technological leadership. Canadians must become more adept at managing technology to enable continued economic growth.

Forecasting

While it is useful to understand the current environment of business, the most useful information for a business manager is the characteristics of the *future* environment of business that are relevant to the firm.

The most relevant environmental characteristics will vary for different types of firms. For example, a public utility would be very interested in the demographic characteristics of its customers. A retail operation would be very interested in information about competitors' processes and product lines.

In making a decision about allocating resources, the business manager is always making an assumption (implicitly if not explicitly) about what the future environment will be. In business, as in betting on a horse race, the more accurate your assumptions are about what will happen (i.e., your forecast), the better your chances are of making money, or the lower your chances are of losing it.

forecasts **Forecasts are assumptions about what the future environment of business will be.** A forecast can be based on intuition or on studies which cost hundreds of thousands of dollars. It is never possible to forecast the future with absolute certainty. However, it is possible to gain a better appreciation of what environmental developments might occur in the future. There are a variety of forecasting techniques which can be used. These are discussed below in terms of the physical, ecological, and technological environments. However, they can also be utilized for forecasting the other environments of business as well.

forecasting techniques	**Forecasting techniques are specific methods used for making predictions about the future of business environments.** Some of the techniques for environmental forecasting include: vision, intuition, extrapolation, correlation, scenarios, simulation, content analysis, and informed judgments.
vision	**Vision is when a person decides that he or she wants something to happen and goes out and does it.** This was essentially the case with the United States' effort to put a man on the moon. In the early 1960s the commitment was made to walk on the moon within a decade, and the vision became a reality in July 1969.
intuition	**Intuition is a judgment by an individual or a group based on limited information.** Brainstorming is another way of describing this method of formulating assumptions about the environment. If you hear someone say that it is their "gut feel" that a certain event will occur, you are listening to a prediction based on intuition. Many decisions are made this way.
extrapolation	**Extrapolation is the projection of past and present circumstances into the future.** This could involve projection of past trends. For example, because resource use per capita and pollution had been increasing in the past, it might be assumed that they will continue to increase. Sophisticated extrapolation involves use of time series regression analysis. An example would be the projection by representatives of government that the automobile industry's technological efforts will be able to meet new pollution emission standards. Extrapolation could also involve anticipation of the same conditions in the future that have prevailed in the past.
correlation	**Correlation involves making a prediction about one outcome based on knowledge of other outcomes.** For example, the cost of producing a new technologically advanced product can be related to the length of time the product will be in production. Experience curve data compiled by the Boston Consulting Group indicate that for every doubling of the time of production, costs decrease by 20 to 30 percent. A forecast that inflation will occur as a result of an increase in the money supply is another example of a correlative prediction.
scenarios	**Scenarios are statements of how an event could unfold.** One weather scenario is that within the next century our average annual temperature will drop by three degrees. Another is that it will increase by three degrees, and still another is that it will remain the same. The most likely scenario is that the average annual temperature will remain the same, and we can plan on that basis. However, if the possibility is recognized that the other scenarios *could* also happen, contingencies can be developed for them. The time and resources allocated to developing contingencies would have to relate to the probability that an alternative scenario would develop. Scenarios can be developed for a wide variety of things. Examples include: future resource availability; future sources of energy; future levels of pollution; and technology for preventing undesirable atmospheric emissions and weather emergencies such as hail, hurricanes, or tornados.
simulation	**Simulation involves developing a model of an actual situation and working through the simulation to see what kind of outcome results.** Simulation models were used by the "Club of Rome" analysts to predict future high levels of pollution and exhaustion of resources on this planet.

WHAT DO YOU THINK?

Physical, Ecological, and Technological Forecasts

Many different forecasts can be made. Some may occur; others probably will not. How might you check some of these forecasts?

1. By the early part of the twenty-first century our natural resources in North American will be so depleted and our environment will be so polluted that our standard of living will be reduced to that of the late 1800s.
2. By the year 2025 nuclear fission as a source of energy will be an economic reality.
3. Within ten years our dependence upon the United States for technological assistance will make us an economic slave of that country.
4. Cable television companies will replace the current television networks as the prime producers of home entertainment.
5. Solar energy will be economically feasible for individual homes by the year 2000.
6. Technology will solve all pollution problems within the next thirty years.
7. Within the next fifty years the amount of effluent reaching the world's oceans will put them in danger of a pollution crisis.
8. The trend to technological obsolescence of products will be reversed and replaced with a trend toward higher-quality, longer-lasting, more expensive products.
9. Our weather will become more and more severe.
10. We will deplete our natural oil, mineral, and forest resources by the year 2050.
11. After 1995 we will be unable to further increase agricultural productivity because chemical fertilizers, herbicides, and insecticides will be restricted due to pressure from environmentalists.
12. We will continue indefinitely to find technological solutions to ecological and physical resource shortage problems.

WHAT DO YOU THINK? What forecasts would you accept? What methods would you use to check them?

---

content analysis

Content analysis is examination of the content of publications for reference to specific items. Content analysis of patent publications or of scientific and trade publications for reference to certain types of technological advances could be used to predict breakthroughs with respect to the development of certain types of products.

informed judgment

Informed judgment is expert opinion on a subject. It is based on a thorough understanding of all the facts in a given situation. It could also be referred to as a projection based upon an analysis of a situation. In most cases, the informed judgment of someone is probably the last thing done prior to acceptance of a forecast. **A method of combining the informed judgments of a number of experts on a subject is**

Delphi technique

known as the Delphi technique. This involves getting opinions on a subject from a group of experts and then going through a process of giving them feedback about what other experts in the group said and allowing them to reformulate their own opinions.

Different forecasting methods will be used for different purposes by different people. In some cases a variety of methods will be used.

CAREER PROFILE

MY NAME IS BILL BENNETT AND I AM THE owner and manager of Bennett's Lodges Ltd. I run three fly-in fishing camps on Nueltin Lake which is situated on the border of Manitoba and the Northwest Territories.

Like many young Canadians I worked in mining and lumber camps as a teenager. I also worked as a guide at fishing camps in Ontario and Saskatchewan during the summer months. In 1972 I was admitted to the University of Guelph as a mature student; I received a B.A. (Honours) in English in 1976. I originally intended to be a teacher, but after several summers of guiding I was asked to be a camp manager. That line of work appealed to me, and I decided to make it my career upon graduation.

In 1977, after searching Canada's North for the right camp, I bought Treeline Lodge and began operations. Financing the purchase was difficult because of my youthful age and lack of equity, but eventually it was arranged through the Federal Business Development Bank and Treeline's previous owners.

I find the job of owner-manager to be interesting and demanding. The most important skill needed is the ability to plan and organize. The key to successful planning and organiza-

tion in my business is the cost-efficient management of the air freight process, but there are many other important areas as well. Advertising copy must be written and circulated, reservations must be made, personnel must be hired, and many other details of the total operation must be planned and carried out in

---

SUMMARY AND LOOK AHEAD

In this chapter we considered the physical, ecological, and technological environments of business. The physical environment is our natural resource endowment. Technology allows us to develop the physical environment both for the benefit of society and to make ourselves less dependent upon it.

The ecological environment has become an issue of great concern in the last two decades. That is, people have become more concerned with not altering the natural balance of the physical environment, for aesthetic reasons and because they believe that the natural physical environment may be less able to serve our needs in the future.

Technology is the application of knowledge to enable people to do entirely new things or to do old things in a better way. Technology has added

a coordinated way so that the guests are happy and the business makes a profit.

There are many rewards in running a fly-in fishing camp. First, the work is never boring. I have to be a combination of motor mechanic, carpenter, typist, office manager, bookkeeper, salesman, labour relations specialist, amiable host, and amateur biologist. There is never a dull moment. Second, I meet people from all walks of life and from many different places. Interesting conversations result and some good friendships are formed. Third, I have some freedom during the winter months and enjoy travelling to sportsmen's shows across North America. At these shows I promote my business and in my spare time I get to see some of the local attractions. Finally, the business, if run properly, allows me to make a good living.

As with any business there are some problems that must be dealt with. Weather is a major one. I am selling a specialized product, but the weather in the Far North can interfere with even my best plans to do this successfully. If the ice goes off the lake later than expected, or if it rains or snows excessively, or if it is too windy, tourists can't fish the way they want to and they are understandably disappointed. I can overcome these problems to some extent (by providing large boats, by showing guests sheltered fishing spots, and by providing roomy accommodations), but the weather is an uncontrollable factor.

I am also very dependent on the transportation and communication systems that service the camp. When people come to the Far North they want to be able to get in and out of the camp on time so they can make flight connections on commercial jets. Also I must be able to communicate clearly with our suppliers "outside" to ensure that all critical supplies are put on the next airplane. Once again, weather can interfere in both these areas. If the ceiling is too low, float planes can't fly; if the weather is bad, radio communication may be blocked out.

Another problem to be recognized is that the ecosystem of the North is very fragile. Fish grow very slowly here, so I have had Nueltin Lake declared a "trophy lake." This means that each guest may keep only one fish per week; all others must be released. We encourage guests to use only barbless hooks so that fish can be released unharmed. If these two practices are followed, good fishing will be available in the lake for years to come. This in turn improves the prospects of my staying in business for a long time.

Overall, operating a fishing camp has been a positive and satisfying experience for me. With proper long-range planning and a realistic view of the natural resources available, I hope to continue selling this service to customers for many years.

---

immeasurably to our standard of living. Management of technology is an important task. The two main aspects of managing technology are developing, or acquiring, the technology and implementing it. Technological development is important to the Canadian national interest. It is the subject of much discussion, since so much technology is imported from the United States.

Environmental forecasting is predicting the future state of all environments which are important to business (including the physical, ecological, and technological environments). Assumptions about what these environments will be in the future are very useful in management decision making. There are a variety of techniques for environmental forecasting.

In the next chapter we look at characteristics of the economic and social environments of business. ■

1. What are the physical, ecological, and technological environments of business?
2. What steps can a tourist camp operator and a mine manager take to deal with the physical environment?
3. Does business have a responsibility to not pollute the physical environment?
4. Is business the only contributor to environmental pollution?
5. How would you decide whether to allocate resources to cleaning up weed growth in a lake or to building a new sewage system for a town on the edge of the lake?
6. What are the primary tasks involved in management of technology?
7. Can you give ten examples of technological developments which are important to our way of life?
8. How important is technological development to industry in Canada?
9. Should government support technological development?
10. Does technology contribute to unemployment?
11. How can R&D increase the competitive strength of a manufacturer?
12. Identify five important environmental variables and illustrate how you would forecast each of them for five years from now.
13. What are the differences between the various forecasting methodologies?

INCIDENT

Blakley, Inc.

Blakley, Inc., a manufacturer of washing machines for the home, is the smallest of the major competitors in its market in Canada. Among its competitors are the U.S.-based giants, Maytag, RCA Whirlpool, and General Electric. Rumours persist that a new washer based on "sound waves without water" is nearing perfection in the laboratories of one of the big firms.

Questions:
1. What should Blakley do? Why?
2. Explain how the concept of the product life cycle fits in here.
3. Could any social problem follow from this invention? Explain.

CASE STUDY

ARSENIC STORAGE

IN JUNE 1978, A TORNADO TOUCHED DOWN BRIEFLY IN A SMALL town in southern Manitoba. Fortunately, it did not damage a dilapidated storage shed containing 300 tons of arsenic trioxide—a deadly chemical used for killing rats and insects before it was banned by the federal government a number of years ago. Some of the material had been stored there for twenty years.

There was fear, even prior to the tornado, that the chemical could be dangerous. The one-storey frame building housing the chemical was old and insecure. At one end of the building the wooden siding could easily be forced open. On hot days fumes could be seen rising from the building.

The company that owned the material did not feel it was responsible for removing the chemical. The company's general manager said that the banned chemical had been in the firm's inventory when he bought the firm and that the change in government regulation was what made it unusable. He indicated that the ideal solution was to transport the chemical and store it in an old missile silo in Idaho. The cost of this, however, was estimated at between $60,000 and $80,000, a very large amount for a small firm.

Just prior to the tornado, the provincial minister of mines, resources, and environmental management had indicated in the legislative assembly that the government was planning to see that the arsenic was moved but that it was an extremely complicated situation.

The issue has been under discussion by the village council, the provincial and federal governments, and the company for six years. A company representative said he had a "five-inch stack of letters" from various provincial and federal governments.

A councillor of the town said the villagers were angry because they felt the company and the federal and provincial governments were "first considering who will get stuck with the bill" rather than considering the safety of the community. The townspeople weren't optimistic about the province's plans to have the arsenic removed. "We've heard that so many times before. What we want now is action, not more promises."

Questions:
1. Who is responsible for the situation?
2. Should action be taken? When?
3. What should the company do?
4. What should the provincial government do?
5. What should the federal government do?
6. What should residents of the town do? ∎

CASE STUDY

TECHNOLOGICAL ENTREPRENEURSHIP: HOME COMMUNICATIONS SYSTEMS

MATHEW DERKATCH HAD DEVELOPED A NEW HOME COMMUNICATIONS system concept. His approach involved taking a number of existing products and combining them, utilizing a patented control and switching system that he had invented. The home communications system combined in one set of components: television, telidon, computer, radio, stereo, telephone, voice message receiving and sending, and text messaging or electronic mail. He felt this system, when fully developed, could sell for about $3500, compared to much more for all the items individually.

Mathew was a 42-year-old design engineer for a major telecommunications company. His wife Angela also worked and they had no children. Their total family income was $85,000 annually, and they had savings of $50,000 and a borrowing potential of $150,000.

His company had expressed no interest in developing the home communications system concept. In fact, Mathew was concerned that the management of the company he worked for would "kill" the idea if he turned it over exclusively to them.

Mathew was seriously considering whether he should attempt to develop the system himself or approach some other company with his concept and patents.

A general consideration was whether there really was a substantial market for the product or whether Mathew was overestimating the potential for it. The technical adequacy of his system was also a concern, but he had received advice from independent technical experts who were impressed with the commercial potential for his concept and had encouraged him to proceed.

Specifically, Mathew was concerned that it would cost $400,000 to develop the system himself before even limited sales could be made. He would also have to quit his current job in order to do this and there was no guarantee of revenue. On the other hand, he was sure that he could raise the money by borrowing and by bringing in some other shareholders.

Taking his idea to other possible manufacturers was seen as difficult. He did not know the top management people in many other companies. He also had to consider the appropriateness of dealing with the competitors of his current employer.

Mathew Derkatch felt deep down that more than anything else he wanted to see his idea developed into a commercial reality.

Questions:
1. What technological issues face Mathew Derkatch?
2. What are his major choices?
3. What are the pros and cons of each of the choices he has?
4. What should Mathew Derkatch do? ∎

After reading this chapter, you should be able to:

1. Understand the components and importance of the economic environment of a firm.
2. Discuss the differences between microeconomic and macroeconomic influences on business.
3. Describe the economic theory of the firm and how it is useful in understanding microeconomic influences on the firm.
4. Indicate the various types of macroeconomic environmental influences and how they can affect a firm.
5. Describe various microeconomic and macroeconomic concepts such as demand, supply, productivity, competition, economic growth, income distribution, stagflation, and the balance of payments.
6. Understand the importance of economic forecasting.
7. Understand the components and the importance of the social environment of a firm.
8. Describe the characteristics of the individual, small-group, institutional, and societal variables.
9. Discuss the differences between individual, small-group, institutional, and societal variables.
10. Indicate the differences between "traditional values" and "new values."
11. Explain the differences between the traditional managerial ethic and the professional-managerial ethic.
12. Discuss the concept of social responsibility and indicate the arguments for and against it.

In reading this chapter, look for and understand these terms:

economic environment	small groups
economic theory of the firm	norm
microeconomic environment	institutions
productivity	power
macroeconomic environment	demography
economic development	values
economic growth	traditional values
distribution of income	new values
progressive income tax	social responsibility of business
stagflation	traditional business ethic
social environment	professional-managerial ethic
individual social environment variables	

THE CONDITION OF THE CANADIAN economy in the early 1980s created social hardships for many people. Some members of the labour force were unemployed; it was difficult for graduating students to find jobs; and layoffs of middle- and upper-level executives were frequent.

The social problems created a base for considerable debate about what would be the most appropriate means to revive the

CHAPTER EIGHTEEN

The Economic and
Social Environments

economy. Some economists advocated significantly greater government debt levels. Others recommended restraint in government spending in order to prevent inflation from returning to its previous record-high levels. One argument was that people's attitudes must change before economic recovery would be possible. The advocates of this point of view said that inflationary psychology must be broken.

The interrelationships of economic and social factors were never more clearly demonstrated than during this period.

THIS CHAPTER CONTAINS A DISCUSSION OF THE ECONOMIC AND SOCIAL environments of business. These two environments have a big influence on business firms. The economic environment determines the prices firms must pay for supplies and the prices they can charge for their products. There are many microeconomic and macroeconomic factors which influence a firm.

The social environment is composed of all human factors which are external to the firm. The social environment influences marketing, production, and personnel decisions in many ways. The social environment is analyzed in terms of individuals, small groups, institutions, and societal variables.

The final section of the chapter is devoted to a discussion of the responsibilities of Canadian business firms. The main issue is whether or not firms have a social responsibility which goes beyond the simple pursuit of profit.

THE ECONOMIC ENVIRONMENT

economic environment

The economic environment is composed of external influences which result in changes in prices of inputs used by firms or of products sold by firms. The economic environment must be considered when making decisions about methods of production, location of production, advertising, pricing, volume of output to produce, and selection of inputs. The effect of the economic environment on these decisions is shown in Table 18.1.

One way of categorizing the multitude of economic factors, and at the same time relating the discussion to basic economics courses you have taken, is to divide it into microeconomic and macroeconomic influences on business decision making. Microeconomic factors are those that relate directly to the firm's cost of production and revenues from production, while macroeconomic factors are those related to the economy in general.

Table 18.1   Some Economic Environmental Influences on Business Decision Making

Business Decisions	Examples of Economic Environmental Considerations
What products to produce	(a) selling prices of products in relation to cost of production (b) actions by competitors
Investment in new production process	(a) outlook for economic growth and inflation (b) cost of new process in relation to revenues it will generate (c) savings in cost of production
Decision about what volume of output to produce	(a) current inventories (b) expected growth in demand (c) outlook for economic growth and inflation
What price to sell products at	(a) prices charged by competition (b) anticipated inflation (c) anticipated demand for product (d) cost of production

MICROECONOMIC ENVIRONMENTAL FACTORS

economic theory
of the firm

The economic theory of the firm (microeconomics) is that a firm will choose the level of output which results in the maximum profit for the firm. Profit is what remains after costs are deducted from revenues. Figure 18.1 on page 616 indicates how the relationship between cost and revenue (profit) changes as the level of output changes. **Therefore, the**

microeconomic
environment

microeconomic environment is composed of those factors that directly affect a firm's input and output prices. These factors include demand and price for a product, supply and price of inputs, productivity of inputs, and competition.

Demand and Price for a Product

The demand for and price of a product will influence the level and shape of the revenue curve for a firm's product. We discussed demand and price and factors that influence them in Chapter 2. Some examples will clearly illustrate the effect of changes in demand or price on a firm's revenue.

The traditional example is the buggywhip manufacturer whose market evaporated with the introduction of automobiles. The demand for the product declined and the firm's revenue likewise declined. More recently, the oil-price increase in the mid-1970s resulted in a significant increase in revenue for oil-producing firms.

There are a multitude of factors which can result in changes in demand and/or price for the products of a firm. In many instances a firm's managers have no influence over these external factors.

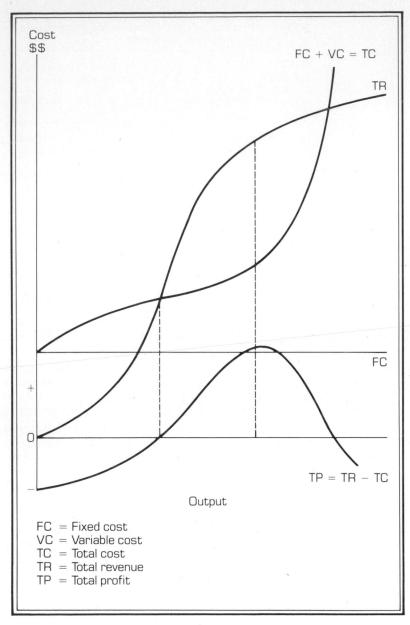

Figure 18.1
Theory of the firm

Supply and Price of Inputs

Just as the demand for and price of products influence the *revenue* curve of a firm, the availability of the inputs required by a firm influences its *cost* curve. If, for example, petroleum products such as heating oil and gasoline are a major input factor for a firm, an oil-price increase would have the effect of raising its costs and lowering profits unless there was a compensating increase in price.

Similarly, if the price of labour increases, the effect is to raise the cost curve of a firm. Again, the managers of firms have little influence over the cost of most inputs they require. Changes in the environment which alter input prices can have a major effect on the profit position of a firm.

Productivity of Inputs

productivity

The productivity of inputs is the number of units of output per unit of input. Increases in productivity which result in lower costs per unit of product increase the profit of a firm. For example, when automation makes it possible to produce a given amount of output with less hours of labour, we say that the productivity of labour has been improved. Productivity of any of the factors of production — land, labour, or capital — is normally increased by technological improvements. With any new product there is usually an improvement in productivity as experience is gained with its production. This is referred to as a learning curve. Productivity of all inputs for a new product improve after the product has been in production for a period of time.

A firm must be able to remain competitive with other firms which introduce new technology to improve their productivity. Each firm must therefore make efforts to improve its own productivity.

Competition

Competition is a very real and significant factor in the microeconomic environment of most firms. Competition forces business managers to keep their product prices at a level comparable to those of other firms in the industry. Similarly, competition keeps the price of required inputs up. Competition also forces managers to adopt the most modern management and production techniques in order to keep costs of production down at the lowest level possible. Competition provides excellent discipline in the privately operated portion of our mixed economy. It is harsh discipline, too. The ultimate penalty for not maintaining revenues, or for letting costs rise to the point where operations become unprofitable, is bankruptcy.

Although it is not as direct, competition also provides discipline for publicly owned firms. A government can only afford to provide so much support for an agency whose expenses exceed its revenues.

There are different types of competitive structures in different industries. These create somewhat different competitive environment situations. Three types of market structures are perfect competition, oligopoly, and monopoly. In perfect competition, there are a large number of firms and prices are set by the market. In oligopoly there are a limited number of firms and prices are normally set by a price leader among the firms. In monopoly there is only one firm and it sets its prices so as to maximize profits.

When we think about the competitive structure of an industry it is necessary to take note of:

- the nature and extent of competition among firms in the industry
- the likelihood of entry of new competitors
- the degree of influence of industry suppliers
- the degree of influence of industry customers
- the emergence of new substitute products

MACROECONOMIC ENVIRONMENTAL FACTORS

macroeconomic environment

The macroeconomic environment is the general economic situation in the country or countries in which a firm operates. It includes factors such as economic development, income distribution, the business cycle, and the balance of payments and exchange rates. These macroeconomic factors are not controllable by business managers, but like many other environmental factors they can have a significant influence on the operation of a firm.

Economic Development

economic development

A nation—even a region within a nation—goes through certain stages of economic development. **Economic development means that a nation grows in terms of the amount its average citizen produces.** Canada has evolved from a simple farm economy to a highly developed, urban, manufacturing and service economy.

Some parts of our country are still relatively underdeveloped, largely because of geographic and climatic factors. However, the least-developed parts of Canada are at a more advanced stage of economic development than many of the nations of Asia, Africa, and South America. Some of these nations cannot even feed and clothe their people.

economic growth

The most common measure of a nation's level of economic development is per capita Gross National Product (GNP). **Economic growth refers to the year-to-year increase in GNP.** If there is rapid economic growth, the prospects for business are normally better than if there is little economic growth.

Canada is rich in resources such as iron, coal, oil, forest products, and nickel. We have relied heavily upon natural resource development for economic growth. Some other countries have few natural resources. They must either import them or do without them. Japan, one of the largest manufacturing nations in the world, has few natural resources. Because of this, Japan has had to follow a different approach to economic development. By importing resources and by developing capital, Japan has overcome the handicap.

Other nations, such as Colombia and Nigeria, have substantial natural wealth but low levels of economic development. These nations can develop their great economic potential if they can bring in more capital and "know-how."

Since our country is rich in natural resources, our firms need not depend on foreign suppliers for most raw materials. This is a strength of the economy.

Income Distribution

distribution of income

progressive income tax

The general economic health of a nation and the wealth of its people depend on how the nation's income is distributed among the people and how taxes are levied. The continued economic health of a mature economy like Canada's requires a distribution of income which permits a high level of consumption and investment in business. **Distribution of income means the way in which the people share in the total income of a nation or region.**

The progressive income tax means taxing people with higher incomes at a higher rate. Jack pays $1,000 on $10,000 income while Jerry

---

THE INTERNATIONAL ECONOMIC ENVIRONMENT

The economic systems of some countries are simple when compared with the Canadian economy. In many, people live at a subsistence level. Perhaps more important to businesspeople is what the country is doing to advance. Some "backward" countries do not appear to want change. This may be based on religious beliefs which look down on material progress.

Underdeveloped countries that are rich in natural resources have the potential to develop faster than those that are poor in natural resources. Valuable natural resources attract foreign investment to a country. This brings its people into closer contact with people from more developed nations. This may encourage them to pursue economic growth. But as the world's supply of natural resources dwindles, many countries which export them want to use them to help industrialize their own countries.

The fact that a country is rich in natural resources does not mean that it can be economically exploited. Brazil is rich in natural resources, but it is largely unexploited. One reason is its poor transportation facilities. Japan, on the other hand, is rather poor in natural resources. Because of an efficient transportation system and business know-how, the Japanese can import natural resources and convert them into finished goods for export.

The tax structure affects a country's appeal to the multinational firm. Because most of the people in underdeveloped countries are poor, their governments rely heavily on business taxes. This sometimes discourages foreign business. The same is true of inflation. High rates of inflation are common in many underdeveloped countries.

YOU BE THE JUDGE!

When Does a Progressive Income Tax Become Too Progressive?

During recent years, some well-known entertainers have left England to live elsewhere.

One reason given by some of those leaving is the high income taxes they pay. Some were in the 90 percent and over tax bracket. When does a progressive income tax become "too progressive"? YOU BE THE JUDGE!

pays $1,500 on $12,000 income. A progressive income tax has the effect of increasing total consumption, because poor people spend more of their income than rich people do. Tax policy, however, must avoid being too progressive. This would leave little incentive for wealthy people to invest. Why take a risk if most of your reward will have to be turned over to the tax collector?

The economic environment is greatly affected by the tax policy and the distribution of income. Business today depends on our large middle class for customers. This group is made up of families in the $15,000 to $30,000 annual income bracket. (See Table 18.2.) Only families with reasonable incomes can buy all the appliances, furnishings, conveniences, and amusements which keep factories and stores open. If our nation's wealth were concentrated in the hands of a few, this vast market and the thousands of firms which serve it would not exist. On the other hand, large individual incomes and wealth accumulations are vital to the environment of busi-

Table 18.2   Progressive Federal Taxation in Canada, 1979 Taxation Year

Total Income ($000's)	Number of People	% of People	Taxable Income (millions)	% of Taxable Income	Federal Tax Paid	% of Tax Paid	Effective Rate of Federal Tax on Taxable Income
Loss and Nil	1,022,263	6.96	—	—	—	—	—
0–5	3,405,424	23.20	865.2	0.80	1.6	0.01	0.18
5–10	3,111,297	21.19	9,779.7	8.97	730.9	4.29	7.47
10–15	2,602,489	17.73	18,881.1	17.32	2,397.0	14.09	12.70
15–20	1,917,774	13.06	21,693.6	19.90	3,270.9	19.22	15.08
20–25	1,210,498	8.25	18,508.0	16.98	3,025.2	17.78	16.35
25–30	631,569	4.30	12,202.0	11.20	2,110.3	12.40	17.29
30–40	474,724	3.23	11,741.2	10.77	2,153.6	12.65	18.34
40–50	143,694	0.98	4,799.6	4.40	920.3	5.41	19.17
50–100	134,150	0.91	6,862.9	6.30	1,449.6	8.52	21.12
100–200	23,278	0.16	2,287.0	2.19	591.0	3.47	25.84
200 and over	4,995	0.03	1,276.3	1.17	367.6	2.16	28.80
TOTAL	14,682,155	100.0%	108,996.6	100.0%	17,018.0	100.0%	15.61

Source: Revenue Canada Taxation, 1981 Taxation Statistics, p. 30.

ness. The opportunity to accumulate a fortune is an incentive for risk taking, which is essential to the capitalist system.

The regional distribution of income is an important issue in Canada. The federal government is trying, through the Department of Regional Industrial Expansion (DRIE), to balance economic growth in different parts of Canada. In one DRIE program, companies establishing plants in "designated areas" are eligible for grants from DRIE. This lowers the cost of establishing plants.

The Business Cycle

Although the long-term trend in our economy has been one of economic growth, the level of economic activity and the rate of growth vary over time. The long-term, recurring part of such change is called the business cycle. (See Figure 18.2.) A period of great volume of business activity is called a boom. During boom periods, profits, consumer confidence, capital investment, and employment are high and interest rates are low. But no boom is permanent. For any of a number of reasons, businesses begin to cut back on expansion plans. The economy enters a period of decline. Confidence in the economy fades and consumers cut back on spending. This causes unemployment to rise. If this period is brief, it is called a recession. If it

Figure 18.2
The business cycle

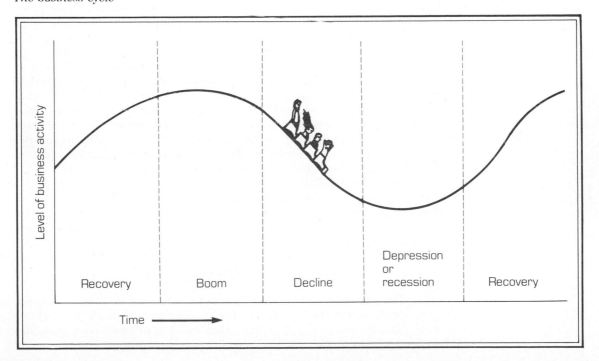

continues so that unemployment and the rate of business failures get very high, it is called a depression. Such a depression last occurred in Canada in the period 1930–1939. It led to a rise in the role of government as a stabilizer of the Canadian economy.

As a recession or depression turns into recovery, inventories begin to decline, businesses begin to build factories, households begin to buy cars again, banks expand loans, employees are rehired, and production returns to higher levels. The economy approaches a boom again.

Human psychology, of course, plays a large role in the business cycle. It has a kind of "snowball" effect. During the downturn pessimism is "catching," and because people expect the worst, things actually get worse. Fortunately, the same kind of thing occurs in reverse during recovery. Optimism becomes contagious.

For a small business, the environmental effect of the business cycle can be crucial. Consider the case of Smitty's Restaurant. This restaurant was opened in a neighbourhood made up mostly of factory workers and their families. A recession occurred soon after Smitty's opening. It led to cutbacks at a large production plant and high unemployment in the neighbourhood. Many of Smitty's regular customers lost their jobs and stopped eating out. Other workers, too, who were fearful of being laid off, started to save their money instead of dining out. Smitty's sales soon fell off 30 percent. The local banks refused to lend him enough to meet current payrolls because they feared he would fail. Within six months after the initial employment cut, Smitty was out of business. If he had opened during a period of recovery, he would have had a much better chance to succeed.

In periods of prosperity prices traditionally rise. We call these price increases inflation. Since the Great Depression of the 1930s, the economic policy followed by the federal government has included a general willingness to permit inflation in order to avoid a recession. **In the 1970s and early 1980s our economy began to suffer from "stagflation." This was a peculiar situation in which we had both a recession and a high rate of inflation.** Economists do not agree on why we experienced stagflation for the first time and for so long a period. It shows that there are still many things that we don't know about managing an economy. We're not sure about the economic effects of welfare programs, the energy shortage, defence cutbacks, and consumer credit expansion, to name a few factors which probably contributed to stagflation.

Inflation affects different groups in our society in different ways. A worker whose union contract provides for increases in wages as the price level increases (an escalator clause) suffers no loss in buying power. The same is true of many businesses which can raise the price of the goods they sell. The groups which suffer are those whose money income doesn't rise, such as those living on fixed-dollar pensions and stable salaries. They find it harder and harder to live as prices rise. Table 18.3 shows how prices have changed in recent years.

The effect of inflation on business varies. Most firms pass on higher costs to their customers. But some, for competitive or market structure reasons, cannot raise prices. They must pay inflated prices for supplies and inflated wages to employees. Their profits are "squeezed."

stagflation

Table 18.3   Canadian Consumer Price Index (1971 = $1.00)

Year	CPI
1970	97.2
1971	100.0
1972	104.8
1973	112.7
1974	125.0
1975	138.5
1976	148.9
1977	160.8
1978	175.2
1979	191.2
1980	210.6
1981	236.9
1982*	269.2

*October 1982

Balance of Payments and Exchange Rates

The balance of payments, the difference (in dollars) of goods and services which our country buys from and sells to other countries, was explained in Chapter 16. The balance of payments affects our exchange rate. If Canadians are buying more abroad than they are selling, we run up a balance of payments deficit. This puts downward pressure on our currency, and our currency goes down in value relative to the currency in other countries. If our balance of payments is positive, our currency can appreciate relative to that of other countries.

Changes in the exchange rate can have a big effect on companies which buy, sell, or have plants and offices abroad. A decline in our exchange rate will make imported goods more expensive to purchase. It will also reduce the cost of exports. This will aid exporting firms and hurt importing firms.

Another problem created by exchange rate fluctuations is change in the value of assets in different countries. This is particularly significant for a multinational corporation. It must make decisions about what country's currency to hold its cash in. For example, in 1982 the Canadian dollar fell to less than 75 cents relative to the U.S. dollar. If a company had held its cash in U.S. rather than Canadian dollars during this period, it would have been much better off.

THE SOCIAL ENVIRONMENT

social environment

The social environment also influences decisions made by business managers. **The social environment is the total of all human variables that are external to the firm.** We will analyze the social environment in terms

Table 18.4   Four Types of Social Environment Variables

I. Individual Variables
 A. Consumer needs and wants
 B. Consumer talents and abilities
 C. Consumer values
II. Small-group Variables
 A. Group norms
 B. Informal work groups
 C. The role of groups in the socialization of individuals
 D. The role of the family
III. Institutional Variables
 A. Business
 B. Government
 C. Labour
 D. Consumers
IV. Societal Variables
 A. Demographic variables
 B. Societal values
 C. Social responsibility

of individual, small-group, institutional, and societal variables. There are certain environmental variables associated with each of these four groupings of social factors. (See Table 18.4.)

Social environmental variables must be taken into account in many management decisions (Figure 18.3). These include, as examples, product design, promotion, decisions with social responsibility overtones, personnel and employee relations decisions, plant location, and production process decisions. The social environment is important to many managers in a firm. These include the marketing manager, the personnel manager, the production manager, and the general manager.

Individual Variables

individual social environment variables

Individual social environment variables are those that relate specifically to important individuals in the environment of the firm. There are many important individuals in the firm's environment. These include (1) the customer who decides whether or not to purchase a firm's product, (2) members of the labour force who choose to work or continue to work for a firm, (3) individuals in competitive firms, and (4) government officials who make decisions which affect a firm.

It is important that the management of a firm have as good an understanding as possible of the characteristics of individuals in the firm's environment. The more intimate the contact with individuals, the greater the importance of having a full understanding of the individual.

Figure 18.3
Illustration of how social environmental variables can influence management decisions

Social environment variables	Selected Management Decisions				
	Product design	Promotion	Personnel and employee relations decisions	Plant location	Production process design
Individual Variables (a) motivation of people		The motivation to make a purchase decision affects the way promotions are designed.	People's motivation affects how they should be managed.		Should attempt to take the needs and motivation of people into account in designing jobs.
(b) talents and abilities of people	Products can be designed for people of certain skills and abilities (e.g., tools for professionals).	Design promotions to appeal to people with certain talents.	Will hire people with talents appropriate for jobs.	Will locate plant where it is possible to hire people with talents appropriate for jobs.	Talents and skills of work force can affect design of the production process.
Small-group Variables (a) group norms	People with common skills (e.g., athletes may desire similar products).	Promotion can attempt to convince people that they should use a product because others are using it.	Group norms can affect the decisions of employees.	Community group norms can result in massed opposition to a plant location.	The norms of a work group (e.g., pride in what they produce) can be important in design of a production process.
Institutional Variables (a) institutions other than business	Consumer organizations affect product design.	Consumer organizations affect promotion techniques (e.g., advertising for children).		Conserver and ecological movements can affect plant location and production process.	
Societal Variables (a) societal values and attitudes	Attitudes affect the types of products which appeal to people (e.g., fashion in clothing and entertainment).	Attitudes of potential consumers affect design of promotional campaigns.	Change in values and attitudes affect hiring decisions (e.g., business now hires more women)	Residents may have preferences that firms not locate in some areas.	Must now take greater account of pollution control in designing production processes.
(b) Demographic characteristics (e.g., location, age, sex, occupation, income)	Demographics affect the types of products in high demand (e.g., if more babies are born, there will be more baby food and other baby products sold).	Promotion must take demographic characteristics into account.	Demographic characteristics of an area affect the supply of labour.	Will locate after consideration of the demographics of the market and the work force.	Availability and type of work force can affect decisions about production processes.

The characteristics of individuals which may be of interest include people's needs and wants, their motivation, their values, and their talents and abilities. Students taking, or who have taken, psychology courses will find them of benefit in understanding individuals in a firm's environment.

Customers As Individuals

Customers make their decisions to purchase in order to satisfy personal needs or wants. An automobile or a dress may be purchased to satisfy a functional need, but it will often be purchased to satisfy social or ego needs as well. If a firm, through the attractiveness of its product or its advertising, can stimulate individuals to need or want its product, it will increase its sales.

Understanding a customer's motivation to make a purchase is important to firms. Certain types of firms use personal selling to motivate customers to make a purchase, while others use mass advertising. It is important for firms to have an understanding of how customers make purchase decisions and what factors are important to them when they make them. Courses you may take in buyer behaviour will go more deeply into this subject.

Labour Force As Individuals

People work to satisfy important needs and wants which they have. They agree to contribute their skills and abilities to an employer in return for things which will satisfy their needs. One thing employees receive is money; this allows them to purchase goods and services. In addition, however, a job can satisfy many other needs and wants. Employees can achieve a sense of pride and achievement in their work. People can also satisfy social needs at work through their affiliations with others.

The needs and wants of employees can change over time, as can those of customers. As our level of affluence increases, people develop higher expectations about what they would like to receive from a job, in terms of both financial rewards and working conditions. Failure by a manager to respond to the needs and wants of current or prospective employees can result in labour relations difficulties.

Competitors As Individuals

Competitors are a very important part of the environment of a firm. Competitors are also individuals, whether they are managers of competing firms or salespeople from another firm who are attempting to convince a customer to buy their product rather than yours. If you think of competitors as individuals and are able to understand them to the point where you feel you can predict their moves with some confidence, you will improve your ability to compete against them.

Government Representatives As Individuals

When you deal in the political environment, you do not deal with an abstract entity called "the government." You deal with individuals, whether they be clerks behind a counter, government inspectors, advisors, senior civil servants, or elected officials. Business managers deal with government representatives when existing government policies are implemented or when new government policies are formulated. In both cases, it is wise to remember that government officials are individuals with needs, wants, and feelings.

Government officials are responsible for implementing government policy. It is not wise to belittle or harass them in the performance of their job. Such attitudes, if expressed openly, can create resentment in government officials and cause them to look particularly hard for rule violations by the company.

Government representatives are important in the formulation of new government policies. Government employees make crucial decisions about changes in the policies under which businesses operate. They make them after consideration of all available facts as they understand them. They also make decisions which will satisfy government objectives. The task for the business manager who wants to influence government policy is to first understand the government decision maker as a person in a specific job. The business manager must then frame alternatives which will allow the government official to meet his or her objectives without seriously affecting the business manager's firm. (The interaction between business and government is discussed in detail in the next chapter.)

Small Groups

Small groups have a big impact on people's attitudes and behaviour. An understanding of significant small groups in a firm's environment and of the dynamics of small-group activity is of value to the business manager.

Some small groups of importance to business managers include families, social groups, and recreation groups. Members of these types of small groups are prospective customers, employees, suppliers, and competitors of a firm.

small groups

Small groups are composed of members who have some common goal and a structure for achieving it. The real importance of groups is that they have norms to which group members conform. **A norm is a**

norm

standard way of thinking or behaving which group members feel is reasonable. The importance of this type of conforming behaviour for business managers can easily be understood.

A group norm to wear a certain style of clothing, or to listen to a certain performer's music, will have positive effects upon sales of these products. Such "fads" as hair length or wearing blue jeans are reflections of our tendency as consumers to conform to group norms.

We can all think of examples of different members of a family, or different people in a community, acquiring major items such as microwave ovens or swimming pools after they had been initially acquired by someone generally respected by other members of the group. Some call it "keeping up with the Joneses"; what it really amounts to is conforming to norms of a group the consumer would like to identify with.

The norms of a group will also dictate whether certain restaurants or cabarets will be frequented. An eating or entertainment establishment which can appeal to a group can become very successful rapidly. If for some reason, however, the appeal of the establishment to the group is lost, sales can decrease rapidly.

The norms of groups of the current employees of a firm, or of groups from which potential employees will be drawn, are important to a firm. It is desirable that current employees' group norms reflect a constructive, satisfied attitude toward their firm. If, on the other hand, current employees' norms reflect dissatisfaction, distrust, and unrest regarding their employer, labour relations difficulties are almost inevitable.

If prospective new employees, such as college students, have a positive attitude toward a firm or industry, it makes it easier for that firm or industry to recruit new employees. If student norms are to shun a prospective employer, it is much more difficult for that firm to recruit the type of people they want.

Company managers should not underestimate the importance of group norms among important groups of consumers and employees. If group norms are favourable to, or can be harnessed by, managers, a business can benefit greatly from sales increases or good labour relations. If norms of important groups are unfavourable, the negative effects on a business can be serious.

Institutional Variables

institutions

We live in a society of large organizations and institutions. **Institutions are organizations, or groups of organizations, having an economic, social, educational, religious, or other recognized purpose in society.** Thus, we can talk of labour, business, government, consumers, religions, or charities as examples of institutions. The recognized and established purposes of the institutions are reflected through laws, practices, customs, or traditions. Different institutions have different purposes. They all play important roles in society. Because their objectives differ, there can be conflict between them.

A business manager must be aware of the characteristics, objectives, and views of representatives of different institutions. This is necessary because some of the actions of businesses can be in conflict with the objectives of other institutions. It would be unwise for business managers to take action on certain issues without considering other institutions. For example, the reactions of environmentalists must be taken into account in decisions with pollution implications. Labour's reaction must be considered in decisions about employee salaries. A firm's managers certainly cannot make decisions affecting labour without taking the possible labour reaction into account. Such decisions inevitably lead to labour relations problems.

Business managers also must understand and relate to various government agencies. This relationship is so important that the next chapter is devoted to discussion of it. Business managers must also understand and relate to the media. Many large firms employ people with previous media experience to handle their relations with radio, television, and the press.

Developments in education and research can also affect business decisions. In the previous chapter we saw how important the technological environment could be to a firm.

power

Business managers must know how much they are able to influence decisions of the various institutions. **Power is the ability to induce others to behave the way you want them to.** The power of some groups is increasing, while that of others is decreasing. The power of the Church, for example, has decreased in the last century. The power of both business and labour has also decreased relative to that of government. Governments have become relatively more powerful and important in economic decision making. It is likely that this trend will continue.

THE INTERNATIONAL SOCIAL ENVIRONMENT

International business requires people of different cultures to interact. Business transactions involve the written and/or spoken language. Unless the parties really understand each other, there can be no basis for business. This problem exists even when people in different countries use the same language. For example, people from England and English Canadians speak the same language but give different shades of meaning to the same words.

Canadian executives overseas should have a basic understanding of the language(s) of the land. Many global firms find it helpful to hire and train local nationals for management jobs. This helps reduce the language gap. Furthermore, many governments demand this.

There are also differences in cultural values. Canadian ideas about getting ahead are rejected in some cultures. Our emphasis on convenience is equated with laziness in some cultures. Although cultural values do change over time, there is cultural resistance to change. For example, Japan accepted a cultural value of fewer children and legalized abortion long before many other cultures accepted family planning. But the Japanese are reluctant to adopt a new alphabet, even though their alphabet contains too many symbols to make use of the typewriter practical.

Tastes also vary. The colours which are considered lucky by one people, for example, often depend on the religious beliefs or superstitions held by that group of people. Western cultures associate black with mourning, whereas Eastern cultures associate white with mourning. This affects a global firm's advertising and packaging decisions.

The religious beliefs of a people influence their ideas of what is ethical behaviour. Our "affluent" society is rejected by devout followers of Buddhism and Hinduism. Employers who favour their relatives in hiring and promotions are frowned on in Canada. Such favoured treatment is part of the religious teaching of Hinduism.

There are other differences in the social environments as well. In extremely class-conscious societies, a person is born into a particular social class and remains there. Ad campaigns built around the idea of "moving up" are not effective, nor are personnel policies which encourage employees to move up the job ladder.

Social customs also vary. In Oriental societies extreme politeness and formality are part of doing business, unlike the more informal approach in Western countries. A Canadian who wants to get down to business without engaging in the proper social behaviour is headed for trouble.

Some people feel there is an elite "establishment" in Canada which possesses disproportionate power and is self-perpetuating. While there is a group of senior executives of major companies and governments who have more power than other Canadians, they do not have anything approaching absolute power. Furthermore, they cannot automatically pass this power on to someone of their choosing, such as their children. Possession of power at any point in time is primarily a function of competence and outstanding job performance.

Another institutional fact of life is that Canadian institutions are getting larger and larger. We have big government, big business, big labour, big universities, and big religious organizations. Large organizations have developed for a variety of reasons, but the primary one is that they are able to perform large tasks. The main concern, however, is not how and why they have developed but that they exist and that Canadian society will continue to be characterized by large organizations. For example, we see efforts by consumer, environmental, and other institutions to become larger and better staffed and financed in order to increase their power.

The fact that there are increasing numbers of large organizations is important for business managers and for you as future managers. In spite of this, there are still many opportunities for smaller organizations. There will always be things which smaller organizations can do better than large ones, such as producing customized products and providing personalized services.

An implication is the need for detailed planning within organizations, with an emphasis on forecasting the effects of major decisions before they are made. There will also be more emphasis on joint planning by different institutions. An example of joint plans are those undertaken by business and government to improve the Canadian industrial society. When joint decision making is used, the consequences of making bad decisions can be very expensive to firms.

A further implication of working for large organizations is that more people have input into decisions which are made. This is unlikely in small organizations where major decisions are made by one person or a small group of people. Managers in a large organization must understand the process of policy formulation in order to be able to contribute to it effectively.

Societal Variables

In addition to looking at the needs and wants of individuals and the characteristics of small groups and institutions, business managers should also examine the overall social environment of the country. This includes demographic characteristics and the values of Canadians.

Demographic Characteristics of Canadians

demography

Demography is the branch of anthropology that deals with population statistics, primarily the size and characteristics of the population.
The total population size and distribution is important to the Canadian business manager. The relatively small size of the Canadian population in

comparison with that of the United States, Europe, or Japan gives Canadian business managers a smaller domestic market to serve. Because the domestic market is not as large, plants in Canada cannot be as large as those in other countries. Consequently, these smaller Canadian plants do not have the economies of scale of plants in other countries. This means that Canadian plants have higher costs and are less able to compete on a cost basis with production from plants in other countries.

In addition to the smaller Canadian market, the population is widely dispersed. The transportation costs associated with this population distribution make it even more difficult to have one large plant to serve the entire population.

The major areas of population growth are projected to be Ontario, Alberta, and British Columbia. In absolute numbers, the greatest growth in population will occur in Ontario. In percentage terms, the most significant population growth will occur in the Northwest Territories, British Columbia, and Alberta.

The age distribution of the population is also changing. The average age of Canadians is increasing. People born in the post-World War II baby boom are growing older. This "bulge" of people is moving through the age distribution of the population. This has implications for firms which sell products directed at specific age groups. For example, soft drinks are most heavily consumed by people in the under twenty-five age category. This age group is not forecasted to increase in size. In order to increase sales, efforts must be directed at encouraging consumption by older persons. A future concern is care of the aged. The proportion of people in the over sixty-five age group will increase in the future. This presents problems in providing public health services. It will also represent an opportunity for firms which provide services and products for people of this age group.

Another important demographic characteristic of the Canadian population is its bilingual nature. The majority of the population of Canada is English-speaking. However, the majority of Quebecers speak French, and there are also significant pockets of French-speaking people in provinces such as New Brunswick and Manitoba.

These language differences have implications for business managers. Advertising must be different in the two languages. English labels must be translated into French for products sold in Quebec. Firms from other parts of Canada with plants and offices in Quebec must be prepared to conduct operations in that province in French.

The Values of Canadians

values

We have already discussed individuals and their needs, wants, and attitudes. Individuals also have values. **Values are simply what people think is important.** If we could combine the values of all Canadians, we would have a statement of Canadian societal values of the Canadian culture.

There has been considerable discussion in recent years about whether Canadian societal values have been changing. In a book entitled *Canada Has a Future,* prepared for the Hudson Institute of Canada, "traditional" values and "new values" are discussed.

traditional values

Traditional values are "regard for duty, honour, custom, order, restraint, prudence, loyalty to family, church, and nation, and the pursuit

new values

of knowledge, technology. and economic growth." New values refer to "spontaneity, self-actualization, sensory awareness, equality, concern for self, humanity, and nature, and indifference or opposition to traditional values" (Marie-Josee Drouin and B. Bruce-Briggs, *Canada Has a Future* (Toronto: McClelland and Stewart Ltd.), 1978, p. 233).

In the decade of the 1960s there was considerable emphasis on the new values. In the 1970s and 1980s, particularly after the economic difficulties caused by the energy crisis and possibly as a reaction to the liberal views of the 1960s, there was a resurgence of the traditional values. We saw a definite conservative trend in elections in many of the provinces, including Manitoba, Nova Scotia, British Columbia, Prince Edward Island, Alberta, and Ontario. There was also talk of restraint and financial conservatism at the federal level of government.

The conservative reaction of the 1970s and 1980s and the return to more traditional values was associated with economic difficulties and uncertainty. Many of the attitudes associated with the "new values" are being incorporated into the decisions of many individuals and firms. As economic conditions improve and the long-term outlook again looks more favourable, there may be a reemergence of the new values.

The societal values of a country influence the decisions which business managers make. These values are incorporated into business decisions because they influence the criteria which managers apply to the decisions they make.

THE SOCIAL RESPONSIBILITY OF BUSINESS

Business firms exist to produce economic goods and services which people want. In a really competitive situation business firms must produce useful goods and services or they will not survive. When they produce, businesses also create jobs and income for people. This creates a healthy economic base for the society. Without a healthy economic base, social problems would probably be much more serious than they are at present. The federal and provincial governments would also have much smaller tax revenues with which to attack social problems.

To some people, this means that business should not worry about social problems. An increasing number of people, however, feel that business firms should go beyond the mere pursuit of profit and should be truly socially responsible. **A firm demonstrates social responsibility when, in the process of making decisions, it takes things in addition to profit into consideration.** For example, a firm might decide to start a training program for the hard-core unemployed, even though in the short run the costs of the program will mean less profit for the firm.

social responsibility of business

There are two opposing points of view about the obligations of business to Canadian society, depending upon whether the "traditional" or the "new" societal values are emphasized. One view is called the traditional ethic. The other is the professional-managerial ethic. Let's examine both of them. (See Table 18.5.)

Table 18.5 Two Opposing Ethics in Business

Traditional Business Ethic	Professional-Managerial Ethic
1. Maximum short-term profits	1. Satisfactory long-term profits; other values are weighed
2. Minimum government control	2. Government-business "partnership"
3. Protectionism	3. Internationalism
4. Stockholder-oriented	4. Serves several masters, including stockholders, customers, citizens, and employees

The Traditional Business Ethic

traditional
business ethic

In the traditional business ethic, business decisions are based only on how they affect the short-term profit for owners. Profit is measured in the short run. What is "best" for the firm means what provides measurable profit soon.

This position has dominated our business climate for many decades. It is still supported widely by many business managers. Most small- and medium-size firms still feel pretty much this way. This ethic calls for minimum government control of business, and it serves the interest of the business's owners or stockholders almost exclusively. All in all, it is rather conservative and is in sharp contrast to the professional-managerial ethic.

The Professional-Managerial Ethic

The professional-managerial ethic has become accepted in recent years by an increasing number of the largest corporations and many smaller firms.
professional-managerial
ethic
The professional-managerial ethic holds that managers represent the interests of stockholders, customers, employees, and the general public. Decisions are weighed in terms of longer-range company welfare, not immediate profit. Also, it is assumed that what is good for the employees and the general public is good for the company. For example, a firm which participates voluntarily in training and hiring the disadvantaged may not expect increased profits to result in the next year or two. However, the firm may expect that such activity will "pay off" in the long run. The society gains, and a stable, healthy society is presumed to have long-run beneficial effects on the firm. There are also indirect benefits in the form of good public relations from such activities.

Another important part of this ethic is the belief in a cooperative "partnership" relationship between business and government instead of the traditional hostility. This thinking fosters business participation in solving social problems.

The modern professional-managerial ethic has developed since World War II. It is a product of changing political ideas and of people's acceptance of a greater social consciousness. It is an extremely practical, long-run view.

WHAT DO YOU THINK?

Should Business Be Socially Responsible?

Arguments in Favour of Social Responsibility

1. The public supports business by purchasing its output. If the public expects business to be socially responsible, business must be or it will lose customers.
2. If business does not voluntarily behave in a socially responsible way, government legislation will be passed in order to force business to be responsible.
3. Business has a great deal of power. In a democracy, the possession of power means acceptance of responsibility for the way the power is exercised.
4. If a company is socially responsible, it will benefit from good public relations.
5. If business is socially responsible, all companies will benefit because the work force will be more capable, the air and water will not be polluted, and consumers will think highly of the business community.

Arguments against Social Responsibility

1. Business makes its greatest contribution to society by producing goods and services as efficiently as possible. Worrying about whether decisions are socially responsible distracts business managers from their primary goal—making a profit. If profit is not made, the business will go out of existence and many jobs will be lost.
2. The owners of the company (the stockholders) take all the risks, and they must decide if they want company funds spent on socially responsible projects such as hiring the disadvantaged or contributing to charities. If they decide not to do these things, the company should not be forced to do them.
3. When business is socially responsible, the cost of the company's products increases. This is detrimental to consumers and causes inflation.
4. Since business managers are not elected by the people, they have no right to make decisions about social issues. This amounts to them imposing their value system on the public, and in a democracy this is not tolerated.
5. Government agencies have been set up to ensure that various segments of society behave in a responsible way. Business managers therefore do not need to be concerned about whether their actions are socially responsible, since government agencies will make that decision.

It says that a firm is successful when it is accepted by society as a contributor to social welfare. It presumes that stockholders themselves will recognize the wisdom of sacrificing short-run profits for the long-run stability of the society. This kind of thinking led Xerox Corporation to spend half a million dollars a year to release employees with full pay to work at socially oriented tasks in their communities.

It is harder to evaluate managers when values other than the direct economic interests of the firm are brought into the decision-making process. Deciding which noneconomic values are to be considered is tough—especially when executives and board members disagree. There is also the added problem of weighing these noneconomic values along with the economic ones. Economists and accountants are working on methods of evalu-

THINK ABOUT IT!

A Contemporary View of Social Responsibility

A well-known analyst of the role of business in society offers a "model" for business to follow (Keith Davis, "Five Propositions for Social Responsibility," *Business Horizons* (June, 1975), pp. 19–24). It consists of five guidelines which may keep businesses in harmony with the will of society: (1) We must remember that social responsibility arises from social power. (2) Business must exchange information openly with the general public. (3) Business must weigh every decision in terms of its social cost. (4) Business should pass on to consumers the full cost of including the social goods in its decisions. (5) Businesses are responsible to help solve social problems not of their own making when they have the special abilities to do so.

ating such activities. These methods fall under the general heading of "social auditing."

The professional-managerial ethic is described in a booklet published by the Committee for Economic Development, *Social Responsibility of Business Corporations* (New York: Committee for Economic Development, 1971).

The difference between the two ethics is clear. Some say that a capitalist system cannot survive if firms bring noneconomic values into their decision making. Others say that if business (especially large corporations) does not assume social responsibilities, the entire society could perish.

WHAT WOULD YOU DO?

Being Socially Involved

The board of directors of the Wranston Department Store is considering the complaint of two of its major stockholders that the dividends for the last two years have been too small. A review of the firm's operations over the last two years showed that the two largest stores, usually major profit contributors to the corporation, have each made only a 2 percent return on investment. Further study showed that the major cause of this was their participation in a massive training program for the disadvantaged unemployed.

Wranston's president, Will Carter, was the force behind the employment program. He believes that such social programs are essential in the long run for the big-city stores to survive. He, along with some other board members, believes that reduced short-term earnings are unfortunate, but necessary, in the interest of social stability for the urban environment.

Other directors feel that endangering the corporation's ability to attract investors is too risky. Low profits drive investors away and the basic economic health of Wranston is at stake. The issue is to be resolved at the next board meeting. Assume that you are on the board. WHAT WOULD YOU DO?

CAREER PROFILE

MY NAME IS JOHN McCALLUM. I AM A professor of finance in the Faculty of Administrative Studies at the University of Manitoba. I teach and do research in corporation finance, monetary economics, investments, and international finance.

I have a Ph.D. in finance from the University of Toronto, an M.B.A. in operations research from Queen's University, a B.Sc. in mathematics and physics from the University of Montreal, and a B.A. in economics also from the University of Montreal. I have worked five years with the Bank of Montreal and two years with Shell Oil.

In my job I teach university students, conduct research, consult to business and government, and write for a number of periodicals including the *Journal of Finance,* the *Journal of Bank Research,* and the *Business Quarterly.* I also have a regular radio broadcast on CBC, and publish articles in the *Financial Post* and *Winnipeg Free Press* on a weekly basis.

These activities are all related to each other. Writing and broadcasting are teaching but in a different way. Consulting is partly teaching and partly research. It really comes down to people wanting me to address a problem they have. I research it and make recommendations.

My initial involvement in finance came because I had focused on operations research and marketing for my M.B.A. When I decided to get a Ph.D. in business I wanted to do it in a different area so that I could broaden my field of understanding. I had always been interested in financial markets, so finance was a natural choice.

Issues I deal with in my teaching, research, consulting, broadcasting, and journalism include:

- forecasting economic variables like interest rates, exchange rates, and growth of the economy
- where capital is going to come from for undertaking different projects
- how to put together financial packages for different specific tasks
- how to deal with liquidation of assets
- what types of securities to hold in an investment portfolio
- what basic factors determine things like interest rates and other financial variables

The major problems in addressing these very interesting issues derive from the fact that the world is so uncertain. For example, when you are putting together a deal or a financial package, you don't know all the things that could happen. Technology could change; there could be an unexpected rapid increase in interest rates; or other environmental conditions could change. Lack of good data is also a

---

SUMMARY AND LOOK AHEAD

This chapter has dealt with the economic and social environments of business. The economic environment includes all the factors that influence the prices a firm must pay for its inputs (land, labour, capital, and management) or the prices it will charge for its output. We discussed the

problem. This is a problem, particularly in conducting academic research.

In journalism, what it comes right down to is the ability to write under pressure. For example, when a Manitoba provincial or federal budget is published, there are about five or six organizations and/or publications that expect something written from me within twenty-four hours. This requires not only the ability to work under pressure but also an ability to organize things well. I write much of the material by dictating it into a tape recorder first.

I enjoy doing what I do immensely, and get great personal satisfaction from my occupation. Some of the particular highs, or pleasures, include things like getting a forecast right. I also get well paid for what I do. I like being involved with a large number of people. Another advantage to being as diversified in my activities as I am is that, when you work on a lot of projects, it is likely that something good is happening in one or more of them at almost any particular point in time. Another advantage to being so involved and so busy is that you always have something to look forward to on any one day. Very seldom do you look back or dwell on mistakes that everyone inevitably makes. Another aspect of my university career which I value is the freedom I have. I am able to write and speak on issues as I wish. I consider it an ideal type of occupation.

Each day is different, and each time the phone rings I don't know who it will be or what they will want. Although I am very involved in my activities and probably actively work at them sixty or more hours a week, I don't feel I work hard at all. In fact, I don't even view what I do as work. I can do it day after day and never get sick or tired of it at all.

In summary, there are a few points I would like to make. The first is that, next to being happy in your family, the most important thing is to be happy in your work. I recommend to students that they spend a lot of time thinking about a career and experiment with a number of different options until they discover what it is they really enjoy doing. Second, regardless of what career path students choose, changes in technology will probably lead to three or four career changes over a lifetime. Students should make every effort to learn to cope with this eventuality by educating themselves well, by trying to keep an open mind, by committing themselves to doing a good job on whatever they do, and by not being afraid to try new things.

Another thing I observe is that a common characteristic of successful people is patience, or the willingness to invest time in developing things and waiting for the rewards. A further observation is this: Students should realize that the most important power they will have in their career will come from the knowledge they acquire and, with that knowledge, the ability to do something the public values. This kind of power is worth much more than positional power over someone in an organizational hierarchy.

On a personal note to each student — you should realize that the education you are getting makes you special. It gives you knowledge and earning power; and commensurate with these benefits it makes you responsible for attempting to improve the way people live. You should have the willingness to speak out on issues that you know well. You have been educated and exposed to the history of thought; you shouldn't be afraid to speak out when you see an injustice or a problem, even if it creates some short-term problems for you.

Finally, do not be afraid of not knowing what you want to do. You have lots of time and lots of opportunity to experiment and find the thing that is precisely correct for you.

microeconomic environment of the firm, which includes supply, demand, productivity, and competition.

The macroeconomic environment of business is the general economic situation in the country in which a firm operates. Macroeconomic variables discussed include economic development and growth, income distribution, the business cycle, inflation, and exchange rates.

The social environment is the total of all human variables external to the firm. Individual, small-group, institutional, and societal variables were discussed.

Individuals external to the firm, but relevant to it, include customers, competitors, labour force members, and government representatives. Small groups of importance include informal work groups and the family. Group norms can have an impact upon the success of business operations.

Institutions in society are very important. Business managers often have objectives that conflict with the objectives of other institutions. The relative power of different institutions will determine how much influence they have and to what extent they will be able to impose actions on society.

The values of society were also discussed. A distinction was made between traditional values and new values. Values also influence the ethics which business managers apply in making decisions. The traditional management ethic and the professional-management ethic were discussed.

The question of social responsibility was also raised and the advantages and disadvantages of socially responsible behaviour were noted.

In the next chapter the political environment of business is outlined. Various federal, provincial, and municipal influences on business are indicated. ■

QUESTIONS FOR REVIEW AND DISCUSSION

1. What is the economic environment of the firm? How can the economic environment be important to a firm?
2. What type of environmental change would you call a change in ocean conditions which resulted in a shortage of a certain species of fish which subsequently raised the price of this fish to processors and consumers? Discuss.
3. What are the microeconomic variables which can influence a firm?
4. What is the competitive environment of Bell Telephone? Of a provincial telephone utility? Of a travel agency? Of a large mining company?
5. Are macroeconomic or microeconomic environmental factors more important to a firm?
6. What can the consequences be for a firm if one of its competitors makes major improvements in the productivity of labour?
7. What are the implications of stagflation for a Canadian manufacturing firm?
8. What is the difference between individual, small-group, institutional, and societal variables in the social environment of a firm?
9. How can individual social environmental factors affect a firm that manufactures dresses and pantsuits?
10. What is the role of business as an institution in Canadian society? Illustrate how the power of business has changed relative to that of consumers and the government.

11. Should business managers attempt to impose their views on other social institutions?
12. Do you think there will be a shift from traditional values to new values?
13. Is the traditional managerial ethic more appropriate in times of economic recession than the professional-managerial ethic?
14. Can you think of five types of decisions by business managers which are not influenced by either the economic or social environments?
15. How can a person decide whether a given business decision was a socially responsible one?

INCIDENTS

Roberts' Implements Ltd.

Jim Roberts, the president of Roberts' Implements Ltd., contemplated his situation in mid-December, 1983. His firm manufactured a specialized line of farm implements—the Roberts cultivator—in a rural Saskatchewan community of approximately 2,000 people. He employed forty-seven people on a two-shift basis. The cultivator was sold primarily in Manitoba, Saskatchewan, and Alberta.

After increasing dramatically from $320,000 and $15,000 in 1976 to $810,000 and $90,000 in 1982, sales and profits levelled off in 1983 as farm incomes, with which farm implement sales were directly correlated, stabilized. Because of these good years the firm was in very solid financial shape. The outlook for 1984, however, was uncertain. Agricultural experts were divided, although the balance felt that grain prices would remain low for 1984. Furthermore, there was concern about a very dry growing season in 1984 which, if it occurred, would adversely affect yields. There was evidence that inventories of competitive firms were increasing. In addition, there was pending legislation on farm implement warranties which would increase manufacturing costs.

Mr. Roberts was considering whether he should reduce his planned output for the coming year. It would mean cutting back to a work force of thirty men. He anticipated that if he did do this the men laid off would have difficulty finding other jobs, and this would affect the community's image of his firm. On the other hand, if he did not decrease production, there was an opportunity to increase market share if the anticipated market decline did not occur.

Questions:
1. What economic environment factors have influenced Roberts' Implements Ltd.?
2. What social environment factors have influenced the firm?
3. How have these environmental factors created problems for Mr. Roberts?
4. After assessing his problems and options, what is your recommendation to Jim Roberts?

Jones' Carpets

Jim Hannesson, his wife Doreen, and their three teenage children lived in Halifax. Jim had worked as an accountant for a plumbing supply firm in the city for a number of years. His last year's pay, including a bonus of $3,400, was $33,248.18. He had recently become aware of an opportunity to purchase a retail carpet business.

The firm, belonging to a long-time friend of the Hannessons, Harold Jones, was apparently in difficulty because personal and family problems were preventing him from devoting appropriate attention to the business. As a last resort Mr. Jones was considering sale of the firm. He had indicated that he felt the business was worth about $50,000, plus inventory. However, Jim Hannesson had heard the opinion expressed by a mutual friend that the price could probably be bargained down to under $40,000. Jim had $30,000 in savings available for investment and could borrow at least an equivalent amount.

Sales of the carpet store in the previous year had been $200,000. The cost of goods sold was $125,000. Expenses were $25,000 for two full-time salespersons; advertising expenditures of $23,000; building rental and maintenance of $6,000; and administrative expenses of $15,000. Harold Jones was drawing a salary of $2,000 a month for himself.

Jim Hannesson was planning, if he did decide to purchase the firm, to increase advertising expenditures by $15,000. It was his hope that this would increase sales by 50 percent. His reasoning for this was that the store was located in a growing area of the city. Jim Hannesson also felt that potential sales for a store in the area with adequate management would be over $500,000 within three years. The size of the store would require expansion for sales of over $400,000.

Jim was concerned about how beneficial his past experience would be for operation of a retail store. There had been recent complaints from consumer groups to the Carpet Association concerning the difficulty of distinguishing between different qualities of carpet. Jim did not know what effect, if any, this would have upon the operation of a carpet store.

Jim was also concerned about Harold Jones' alcohol problem. He wondered if it was proper to consider buying a business from a friend who was selling because of this type of problem. He also felt that Mr. Jones would ask to be retained to work for the firm on a part-time sales and advisory basis at $1,000 per month.

Questions:
1. What economic, environmental, and social factors are reflected in the case?
2. What problems do they create for Mr. Jones? For Mr. Hannesson?
3. What would you recommend to Mr. Jones? To Mr. Hannesson?

CASE STUDY

SEX BANTER GROUND FOR FIRING, ARBITRATOR SAYS

WORKPLACE ROMEOS HAVE BEEN WARNED BY AN ARBITRATOR THAT sexist remarks are grounds for discharge and are no longer acceptable.

The only saving factor for an electrician in an Ottawa hospital who was fired for his comments to female employees was the lack of a previous reprimand and a warning he would be fired for any repetition of his conduct.

The grievor, who had been dismissed at St. Vincent Hospital, said of himself to female employees, "Je suis Fabien L'Amour."

Arbitrator Walter Little, a former judge, said that, translated figuratively, it meant, "I make good love," or colloquially, "I am a good lover."

The grievor's supervisor said he had overheard such comments as "Is your husband home tonight?" and "Are you going to take me out for supper?" Other commends included "Did you bring my bottle of wine for tonight?" and "I'll fix that for you if you will give me a kiss."

A desk clerk, described by the arbitrator as a naturally cheerful person, entered the elevator one morning with the comment, "It's a wonderful day."

The grievor, who was on the elevator, responded, "God, you have a big smile today. Have you got yours last night?"

The woman testified that on another occasion he told her, "Don't forget to bring my bottle of wine and some kisses."

As a result of complaints, the grievor was fired. At the arbitration hearing, he said he had been joking.

Mr. Little said he had no hesitation in concluding that statements of a sexist nature had been made repeatedly to female employees and that the employer was entitled to discipline the grievor.

The issue was whether discharge was the proper penalty.

Mr. Little said the grievor's conduct was reprehensible and cannot be tolerated in the workplace.

"Unfortunately, it is the type of conduct which was tolerated, and almost accepted, privately and publicly, over the years as an example of male chauvinism."

Questions:

1. Do you agree with the statement in the last paragraph that this "type of conduct . . . was tolerated, and almost accepted, . . . over the years"?
2. Was the hospital electrician treated fairly?
3. What are your projections concerning future roles for men and women in business? ∎

Source: Wilfred List, *Globe & Mail*, June 15, 1983.

After reading this chapter, you should be able to:

1. Indicate the three different forms of business-government interaction.
2. Discuss the various levels of government and their responsibilities.
3. Understand and describe the various aspects of an economic decision.
4. Explain how governments can influence business decision making.
5. Indicate the specific tools available to government to influence business decision making.
6. Discuss how government and business interact in the day-to-day administration of government programs.
7. Describe the stages involved in the process of government policy formulation.
8. Indicate the different people who are involved in government policy formulation.
9. Describe the ways that business executives can get involved in changing government policy.

KEY CONCEPTS

In reading this chapter, look for and understand these terms:

distribution of government powers

cooperative federalism

Crown corporation

FIRA

CRTC

CTC

NEB

provincial boards

competition policy

Hazardous Products Act

Food and Drug Act

Consumer Packaging and Labelling Act

Weights and Measures Act

Textile Labelling Act

royalties

incentive programs

administration of government programs

government policy formulation

IN EARLY 1983 THE OIL MINISTERS from the Organization of Petroleum Exporting Countries (OPEC) were attempting to negotiate an agreement on oil price and production levels. Their objective was to prevent a further erosion in world oil prices.

Concurrently, the Prime Minister of Canada — Mr. Trudeau — and the Premier of Alberta — Mr. Lougheed — were exploring their options for changing their previous energy pricing agreement. This agreement stipulated that the price of oil would not exceed 75 percent of the world level. It was negotiated at a time when the expectation was that the world oil price would continue to increase and would not decrease.

Many economic observers were waiting with anticipation to see what the OPEC agreement would be and also what the agreement between the two Canadian political leaders would be. These included consumers, oil company executives, business consumers, and bankers. The importance of government to Canadian business practitioners was never more clearly illustrated.

CHAPTER NINETEEN

FROM SEA TO SEA

BRITISH COLUMBIA

ALBERTA

SASKATCHEWAN

MANITOBA

ONTARIO

CANADA

Coat-of-arms of Canada and
the ten Canadian Provinces

QUEBEC

NEWFOUNDLAND

PRINCE EDWARD ISLAND

NOVA SCOTIA

NEW BRUNSWICK

The Political Environment

THE POLITICAL ENVIRONMENT IS IMPORTANT TO BUSINESS IN Canada. Governments influence many of the economic decisions mentioned in Chapter 1 about what to produce, how to produce, and how to distribute income. Some of these economic decisions are made directly by government. Others are made by private sector firms, but are influenced by government. We begin this chapter with a description of how the government is organized. We then discuss the role of government as a decision maker in the economic system and as an influencer of decisions made by private companies. This role of government in the economic system is one concern of business. There are two other interactions of business and government. One of the interactions occurs when government policies are implemented (e.g., administration of the tax laws or obtaining a licence to do business). Another interaction occurs when new government policy is formulated.

The major part of this chapter deals with the first of these concerns, the role of government in the economic system. The administration of existing government policy and the way government policy is changed are also examined.

THE GOVERNMENT OF CANADA

The political environment of Canadian firms is composed of a number of different governing bodies. These include the Canadian federal government, the provincial and territorial governments, and the nearly 5,000 municipal governments. Foreign governments are also part of the political environment of those Canadian firms that have operations in other countries, or that buy from or sell to firms located in other countries.

The Structure of Government

distribution of government powers

Canada has a federal structure of government, as outlined in the British North America (BNA) Act. Powers are distributed between the national government and the provincial governments. **The distribution of government powers means that different levels of government have responsibilities for different matters.** The federal government has legislative jurisdiction over all matters of general or common interest. Provincial governments have jurisdiction over all matters of local or common interest. The specific areas of jurisdiction for federal and provincial governments are indicated in the boxed inserts.

The sharing of responsibilities between federal and provincial governments has been a controversial matter. Negotiations between the provinces

FEDERAL GOVERNMENT CONSTITUTIONAL RESPONSIBILITIES

The legislative authority of the Parliament includes:

- the amendment of the Constitution of Canada
- the public debt and property
- the regulation of trade and commerce
- unemployment insurance
- the raising of money by any mode or system of taxation
- the borrowing of money on the public credit
- postal service
- the census and statistics
- militia, military and naval services, and defence
- the fixing of and providing for the salaries and allowances of civil and other officers of the government of Canada
- beacons, buoys, lighthouses, and Sable Island
- navigation and shipping
- quarantine and the establishment and maintenance of marine hospitals
- seacoast and inland fisheries
- ferries between a province and any British or foreign country or between

two provinces
- currency and coinage, banking, incorporation of banks, and the issue of paper money
- savings banks
- weights and measures
- bills of exchange and promissory notes — interest
- legal tender
- bankruptcy and insolvency
- patents of invention and discovery
- copyrights
- Indians and lands reserved for the Indians
- naturalization and aliens
- marriage and divorce
- the criminal law, except the constitution of courts of criminal jurisdiction, but including the procedures in criminal matters
- the establishment, maintenance, and management of penitentiaries
- agriculture and immigration
- old-age pensions

Source: Reproduced by permission of the Minister of Supply and Services Canada.

and the federal government regarding patriation of the Canadian Constitution and the Charter of Rights illustrate the degree of controversy very clearly. The tasks outlined in the boxed inserts sometimes overlap, as in the case of agriculture, immigration, and old-age pensions. Social, technological, economic, and political developments have created new problems to be dealt with. Some of these problems have included aviation, broadcasting, telecommunications, and energy shortages.

Problems have arisen over provincial control of natural resources. This was a factor in disputes about how mining tax revenues were to be collected and allocated between the federal and provincial levels.

Broadcasting is another area of concern. The Quebec government, in particular, had wanted provincial control over broadcasting to assure consistency between programming and the cultural aspirations of Quebec citizens. The government of Canada, on the other hand, refused to give up control of broadcasting.

PROVINCIAL GOVERNMENT CONSTITUTIONAL RESPONSIBILITIES

The legislature of each province may make laws in relation to the following:

- amendment of the constitution of the province except as regards the lieutenant governor
- direct taxation within the province
- borrowing of money on the credit of the province
- establishment and tenure of provincial offices and appointment and payment of provincial officers
- the management and sale of public lands belonging to the province and of the timber and wood thereon
- the establishment, maintenance, and management of public and reformatory prisons in and for the province
- the establishment, maintenance, and management of hospitals, asylums, charities, and eleemosynary institutions in and for the province, other than marine hospitals
- municipal institutions in the province
- shop, saloon, tavern, auctioneer, and other licences issued for the raising of provincial or municipal revenue
- local works and undertakings other than inter-provincial or international lines of ships, railways, canals, telegraphs, etc., or works which, although wholly situated within one province, are declared by the federal Parliament to be for the general advantage either of Canada or of two or more provinces
- the incorporation of companies with provincial objects
- the solemnization of marriage in the province
- property and civil rights in the province
- the administration of justice in the province including the constitution, maintenance, and organization of provincial courts, both of civil and of criminal jurisdiction, including procedure in civil matters in these courts
- the imposition of punishment by fine, penalty, or imprisonment in enforcing any law of the province relating to any of the aforesaid subjects
- generally all matters of a merely local or private nature in the province
- education
- agriculture and immigration

Source: Reproduced by permission of the Minister of Supply and Services Canada.

The BNA Act granted the federal government far more extensive taxing powers than the provincial governments. Since the costs of some provincial responsibilities such as education and health care exceed their revenue-raising capabilities, revenue sharing has been instituted by the federal government. Education expenses, for example, are shared by the federal, provincial, and municipal governments.

The federal government, through the Department of Regional Industrial Expansion, also makes funds available in various provinces for economic development. Examples of other programs for which the federal government transfers money to the provinces include medical care, agriculture, tourism, crop insurance, and pest control. **The techniques and arrangements for dealing with federal-provincial economic relations have come to be known as cooperative federalism.**

cooperative federalism

Local authority covers areas such as transportation, police protection, environmental health and development, recreation, community services, and education.

The major source of revenue for local governments is taxation of real property. Revenue is also obtained from licences, permits, rents, concessions, franchises, fines, and surplus revenue from municipal enterprises such as transit systems.

The Canadian Parliamentary System

Our federal and provincial governments are characterized by a parliamentary system of government. We have an executive branch of government headed by the Queen, whose representative in Canada is the Governor General. (See Figure 19.1.) The Queen's representative in each of the provinces is the Lieutenant Governor. At the federal level, the Prime

Figure 19.1
Structure of the Canadian parliamentary system

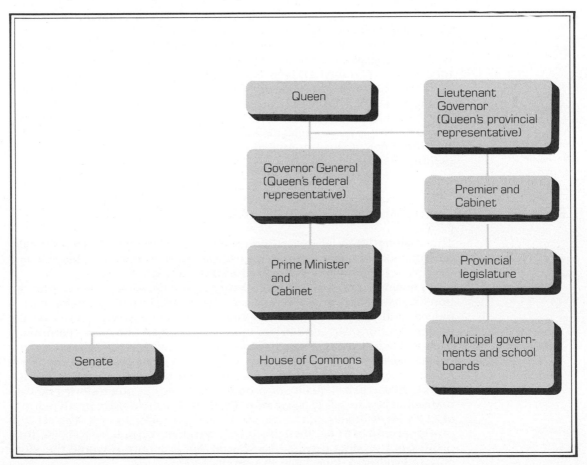

Minister and his Cabinet are formally the Queen's advisors. In the provinces, the provincial premier and the cabinet perform this function.

The Cabinet plays a key role in this system at the federal and provincial levels. It determines what executive actions will be taken by the government. It also places legislative proposals before the House of Commons, Senate, or relevant provincial legislatures.

The unit of local government is usually the municipality, which is normally incorporated as a city, town, village, district, or township. The powers and responsibilities of municipalities are delegated to them by the provincial governments.

Government Departments and Agencies

We cannot simply talk about the federal, provincial, and municipal governments as single units. Each of them is composed of various departments and agencies. Different departments and agencies affect business decision making in very different ways.

Some idea of the number and diversity of federal government departments and agencies is given in the boxed insert.

Each provincial and territorial government has a number of departments and agencies. A study published by the Ontario Economic Council, for example, identified 292 boards, commissions, and advisory and research bodies in that province. Other provinces also delegate authority to many agencies, boards, and commissions.

Municipal governments, particularly the larger ones, also have numerous departments, agencies, boards, and commissions. City planning commissions, environmental boards, licensing agencies, and zoning commissions are examples.

THE ROLE OF GOVERNMENT IN THE ECONOMIC SYSTEM

The various levels of governments with their many agencies and departments have a definite role in business decision making. This role and the forms it can take are discussed in this section.

A business decision has four elements: the decision maker(s), the options available to the decision maker(s), the criteria by which the options are judged, and the payoffs of the options. A simple example would be the owner of a store, Mr. Lamoureux, who has to choose one of two competing products to sell in his store. His objective is to make as much profit on the product as possible. The criteria he will apply in judging the two brands will be the anticipated profitability of each. Based upon his knowledge of the brand, image, price, quality of product, and sales in other stores, he estimates that he can sell 12,000 units of Product A at an average profit per unit of $2.73. He estimates that he can sell 15,000 units of Product B at an average profit per unit of $1.68. Total profit from Product A would be $32,760. Total profit from Product B would be $25,200. Mr. Lamoureux would therefore choose Product A. (See Table 19.1 on page 652.)

FEDERAL GOVERNMENT MINISTRIES AND THE DEPARTMENTS, AGENCIES, AND CROWN CORPORATIONS THAT REPORT TO PARLIAMENT THROUGH THEM (AS OF JUNE 1983)

Department of Agriculture
Agriculture Stabilization Board
Canadian Dairy Commission
Livestock Feed Board of Canada
Farm Credit Corporation
Canadian Grain Commission
Agricultural Products Board
National Farm Products Marketing Council

Department of Communications
National Museums of Canada
Canadian Film Development Corporation
Canadian Broadcasting Corporation
Teleglobe Canada
Canada Council
National Arts Centre Corporation
Canadian Radio-Television and
    Telecommunications Commission
Communications Research Advisory Board
Cultural Property Export Review Board
National Film Board
Social Sciences and Humanities Research
    Council
National Library
Public Archives
Telesat Canada

Consumer and Corporate Affairs Canada
Restrictive Trade Practices Commission
Copyright Appeal Board
Standards Council of Canada

Economic Development, Ministry of State
Northern Pipeline Agency

Canada Employment and Immigration Commission
Department of Employment and
    Immigration
Employment and Immigration Special
    Advisory Board
Immigration Appeal Board

Department of Energy, Mines and Resources
Atomic Energy Control Board
Atomic Energy of Canada Limited
Petro-Canada Limited
Uranium Canada Limited
Eldorado Aviation Limited
Eldorado Nuclear Limited
Canertech
Board of Examiners for Dominion
    Land Surveys
Canadian Permanent Committee on
    Geographical Names
Energy Supplies Allocation Board
National Energy Board
Petroleum Compensation Board
Petroleum Monitoring Agency

Environment Canada
Atmospheric Environment Service
Environmental Conservation Service
Canadian Forestry Service
Federal Environmental Assessment
    Review Office
Parks Canada
Historic Sites and Monuments Board
    of Canada
National Battlefield Commission

External Affairs Canada
Canadian Commercial Corporation
Export Development Corporation
Foreign Claims Commission
International Boundary Commission
International Joint Commission
Roosevelt Campobello International
    Park Commission
Canadian International Development Agency
Grains Group
International Development Research Centre

FEDERAL GOVERNMENT MINISTRIES AND THE DEPARTMENTS, AGENCIES, AND CROWN CORPORATIONS THAT REPORT TO PARLIAMENT THROUGH THEM (AS OF JUNE 1983) (*continued*)

Department of Finance
Inspector General of Banks
Foreign Claims Commission
Tariff Board
Anti-Dumping Tribunal
Department of Insurance
Bank of Canada

Fisheries and Oceans
Fisheries Price Support Board
Canadian Saltfish Corporation
Freshwater Fish Marketing Corporation
Fisheries and Oceans Research
   Advisory Council
International Fisheries Commissions

Indian and Northern Affairs
National Canada Power Commission
Canadian Indian Rights Commission
Water Boards
Commissioner of the Northwest Territories
Commissioner of the Yukon Territory
Eskimo (Inuit) Arts Council

Industry, Trade and Commerce/ Department of Regional Economic Expansion (Name Changed to Department of Regional Industrial Expansion in November 1983)
Canadian Patents and Developments Ltd.
Federal Business Development Bank
Machinery and Equipment Advisory Board
Metric Commission Canada
Textile and Clothing Board
National Design Council
Standards Council of Canada
Canadian International Grains Institute
Canadian Trade and Tariffs Committee
Foreign Investment Review Agency
Cape Breton Development Corporation
Atlantic Development Council

Department of Justice
Supreme Court of Canada
Federal Court of Canada
Canadian Human Rights Commission
Federal Judicial Affairs, Office of
   the Commissioner
Law Reform Commission
Statute Law Revision Commission
Tax Review Board
Canadian Judicial Council

Labour Canada
Canada Labour Relations Board
Merchant Seaman Compensation Board
Canadian Centre for Occupational Health
   and Safety

Department of National Defence
Defence Construction (1951) Limited

National Health and Welfare Canada
Medical Research Council
National Advisory Council on Aging

Canada Post Corporation
   Reports to Parliament through a designated Minister.

Public Works
Fire Commissioner of Canada
Canada Mortgage and Housing Corporation

Revenue Canada—Customs and Excise and Taxation
Anti-Dumping Tribunal

Science and Technology
National Research Council
Science Council of Canada
Natural Sciences and Engineering
   Research Council

Secretary of State
Public Service Commission of Canada
National Advisory Council on Fitness
  and Amateur Sport

Social Development, Ministry of State

Solicitor General
National Parole Board
Correctional Investigator
Correctional Services of Canada
Royal Canadian Mounted Police

Supply and Services Canada
Canadian Arsenals Limited
Canadian Commercial Corporation
Crown Assets Disposal Corporation
Royal Canadian Mint
Statistics Canada
Canadian General Standards Board

Transport Canada
Harbours Board Canada
Air Canada
Atlantic Pilotage Authority
Great Lakes Pilotage Authority
Laurentian Pilotage Authority
National Railways
Northern Transportation Company Ltd.
Pacific Pilotage Authority
St. Lawrence Seaway Authority
Seaway International Bridge Corporation Ltd.
Via Rail Canada Incorporated
Canada Ports Corporation
Canadian Transport Commission
Aircraft Accident Review Board

Treasury Board
Statistics Canada

Veterans Affairs Canada
Canadian Pension Commission
Commonwealth War Graves Commission
  Review Board
War Veterans Allowance Board
Army Benevolent Fund
Bureau of Pensions Advocates

MISCELLANEOUS

Canadian Wheat Board
  The Governor in Council designates a member of the Cabinet to act as Minister for the Canadian Wheat Board.

Economic Council of Canada
  The Economic Council of Canada reports to Parliament through the Prime Minister.

Commissioner of Official Languages
  Reports directly to Parliament.

Canadian Industrial Renewal Board
  Works under the direction of a Special Committee of Ministers chaired by the Prime Minister.

Public Service Staff Relations Board
  Reports to Parliament through such ministers of the Crown, other than a member of the Treasury Board, as may be designated by the Governor in Council. The President of the Privy Council was designated for this purpose in 1972.

Advisory Council on the Status of Women
  Reports to Parliament through the Minister responsible for the Status of Women.

**Canadian Consultative Council
on Multiculturalism**
  Reports through Minister of State—Multiculturalism.

Auditor General's Office
  Reports directly to Parliament.

Emergency Planning Canada
  Reports through Privy Council Office and Department of National Defence.

Source: CCH Canadian Ltd.—Topical Law Reports. The CCH law reports are kept updated on a monthly basis.

Table 19.1 Four Elements of the Decision about What Product to Sell

The Decision Maker	The Options	The Criterion	The Anticipated Payoffs
Mr. Lamoureux	1. Product *A*	Profit for the	12,000 × $2.73 = $32,760.00
	2. Product *B*	store	15,000 × $1.68 = $25,200.00

The political environment (government) can influence the way this decision is made. It could change the decision maker, the options available to the decision maker, the criteria used to make the decision, or the anticipated payoffs from one or more of the decision options.

Governments Can Change the Decision Maker

In this example, Mr. Lamoureux is the only decision maker. He is an entrepreneur. This would be changed if there were a government decision to nationalize the sale of the product. The decision maker in that case would not be Mr. Lamoureux. He would simply be a representative of the government. The authority and responsibility to make the decision shift from the private sector to the public sector.

WHAT DO YOU THINK?

The Saccharin Ban

In mid-1977 it was announced that products containing saccharin (an artificial sweetener) would have to be removed from retail shelves by September, 1977.

The reason for the ban was because experimental results had linked saccharin with cancer. In order to give retail operators time to comply, the deadline was subsequently extended to December, 1977.

Retailers and food processors were upset by the ban. They claimed that the experimental results did not clearly show saccharin to be a health hazard. They pointed to the fact that saccharin had not been banned in the United States.

Food industry representatives were also concerned about the way in which the ban was enforced. They claimed that government bureaucrats were "overzealous" because in early January, 1978, they began visiting stores and breaking open packages of products containing saccharin, rendering them unsaleable. WHAT DO YOU THINK? Is it proper for a government to control the options available to business decision makers in this way?

Source: Government of Canada, *Report by the Sector Task Force on the Canadian Food & Beverage Industry,* 1978, Appendix C-5, p. 6. Reproduced by permission of the Minister of Supply and Services Canada.

Another way in which the authority and responsibility for making the decision could shift away from Mr. Lamoureux would be if a government appointed a board or tribunal to review and approve decisions about what products could be sold. If this type of body was introduced, it would mean that Mr. Lamoureux would no longer be free to decide what product to sell. The government, through its board, would have control over the decision. When the government control over the decision increases, so does the government responsibility for the decision.

Governments Can Change Options

The options currently available to Mr. Lamoureux are to sell either Product *A* or Product *B*. Government action could affect these options. This could be done by making it illegal to sell one or the other, or both, of the products; this can certainly happen.

Governments Can Change Decision Criteria

Government actions can change the criteria which will be applied to the making of economic decisions. This occurs when government becomes involved as a decision maker, either through Crown corporation ownership or through operation of a regulatory board or tribunal.

The traditional decision criteria or goals for private economic activity are some combination of profit, growth, and survival. We have assumed in Mr. Lamoureux's case that his primary goal is profitability.

Imagine a situation where Mr. Lamoureux calculated that he could increase his profitability by manufacturing Product *A* himself rather than purchasing it from someone else. He decides that he will go into a joint venture with a U.S.-owned firm to buy out the Canadian-owned manufacturer of Product *A*. Because a foreign-owned firm is involved in the takeover, the transaction must be approved by the Foreign Investment Review Agency (FIRA).

The criteria that the purchase must satisfy for FIRA are more complex than the original profitability criterion that motivated the transaction. (The criteria that are applied by FIRA were discussed in the chapter on international business.)

Governments Can Affect Payoffs

There are many government policies that can affect the anticipated payoffs from decision options. Taxes, incentive grants, and tariffs are some of these. Government purchasing decisions can also affect the anticipated payoffs.

Let's assume that Product *B* was imported from France and the federal government decided to impose an import tariff of $1.00 per unit on it. This would have the effect of reducing the profit per unit by $1.00 if the selling price were not raised by $1.00. This would reduce the potential profit on

Product *B* to $10,200.00. This would make it even less attractive in relation to Product *A* than it previously had been.

Assume that Mr. Lamoureux has just received an order from the government for 12,000 units of Product *B* in addition to the initial 15,000 units he had estimated could be sold. Suppose also that Mr. Lamoureux could make the same profit per unit on these 12,000 units that he could on the initial 15,000. He was also aware that the government would not purchase Product *A*. He has to recalculate the estimated profitability of Product *B*. Instead of $1.68 × 15,000 units or $25,200.00, it is now $1.68 × 27,000 units or $45,360.00. This would make Product *B* more profitable than Product *A*, and Mr. Lamoureux would decide to sell it if he wished to maximize his profits.

In addition to specific policies like the ones mentioned, government policies can have a general influence upon the payoffs of decision options. Two items are the cost of implementing government regulations and collecting statistics on business activity.

Government intervention in the macroeconomy also affects payoffs. The exchange rate can influence costs. In our example, Product *B* is imported. If the value of the Canadian dollar decreases, the cost of Product *B* to Canadian firms increases. Interest rate changes which are influenced by the government through the Bank of Canada can also affect the anticipated payoffs of decisions, because, if a firm is borrowing money, interest rate fluctuations affect its interest costs.

GOVERNMENT INFLUENCE IN BUSINESS DECISIONS

There are many specific ways the government directly or indirectly participates in or influences decisions made by business firms. These can be grouped into four basic categories. First, government can get directly involved in business decision making by forming corporations to produce products or services. When this is done, government may become a competitor to firms in the private sector. Second, government can set up agencies which must give approval before certain business activities are allowed. Third, the government may introduce legislation which prohibits certain business activities. Finally, the government can take actions which will

WHAT DO YOU THINK?

What types of economic decisions, do the following organizations, which are Crown corporations of the federal government, make that could not be made by privately owned firms?

•Air Canada

•Canadian Broadcasting Corporation
•Export Development Corporation
•Federal Business Development Bank
•Freshwater Fish Marketing Corporation
•Canadian National Railways
•Petro-Canada

change the payoffs of various business activities. These four categories are discussed below, and the various roles that comprise these categories can be summarized as:

- direct competitor
- economic administrator
- regulator
- taxation and incentive programs
- customer
- "housekeeper"

Government Corporations

Crown corporation

Crown corporations are used by government in Canada to participate directly in business decision making. **A Crown corporation is one that is accountable, through a minister, to Parliament for the conduct of its affairs.** The federal government utilizes three types of Crown corporations: departmental corporations, agency corporations, and proprietary corporations. These were discussed in Chapter 3.

Crown corporations exist at both the provincial and federal government level. In the mid-1970s, over 70 percent of the electricity in Canada was generated by provincial government utilities. A number of provinces also own the telephone utilities within their borders. In addition, various provincial governments are involved in ownership and operation of other types of businesses. Manitoba, Saskatchewan, and British Columbia have provincial automobile insurance operations. Saskatchewan has taken over operation of much of the potash industry in that province. The Alberta government owns Pacific Western Airlines. Government-owned and government-operated enterprises account for a significant amount of economic activity in Canada.

Government Review Boards: Economic Administration

For governments wishing to control business decisions there are alternatives to Crown corporations. Governments can, as we saw earlier, use administrative boards, tribunals, or commissions to screen decisions of private companies before they can be implemented. There are many examples of such boards, including the Foreign Investment Review Agency (FIRA), the Canadian Radio-Television and Telecommunications Commission (CRTC), the Canadian Transport Commission (CTC), the National Energy Board (NEB), and provincial boards.

FIRA

The Foreign Investment Review Agency (FIRA) reviews proposed acquisitions of Canadian businesses by non-Canadians. A non-Canadian cannot complete a takeover transaction until approval has been received from FIRA.

CRTC   **The Canadian Radio-Television and Telecommunications Commission (CRTC) regulates and supervises all aspects of the Canadian broadcasting system. The CRTC issues broadcasting licenses and renews licenses of existing broadcasting outlets subject to certain conditions.** For example, a licence may stipulate the type of programming, the power of the station, or the minutes of commercial messages which can be broadcast. **The CRTC also decides upon applications for rate changes submitted to it by federally regulated telecommunications carriers such as Bell Canada.**

CTC   **The Canadian Transport Commission (CTC) makes decisions about route and rate applications for commercial air and railway companies.** For example, before rail service can be expanded or contracted, the changes must be approved by this agency. **The same holds true for other transportation activities (e.g., trucking and airlines). Proposed changes in rates must also be approved.**

NEB   **The National Energy Board (NEB) is responsible for regulating the construction and operation of oil and gas pipelines which are under the jurisdiction of the Canadian government. This includes decisions about routes of pipelines and the size of pipe to be used in the lines. The NEB also decides on the tolls to be charged for transmission by oil and gas pipelines and the levels of export and import of oil and gas. It also issues guidelines on internal company accounting procedures and allowable rates of return.**

provincial boards   **There are also certain provincial boards which consider and pass judgment on proposed decisions by private companies. One example of such boards is provincial liquor boards or commissions.** They must authorize price changes by breweries within provinces. Milk prices charged by farmers, dairies, and supermarkets are also regulated in a number of provinces. Other marketing boards for commodities such as pork, eggs, and vegetables have important roles in establishing prices and/or production levels of producers.

Government Regulation

One effect of government regulation is to limit the options available to business managers. According to the Economic Council of Canada in their November 1979 Interim Report, about one-third of all the federal and provincial statutes in force are regulatory. This means that these statutes seek to alter the economic behaviour of individuals in the private sector. The Consolidated Regulations of Canada contained 9,475 pages of statutory instruments in 1979; of these, 140 federal statutes can be identified as regulatory.

Governments use regulations to protect property rights (e.g., patents and copyrights); to stop abuses of market power (e.g., competition policy); and to set standards for consumers and/or producers in the health, safety, and fairness areas.

Three important areas of regulation are (1) competition policy, (2) consumer protection, and (3) environmental policies.

Competition Policy

competition policy

Canada's competition policy has been the subject of much discussion, with supporters arguing it is necessary for a healthy economy and critics claiming it is not effective. **Competition policy seeks to eliminate restrictive trade practices and thereby stimulate maximum production, distribution, and employment through open competition.**

The guidelines for competition policy are contained in the Combines Investigation Act, a comprehensive document which regulates the practices of Canadian business firms (the act does not apply to labour unions). The act is divided into forty-nine sections; these deal either with the actual laws or with activities that are necessary to administer them. The act is designed to encourage competition among business firms. If competition exists, all Canadians should benefit from efficient production systems, lower prices, and a healthier economy. (See boxed insert.)

THE COMBINES INVESTIGATION ACT

Section 32. Prohibits conspiracies and combinations which are formed for the purpose of unduly lessening competition in the production, transportation, or storage of goods. Persons convicted may be imprisoned for up to five years or fined up to $1 million or both.

Section 33. Prohibits mergers and monopolies which substantially lessen competition. Individuals who assist in the formation of such a monopoly or merger may be imprisoned for up to two years.

Section 34. Prohibits illegal trade practices. A company may not, for example, cut prices in one region of Canada while selling at a higher price everywhere else if doing this substantially lessens competition. A company may not sell at "unreasonably low prices" if this substantially lessens competition. (This section does not prohibit credit unions from returning surpluses to their members.)

Section 35. Prohibits giving allowances and rebates to buyers to cover their advertising expenses, unless these allowances are made available on a proportionate basis to other purchasers in competition with the buyer given the rebate.

Section 36. Prohibits misleading advertising. There are many types of misleading advertising which are prohibited, including (1) false statements about the performance of a product, (2) misleading guarantees, (3) pyramid selling, (4) charging the higher price when two prices are marked on an item, and (5) referral selling.

Section 37. Prohibits bait-and-switch selling. No person can advertise a product at a "bargain price" if there is no supply of the product available to the consumer. This is usually done to "bait" prospects into the store and then "switch" them to higher-priced goods. This section also controls the use of contests to sell goods and prohibits the sale of goods at a price higher than that advertised.

Section 38. Prohibits resale price maintenance. No person who produces or supplies a product can attempt to influence upwards, or discourage reduction of, the price of the good in question. It is also illegal for the producer to refuse to supply a product to a reseller simply because the producer believes the reseller will cut the price.

Consumer Protection

A number of government programs related to consumer protection have been implemented. Many of them are administered by the federal Department of Consumer and Corporate Affairs. The department initiates programs to promote the interests of Canadian consumers. Some of the programs which the department administeres are indicated below.

Hazardous Products Act

The Hazardous Products Act regulates two categories of products. The first category comprises products that are banned because they are dangerous. Some examples are: toys and other children's articles painted with coatings containing harmful amounts of lead and other chemical compounds; certain highly flammable textile products; and baby pacifiers containing contaminated liquids. **The second category comprises products that can be sold but must be labelled as hazardous. Standard symbols which denote poisonous, flammable, explosive, or corrosive properties must be attached to certain products.**

Food and drug regulations are another important area. These regulations are designed to protect the public from possible risk to health, fraud, and deception in relation to food, drugs, cosmetics, and therapeutic devices. **For example, the Food and Drug Act prohibits the sale of a food that contains any poisonous or harmful substances; is unfit for human consumption; consists in whole or in part of any rotten substances; is adulterated; or was manufactured under unsanitary conditions. The act also provides that no person can sell or advertise a food in a manner that is misleading or deceptive with respect to its value, quantity, composition, or safety.**

Food and Drug Act

Consumer Packaging and Labelling Act

The Consumer Packaging and Labelling Act has two main purposes. The first is to provide a comprehensive set of rules for packaging and labelling of consumer products. The second is to ensure that full and factual information is provided on labels by the manufacturer. All pre-packaged products must state the quantity enclosed in French and English, in metric as well as traditional units. The name and description of the product must also appear on the label in both French and English.

Weights and Measures Act

Regulations under the Weights and Measures Act complement the packaging and labelling regulations. The Weights and Measures Act sets standards of accuracy for weighing and measuring devices.

Textile Labelling Act

The Textile Labelling Act regulates the labelling, sale, importation, and advertising of consumer textile articles. The National Trade Mark and True Labelling Act provides that products authorized under the regulations can be designated by the term "Canada Standard." A familiar application is with children's garments which bear the Canada Standard trademark.

Environmental Regulations

Most of the industrial sources of environmental pollution are subject to provincial regulation. The federal role is limited to areas where there are inter-provincial or international implications.

One of the major pieces of federal government environmental legislation is the Canada Water Act. Under it the federal government can control water quality in fresh and marine waters, when there is a formal federal-provincial agreement, when federal waters are involved, or when there is sufficient national urgency to warrant federal action. The acid rain situation is handled by the federal government because international dealings are necessary.

Two other important environmental regulations are the Fisheries Act, which controls the discharge of any harmful substance into any water, and the Environmental Contaminants Act, which establishes regulations for airborne substances that are a danger to human health or the environment.

Government Action That Changes Payoffs

Some of the regulations indicated above can affect the payoffs of certain options. This occurs if there are fines for certain actions, or if significant investment is required to comply with new regulations.

There are other government actions that affect the payoffs of certain options, making them either more or less attractive. These include taxes and tariffs, incentive programs (grants), low-cost or free governmental services, government demand for products and services, and macroeconomic policy management.

Taxes and Tariffs

These charges, which governments levy on business firms, can have a big influence on the payoffs of business decisions. Taxes paid are a cost of doing business. Differences in tax levels in different countries or provinces can affect a company's decision about initial investment or increases in investment in those areas.

Canada imposes federal and provincial income taxes on profits of corporations. Profits of proprietorships and partnerships are taxed at the same rate as personal income. Corporate income taxes accounted for more than 14 percent of total federal government revenues in 1980.

Local property taxes and provincial royalties are other forms of taxes. Companies pay property taxes directly on property they own and indirectly on property they rent. **Royalties are government charges levied for the use of Crown property.** Royalties on natural resources are levied by provincial governments because they control resources. The major source of royalties is from mining, oil, and timber properties.

royalties

The federal Excise Tax Act imposes a retail sales tax on most goods produced in Canada or imported into Canada. A tax of 12 percent is imposed on the manufacturer's sales price of goods produced in Canada and on the duty-paid value of imports. Certain goods, such as production machinery and equipment, food products, and all exports, are exempt from the tax.

All provinces except Alberta impose a retail sales tax. Rates of sales tax varied from 10 percent in Newfoundland to 5 percent in Manitoba and Saskatchewan.

Canada has traditionally had high tariffs. These contributed to the centralized, small-scale, high-cost, and largely foreign-controlled manufacturing firms in Canada. Canada's tariff rates have been progressively lowered through seven post–World War II rounds of trade negotiations among the Western trading nations, known as the General Agreement on Tariffs and Trade (GATT).

Canada has also negotiated certain bilateral (two-country) agreements which have influenced business activity in Canada. These include the Auto Pact and the Defence Production Sharing Agreement with the United States. These are agreements for the reduction of duties on automobiles and defence products between the two countries.

Incentive Programs

incentive programs

Federal, provincial, and municipal governments offer incentive programs which business managers should take into account when they make decisions. Incentive programs can be very important in stimulating economic development. **Incentive programs are designed to encourage managers to make certain decisions and take certain actions desired by governments.** For example, they are designed to encourage managers to locate in one region rather than another, to invest in new product development, or to engage in export activities. Incentive programs improve the payoff from a certain option and hence encourage a manager to select that option.

An example of grant incentive programs is the one offered by the federal Department of Regional Industrial Expansion (DRIE). These grants are designed to stimulate increased manufacturing investment and employment in slow growth areas.

Direct regional incentives are available to you if you are in a "designated region." These are slow-growth areas for which special assistance is available. They include the Atlantic provinces; most of Quebec, except for the Montreal Special Areas (which are covered by a separate program of their own); Northern Ontario, including the district of Parry Sound and most of Nipissing; Manitoba; Saskatchewan; Northern Alberta (beginning sixty miles north of Edmonton); Northern British Columbia (beginning sixty miles north of Kamloops); and the Yukon and Northwest Territories.

Grants and loan guarantees are provided through the Regional Development Incentives Program to encourage entrepreneurs to locate in the designated regions and industries already established there to expand or modernize. Most manufacturing and processing industries are eligible for grants and loan guarantees. The major exceptions are initial processing operations such as petroleum refining and certain parts of the pulp and paper industry, mining, and the growing, harvesting, or extracting of natural products. Industries that process natural products, such as sawmills, fish processing plants, or food processing plants, are eligible.

The main legislative ceilings on incentive grants are 20 percent of approved capital cost for plant modernization and/or volume expansion; and 25 percent of approved capital cost plus $5,000 per direct job created for new plants or new product expansions.

An example of a grant program that encourages development of pollution control equipment is one administered by the federal Department of Fisheries and the Environment. This is the program for the Development and Demonstration of Pollution Abatement Technology. It is intended to assist in the development of new methods, procedures, processes, and equipment to prevent, eliminate, or reduce the release of pollutants into the environment. The program pays a percentage of the capital and operating costs incurred by firms and municipalities in such developments.

There are many other examples of grant programs. Some of these include municipal tax rebates for locating in certain areas, design assistance programs, and remission on tariffs on certain advanced technology production equipment.

Low-Cost or Free Services

Governments offer many services of value to business firms. One example of such a program is the Trade Commissioner Service of the federal government. The Department of External Affairs has approximately 300 trade commissioners in 70 countries. The Trade Commissioner Service responds to requests for assistance from Canadian exporters and assists foreign importers to locate Canadian sources of supply for products they wish to buy. Trade commissioners also participate in the development of programs to improve Canadian exports. This requires identification of market opportunities and the development of export programs.

Some provinces, such as British Columbia, Alberta, Ontario, and Quebec, also have very active programs to encourage exports.

The Export Development Corporation was designed to improve Canadian exports by offering export insurance for Canadian exporters against non-payment by foreign buyers; long-term loans to foreign purchasers of Canadian products or guarantees of private loans to purchasers; and insurance against loss of, or damage to, a Canadian firm's investment abroad arising from expropriation, revolution, or war.

There are many other grants and low- or no-cost incentive programs available to Canadian firms. Information on these programs is available from the relevant departments or from centralized federal government information services.

Information on provincial incentive programs is available from the various provincial governments. Similarly, information on municipal incentive programs is available from the various municipal governments. CCH Canadian Limited publishes a book entitled *Industrial Assistance Programs in Canada* which is updated on a regular basis.

The federal Department of Energy, Mines and Resources provides geological maps of Canada's potential mineral-producing areas. This service gives companies interested in mineral exploration much better geological information about Canada than is available about most other countries. Provincial governments also provide geological services to the mining industry.

Statistics Canada is yet another valuable service to business firms. The prices charged are below the actual cost of providing the service.

Government Demand for Goods and Services

Government spending can also influence business decisions such as where to locate or what type of product to produce. Government purchases range from paper clips and pencils to warships, highways, and high-rise office buildings. Many firms and industries are dependent upon govern-

WHAT DO YOU THINK?

Paper Burden

The following list indicates some of the different types of government programs that require companies or individuals to complete paperwork.

federal sales tax collection
excise duties
customs clearance
unemployment insurance commission
   deductions
workmen's compensation
hospitalization
loan applications
building permits
equipment operating licences
property taxes
vehicles registration
transport operating licences
communication licences
income tax forms
detailed household surveys
business licences
drivers' licences
restaurants and liquor taxes
CMHC housing surveys

safety inspections
tax audits
FIRA requirements
elevator licences
boiler licences
subsidy applications
development permits
waste control
minimum wage guidelines
Statistics Canada Surveys
manpower training programs
employee hiring procedures
government contracts — procurement
grants and incentive programs
census of population
welfare and health benefits

This paper burden is one of the subtle ways which government changes the payoffs for certain options. The costs to all Canadians for completing all this paperwork have not been estimated. However, one U.S. estimate is that completion of government paperwork in that country costs the equivalent of $500 for each citizen. If Canadian costs are that high, can they be justified?

ment purchasing decisions, if not for their survival, at least for their level of prosperity. Examples include construction and architectural firms and companies in the aerospace industry. Government expenditures on goods and services amount to billions of dollars per year.

Macroeconomic Management

Government is important to business in its role as manager of macroeconomic policy. This is done primarily through changes in monetary and fiscal policy. Macroeconomic conditions such as inflation, economic growth, exchange rates, and employment levels can, as we saw in the previous chapter, have a significant effect upon economic decisions.

The macroeconomic climate, and the level of confidence it generates, are significant contributors to investment decisions made by company managers. They therefore affect the payoffs of decisions. The level of confidence is important because, when business managers make a decision based on the expectation of some level of return, they want to feel reasonably sure that the return will be realized. If there are uncertainties about exchange rates, the rate of economic growth, or rates of income tax, it can result in deferral of investment decisions, or even decisions to not invest in Canada.

ADMINISTRATION OF GOVERNMENT PROGRAMS

administration of
government programs

The previous section on the role of government in the economic system illustrates the many government programs that are important to business decision makers. For these programs to be effective they must be put into practice and managed properly. **Administration of government programs involves the day-to-day activities that are required in the implementation of government programs.** This creates the need for business decision makers and those responsible for implementation of government programs to relate to each other. This is important in the operation of Crown corporations and in understanding and administering government regulations, taxation, tariffs, incentive programs, and government purchasing programs.

For government representatives this implies a need to understand business strategy and how it is formulated and implemented. It also requires an emphasis on the design of efficient systems for administering government policies.

Business managers, on the other hand, must have a thorough knowledge of government programs and how they are implemented. This allows business to deal effectively with government and to keep their costs for this activity as low as possible. Failure to understand government programs or regulations can be costly. One firm which developed a new product and spent money developing a media campaign for it found that under Food and Drug Act regulations they could not sell it. This firm could have avoided thousands of dollars of costs if it had taken the time and effort to check out the regulations.

Business firms working in a mixed economy must develop the capacity to deal with government. This includes the ability to make effective representations to regulatory tribunals such as the CRTC. The case presented by the firm may determine whether a price increase is granted or whether a firm will be able to keep its licence to conduct business.

Firms must also develop an ability to understand and work within a maze of government regulations. A part of this is the ability to deal with the tax laws of the country. Many large firms employ one or more full-time specialists who do nothing but work on tax problems. Similarly, firms involved in import and export operations must have specialists who understand tariffs and how to deal with the customs officials who administer them.

A thorough understanding of the available government incentive programs and how to utilize them to the best advantage of the firm is also necessary. With the many reporting requirements facing companies, an ability to deal efficiently with them is a capacity which must be developed by a firm.

Firms which sell products to the government must develop special skills. Some large firms such as IBM have sales groups which work only with government clients. For large multi-billion-dollar projects like the recent purchase of new fighter aircraft by the Canadian government, specialized sales efforts are required, in this case by airplane manufacturers.

CHANGE IN GOVERNMENT POLICY

government policy formulation

Another type of interaction between business and government representatives is that which accompanies the process of changing government policy. **Government policy formulation is the process by which changes are made in current government policies.**

Some general characteristics of this process can be identified. First, there are a number of stages in the process. Second, there will typically be a number of people involved; these people will change at different stages of the process. Third, decisions will be made at each stage of the process, and these decisions will depend on the power of the people involved at each stage. (See Table 19.2.)

No one person controls the process through all of the stages. The primary determiners of outcome vary from politicians at the "decision to proceed with legislation" stage, to civil servants at the "drafting of

THE INTERNATIONAL POLITICAL ENVIRONMENT

When a government owns the means of production, foreign firms doing business in that country must deal with that government. A firm may have to enter into a "partnership" arrangement with a government before the firm can begin operations there.

A Canadian firm that deals with foreign governments and/or businesses gets involved in politics. It's hard to keep sharp dividing lines between politics and ethics. This often poses a dilemma for managers. What is illegal in one country may be acceptable activity in another country.

The governments of many of the emerging nations try to instil in their people a strong feeling of nationalism. This sometimes leads them to distrust "foreigners." This can hurt multinational business.

Business activity thrives under conditions of political stability. Management should study the past history of political stability and current trends before committing itself to operations in a given country.

Many laws restrict a parent firm's control of its overseas operations. These include laws that require a subsidiary to hire local nationals or restrict how much profit can flow out of the country. A multinational firm takes on a considerable risk, much of which is political.

A firm operating in different countries is subject to different legal and tax systems. Quite often an item that is tax deductible in one country is not in another. The firm is caught in the middle but must be careful not to violate the laws of any country in which it operates.

Table 19.2 The Process of Government Policy Formulation

Stage of Process	Outcome of Stage	Primary Determiner of Outcome (Decision Maker)	Possible Influencers
1. Societal need	The existence of a problem	Created by changes in technology or attitudes (economic or ecological)	
2. Perception of need	General awareness of a problem	Researchers, media, politicians	
3. Articulation of demand	Different groups with different ideas about what to do	Leaders of different groups; e.g., political parties, media, interest groups, businesses	Members of various groups
4. Decision to proceed with legislation	Government commitment to deal with the problem	Cabinet ministers	Political party members Civil servants Public Media Researchers Interest groups Etc.
5. Determination of the nature of the legislation	A decision about what type of legislation to introduce	Civil servant teams Cabinet	Same influencers as for No. 4
6. Drafting of legislation	A draft of new legislation	Public service drafting expert	Cabinet minister Civil servant study team
7. Legislative consideration	Royal assent to legislation	Parliament or legislative assembly	Party loyalties Pressure groups Media
8. Formulation of regulations	The completed set of regulations	Civil servants	Industry representatives Politicians Interest groups
9. Implementation	The new policy in practice	Civil servants	Groups being affected

legislation" stage. Similarly, the people and groups with access to the decision maker, and, therefore, an opportunity to influence her or him, vary from stage to stage.

The primary determiners of outcomes at the various stages are not business managers. They are government representatives.

Understanding the process of change in government policy is important for business managers or others who wish to influence government policy. A major implication is that the would-be influencer should attempt to undertake appropriate activities at all stages of the process. He or she should not restrict efforts to one point in the process, such as the "legislative consideration" stage.

CAREER PROFILE

MY NAME IS KEITH O'BRIEN, AND I AM Director of Government Affairs for Inco Limited, an integrated, transnational company primarily involved in metals exploration, mining, smelting, refining, processing, and fabrication. Inco's head office is in Toronto.

By way of personal background, I was raised in Timmins, a northern Ontario mining town. After obtaining my designation as a Chartered Accountant I was with Revenue Canada for ten years and then with a major accounting firm, Deloitte, Haskins and Sells, prior to joining the Inco Canadian tax group in 1970.

In the mid-1970s, mineral taxation underwent radical change in a number of political jurisdictions. Dealing with the taxation and mining departments of the federal, Ontario, Manitoba, Saskatchewan, New Brunswick, and British Columbia governments during that 1974–1977 period gave me the opportunity to meet and establish a rapport with many of the people who have direct influence on legislation that affects the operations of the mining industry. This base of experience and the network of contacts it fostered, combined with a long-standing interest in politics, were important qualifications for my current position which commenced in 1979. In discharging responsibilities relating to this position Inco's corporate goals and objectives are paramount, and my department and I have these in mind, first and foremost.

These responsibilities include extensive involvement with the Canadian federal and provincial governments. Because Inco is an international company, international concerns are also a large part of my mandate. For example, I advise and/or seek the counsel of officials in External Affairs relating to our activities

in Guatemala, Indonesia, and so on, where Inco has substantial investments. I have also been very involved in monitoring the progress of the ongoing United Nations Conference on Law of the Sea (UNCLOS), and in industry and government discussions related to the mining of seabed minerals.

In a large company like Inco a great deal of contact takes place on a regular basis between virtually all company departments and numerous government agencies. My job is not to take over or interfere with this dialogue, although I must monitor activities and be satisfied that they are taking place when and where they should and that there are no problems. I also get involved in activities when there is no easily identifiable person or department to handle a particular issue. Often, circumstances are unique — one-of-a-kind issues. Activities may require the coordinated input of a number of company departments, or require the coordination and development of an overall company position or policy. Some recent examples include the Law of the Sea Conference; the presentation of a company position to parliamentary subcommittees (Latin America, acid rain, pension reform); a company position on the National Mineral Policy, and dealing with the Foreign Investment Review Agency (FIRA) concerning the sale of Inco's Canadian battery divisions.

In addition to single-issue activities, my department coordinates for Inco regular meetings with various political and government groups. There may be fifteen or more formal presentations a year to various government departments and to government and opposition caucuses.

A general goal I work toward is a better understanding of business by governments in order to achieve better policy directions. This necessitates business and government working together, each making their own contribution. As I work at the interface between business and government, a few general problems present themselves. First, getting politicians and civil servants to understand Inco — the kinds of problems the company faces, what we are doing about them, and why it is important that a private enterprise company like Inco have a strong role in the economy.

Correspondingly, another major challenge is ensuring that the appropriate people in the company, often the top management, are aware of and understand the political issues of importance to us. Management must be politically sensitized and must have a good understanding of politicians and the political process. Out of necessity, Inco management,

like that of many other Canadian companies, has become much more politically sensitive in the last decade.

Another general problem is that it is often difficult to anticipate when events will take place. When events do crystalize response is often required within a very short time frame.

One of the most rewarding times in my job comes when I can combine the company's capabilities with government programs, and initiate action that results in company profitability. For example, the Canadian government recently instituted a new program which was identified as one that would enable us to open a certain gold mining property. Negotiations resulted in a profitable situation for the company and fulfillment of the public interest in terms of employment.

I also took a great deal of satisfaction from a recent statement made by a politician — a well-known critic of the company — when he praised Inco for its progress in reducing its sulphur dioxide emissions in Canada. His publicly acknowledged change in attitude took place after my colleagues and I had met with him and his associates and explained the major efforts that Inco was making in this area.

In summary, let me observe that government involvement in busines in Canada is not going to go away. The Canadian psyche seems to desire government participation in the economy. This is a political fact which business people must accept, even if it grates on their free enterprise attitudes. There will be tensions between government and business, but we must live with them and use them to our advantage. The attitude in Canada is different from that in the U.S. where the free enterprise attitude dominates. We should accept that. Perhaps we should begin to compare the relations between business and government in Canada to those in some European countries, rather than to those in the United States.

STAGES IN THE PROCESS OF GOVERNMENT POLICY FORMULATION*

1. Societal need. Where for whatever reason, or combination of reasons, some problem of significance to society arises. For example, advances in technology which create a new form of environmental pollution.
2. Perception of need. Where certain people come to be aware that there is a problem of significance to society, and that it requires attention.
3. Articulation of demand. Where people begin to demand that the problem be addressed. At this stage different people will likely advocate different solutions to the problem. For example, some may advocate that the technology be banned; others will say that it really creates no problems and should be continued; others will advocate measures to reduce the level of pollution created by the new technology.
4. Decision to proceed with legislation. Will be made at some stage if the pressures from the first three stages are great enough. The first three stages can stretch over a long period of years. The decision to proceed with legislation may be precipitated by some event. Such an event could be a sudden worsening of a situation, a change in the elected government, or the appointment of a new elected or civil service official who is to be responsible for the problem.
5. Determination of the nature of the legislation. This could involve an appointed task force or royal commission. Most likely some person or group will be appointed to study the problems and the solution options and to make recommendations to the Cabinet minister responsible. The Cabinet minister in consultation with his officials and other Cabinet ministers will arrive at the recommended course of action.
6. Drafting of legislation. Will be the stage after it is decided what the characteristics of the program are to be.
7. Legislative consideration. Involves the first, second, and third reading by the Canadian Parliament or a provincial legislature. It also involves committee consideration between second and third reading. Federal legislation must also be considered by the Senate. Royal assent, or signing of the bill, by the Queen's represenative (i.e., the Governor General or a Lieutenant Governor) is the final aspect of legislative consideration.
8. Formulation of regulations. The regulations may be necessary to put the legislation into effect. After regulations are formulated, the legislation will be proclaimed to be in effect.
9. Implementation. The way in which the legislation and regulations are interpreted and administered by government departments, agencies, and the courts will ultimately determine exactly what effect the new policy has on economic decision making.

---

*The stages in the process of government policy formulation outlined here were presented in Brian E. Owen's article, "Business Managers Influence (or Lack of Influence) on Government," Autumn 1976, *The Business Quarterly*. Published by the School of Business Administration, The University of Western Ontario.

Business managers should also recognize that the decisions made at various stages of the process have a cumulative effect. Decisions at an early stage can have a profound effect on the ultimate outcome of the process.

The fact that different people are involved at different stages is also important. These people must be identified, and the appropriate method by which to approach them must be considered. Recognition of the stages of the process of government policy formulation and some thought about the best way to participate at each stage can result in an improved ability to influence the process.

Some motivation is required to move the process from stage to stage, for example, from societal need to perception of need to articulation of demand. In the early stages the movement from stage to stage is caused by a discrepancy between industry practice and the public perception of what proper industry practice should be.

SUMMARY AND FINAL WORD

This chapter has discussed the political environment of business. Initially, three ways of viewing the relationship between business and government were identified. These are: (1) the role of government in the structure of the economic system; (2) the roles of government and business in the ongoing day-to-day administration of government programs, and (3) the interactions between business and government in the process of changing government policies.

Governments can participate in and influence economic decisions by actually making the decision (by using a Crown corporation or a regulatory tribunal), by limiting the options available to business managers, by specifying goals for the decision, or by influencing the payoffs associated with available options. The wide range of tools available to governments to influence economic decisions was indicated, including Crown corporations, administrative (regulatory) tribunals, regulations, taxes, tariffs, incentive programs, government purchases, information collection, and macroeconomic management.

Activities of government and business representatives involved in the administration of government policies were briefly indicated.

The formulation of new government policy was also discussed briefly. The stages involved in the process were identified, as were the types of people involved at various stages.

You now have a taste of what the business world is like. It is such a huge and complicated set of industries and firms that it is almost impossible to describe adequately. Even if we could describe it well, you would still have to become a part of it to begin to really appreciate it. And even after you're in it for a while, you'll realize that because it's changing so rapidly, you'll never really learn all there is to know. You'll probably take other business courses in school which will concentrate on specific aspects of operating businesses to prepare you more completely for a specific job. They will also help you in choosing a career.

No matter what you choose as a career, the essential ingredients will be flexibility and willingness to learn. At some time in your career, you may have to be completely retrained if your job becomes obsolete. This is one of the bad features of technical advance. This specific kind of insecurity can be overcome if you have the right attitude. Think of your education as a process of learning how to learn, learning to keep an open mind, and learning about the relationships between yourself and your environment.

Such an attitude towards your education will sharpen your appreciation of it. How you approach the rest of your college experience will set a pattern for your lifetime. You should make sure that it is a pattern which includes the appreciation of learning as a continuing and unending process. ■

QUESTIONS FOR REVIEW AND DISCUSSION

1. What are three different forms which business-government interaction can take?
2. What are the various levels of government in Canada and what are their characteristics?
3. What are the responsibilities of the various levels of government?
4. What are the elements of a business decision? How are goals an important element of an economic decision?
5. What are the tools government can use to influence business decisions?
6. How can these tools actually affect business decisions?
7. What is the difference between taxes and incentive programs? Can taxes ever be used to provide incentives to business decision makers?
8. Should the use of Crown corporations be limited? Why?
9. What different roles are business managers required to play as government programs are implemented on a day-to-day basis?
10. What are the stages in the process of government policy formulation?
11. Why is the political environment important to business managers?
12. How important to business is government as a manager of macroeconomic policy?
13. Do you regard the physical, ecological, technological, economic, social, or political environment as most important to business? Why?

INCIDENTS

Baumann's Ltd.

James Baumann, president of Baumann's Ltd., a manufacturer of bakery products, was considering what actions he should take about what he considered to be the maze of government regulations he operated within. There were relevant Food and Drug laws, packaging, environmental, consumer protection and competition regulations, and taxes to be paid and incentive programs to consider.

In recent months many changes in environmental and consumer protection legislation had been proposed by the provincial and federal governments. This had placed heavy demand upon Mr. Baumann as, in his small company, he could not afford to hire someone to deal exclusively with such matters. He was uncertain whether to fight the changes in regulation or to accept them and adapt his operation accordingly. He wondered whether his membership in the local chamber of commerce would help in this regard.

Questions:

1. What type of business-government interaction is Mr. Baumann participating in?
2. Should he concentrate on trying to prevent change in government policy, on adapting his operation to the proposed new regulations, or on looking for another option?

Government Involvement: Aerospace and Steel*

"As in most other countries, the Canadian aerospace industry has always been, and is, heavily supported by government. It is a magnificent success as a technological leader, as an employer of skilled manpower and in terms of export orders. It has, moreover, responded brilliantly to our woeful defence policy and has diversified effectively from a primarily military base to commercial successes such as the de Havilland Dash-7 and Dash-8 and the Canadair Challenger. Canadian aerospace has an international reputation to be proud of and is in many respects the kind of model industry that we try to emulate in other sectors. Yet it is a perpetual recipient of government support, and the support seems to rise in correlation with its growth . . . .

"Yet in another sector, steel, Canada is almost unique in the world, enjoying private-sector ownership, a high level of technological intensity, highly competitive with state-supported steel industries elsewhere requiring little direct support from government, and relying for its capital largely on the financial markets.

"If steel can achieve this genuine entrepreneurial capacity, why cannot aerospace? Why should not aerospace? And why should not government, within the conceptual framework of the economic contract, force an answer to that question? We should articulate a ten- or fifteen-year program of support in return for viability by the end of that period, including the return to private ownership of de Havilland and Canadair, and we should be ready to accept the consequences of success or failure."

Questions:

1. Can government involvement in the Canadian aerospace industry be decreased?
2. What possible reasons might account for the success of the steel industry compared to aerospace?
3. If you were a member of the Cabinet of the Government of Canada, what would you do with the aerospace industry?

*Source: John J. Shepherd, "Government Aid to Industry," *Canadian Public Administration*, as quoted in the *Globe & Mail*, June 1983.

CASE STUDY

SANAK INDUSTRIES LTD.

BILL HARMAN IS THE NEW PRODUCT DEVELOPMENT MANAGER FOR Sanak Industries Ltd., an Ontario company which is a Canadian leader in the major household appliances manufacturing business. The company was considering development of a line of microwave ovens. Bill Harman had been presented with a new rotary-wave oven feature, which was felt, by its developer, to represent a significant improvement over previous microwave ovens. He felt that microwave ovens were becoming increasingly popular. One prediction was that in five years time microwave oven sales would exceed conventional oven sales. The new rotary-wave oven feature was so unique that, if developed to its full promise, it could make Sanak a Canadian and world leader in the microwave oven industry. On the other hand, if not developed to its full potential it would cost the company a lot of money and would divert attention away from the company's other products.

Sanak Industries did not have the financial resources to be able to easily handle the estimated $1.5 million development cost of the project. Mr. Harman felt there might be certain federal government programs that would support initial feasibility testing and development for the product. He seemed to recall specific reference to programs offered by the Department of Regional Industrial Expansion and the National Research Council that might be applicable. He wondered if it would be worth his while to collect additional information on these agencies and see if there were specific programs that could be of use.

Questions:
1. Do you think that Bill Harman should further investigate available government programs?
2. Identify the federal government programs available to Sanak Industries Ltd. by contacting the appropriate government departments.
3. What program or programs, if any, would you recommend that Bill Harman apply for? ■

CASE STUDY

IN THE THRONE SPEECH ON DECEMBER 3, 1982, THE NDP
government of Manitoba announced that it was going to undertake a
study of the possible entry of the Manitoba Public Insurance Corporation
(MPIC) into the field of life insurance and pension services. MPIC was the
publicly owned, monopoly supplier of automobile insurance in Manitoba.
MPIC also competed in the field of general insurance in Manitoba.

The announcement was indicated by the press to be one of the
only surprises in the Throne Speech. The proposal that the government
enter the life insurance and pension fields was similar to a plan that
had been under consideration in Saskatchewan the year prior. The
Saskatchewan plan had been discontinued after the progressive
conservative government was elected in Saskatchewan in the spring
of 1982.

Members of the government, and supporters of the entry into these
fields, felt that it would create more opportunity for investment in
areas requiring public funding or investment. There was also a concern
that the major life insurance companies in Manitoba were not investing
an amount proportionate to their Manitoba revenues into public and
government areas. Investment of the funds collected under a public
program, it was stated, would be in the areas of home mortgages as
well as school, hospital, and municipal finance. A major aspect of the
proposal was that the proposed company would participate in the life
insurance and pension management business in all of Canada, not just
in Manitoba.

Initial reaction from private life insurance company executives was
that government involvement in life insurance and pension management
would cost a lot of money. There was a feeling that a government
operation could not be profitable if it concentrated only on the Manitoba
market. There was concern that the operation would be subsidized out
of government expenditures in order to get it started. One private life
insurance company executive asked, "Why don't they get into the milk
businesss instead?"

Beyond the initial statement in the Throne Speech the government
did not communicate any further intention to the public or to industry
for a number of months. When contact was made by industry
representatives, it was stated that the government would be undertaking
a study and review of the area in the upcoming months.

Questions:
1. As an advisor to a life insurance company president in Canada, what would you suggest as a plan of action in response to the Throne Speech?
2. What plan of action would you recommend to your life insurance company president in response to the indication that the study of the feasibility of entering this area was going ahead? ■

GLOSSARY

absolute advantage A country enjoys an absolute advantage in producing a good when either (1) it is the only country which can provide it, or (2) it can produce it at lower cost than any other country.

account A basic idea in accounting is that of an account. This is a register of financial value. The set of accounts kept by a firm represents all those separate classes of values, both positive and negative, and the changes in value that occur.

accountability Accountability is the act of holding subordinates, who have been delegated adequate authority to fulfill their responsibilities, liable for performing their assigned tasks and for reporting results to their superiors.

accountants Accountants are individuals who have satisfied the knowledge and experience requirements of a professional group and have been admitted as members of the profession.

account executive An account executive is in charge of the entire relationship between the agency and a particular client (account) and coordinates the work of the group of professionals involved in the client's ad program.

accounting Accounting has been defined in many ways. We will define it as a process of recording, gathering, manipulating, reporting, and interpreting information which describes the status and operation of a firm and aids in decision making.

accrued expense Accrual is a major accounting principle. Expenses are charged against revenue in the period in which the firm benefits from them. An accrued expense is used up but not paid for yet.

Ada Ada is a programming language recently developed by the U.S. military in an attempt to design a language that is more efficient than any of the other major programming lan-

guages. It is suited to both scientific and business applications.

administration of government programs Administration of government programs involves the day-to-day activities that are required in the implementation of government programs.

advertising Advertising includes all nonpersonal promotional activity for which a fee is paid.

advertising agency The principal creative centres for advertising for most medium-sized and large firms are their advertising agencies. An advertising agency specializes in performing advertising functions for other firms.

advertising media The advertising media carry the message designed by firms and their agencies to many receivers (customers or potential customers). The most important media are newspapers, television, direct mail, and magazines, in that order.

agency shop In an agency shop, all employees for whom the union bargains must pay dues, but they need not join the union.

AIDA process A promotional process can be thought of in terms of how it works on a particular receiver or prospective customer, leading him or her through the stages of attention, interest, desire, and action—the AIDA process.

amalgamation In an amalgamation both firms lose their identity. A new corporation is formed, and shareholders of both former firms receive stock in the new corporation in exchange for their old shares.

arithmetic mean The arithmetic mean is an average computed by first adding numbers, finding the total, and then dividing that total by the number of numbers that were added together.

assembly language Systems software programs are usually written in assembly language. This

675

is called an intermediate level language because it lies between machine language and the higher-level (English-like) languages used in writing applications programs.

asset An asset is something of a positive dollar value to a firm.

authority Authority is the right to take the action necessary to accomplish an assigned task.

automation The process, as in the case of most continuous processes, is highly automated. This means that little human supervision is needed because computers and machines can deal with nearly everything that could happen to interrupt operation.

background investigation In a background investigation, the applicant's past employers (if any), neighbours, former teachers, etc., are questioned about their knowledge of the applicant's job performance, character, and background.

balance of payments A country's balance of payments is the difference between its receipts of foreign money and the outflows of its own money due to imports, exports, investments, government grants and aid, and military and tourist spending abroad.

balance of trade A nation's balance of trade is the difference between the money values of its exports and its imports.

balance sheet A balance sheet (also known as a statement of financial position) presents a financial picture of a firm at one point in time.

bank rate The rate at which chartered banks can borrow from the Bank of Canada is called the rediscount, or bank rate.

bankruptcy If its liabilities are greater than its assets, the firm is bankrupt. Such a firm is said to be in bankruptcy.

bargainable issues Bargainable issues are aspects of the work or job environment that are subject to collective bargaining between union and management representatives.

BASIC BASIC was originally designed to teach students how to program. Because it is easy to use, it has become the most widely implemented language for microcomputers.

basic accounting equations Basic accounting equations are equations that explain the basic system of relationships in financial accounting.

Better Business Bureau (BBB) A BBB is a non-profit organization of business firms which join together to help protect consumers and businesses from unfair business practices. Businesses "police" themselves through the workings of the BBB.

blacklists Blacklists contained the names of workers who were known to be in favour of unions.

board of directors The board of directors is a group of people who are given the power to govern the corporation's affairs and to make general policy. This power comes from the corporate charter and the corporation's stockholders.

bond A bond is a written promise to pay. It indicates that the borrower will pay the lender, at some stated future date, a sum of money (the principal) and a stated rate of interest.

boycott In a boycott a union tries to get people to refuse to deal with the boycotted firm.

brand A brand is "a name, term, symbol, or design, or a combination of them, which is intended to identify the goods or services of one seller or group of sellers and to differentiate them from those of competitors."

breakeven analysis A useful management tool in both production planning and pricing of products is breakeven analysis. Breakeven analysis demonstrates the profitability of various levels of production.

breaking down Breaking down means removing or at least separating some of the original input, usually a raw material.

British North America Act This act allocated certain activities to the federal government (e.g., labour legislation for certain companies operating inter-provincially) and others to individual provinces (labour relations regulations in general).

brokerage function The brokerage function involves buying and selling securities which previously have been issued by businesses and governments.

budget A budget is a formal dollar-and-cents statement of expected performance.

business firm A business firm is an entity (thing) which seeks to make a profit by gathering and allocating productive resources to satisfy demand.

business policy The study of top management of business firms is the subject of business policy.

Canada Labour Code The Canada Labour Code is a comprehensive piece of legislation which applies to the personnel practices of firms operating under the legislative authority of Parliament.

capital Capital, as a factor of production, means tools and machinery or anything made by humans that aids in producing and distributing goods. It is humanmade productive capacity.

capital budget This projects the expected need for fixed assets for a period of five to ten years.

capital formation Capital formation is the process of adding to an economy's productive capacity.

capital-intensive This takes place when people may have little to do with production. Instead, investment in machinery is great.

capitalism Capitalism is an economic system based on private ownership of the factors of production.

cartel A cartel is a group of business firms or nations which agree to operate as a monopoly.

cash discount It is common for a firm to offer small discounts for prompt payment of bills. These are called cash discounts.

cash trading Cash trading involves the actual buying and selling of commodities for delivery.

centralization Centralization of authority means that decision-making authority is concentrated in the hands of a few people at the top level of a firm. Such a firm is said to be relatively centralized.

central planning Central planning means that the government drafts a master plan of what it wants to accomplish and directly manages the economy to achieve the plan's objectives.

central processing unit (CPU) The heart of any computer is its central processing unit (CPU). The CPU includes an internal memory for storing data, an arithmetic unit for performing calculations, a logic unit for comparing values and helping to "make decisions," and a control unit that actually operates the computer and sends instructions for controlling all of the other components.

Chamber of Commerce The Chamber of Commerce is a national organization of local chambers of commerce in cities and provinces throughout Canada. Its purpose is to improve and protect the free-enterprise system.

channel of distribution A channel of distribution is the firm, or usually the set of firms, directly involved in selling a product.

chartered bank A chartered bank is a privately owned, profit-seeking firm which serves individuals, nonbusiness organizations, and businesses.

closed shop In a closed shop an employer can hire only union members.

COBOL COBOL (Common Business Oriented Language) is specially designed for conventional commercial applications. COBOL is especially good for handling large files of alphabetic and numerical data such as payrolls.

COLA clause A COLA, or escalator, clause means that, during the period of time covered by a labour contract, wage hikes will be granted on the basis of changes in the cost of living. These hikes are called cost-of-living adjustments (COLA).

collective bargaining Collective bargaining is the process of negotiating a labour agreement between union representatives and employer representatives.

collectivism Collectivism means government ownership of the factors of production and government control of all economic activities.

combination Combination means putting parts together.

combination export manager The combination export manager is a middleman who represents several exporters and handles all the work involved in moving their goods overseas.

commodity exchanges Commodity exchanges provide a market for commodities much as securities exchanges provide a market for stocks and bonds.

common carrier A common carrier offers its services to the general public at uniform, published rates.

common stock Common stock is a certificate showing ownership in a corporation. All shares of common stock are equal in value, and all common stockholders enjoy the same rights. Common stock is voting stock.

communication Communication is a transfer of information between people that results in a common understanding between them.

comparative advantage Comparative advantage means that a country should specialize in producing those goods in which it has the greatest comparative advantage or the least comparative disadvantage in relation to other countries.

competition policy Competition policy seeks to eliminate restrictive trade practices and thereby stimulate maximum production, distribution, and employment through open competition.

compulsory arbitration Compulsory arbitration may be compelled by federal or provincial law in certain cases. If labour and management cannot reach an agreement during contract negotiations, they must submit their dispute to an arbitrator. The arbitrator's decision is binding on both parties.

computer A computer or, more exactly, a computer system is an electronic machine capable of storing and retrieving huge amounts of data and performing mathematical calculations very quickly.

computer program A computer program is a detailed set of instructions in a special computer language.

conciliation In conciliation the neutral third party's task is to prevent negotiations from breaking down. If negotiations break off, the conciliator tries to get the two parties back to the bargaining table.

Conciliation Act The act was designed to assist in the settlement of labour disputes through voluntary conciliation and was a first step in creating an environment more favourable to labour.

confiscation Confiscation means that the government does not compensate the owner for the expropriated property.

conspicuous consumption For some people there has been a lot of conspicuous consumption. This means spending in a visible way so that your neighbours will be aware of your wealth and "good taste."

consumer finance company A consumer finance company makes personal loans to consumers.

consumer goods Consumer goods are goods and services that people buy for their own use — to wear, to eat, to look at, or to live in.

consumerism Consumerism is a movement to strengthen the power of product users in relation to the power of product makers and sellers.

Consumer Packaging and Labelling Act The Consumer Packaging and Labelling Act has two main purposes. The first is to provide a comprehensive set of rules for packaging and labelling of consumer products. The second is to ensure that full and factual information is provided on labels by the manufacturer.

consumer power The consumer power concept means that, because consumers are free to do business with whomever they choose, businesses must consider consumer needs and wants in making decisions.

containerization Containerization is the practice of using standard large containers, preloaded by the seller, to move freight.

content analysis Content analysis is examination of the content of publications for reference to specific items.

continuous production A continuous production process, as the name implies, goes on and on.

contract carrier A contract carrier is a firm, such as a trucking company, that negotiates long- or short-term contracts with shippers to handle their freight.

contract manufacturing In contract manufacturing the firm that wants to do business in a foreign country enters into a contract with a firm there to produce the product.

control chart A control chart is a device which shows the standard set of steps to be taken in the performance of a procedure.

controllers Devices known as controllers regulate the "traffic" of peripheral hardware into the computer's central processing unit.

controlling Controlling involves — setting standards of performance; measuring actual performance and comparing it to performance standards to detect deviations from standards; taking corrective action when significant deviations exist.

convenience goods Convenience goods are items bought frequently, demanded on short notice, and often purchased by habit.

co-operative A co-operative is an organization which is formed to benefit its owners in the form of reduced prices and/or the disbursement of surpluses at year-end.

cooperative federalism The technique and arrangements for dealing with federal-provincial economic relations have come to be known as cooperative federalism.

corporation A corporation has been defined as "an artificial being, invisible, intangible, and existing only in contemplation of law."

corporation bylaws Corporation bylaws are the rules by which the corporation will operate. They include: place and time of meetings; procedure for calling meetings; directors' pay;

duties of the corporate officers; regulations for new stock issues; procedure for changing the bylaws.

correlation Correlation involves making a prediction about one outcome based on knowledge of other outcomes.

Counselling Assistance to Small Enterprises (CASE) As far as management aid is concerned, firms with fewer than seventy-five employees are eligible to use the Counselling Assistance to Small Enterprises (CASE) services. The CASE program is designed to help owner-managers more effectively manage their business in all areas, not simply the financial end of the organization.

countervailing duties Countervailing duties are tariffs or non-tariff barriers introduced by a nation to offset an artificial advantage gained by another nation as a result of trade barriers.

countervailing power In order to counter the power of big business, big labour and big government also are part of our business system. The overall balancing of power between them is called countervailing power.

CPM CPM is much like PERT except that specific estimates rather than variable estimates of elapsed time in operations are used.

craft unions Craft unions are organized by crafts or trades—plumbers, barbers, airline pilots, etc. Craft unions restrict membership to workers with specific skills.

credit union A caisse populaire, or a credit union, is a cooperative savings and lending association formed by a group with common interests.

Crown corporation A Crown corporation is one that is accountable, through a minister, to Parliament for the conduct of its affairs.

CRTC The Canadian Radio-Television and Telecommunications Commission (CRTC) regulates and supervises all aspects of the Canadian broadcasting system. The CRTC issues broadcasting licences and renews licences of existing broadcasting outlets subject to certain conditions. The CRTC also decides upon applications for rate changes submitted to it by federally regulated telecommunications carriers such as Bell Canada.

CTC The Canadian Transport Commission (CTC) makes decisions about route and rate applications for commercial air and railway companies. The same holds true for other transportation activities (e.g., trucking and airlines). Proposed changes in rates must also be approved.

cumulative voting With cumulative voting the number of votes a stockholder has is the number of his or her shares times the number of directors to be elected.

current asset A current asset is one that the firm normally expects to hold no longer than a year.

current liability Current liabilities are those that must be paid off within a year.

current ratio A short-term key credit ratio which is widely used is the current ratio. It is computed by dividing current assets by current liabilities.

data processing All businesses need to collect, store, manipulate, interpret, and report data. This is called data processing.

debt financing Debt financing is the use of borrowed funds.

decentralization Decentralization of authority means that decision-making authority is given to people in addition to those in top management. Such a firm is said to be relatively decentralized.

decision-making process The stages in the decision-making process are as follows: recognizing an opportunity or a problem; gathering information; developing alternatives; analyzing alternatives; choosing the best alternative; implementing the decision; evaluating the decision.

delegation Delegation means entrusting part of a superior's job (or activities) to a subordinate. Three actions are involved in the delegation process: assigning responsibility; granting authority; establishing accountability.

Delphi technique A method of combining the informed judgments of a number of experts on a subject is known as the Delphi technique.

demand Demand for a good or a service exists when there are people who desire the good or service; have the buying power to purchase it; are willing to part with some buying power in order to buy it.

demand curve A demand curve is a line that shows the number of units that will be demanded (bought) at each price at a given point in time. Fewer units are demanded at higher prices than at lower prices.

demand deposit One type of deposit a customer can make in a bank is a demand deposit. A demand deposit is a chequing account.

demography Demography is the branch of anthropology that deals with population statistics, primarily the size and characteristics of the population.

departmentation Departmentation means identifying, grouping, and assigning activities to specialized departments within an organization.

depreciation As an asset loses value, it suffers depreciation. This loss of value is charged off as an expense and the stated value of the fixed asset is reduced on the balance sheet.

devaluation Devaluation means reducing the value of a currency in relation to gold or in relation to some other standard.

directing Directing means encouraging subordinates to work toward achieving company objectives. It sometimes is called leading, guiding, motivating, or actuating.

discharge Discharge is a permanent type of involuntary separation due to a permanent layoff or outright firing of an employee.

discretionary income Discretionary income is what remains of your disposable income after you have bought your necessities.

dismissal Dismissal is an involuntary temporary or permanent type of separation of the employee.

Disposable Personal Income (DPI) Disposable Personal Income is a smaller amount than GNP. It indicates the total amount of buying power from current sources available to the nation's people. It is equal to their incomes minus the taxes they pay.

distributed data processing (DDP) DDP is a multiple systems approach to information handling. It puts computer power in many different places.

distribution Distribution (place) means getting things from where they are made to where they are used.

distribution of government powers The distribution of government powers means that different levels of government have responsibilities for different matters.

distribution of income Distribution of income means the way in which the people share in the total income of a nation or region.

documentation An important part of software is known as documentation. This means an explanation either in English (or other spoken languages) or in diagram form of what a program does, how it is used, and how it works.

echelons of management The different layers, or levels, of management in an organization are called the echelons of management.

ecology Ecology is the branch of biology that deals with the relations between living organisms and their environment.

economic development Economic development means that a nation grows in terms of the amount its average citizen produces.

economic development council An economic development council is an organization of business firms and local government officials. It seeks to further the economic development of the area in which it is located.

economic environment The economic environment is composed of external influences which result in changes in prices of inputs used by firms or of products sold by firms.

economic growth Economic growth refers to the year-to-year increase in GNP.

economic problem The economic problem is concerned with how we can satisfy our unlimited wants with our limited resources.

economic theory of the firm The economic theory of the firm (microeconomics) is that a firm will chose the level of output which results in the maximum profit for the firm.

embargoes Embargoes prohibit the import and/or export of certain goods into or out of a country.

employee orientation Employee orientation (induction or indoctrination) involves introducing the new employee to the job and to the firm. It is the first, and probably most critical, phase of the employee's training.

entrepreneur An entrepreneur is a person who assumes the risk of organizing and managing a business in the hope of making a profit.

entrepreneurship Bringing land, labour, and capital together and managing them productively to produce a good or service to make a profit is entrepreneurship.

equipment trust certificates Some firms have issued equipment trust certificates of five- to ten-year maturity. These are like short-term bonds backed by the equipment purchased with revenues from their sale.

equity An equity account is a register of claims or rights of different groups to a firm's assets.

equity financing Equity financing means the provision of funds by the owners themselves.

exchange Exchange means trade, or giving up one thing to get another thing.

exchange control Exchange control means government control over access to its country's currency by foreigners.

exit interview The purpose of an exit interview is to determine the reasons why an employee is leaving.

expense Expense accounts are measures of the using up of resources in the normal course of business in a given time period.

expropriation Expropriation means that the government of a country takes over ownership of a foreign-owned firm located in its country.

extrapolation Extrapolation is the projection of past and present circumstances into the future.

extraterritoriality The Watkins Report in 1968 dealt with extraterritoriality, that is, the application of U.S. laws to the subsidiaries of U.S. companies in other countries.

factoring company A factoring company (or factor) buys accounts receivable (amounts due from credit customers) from a firm.

factors of production These limited resources are the factors of production: (1) land, (2) labour, (3) capital, and (4) entrepreneurship. The factors of production are the inputs of the productive system.

Federal Business Development Bank The Federal Business Development Bank encourages loans to small business by charging increasingly higher interest rates as the amount borrowed increases.

final selection interview In the final selection interview, all company personnel who have interviewed the prospect are present, along with the manager under whom the applicant will work. The manager is the person who makes the decision whether or not to hire the applicant.

financial accounting Financial accounting helps the manager to "keep score" for the firm. It watches the flow of resources and lets those who have an interest in them know where they stand.

FIRA The Foreign Investment Review Agency (FIRA) reviews proposed acquisitions of Canadian businesses by non-Canadians. A non-Canadian cannot complete a takeover transaction until approval has been received from FIRA.

fixed asset A fixed asset is a tangible resource that is expected to remain useful for more than a year.

floor planning A special kind of secured financing is called floor planning. An auto dealer who gets a shipment of new cars signs a note to a bank or other financing agency for the amount due. Title passes to the lender who pays the bill.

focus group interview A focus group interview entails listening to eight to twelve people at one time with very little formal questioning by the interviewer. The idea is to provide a natural conversational setting in which a group of similar people frankly exchange opinions and attitudes toward a product, store, or idea.

Food and Drug Act The Food and Drug Act prohibits the sale of a food that contains any poisonous or harmful substances; is unfit for human consumption; consists in whole or in part of any rotten substances; is adulterated; or was manufactured under unsanitary conditions. The act also provides that no person can sell or advertise a food in a manner that is misleading or deceptive with respect to its value, quantity, composition, or safety.

forecasting techniques Forecasting techniques are specific methods used for making predictions about the future of business environments.

forecasts Forecasts are assumptions about what the future environment of business will be.

foreign assembly In foreign assembly the parent firm exports parts overseas where they are assembled into a finished product by its overseas subsidiary or a licensee.

foreign direct investment Foreign direct investment, defined in the *Report of the Royal Commission on Corporate Concentration*, is the transfer of a package of assets from a foreign-domiciled corporation through corporate channels into an enterprise in Canada, either by acquisition of an existing firm or by the creation of a new enterprise, which thereafter becomes a subsidiary of the foreign corporation and subject to its control.

form utility   Form utility is utility resulting from a change in form.

FORTRAN   FORTRAN has for years been the most widely used language for scientific and engineering programming applications. FORTRAN is short for FORmula TRANslator.

franchised retailer   A franchised retailer is tied closely by contract to a manufacturer, and its operations are strictly supervised. Examples of franchised outlets include McDonald's and other fast-food firms, as well as auto dealers and many gasoline stations.

franchisee   A franchisee has an exclusive right to sell the franchiser's product or service in his or her specified territory. Each franchisee is an independent business owner.

franchiser   The franchiser is the firm that licenses other firms to sell its products or services.

franchising agreement   A franchising agreement is a contract between a franchiser and its franchisees which spells out the rights and obligations of each party.

frequency distribution   A frequency distribution is a table that shows how many members of a larger group fall within various classes or subgroups.

functional authority   The staff has authority to issue orders directly to line personnel. This is functional authority. It is granted only in the staff's area of expertise and only if it will benefit the firm.

functional discount   Sometimes a functional discount is granted to a customer in return for services rendered.

functions of management   Managerial work consists of performing the functions of management: planning, organizing, staffing, directing, and controlling.

futures markets   In futures markets, traders buy and sell contracts to receive or deliver a certain quantity and grade of commodity at a specified future date.

government policy formulation   Government policy formulation is the process by which changes are made in current government policies.

grievance procedures   Grievance procedures spell out the sequence of steps a grieved employee should follow in seeking to correct the cause of the grievance.

Gross National Product (GNP)   The Gross National Product is the sum of the values of all goods and services produced in a nation during a given year.

gross profit   The difference between net sales and cost of goods sold is gross profit.

guaranteed annual wage   The guaranteed annual wage is a provision in a labour contract which maintains the workers' income level during a year.

hardware   Computer hardware consists of the machinery and electronic components.

Hazardous Products Act   The Hazardous Products Act regulates two categories of products. The first category comprises products that are banned because they are dangerous. The second category comprises products that can be sold but must be labelled as hazardous. Standard symbols that denote poisonous, flammable, explosive, or corrosive properties must be attached to certain products.

hierarchy of needs   We all have certain basic needs. Abraham H. Maslow arranged these needs in a hierarchy of needs. The hierarchy is based on the prepotency (superiority) of needs. They emerge in the following order: physiological needs, safety needs, belonging needs, esteem needs, self-actualization needs.

hierarchy of organizational objectives   This concept involves breaking down broad company goals into specific goals for each person in the organization.

histogram   The histogram, or bar chart, portrays a frequency distribution in vertical or horizontal columns whose length, measured on an accompaying scale, indicates the number or percent in each class.

holding company   A holding company owns the stock of one or more other corporations and controls them.

human resource   The human resource is the personnel who staff the firm—its workers and managers.

implementation of strategy   Top management can influence implementation of strategy by design or organizational structure; by design and management of various organizational systems such as accounting and control, planning, reward/punishment, staffing, training, and the like; and by the personal leadership style used in dealings with others in the firm.

incentive pay To encourage greater worker productivity, some firms offer incentive pay. For those units produced by a worker above the normal output per day (the quota), the piece rate is increased.

incentive programs Incentive programs are designed to encourage managers to make certain decisions and take certain actions desired by governments.

income statement The income statement shows what actually happened over a period of time to explain some of the differences between successive balance sheets. It summarizes the revenue and expense accounts, just as the balance sheet summarizes the asset and equity accounts.

independent local union An independent local union is one which is not formally affiliated with any labour organization.

in-depth interview An in-depth interview is one conducted by trained specialists to shed light on the applicant's motivation, ability to work with others, ability to communicate, etc.

individualism Individualism is the idea that the group, the society, and the government are necessary but are of less importance than the individual's self-determination.

individual social environment variables Individual social environment variables are those that relate specifically to important individuals in the environment of the firm.

Industrial Development Bank The Industrial Development Bank (IDB), a subisidary of the Bank of Canada, makes loans to business firms. The Federal Business Development Bank (FBDB) took over operation of the IDB in 1975.

Industrial Disputes Investigation Act In 1907 the Industrial Disputes Investigation Act provided for compulsory investigation of labour disputes by a government-appointed board before a strike was allowed.

industrial goods Industrial goods are goods or services that will be used by a firm or an institution to make another product or to provide a service.

industrial unions Industrial unions are organized according to industries — steel, auto, clothing, etc. Industrial unions include semiskilled and unskilled workers.

inflation Inflation means an increase in the prices of goods and services over a period of time that effectively reduces the purchasing power of a nation's currency.

informal groups Informal groups are small, face-to-face groups which spring up naturally as a result of human interaction on the job. They are created by their members to satisfy wants which are not being satisfied on the job by management.

informal organization The informal organization is the entire complex of informal groups which exists within the framework of the formal organization.

information labelling One of consumerism's goals is the informative labelling of products. This would help a buyer to make a more informed choice among products — particularly when self-service is involved. The label could describe in simple terms the content, nutrition, durability, precautions, and other special features of a product.

informed judgment Informed judgment is expert opinion on a subject. It is based on a thorough understanding of all the facts in a given situation. It could also be referred to as a projection based upon an analysis of a situation.

injunction The injunction is a court order forbidding union members from carrying on certain activities such as intimidating workers or impeding other operations of the company.

input-output (I-O) devices Input and output (I-O) devices are the hardware used in getting information in and out of the computer.

institutions Institutions are organizations, or groups of organizations, having an economic, social, educational, religious, or other recognized purpose in society.

intermediate-term financing Between the short-term borrowing period (one year or less) and the long-term period (usually ten years or more) there is intermediate-term financing.

intermittent production An intermittent production process starts and stops and starts again, maybe several times.

international trade International trade involves the exchange of goods and services between one country and other countries.

international union A union which has members in more than one country is called an international union.

intuition Intuition is a judgment by an individual or a group based on limited information.

inventory turnover rate The inventory turnover rate in a particular period of time is determined by dividing cost of goods sold by the average inventory value.

isolationism Isolationism is the tendency of a country (or a group of countries) to limit social and economic contact with other countries.

job analysis Job analysis involves defining the jobs that must be done if the firm is to reach its objectives.

job application form The job application form (application blank or biographical inventory) is prepared by an employer and filled in by a job applicant. The applicant provides job-related information that helps the employer to determine if the applicant has the needed education, experience, training, etc., for the job.

job description A job description outlines the nature of a given job—how the job relates to other jobs; the specific duties involved; and the tools, machinery, and supplies needed.

job enrichment Job enrichment is the process of redesigning jobs to satisfy higher-level needs and organizational needs by improving worker satisfaction and task efficiency. It gives workers more responsibility, authority, and autonomy in planning and doing their work.

job-skill training Job-skill training teaches employees specific jobs skills. It can be done on the job or away from the job.

job specification A job specification states the personal qualifications needed by the person who is to fill each job—education, skills, experience, etc.

job venture A joint venture involves some ownership and control of the foreign firm by the firm wanting to do business there.

key ratio A key ratio is a value obtained by dividing one value on a financial statement by another value. A particular firm's financial condition can be judged by comparing several important key ratios of items from its financial statements with typical key ratios of similar types of firms.

labour Labour means human mental and physical effort.

labour contract A labour contract sets forth the terms and conditions under which union members will offer their labour services to an employer.

labour-intensive Labour-intensive processes depend more on people than on machines.

labour union A labour union is an organization of employees formed for the purpose of dealing collectively with their employers in order to further the interests of those employees.

laissez faire Laissez faire means let people do as they please. When applied to business, it means let the owners of business set the rules of competition without government regulation or control.

land Land, as a factor of production, means natural resources.

law of demand The inverse relationship between price and quantity demanded is the "law of demand"—as price goes up, the quantity demanded goes down.

law of large numbers If an insurance firm has a large number of policyholders, it can pretty well predict how many of them will die in a year from the mortality tables. This is the law of large numbers.

law of supply As price goes up, the quantity supplied goes up—this is the "law of supply."

leadership Leadership is a manager's ability to get subordinates to develop their capabilities by inspiring them to achieve. It is a means of motivating them to accomplish goals.

lease A lease is an agreement to grant use of an asset for a period of time in return for stated regular payments.

liability The claims of outsiders are called a firm's liabilities.

licensing In a licensing arrangement, licensees are licensed to manufacture and market products in their countries. The licensor gets an agreed-upon percentage of the licensee's sales revenues.

life insurance company A life insurance company is a mutual or stock company which shares risk with its policyholders for payment of a premium.

linear programming Linear programming is a mathematical tool used to allocate resources in the "best way" so as to maximize or minimize a desired objective.

line authority Line authority is the right to direct subordinates' work.

line functions Line functions contribute directly to reaching primary firm goals.

line of credit When a line of credit is set, the bank

stands ready to lend up to this amount to the borrower with some restrictions.

liquidity A firm needs to have enough cash coming in to meet bills, wages, and other current payments. This ability to make payments which are due is the test of a firm's liquidity.

local union The local union (or local) is the basic unit of union organization.

lockout In a lockout employees are denied access to the plant until they accept the employer's terms of employment.

long-term capital Long-term capital is the firm's investment in fixed assets. Such capital is committed for at least one year (usually much longer), and it requires a different perspective.

machine language Machine language consists of binary (1 and 0 digits only) code and relates to a specific computer or set of computers.

macroeconomic environment The macroeconomic environment is the general economic situation in the country or countries in which a firm operates.

make-or-buy decision One question that often arises in planning the product is the decision whether to make a product or a component part or to buy it — the "make-or-buy" decision.

management Our primary definition of management is the process of achieving goals through the efforts of others.

management by exception According to the concept of management by exception (or the exception principle), routine decisions should be pushed as far down in the firm as possible. By granting authority to lower-level managers to make routine decisions, higher-level managers can devote more time to nonroutine decisions.

management by objectives (MBO) Recently, many managers have been adopting the management by objectives (MBO), or managing by results, approach. The manager meets with each subordinate to set his or her objectives. The subordinate participates in goal setting and, if the objectives are accomplished, the subordinate is considered to have performed well.

management development Management development refers to efforts to prepare people for managerial positions and to improve the managerial skills of present managers.

manager A manager is a person who works through other people (subordinates), and

"brings together" their efforts to accomplish goals.

managerial accounting Managerial accounting calls attention to problems and the need for action.

managerial approach to marketing This approach takes the point of view of a firm which must make a variety of marketing decisions, each of which may affect the profit of that firm.

managerial skills All managers, regardless of their level, must have three basic managerial skills: conceptual skills, "people" skills (human relations, communication, motivation, and leadership skills), and technical skills.

manufacturers' agent Manufacturers' agents are paid a commission to represent manufacturers of several noncompetitive lines in a limited geographic territory. Without taking possession of products, such agents aggressively seek to establish these products in this territory.

margin trading Margin trading enables speculators to buy more shares for a given amount of money because they are buying partly on credit.

market economy A market economy is an economic system in which prices determine how resources will be allocated and how the goods and services produced will be distributed.

marketing Marketing is the set of activities needed to find, build, and serve markets for products and services. It is the performance of activities that are necessary to get goods and services from producer to consumer, and that result in satisfaction to consumers and profit for the company.

marketing concept This means that the whole firm is coordinated to achieve one goal — to serve its present and potential customers and to do so at a profit.

marketing mix To apply the marketing concept effectively, a firm must understand the major factors or tools it may use to meet (and to influence) consumers' wants. These factors are called the marketing mix. The marketing mix includes four elements: product, price, promotion, and distribution.

marketing research Marketing research means applying methods of science to marketing problems. These techniques are largely directed at the people who make up the market.

market penetration pricing   To feature low price when introducing a new product is called market penetration pricing. The firm's goal is to build a large initial market share and to build brand loyalty before competitors can enter the market.

market segmentation   A strategy of market segmentation calls for making a special marketing mix for a special segment of the market or several different mixes for several different segments.

market skimming pricing   To feature a high price when introducing a new product is called market skimming pricing. The goal is to get the greatest early revenue from sales to recover product development costs before competitors enter the market.

markup   A markup is an addition to cost to reach a selling price.

Materials Requirements Planning   A Materials Requirements Planning (MRP) system shows which parts and materials will be needed in a finished product and then calculates when the orders for these parts should be placed.

matrix organization   A matrix organization includes horizontal reporting requirements in addition to the traditional vertical chain of command. Organizational activities are structured in both functional and project arrangements and functional and project managers have authority over the same subordinates.

maturity   Maturity is the factor of time of repayment. When a debt matures, it must be paid.

median   Another measure of an average is called a median. It means the middle number when numbers are listed in rank—from smallest to largest or vice versa.

mediation   In mediation, there is a neutral third party, whose task is to suggest a possible compromise.

mercantilism   Mercantilism is an economic philosophy which advocates building strong national states (nations) from warring feudal kingdoms. A major goal of mercantilism is to increase the government's holdings of precious metals.

merger   In a merger one firm (the absorbing firm) keeps its identity, and another firm is absorbed and loses its identity.

merit rating system   Traditional performance appraisal systems require a manager to appraise a subordinate's work habits and personal traits. In the merit rating system, each employee's job performance is appraised every six months or every year.

microeconomic environment   The microeconomic environment is composed of those factors that directly affect a firm's input and output prices.

middlemen   Besides industrial buyers and ultimate consumers, firms must also consider a third kind of customer. These are called middlemen because they usually hold products briefly during the process of bringing them from their producer to their user.

mixed economic system   In Canada we have a "mixed" economic system, characterized by an active market economy with significant direct and indirect involvement by government in economic decision making.

mode   A third average is called a mode. It is the most common or frequent number in a list.

modem   This is the device by which terminals are often connected to the central processing unit by means of telephone lines. A modem modulates or converts direct current (DC) signals to tones and demodulates or converts tones back to DC signals.

money   Money means paper currency, coins, and chequing account balances.

monopolistic competition   Monopolistic competition is a market in which many somewhat differentiated products or services are sold.

motivation   Motivation is the result of the drive to satisfy an internal urge. Managers must structure jobs so that they provide incentives that will satisfy workers' needs if those workers apply effort on the job. By doing this, managers can motivate their subordinates to work toward company objectives.

multinational company   A multinational company is a firm that is based in one country (the parent country) and has production and marketing activities spread in one or more foreign (host) countries.

mutual fund   The owners of a mutual fund pool their investment dollars and buy securities in other businesses. Buying one share in a mutual fund makes you part owner of all the securities owned by the fund.

nationalization   Nationalization means that the expropriating government keeps ownership and runs the firm.

national union   A national union is one which has members across Canada.

NEB The National Energy Board (NEB) is responsible for regulating the construction and operation of oil and gas pipelines which are under the jurisdiction of the Canadian government. This includes decisions about routes of pipelines and the size of pipe to be used in the lines. The NEB also decides on the tolls to be charged for transmission by oil and gas pipelines and the levels of export and import of oil and gas. It also issues guidelines on internal company accounting procedures and allowable rates of return.

net profit Current revenue minus the expenses incurred in gaining that revenue equals net profit. Net profit measures the success of the firm's current operations during the period.

new product committee In many larger firms the task of developing new products is performed by a new product committee. This committee, an example of the matrix form of organization which we discussed in Chapter 5, consists of personnel from several different departments, such as production, marketing, finance, and R&D.

new values New values refer to "spontaneity, self-actualization, sensory awareness, equality, concern for self, humanity, and nature, and indifference or opposition to traditional values."

nonroutine decision A nonroutine decision is a nonrecurring decision.

non-tariff barriers The measures to restrict trade, other than tariffs, are referred to as non-tariff barriers. These can include things such as bilingual labelling requirements, package size or characteristics, product safety requirements, requirements for import licences, inspection of perishable products and emission standards, to name a few.

norm A norm is a standard way of thinking or behaving which group members feel is reasonable.

obsolescence Inventory goods also may be subject to obsolescence. This is what happens when something is out-of-date or not as efficient as newer products.

oligopoly An oligopoly means there are only a few sellers of the same or slightly different products.

online real-time system When those using the software system are in direct communication with the computer, either by telephone or directly wired in, the system is called an online system. When such a system can respond immediately it is called a real-time system. A large proportion of the computers in use today are online real-time systems.

open shop In an open shop, an employer may hire either union and/or non-union labour. Employees need not join or pay dues to a union in an open shop.

operational planning Operational planning is planning for the day-to-day survival of the firm. Middle and lower-level managers engage mainly in this type of planning.

operations research (OR) The various quantitative techniques used to solve problems of scheduling or allocation are called operations research (OR).

opportunity An opportunity exists where there is a "set of circumstances" which may enable a firm to make a profit.

opportunity costs Opportunity costs are costs of losing the option to use the funds in another way.

organization When a group of people and things interact to reach objectives and their behaviour is structured, we call this an organization.

organization chart An organization chart graphically depicts a firm's formal structure at a given point in time.

organization development Organization development (OD) is a re-education process that is used to change the values and behaviour of the entire organization in order to improve its effectiveness in reaching its objectives and in solving problems.

organizing Organizing is the management function of relating people, tasks (or activities), and resources to each other so that an organization can accomplish its objectives.

outside data storage systems A computer's internal memory can be added to by means of outside data storage systems. These are separate systems for storing information, such as magnetic disks, floppy disks, cassette tape, magnetic tape, and decks of punched cards.

over-the-counter market The over-the-counter market is a complex of dealers who are in constant touch with one another.

owners' equity The claims of insiders, or owners, are kept in owners' equity or capital accounts.

ownership utility Ownership utility is that aspect of the usefulness of a product related to the passage of legal title to the final user.

participative management Participative management means that the manager encourages and allows his or her subordinates to involve themselves directly in the decision making that will affect them.

partnership A partnership comes into being when two or more individuals agree to combine their financial, managerial, and technical abilities for the purpose of operating a company for profit.

Pascal Pascal is a relatively new language that uses most of the modern techniques of good programming design. It features an important software design technique called *structured programming*. It is powerful in its data description and in its ability to process that data.

patent A patent protects an invention, a chemical formula, or a new way of doing something from imitation.

pension fund Pension plans accumulate money which will be paid out to plan subscribers at some time in the future.

performance appraisal system The personnel department often helps to develop a formal performance appraisal system to enable supervisors to rate their subordinates' job performance. A good performance appraisal system provides a basis for measuring an employee's contribution to the firm.

personal selling Personal selling includes any direct human communication for the purpose of increasing, directly or indirectly, a firm's sales.

personnel department A personnel department is a staff department which is headed by a personnel manager. It advises and helps line managers to manage their personnel by performing specialized activities which are assigned to it.

personnel management Personnel management consists of recruiting, selecting, training, developing, compensating, terminating, and motivating employees to good performance.

PERT Pert is a planning and control tool focusing on the timing of the occurrence of many operations included in a project.

physical distribution Physical distribution is concerned with the physical movement of raw materials into the plant, the in-plant movement and storage of raw materials and semi-manufactured goods, and the movement of finished goods out of the plant to the ultimate consumer or industrial user.

physical environment The physical environment is our natural resource endowment and includes minerals, vegetation, animal, and water resources. The weather, as part of our natural resource endowment, is also an extremely important part of the physical environment of business.

picketing Picketing means that people (pickets) form a picket line and walk around a plant or office building with placards (signs) informing other workers and the general public that the employer is held unfair to labour.

piece rate Some workers are paid a piece rate. Each worker is paid a certain rate for each acceptable unit of output produced.

piggyback exporting In piggyback exporting, one firm (the carrier) uses its overseas distribution network to sell noncompetitive products of one or more other firms (riders).

place (or distribution) Place (or distribution) is an element of the marketing mix concerned with the movement of products through a channel from producer to consumer or industrial user.

place utility Place utility is that aspect of usefulness determined by location.

planned obsolescence When a firm intends to replace a product, it is called planned obsolescence.

planning Planning means preparing a firm to cope with the future. It involves setting the firm's objectives over different time periods and deciding on the methods of achieving them.

plant capacity Plant capacity is the production output limit of the facility.

plant layout Plant layout describes the relative location of the different parts of the production process in the building or buildings.

portfolio investment Another type of foreign investment, portfolio investment, is purchase of the stocks and bonds of Canadian corporations by non-residents.

power Power is the ability to induce others to behave the way you want them to.

preferred stock Preferred stock is a certificate that shows ownership in a corporation. Preferred stockholders usually cannot vote their shares, but they do enjoy certain preferences with respect to dividends and assets.

preliminary employment interview The preliminary employment interview is the first time that the employer and the applicant meet face-to-face. The employer is usually represented by an interviewer who informs the applicant of job openings and the applicant has an opportunity to ask questions and to discuss skills, job interests, and so on.

preventive maintenance Many firms practise preventive maintenance. This means that they inspect and/or replace certain critical machines and parts on a regular basis to avoid downtime.

price Price is the amount of money for which the product sells.

price leadership In oligopoly, one of the stronger competitors may sometimes raise price, and it is likely that others will follow suit. This is called price leadership.

price lining Partly to simplify choices for customers and partly to simplify the job of the salespeople, the retailer may use price lining—grouping the costs at three or four sales price levels.

pricing model A pricing model is an equation or set of equations that represents all the important things in a pricing situation that help decide on the "best" price.

primary research Primary research is getting new facts for a specific purpose.

prime rate of interest The prime rate of interest is the lowest rate charged to borrowers.

private carrier If a manufacturer or middleman owns and operates its own transportation, it is called a private carrier.

private trading company A private trading company is a privately owned business that buys and sells goods in many different countries, either in its own name or as an agent for its buyer-seller clients.

Privy Council Order 1003 The current positive environment for labour did not come into being until 1943 when Privy Council Order 1003 was issued which (1) recognized the right of employees to collectively bargain, (2) prohibited unfair labour practices on the part of management, (3) established a labour board to certify bargaining authority, and (4) prohibited strikes and lockouts except in the course of negotiating collective agreements.

product The product includes much more than a physical product. It includes the guarantee, service, brand, package, installation, alteration, etc., which go with it. The product can best be thought of as a bundle of utilities.

product cost accounting Product cost accounting systems also use cost centres to allocate all costs to the various products made by a firm. This gives a firm a better idea about which products are profitable and which are not.

product differentiation Product differentiation is a process of convincing target customers that one brand is different from, and better than, the competition's.

production Production activity results in the creation of goods and services. Someone or something is "better off" because of production.

productivity The productivity of inputs is the number of units of output per unit of input.

product life cycle The life history of a product is called the product life cycle. The cycle has four phases: introduction, growth, maturity, and decline.

product mix A manufacturer's or a retailer's product mix is the combination of products it produces or sells.

professional-managerial ethic The professional-managerial ethic holds that managers represent the interests of stockholders, customers, employees, and the general public.

professional managers Professional managers are people whose profession or career is management. Such a person participates in managing a firm in which he or she is not a major owner.

profit Profit is the difference between the cost of inputs and the revenue from outputs.

progressive income tax The progressive income tax means taxing people with higher incomes at a higher rate.

promotion In personnel management, promotion means moving up to a higher position in the firm, usually one that involves more pay and more challenge. In marketing, promotion is probably the most dynamic, aggressive, and persuasive element of the marketing mix. Promotion includes all communication by a firm with its customers or potential customers for the purpose of expanding sales, directly or indirectly.

prospectus A prospectus is a detailed registration statement which includes information about the firm, its operation, its management, the purpose of the proposed issue of stock, and any other things which would be helpful to a potential buyer of these securities.

Protestant ethic The Protestant ethic is a tradition which emphasizes the value of hard work, accumulation of property, and self-reliance.

provincial boards There are certain provincial boards which consider and pass judgment on proposed decisions by private companies. One example of such boards is provincial liquor boards or commissions.

proxy A proxy is a person who is appointed to represent another person. By signing a proxy form, a stockholder transfers his or her right to vote at a stockholders' meeting to someone else.

publicity Publicity is a communication through the news media as a legitimate part of the news.

public market The public market is made up of millions of people who buy stocks and bonds and the business and nonbusiness organizations which also invest in corporate securities.

public relations Public relations includes any personal communication with the public or with government (lobbying) that seeks to create goodwill for the firm. Its effect on sales is usually indirect and long-run.

pure risk Pure risks are those which offer only a chance of loss. There is no chance of gain.

quality control A quality control system sets up a standard for an input or output and makes comparisons against this standard to prevent nonstandard items from going into or coming out of the production process.

quality-of-work-life (QWL) program Quality-of-work-life (QWL) programs have received a lot of attention in recent years. The underlying idea is that worker and manager participation in decisions at the bottom level of the organization through problem-solving committees will result in increased job satisfaction and raise product quality and labour productivity.

quantitative tools Many of the mathematical and statistical tools depend on computers for their practical application. We refer to this whole set of mathematical and statistical applications to business as quantitative tools.

quantity discount Another common discount is the quantity discount which involves reduced unit prices as the size of the order increases.

real income Real income is your income expressed in terms of buying power; it is your income adjusted for the decline in buying power due to inflation.

recapitalization Recapitalization occurs when a firm changes its capital structure to meet changing conditions.

reciprocity A common purchasing policy involves reciprocity—"you buy from me and I'll buy from you."

recruiting Recruiting is the task of attracting potential employees to the firm. It should be a continuous process for most medium- and large-sized firms.

regional trading bloc A regional trading bloc is a group of countries which agree to eliminate restrictions which limit trade among member nations.

research and development (R&D) R&D is a general name applied to activities which are intended to provide new products and processes.

reserve requirement The reserve requirement is the percentage of its deposits member banks have to keep in vault cash or as deposits with the Bank of Canada.

resignation Resignation occurs when an employee voluntarily leaves the employer's service.

responsibility Responsibility is the obligation of a subordinate to perform an assigned task.

responsibility accounting Responsibility accounting involves setting up responsibility centres in a firm. These are used to classify cost information so as to evaluate the performance of various parts of the firm and their managers.

revenue A revenue account is a register of gross earnings or inflows of value to a firm during a given time period.

revolving credit A revolving credit agreement is a very formal and specific agreement which guarantees funds for a period of time with strict rules limiting the borrower.

risk Risk is the chance of loss.

rolling over Rolling over means successive renewals of short-term notes as a substitute for longer-term financial commitments.

routine decision A routine decision is a recurring decision. It is a decision which must be faced over and over.

royalties Royalties are government charges levied for the use of Crown property.

salary A worker paid a fixed amount on a weekly, biweekly, or monthly basis receives a salary.

sales finance company A sales finance company specializes in financing instalment purchases made by individuals and firms.

sales forecast The sales forecast is the starting point for a general (master) budget. It predicts what sales will be over a certain period of time. This forecast depends on what effect the marketing manager thinks the planned changes in the marketing mix will have on sales. Sometimes the sales forecast is tied to a projection of Gross National Product or to industry sales forecasts.

sales promotion Sales promotion includes special events directed at increasing sales. Special sales, coupon offers, contests, games, entertainment features, and trading stamps are examples.

sample A sample is a part of a larger group called a universe or population. It is intended to take the place of the larger group and to convey some information about that larger group.

scenarios Scenarios are statements of how an event could unfold.

secondary research Assume that a firm decided which characteristics are related to consumption of its product. Now it seeks information about the number of such prospects in the area to be served. A firm may find this additional demographic information on consumers in Canadian census publications or other government or private sources. This is called secondary research.

secured loans Many commercial loans to smaller firms and to firms with lower credit ratings are "secured" loans. Here, the lender is protected by a pledge of the borrower's assets.

securities exchanges Securities exchanges are placed where buyers and sellers deal with each other through members of the exchanges.

selection tests Selection tests are used to measure the applicant's potential to perform the job for which he or she is being considered. These tests include intelligence tests, aptitude tests, performance tests, interest tests, and personality tests.

self-insurance Many firms practise self-insurance of certain types. This means assuming your own risk and preparing for loss.

seniority Seniority refers to an employee's length of service. The longer that service, the more seniority an employee has.

shipper's export declaration An export declaration is required for all goods exported from Canada. This document declares the quantity and dollar value of the goods and must be filed with the collector of customs at the port of exportation.

shopping goods Shopping goods are items which are taken seriously enough to require comparison and study.

short selling Short selling means selling a security which you do not own by borrowing it from your broker.

simulation Simulation involves developing a model of an actual situation and working through the simulation to see what kind of outcome results.

sinking-fund Firms set up a sinking-fund to retire maturing bonds. This means putting aside money each year from profits to pay them off.

Small Business Loans Act The Small Business Loans Act helps proprietors get loans to purchase and/or update fixed assets and to improve facilities in general.

small groups Small groups are composed of members who have some common goal and a structure for achieving it.

social environment The social environment is the total of all human variables that are external to the firm.

social responsibility of business A firm demonstrates social responsibility when, in the process of making decisions, it takes things in addition to profit into consideration.

software Computer software complements hardware by giving instructions and setting hardware into motion.

sole proprietorship A sole proprietorship is a business owned and managed by one person.

That person, however, may have help from others in running the business.

span of management Span of management refers to the number of persons an individual manager supervises.

specialization Specialization means concentrating effort on a specific task instead of dividing one's effort among a greater number of tasks.

specialty goods Specialty goods are those for which strong conviction as to brand, style, or type already exists in the buyer's mind. The buyer will make a great effort to locate and purchase the specific brand.

speculative risk Speculative risks are "gambles" in which there is possible gain as well as loss.

speculative trading Speculative trading means buying or selling securities in the hope of profiting from near-term future changes in their selling prices.

staff Staff are people who advise and assist line managers in their work of achieving company objectives.

staff functions Staff functions help the line to achieve primary firm goals.

staffing Staffing includes the recruitment, selection, training, and promotion of personnel to fill both managerial and nonmanagerial positions in a company.

stagflation In the 1970s our economy began to suffer from "stagflation." This was a peculiar situation in which we had both a recession and a high rate of inflation.

standard of living The standard of living is a measure of economic well-being.

state trading company A state trading company is a government-owned operation that handles a country's trade with other governments or firms in other countries.

statistics Managers have dealt with numerical data in their decision making for many years. These numerical data and methods of summarizing them are called statistics.

stockholders Stockholders are persons who own the common and preferred stock of a corporation.

strategic planning Strategic planning is concerned with a firm's long-range future and its overall strategy of growth. This is the type of planning for which top-level managers are responsible.

strategy A firm's strategy is what it is currently doing, what it intends to do in the future (its goals), and how it intends to achieve these goals.

strategy formulation Strategy formulation is the activities (formal and/or informal) determining what a firm's strategy is to be. Formulating a strategy involves matching company strengths with environmental opportunity.

strike A strike is a temporary withdrawal of all or some employees from the employer's service.

supply The supply of a good or a service results from the effort of producers. The quantity supplied is the number of units of a good or a service that producers will offer for sale at a certain price.

supply curve A supply curve is a line that shows the number of units that will be supplied (offered for sale) at each price at a given point in time. Fewer units are supplied at lower prices than at higher prices.

systems concept According to the systems concept, a firm is not the accounting department or the marketing department. It consists of a network of interrelationships among the various departments and their environment.

tangible net worth Tangible net worth is equal to stockholders' equity minus goodwill (goodwill is an intangible asset).

target market If a firm is to adopt the marketing concept, it must define the characteristics of its customers. This set of customers is called the target market.

tariffs Tariffs are duties or taxes which a government puts on goods imported into or exported from a country.

tax control A country practises tax control when it uses its tax authority to control foreign investments in that country.

technological environment The technological environment includes all applications of knowledge which have an impact upon a business firm.

technology Technology is the application of knowledge so that people can do entirely new things or do old things in a better way.

Textile Labelling Act The Textile Labelling Act regulates the labelling, sale, importation, and advertising of consumer textile articles.

time deposit A time deposit is one which is to remain with the bank for a period of time.

Interest is paid to depositors for the use of their funds.

time sharing System software may enable a computer to permit many users to interact with the computer at the same time. Such a process is called time sharing.

time utility Time utility is hard to explain. It is that aspect of utility determined by the passage of time as it relates to consumption.

total cost concept Modern firms apply the total cost concept, which considers all costs related to a particular means of physical distribution. Their goal is to minimize their total costs without sacrificing their desired level of customer service.

trade barriers Trade barriers are natural and "created" obstacles which restrict trade among countries.

trade credit Trade credit or "open-book account" differs from other types of short-term credit because no financial institution is directly involved. It is simply credit extended by sellers to buyers.

trademark The patent office protects a name or symbol which, when registered, is called a trademark.

trade position discount Any discount granted because of a difference of position in the distribution channel is called a trade position discount.

traditional business ethic In the traditional business ethic, business decisions are based only on how they affect the short-term profit for owners.

traditional values Traditional values are "regard for duty, honour, custom, order, restraint, prudence, loyalty to family, church, and nation, and the pursuit of knowledge, technology, and economic growth."

transaction The term *transaction* is used to describe any change in an asset or an equity.

treatment Treatment is doing something to an input without adding to it or subtracting from it.

trust company A trust company safeguards property—funds and estimates—entrusted to it. It also may serve as trustee, transfer agent, and registrar for corporations and provide other services.

underwriting Underwriting involves helping corporations and governments to sell new issues of stocks and bonds.

unfair lists Unfair lists contained the names of employers whom unions considered unfair to workers because these employers would not hire union members.

union shop In a union shop, an employer may hire non-union workers even if the employer's present employees are unionized.

unlimited liability Unlimited liability means that a proprietor is liable for claims against the business that go beyond the value of his or her ownership in the firm. The liability extends to his or her personal property (furniture, car, and personal savings) and, in some cases, real property (home and other real estate).

utility Utility means usefulness.

value analysis Value analysis starts by reviewing existing product specifications as set by user departments. Attention then focuses on identifying and eliminating nonessential cost factors.

value in exchange Something has value in exchange when it can command something else in return for it.

values Values are simply what people think is important.

vendor analysis Vendor analysis evaluates and rates the technical, financial, and managerial abilities of potential suppliers in terms of their past performance. It is a method of substituting facts for feelings in the selection of suppliers.

venture capital firm A venture capital, or development firm will provide funds for new or expanding firms which are thought to have significant potential.

venture capitalists Venture capitalists are individuals or businesses that are willing to provide equity capital to entrepreneurs who have new products or new product ideas that are as yet unproven on the market but that have a good chance of becoming successful.

vision Vision is when a person decides that he or she wants something to happen and goes out and does it.

voluntary arbitration In voluntary arbitration the neutral third party hears both sides of the dispute and settles the issue.

wage A worker paid on an hourly rated basis receives a wage.

wage and salary administration Wage and salary administration is the process of developing and implementing a sound and fair method of compensating employees. It involves setting pay ranges for all jobs in the firm and setting a specific amount of pay for each employee.

Weights and Measures Act Regulations under the Weights and Measures Act complement the packaging and labelling regulations. The Weights and Measures Act sets standards of accuracy for weighing and measuring devices.

word processing system A word processing system is a computer that is programmed to manipulate letters, words, and paragraphs. It is a text-editing computer.

working (short-term) capital Working capital is a term applied to a firm's investment in short-term assets — the current assets we discussed in Chapter 11.

work-to-rule When workers meticulously follow all rules and regulations in the collective agreement, they are using a work-to-rule strategy to get management's attention.